THE KENNEDY TAPES

THE
KENNEDY TAPES

INSIDE THE WHITE HOUSE
DURING THE CUBAN MISSILE CRISIS

EDITED BY

Ernest R. May and Philip D. Zelikow

THE BELKNAP PRESS OF
HARVARD UNIVERSITY PRESS

Cambridge, Massachusetts, and London, England

First Harvard University Press paperback edition, 1998

Library of Congress Cataloging-in-Publication Data

The Kennedy tapes : inside the White House during the Cuban missile
  crisis / edited by Ernest R. May and Philip D. Zelikow.
    p.   cm.
  Includes index.
  ISBN 0-674-17926-9 (cloth)
  ISBN 0-674-17927-7 (paper)
    1. Cuban Missile Crisis, 1962—Sources. 2. Kennedy, John F. (John
Fitzgerald), 1917–1963—Archives. I. May, Ernest R. II. Zelikow,
Philip D; 1954–.
E841.K4655   1997
973.922—dc21   97-14216

To Graham Allison

CONTENTS

Illustrations follow page 188.

By mid-October 1962, the Cold War had intensified in numerous ways. Cuba, which had long been a virtual colony of the United States, had recently moved into the Soviet orbit. In late September U.S. newspapers had begun reporting shipments of Soviet weapons to Cuba. President John F. Kennedy told the American public that, to the best of his understanding, these weapons were defensive, not offensive. Soviet Premier Nikita Khrushchev had given him absolute assurances that this was the case. "Were it to be otherwise," Kennedy said, "the gravest issues would arise."

Shortly before 9:00 A.M. on Tuesday, October 16, Kennedy's Assistant for National Security Affairs, McGeorge Bundy, brought to his bedroom photographs showing that the "gravest issues" had indeed arisen. Taken from very high altitude by a U-2 reconnaissance plane, these photographs showed the Soviets in Cuba setting up nuclear-armed ballistic missiles targeted on cities in the continental United States.

For Kennedy, the presence of these missiles was intolerable. So was the fact that Khrushchev had lied to him. For the next 13 days, Kennedy and a circle of advisers debated how to cope with the challenge. They knew that one possible outcome was nuclear war, and during their discussions Kennedy's civil defense expert offered the chilling information that the U.S. population was frighteningly vulnerable: "the only protection that exists today is in the cities, and there's little or no protection in the rural areas." Those rural areas contained more than 50 million people, but city dwellers would find little comfort in the protection they had against missile warheads each of which carried the explosive power of 2 or 3 million tons of TNT.

Throughout the crisis, American decision-making was centered in the White House, and during much of that time, a tape recorder was running. Except for President Kennedy and possibly his brother Robert, no one taking part in the discussions knew this. As records of frank deliberation in a time of crisis, these tapes have no parallel at any other time or place in history.

President Kennedy had only installed the recording apparatus during the summer of 1962. As both a reader and writer of history, he may have been looking toward future memoirs. We do not know his motives. The practice had precedents. Franklin Roosevelt recorded a few conversations by means of a Dictaphone hidden in his desk. Kennedy, like his predecessors, authorized wiretapping and bugging by the Federal Bureau of Investigation. Most legal limitations on such activities came later, and Kennedy's White House taping system was probably lawful at the time, so long as he did not make his recordings public.

The taping system was simple. It involved microphones concealed in unused light fixtures in the Cabinet Room and one concealed in the President's desk in the Oval Office. These microphones transmitted to a reel-to-reel tape recorder in the White House basement. The President had to flip hidden switches to start the system running. From the Oval Office, he could also record telephone calls, but on a separate machine called a Dictabelt. Kennedy would signal his private secretary, Evelyn Lincoln, to turn on this machine. Almost all Kennedy administration recordings, more than 95 percent, are of meetings, not telephone calls.

This book includes no transcripts of taped telephone calls. Kennedy seldom discussed sensitive matters over telephone lines that might be tapped by foreign governments or by the FBI. He broke this rule, however, when talking over a special line with British Prime Minister Harold Macmillan. Though Kennedy did not record these conversations, Macmillan's staff in London monitored them and prepared stenographic, verbatim transcripts. These have been recently declassified by the United Kingdom's Public Record Office. We include these transcripts in our book because they resemble the White House tape recordings in literal authenticity.

President Kennedy began recording meetings at the end of July 1962, and telephone calls in September. Since he had to make a positive, conscious decision to activate a recorder, we can assume that he recorded only conversations he wished to record and that he was conscious of recording those transcribed here. If Robert Kennedy was aware of being recorded, the fact did not restrain his candor. On the tapes, both he and President Kennedy make many remarks that appear unguarded and that could have been damaging politically, if disclosed.

After President Kennedy was assassinated on November 22, 1963, Evelyn Lincoln had only hours to clear out before President Lyndon Johnson's secretaries took her place. At the time, with the possible exception of Robert Kennedy, only three people knew of the taping system: Lincoln and two agents of the U.S. Secret Service who had installed the system and then maintained it, mainly by changing reels of tape as needed. Mrs. Lincoln's loyalty to Kennedy was legendary. Kennedy once said to his chief speechwriter, Theodore Sorensen, that, if he had told Lincoln he had cut off his wife's head and needed a box, she would have responded, "That's wonderful, Mr. President, I'll send it right away . . . Did you get your nap?"[1] She arranged for the Secret Service agent to remove the microphones and dismantle the taping system. She then took the tapes to her newly assigned office in the Executive Office Building, just west of the White House.

Robert Kennedy later asked Lincoln to transcribe the tapes. She apparently began doing this with the help of an Army sergeant named George Dalton. The rough transcripts are reported to be very poor, and at some point the effort was abandoned. (The "Dalton transcripts" are in the custody of the John F. Kennedy Presidential Library, Boston, and will eventually be made available to researchers.) Although Lincoln kept the tapes near her as long as she lived, they eventually migrated to a federal records depository in Waltham, Massachusetts, along with other Kennedy relics.

In the summer and fall of 1967, when Robert Kennedy drafted a memoir of the missile crisis, he may have used some of the rough transcripts and possibly the tapes themselves. After Robert Kennedy's murder in June 1968, Sorensen, one of his close friends, edited the manuscript memoir, eventually published under the title *Thirteen Days*.[2] Sorensen described it as based in part on "personal diaries," yet he did not claim to have seen such diaries. Robert Kennedy wrote or dictated a few memos about the events as they were happening; nothing else (besides the tapes) has been found.

After 1968, the circle of those who knew of the tapes widened. It came to include Senator Edward Kennedy, former Assistant Attorney General Burke Marshall, and a representative of the National Archives, who were formally the joint custodians of President Kennedy's public and private papers. It probably included others. Despite occasional rumors, however, the secret of their existence held until 1973.

On July 16, 1973, in nationally televised hearings before the Senate committee investigating the "Watergate" scandals, an aide to President Richard M. Nixon made the sensational disclosure that the White House had a sophisticated, voice-activated taping system. Congress subpoenaed the Nixon tapes for use in impeachment proceedings. With rumors reviving of similar taping systems in previous administrations, Senator Kennedy and the other custodians of President Kennedy's papers decided to confirm the existence of Kennedy tapes. They publicly promised to turn these tapes over to the National Archives.

During the next two years, they negotiated a deed of gift that transferred to archivists at the John F. Kennedy Presidential Library all tapes except those dealing with private, family affairs.

In 1975, tapes recording 248 hours of meetings and 12 hours of telephone conversations became part of the President's Office Files at the JFK Library. Soon afterward the Library made available for research about 26 hours of recordings, accompanied by 500 pages of transcripts. Almost all dealt with domestic issues and involved no problems of security classification.

The Library first released material on the Cuban missile crisis in 1983. It consisted of a 33-minute sample of actual recordings from October 16, the first day of the crisis, and a heavily sanitized transcript covering an additional two hours of that day's tapes. McGeorge Bundy exercised his privilege as a former official and listened to recordings for October 27, the last day of the crisis. He prepared a rough transcript, of which the Library released a summary, again with many sections blacked out. The Library released no actual recordings for that day.

Short of money and people, the Library prepared no further transcripts. Without transcripts, agencies in Washington could not review the tape recordings for declassification. There matters stood for 10 years.

In 1993 the Library acquired new equipment and began copying some of the original tapes onto Digital Audio Tape (DAT). Washington agencies could review these copies without transcripts. Changes in procedures and standards for declassification review meanwhile made the process easier, as did greater delegation of review authority to the Library's archivists and coincidental release by the Central Intelligence Agency of large quantities of material previously regarded as highly sensitive.[3] All these developments opened the way for faster action on the tapes. Cuban missile crisis material had a high priority. In 1994 the Kennedy Library declassified some previously sanitized passages from the Bundy summary for October 27. In the same year the Library released about $5\frac{1}{2}$ hours of recordings from meetings that took place from October 18 through 22. But no transcripts. In late 1996 and early 1997, the Library released all remaining missile crisis recordings for October 16 through October 29, including material for October 16 previously withheld. But still no new transcripts.

The reason for the nonproduction of transcripts becomes apparent the minute one actually listens to a tape. Though the recording quality is occasionally excellent, the large majority of tapes crackle, rumble, and hiss. Conversation is as hard to make out as on a factory floor or in a football stadium during a tight game. The listener has trouble distinguishing words and sentences and separating or identifying speakers. Reliable transcribing therefore takes much time and effort. Yet reliable transcripts—ideally, annotated transcripts—are essential to make the tapes intelligible.

As a first step toward producing such transcripts, we commissioned a team of court reporters from the firm of Atlantic Transcriptions, Inc. Under the leadership of Steve Fuller, they produced draft transcripts from the recordings released by the JFK Library. We then asked an expert in audio techniques to improve the sound quality of most of the tapes. Using the Sonsonic method, he cut down background interference.[4] The court reporting team then went back over all their draft transcripts to exploit the benefits of the enhancement and to check that nothing had been lost.

The two of us then worked with the tapes and the court reporters' drafts to produce the transcripts printed here. The laboriousness of this process would be hard to exaggerate. Each of us listened over and over to every sentence in the recordings. Even after a dozen replays at varying speeds, significant passages remained only partly comprehensible. For example, on Friday, October 26, one of the days of highest tension, President Kennedy concludes a comment, apparently about Khrushchev, with the words ". . . in 48 hours, if he would agree to that, I would agree to that." For the life of us, we cannot make out how Kennedy begins this comment.

Notwithstanding the high professionalism of the court reporters, we had to amend and rewrite almost all their texts. For several especially difficult sessions, we prepared transcriptions ourselves from scratch. In a final stage, we asked some veterans of the Kennedy administration to review the tapes and our transcripts in order to clear up as many as possible of the remaining puzzles. The reader has here the best text we can produce, but it is certainly not perfect. We hope that some, perhaps many, will go to the original tapes. If they find an error or make out something we could not, we will enter the corrections and enhancements in subsequent printings of this volume.

When preparing our final transcriptions, we cleaned up the tapes. We did not censor the language. The reader will find none of the "bleep" entries so common in the Nixon tapes. But any serious conversation involving several people is full of verbal debris. This includes the omnipresent "uh," fragments of words, phrases uttered when two or more persons are interrupting one another. Where a pause or the substitution of one word or phrase for another seems a reflection of uncertainty or of second thoughts, the transcript shows it. What we omit are the noncommunicative fragments that we believe those present would have filtered out for themselves. We believe that this gives the reader a truer sense of the actual dialogue as the participants themselves understood it.

Through an Introduction and through scene-setters preceding each chapter, we try to place the reader in the setting of October 1962. We stress what was known or knowable to Kennedy and those around him. We reserve for a final chapter secrets from the Soviet side not known till later and comments on what happened after the crisis and on lessons that have been drawn from it. We do this in hope that someone reading the transcripts will come to the crisis as did Kennedy and those around him. With verbal debris cleared away, these transcripts have some qualities of a screenplay. Since this volume traces almost minute by minute what may be the most harrowing episode in all of human experience, we hope that the reader will experience it not only as history but as drama.

We are grateful for financial support from Harvard University's Center for Science and International Affairs; Harvard University's Intelligence and Policy Project, which is sponsored by the Central Intelligence Agency's Center for the Study of Intelligence; and the Charles Warren Center for Studies in American History, also at Harvard. We are further grateful for the help we received from the staff of the John F. Kennedy Library in Boston, especially archivist Stephanie Fawcett, and to our friends at the National Security Archive and the Cold War International History Project, notably Peter Kornbluh and James Hershberg. We benefited from wise advice, as well as encouragement, from the superb editorial and production staff at Harvard University Press—especially Aida Donald and our thoughtful manuscript editor, Ann Hawthorne. Useful comments on draft transcripts were offered by Carl Kaysen, Theodore Sorensen, and William Smith. Our warm thanks also go to John Hermon (who helped with the British research), Sally Makacynas, Sarah Peterson, Eric Baudelaire, Philip Nash, Nigel Gould-Davies, and Enmi Sung.

Our sources for assertions in the Introduction and Conclusion are cited in endnotes. In the main body of the book, we prefer not to divert the reader's attention. Accordingly, there we provide footnotes instead of endnotes and include citations of other sources only when absolutely necessary. In addition to the various memoirs and other writings cited, we have relied upon the relevant archival holdings for the White House and the various agencies of the U.S. government, held mainly in the John F. Kennedy Library in Boston (cited throughout as JFKL), which also furnished the photographs; and the National Archives, Washington D.C. We have also relied on the less formal holdings of that useful private institution the National Security Archive, Washington D.C., as well as its cousin, the Cold War International History Project, headquartered at the Woodrow Wilson International Center in Washington. At those institutions, we are particularly grateful for help received from Peter Kornbluh and James Hershberg. The Cold War International History Project has helped us locate various Soviet and Cuban documents. We have also examined the relevant archives of the British government, held at the Public Record Office in Kew.

Many primary sources pertaining to the Cuban missile crisis have recently been published in several useful collections, which we cite in short form throughout this volume:

McAuliffe, *CIA Documents* = Mary S. McAuliffe, ed., *CIA Documents on the Cuban Missile Crisis, 1962* (Washington, D.C.: Central Intelligence Agency, 1992)

FRUS 1961–1963 = U.S. Department of State, *Foreign Relations of the United States,* 25 vols. (Washington, D.C.: Government Printing Office, 1988–1997)

Larson, *"Cuban Crisis"* = David L. Larson, ed., *The "Cuban Crisis" of 1962: Selected Documents, Chronology, and Bibliography,* 2d ed. (Lanham, Md.: University Press of America, 1986).

THE KENNEDY TAPES

INTRODUCTION

On the morning when he first saw photographs of Soviet missiles in Cuba, John Fitzgerald Kennedy was 4 months and 18 days past his forty-fifth birthday. During the 13 days of crisis that followed, he would ask advice from some men older than he and from a few who were younger. (From no women, so far as we know.) All had been molded by World War II and the Cold War. "Munich," "Pearl Harbor," "the iron curtain," "containment," "the Berlin blockade," "Korea," "McCarthyism," "Suez-Hungary," "Sputnik," and other such shorthand references to recent history called up shared memories and shared beliefs. A reader for whom those terms have only faint associations may misunderstand some of the dialogue recorded here. This introductory chapter aims at providing such a reader a sense of the framework of experience within which Kennedy and his advisers interpreted the crisis.

"Munich" captured a world of meaning, especially for Kennedy. His father had played a role in the drama. He himself had published a book analyzing it. "Munich," of course, referred not to a single event but to a series of events and to their supposed lesson or lessons. The Munich conference of 1938 capped efforts by Britain to appease Nazi Germany, arguably making up for too-harsh peace treaties imposed after World War I. Czechoslovakia had been created by those treaties. At Munich, Britain compelled Czechoslovakia to cede to Germany borderlands populated by German speakers. When the Nazi dictator, Adolf Hitler, subsequently seized non-German Czechoslovakia and invaded Poland, Britain changed policy. World War II commenced. "Munich" and "appeasement" became synonyms for failure to stand firm in the face of aggression.

Kennedy's father, Joseph Patrick Kennedy, a famous stock speculator and one of the few millionaires openly to back Franklin Roosevelt, was Roosevelt's ambassador to Britain at the time of the Munich conference.[1] Both in cables to the State Department and in public speeches and interviews, Joe Kennedy backed Britain's appeasement of Germany. He continued to do so. Well into World War II, he argued that Britain had been right to conciliate Hitler and that the best interests of the world would be served by a compromise peace. Joe Kennedy also spoke out against any action by his own government that might embroil the United States in the war. He thus marked himself as both an appeaser and an isolationist. (In his 1992 novel, *Fatherland*, Robert Harris imagines the world as it might have been had Britain actually come to terms with Hitler. One plot line concerns a visit to Europe in the 1960s by President Kennedy. But the President is Joe Kennedy, not John.)

John Kennedy was twenty-one and a third-year undergraduate at Harvard at the time of the Munich conference.[2] During the actual period of the conference, he seemed to agree with his father. The coming of war gave him second thoughts. Previously a desultory student, preoccupied with games and girls, he turned in his final college year to writing a long honors thesis, with the laborious title "Appeasement at Munich (the Inevitable Result of the Slowness of Conversion of the British Democracy to Change from a Disarmament Policy to a Rearmament Policy)." Family friends helped him polish the manuscript and publish it under the improved title *Why England Slept*. Appearing in 1940, only weeks after the fall of France, it became a surprise best-seller. It did not entirely contradict his father's line. Indeed, Joe Kennedy read and approved the final draft. But the book struck a different stance. Declaring "appeasement" a weak policy forced upon British governments by British public opinion, it called on America to arm so as not to have to follow a similar policy if challenged by totalitarianism.

All his life, Kennedy would carry the burden of being Joe Kennedy's son. Robert Lovett, Truman's Secretary of Defense and one of the elder statesmen whom Kennedy would consult during the missile crisis, voted against Kennedy in 1960 because Joe Kennedy was his father.[3] George Ball, who would be Under Secretary of State and a regular member of Kennedy's missile crisis circle, writes in his memoirs that he joined the Kennedy administration only after assuaging doubts similar to Lovett's: "I had long despised the elder Kennedy, who represented everything I disliked and mistrusted. He had been a buccaneer on Wall Street, an opportunist in politics, and a debilitating influence when our civilization was fighting for its life; now we were once more engaged against an enemy with the same face of tyranny. Before I could wholeheartedly support the new President, I had to satisfy myself that he was free of his father's views and influence. Just after the election I had carefully analyzed his writings and speeches—and had found reassurance that the father's noxious views had not infected the son."[4] So, for Kennedy, "Munich" and "appeasement" connoted not only past events and their supposed lessons but also his own need continually to prove that his views were not his father's.

Another member of the missile crisis circle in whose words one can hear echoes of the 1930s is Secretary of State Dean Rusk. Eight years older than Kennedy, Rusk had grown up in circumstances that Kennedy could scarcely imagine. The son of a poor Georgia farmer, he could remember running through the cold night to reach an outdoor privy and wearing underwear stitched from flour sacks. But he had managed to go to Davidson College in North Carolina. From there he had gone on to a Rhodes Scholarship. Studying at Oxford from 1931 to 1934 and spending several months in Germany, he had seen at firsthand not only Hitler's dictatorship but an event highlighted in Who Knows What— an Oxford Union debate of February 1933 that resulted in a 275 to 153 vote in favor of the resolution "This House will in no circumstances fight for King and Country." Rusk remembered ruefully how he himself, back in the United States teaching at a women's college in northern California, had argued for giving Hitler some leeway. His subsequent conversion was so complete that tears could come to his eyes when he pleaded with students not to be seduced by appeasement and isolationism.[5]

"Pearl Harbor" was another historical reference point for Kennedy and his advisers. Practically all Americans had been shocked to learn on December 7, 1941, that Japanese planes had bombed the American naval base at Pearl Harbor and sunk or severely damaged the warships anchored there. Most could recall ever afterward exactly where they had been when they heard this news. Kennedy and a friend with whom he shared an apartment in the District of Columbia had just finished a pickup game of touch football on the grounds near the Washington Monument. They heard the first bulletins on their car radio while driving home.[6]

On Kennedy himself, the Pearl Harbor attack had no immediate effect. During the previous year, as the nation moved further and further away from isolationism, the armed forces had expanded. Concealing chronic ailments that should have exempted him, Kennedy had wangled a commission in the naval reserve. As one team of biographers comments, "Thus, a young man who could certainly not have qualified for the Sea Scouts on [the basis of] his physical condition, entered the U.S. Navy."[7] He was serving as an ensign in the Office of Naval Intelligence when the Pearl Harbor attack occurred. Rusk, having been in ROTC and remained in the reserve, had been called to active duty in 1940. He was a captain in the Army, also in Washington, serving in Army intelligence.

And in the same building with Kennedy was Adlai E. Stevenson, who would be Kennedy's ambassador to the United Nations in October 1962. Eight years older than Rusk and seventeen years older than Kennedy, Stevenson was a prominent Chicago lawyer serving as a civilian assistant to the Secretary of the Navy. In Chicago, he had been a conspicuous critic of the positions espoused by Joe Kennedy. Ironically, he would be the person in Kennedy's missile crisis circle regarded as most nearly an advocate of "appeasement."

President Roosevelt's address to Congress on Pearl Harbor had breathed moral outrage. He declared December 7, 1941, "a date which will live in infamy," remembered for an "unprovoked and dastardly attack." The two members of Kennedy's missile crisis circle whose references to Pearl Harbor would echo some of Roosevelt's indignation were two not then in uniform or in government service—George Ball and Kennedy's younger brother Robert Francis (or Bobby), who would be his Attorney General. Ball, approximately the same age as Rusk, was a wealthy Chicago lawyer, friendly with Stevenson. He had worked in the Treasury Department during the early New Deal but then returned to private practice. Though he had been, if anything, more critical than Stevenson of the isolationism identified with Joe Kennedy, he had stayed away from Washington, and he would continue to do so until the spring of 1942. Robert Kennedy, at the time of Pearl Harbor, was barely sixteen years old and a third-year student at a Rhode Island preparatory school, struggling for passing grades.[9]

In the debates recorded on Kennedy's tapes, Pearl Harbor has a presence as pervasive as Munich. Recollections of Pearl Harbor had helped to make worst-case worry about surprise attack a guiding theme for postwar U.S. military planning and procurement. Absent Pearl Harbor, the whole debate about the Soviet missiles in Cuba might have been different, for supposed lessons from the Pearl Harbor attack shaped the intelligence collection apparatus that informed Kennedy of the missiles and kept him and his advisers abreast of day-to-day developments. Most important of all, Pearl Harbor served as a conclusive example of the proposition that a secretive government might pursue its ambitions, or relieve its frustrations, by adopting courses of action that objectively seemed irrational or even suicidal. This proposition haunts discussion of Soviet motives and possible Soviet reactions during the missile crisis.

Though Kennedy and his advisers carried away from World War II itself memories that influenced their thinking in October 1962, the memories were not counterparts to Munich or Pearl Harbor. They were individual, not collective. Kennedy, continuing to hide his ailments, was assigned combat duty as skipper of a twelve-man patrol torpedo boat in the southwest Pacific. When the boat was rammed by a Japanese destroyer, Kennedy managed to save most of his crew. He towed one man ashore by keeping his teeth clenched on the man's lifejacket strings. Graphically recounted in a *New Yorker* article by John Hersey (and later in a book by Robert Donovan), the story of PT 109 made young Kennedy famous once again. The experience may also, however, have contributed to the caution he would exercise during the missile crisis. He wrote to his father at the time: "When I read that we will fight the Japs for years if necessary and will sacrifice hundreds of thousands if we must—I always like to check from where he is talking—it's seldom out here. People get so used to talking about billions of dollars and millions of soldiers that thousands of dead sounds like drops in the bucket. But if those thousands want to live as much as the ten I saw—they should measure their words with great, great care."[10]

Invalided out after his return from the Pacific, Kennedy did a brief stint as a newspaperman. He covered the San Francisco conference of April 1945, from which came the final Charter of the United Nations organization. Adlai Stevenson, who was there as a senior adviser to the U.S. delegation, had responsibility for press relations. "It was all a little ridiculous," Stevenson remarked later, "me interpreting developments play by play in a secret room at the Fairmont Hotel, whose number was known to not less than 50–75 U.S. correspondents."[11] Kennedy, one of the fifty to seventy-five, wrote for his newspaper, in the vein of his earlier, private letter:

> The average GI on the street . . . doesn't seem to have a very clear-cut conception of what this meeting is about. But one bemedaled marine sergeant gave the general reaction when he said: "I don't know much about what's going on—but if they just fix it so that we don't have to fight any more—they can count me in."
>
> Me, too, sarge.[12]

The Pacific War that had commenced at Pearl Harbor ended with Japan's surrender in August 1945. Two other men who would be around Kennedy during the missile crisis had also seen service in that war. Curtis LeMay, who would be Chief of Staff of the Air Force in October 1962, and Kennedy's most hawkish adviser, had been transferred from the European theater to take over the 20th Air Force, based on Guam. Slightly older than Rusk, he had joined the Army Air Corps in 1928, leaving Ohio State University without a degree. The mission of LeMay's command was strategic bombing of the Japanese home islands. After analyzing the command's operations, LeMay ordered a complete change in tactics. The B-29s had been flying at high altitude in order to be safe from antiaircraft fire. LeMay calculated that at much lower altitudes there might be somewhat greater loss of aircraft, but that this disadvantage would be more than offset by increases in bomb loads and in bombing accuracy. Experience seemed to prove him right. In a low-level attack on Tokyo in March 1945, his 325-plane force lost only 14 aircraft and hit a much higher-than-usual percentage of its targets.

An admiring observer of LeMay's management of the 20th Air Force was Army Air Forces Lt. Colonel Robert S. McNamara, who would later be Kennedy's Secretary of Defense and LeMay's civilian boss. McNamara was less than a year older than Kennedy. He, too, came of Irish immigrants, but his forebears had taken the Panama route to California. Although his parents were never as poor as Rusk's, and he grew up in a city rather than on a farm, he remembered money's being scarce in his family. While attending the University of California at Berkeley, he had had to live at home in Oakland, and he and a classmate would drive to school, hoarding gas by coasting downhill whenever possible.[13] He majored in economics, had a superb record, and graduated at twenty-one but, to his lasting vexation, failed to win a Rhodes Scholarship. He went on instead to the Harvard Business School. During the period of the Munich conference and *Why England Slept*, McNamara was studying management just across the Charles River from Kennedy. After graduation, he was one of a group kept on at the Business School to teach the new subject of financial control. Early in 1942, the Air Forces appropriated the entire group and gave McNamara a commission. He served in Europe until late in 1944, urging on commanders exactly the type of benefit-versus-cost calculation that he saw exemplified by LeMay.

McNamara and LeMay were not to see eye to eye during the missile crisis. Indeed, they may not have seen eye to eye in 1945, when LeMay was clearly gratified not only by the cost-effectiveness of his operations but by their consequences. Of the March 1945 raid, LeMay boasted later: "We burned up nearly sixteen square miles of Tokyo," then quoted the official report from the time: "There were more casualties than in any other military action in the history of the world."[14] LeMay had also had command responsibility for the special bomber group that attacked Hiroshima and Nagasaki, and his attitude toward the first atomic bombs was dismissive. He rejected the notion that they were somehow special, morally or otherwise. "The assumption seems to be," he wrote, "that it is much more wicked to kill people with a nuclear bomb, than to kill people by busting their heads with rocks."[15] At least in later years,

McNamara would come to argue vehemently that nuclear weapons were special and ought never to be used.

During the final year of World War II and the early postwar years, Kennedy and the men who would surround him during the missile crisis moved into the era of the Cold War.[16] The syndicated columnist Walter Lippmann popularized that term as early as 1946. Winston Churchill contributed another enduring one when he declared, also in 1946: "From Stettin in the Baltic to Trieste in the Adriatic, an iron curtain has descended across the continent." Yet another new term—"containment"—came into wide use in 1947. George F. Kennan, a professional diplomat, later an eminent historian, gave "containment" currency through an article published in 1947 under the pseudonym "X" in the quarterly Foreign Affairs. He called for "a long-term, patient but firm and vigilant containment of Russian expansive tendencies," particularly through "adroit and vigilant application of counter-force at a series of constantly shifting geographical and political points, corresponding to the shifts and maneuvers of Soviet policy."

Kennedy's attitudes evolved much as did those of most other Americans. When reporting on the San Francisco conference and its aftermath, he had expressed some wariness about the future. Explaining to the editor of the *Atlantic Monthly* why he could not complete a projected article in favor of arms limitation, Kennedy wrote: "The Russians . . . have demonstrated a suspicion and lack of faith in Britain and the United States which, while understandable in the light of recent history, nevertheless indicates that in the next few years it will be prudent to be strong."[18] These comments from the 1940s foreshadow the wary empathy with which he would approach the Soviet Union as President.

Kennedy ran successfully for Congress in 1946. There he supported President Truman's efforts to put containment into practice by giving aid to European countries threatened either by the Soviet Union or by domestic Communist parties. While his father spoke out publicly against wasting money or running risks on behalf of foreigners unable to solve their own problems, Kennedy made a well-publicized speech in the House, declaring that the United States had a duty not only "to prevent Europe and Asia from becoming dominated by one great military power" but to prevent "the suffering people of Europe and Asia from succumbing to the soporific ideology of Red totalitarianism."[19]

As the language of Kennedy's speech attests, Americans had come increasingly to see Soviet totalitarianism as a threat comparable to that of Nazi totalitarianism. One seeming lesson of the 1930s was that the United States should not do what it had done then. The U.S. government should instead make clear that, in case of aggression in any way resembling Hitler's, the United States would be in the front line from the very first day.

In 1948 the Truman administration set an example. Berlin, the former German capital, lay well inside eastern Germany, occupied by the Soviets under wartime agreements. Berlin itself, however, had American, British, and French sectors too, creating a populous Western island within the Soviet zone. In June the Soviets suddenly imposed a blockade, stopping all rail and road traffic from the West into Berlin. After reflecting on alternatives, President Truman ordered a round-the-clock airlift to deliver food and supplies to the city. If the Soviets had interfered, the result could well have been war. The Soviets let the planes go through. After some months, they suspended the blockade. From then on, Berlin stood as a symbol of U.S. determination to put American lives on the line against forceful Soviet takeover of any part of Europe.

In 1949 the United States signed with Canada, Britain, and various West European states the North Atlantic Treaty. The Senate as well as the executive branch thus committed the United States to the principle that an attack on any European signatory would be treated by the United States as an attack on itself. At the time, the commitments to Berlin and to the North Atlantic Treaty were made easier by the American monopoly on nuclear weapons and by misplaced confidence that that monopoly would last.

Despite the vigor of his initial support for containment, Kennedy seemed a mere observer of these events. Others who would be around him in October 1962 were, however, deeply engaged. Robert Lovett was Under Secretary of State and a key adviser to Truman and Secretary of State George Marshall on the Berlin blockade. Rusk, who had become a colonel during the war and ended up on Marshall's Pentagon staff, had followed Marshall to the State Department and was Assistant Secretary for UN Affairs. LeMay, a three-star general in the newly independent Air Force, was commander of U.S. Air Forces in Europe. He thus organized and ran the airlift, and did so with the same driving efficiency he had shown in the Pacific.

Time and again during the missile crisis debates, one person or another would make reference to the blockade and airlift. For some reason, everyone tended to misdate it, placing it in 1947–48 instead of 1948–49. But Kennedy and Rusk, in particular, would mention the blockade as the one example in the past of a direct Soviet challenge to the West. And Kennedy would cite the episode as one in which the United States had been free to use nuclear weapons and had chosen not to do so.[20]

After the Berlin blockade crisis, the Cold War intensified. In 1949 the Soviets surprised the West by testing an atomic bomb. It became clear that Soviet dictator Joseph Stalin, instead of giving priority to repairing war damage, was pouring resources into military modernization. In late June 1950 came the Korean War. Soviet-backed North Korea suddenly launched a major offensive against U.S.-backed South Korea. Interpreting this as a challenge to the principles of the UN Charter and possibly as a rehearsal for a similar offensive in divided Germany, Truman immediately sent in U.S. military forces. Before the year was out, North Korea had been defeated, but Communist China had intervened and pushed the battle line back to the prewar boundary.

The then commander of U.S. and UN forces, General Douglas MacArthur, declared that China's intervention created "a new war." He proposed various operations against China proper. When the Truman administration remained adamant against extending the war beyond the Korean peninsula, MacArthur appealed for support from Truman's political opponents in Congress and elsewhere. Truman relieved MacArthur of his command. MacArthur then came home, greeted by huge crowds in city after city and received with a standing ovation by a joint session of Congress. Protracted hearings followed, calling into question the wisdom of Truman's policy and stirring speculation about Truman's possible impeachment. Passions eventually died down, but only after a parade of other World War II military leaders joined in testifying that MacArthur's position was unsound. Meanwhile, the Soviets had initiated truce talks, and eventually all parties accepted an armistice, leaving the country divided very much as previously.

This long and decidedly unpopular war was another important landmark for men in Kennedy's missile crisis circle. Shortly before the 1950 North Korean offensive, Rusk voluntarily left his job as Deputy Under Secretary of State to assume the lower-ranking post of Assistant Secretary for Far Eastern Affairs. The Communists' success in the Chinese civil war had stirred domestic furor; many in Congress and elsewhere alleged that the United States had "lost" China, possibly because of Communist subversives within the U.S. government. (One of the attackers was Congressman John Kennedy, who declared in 1949 that America's China policy had "reaped the whirlwind . . . What our young men had saved, our diplomats and our President have frittered away.")[21] The Far Eastern Bureau thus became the hottest spot in the State Department, if not in the executive branch, and hence a challenge to Rusk's strong sense of duty. Looking back, Rusk took pride in having fended off such charges and especially in having been one who counseled patience and restraint during the Korean War.

LeMay's retrospect on the Korean War was exactly the opposite of Rusk's.

After initiating the Berlin airlift, LeMay had returned to the United States to take over the U.S. Strategic Air Command (SAC). Technically a unified command directly under the Joint Chiefs of Staff (JCS), it was, for practical purposes, an all Air Force command with the mission of preparing to destroy the Soviet homeland. LeMay made it one of the most efficient and dedicated organizations in military history. When the Korean War opened, LeMay urged that SAC attack North Korea "immediately with incendiaries and delete four or five of their largest towns."[22] He remained bitter ever afterward that his proposal was rejected. He also favored bombing China once the Chinese intervened, and he argued gruffly that they never would have intervened had they been presented with a credible threat that the result would be incendiary raids on their cities.

Maxwell Taylor, who would be Chairman of the Joint Chiefs of Staff during the missile crisis, also had a part in the Korean War.[23] About the same age as Adlai Stevenson, Taylor was a Missouri-born West Pointer. A linguist who had gone back to the Academy to teach French and Spanish and served a tour in Asia as a Japanese language officer, he had been on General Marshall's staff in Washington early in World War II, then been a distinguished paratroop commander in Europe. Analyzing the Korean War for the Army staff, he concluded that the war's military objectives had been poorly defined. Shortly before a final truce agreement was reached, Taylor assumed the principal U.S. military command in Korea. From this experience as a whole, he concluded that the U.S. government had made a mistake in treating diplomatic negotiations and military pressures as alternatives rather than as complementary courses of action, best pursued simultaneously. As to whether the United States had been right or wrong to keep the war so limited, he remained of two minds—not of Rusk's but also decidedly not of LeMay's. These lessons—and this past ambivalence—would influence his thinking when he sat with Kennedy in October 1962 and interpreted for him the advice of LeMay and the other chiefs of staff.

Apart from its particular lessons for individuals, the Korean War had lasting effects on American policymaking. Until World War II, the military establishment had had almost no voice in foreign policy decisions. After the war, Congress made provision for a National Security Council, intending it to ensure that Presidents would not totally ignore military considerations when making decisions about international relations. Besides the President, the principal members were the Secretary of State and the civilian Secretary of Defense. The Chairman of the Joint Chiefs of Staff was later designated as an adviser to, but not a member of, the NSC. Until the Korean War, the Secretary of State remained the pivotal member of the NSC and the principal framer of foreign policy.

During and after the Korean War, the military establishment gained a much stronger voice.[24] Dwight Eisenhower, who succeeded Truman, had the advantage of being himself a five-star general and a hero of World War II. He sought to reduce the influence of the uniformed military largely because of concern lest they use that influence to increase military spending. Despite his background and the force of his personality, he was only partially successful. Military leaders who criticized his policies found ready supporters on Capitol Hill and in the press. Kennedy was among them.

During the missile crisis, Kennedy would hold only one formal meeting with the Joint Chiefs of Staff. He and the others would usually rely on Taylor to report their views, but that did not make their views any less weighty. Kennedy and his civilian advisers recognized that it would be inadvisable—to say no more—to adopt a line of action that leaders in the uniformed military would unite in opposing. During the spring of 1962, Kennedy's light reading would include a novel by Fletcher Knebel and Charles Bailey, *Seven Days in May*, in which military leaders engineer a coup against a President who seems to them too pacifistic. Asked by a friend whether something of the sort could actually happen, Kennedy said he thought it could.[25] The fact that such a contingency did not seem totally unrealistic in 1962 was traceable in large part to the Korean War and the MacArthur affair.

The period of the Korean War had also been the high phase of "McCarthyism."[26] The label came from Joseph R. McCarthy, a loutish Senator from Wisconsin, who had taken to its outer limit the tactic of detecting domestic U.S. Communists and Communist sympathizers as the chief sources of trouble both in the United States and in the world. But McCarthy's success in capturing headlines and terrorizing individuals and agencies reflected widespread public anxiety fed by, among other things, proof that prominent officials of the Roosevelt administration had been secret Soviet agents. Alger Hiss, Rusk's immediate predecessor in managing UN affairs in the State Department, had gone to the penitentiary.

To assuage public anxiety, the executive branch, Congress, and officials in state and local governments and in private bodies such as colleges and churches established rules and procedures that did in fact resemble earlier efforts to find witches or to punish heretics. Many rules and procedures inhibiting if not barring free speech remained commonplace in 1962.

Kennedy's father was a strong and an unrepentant supporter of McCarthy.

Kennedy, who moved from the House to the Senate after the election of 1952, was on good terms with McCarthy. Robert Kennedy went to work on McCarthy's staff. After finishing Harvard during World War II, he had served briefly in the Navy as an enlisted man and had just graduated from the University of Virginia Law School. After a row with McCarthy's chief staffer, Roy Cohn, he quit. He later worked with Senators who were critical of McCarthy and Cohn and helped draft a report that led to formal Senate censure of McCarthy in 1954, a censure that effectively ended McCarthy's career.

John Kennedy did not vote for or against the McCarthy censure. He was in a hospital undergoing a series of life-threatening operations to arrest one of his disabilities—spinal degeneration that kept him in constant and increasing pain. He could, of course, have recorded a position by pairing with another Senator. He was the only Democrat not to do so. This fact, together with his brother's work for McCarthy, helped to keep alive suspicion of John Kennedy—like father, like son, like brother.

By October 1962 McCarthyism itself would seem far in the past. Memories of its virulence, however, persisted. So did public anxiety. A hit film of 1962, John Frankenheimer's *The Manchurian Candidate*, starring Kennedy's friend Frank Sinatra, was based on the premise that Communists could manipulate American political processes through their own mind-controlled puppets. When Kennedy and his advisers talked at the White House about possible public reactions to one option or another, many of them had in the backs of their minds hysteria such as that which had risen during the first decade of the Cold War. This recollection would increase their sensitivity to opinions such as those of LeMay.

During the 1950s the careers of Kennedy and Stevenson had intersected again. After World War II, Stevenson had gone back to Illinois to practice law, oversee a small-town newspaper, and manage a farm in the village of Libertyville. (His friend George Ball observed: "He had the normal equipment of any good farmer of the area: a tennis court, a swimming pool, a horse or two, and a few sheep.")[27] In 1948 the Illinois Democratic machine enlisted Stevenson as its clean-government candidate for governor. Eloquent, obviously sincere, and running against a Republican tarred by scandal, he swept the state. Though Stevenson wanted to seek a second term as governor, Truman and others talked him into becoming the presidential nominee. Again, he was eloquent and obviously sincere. All the Kennedys supported him. He garnered many more votes than Truman had in 1948, but not enough to avoid being overrun by Eisenhower.

Four years later, Stevenson was again the candidate against Eisenhower. Before the Democratic convention, Kennedy decided to seek the vice-presidential nomination. He had in the meantime again achieved celebrity through a book. Titled *Profiles in Courage*, it sketched biographies of Senators, from the early republic on, who had risked their careers for unpopular principles. Kennedy's work on it had kept him occupied while recuperating from back surgery. It not only became a best-seller; it won a Pulitzer Prize. (Given his failure to vote on the McCarthy censure, his book and his prominence among the Democratic left a rebuke that he needed less prominence. Eleanor Roosevelt was usually the person credited.)

For the vice presidential nomination, Kennedy's chief opponent was Senator Estes Kefauver, who had unsuccessfully opposed Stevenson in the presidential primaries. Stevenson disappointed Kennedy by deciding to support neither candidate but to let the delegates make their own choice, and Kefauver won. Robert Kennedy joined Stevenson's campaign train and suffered even greater disappointment by watching the candidate in action. "Stevenson just did not seem to be able to make any kind of decision," he commented later.[28]

At some point after Stevenson's second defeat, Kennedy decided that he would try himself to be the Democratic presidential nominee in 1960. This effort would preoccupy him and his brother from then until the 1960 election.

In the course of seeking the presidency, Kennedy confronted three clusters of issues that would become central concerns for him after being elected and that would bear critically on his management of the missile crisis. Their catchwords were "the strategic balance," "European security," and "the Third World."

"Strategic balance" referred to the relationship between the U.S. and Soviet nuclear arsenals.[29] The years between Hiroshima and Kennedy's swearing-in as President saw dizzying advances in nuclear weapons and related military technologies. Having cracked the secret of making bombs based on the power of nuclear fission, scientists and engineers in both the West and the Soviet Union turned successfully to exploiting the vastly greater potential energy of nuclear fusion. The blast of an atomic bomb, a fission weapon, had been calculated in kilotons, each kiloton equivalent to 1,000 tons of TNT. The blast of a hydrogen bomb, a fusion weapon, was calculated in megatons, each equivalent to 1,000 kilotons, or a million tons of TNT.

Before long, both Soviet and Western weapons laboratories became able to mass-produce both fission and fusion weapons and to increase explosive power while reducing both size and weight. The bombs used against Hiroshima and Nagasaki had been huge, hand-crafted devices, so delicate and so difficult to engineer that it had been hard to imagine their ever existing in large numbers. The Hiroshima bomb had been 10 feet long, weighed almost 5 tons, and, to be loaded in an airplane and armed to explode, required a crew of experts, working several days. By the time of the missile crisis, bombs twenty times more powerful were 3 feet long, shaped like ordinary TNT bombs, and easily slapped onto the wing of a ground-based or carrier-based fighter-bomber.[30]

During the 1950s both camps increased the range, speed, and accuracy with which they could deliver nuclear weapons. In 1957 Soviet Sputnik rockets put objects in space orbit, demonstrating an apparent capability for intercontinental ballistic missiles (ICBMs), which would be in flight only about thirty minutes and against which there was no known defense.

The Sputnik flights sparked panicky debate in the United States about an impending "missile gap." Democrats, with Kennedy one of the leaders, charged that Eisenhower administration penny-pinching had allowed the Soviets to gain a lead that not only compromised containment but also possibly jeopardized national survival.

To appease critics, the Eisenhower administration stepped up work on high-thrust rockets and large-capacity reentry vehicles. It was for the same purpose and also to placate allies that the administration arranged to place intermediate-range ballistic missiles (IRBMs) abroad—Thors in Britain, Jupiters in Italy and Turkey. By the time of the 1960 presidential election, the Eisenhower administration had moved far along in development of several models of ICBM, with a solid-fueled Minuteman the most promising. It was also well along on Polaris, a missile of intermediate range but classified as an SLBM (submarine-launched ballistic missile) rather than an IRBM.

As of 1960 the actual nuclear arsenal of the United States was enormous. That of the Soviet Union, according to calculations by the U.S. intelligence community, was smaller but also huge. With competition spurred by the Sputniks, the arsenals grew almost by the day. When Eisenhower yielded the presidency to Kennedy, the United States would have around 18,000 nuclear weapons. The most powerful were 10-megaton bombs carried by intercontinental bombers (B-52s). The least powerful were tactical weapons that could be fired from 8-inch guns or even from jeep-mounted mortars. The gross yield of all these weapons probably equaled one million times that of the bomb that had obliterated Hiroshima, dry roasted most of its 85,000 people, and irradiated tens of thousands more. Though U.S. intelligence analysts doubted that the total Soviet arsenal yet matched America's, they had no question that the Soviets, too, possessed what critics already decried as "overkill." To generals and admirals who talked of nuclear victory over the Soviet Union, President Eisenhower, according to notes of one White House meeting, "expressed his concern that there just might be nothing left of the Northern Hemisphere."[31]

The rationale for continuing to accumulate new and improved nuclear weapons resided in another watchword of the Cold War: "second strike." During the 1950s some of the best minds in the world tried to untangle the logic of using nuclear weapons to defend territory despite the likelihood that their actual use would obliterate the territory and be suicidal for the defender. One early insight was that a nuclear arsenal might not achieve any deterrent effect—indeed, might encourage both aggression and nuclear war—if it could be destroyed in a disarming first strike, for a state might be tempted to rid itself at once of resistance to its aggression and any danger of its own annihilation. It followed that a nuclear arsenal served as an effective deterrent if so configured that significant forces would survive any attempt at a disarming first strike. This "second strike" capability would guarantee the attacker's devastation, no matter what.

From the concept of second strike came arguments for large and diversified nuclear forces and for comparatively invulnerable nuclear weapons-delivery systems. Hence came routines under which the U.S. Strategic Air Command, when put on alert, as in October 1962, would keep approximately 180 bombers in the air at all times. Fully loaded with thermonuclear bombs, these bombers would fly to a preassigned line a certain distance from the Soviet Union and then, unless ordered to proceed, would turn around and fly back. (Two of the decade's biggest movies, *Fail Safe* and *Dr. Strangelove*, end with such a plane not turning back.) Hence came also a crash effort to produce nuclear-powered submarines able to carry and fire SLBMs. Moving silently near the ocean floor, they probably could not be targeted for a disarming first strike. Hence, too, came programs for putting ground-based missiles in underground silos, surrounded by thick concrete, where they would be vulnerable only to enemy missiles of extraordinary power and accuracy.

On the missile crisis tapes, the language of nuclear strategic debates rarely appears. Kennedy and many of those around him had, however, steeped themselves in those debates. The inherent dilemmas that many had studied but that no one had resolved can be heard in insistent undertone in what they said to each other during the Cuban crisis. "Do they really believe that they can cow us into not using our nuclear weapons?" they are often asking implicitly about the Soviets. "Are we willing to take actions that could set in train a nuclear war?" they are continually asking of themselves. And one cannot fully comprehend their discussions without awareness of these unspoken questions and of their perception that hundreds of millions of lives hung on the answers.

Though there was evident public support for racing the Russians in building missiles and accumulating nuclear weapons, there was also evident public enthusiasm for possibly turning the arms race around. During the mid-1950s the public learned that radioactive fallout from nuclear weapons tests could affect areas far from the test sites. Strontium-90 generated by tests in Nevada showed up in milk in New Jersey. *Newsweek* in 1957 devoted a special section to "this insidiously invisible powder" of which "a concentrated teaspoonful could kill 30 million people."[32] All over the country, schoolchildren had already become accustomed to crouching under desks or running for fallout shelters in nuclear-attack drills. Pressure from scientists and concerned parents caused the Eisenhower administration to enter negotiations with the Soviets about a possible test-ban treaty. At the end of Eisenhower's presidency, these negotiations had gone far enough to offer at least faint promise of an agreement that might conceivably be a first step toward slowing the nuclear arms competition.

American public attitudes toward nuclear weapons loom large in the background of the missile crisis. These attitudes were clearly ambivalent. The public wanted the United States to be number one in nuclear weapons as in other spheres. Kennedy struck fire with audiences during the 1960 campaign by declaring: "Our defense policy can be summed up in one word: first. I do not mean first but. I do not mean first when. I do not mean first if. I mean first, period."[33] At the same time, there was a sense of despair, probably best caught in the hugely popular 1959 film *On the Beach*. Based on a best-selling novel by Nevil Shute, directed by Stanley Kramer, the film starred Gregory Peck as an American submarine commander. Peck's boat surfaces in Australia after a U.S.-Soviet nuclear war. There is no communication with the rest of the planet. The Australians understand that they are doomed by a slowly approaching radioactive cloud. No one can explain the war. People line up for suicide pills. Peck sails his submarine back to the California coast to see if anything survives. Nothing does. What seemed a sign of life turns out to be an empty Coca-Cola bottle dangling among telephone wires.

The second key issue complex—European security—linked inseparably with the strategic balance. The United States had become engaged in the Cold War primarily from concern lest the Soviet Union expand into Western Europe. Increased concern, fueled by evidence of the Soviet arms buildup and especially by the Korean War, caused the United States in the 1950s to station American military forces in Europe and to press successfully for West German membership in NATO and for West Germany to provide troops and other forces for NATO.

Always anxious as to whether the Americans would actually live up to their promises of military support, given the history of the two world wars, Europeans became newly nervous as they observed the accelerating nuclear arms race. On the one hand, they feared that the Americans would decide to save themselves and let Europe go—would refuse, as the phrase went, to risk Chicago for Bonn. On the other hand, Europeans feared that the United States might either take some rash action that would precipitate a Soviet attack on Europe or, trying to protect the American homeland while at the same time sticking by the commitment to Europe, would make a war for the people of Europe a nonnuclear war, the result of which would be a replay of World War II. While Americans made their calculations chiefly about future wars, Europeans remembered the tens of millions lost between 1914 and 1945. For many of them, a one in one thousand chance of a nuclear war that would kill 500 million looked better than a one in one hundred chance of a war that killed only 50 million.

For Europeans, the Suez crisis of 1956 provided the strongest evidence that the United States might put its own national and global interests ahead of the interests of its NATO allies. This crisis, which would be cited repeatedly in missile crisis debates, originated with Egypt's nationalization of the Suez Canal. Ignoring advice to the contrary from Eisenhower, the British and French conspired with the Israelis and commenced military operations that surprised Washington no less than Cairo. Through ruthless use of diplomatic and economic pressure, Eisenhower forced the British and French to desist. Meanwhile, the Soviets sent tanks into Hungary to suppress a rebellion that had briefly offered promise of that country's liberation from tight Soviet control. References to "Suez-Hungary" in missile crisis debates implied that the Soviets might use a crisis over Cuba to achieve an objective somewhere else, possibly in Berlin. For Europeans, "Suez" stood for the moment when they had been shocked into awareness of how much inferior in power they were to the United States, and how dependent on that power.

From that time onward, the U.S. government had increasing difficulty coping with the question of how credibly to assure Europeans that it would actually defend them and would do so without bringing on their ruin. As the Soviets acquired more and more capacity for attacking the continental United States, Americans searched for strategies that would continue to reassure Europeans but also reduce the risk of nuclear cataclysm. For the Eisenhower administration, NATO ground forces constituted a trip wire. If the Soviets moved against them, the next event would be a U.S. nuclear strike on the Soviet Union. Especially after the Sputnik shots, Americans cast about for possible intermediate steps, such as a period of nonnuclear combat or of use only of "tactical" nuclear weapons. Under the label "flexible response," the introduction of plans for such intermediate stages would be a central element in the Kennedy administration's revamping of U.S. strategic planning.

At the same time, U.S. officials remained sensitive to European concerns and eager to allay them. General Lauris Norstad, who commanded NATO forces at the end of the Eisenhower administration and well into the Kennedy administration, proposed creation of a European nuclear force, the object being to assure Europeans—and caution the Russians—that a Soviet attack on Europe could bring nuclear retaliation regardless of American concern about the safety of the continental United States. Variants of this idea were to be debated throughout the Kennedy administration.

The U.S. positioning of IRBMs in Britain, Italy, and Turkey was part of this effort to allay European fears of being left in the lurch. But so fast was the evolution both of missile technology and of thinking about nuclear weapons that the Thors and Jupiters were to seem obsolete before they became operational. In part, this was because more accurate, longer-range missiles came along. In larger part, it was because of "second strike" reasoning. Maxwell Taylor had become Chief of Staff of the Army after his Korean tour. He had been a dissenter within the Eisenhower administration, criticizing overreliance on strategic nuclear weapons. After retiring in 1959 he made his dissent public in a long essay, *The Uncertain Trumpet*, a book that caught Kennedy's attention. In this book Taylor described the Jupiter missiles as "a sterile asset" because, being "fixed and without mobility," they became "stationary bulls-eyes."[34] After the British had arranged for the Thors to be replaced by less vulnerable systems, members of the Kennedy administration would discuss among themselves removing the Jupiters from Italy and Turkey and perhaps replacing them with Mediterranean-based Polaris SLBMs. But Norstad and the Turks themselves counseled against such action. After Kennedy's June 1961 confrontation with Khrushchev, the issue subsided. The Jupiters would go in, under the 1959 agreements, at least until something better was arranged. During the missile crisis analogies would often be pressed between U.S. IRBMs in Turkey and Soviet IRBMs in Cuba.

From the late 1950s into the early 1960s, the key pressure point testing the firmness of American guarantees to Europe was, as early in the Cold War, Berlin. Stalin's successor, Nikita Khrushchev, threatened in 1958 to sign a separate peace treaty with East Germany, turn over to the East Germans control of Berlin, and declare that, so far as he was concerned, Westerners no longer had any legal rights within the city. Meeting unbending opposition from Eisenhower, Khrushchev postponed action. He revived the threat during 1960, then let it be known that he would hold off action until the United States had a new President. Kennedy would therefore take office under warning that difficulties over Berlin, possibly a crisis, loomed ahead.

The term "Third World" came into use to describe those nations that had not aligned themselves with either the Soviet Union or the West. Since most were comparatively poor and a number were new nations, previously European colonies, "Third World" often applied to nations that were aligned but that happened to be poor—as, for example, those in Latin America.

The so-called Third World had by 1960 become a major theater of East-West competition. Khrushchev spoke of sponsoring "wars of national liberation." The Eisenhower administration had countered with modest programs of economic aid for non-Communist states and, on occasion, with covert action aimed at overturning regimes believed to be aligning themselves with the Soviets. At the same time that they took the administration to task for the "missile gap," Democrats criticized the scale and direction of its competition for the Third World.

This criticism became stronger and attracted wider attention within the United States as a result of several developments late in the 1950s. One was a civil war in the former Belgian Congo, where one faction sought and obtained Soviet aid while others obtained U.S. aid. Though the Soviet-backed faction lost, the contest went on for some time, and the durability of the victory by the American-backed faction remained in doubt. A second development was a civil war of sorts in the landlocked kingdom of Laos. Because the Communist North Vietnamese supported the Pathet Lao faction and the Soviets airlifted some supplies to the Pathet Lao, the contest was interpreted in the United States as one in which Khrushchev aimed at winning one of his wars of national liberation.

A third development, of signal importance for understanding the debates recorded here, was the revolution in Cuba.[35] It originated with a relatively small band of guerrillas operating from mountain bases in eastern Cuba. The existing Cuban government, headed by Fulgencio Batista, had become more and more corrupt, partly as a result of alliances with American gangsters who operated casinos in Havana. Whatever popular support Batista had once possessed he lost. Though his regime had been generally incompetent, his police had been relatively successful in rooting out all organized opposition other than that of the guerrillas and of underground factions such as the Cuban Communist

Party. The result was that the Cuban populace had no one to whom to turn as an alternative to Batista other than the flamboyant guerrilla leader, Fidel Castro.

When Batista's regime collapsed at the very end of 1958, Castro easily took control of Havana. At the time, many Cubans and many Americans looked upon Castro as essentially a radical reformer but not necessarily either anti-American or pro-Soviet. Some of the most prominent American news correspondents in Cuba encouraged such a view. As a result, for a year or more Castro had some support in the United States. At one point he gave a talk at Harvard University, where he was welcomed by the then dean, McGeorge Bundy, and applauded by a throng of faculty and students.

By mid-1959, if not earlier, U.S. feeling toward Castro had cooled. He was not only expropriating American property without compensation; he was also taking property from and jailing Cubans who criticized him. He had developed a working alliance with the now largely aboveground Communist Party, and the very long speeches to which he was prone became increasingly critical of the United States. During the following year he began openly to align himself with the Soviet Union and to accept Soviet aid. The Eisenhower administration retaliated with economic sanctions. American ports, particularly in Florida, received streams of refugees, mostly members of the middle class and intellectuals whom Castro had either dispossessed or silenced. Castro's Cuba came increasingly to be characterized in the United States as a base for Communist subversion in the hemisphere.

Latin Americans, long envious of the extent of U.S. support for and attention to Europe, clamored for aid from Washington to help them combat Cuban propaganda and avoid acquiring Castros of their own. The Rio Treaty of 1947 had set a precedent for the North Atlantic Treaty. It committed the United States and other independent states of the Americas to one-for-all, all-for-one mutual defense, coordinated through an Organization of American States (OAS). Subsequently, in the global Cold War, the United States had seemed to forget about the Western Hemisphere. The success of Castro in Cuba revived Washington's interest in the Americas. It made Latin American nations honorary members of the Third World.

The emergence of the loosely defined Third World as a major arena of East-West competition revived some conditions of the early Cold War. Back then, many Americans had seen the contest with the Soviets as something like a holy war. In 1950 Truman's advisers composed a statement of basic U.S. national security policy—number 68 in a series of National Security Council papers; hence, NSC 68. Formally endorsed by Truman, this document pro-

nounced the issues of the Cold War to be "momentous, involving the fulfillment or destruction not only of this Republic but of civilization itself" and
declared the Cold War to be "in fact a real war in which the survival of the
free world is at stake."[36] (The chief drafters of NSC 68 were Secretary of State
Dean G. Acheson and the chief of his Policy Planning Staff, Paul H. Nitze, both
of whom would be advisers to Kennedy during the missile crisis.) A decade of
a nuclear arms race and other experiences had produced a calmer outlook,
reflected by Kennedy in his inaugural address, when he spoke of sounding a
trumpet "not as a call to battle . . . but a call to bear the burdens of a long
twilight struggle."

With regard to the Third World, American rhetoric could return to the level
of the era of NSC 68. Kennedy devoted three paragraphs of his inaugural
address to "those new states whom we welcome to the ranks of the free," to
"those peoples in the huts and villages of half the globe struggling to break
the bonds of mass misery," and to "our sister republics south of our border."
To the last he offered "a new alliance for progress—to assist free men and free
governments in casting off the chains of poverty." He supplemented that offer
with a vow "to oppose aggression or subversion anywhere in the Americas."
The Third World seemed at the time to be a theater for replaying "containment." The risk that the Congo or Laos or Cuba would become the tinderbox
for a nuclear war seemed small—until October 1962.

Kennedy won the Democratic nomination in July 1960 and went on to win
the presidency in November. Four facts about that campaign year testify to
peculiarities of the period and illuminate the crisis that occurred less than two
years later. First, both Kennedy and his opponent, Vice President Richard
Nixon, were in their forties. As Kennedy would say in his inaugural, the torch
had passed to a new generation. Truman, Eisenhower, and those around them
had been molded by the Progressive Era, World War I, and the 1920s. For
Kennedy and Nixon alike, remembered history began with the 1930s and World
War II. Second, Kennedy won nomination and election despite strong opposition on the ground of his being a Roman Catholic. His success indicated the
ebbing strength of the religious bigotry that had previously been a strong strain
in American culture. Third, Kennedy's thin margin of success over Nixon—
fewer than 120,000 votes out of more than 68 million—was widely attributed
to his successful use of television, particularly in face-to-face debates staged by
the networks. The 1960 election helped to seal the primacy of television as the
key medium of communication between Presidents and would-be Presidents
and the public.

Lastly, and most importantly for the context of the missile crisis, the 1960 election was a referendum on nuances of the Cold War. Neither candidate talked about much else. When Kennedy promised pocketbook benefits, he did so on the ground that faster economic growth would enable the United States to compete more successfully with the Soviet Union, to demonstrate the superiority of capitalism over Communism, and to prevail in the arms race. Kennedy and Nixon vied to prove which would be better able to stand up against Khrushchev. For example, Kennedy (or at least his campaign staff) attacked Nixon and the administration of which he was part for failing to support exile "freedom fighters" seeking to return to Cuba and overturn Fidel Castro. At the same time, Kennedy and Nixon vied for the mantle of prudent guardian of nuclear peace. Both men called insistently for somehow limiting what Kennedy would describe in his inaugural as "the steady spread of the deadly atom."

Kennedy's inauguration on January 20, 1961, can be seen as portending the crisis recorded in this book. On the preceding day, Washington was hit with one of the heaviest snowfalls in its history. The only surface traces of highways leading into the city were columns of abandoned cars and trucks. But inauguration morning, though still more than freezing cold, came with glittering sunshine. Not long before, the nation had heard from Eisenhower a gloomy farewell warning, including a caution about a "military-industrial complex" emerging in control of society. Now people saw on television the new President, young, topcoatless, bareheaded, asserting that energy, faith, and devotion "will light our country and all who serve it—and the glow from that fire can truly light the world."

By that day, Kennedy had assembled most of the circle that would surround him during the missile crisis. Despite predictable outrage and ridicule, he made his 35-year-old brother Bobby Attorney General. He brought into the White House as all-purpose aide and chief speechwriter his longtime Capitol Hill assistant Theodore Sorensen. Even younger than Robert Kennedy, Sorensen was a Nebraska liberal, originally interested only in domestic issues. He had developed such rapport with Kennedy that he could speak as well as write in Kennedy's natural cadences.

Most of the others were comparative strangers to Kennedy at the beginning of his administration. Kennedy complained to his transition adviser, Richard Neustadt, "I don't know any people. I only know voters."[37] To complement Sorensen, Kennedy picked as staff aide for National Security Affairs Harvard dean McGeorge Bundy. Two years younger than Kennedy, Bundy had been an academic star at Yale, served in the Navy in the European theater during World

War II, and afterward coauthored a book with Henry L. Stimson, who had been Roosevelt's (and William Howard Taft's) Secretary of War and Herbert Hoover's Secretary of State. Bundy's bloodline was Republican, and he had done campaign work for Republican candidates in both national and state elections. He and Kennedy had become acquainted after Kennedy was elected to the Harvard Board of Overseers in 1956. They matched each other in quickness of mind and taste for irony, and Kennedy gambled that they would work well together in the intimacy of the White House.

Kennedy asked Robert Lovett to take a Cabinet post, but Lovett pleaded ill health. He did, however, nominate the men whom Kennedy eventually chose as Secretary of State and Secretary of Defense, Rusk and McNamara.

Kennedy had known that he did not want Stevenson as Secretary of State. Not only had he and his brother developed qualms about Stevenson during the 1956 campaign; both were angry at Stevenson for having taken himself out of the 1960 race but then allowed the anti-Kennedy left, led by Eleanor Roosevelt, to try to draft him. Kennedy used flattery to induce Stevenson to accept the post of ambassador to the UN. Kennedy's own preference for State was Senator J. William Fulbright of Arkansas, a Rhodes Scholar and former university president, with whom Kennedy had been close on Capitol Hill, but Fulbright's advocacy of racial segregation made him too vulnerable. So Kennedy turned to the stranger suggested by Lovett, and Rusk, who had been president of the Rockefeller Foundation since leaving the State Department in 1953, accepted without condition.

McNamara, Lovett's nominee for Defense, was president of the Ford Motor Company, where he had gone after World War II. At Ford he had achieved several design and production successes and had stanched losses due to spectacular failure of the Edsel. Though he was a nonconformist among Ford executives, living in Ann Arbor instead of Grosse Pointe and skiing instead of golfing, McNamara had lived in a cocooned, nonpolitical world. He had become attuned to the Cold War, he testified in 1961, by reading some quotations from Stalin published in *Foreign Affairs* in 1949. The Korean War intruded on his life by disrupting Ford's production schedule. His only known public allusion to McCarthyism was elliptical and occurred a year after McCarthy's censure. Overriding objections from company headquarters, McNamara spoke at the University of Alabama, condemning the current "grave pressure to conformity." When Kennedy interviewed him, liked him, and offered him a Cabinet post, McNamara not only hesitated but, unlike Rusk, set conditions. Chiefly, McNamara asked for a guarantee that he would control appointments in his department. Though surprised, Kennedy acceded.[38]

For Secretary of the Treasury, Kennedy chose C. Douglas Dillon, who had been a fellow Harvard Overseer. The son of a financier who had been as much a buccaneer as Joe Kennedy, Dillon had headed his father's firm, Dillon Read. Though thirty-two at the time of Pearl Harbor, he had become a Navy flier and won an Air Medal in the Southwest Pacific. He had served Eisenhower in various diplomatic posts, ending up as Under Secretary of State. His being an unregenerate Republican was an asset because it offered reassurance to the financial community and also, more broadly, symbolized continuity. Kennedy hesitated only because his father expressed skepticism as to whether Dillon really understood money. What probably tipped the scale was Dillon's evident fit with the likes of Bundy and McNamara. Both Dillon and Bundy had gone to the exclusive Groton preparatory school, where school legend had it that the headmaster's reports on Dillon always said "Can do better," even when Dillon's grades were A-pluses.

On the day before inauguration, Kennedy and his prospective national security team met with Eisenhower and members of the outgoing administration. Though Eisenhower had deliberately built an image as an aloof, grandfatherly President who exercised authority reluctantly and only when necessary, and though he had aged in office, no one long in his company failed to see the steeliness, shrewdness, and sheer brain power that had made him earlier the most effective commander of allied armies in the entirety of history. Kennedy and his entourage went away from this meeting having heard from Eisenhower warnings that war could be ignited in any of a number of places around the globe, especially Berlin. Kennedy said to his brother afterward that he was shaken by the "equanimity" with which Eisenhower spoke of the nuclear arsenal.[39]

However much they might discount voices from the past, Kennedy and the others could not ignore what they heard from Eisenhower. Eisenhower's views would continue to carry weight with a large part of the public, and the new administration would often need his support or at least his silence. During the missile crisis, Kennedy would keep in regular touch with Eisenhower, sending intelligence data to his farm in Gettysburg, Pennsylvania, and inviting his counsel. And readers of these tape transcripts should bear in mind that an often unspoken question in Kennedy's mind regarding recommendations before him must have been, "If I do this, will General Eisenhower back me?"

The first crisis of the Kennedy administration concerned Cuba. It was the Bay of Pigs affair.[40] When Kennedy had charged that the Eisenhower administration was doing far too little for Cuban exile "freedom fighters," he had done so in ignorance that the Central Intelligence Agency, with active encouragement from Vice President Nixon, was arming and training Cuban exiles for an effort to unseat Castro. (Nixon never believed that Kennedy did not know this; he died convinced that Democrats in the CIA had told Kennedy what was afoot and that Kennedy had taken advantage of Nixon's being honor bound to guard the secret.) After being elected, Kennedy received a briefing on the plan. After becoming President, he learned that the plan had been expanded. Originally envisioning only establishment of a guerrilla base in the Cuban highlands, it now called for a brigade-size amphibious landing and a march toward Havana in expectation of internal uprisings.

Kennedy approved the expanded CIA plan, but with misgivings. The Alliance for Progress announced in his inaugural address aimed at helping non-Marxists gain the initiative in Latin American reform movements. He feared that evident U.S. intervention in Cuba would revive denunciation of Yankee imperialism and frustrate the Alliance. He also feared that U.S. military engagement in Cuba might encourage Khrushchev to make a move somewhere else, perhaps against Laos or Berlin. The Director of Central Intelligence, Allen Dulles, had, however, an impressive reputation as an engineer of covert action. The actual man in charge was Richard Bissell, whom Kennedy knew as creator and manager of the program for U-2 reconnaissance, and with whom Bundy had studied economics as an undergraduate at Yale. After repeatedly saying to Dulles and Bissell that he wanted the noise level kept down and that he would in no circumstances commit U.S. military forces, Kennedy gave a final go-ahead.

On April 17, 1961, 1,400 Cubans arrived off the south coast of Cuba and embarked in small boats for the nearby beach around the Bay of Pigs. Everything that could go wrong had already started to go wrong. B-26 aircraft that had bombed Cuban airfields landed in Miami, with the pilots claiming to be defectors from the Cuban air force. Their story came apart almost at the moment reporters began to quiz them. They and their planes were identified as belonging to the CIA. In Cuba, they had missed most of their targets. Much of Castro's air strength survived. Its planes strafed the landing parties and sank 2 of the exiles' 4 freighters, including the one with most of their communications equipment. Meanwhile Castro's land forces arrived in the area in overwhelming force. And the rest of Cuba remained free of any uprisings. The 1,000 survivors soon surrendered.

Even though U.S. sponsorship of the landing had been effectively proved by the unmasking of the pilots, Kennedy stuck to the position he had taken earlier. He rejected pleas from Bissell and others that he order U.S. Navy and Air Force units into action to support the exiles. When asked at a press conference, he declined to criticize the CIA. "There's an old saying that victory has a hundred fathers and defeat is an orphan," he replied. "I am the responsible officer of this government." Later he told Dulles and Bissell that, after a decent interval, they would have to leave. "In a parliamentary system I would resign," he said. "In our system the President can't and doesn't. So you . . . must go."[41]

The Bay of Pigs affair had many consequences important for the subsequent missile crisis. First of all, it damaged severely Kennedy's standing among groups previously attracted to him by his father's reputation and by the fact that he had not voted to censure McCarthy. Hard-line Cuban exiles never came close to forgiving him. Nor did Americans who were as much old-fashioned nationalists as anti-Communists. For them, Cuba was as American as apple pie. Its being Communist was intolerable. In their eyes, Kennedy was a gutless appeaser. In varying degrees, this was also a common verdict among senior military officers, particularly in the Navy and Air Force, and in the CIA's Clandestine Service. Awareness of anger and contempt carrying over from the Bay of Pigs affair would affect Kennedy and others during the crisis of October 1962.

A second, closely related consequence of the affair was the development within Kennedy's inner circle of personal animus against Castro. Kennedy, and his brother even more, longed for some redeeming opportunity. They organized a new set of covert operations, code-named Mongoose, to stir up trouble in Cuba and, if opportunity offered, to bring down Castro. Some looked to assassination of Castro. The governing directive, issued in November 1961, said that the United States would "help the people of Cuba overthrow the Communist regime from within Cuba and institute a new government with which the United States can live at peace." An update of March 14, 1962, added: "the U.S. will make use of indigenous resources, internal and external, but recognizes that final success will require decisive U.S. military intervention." Under constant badgering from the younger Kennedy, the CIA came up with a number of what veteran intelligence officer Richard Helms later termed "nutty schemes."[42]

Anxious to be ready in case anything came of Mongoose, the President and the Attorney General saw to it that the military services prepared for possible intervention. As a result, the JCS put on a "first priority basis" the drafting of contingency plans. The U.S. Air Force's Tactical Air Command, which had responsibility for providing air support for ground operations, drew up specifications for an air campaign designed to precede amphibious landings. LeMay, as Chief of Staff of the Air Force, approved it. On October 6, 1962, his government agitated by shipments of Soviet arms to Cuba, the Commander-in-Chief of U.S. Forces in the Atlantic (CINCLANT), Admiral Robert L. Dennison, ordered urgent preparations to carry out the landings themselves.[43] Thus, when Kennedy and his advisers considered invasion of Cuba, it was an option that the military services were much better prepared to carry out than might have been the case, absent the earlier Bay of Pigs affair.

The Bay of Pigs affair affected the missile crisis in another way. It made Kennedy sharply aware of shortcomings in his decision-making processes. Kennedy concluded, for one thing, that he should not make decisions about national security issues by relying exclusively on advisers with national security portfolios. Thereafter, he almost always consulted Sorensen and Bobby and sometimes others whose primary loyalty was to him and who would think above all of his interests.

Kennedy also came to recognize that naive brain power did not entirely make up for lack of experience. He had relied on the presumed expertise of Dulles and Bissell. When he took the precaution of checking their plan with the Joint Chiefs of Staff, he had been assured that it had "a fair chance of success." Only through post hoc review did Kennedy discover that Dulles and Bissell had shut out many of their CIA colleagues, thus keeping him from learning that many others in the Agency had had doubts, especially about the premise that the exiles' landing would spark a popular uprising. Only then did he learn that the JCS response had been a dodge to avoid taking issue with the CIA. Among themselves, he was told, the JCS interpreted "fair chance" to mean three-to-one against.

When Kennedy effected the removal of Dulles and Bissell, he replaced Dulles with John McCone. A 58-year-old steel industry executive, McCone had served in the Defense Department during the Truman administration and become head of the Atomic Energy Commission under Eisenhower. Since McCone was a Republican personally close to Eisenhower, Kennedy had no reason to expect personal loyalty. While in the Senate, however, he had observed and applauded the firmness with which McCone controlled the supersecret nuclear weapons bureaucracies and the candor with which he had answered questions about sensitive test-ban issues. He could trust McCone not deliberately to mislead him. Meanwhile, Bundy added some CIA veterans to his White House staff and began in other ways to reach directly into the intelligence community. By the time of the missile crisis, Kennedy and Bundy and others in the circle would have an understanding of intelligence not only far beyond what they had had in 1961 but well beyond that in most subsequent administrations.

Kennedy also made changes in his relationship with the military establishment. The behavior of the JCS regarding the Bay of Pigs affair enraged him. "Those sons-of-bitches with all the fruit salad just sat there nodding, saying it would work," he complained.[44] Kennedy was particularly angry at the JCS Chairman, Army General Lyman Lemnitzer. He added Maxwell Taylor to his White House staff as someone to interpret for him communications from the Chiefs. As soon as Lemnitzer's term ran out, Kennedy made Taylor JCS Chairman. During the missile crisis, Kennedy could know that what he heard about the views of military leaders came from a man whom he had chosen and whom he had calibrated.

The Bay of Pigs affair also had effects on Kennedy's style of decision-making. Afterward, he recognized that he had not only listened to too few advisers but that he had given the issues too little time. Eisenhower, before giving him the public backing that he sorely needed, subjected him to a staff school quiz. "Mr. President," Eisenhower asked, "before you approved this plan did you have everybody in front of you debating the thing so that you could get the pros and cons yourself and then made the decision . . . ?" Kennedy had to confess that he had not. Bundy, whose offer to resign Kennedy rejected, also counseled that he become much more deliberative.[45]

When the missile crisis arrived, Kennedy applied the lessons taught him by the Bay of Pigs affair. From the outset, he assembled a comparatively large circle of advisers, not all of whom were obvious choices. He included Treasury Secretary Dillon. He brought in State Department experts on both the Soviet Union and Latin America. To be sure that knowledge and wisdom from the past were not ignored, he also brought in Dean Acheson, Robert A. Lovett, and John J. McCloy, key figures from the Truman administration. And, as the records in this volume testify, he squeezed from these advisers everything they could say about the options open to him. If there were flaws in Kennedy's decision-making during the missile crisis, they are the exact opposite of those in the Bay of Pigs affair. The reader of these records may conclude that, if anything, he listened to too many people and listened to some of them too long.

Other events of the Kennedy presidency prior to the missile crisis also bore on the deliberations documented here. All during the spring of 1961, both before and after the Bay of Pigs affair, Kennedy dealt with the problem that had headed Eisenhower's agenda during the pre-inaugural conference—Laos. After acquiring some detailed knowledge about that isolated, sparsely settled kingdom, Kennedy concluded that it was not a good place in which to draw a hard and fixed line.

To act on this conclusion without compromising his residual credentials as a hard-line Cold Warrior, Kennedy engaged in sleight of hand. He made tough speeches about stopping the spread of Communism in Southeast Asia, and he deployed warships and troops so as to create an impression that he was prepared to make Laos a theater of war. Subtly in his speeches, and more explicitly in secret communications to Moscow, Kennedy meanwhile indicated that, though he was not prepared publicly to abandon Laos to Communist rule, he would not be adverse to a deal that made Laos neutral, with its pro-Communist faction participating in a coalition government.

Time magazine took Kennedy to task at one point. Predicting that Laos would soon disappear behind an iron curtain, the magazine's editors wrote: "Kennedy declared he would 'pay any price to assure the survival and success of liberty.' But the price in Laos seemed too high."[46] In the end, however, Kennedy got his way. He managed to seem uncompromising while in reality seeking and obtaining an accommodation that averted a genuine crisis.

In June 1961 Kennedy

territory. Khrushchev then triumphantly produced not only wreckage of the plane but the living pilot, Gary Powers. A Soviet SA-2 SAM had shot it down, and Powers had ejected safely instead of taking the cyanide capsule he was supposed to. This U-2 affair destroyed the projected Paris summit. It also made American diplomats thereafter very sensitive about intelligence overflights, a fact that would affect the timing of the missile crisis.[47]

Kennedy had wanted an early meeting with Khrushchev, hoping to resume the progress toward détente that had been broken by the U-2 affair. He jumped at Khrushchev's indication that he, too, wanted such a meeting. As the time for it arrived, however, Kennedy was of two minds about this meeting. He worried, on the one hand, that it might be too soon after the Bay of Pigs affair, and that Khrushchev, thinking him weak, might make impossible demands. On the other hand, he thought that only through a face-to-face encounter could he convince Khrushchev that he was tough but not intransigent. In Vienna Kennedy spent many hours with Khrushchev. He had already, before inauguration, set up a secret channel for personal correspondence. There would eventually be enough material that, when finally released and published in

1996, it filled more than 300 printed pages. But Kennedy's image of Khrushchev was probably shaped by the Vienna meeting more than by anything he later saw on paper or heard from his Soviet experts. Though that image would become more nuanced later, it never entirely ceased to be as Kennedy described it to British Prime Minister Harold Macmillan in a London stopover on the way home. "The President," noted Macmillan, "was completely overwhelmed by the ruthlessness and barbarity of the Russian Chairman. It reminded me in a way of Lord Halifax or Neville Chamberlain trying to hold a conversation with Herr Hitler."[48]

At Vienna Khrushchev revived his earlier threat to sign a separate peace treaty with East Germany and thus to call into question the legitimacy and perhaps the survival of West Berlin. Kennedy did his utmost to convince Khrushchev that his position on Berlin was not comparable to his position on Laos. He said specifically: "Here, we are not talking about Laos . . . if we were to accept the Soviet proposal US commitments would be regarded as a mere scrap of paper. Western Europe is vital to our national security . . . If we were to leave West Berlin, Europe would be abandoned as well . . . We cannot accept that."[49] Kennedy returned to Washington, however, unsure that Khrushchev had absorbed the message, fearful that he had not convinced the Soviet leader that he was not the weakling of the Bay of Pigs affair, and hence anxious about the future.

During the summer of 1961, the possibility of a major Berlin crisis preoccupied the Kennedy administration. Kennedy and his advisers reviewed innumerable proposals and plans, most of which sketched scenarios that ended in nuclear war. The scenarios differed chiefly in the number of intermediate steps envisioned between a Soviet challenge and a presidential order releasing nuclear weapons for operational use. One of the more ingenious, emanating from Harvard economist Thomas C. Schelling, called for replying to a Soviet move against Berlin with a demonstration nuclear drop on a Hiroshima-sized Soviet city.[50]

Applying lessons from the Bay of Pigs affair and acting somewhat as he would in the missile crisis, Kennedy searched widely for advice, insisted on going over and over alternative courses of action, and pressed for imagination to expand the menu. For a July 1961 meeting that Bundy characterized as perhaps the most important yet held, Kennedy called in no fewer than 25 people.[51]

Even though Kennedy meant what he said to Khrushchev about Berlin's being qualitatively different from Laos, his tactics were not altogether unlike those applied to Laos. He and his advisers came gradually to recognize that the most immediate problem for Khrushchev was a huge outflow of the best-educated and most highly skilled East Germans. They simply walked or took a streetcar from East to West Berlin and from there went on to West Germany.

By word and act, Kennedy tried to erase from Khrushchev's mind any doubt that the United States would risk its own existence, if necessary, to protect West Berlin. In a televised address to the nation on July 25, Kennedy said: "we have given our word that an attack upon that city will be regarded as an attack upon us all . . . if war begins, it will have begun in Moscow, not Berlin." He asked for and obtained from Congress additional money and authority to call up reservists. But in his speeches and in diplomatic comm... ...was careful to speak of West Berl... ...simply of B...

...wall with ...area that machine guns and guard ...ing ground. The Berlin Wall would stand for the next 28 years as a grotesque monument of the Cold War.

As the Wall went up, Kennedy and other Western leaders repeated in stronger and stronger language their determination to stand by the people of West Berlin. Neither Kennedy nor any other responsible leader seriously suggested acting to reverse the closing off of East Berlin. Gradually, the atmosphere of crisis lightened. But no one in the West regarded the erection of the Wall as a culmination or even a caesura in the long-building Berlin crisis. It was a common assumption that the Wall was a temporizing device and that Khrushchev would soon resume an effort to take possession of West Berlin. Kennedy administration officials continued to work out elaborate plans for countering possible Soviet moves. They were to be especially surprised by the Cuban crisis because, on its eve, they were seeing indications that another serious Berlin crisis might be about to break.

After the Berlin crisis of 1961 and before the missile crisis, three developments changed the light in which Kennedy and his advisers perceived U.S.-Soviet relations. The first was the complete disappearance of "the missile gap," with the Kennedy administration becoming certain—and advertising to the Soviets—that, far from being at a disadvantage, the United States held an enormous lead in capacity to deliver nuclear weapons at intercontinental range, and in a second strike no less than in a first. The second, which was closely correlated, was a surge within the administration of hope for some kind of détente with the Soviets, which would reduce the danger of nuclear war. The third was a nagging reemergence, in connection with the congressional elections of 1962, of public debate about the role of Cuba in the global Cold War.

From the beginning, there had been doubts about "the missile gap." U-2 photography had never found ICBM launchers in numbers corresponding to Khrushchev's boasts. Because the capabilities of the U-2 remained secret even after the May 1960 affair, Eisenhower could only hint that he had evidence calling into question the "missile gap" thesis. Kennedy and other Democrats paid no attention. Moreover, some insiders supported them. Air Force intelligence estimates discounted U-2 imagery, pointing out that it covered only a fraction of the Soviet Union, noting that Soviet radar had detected every U-2 flight from the first one on, and arguing that the Soviets would therefore base their ICBMs where clouds would ordinarily mask them.

Soon after taking office, Kennedy and his principal aides learned that most of the intelligence community apart from the Air Force doubted the existence of a wide "missile gap." Coping with competing service budgetary claims, the new administration also found itself in need, like its predecessor, of questioning service estimates of the Soviet threat. Hence Kennedy, McNamara, and others increasingly moderated their language about U.S.-Soviet competition in long-range missiles. They did sponsor, and obtain congressional approval for, substantial increases in strategic and other defense programs. They did not, however, agree to anything like the ICBM deployments advocated by the Air Force. LeMay's protégé and successor as head of the Strategic Air Command, General Thomas Power, urged acquiring 10,000 Minuteman ICBMs. White House analysts concluded that a few hundred would be ample. McNamara set a ceiling of 1,000, acknowledging that the extra hundreds would go primarily to appeasing Air Force friends on Capitol Hill.

From 1957 on, the CIA had attempted to top its accomplishments with the U-2 by putting up a satellite that would take pictures of the Soviet Union from space. This effort, code-named CORONA, suffered 13 successive failures. In the summer of 1961 it finally scored the first of what would be an extraordinary series of successes. The very first imagery recovered from a CORONA reentry vehicle provided more photographic coverage of a greater area than had all the U-2 flights combined. Though it showed the Soviets hard at work on new versions of an ICBM, it provided convincing evidence that their existing ICBM arsenal numbered at most six.

By coincidence, the CIA's human intelligence collectors had meanwhile acquired a prime agent high in the Soviet military bureaucracy. Colonel Oleg Penkovsky smuggled to them microfilm of numerous Soviet Defense Ministry documents. He also told his handlers in great detail about what he heard and saw by virtue of his status as a senior officer well connected not only in the Strategic Rocket Forces but in Soviet military intelligence.[52] All this jibed neatly with what appeared in U-2 and CORONA imagery.

Although the intelligence community phrased its conclusions in characteristically guarded language, these conclusions were much more reassuring than in the past. A year later, in July 1962, a National Intelligence Esti would say: "By the mid-1960's, the USSR will h missile capability to deliver nucle Soviets could sti

in Moscow with- public said: "The fact is that this nation force of such power that an enemy move which brought into play would be an act of self-destruction . . . Our forces are so deployed and protected that a sneak attack could not effectively disarm us . . . In short, we have a second strike capability which is at least as extensive as what the Soviets can deliver by striking first."[54]

Armed with this knowledge about the favorable strategic balance, Kennedy and his advisers became modestly hopeful that the Soviets would perceive how far behind they were, calculate how much it would cost them to catch up, and conclude that their best interests would be served by arms-control arrangements that put a stop to or at least braked the nuclear arms race. Just before the missile crisis, Kennedy and Khrushchev exchanged messages about a possible meeting in November, when Khrushchev planned to come to New York for the opening of the UN General Assembly. Kennedy wrote that he thought they might be "within striking distance" of a test-ban agreement, which might be a harbinger of yet greater accomplishments.[55]

Troubling Kennedy also were continuing questions about Cuba. Robert Kennedy, who had learned about the Bay of Pigs plan only at the last moment, expressed concerns immediately afterward lest the fiasco have wider effects on the Cold War. He wrote his brother: "if we don't want Russia to set up missile bases in Cuba, we had better decide now what we are willing to do to stop it."[56] This concern, as well as anger in his brother's behalf, probably had something to do with his zeal in promoting Mongoose. But Khrushchev had long before denied that he had any such intention. He did so again in a private letter to President Kennedy, upbraiding him for having supported the exiles' operation and asserting vehemently that the United States had no cause for trying to unseat Castro. He wrote: "we have stated on many occasions, and I now state again, that our Government does not seek any advantages or privileges in Cuba. We have no bases in Cuba, and we do not intend to establish any."[57]

By early 1962, Kennedy's own feelings about Castro and Cuba seemed to have cooled. At the very beginning of the year, his brother was pushing Mongoose with undiminished energy. The overthrow of Castro had "top priority," Robert Kennedy reportedly told the Mongoose team; "No time, money, effort—or manpower is to be spared."[58] But the operating head of the team, General Edward Lansdale, complained not long afterward that there had actually been no high-level decision for follow-on military intervention. By the beginning of March, Lansdale understood that he was to cut back to a program of limited action not inconsistent with stated U.S. policy, which denied any intention of going beyond isolating Cuba and limiting Cuban influence.[59] At the end of April Kennedy held a meeting—the last of 1962, so far as we know—with Cuban exile leaders who were supposed to have formed a government, had the Bay of Pigs landing succeeded. They went away frustrated, because Kennedy refused either to set up training camps for a new landing attempt or to indicate that he would eventually approve an armed invasion.[60]

The probable reason for Kennedy's lessened interest in Cuba was rising concern about Berlin. In mid-February 1962 he had a difficult conversation with the German ambassador, Wilhelm Grewe. Parts of the memorandum for the record show Kennedy's personal views on the problem of European security, which were frequently central in the missile crisis debates:

> The President stated that the situation which might develop over Berlin deserved serious thought. We wanted to convince the Soviets, in the event of a major confrontation, that the US was prepared to go all out and that this deserved a last thought on their part. No one expected to fight a conventional war in Europe, which we could not do without being overwhelmed . . . if we face a major defeat in Europe, then nuclear weapons will be used, but we must exhaust the full battery of other possibilities before pressing the button . . . The US took this question quite seriously. We felt our survival was tied up with that of Western Europe.[61]

Speaking soon afterward with congressional leaders, Kennedy confessed his puzzlement about Khrushchev. "We are not convinced," he said, "that the Soviets themselves are sure of what course of action they are going to follow . . . We just don't know."[62]

In March 1962 Khrushchev returned to the attack, telling Kennedy in a private communication that, in his view, Berlin had to become a demilitarized free city. State Department experts told the President that they thought Khrushchev had given up hope of negotiating satisfactory terms for Berlin. In July Kennedy received another private letter from Khrushchev, in which the Soviet leader rambled on about possibly replacing Western military forces in Berlin with UN police units. The U.S. ambassador in Moscow and experts in the State Department voiced worry, as did European leaders.[63]

Kennedy answered Khrushchev with public releases. He allowed reporter Stewart Alsop to interview him for a feature article in the *Saturday Evening Post*.

, Defense Minister, Castro's brother, Raul, spent two weeks in Moscow. Not long afterward the CIA reported Soviet freighters steaming for Cuba with what appeared to be military cargo on board, and CIA informants in Cuba relayed numerous reports of military equipment arriving at Cuban ports and moving to interior areas under Soviet guard.[65]

Noting that the reports from informants were scattered and contradictory, CIA analysts offered a cautious judgment that the Soviet shipments were probably surface-to-air air defense missiles (SAMs) and that some of the other equipment consisted of radar and electronic gear associated with such missiles. McCone, the Director of Central Intelligence (DCI), nevertheless began to send Kennedy, Rusk, and others a stream of communications stating his personal opinion that the Soviets might be planning to base medium-range ballistic missiles (MRBMs) in Cuba. He made the point that the longest range Soviet SAMs, the SA-2s, were indistinguishable from MRBMs with a 350-mile range. McCone's telegraphic-style notes on a meeting at the White House on August 23, attended by Kennedy, Rusk, McNamara, Taylor, and Bundy, show early indications of thoughts that would become better articulated when the missile crisis broke:

3. President requested analysis of the danger to the United States and the effect on Latin America of missile installations . . .

4. President raised the question of whether we should make a statement in advance of our position, should the Soviets install missiles and the alternative actions open to us in such event. In the course of the discussion, apparent many in the room related action in Cuba to Soviet actions in Turkey, Greece, Berlin, Far East and elsewhere. McCone questioned value of Jupiter missiles in Turkey and Italy. McNamara agreed they were useless but difficult politically to remove them . . .

5. President raised question of what we should do against Soviet missile sites in Cuba. Could we take them out by air or would a ground offensive be necessary . . .

6. President raised question of what we should do in Cuba if Soviets precipitated a Berlin crisis.[66]

Even if Kennedy felt as much concern about Cuba as McCone's memorandum suggested, that concern was probably short-lived. Two contemporaneous reports dampened whatever residual enthusiasm he might have had for Mongoose, for, independently, a CIA group and an operational group headed by Taylor concluded that there was no real hope of Castro's being overthrown, absent large-scale U.S. military intervention. As for the possibility broached by McCone—that the Soviets were preparing to put surface-to-surface missiles in Cuba—Kennedy learned that U-2 flights over Cuba had discerned nothing except work on SAM sites and emplacements of short-range cruise missiles (or pilotless aircraft) designed for shore defense. Intelligence data thus reinforced the earlier assurances from Khrushchev. And these assurances were repeated by the amiable Soviet ambassador, Anatoly Dobrynin, who spoke with Robert Kennedy and soon afterward with U.S. Ambassador to the UN Adlai Stevenson, saying flatly to each that the Soviet government had no intention whatever of using Cuba as an offensive military base. What Dobrynin said privately was then said publicly out of Moscow by the authoritative official TASS news service.[67]

Kennedy now had reason for wanting to believe what the Russians were saying, for Republicans had begun to charge the administration with looking the other way while the Soviets converted Cuba into a missile base. Probably on the basis of human intelligence reports leaked to or summarized for him by a disgruntled Navy intelligence officer, Republican Senator Kenneth Keating of New York charged on the floor of the Senate that there were "Soviet rocket installations in Cuba."[68] This charge by Keating provoked Kennedy's public declaration that Soviet weaponry in Cuba was all defensive but that, were it to be otherwise, "the gravest issues would arise." Given what he had been told by the CIA and by the Russians themselves, he probably felt confident then that Keating was wrong and that his statement was safe.

With Republicans remaining on the offensive, Kennedy felt obliged to make yet another statement. Keating and others and a number of newspapers talked of military action against Cuba both as a means of preventing its use by the Soviets as a military base and simply as a means of getting rid of Castro. Bundy outlined a rationale for Kennedy to use with the press, commenting early in his memorandum that if the President intended to invade Cuba, he need read no further. In fact Kennedy followed Bundy's cues and apparently did not want to invade, because he said to the press regarding Cuba: "unilateral military intervention on the part of the United States cannot ~ required or justified." Underscoring ~ ~ ever, that if ~ ~

~ ~ for Senate

~ ~ Keating and Republican Senator ~ ~ Indiana, the Senate on September 20 passed by 86 to 1 a resolution authorizing use of force against Cuba "to prevent the creation or use of an externally supported offensive military capability endangering the security of the U.S." On October 10 Keating rose in the Senate to charge that the Soviets were establishing intermediate-range missile bases in Cuba.

Kennedy knew of no intelligence data that warranted the Senate resolution or supported Keating's allegations. He had learned that, in addition to SAMs, the Soviets were sending to Cuba crates containing unassembled IL-28 bombers. These bombers, though capable of carrying nuclear weapons, were being phased out of the Soviet air force as obsolete. In themselves, they were not causes for worry. Moreover—though before evidence came in regarding the IL-28s—the CIA's top analytic group, its Board of National Estimates, produced a Special National Intelligence Estimate. Use of Cuba by the Soviet Union as a base for offensive ballistic missiles, said the Board, "would be incompatible with Soviet practice to date and with Soviet policy as we presently estimate it. It would indicate a far greater willingness to increase the level of risk in US-Soviet relations than the USSR has displayed thus far."[70]

Kennedy not only had reason to feel justified in discounting the Republicans' charges; he also felt quite clearly that he had a right to curb suspected leaks feeding those charges. Recording that he had shown Kennedy photographs of the crates containing IL-28 bombers, McCone noted: "The President requested that such information be withheld at least until after the elections as if the information got into the press, a new and more violent Cuban issue would be injected into the campaign and this would seriously affect his independence of action."[71]

That Kennedy could make such a request of McCone, a Republican, should probably not be taken simply as an instance in which Kennedy let his own partisanship override good judgment. The final phrase, about his "independence of action," may well have had significance only partially related to the particular matter that he and McCone were discussing. A letter from Khrushchev dated September 28 had brought Kennedy potentially ominous news about Berlin. In it Khrushchev said: "the abnormal situation in Berlin should be done away with . . . And under present circumstances we do not see any other way out but to sign a German peace treaty." Moreover, Khrushchev commented angrily on agitation in the United States for action against Cuba. The congressional resolution, he said, "gives ground to draw a conclusion that the U.S. is evidently ready to assume responsibility for unleashing nuclear war." Khrushchev asserted that he would not force the Berlin issue until after the U.S. congressional elections, but he seemed to say that by the second half of November time would have run out.[72]

Other members of the administration were alarmed about Berlin. Defense Secretary McNamara returned from a trip to Europe and said at a press conference that conditions in Berlin were as tense as any since those in Korea during the Korean War. He added bite to the by then well-worn assertion of U.S. interest in Berlin by saying that the United States would "utilize whatever weapons are needed to preserve our vital interests" and then saying: "Quite clearly, we consider access to Berlin a vital interest."[73]

By mid-October Kennedy and members of his circle had reason to expect a crisis. To them, Khrushchev remained a mystifying figure. In early 1962, they knew, Khrushchev had suffered domestic setbacks. He had had to admit to shortfalls in his announced goals for increased food production and, indeed, to raise state-controlled food prices. He had also backed away from previously announced plans to reduce spending on traditional branches of the armed forces in order to strengthen the new Strategic Rocket Forces.[74] This evidence suggested that Khrushchev might need an offsetting foreign policy success. Other evidence suggested that he might not have taken at full value U.S. efforts to demonstrate determination not to yield on Berlin.

Just recently, Khrushchev had granted long interviews to two Americans. In early September he had invited Kennedy's Interior Secretary, Stewart Udall, to visit him at Petsunda, in Georgia. Perhaps assuming that Udall's functions resembled those of interior ministers in Soviet states, who usually had large police and internal security functions, Khrushchev harangued him about Berlin, saying that he intended to put Kennedy in a position in which he would have to settle the Berlin problem: "We will give him a choice—go to war or sign a peace treaty." Delivering his own counterpart to the Gilpatric speech, in his own vernacular, Khrushchev said: "It's been a long time since you could spank us like a little boy—now we can swat your ass." He assured Udall that he would not act until after the U.S. congressional elections. "Then," he said, "we shall see whether you bring us to the brink of war."[75]

More disturbingly, Khrushchev told the poet Robert Frost th
the United States and Western Europe to be w
Tolstoy's legendary comment to
desire is the same

_____nev said to Udall and
_ne really believed that they would prove
_wuown. They had many reasons for fearing that he
_,. but what was uppermost in their minds was Berlin. That the focus of crisis turned out to be Cuba must have come as a shock to all of them, except possibly McCone.

In the Cabinet Room, during the missile crisis, President Kennedy would sit in the center of a long oblong table, tall windows at his back and book alcoves on the wall opposite. The hidden microphones were positioned so as to catch his voice better than those of others. Also, though he would often use a word, then check himself and substitute another, and would frequently leave sentences unfinished, he was usually both precise and clear. On the tapes, his accent and cadence can be recognized by anyone who has ever heard a sound recording of one of his speeches.

Kennedy was, of course, almost two years older than when he took office, promising "to bear any burden." He had the same bush of brown hair, the same calm, ruddy face, the same penetrating blue eyes. In his voice, a listener can hear surviving traces of his earlier personae, even of the 23-year-old author of *Why England Slept.* But the shadows around his eyes had darkened, and the lines there and at the corners of his mouth were more deeply etched. A listener can detect on the tapes some of the wariness induced by the Bay of Pigs experience, the combination of puzzlement and fear induced by Vienna, the Berlin Wall, and other dealings with the Soviets, and, above all, a sense of the responsibility symbolized by the military aides, always within a 90-second hail, who handed off to one another every 8 hours the black vinyl satchel known as "the football," which contained the codes that the President alone had authority to use and which, if used, would unleash a rain of nuclear bombs and missiles.

On the President's right sat the team from the State Department: Secretary Rusk, Under Secretary Ball, and, in due course, Edwin Martin, the Assistant Secretary for American Republics Affairs; U. Alexis Johnson, the Deputy Under Secretary for Political-Military Affairs; and Llewellyn "Tommy" Thompson, who had recently been U.S. Ambassador in Moscow.

Tall, portly, and almost completely bald, Rusk had an impassive face. He resembled distantly a statue of the Buddha. His manner conveyed both authority and insecurity. More experienced than most others at the table, he sometimes spoke as if coaching amateurs. But he also spoke as someone who had never achieved as much independence as some of the others, or as much rapport with the President. Unlike McNamara, he had set no conditions for taking his post. As a result, he had had one unwanted assistant after another pushed on him by the White House. He had recently pulled Martin out of Economic Affairs to take over the American Republics bureau so that Martin could sit on a former White House staffer, Richard Goodwin, sent over to ramrod the Alliance for Progress.[77] Other White House staffers made fun of Rusk for his formality and his reluctance or inability to act as a McNamara-like manager, and Rusk almost certainly knew that this was so.

In the missile crisis debates, Kennedy addresses McNamara as "Bob" and Dillon, Rusk's near contemporary, as "Doug," but Rusk is always "Mr. Secretary," and rarely would others say "Dean." Though Rusk's interventions are often lengthy and appear well organized and well prepared, his soft Georgia accent, with a slight overlay of Oxford drawl, is not always easy to understand, and he often gropes for words.

Ball, by contrast, was more assertive than is always apparent to a reader. His interventions were often well organized—briefs prepared by a skilled litigator—and Ball often spoke with table-thumping emphasis and not a trace of inner uncertainty. But Ball lacked experience comparable to Rusk's, for he had dealt mostly with economic issues. Also, he had the disability of having been, and seeming still, more identified with Stevenson than with Kennedy.

Martin is a minor figure in the debates. So is Alexis Johnson. Thompson, by contrast, is one whom Kennedy continually consults and heeds. He was the one person at the table who had known and studied Khrushchev. About the same age as Rusk, he had grown up on a ranch in Colorado, graduated from the state university, and entered the Foreign Service. He was sent to the Soviet Union in World War II after a rush course in Russian (which he never spoke with the facility of old Russia hands like Kennan). Although he was away from Soviet affairs for much of the time between the end of the war and 1957, when he went back to Moscow as ambassador, he established closer relationships with Soviet leaders than had any of his predecessors, and especially with Khrushchev.[78] When interpreting or predicting Soviet actions, Thompson does not hesitate to contradict anyone, including the President. Nor d~ ~ back from saying what he thinks Kennedy should d~ ~ dry voice is heard on the tapes, one ~~ ~ was paying attention

On th~ ~

~~ger

~~ in human form,

~~ middle, wearing rimless glasses,

~~ny almost any group he joined. On the tapes, ~~ near him keeping impatience barely under control, then ~arging in to catalogue his own points. "Number one . . . number two . . . number three . . . ," he would say, slapping first one bony finger, then another against the palm of his right hand. Though his intensity seldom lightened, associates remembered one occasion when he reached "number six . . ." and laughed at discovering that he was out of fingers.[79]

Unlike Rusk, McNamara had gained confidence from experience in office. (And he had not lacked confidence when he started.) He had won most of his battles in the Pentagon and on Capitol Hill. He was conscious of having the complete trust of the President and respect, if not awe, from all the others who would be in the missile crisis circle. McNamara's voice, in contrast to that of Rusk, was always more forceful than may be evident to someone reading the transcripts but not hearing the actual tapes.

Gilpatric, a studious Wall Street lawyer, commanded respect when he spoke, but rarely spoke. While Taylor entered the discussion frequently, he did so less often as the President's personal friend and former staff aide than as spokesman for the Joint Chiefs. Someone listening to the tapes, unaware of the past relationship between Kennedy and Taylor, might be inclined to discount Taylor's interventions in part because they so often summarize what the chiefs have been saying or what they are likely to say. Also, a slight lisp and a tendency to fumble for words cause Taylor to seem less articulate than many of the others. But the reader should bear in mind that, when Taylor speaks, he conveys to those in the room a sense not only of what the chiefs say but of what they could conceivably say—eventually—to Congress and the public.

Nitze brought to the Pentagon team experience that almost matched Rusk's.[80] A Wall Street financier who had shifted to public service during World War II, Nitze had continued to head the Policy Planning Staff in the State Department during the Korean War. But Nitze made most of his contribution to missile crisis decision-making in small groups working outside the White House, chiefly on Berlin contingencies. He is seldom heard on Kennedy's tapes.

Across the table from the President sat, from his left to his right, his two key assistants, Sorensen and Bundy, Secretary of the Treasury Dillon, the Attorney General, and the Vice President. On the tapes, although Sorensen speaks only occasionally, he is a constant presence because he is usually the last crafter of words that the President is going to voice or include in a letter or cable. Bundy speaks more often but always briefly and crisply. He never offers extended analyses in the manner of Rusk or McNamara. As a rule, the rest of the table quietens for both Sorensen and Bundy, for, except for Robert Kennedy, Sorensen is the person there who best knows the President's mind and habits of thought, while Bundy is the clarifier—the person who frames in precise language the issue that the President must decide. In Sorensen's voice, one can still hear a touch of the onetime University of Nebraska debater; in Bundy's, the patrician intellectual who would cut off fellow professors and finish their sentences in language clearer than their own.

Dillon's speaking style is very much like Kennedy's, though the accent is upper-class New York, faintly reminiscent of Franklin Roosevelt. Like Kennedy, Dillon leaves sentences unfinished if his meaning is clear; he does not use 10 words where 8 will do. And his customary lead-in has no trace of diffidence. He says: "It seems to *me-e*," conveying the impression that he believes it must seem so to anyone.

Robert Kennedy's voice is like his brother's but more crisp, more urgent, more combative. And Lyndon Johnson's is in his small-group style, not in the flat, wooden, somewhat unctuous tones of his public addresses, where the microphone or camera seems to make him self-conscious about having grown up poor, gone to Southwest Texas State Teachers College, and never learned the manners of the Eastern elite. On Kennedy's tapes, one hears the former

Senate majority leader with the legendary capacity for personal persuasion. When the Kennedys are out of the room, Johnson takes command. Sometimes he even asserts himself when one or both are there.

Often, DCI McCone is present. His voice is flat, confident, occasionally opinionated or quarrelsome. Adlai Stevenson occasionally comes down from New York. Mostly, however, he is present by virtue of what he writes or says over the phone. Senators, Congressmen, and service chiefs, including LeMay, make cameo appearances. However, their reactions, and possible reactions around the country, weigh on the minds of Kennedy and his advisers much more frequently than their words acknowledge. For all of their being kept secret by Kennedy and kept under lock and key by the government for almost 35 years, these tapes record the decision-making of a democracy.

TUESDAY, OCTOBER 16

11:50 A.M.

CABINET ROOM

On October 14 a high [...] Strategic A[...]

[...]ted

[...]out U.S. overflights

[...]te delicate ongoing negotiations.

[...]st Soviet experts, including those in McCone's

[...]t McCone wrong. When Soviet surface-to-air missiles (SAMs) [...]e spotted in Cuba at the end of August, McCone pressed harder for U-2 flights, for he interpreted these SAMs as harbingers of offensive surface-to-surface missiles. Rusk's and Bundy's resistance also hardened, for the Soviet SAMs were SA-2s, which had shot down Gary Powers' U-2 in 1960. The shootdown of a Taiwanese U-2 over western China on September 8 added to Rusk's fears. Robert Kennedy, however, weighed in on McCone's side, and McCone finally won compromise approval for the flight that ultimately occurred on October 14.

During October 15, experts at the CIA's National Photographic Interpretation Center (NPIC), in a nondescript building at 5th and K in Washington, pored over photos from the October 14 U-2 flight over Cuba. Seeing images of missiles much longer than SAMs, they leafed through files of photos from the Soviet Union and technical data microfilmed by their Soviet informant Oleg Penkovsky and came up with a perfect match. These were medium-range ballistic missiles (MRBMs) of the SS-4 family. At about 5:30 in the afternoon,

Arthur Lundahl, the head of NPIC, passed the news to CIA headquarters out in Langley, Virginia.[1]

In ignorance of what was in progress at NPIC, McNamara had met that afternoon with the Joint Chiefs of Staff, dozens of lower-level officials, and presidential assistant Bundy. Although McNamara explained that Kennedy had decided not to take any military action against Cuba during the next 3 months, the group reviewed plans for a massive air strike on Cuba and for an invasion. For McNamara and Bundy, it was a contingency plan if Kennedy's September 13 warning was defied. For many of the military officers present, it may have seemed preparation for something actually to happen.

That evening, Bundy and his wife gave a small dinner at their home on Foxhall Road for Charles and Avis Bohlen. Though a veteran Soviet expert, formerly ambassador in Moscow, "Chip" Bohlen was going off to be U.S. Ambassador to France. Called away to the telephone, Bundy heard CIA Deputy Director for Intelligence Ray Cline say cryptically, "Those things we've been worrying about—it looks as though we've really got something." "It was a hell of a secret," Bundy wrote later. Though he considered immediately calling Kennedy, he concluded that a few hours made no difference. The President had been in New York State, speaking for Democratic congressional candidates, and was expected back in Washington in the early hours of the morning. Bundy, as he also wrote later, "decided that a quiet evening and a night of sleep were the best preparation" the President could have for what lay ahead of him. Kennedy never reproached him for the decision.[2]

Bundy brought his news to the private quarters of the White House at about 9:00 A.M. on Tuesday, October 16. In the major morning papers, the President had seen one front-page story about Cuba. The *Washington Post* reported that "Communist sources" were floating a rumor of a possible trade—the West to make concessions on Berlin in return for a slowdown in the Soviet buildup of Cuba. State Department spokesman Lincoln White had denied having seen any such proposal. The *Post*'s front page also carried, and that of the *New York Times* featured, a Boston address by Eisenhower, attacking the Kennedy administration's "dreary foreign record." In his administration, Eisenhower said, "No walls were built. No threatening foreign bases were established."

1. Full details are in Dino A. Brugioni, *Eyeball to Eyeball: The Inside Story of the Cuban Missile Crisis*, ed. Robert F. McCort (New York: Random House, 1991), pp. 187–217.
2. McGeorge Bundy, *Danger and Survival: Choices about the Bomb in the First Fifty Years* (New York: Random House, 1988), pp. 395–396.

Recognizing that Cuba now had to be *his* preoccupation but hoping to be able to think for a time about what to do without also having to think about what to say to reporters, Kennedy instructed Bundy to have his top advisers come to the White House for a secret meeting to begin at 11:45. Then he contacted his brother Robert. Before the meeting began, Kennedy discussed the missiles with Bohlen, who paid a previously scheduled farewell call as he prepared to depart for Paris.

Kennedy was in the Cabinet Room with his 5-year-old daughter, Caroline, when the advisers filed in, accompanied by Arthur Lundahl from NPIC and another CIA expert, Sidney Graybeal. CIA as a whole was represented by Acting Director Marshall Carter. McCone was on the West Coast of his stepson. As Ca

, in west-central Cuba.

Kennedy: Where would that be?

Lundahl: West-central, sir. That's south of [unclear]. I think this [unclear] represents your 3 dots we're talking about. Have you got the [unclear]?

Unidentified: Yes, sir.

Lundahl: The President would like to see those. On site, one of the encampments contains a total of at least 14 canvas-covered missile trailers measuring 67 feet in length, 9 feet in width. The overall length of the trailers plus the towbars is approximately 80 feet. The other encampment contains vehicles and tents but with no missile trailers.

Carter: These are the launchers here. These are missile bases up the [unclear]. In this instance the missile trailer is backing up to the launch point. The launch point of this particular vehicle is here. The missile [unclear] feet long.

Lundahl: The site that you have there contains at least 8 canvas-covered missile trailers. Four deployed probable missile erector-launchers. These are unrevetted.[3] The probable launch positions as indicated are approximately 850 feet, 700 feet, 450 feet, for a total distance of about 2,000 feet.

---

3. An erector-launcher trailer can carry a missile and then be secured in place at a designated launch point. The missile launcher is then raised to the firing angle, and the missile is fired from

In area 2, there are at least 6 canvas-covered missile trailers, about 75 vehicles, about 18 tents. And in area number 3 we have 35 vehicles, 15 large tents, 8 small tents, 7 buildings, and one building under construction. The critical one—do you see what I mean?—is this one.

Carter: There is [unclear] right there, see? The missile trailer is backing up to it at the moment. It's got to be. And the missile trailer is here. Seven more have been enlarged here. Those canvas-covered objects on the trailers were 67 feet long, and there's a small billet between the two of them. The gate on that side of the particular trailer [unclear]. That looks like the most advanced one.

Then the other area is about 5 miles away. There are no launcher-erectors over there, just missiles.

President Kennedy: How far advanced is this?

Lundahl: Sir, we've never seen this kind of an installation before.

President Kennedy: Not even in the Soviet Union?

Lundahl: No, sir. Our last look was when we had TALENT coverage of [3 seconds excised as classified information][4] and we had a 350-mile [range] missile erected just on hard earth with a kind of field exercise going on. But from May of 60 on we have never had any U-2 coverage of the Soviet Union. So we do not know what kind of a practice they would use in connection with—

President Kennedy: How do you know this is a medium-range ballistic missile?

Lundahl: The length, sir.

President Kennedy: The what? The length?

Lundahl: The length of it, yes.

President Kennedy: The length of the missile? Which part? I mean which—

Lundahl: The missile is—

President Kennedy: Which one is that?

Lundahl: This will show it, sir.

President Kennedy: That?

Lundahl: Yes. Mr. Graybeal, our missile man, has some pictures of the equivalent Soviet equipment that has been dragged through the streets of Moscow. That can give you some feel for it, sir.

Graybeal: There are 2 missiles involved. One of them is our [designation]

---

it. An unrevetted site lacks earthworks or fortifications to protect against attack or the blast from the missile.

4. TALENT was a code word for overhead photography. The briefer was probably describing photography of a particular missile test range in the Soviet Union.

SS-3, which is 630-mile [range] and on up to 700. It's 68 feet long. These missiles measure out to be 67 foot long. The other missile, the 1,100 [-mile range] one, is 73 foot long.

The question we have in the photography is the nose itself. If the nose cone is not on that missile and it measures 67 feet—the nose cone would be 4 to 5 feet longer, sir—and with this extra length we could have a missile that'd have a range of 1,100 miles, sir. The missile that was drawn through the Moscow parade was [unclear] from the pictures, but—

President Kennedy: Is this ready to be fired?

Graybeal: No, sir.

President Kennedy: How long have we got? We can't ⁔ before it can be fired?

Graybeal: No, sir. That depends on ¹ for the missile]—how—

President Kennedy: ᴾ

Graybeal: It ⁔

be pacⁱ ⁔ nard.

ᵗⁱⁱe.

ᴶᵗⁱon of nuclear war-

ᴬᵉ President—when can these

ᵉry hard. We can find nothing that would spell ᴵᵐs of any isolated area or unique security in this ᴵ. The mating of the nuclear warhead to the missile from some ᴼᵗher short-range missiles there would take about a couple of hours—to do this.

McNamara: This is not defensed, I believe, at the moment?

Lundahl: Not yet, sir.

McNamara: This is important, as it relates to whether these, today, are ready to fire, Mr. President. It seems almost impossible to me that they would be ready to fire with nuclear warheads on the site without even a fence around it. It may not take long to place them there, to erect a fence. But at least at the moment there is some reason to believe the warheads aren't present and hence they are not ready to fire.

Graybeal: Yes, sir. We do not believe they are ready to fire.

Taylor: However, there is no feeling that they can't fire from this kind of field position very quickly, isn't that true? It's not a question of waiting for extensive concrete pads and that sort of thing.

Graybeal: The unknown factor here, sir, is the degree to which the equipment has been checked out after it's been shipped from the Soviet Union here. It's the readiness of the equipment. If the equipment is checked out, the site has to be accurately surveyed, the position has to be known. Once this is known, then you're talking a matter of hours.

Rusk: Well, could this be an operational site except perhaps for the fact that at this point there are no fences? Could this be operational now?

Graybeal: There is only one missile there, sir, and it's at the actual, apparently, launching area. It would take them—if everything were checked out—it would still take them in the order of 2 to 3 hours before they could get that one missile up and ready to go, sir.

Lundahl: Collateral reports indicated from ground observers that convoys of 50 to 60 of these kinds of Soviet vehicles were moving down into the San Cristóbal area in the first couple of weeks of August. But this is the first time we have been able to watch them on photography, at a location.

Sorensen: You say there is only one missile there?

Graybeal: There are 8 missiles there. One of them is in what appears to be the position from which they're launched, in the horizontal, apparently near an erector to be erected in vertical position.

Rusk: You have to erect one? You mean something has to be built? Or is that something that can be done in a couple of hours?

Graybeal: Mobile piece of equipment, sir. We haven't any specifics yet on this, but here is the way we believe that it could actually be lifted. Something of this nature. Now this would be the erectors, helping to raise the missile from this transporter up into a vertical position on the ground.

McNamara: Am I correct in saying that we have not located any nuclear storage sites with certainty as yet?

This is one of the most important thoughts we face in properly interpreting the readiness of these missiles. It's inconceivable to me that the Soviets would deploy nuclear warheads on an unfenced piece of ground. There must be some storage site there. It should be one of our important objectives, to find that storage site.

Lundahl: May I report, sir, that 2 additional SAC missions were executed yesterday.[5] They were taken to the Washington area last night. They're currently being chemically processed at the Naval Center in Suitland, and they're due to

5. The Strategic Air Command had taken over responsibility from the CIA for flying U-2 missions over Cuba.

reach us at the National PI Center around 8:00 tonight.[6] Both of these missions go from one end of Cuba to the other, one along the north coast and one along the south. So additional data on activities, or these storage sites which we consider critical, may be in our grasp, if we can find them.

McNamara: And is it correct that there is, outside of Havana, an installation that appears to be hardened that might be the type of installation they would use for nuclear warheads, and therefore is a prospective source of such warheads?

Lundahl: Sir, I couldn't put my finger on that. The Joint Atomic F-people[7] may be looking at that and forming a judgment. But from I cannot attest to that.

Carter: There would appear to be little need in there, however, unless it were assoc

Rusk: Don't you have to a

McNamara: Oh, I

of readiness

bet

_ops is

where these

_e storage of warheads.

_cy are now ready to fire, or may

_ours, or even a day or two.

excised as classified information, apparently refer-

_ collection of electronic intelligence.]

.... If new types of radars, or known associated missile-firing _dars or [radars] associated with missile firing, are coming up on that, that might be another indicator of readiness. We know nothing of what those tapes [of electromagnetic emissions] hold, at the moment.

Taylor: When will those be ready? Sometime today?

Lundahl: They're supposed to be in, sir. I think that's right. Isn't it, General Carter?

Carter: Yes, it is. The readout from Sunday should be available now. We have done some—

---

6. The Naval Photographic Intelligence Center in Suitland, Maryland; and the National Photographic Interpretation Center, directed by Lundahl, which was part of the CIA.

7. The Joint Atomic Energy Intelligence Committee (JAEIC) of the U.S. Intelligence Board. The latter was an interagency body of representatives from various government intelligence bureaus. Though not part of the CIA, the Board was under the purview of the Director of Central Intelligence in his capacity as (at least nominal) head of the U.S. intelligence community.

Taylor: Weren't there flights yesterday as well, too?

Carter: Two flights yesterday.

Taylor: You don't have the results from those yet?

Carter: No.

[The room is silent for about 8 seconds.]

President Kennedy: Thank you.

Lundahl: Yes, sir.

President Kennedy: Well, when is there any further flights scheduled?

Lundahl: There are no more scheduled, sir.

President Kennedy: These flights yesterday, I presume, cover the . . .

Bundy: We hope so, sir, because the weather won't have been clear all along the island. So we can't claim that we will have been—certainly we surely do not have up-to-date photographic coverage on the whole island. I should think one of our first questions is to consider whether we should not authorize more flights on the basis of COMOR priorities.[8]

There's a specific question of whether we want a closer and sharper look at this area. That, however, I think should be looked at in the context of the question [of] whether we wish to give tactical warning—any other possible activities.

McNamara: I would recommend, Mr. President, that you authorize such flights as are considered necessary to obtain complete coverage of the island. Now, this seems to be ill-defined. But I purposely define it that way because we're running into cloud cover on some of these flights, and I would suggest that we simply repeat the flight if we have cloud cover and repeat it sufficiently often to obtain the coverage we require.

President Kennedy: Are your thoughts good on that?

Carter: Yes, sir.

McNamara: Now, this is U-2 flying.

Carter: U-2, sir.

McNamara: This specifically excludes the question that Mac [Bundy] raised of low-level flying,[9] which I think we ought to take up later, after our further discussions on these possibilities here.

---

8. The interagency Committee on Overhead Reconnaissance, also a part of the U.S. Intelligence Board. Chaired by James Reber, COMOR set guidelines and priorities for American surveillance overflights of other countries.

9. Low-level reconnaissance overflights went underneath clouds, low and fast, over their targets. These flights were carried out by Air Force or Navy tactical reconnaissance units. In September the CIA had asked McNamara to dispatch low-level overflights over Cuba, but at that time he had declined, preferring to leave the work to the U-2.

Lundahl: I have one additional note, sir, if I may offer it.

Of the collateral information from ground observers as to where these kinds of trailers have gone, we don't have any indications elsewhere on the island of Cuba except for this San Cristóbal area, where we do have coverage. So we have no ground collateral which indicates there might be an equivalent thing going on somewhere else.

President Kennedy: In other words, the only missile base—

Carter: Intermediate-range missile.

President Kennedy: —missile base that we now know about is this one?

Carter: That is correct.

President Kennedy: Is this one or 2? Th

Carter: There's 3 of th

...so that ...has 8 missiles. That'd be 2 ...ze. This one in front of the table is a second ...allation from which we can see 6 missiles. So there are probably 2 more battalions there. The other missiles may be under the tree. The third installation has the tents, but there are no missiles identified anywhere in that area.

President Kennedy: These are the only ones we now know about?

Graybeal: Yes, sir.

Lundahl: Other than those cruise missiles that you're familiar with, those coastal ones. And the surface-to-air missiles.[10]

Unidentified: Any intelligence on that thing?

---

10. The Soviet SAM sites in Cuba were first identified after a U-2 overflight of Cuba on August 29; the White House was briefed about this discovery on August 31. The discoveries prompted the first U.S. warning to the Soviets on September 4 against deploying "offensive weapons." The same U-2 mission revealed another kind of missile site, near Banes, in eastern Cuba, which CIA analysts needed more time to analyze. They finally judged (correctly) that this missile was a cruise missile (more akin to a small unguided jet aircraft, without a ballistic trajectory) with a range of 20–40 nautical miles, apparently designed for coastal defense. President Kennedy was briefed in person about this finding on September 7. See Brugioni, *Eyeball to Eyeball,* pp. 120–127.

President Kennedy was concerned that the nature of this arguably defensive system not be misunderstood, and that news about it not leak out into the ongoing, volatile domestic debate over his response to the Soviet buildup in Cuba. A new code-word classification, PSALM, was thereupon created—with a tightly restricted distribution—for future reports on Soviet deploy-

President Kennedy: Mr. Rusk?

Rusk: Mr. President, this is, of course, a very serious development. It's one that we, all of us, had not really believed the Soviets could carry this far. They seemed to be denying that they were going to establish bases of their own in this hemisphere. This is a Soviet base, essentially, from a Cuban point of view. The Cubans couldn't conflict with it anyhow.

Now, I do think we have to set in motion a chain of events that will eliminate this base. I don't think we can sit still. The question becomes whether we do it by sudden, unannounced strike of some sort or that we build up the crisis to the point where the other side has to consider very seriously about giving in, or even the Cubans themselves take some action on this.

The thing that I'm of course very conscious of is that there is no such thing, I think, as unilateral action by the United States. It's so intimately involved with 42 allies and confrontation in many places that any action that we take will greatly increase the risks of a direct action involving our other alliances and our other forces in other parts of the world.

So I think we have to think very hard about *two* major courses of action as alternatives. One is the quick strike. The point where we make it, that is the overwhelming, overriding necessity to take all the risks that are involved in doing that. I don't think this in itself would require an invasion of Cuba. I think that with or without such an invasion—in other words, if we make it clear that what we're doing is eliminating this particular base or any other such base that is established. We ourselves are not moved to general war. We're simply doing what we said we would do if they took certain action.[11] Or we're going to decide that this is the time to eliminate the Cuban problem by actually eliminating the island.

The *other* would be, if we had a few days from the military point of view, if we have the whole time, then I think that there would be another course of action, a combination of things, that we might wish to consider. First, that we stimulate the OAS procedure immediately for prompt action to make it quite clear that the entire hemisphere considers that the Rio Pact has been violated, and actually what action should we take under the terms of the Rio Pact.[12] The

---

ments in Cuba. A new, even more explicit, public warning against deployment of "offensive weapons" was issued by the White House on September 13.

11. Rusk is apparently referring to the White House's public warnings of September 4 and 13.

12. Organization of American States. The OAS was created after World War II as a collective organization of nations in the Western Hemisphere for several cooperative purposes, including the task of responding (by a two-thirds vote) to aggression from a member or nonmember state,

OAS could constitute itself as an organ of consultation promptly, although maybe it may take 2 or 3 days to get instructions from governments and things of that sort. The OAS could, I suppose, at any moment take action to insist to the Cubans that an OAS inspection team be permitted to come and, itself, look directly at these sites, provide assurances to the hemisphere. That will undoubtedly be turned down, but it will be another step in building up the position.

I think also that we ought to consider getting some word to Castro, perhaps through the Canadian ambassador in Havana or through his r~ the UN. I think perhaps the Canadian amb~~~ ' channel to get to Castro ~ ' long~~ ~

...ptable.

...~~~ ot the Cuban people, ... ~oviet Union and prevent this missile base ...~ operational.

And I think there are certain military actions that we might well want to take straight away. First, to call up highly selected units, no more than 150,000, unless we feel that it's better, more desirable, to go to a general national emergency so that we have complete freedom of action. If we announce, at the time that we announce this development—and I think we do have to announce this development sometime this week—we announce that we are conducting a surveillance of Cuba, over Cuba, and we will enforce our right to do so. We reject the condition of secrecy in this hemisphere in any matters of this sort.

We reinforce our forces in Guantanamo.[13] We reinforce our forces in the southeastern part of the United States—whatever is necessary from the military point of view to be able to give, to deliver, an overwhelming strike at any of these installations, including the SAM sites. And also to take care of any MiGs or bombers that might make a pass at Miami or at the United States. Build up heavy forces, if those are not already in position.

---

including economic or political sanctions. The founding documents were signed in Mexico City in 1945. The Inter-American Treaty of Reciprocal Assistance, signed in Rio de Janeiro in 1947, was usually referred to as the Rio Pact. The OAS, spurred by the United States, had adopted sanctions against Cuba in early 1962.

13. Guantanamo was, and is, a U.S. naval base on the eastern end of Cuba, with American rights secured by a long-term treaty signed in 1903.

Then we would move more openly and vigorously into the guerrilla field and create maximum confusion on the island [of Cuba]. Won't be too squeamish at this point about the overt/covert counterpart of what is being done.[14] We review óur attitude on an alternative Cuban government and get Miró Cardona and his group in, Manuel Ray and his group,[15] and see if they won't get together on a progressive junta that would pretty well combine all principal elements, other than the Batista group, as the leaders of Cuba. And we have them, give them, more of a status—whether we proceed to full recognition or not is something else. But get the Cuban elements highly organized on this matter.

I think also that we need a few days to alert our other allies, for consultation in NATO. I'll assume that we can move on this line, at the same time, to interrupt all air traffic from free-world countries going into Cuba, insist to the Mexicans, the Dutch, that they stop their planes from coming in. Tell the British, and anyone else who's involved at this point, that if they're interested in peace they've got to stop their ships from Cuban trade at this point. In other words, isolate Cuba completely without, at this moment, a forceful blockade.

I think it would be important to consider calling in General [and former President] Eisenhower, giving him a full briefing before a public announcement is made as to the situation and the courses of action which you might determine upon.

But I think that, by and large, there are these two broad alternatives: one, the quick strike; the other, to alert our allies and Mr. Khrushchev that there is an utterly serious crisis in the making here, and that Mr. Khrushchev may not himself really understand that, or believe that, at this point.

I think we'll be facing a situation that could well lead to general war. Now with that we have an obligation to do what has to be done, but to do it in a way that gives everybody a chance to pull away from it before it gets too hard.

---

14. Rusk is referring to debates a few months earlier about how much to expand the existing program of covert action against Cuba, code-named Mongoose.

15. Manuel Ray had fought with Castro against the dictator Fulgencio Batista, had broken with Castro over alignment with Communism, and had organized underground activities against him before escaping to the United States in late 1960. He and his group supported anti-Castro activities but had an uneasy relationship with the CIA because they were identified as wanting "Fidelisma without Fidel [Castro]." Ray, however, had also joined a broad, CIA-supported, anti-Castro coalition, the Cuban Revolutionary Council, led by Dr. José Miró Cardona, a lawyer and former professor at the University of Havana who had helped lead the civil opposition against Batista and been appointed in 1960 as Castro's ambassador to Washington. Miró Cardona grew disillusioned with Castro and became an exile to the U.S. in the winter of 1960–61.

Those are my reactions of this morning, Mr. President. I naturally need to think about this very hard for the next several hours; what I and my colleagues at the State Department can do about it.

McNamara: Mr. President, there are a number of unknowns in this situation I want to comment upon, and, in relation to them, I would like to outline very briefly some possible military alternatives and ask General Taylor to expand upon them.

But before commenting on either the unknowns or outlining som[illegible] alternatives, there are two propositions I would sug[illegible] as foundations for our further thi[illegible] an air strike ag[illegible] they [illegible] *before* the air strike, [illegible] knock them out before they can be [illegible] launched there is almost certain to be chaos in part [illegible] East Coast or the area in a radius of 600 to 1,000 miles from Cuba.

Secondly, I would submit the proposition that any air strike must be directed not solely against the missile sites, but against the missile sites plus the airfields, plus the aircraft which may not be on the airfields but hidden by that time, plus all potential nuclear storage sites. Now this is a fairly extensive air strike. It is not just a strike against the missile sites, and there would be associated with it potential casualties of Cubans—not of U.S. citizens, but potential casualties of Cubans—in, at least in the hundreds, more likely in the low thousands—say two or three thousand. It seems to me that these two propositions should underlie our discussion.

Now, what kinds of military action are we capable of carrying out, and what may be some of the consequences? We could carry out an air strike within a matter of days. We would be ready for the start of such an air strike within a matter of days. If it were absolutely essential, it could be done almost literally within a matter of hours. I believe the [Joint] Chiefs would prefer that it be deferred for a matter of days, but we are prepared for that quickly.

The air strike could continue for a matter of days following the initial day, if necessary. Presumably there would be some political discussions taking place either just before the air strike or both before and during.

In any event, we would be prepared, following the air strike, for an invasion, both by air and by sea. Approximately 7 days after the start of the air strike that would be possible, if the political environment made it desirable or necessary at that time.

Fine. Associated with this air strike undoubtedly should be some degree of mobilization. I would think of the mobilization coming not before the air strike but either concurrently with or somewhat following, say possibly 5 days afterwards, depending upon the possible invasion requirements. The character of the mobilization would be such that it could be carried out in its first phase at least within the limits of the authority granted by Congress. There might have to be a second phase, and then it would require a declaration of a national emergency.

Now, this is, very sketchily, the military capabilities, and I think you may wish to hear General Taylor outline his.

Taylor: We're impressed, Mr. President, with the great importance of getting a strike with all the benefit of surprise, which would mean *ideally* that we would have all the missiles that are in Cuba above ground, where we can take them out. That desire runs counter to the strong point the Secretary made, if the other optimum would be to get every missile before it could become operational. Practically, I think, our knowledge of the timing of the readiness is going to be so difficult that we'll never have the exact, perfect timing. What we'd like to do is to look at this new photography, I think, and take any additional [photographs], and try to get the layout of the targets in as near an optimum position as possible, and then take them out without any warning whatsoever.

That does not preclude, I don't think, Mr. Secretary, some of the things that you've been talking about. It's a little hard to say in terms of time, how much I'm discussing. But we must do a good job the first time we go in there, pushing 100 percent just as far, as closely, as we can with our strike. I'm having all the responsible planners in this afternoon, Mr. President, at 4:00, to talk this out with them and get their best judgment.

I would also mention among the military actions we should take, that once we have destroyed as many of these offensive weapons as possible, we should prevent any more coming in, which means a naval blockade. So I suppose that, also and also, a reinforcement of Guantanamo and evacuation of dependents.

So really, in point of time, I'm thinking in terms of *three* phases.

One, an initial pause of some sort while we get completely ready and get the right posture on the part of the target, so we can do the best job.

Then, virtually concurrently, an air strike against, as the Secretary said, missiles, airfields, and nuclear sites that we know of. At the same time, naval blockade. At the same time, reinforce Guantanamo and evacuate the dependents. I'd then start this continuous reconnaissance, the list that you handed Mr. Carter, continue over Cuba.

Then the decision can be made as we're mobilizing, with the air strike, as to whether we invade or not. I think that's the hardest question militarily in the whole business, and one which we should look at very closely before we get our feet in that deep mud in Cuba.

Rusk: There are one or two other things, Mr. President. [Soviet ~ Minister Andrei] Gromyko asked to see you Thursday [O of some interest to know what he say~ ` be bringing a messa~~ seeing `

...ion has got quite

...ose missiles, want to shoot them

out by aircraft. So I'm not sure that this is

...e precise element, Bob.

McNamara: Well, I would strongly emphasize that I think our time should be based on the assumption it is, Dean. We don't know what kinds of communications the Soviets have with those sites. We don't know what kinds of control they have over the warheads.

If we saw a warhead on the site and we knew that that launcher was capable of launching that warhead, I would, frankly, I would strongly urge against the air attack, to be quite frank about it, because I think the danger to this country in relation to the gain that would accrue would be excessive. This is why I suggest that if we're talking about an air attack I believe we should consider it *only* on the assumption that we can carry it off before these become operational.

President Kennedy: What is the advantage? Must be some major reason for the Russians to set this up. Must be that they're not satisfied with their ICBMs. What'd be the reason that they would . . .

Taylor: What it'd give them is, primarily, it makes the launching base for short-range missiles against the United States to supplement their rather defective ICBM system, for example. That's one reason.

President Kennedy: Of course, I don't see how we could prevent further ones from coming in by submarine. I mean, if we let them blockade the thing, they come in by submarine.

McNamara: Well, I think the only way to prevent them coming in, quite frankly, is to say you'll take them out the moment they come in. You'll take them out, and you'll carry on open surveillance. And you'll have a policy to take them out if they come in.

I think it's really rather unrealistic to think that we could carry out an air attack of the kind we're talking about. We're talking about an air attack of several hundred sorties,[16] because we don't know where these [Soviet] airplanes are.

Bundy: Are you absolutely clear on your premise that an air strike must go to the whole air complex?

McNamara: Well, we are, Mac, because we are fearful of these MiG-21s.[17] We don't know where they are. We don't know what they're capable of. If there are nuclear warheads associated with the launchers, you must assume there will be nuclear warheads associated with aircraft. Even if they are not nuclear warheads associated with aircraft, you must assume that those aircraft have high-explosive potential.

We have a serious air-defense problem. We're not prepared to report to you exactly what the Cuban air force is capable of; but I think we must assume that the Cuban air force is definitely capable of penetrating, in small numbers, our coastal air defense by coming in low over the water. And I would think that we would not dare go in against the missile sites, knock those out, leaving intact Castro's air force, and run the risk that he would use part or all of that air force against our coastal areas—either with or without nuclear weapons. It would be a very heavy price to pay in U.S. lives for the damage we did to Cuba.

Rusk: Still, about why the Soviets are doing this, Mr. McCone suggested some weeks ago that one thing Mr. Khrushchev may have in mind is that he knows that we have a substantial nuclear superiority, but he also knows that we don't really live under fear of his nuclear weapons to the extent that he has to live under fear of ours. Also, we have nuclear weapons nearby, in Turkey and places like that.

President Kennedy: How many weapons do we have in Turkey?

Taylor: We have the Jupiter missiles.

Bundy: We have how many?

McNamara: About 15, I believe it is.

16. A sortie is one mission by one aircraft.

17. The MiG-21 (NATO designation "Fishbed") was a short-range Soviet fighter-interceptor that could, in some configurations, carry a light bombload against nearby targets.

Bundy: I think that's right. I think that's right.

Rusk: But then there are also delivery vehicles that could easily be moved through the air, aircraft and so forth, route them through Turkey. And that Mr. McCone expresses the view that Khrushchev may feel that it's important for us to learn about living under medium-range missiles, and he's doing that to sort of balance that political, psychological flank.

I think also that Berlin is very much involved in this. For the first time, I'm beginning really to wonder whether maybe Mr. Khrushchev is entirely ̶ ̶ ̶ about Berlin. We've already talked about his obsess ̶ ̶ ̶ have to keep our eye on that ̶ ̶ ̶

But they ̶ ̶ ̶

̶ ̶ ̶ making a move

̶ ̶ ̶ really see the rationality of the Soviets pushing it this ̶ ̶ unless they grossly misunderstand the importance of Cuba to this country.

Bundy: It's important, I think, to recognize that they did make this decision, as far as our estimates now go, in early summer, and that this has been happening since August. Their TASS statement of September 12 [actually 11], which the experts, I think, attribute very strongly to Khrushchev himself, is all mixed up on this point. It has a rather explicit statement: "The armaments and military equipment sent to Cuba are designed exclusively for defensive purposes and the president of the United States and the American military, the military of any country, know what means of defense are. How can these means threaten the United States?"

Now, *there,* it's very hard to reconcile that with what has happened. The rest, as the Secretary says, has many comparisons between Cuba and Italy, Turkey, and Japan. We have other evidence that Khrushchev honestly believes, or at least affects to believe, that we have nuclear weapons in Japan. That combination—

Rusk: Gromyko stated that in his press conference the other day, too.

Bundy: Yeah. They may mean Okinawa.

McNamara: It's not likely, but it's conceivable the nuclear warheads for these launchers are not yet on Cuban soil.

Bundy: Now, that seems to me that is perfectly possible that this is in that sense a bluff. That doesn't make them any less offensive to us, because we can't have proof about it.

McNamara: No, no. But it does possibly indicate a different course of action . . .

Bundy: Yeah.

McNamara: . . . and therefore, while I'm not suggesting how we should handle this, I think this is one of the most important actions we should take: to ascertain the location of the nuclear warheads for these missiles. Later in the discussion we can revert back to this. There are several alternative ways of approaching it.

President Kennedy: Doug, do you have any . . .

Dillon: No. The only thing I would say is that this alternative course of warning, getting public opinion, and OAS action, and telling people in NATO and everything like that, would appear to me to have the danger of getting us wide out in the open and forcing the Russians, Soviets, to take a position that if anything was done they would have to retaliate.

Whereas a quick action, with a statement at the same time saying this is all there is to it, might give them a chance to back off and not do anything. Meanwhile, I think that the chance of getting through this thing without a Russian reaction is greater under a quick strike than building the whole thing up to a climax, then going through with what will be a lot of debate on it.

Rusk: That is, of course, a possibility, but . . .

Bundy: The difficulties. I share the Secretary of the Treasury's feeling a little bit. The difficulties of organizing the OAS and NATO. The amount of noise we would get from our allies, saying that they can live with Soviet MRBMs [medium-range ballistic missiles], why can't we? The division in the alliance. The certainty that the Germans would feel that we were jeopardizing Berlin because of our concern over Cuba. The prospect of that pattern is not an appetizing one.

Rusk: Yes, but you see—everything turns crucially on what happens.

Bundy: I agree, Mr. Secretary.

Rusk: And if we go with the quick strike, then, in fact, they do back it up. Then you have exposed all of your allies and ourselves to all these great dangers without the slightest consultation, or warning, or preparation.

Bundy: You get all these noises again.

President Kennedy: But, of course, warning them, it seems to me, is warning everybody. And I—obviously you can't sort of announce that in 4 days from now you're going to take them out. They may announce within 3 days that they're going to have warheads on them. If we come and attack, they're going to fire them. So then what'll we do? Then we don't take them out. Of course, we then announce: "Well, if they do that, then we're going to attack with nuclear weapons."

Dillon: Yes, sir. That's the question that nobody—I didn't understand—nobody had mentioned is whether this "take-out," this mission, was going to be able to deal with it with high explosives.

President Kennedy: How effective can the take-out be, do they think?

Taylor: It'll never be 100 percent, Mr. President, we know. We hope to take out a vast majority in the first strike, but this is not just one thing—one strike, one day—but continuous air attack for whenever necessary, whenever we discover a target.

Bundy: They're now talking about taking out the air force as well.

Speaking in those terms, I do raise again the question whether we can handle the military problem. But there is, I would think, a substantial political advantage in limiting the strike in surgical terms to the thing that is in fact the cause of action.

Gilpatric: I suggest, Mr. President, that if you're involved in several hundred strikes, and against airfields, this is what you would do: pre-invade. And it would be very difficult to convince anybody that this was not a pre-invasion strike.

I think also, once you get into this volume of attack, that public-opinion reaction to this, as distinct from the reaction to an invasion—there's very little difference. And from both standpoints it would seem to me that if you're talking about a general air-attack program, you might as well think about whether we can eradicate the whole problem by an invasion just as simply, with as little chance of reaction.

Taylor: Well, I would think we should be in a position to invade at any time, if we so desired. Hence that, in this preliminary, it's all bonus if we are indeed taking out weapons.

President Kennedy: Well, let's say we just take out the missile bases. Then they have some more there. Obviously they can get them in by submarine and so on. I don't know whether you just can't keep high strikes on.

Taylor: I suspect, Mr. President, that we'd have to take out the surface-to-air missiles in order to get in. To get in, take some of them out. Maybe . . .

President Kennedy: How long do we estimate this will remain secure, this information, till people have it?

Bundy: In terms of the tightness of our intelligence control, Mr. President, I think we are in unusually and fortunately good position. We set up a new security classification governing precisely the field of offensive capability in

Cuba just 5 days ago, 4 days ago, under General Carter.[18] That limits this to people who have an immediate, operational necessity in intelligence terms to work on the data, and the people who have . . .

President Kennedy: How many would that be, about?

Bundy: Oh, that will be a very large number, but that's not generally where leaks come from. The more important limitation is that only officers with the policy responsibility for advice directly to you will receive this.

President Kennedy: How many would get it over in the Defense Department, General, with your meeting this afternoon?

Taylor: Well, I was going to mention that. We'd have to ask for relaxation of the ground rules that Mac has just enunciated, so that I can give it to the senior commanders who are involved in the plans.

President Kennedy: Would that be about 50?

Taylor: No, sir. I would say that, at this stage, 10 more.

McNamara: Well, Mr. President, I think, to be realistic, we should assume that this will become fairly widely known, if not in the newspapers, at least by political representatives of both parties, within, I would say, I'm just picking a figure, I'd say a week. And I say that because we have taken action already that is raising questions in people's minds.

Normally, when a U-2 comes back, we duplicate the films. The duplicated copies go to a series of commands. A copy goes to SAC. A copy goes to CINCLANT.[19] A copy goes to CIA. And normally the photo interpreters and the operational officers in these commands are looking forward to these. We have stopped all that, and this type of information is going on throughout the department.

And I doubt very much that we can keep this out of the hands of members of Congress, for example, for more than a week.

Rusk: Well, Senator [Kenneth] Keating has already, in effect, announced it on the floor of the Senate.

Bundy: Senator Keating said this on the floor of the Senate on the 10th of October: "Construction has begun on at least a half-dozen launching sites for intermediate-range tactical missiles."

Rusk: That's correct. That's exactly the point. I think we can count on announcing it not later than Thursday or Friday of this week.

Carter: There is a refugee who's a major source of intelligence on this, of

18. The PSALM classification for distributing information.

19. Commander-in-Chief, U.S. Forces, Atlantic. Headquartered in Norfolk, CINCLANT at this time was Admiral Robert L. Dennison.

course, who has described one of these missiles in terms which we can recognize, who is now in the country.

President Kennedy: Is he the one who's giving Keating his stuff?

Carter: We don't know.

Bundy: My question, Mr. President, is whether, as a matter of tactics, we ought not to interview Senator Keating and check out his data. It seems to me that that ought to be done in a routine sort of way by an open officer of the intelligence agency.

Rusk: I think that's right.

President Kennedy: You have any thoughts, Mr. Vice President?

Vice President Johnson: I agree with Mac that *that* ought to be done. I think that we're committed at any time that we feel that there's a buildup that in any way endangers, to take whatever action we must take to assure our security. I would think that the Secretary's evaluation of this thing being around all over the lot is a pretty accurate one. I would think it'd take a week to do it. I think they may know it before then.

I would like to hear what the responsible commanders have to say this afternoon. I think the question with the base is whether we take it out or whether we talk about it, and either alternative is a very distressing one. But, of the two, I would take it out. Assuming that the commanders felt that way.

I'm fearful if we . . . I spent the weekend with the ambassadors of the Organization of American States. I think this organization is fine. But I don't think, I don't rely on them much for any strength in anything like this.

And the fact that we're talking about our other allies, I take the position that Mr. Bundy says: "We ought to be living all these years [with missiles and not] get your blood pressure up." But the fact is the country's blood pressure *is* up, and they are fearful, and they're insecure, and we're getting divided, and I don't think that . . .

I take this little *State Department Bulletin* that you sent out to all the congressmen. One of the points you make: that any time the buildup endangers or threatens our security in any way, we're going to do what must be done immediately to protect our own security. And when you say that, why, they give unanimous support.

People are really concerned about this, in my opinion. I think we have to be prudent and cautious, talk to the commanders and see what they say. I'm not much for circularizing it over the Hill or our allies, even though I realize it's a breach of faith, not to confer with them. We're not going to get much help out of them.

Bundy: There is an intermediate position. There are perhaps two or three of our principal allies or heads of government we could communicate with, at least on a 24-hour-notice basis. Certainly ease the—

Vice President Johnson: Tell the allies to stop the planes, stop the ships, stop the submarines and everything else from sending. Just not going to permit it. And then stop them from coming in there.

President Kennedy: What you're really talking about are two or three different potential operations.

One is the strike just on these 3 bases.

The second is the broader one that Secretary McNamara was talking about, which is on the airfields and on the SAM sites and on anything else connected with missiles.

Third is doing both of those things and also, at the same time, launching a blockade, which requires, really, the third and which is a larger step.

And then, as I take it, the fourth question is the degree of consultation. I don't know how much use consulting with the British has been. They'll just object. Just have to decide to do it. Probably ought to tell them, though, the night before.

Robert Kennedy: Mr. President?

President Kennedy: Yes?

Robert Kennedy: We have the fifth one, really, which is the invasion. I would say that you're dropping bombs all over Cuba if you do the second, air, and the airports, knocking out their planes, dropping it on all their missiles. You're covering most of Cuba. You're going to kill an awful lot of people, and we're going to take an awful lot of heat on it. And then—you know the heat. You're going to announce the reason that you're doing it is because they're sending in these kind of missiles.

Well, I would think it's almost incumbent upon the Russians then, to say, "Well, we're going to send them in again. And if you do it again, we're going to do the same thing to Turkey," or "we're going to do the same thing to Iran."

President Kennedy: I don't believe it takes us, at least . . . How long does it take to get in a position where we can invade Cuba? Almost a month? Two months?

McNamara: No, sir. No, sir. It's a bare 7 days after the air strike, assuming the air strike starts the first of next week. Now, if the air strike were to start today, it wouldn't necessarily be 7 days after today, but I think you can basically consider 7 days after the air strike.

President Kennedy: You could get 6 divisions or 7 divisions into Cuba in 7 days?

Taylor: No, sir. There are two plans we have. One is to go at maximum speed, which is the one referred to you by Secretary McNamara, about 7 days after the strike. We put in 90,000 men in 11 days.

If you have time, if you give us more time, so we can get all the advance preparation and prepositioning, we'd put the same 90,000 in, in 5 days. We have the choice of those two plans.

President Kennedy: How would you get them in? By ship or by air?

McNamara: By air.

Taylor: Airdrop and ship.

McNamara: Simultaneous airdrop and ship.

President Kennedy: Do you think 90,000 is enough?

Taylor: At least it's enough to start the thing going. And I would say it would be, ought to be, enough.

McNamara: Particularly if it isn't directed initially at Havana, the Havana area. This is a variant. General Taylor and . . .

President Kennedy: We haven't any real report on what the state of the popular reaction would be to all this, do we? We don't know whether . . .

Taylor: They'd be greatly confused, don't you think?

President Kennedy: What?

Taylor: Great, great confusion and panic, don't you think?

Carter: Well, it's very hard to evaluate the effect [of] what the military consequences might be.

McNamara: Sometime today, I think, at the State Department, we will want to consider that. There's a real possibility you'd have to invade. If you carried out an air strike, this might lead to an uprising, such that in order to prevent the slaughter of the free Cubans, we would have to invade to reintroduce order into the country. And we would be prepared to do that.

Rusk: I would rather think if there were a complete air strike against all air forces, you might as well do it. Do the whole job.

President Kennedy: Well, now, let's decide what we ought to be doing.

Robert Kennedy: Could I raise one more question?

President Kennedy: Yeah.

Robert Kennedy: Is it absolutely essential that you wait 7 days after you have an air strike? I would think that after 7 days, that what you're going to have . . .

Taylor: If you give less, you run the risk of giving up surprise. If you start moving your troops around in order to reduce that . . .

Robert Kennedy: Yeah. The only thing is, there's been so much attention on Berlin in the last . . . Would you have to move them so that everybody would know it was Cuba?

Taylor: Well, it's troops, plus shipping even more so, you know. You're going to have to assemble the ships necessary, and that will be very, very overt, and we can think of no way to cover that up.

McNamara: May I suggest the fact that we mentioned this other plan [that] was talked about. We should be prepared for a series of eventualities after the air strike starts. I think it's not probable, but it's conceivable that the air strike would trigger a nationwide uprising. And if there was strong opposition among the dissident groups, and if the air strike were highly successful, it's conceivable that some U.S. troops could be put in in less than 7 days.

Taylor: That's correct. At first our air, our airdrops, and our Marines. Well, the airdrop at least, beginning in 5 days. That might do the trick if this is really a national upheaval.

McNamara: So we should have a series of alternative plans is all I'm suggesting, other than the 7 days.

Robert Kennedy: I just think that 5 days, even a 5-day period—the United States is going to be under such pressure by everybody not to do anything. And there's going to be also pressure on the Russians to do something against us. If you could get it in, get it started so that there wasn't any turning back, they couldn't . . .

President Kennedy: But I mean the problem is, as I understand it . . . You've got two problems. One is how much time we've got on these particular missiles before they're ready to go. Do we have 2 weeks? If we had 2 weeks, we could lay on all this and have it all ready to go. But the question really is whether we can wait 2 weeks.

Taylor: I don't think we'll ever know, Mr. President, these operational questions because, with this type of missile, it can be launched very quickly with a concealed expedience—

Bundy: Do we have any intelligence—

Taylor: —so that even today, this one, this area, might be operational. I can see that it's highly probable.

Bundy: One very important question is whether there are other areas which conceivably might be even more operational that we have *not* identified.

McNamara: This is why, I think, the moment we leave here, Mac, we just have to take this new authority we have and put it . . .

Bundy: May I ask General Carter whether the intelligence, the collateral intelligence, relates only to this area, as I understood it this morning?

Carter: That's right. That's why we specifically covered this area on the one [U-2 flight] Sunday [October 14], because the [unclear], you see . . .

McNamara: May I go back for a second, however, to the point that was raised a moment ago? Mr. President, I don't believe that if we *had* 2 weeks, if we knew that at the end of 2 weeks we were going in, I don't believe we could substantially lessen the 5- or 7-day period required after the air attack, prior to the invasion, for the size force we're talking about. Because we start with the assumption the air attack must take them by surprise. We would not be able to take the actions required to shorten the 5-to-7-day period and still assure you of surprise in the air attack. And, therefore, we haven't been able to figure out a way to shorten that 5-to-7-day period while maintaining surprise in the air attack.

President Kennedy: What are you doing for that 5 days? Moving ships, or where?

McNamara: Moving ships. And we have to move transport aircraft by the scores around the country. We should move ships. Actually, the ship movement would not be as extensive in the 7-day invasion as it would be in an 11-day [invasion], after the air strike.

Taylor: It would take place after the air strike.

McNamara: We have been moving already, on a very quiet basis, munitions and POL. We will have by the 20th—which is Friday, I guess [actually Saturday]—we will have stocks of munitions, stocks of POL prepositioned in the southeast part of this country. So that kind of movement is beginning.

President Kennedy: What's POL?

McNamara: Petroleum, oil, and lubricants. So that kind of movement has already been taking place and it's been possible to do it quietly.

President Kennedy: What about armor, and so on? What about armor?

McNamara: The armor movement would be noticeable if it were carried out in the volume we require. And hence the point I would make is that, knowing ahead of time, 2 weeks ahead of time, that we would carry out the invasion, would not significantly reduce the 5-to-7-day interval between the strike by air and the invasion time, given the size force we're talking about.

Taylor: I think our point of view may change somewhat because of an adjustment here. The decision would take out only the known missile sites and not the airfields. There is a great danger of equipment dispersal of all the interesting aircraft. You'd be keeping surprise. Missiles can't run off quite as readily.

President Kennedy: The advantage of taking out these airplanes would be to protect us against a reprisal by them?

Taylor: Yes.

President Kennedy: I would think you'd have to assume they'd be using iron bombs and not nuclear weapons. Because, obviously, why would the Soviets permit nuclear war to begin under that sort of half-assed way?

McNamara: I think that's reasonable.

Carter: But they still have 10 IL-28s and 20 to 25 MiG-21s.[20]

President Kennedy: So you think that if we're going to take out the missile sites you'd want to take out these planes at the same time?

Carter: There are 8 airfields that are capable of mounting these jets. Eight—

Bundy: But, politically, if you're trying to get him to understand the limit and the nonlimit and make it as easy for him as possible, there's an enormous premium on having a small, as small and clear-cut, an action as possible, against the hazard of going after all the operational airfields becoming a kind of general war.

President Kennedy: General?

Taylor: I wonder if we could get the number of hours required for each type of air strike, if we were just going for . . .

President Kennedy: Well, now, what is it we have, what is it we want to, need to, do in the next 24 hours to prepare for any of these three? It seems to me that we want to do more or less the same things, no matter what we finally decide.

Bundy: We've authorized, Mr. President, we have a decision, for additional intelligence reconnaissance.

A minor decision that we'll talk to Keating.

President Kennedy: I don't think Keating will be that helpful.

Bundy: Leave that out.

President Kennedy: Yeah.

Robert Kennedy: I think that then he'll be saying afterwards that we tried to [unclear word or words].

---

20. The IL-28 (NATO designation "Beagle") was a twin-engine light/medium jet bomber of early postwar design (production began in 1950) with a cruising radius of about 750 miles, able to carry 6,500 pounds of nuclear or conventional ("iron") bombs. On September 28 a Navy reconnaissance aircraft in the Atlantic had photographed a Soviet freighter carrying 10 fuselage crates for these bombers to Cuba. The Soviet freighter arrived on October 4. As a result of delay in Navy transmission of its photos to CIA interpreters, the IL-28s were not identified until October 9. McCone briefed President Kennedy about this discovery on October 11. At that time Kennedy told McCone: "We'll have to do something drastic about Cuba," and said he was looking forward to the JCS operational plan that was to be presented the following week. See McCone to File, "Memorandum on Donovan Project," October 11, 1962, in McAuliffe, *CIA Documents*, p. 124; Brugioni, *Eyeball to Eyeball*, pp. 172–174.

Bundy: All right. The next. I should think we need to know the earliest readiness for the various sizes of air strike and how long they would take to execute.

President Kennedy: Median probability.

Dillon: One other question is: What, if anything, has to be done to be prepared for an eventuality of a Soviet action?

President Kennedy: And then I think what we ought to do is to figure out what are the minimum number of people that we really have to tell. I suppose, well, there's [French President Charles] de Gaulle.

Bundy: Right. You want de Gaulle. It's hard to say about [West German Chancellor Konrad] Adenauer. You've got to tell, it seems to me, you're going to have to tell SACEUR, and the Commandant.[21]

Dillon: I would think this business about the Soviet reaction, that might be helpful if we could maybe take some general war preparation type of action that would show them that we're ready if they want to start anything—without, what you might, risk starting anything. You just don't know . . .

Bundy: On this track, one obvious element on the political side is: Do we say something simultaneously to the Cubans, to the Soviets, or do we let the action speak for itself?

Rusk: This point, whether we say anything to the Cubans and the Soviets before any, before . . .

President Kennedy: I think, what we ought to do is, after this meeting this afternoon, we ought to meet tonight again at 6:00, consider these various proposals.

In the meanwhile, we'll go ahead with this maximum, whatever is needed, from the flights. And, in addition, we will . . .

I don't think we've got much time on these missiles. They may be . . . So it may be that we just have to. We can't wait 2 weeks while we're getting ready to roll. Maybe we just have to just take them out, and continue our other preparations if we decide to do that. That may be where we end up.

I think we ought to, beginning right now, be preparing to. Because that's what we're going to do *anyway.* We're certainly going to do number one. We're going to take out these missiles.

The questions will be whether, what I would describe as number two, which

---

21. NATO's Supreme Allied Commander, Europe, always an American officer (at that time General Lauris Norstad); and the Commandant of the American Sector of Berlin, Major General Albert Watson.

would be a general air strike. That we're not ready to say, but we should be in preparation for it.

The third is the general invasion. At least we're going to do number one. So it seems to me that we don't have to wait very long. We ought to be making *those* preparations.

Bundy: You want to be clear, Mr. President, whether we have definitely decided *against* a political track. I, myself, think we ought to work out a contingency on that.

Rusk: We'll develop both tracks.

President Kennedy: I think we ought to do the OAS. I think that's a waste of time. But I don't think we ought to do NATO.

We ought to just decide who we talk to, and how long ahead, and how many people, really, in the government. There's going to be a difference between those who know that—this will leak out in the next few days—there are these bases, until we say. For the Pentagon or State it won't be hard. We've already said it on the . . . So we, let's say, we've got 2 or 3 days.

Bundy: Well, let's play it, shall we, play it still harder and simply say that there is no evidence. I mean, we have to . . .

President Kennedy: We ought to stick with that until we want to do something. Otherwise we give ourselves away, so let's.

Bundy: May I make one other cover plan suggestion, Mr. President?

President Kennedy: Yes.

Bundy: There will be meetings in the White House. I think the best we can do is to keep the people with a specific Latin American business black[22] and describe the rest as "intensive budget review sessions." But I haven't been able to think of any other . . .

President Kennedy: Nobody [should be told], it seems to me, in the State Department. I discussed the matter with Bohlen of the Soviet part [of State], and told him he could talk to [Llewellyn] Thompson. So that's those two. It seems to me that there's no one else in the State Department that ought to be talked to about it in any level at all, until we know a little more.

And then, as I say, in Defense we've got to keep it as tight as possible, particularly what we're going to do about it. Maybe a lot of people know about what's there. But what we're going to do about it really ought to be, you know, the tightest of all because otherwise we bitch it up.

22. "Black": to conceal a presence, to keep something undercover, covert.

McNamara: Mr. President, may I suggest that we come back this afternoon prepared to answer three questions.

First, should we surface our surveillance? I think this is a very important question at the moment. We ought to try to decide today either yes or no.

President Kennedy: By "surface our" . . .

McNamara: I mean, should we state publicly that, [as] you have stated we will, we'll act to take out any offensive weapons. In order to be certain as to whether there are or are not offensive weapons, we are scheduling U-2 flights or other surveillance or reconnaissance flights to obtain this information. We'll make the information public.

Carter: What's the skull number, commissar? [Laughs.]

President Kennedy: There may not be one. All right, why not?

McNamara: This is one question. A second question is: Should we precede the military action with political action? If so, on what timing?

I would think the answer is almost certainly yes. And I would think particularly of the contacts with Khrushchev. And I would think that if these are to be done, they must be scheduled, in terms of time, very, very carefully in relation to a potential military action. There must be a very, very precise series of contacts with him, and indications of what we'll do at certain times following that.

And, thirdly, we should be prepared to answer your questions regarding the effect of these strikes and the time required to carry them off. I think—

President Kennedy: How long it would take to get them organized.

McNamara: Exactly. We'll be prepared—

President Kennedy: In other words, how many days from tomorrow morning would it . . . How many mornings from tomorrow morning would it take to get the, to take out just these missile sites, which we need to know now. How long before we get the information about the rest of the island, do you figure, General?

Carter: Could take weeks, Mr. President.

President Kennedy: Weeks?

Carter: For complete coverage of a cloud-covered island.

Taylor: Well, we've got about 80 percent now, don't we?

Lundahl: Yes, sir. It depends much on what we get out of yesterday's flight, sir. They won't be . . .

Bundy: There are clouded areas, Mr. President, as I understand it. And there are areas that are very substantial in permanent, or nearly permanent, cloud cover.

Lundahl: We'll have preliminaries by 6:00 tomorrow morning.

President Kennedy: Well, there is the part of the island that isn't covered by this flight we're [expecting to learn about] by tomorrow morning. What about doing that tomorrow, plus the clouded part, doing low-level? Have we got a plane that goes—

Bundy: We can certainly go low-level, and we have been reluctant to do that. The one thing to worry about on low-level is that that will create a sense of tactical alert in the island. And I'm not sure we want to do that. Our guess is that the high-level ones have not, in fact, been detected.

Taylor: I think that's correct.

Bundy: No reactions.

President Kennedy: I would think that if we are going to go in and take out this, and any others we find, that we would at the same time do a general low-level photographic reconnaissance.

Bundy: You could at the same time do a low-level of all that we have not seen. That would certainly be sensible.

President Kennedy: Then we would be prepared, almost any day, to take those out.

Bundy: As a matter of fact, for evidentiary purposes, someone has made the point this morning, that if we go in on a quick strike, we ought to have a photographic plane take shots of the sites.

President Kennedy: All right. Well, now, I think we've got to watch out for this, for us to be doing anything quickly and quietly and completely. That's what we've got to be doing the next 2 or 3 days. So, we'll meet at 6:00?

Robert Kennedy: How long? Excuse me. I just wondered how long it would take, if you took it and had an invasion.

Taylor: To mount an invasion?

Robert Kennedy: No. How long would it take to take over the island?

Taylor: Very hard to estimate, Bobby. But I would say that in 5 or 6 days the main resistance ought to be overcome. We might then be in there for a month thereafter, cleaning that up.

McNamara: Five or 7 days of air, plus 5 days of invasion, plus—

President Kennedy: I wonder if CIA could give us what state . . . Yeah, so we get some idea about our reception there.

I just hate to waste these 6 hours. So it may be that we will want to be doing some movements in the next 6 hours.

Unidentified: About the execution of the [unclear]?

President Kennedy: Yeah.

[The meeting now begins to break up. Various separate conversations begin as some people leave. President Kennedy's next appointment is for a formal lunch with the Crown Prince of Libya.]

President Kennedy: I want to add [unclear], better also. Are you coming to lunch?

Rusk: I was supposed to, but . . .

President Kennedy: George, are you supposed to come?

[Unclear exchange.]

President Kennedy: 6:00 tonight?

Unidentified: 6:00.

President Kennedy: All right, 7:00.

Bundy: 7:00 is better actually for you, Mr. President. Is 6:30 manageable? That would be still better because you're supposed to be out there [at a dinner party] at 8:00.

President Kennedy: Well, that's all right. That, then, 7:00. Between 6:30 and 7:00. As close to 6:30 as you can, be here.

How many would there be? I'd like to have, if you add the members of the Joint Chiefs of Staff here . . . [unclear]. Well, then, you bring who you think ought to be brought.

Bundy (calling to departing participants): May I urge everybody to use the East Gate rather than the West Gate?[23]

President Kennedy: I think we ought to get . . . What's Mr. McCone doing up here, General?

Carter: He's burying his stepson tomorrow morning, back [unclear].

President Kennedy: So, why don't you discuss [unclear]. Is he familiar with this information?

Carter: Yes, sir. He's aware of what has happened.

Robert Kennedy: I talked with him about an hour ago. He'll be back here tomorrow morning. They're burying the child today, his son.

President Kennedy: Why don't we leave it with his judgment, tonight.

Robert Kennedy: Well, he asked me to [unclear]. I think we might tell him [unclear]. He said he was going to call after the meeting. Maybe just tell him we had a meeting.

President Kennedy: All right. Now, the other question is on the General, Eisenhower. Where is the General now?

Unidentified: I'll take care of that.

---

23. The West Gate, on the same side of the White House as the White House Press Room, was the usual entrance for official visitors. The East Gate, the usual entrance for the residential side of the White House, was used more for social functions and tours.

[Unclear exchange.]

Rusk: George, the President wants you to take my place at lunch.

Ball: All right. But I've got, I'm working on [unclear]. No, but I've got [someone I] want to see about a speech, that's all.

Rusk: Well, well. But maybe they could reschedule that.

[There follow a few minutes of fragmentary conversations around the room. Little of them can be understood. Bundy talks a bit about the seating at lunch and arranges for someone to go over to the Pentagon. Someone talks about low-level reconnaissance. Vice President Johnson asks McNamara to help arrange leasing of a different type of small government jet for Johnson's travels around the country. Then silence, and the recording ends.]

6:30 P.M.

CABINET ROOM

The morning meeting had ended with an understanding that the Pentagon team would analyze possibilities for a quick air strike, possibly followed by an invasion. Rusk and others at State would study how the administration could act promptly and effectively against the missiles without surprising allies in the hemisphere and Europe and possibly losing their support.

While this went on, Kennedy kept to his announced schedule. He presided over a formal lunch for the Crown Prince of Libya. Adlai Stevenson was present. After lunch, Kennedy invited Stevenson to the family quarters. Showing Stevenson the U-2 photos, Kennedy said: "I suppose the alternatives are to go in by air and wipe them out, or to take other steps to render the weapons inoperable." Stevenson exclaimed, "Let's not go into an air strike until we have explored the possibilities of a peaceful solution."

During the afternoon, Stevenson took part in the meetings at the State Department. So did Soviet experts Bohlen and Thompson and the Assistant Secretary for American Republics Affairs, Edwin Martin.

At Justice, Robert Kennedy had meanwhile held in his own office a meeting of those involved in Operation Mongoose. Describing the "general dissatisfaction" of the President with progress thus far, the Attorney General focused discussion on a new, more active, program of sabotage just prepared by CIA. Pressed by the CIA representative (Richard Helms) as to the ultimate objective of the operation and what to promise the Cuban exiles, Robert Kennedy hinted that the President might be becoming less averse to overt U.S. military action. He wondered aloud how many Cubans would defend Castro's regime if the country were invaded. After discussing the possibility of having Cuban émigrés attack the missile sites, he and the rest of the group agreed that that was not a feasible option.

At the Pentagon, the Joint Chiefs of Staff conferred with CINCLANT, the commanders of SAC and the Tactical Air Command, and the general commanding the 18th Airborne Corps. McNamara joined them later. Presuming that the Soviets would not initiate a nuclear war against the United States, the JCS favored an attack, regardless of whether the missiles were operational. They nevertheless approved several prudential steps to increase American readiness for nuclear war. After McNamara left, the JCS agreed that they did not favor use of low-level reconnaissance, fearing that it would "tip our hand." They also agreed they would rather do nothing than limit an air strike only to MRBMs.[1] In the last 40 minutes before returning to the White House, McNamara and Gilpatric worked out an outline of three alternative courses of action, which McNamara would present at the meeting.

As scheduled, Kennedy's advisers gathered in the Cabinet Room at 6:30. Taylor arrived after the meeting began. President Kennedy activated the tape recorder as the meeting opened with the intelligence briefing.

President Kennedy: Find anything new?

Carter: Nothing on the additional film, sir. We have a much better readout on what we had initially.

There's good evidence that there are backup missiles for each of the 4 launchers at each of the 3 sites, so that there would be twice the number, for a total of 8 which could eventually be erected. This would mean a capability of from 16 or possibly 24 missiles.

We feel, on the basis of information that we presently have, that these are solid-propellant, inertial guidance missiles with 1,100-mile range, rather than the oxygen-propellant radar-controlled. Primarily because we have no indication of any radar, or any indication of any oxygen equipment. And it would appear to be logical from an intelligence estimate viewpoint that if they are going to this much trouble, that they would go ahead and put in the 1,100 miles because of the tremendously increased threat coverage. Let me see that map.

President Kennedy: What is this map?

1. These proceedings are based on notes taken from transcripts of JCS meetings in October–November 1962. The notes were made in 1976 before these transcripts were apparently destroyed. They have since been declassified and are available from the National Security Archive, Washington, D.C.

Carter: That shows the circular range capability.

President Kennedy: When was this drawn? Is this drawn in relation to this information?

Carter: No, sir. It was drawn in some time ago, I believe. But the ranges there are the nominal ranges of the missiles rather than the maximum. That's a 1,020[-mile] circle, as against 1,100.

President Kennedy: Well, I was just wondering whether San Diego de los Baños is where these missiles are.

Carter: Yes, sir.

President Kennedy: Well, I wonder how many of these [maps] have been printed out.

Bundy: The circle is drawn in red ink *on* the map, Mr. President.

President Kennedy: Oh, I see. It was never printed?

Carter: No, that's on top.

President Kennedy: I see. It isn't printed.

Carter: It would appear that with this type of missile, with the solid-propellant and inertial guidance system, that they could well be operational within 2 weeks, as we look at the pictures now. And once operational they could fire on very little notice. They'll have a refire rate of from 4 to 6 hours, for each launcher.

President Kennedy: What about the vulnerability of such a missile to bullets?

McNamara: Highly vulnerable, Mr. President.

Carter: They're vulnerable. They're not nearly as vulnerable as the oxygen propellant, but they are vulnerable to ordinary rifle fire.

We have no evidence whatsoever of any nuclear warhead storage near the field launchers. However, ever since last February we have been observing an unusual facility which now has automatic antiaircraft weapon protection. This is at Bejucal. There are some similarities but also many points of dissimilarity between this particular facility and the national storage sites in the Soviet Union. It's the best candidate for a site, and we have that marked for further surveillance. However, there is really totally inadequate evidence to say there is a nuclear storage capability now.

These are field-type launchers. They have mobile support, erection, and checkout equipment. And they have a 4-in-line deployment pattern in launchers which is identical, complexes about 5 miles apart, representative of the deployments that we note in the Soviet Union for similar missiles.

President Kennedy: General, how long would you say we had before these, at least to the best of your ability for the ones we now know, will be ready to fire?

Carter: Well, our people estimate that these could be fully operational within

2 weeks. This would be the total complex. If they're the oxygen type, it would be considerably longer, since we don't have any indication of oxygen refueling there, nor any radars.

McNamara: This wouldn't rule out the possibility that one of them might be operational very much sooner.

Carter: Well, one of them could be operational much sooner. Our people feel that this has been being put in since, probably, early September. We have had 2 visits of a Soviet ship that has an 8-foot hold capacity sideways. And this, about so far, is the only delivery vehicle that we would have any suspicion that they came in on. And that came in late August, and one in early September.

Ball?: Why would they have to be sideways though?

Carter: Well, it's just easier to get them in, I guess.

President Kennedy: Fine.

Rusk: The total readout on the flights yesterday will be ready tonight, you think?

Carter: It should be finished, pretty well, by midnight.

President Kennedy: Now that was supposed to have covered the whole island, was it?

Carter: Yes, sir. In 2 throws [flight paths].

President Kennedy: Except for . . .

Carter: But part of the central and, in fact, much of the central and part of the eastern was cloud covered. The western half was in real good shape.

President Kennedy: I see. Now what have we got laying on for tomorrow?

Carter: There are 7, 6 or 7 . . .

McNamara: I just left General Carroll.[2] We're having ready 7 U-2 aircraft: 2 high-altitude U-2s, 5 lesser-altitude U-2s; 6 equipped with an old-type film, one equipped with a new-type, experimental film, which hopefully will increase the resolution.

We only need 2 aircraft flying tomorrow if the weather is good. We will put up only 2 if the weather is good. If the weather is not good, we'll start off with 2 and we'll have the others ready to go during the day as the weather improves. We have weather aircraft surrounding the periphery of Cuba, and we'll be able to keep track of the weather during the day over all parts of the island. Hopefully, this will give us complete coverage tomorrow. We are planning to do this, or have the capability to do this, every day thereafter for an indefinite period.

---

2. General Joseph Carroll, Director of the Defense Intelligence Agency.

Carter: This is a field-type missile. And from collateral evidence, not direct, that we have with the Soviet Union, it's designed to be fielded, placed, and fired in 6 hours.

It would appear that we have caught this in a very early stage of deployment. It would also appear that there does not seem to be the degree of urgency in getting them immediately into position. This could be because they have not been surveyed. Or it could also be because it is the shorter-range missile, and the radars and the oxygen have not yet arrived.

President Kennedy: There isn't any question in your mind, however, that it is an intermediate-range [actually, medium-range] missile?

Carter: No. There's no question in our minds at all. These are all the characteristics that we have seen with live ones.

Rusk: You've seen actual missiles themselves and not just the boxes, have you?

Carter: No, we've seen . . . In the picture there is an actual missile.

Rusk: Yeah. Sure there is. [Tone is serious, not sarcastic.]

Carter: Yes. There's no question in our mind, sir. And they are genuine. They are not a camouflage or covert attempt to fool us.

Bundy: How much do we know, Pat? I don't mean to go behind your judgment here, except that there's one thing that would be really catastrophic, would be to make a judgment here on a bad guess as to whether these things are . . . We mustn't do that.

How do we really know what these missiles are, and what their range is?

Carter: Only that from the readout that we have now, and in the judgment of our analysts, and of the Guided Missile and Astronautics Committee,[3] which has been convening all afternoon, these signatures are identical with those that we have clearly earmarked in the Soviet Union, and have fully verified.

Bundy: What made the verification? That's really my question. How do we know what a given Soviet missile will do?

Carter: We know something from the range firings that we have vetted for the past 2 years. And we know also from comparison with the characteristics of our own missiles as to size and length and diameter. As to these particular missiles, we have a family of Soviet missiles for which we have all accepted the specifications.

Bundy: I know that we have accepted them, and I know that we've had these things in charts for years. But I don't know how we know.

---

3. The Guided Missile and Astronautics Intelligence Committee (GMAIC) was another interagency committee of the U.S. Intelligence Board.

Carter: Well, we know from a number of sources, including our IRONBARK sources,[4] as well as from range firings which we have been vetting for several years, as to the capabilities. But I would have to get the analysts in here to give you the play-by-play account.

Rusk: Pat, we don't know of any 65-foot Soviet missile that has a range of, say, 15 miles, do we?

Carter: Fifteen miles? No, we certainly don't.

Rusk: In other words, if they are missiles this size, they are missiles of considerable range, I think.

McNamara: I tried to prove today—I am satisfied—that these were not MRBMs. And I worked long on it. I got our experts out, and I could not find evidence that would support any conclusion other than that they are MRBMs. Now, whether they're 1,100 miles, 600-mile, 900-mile is still a guess in my opinion. But that they are MRBMs seems the most probable assumption at the moment.

Bundy: I would apparently agree, given the weight of it.

President Kennedy: Is General Taylor coming over?

McNamara: He is, Mr. President.

President Kennedy: Have you finished, General?

Carter: Yes, sir. I think that's it.

Rusk: We've had some further discussion with people this afternoon, and we'll be working on it, pressing, this evening. But I might mention certain points that some of us are concerned about.

The one is the chance that this might be the issue on which Castro would elect to break with Moscow if he knew that he were in deadly jeopardy. Now this is one chance in a hundred, possibly. But in any event we are very much interested in the possibility of a direct message to Castro, as well as Khrushchev, [which] might make some sense here before an actual strike is put on. Mr. Martin will present you with, outline, the kind of message to Castro that we had in mind.

Martin: This would be an oral note, message through a third party, first describing just what we know about what exists in the missile sites, so that he knows that we are informed about what's going on.

Second, to point out that the issues this raises as far as U.S. security is

---

4. IRONBARK was a code word for information passed to the United States by Colonel Oleg Penkovsky, an officer in Soviet military intelligence. Penkovsky had apparently fallen under suspicion and was arrested 6 days later (October 22, Washington time). He was later executed by the Soviet government.

concerned: It's a breach of two of the points that you have made public. First the ground-to-ground missile and, second, obviously, it's a Soviet-operated base in Cuba.

Thirdly, this raises the greatest problems for Castro, as we see it. In the first place, by this action the Soviets have threatened him with attack by the United States, and therefore the overthrow of his regime—used his territory to put him in this jeopardy. And secondly the Soviets are talking to other people about the possibility of bargaining this support and these missiles against concessions in Berlin and elsewhere, and therefore are threatening to bargain him away. In these circumstances, we wonder whether he realizes the position that he is being put in and the way the Soviets are using him.

Then go on and say that if the Soviets are not being willing to do something to remove this ...... without the action that we intend, we will be compelled, to take.

If Castro feels that an attempt by him to take the kind of action that we're suggesting to him would result in serious difficulties for him within Cuba, we at least want him to know that and to convey to him and remind him of the statement that you, Mr. President, made a year and a half ago, in effect, that there are two points that are nonnegotiable. One is the Soviet tie and presence. And the second is aggression in Latin America. This is a hint, but no more than that, that we might have sympathy and help for him in case he ran into trouble trying to throw the old-line Communists and the Soviets out.

Rusk: Yes.

Martin: We'll give him 24 hours to respond.

Rusk: The disadvantage in that is, of course, the advance notice if he judges that we would not, in such an approach, say exactly what we would do. But it might, of course, lead him to bring up mobile antiaircraft weapons around these missiles themselves, or take some other action that will make the strike that [much] more difficult. But there is that move.

There are two other problems that we are concerned about. If we strike these missiles, we would expect, I think, maximum Communist reaction in Latin America. In the case of about 6 of those governments, unless the heads of government had some intimation requiring some preparatory steps from the security point of view, one or another of those governments could easily be overthrown. I'm thinking of Venezuela, for example, or Guatemala, Bolivia, Chile, possibly even Mexico. And therefore the question will arise as to whether we should not somehow indicate to them, in some way, the seriousness of the situation so they can take precautionary steps, whether we tell them exactly what we have in mind, or not.

The other is the NATO problem. We would estimate that the Soviets would almost certainly take some kind of action somewhere. For us to take an action of this sort without letting our closer allies know of a matter which could subject them to very great danger is a very far-reaching decision to make. And we could find ourselves isolated, and the alliance crumbling, very much as it did for a period during the Suez affair, but at a moment of much greater danger over an issue of much greater danger than the Suez affair for the alliance.

I think that these are matters that we'll be working on very hard this evening. But I think I ought to mention them because it's necessarily a part of this problem.

President Kennedy: Can we get a little idea about what the military thing is? Well, of course, number one, would you suggest taking these out?

McNamara: Yes, Mr. President. General Taylor has just been with the Chiefs, and the unified commanders went through this in detail.

To take out only the missiles, or to take out the missiles and the MiG aircraft and the associated nuclear storage facilities, if we locate them, could be done in 24 hours' warning. That is to say, 24 hours between the time of decision and the time of strike, starting with a time of decision no earlier than this coming Friday [October 19] and with the strike therefore on Saturday [October 20], or anytime thereafter with 24 hours between the decision and the time of strike.

General Taylor will wish to comment on this, but the Chiefs are strong in their recommendation *against* that kind of an attack, believing that it would leave too great a capability in Cuba undestroyed. The specific number of sorties required to accomplish this end has not been worked out in detail. The capability is for something in excess of 700 sorties per day. It seems highly unlikely that that number would be required to carry out that limited an objective, but at least that capability is available in the Air Force alone, and the Navy sorties would rise on top of that number. The Chiefs have also considered other alternatives extending into the full invasion. You may wish to discuss [that] later. But that's the answer to your first question.

President Kennedy: That would be taking out these 3 missile sites, plus all the MiGs?

McNamara: Well, you can go from the 3 missile sites, to the 3 missile sites plus the MiGs, to the 3 missile sites plus MiGs plus nuclear storage plus airfields, and so on up through the potential offensive.

President Kennedy: Just the 3 missiles, however, would be . . .

McNamara: Could be done with 24 hours' notice, and would require a relatively small number of sorties. Less than a day's air attack, in other words

President Kennedy: Of course, all you'd really get there would be would you get there? You'd get the, probably, you'd get the that have to be on the . . .

McNamara: You'd get the launchers

President Kennedy: The la

McNamara: No

Taylor:

ical

e, there was

he Joint Chiefs that, in

this very narrow, selective target

it may be detrimental.

ve been willing to give nuclear warheads to these

just as good reason for them to give a nuclear capability to

bases. We don't think we'd ever have a chance to take them again, so that we lose this first-strike surprise capability.

Our recommendation would be to get complete intelligence, get all the photography we need, the next 2 or 3 days, no, no hurry in our book. Then look at this target system. If it really threatens the United States, then take it right out with one hard crack.

President Kennedy: That would be taking out some of those fighters, bombers, and . . .

Taylor: Fighters, the bombers. IL-28s may turn up in this photography. It's not at all unlikely there are some there.

President Kennedy: Think you could do that in one day?

Taylor: We think that [in] the first strike we'd get a great majority of this. We'll never get it all, Mr. President. But we then have to come back day after day, for several days. We said 5 days, perhaps, to do the complete job. Meanwhile we could then be making up our mind as to whether or not to go on and invade the island.

I'm very much impressed with the need for a time, something like 5 to 7 days, for this air purpose, because of the parachute aspect of the proposed invasion. You can't take parachute formations, close formations of troop-carrier planes in in the face of *any* air opposition, really. So the first job, before there is any land attack including parachutes, is really cleaning out the MiGs and the accompanying aircraft.

McNamara: Mr. President, could I outline three courses of action we have considered and speak very briefly on each one?

The first is what I would call the political course of action, in which we follow some of the possibilities that Secretary Rusk mentioned this morning by approaching Castro, by approaching Khrushchev, by discussing with our allies. An overt and open approach politically to the problem, attempting to solve it. This seemed to me likely to lead to no satisfactory result, and it almost stops subsequent military action. Because the danger of starting military action after they acquire a nuclear capability is so great, I believe we would decide against it, particularly if that nuclear capability included aircraft as well as missiles, as it well might at that point.

A second course of action we haven't discussed, but lies in between the military course we began discussing a moment ago and the political course of action, would involve declaration of open surveillance: a statement that we would immediately impose a blockade against offensive weapons entering Cuba in the future and an indication that, with our open surveillance recon- naissance, which we would plan to maintain indefinitely for the future, we would be prepared to immediately attack the Soviet Union in the event that Cuba made any offensive move against this country.

Bundy: Attack who?

McNamara: The Soviet Union. In the event that Cuba made *any* offensive move against this country. Now this lies short of military action against Cuba, direct military action against Cuba. It has some major defects.

But the third course of action is any of these variants of military action directed against Cuba, starting with an air attack against the missiles. The Chiefs are strongly opposed to so limited an air attack. But even so limited an air attack is a very extensive air attack. It's not 20 sorties or 50 sorties or 100 sorties, but probably several hundred sorties. We haven't worked out the details. It's very difficult to do so when we lack certain intelligence that we hope to have tomorrow or the next day. But it's a substantial air attack. And to move from that into the more extensive air attacks against the MiGs, against the airfields, against the potential nuclear storage sites, against the radar installa- tions, against the SAM sites, means—as Max suggested—possibly 700 to 1,000 sorties per day for 5 days. This is the very, very rough plan that the Chiefs have outlined, and it is their judgment that that is the type of air attack that should be carried out. To move beyond that, into an invasion following the air attack, means the application of tens of thousands, between 90 and over 150,000 men, to the invasion forces.

It seems to me almost certain that any one of these forms of direct military action will lead to a Soviet military response of some type, some place in the world. It may well be worth the price. Perhaps we should pay that. But I think we should recognize that possibility, and, moreover, we must recognize it in a variety of ways. We must recognize it by trying to deter it, which ~~~ probably should alert SAC, probably ~~~ other ~~

_ ~~ prepared, in the event of even a small air strike and certainly in the event of a larger air strike, for the possibility of a Cuban uprising, which would force our hand in some way. [It would] either force us to accept an unsatisfactory uprising, with all of the adverse comment that results, or would force an invasion to support the uprising.

Rusk: Mr. President, may I make a very brief comment on that?

I think that any course of action involves heavy political involvement. It's going to affect all sorts of policies, positions, as well as the strategic situation. So I don't think there's any such thing as a nonpolitical course of action. I think also that we have to consider what political preparation, if any, is to occur before an air strike or in connection with any military action. And when I was talking this morning, I was talking about some steps which would put us in the best position to crack the strength of Cuba.

President Kennedy: I think the difficulty, it seems to me, is . . . I completely agree that there isn't any doubt that if we announced that there were MRBM sites going up that that would change . . . we would secure a good deal of political support after my statement. And the fact that we indicated our desire to restrain, this really would put the burden on the Soviets.

On the other hand, the very fact of doing that makes the military . . . we lose all the advantages of our strike. Because if we announce that it's there, then it's quite obvious to them that we're gonna probably do something about it, I would *assume*.

Now, I don't know that. It seems to me what we ought to be thinking about tonight is: If we made an announcement that the intelligence has revealed that there are . . . and if we did the note, message, to Khrushchev . . . I don't think that Castro has to know we've been paying much attention to it, any more than . . . Over a period of time it might have some effect, have settled back down, change. I don't think he plays it that way. So have a note to Khrushchev?

It seems to me my press statement was so *clear* about how we *wouldn't* do anything under these conditions, and under the conditions that we *would*. He must know that we're going to find out. So it seems to me he just . . .

Bundy: That's, of course, why he's been very, very explicit with us in communications to us about how dangerous this is, in the [September 11] TASS statement and his other messages.

President Kennedy: That's right. But he's initiated the danger, really, hasn't he? He's the one that's playing at God, not us.

Rusk: And his statement to Kohler on the subject of his visit and so forth, completely hypocritical.[5]

[At this point, about 20 minutes into the meeting, the recording was interrupted while the reels were being changed on the tape recorder in the basement. About a minute of conversation appears to have been lost before recording resumed.]

McNamara: . . . Cuba. There is a great possibility they can place them in operational condition quickly unless, as General Carter said, the system may have a normal reaction time, setup time, of 6 hours. Whether it has 6 hours or 2 weeks, we don't know how much time has started.

Nor do we know what air-launch capabilities they have for warheads. We don't know what air-launch capability they have for high-explosives. It's almost certainly a substantial high-explosive capability, in the sense that they could drop one or 2 or 10 high-explosive bombs someplace along the East Coast. And that's the minimum risk to this country we run as a result of advance warning, too.

Taylor: I'd like to stress this last point, Mr. President. We are very vulnerable to conventional bombing attack, low-level bombing attacks, in the Florida area.

---

5. Foy Kohler, the U.S. Ambassador to the Soviet Union, had met with Khrushchev earlier in the morning of October 16 (Moscow time). His report on their long conversation had arrived in Washington during the afternoon (Washington time), so Rusk and others would have read the report just before this meeting. In his initial summary report of that conversation (Moscow 970, 16 October 1962), Kohler reported Khrushchev's promise that he would not do anything to worsen relations until after the American congressional elections in early November. Khrushchev planned to visit New York for a meeting of the UN General Assembly later in November. Then he would renew the dialogue on Berlin and other matters. According to Kohler, Khrushchev said the Americans "could be sure he would take no action before meeting which would make situation more difficult."

Our whole air defense has been oriented in other directions. We've never had low-level defenses prepared for this country. So it would be entirely possible for MiGs to come through with conventional weapons and do some damage.

President Kennedy: Yeah.

If they got

.....al weapon.

...y would use a nuclear weapon unless they're

...rate a nuclear war. I don't think, I just don't see that possibility.

Bundy: I would agree.

Rusk: That would mean that—we could be just utterly wrong—but we've never really believed that Khrushchev would take on a general nuclear war over Cuba.

Bundy: May I ask a question in that context?

President Kennedy: We certainly have been wrong about what he's trying to do in Cuba. There isn't any doubt about that. Not many of us thought that he was going to put MRBMs on Cuba.

Bundy: Yeah. Except John McCone.

Carter: Mr. McCone.

President Kennedy: Yeah.

Bundy: But the question that I would like to ask is, quite aside from what we've said, and we're very hard-locked on to it, I know: What is the strategic impact on the position of the United States of MRBMs in Cuba? How gravely does this change the strategic balance?

McNamara: Mac, I asked the Chiefs that this afternoon, in effect. And they said: "Substantially." My own personal view is: Not at all.

Bundy: Not so much.

McNamara: And I think this is an important element here. But it's all very . . .

Carter: The reason our estimators didn't think that they'd put them in there,[6] because of—

***

6. Carter is referring to a Special National Intelligence Estimate, "The Military Buildup in Cuba," 19 September 1962, prepared by the Board of National Estimates, chaired by Sherman Kent. The estimate concluded that the Soviet Union "could derive considerable military advan-

McNamara: That's what they said themselves in [the] TASS statement.

Bundy: That's what they said themselves.

Carter: But then, going behind that—

President Kennedy: But what did it indicate? Being valuable enough?

Bundy: Doesn't improve anything in the strategic balance.

Carter: Doesn't improve anything. That was what the estimators felt, and that the Soviets would not take the risk.[7]

Mr. McCone's reasoning, however, was: If this is so, then what possible reason have they got for going into Cuba in the manner in which they are, with surface-to-air missiles and cruise-type missiles. He just couldn't understand *why* the Soviets were so heavily bolstering Cuba's defensive posture. There must be something behind it. Which led him then to the belief that they must be coming in with MRBMs.

Taylor: I think it was cold-blooded from their point of view, Mr. President. You're quite right in saying that these are just a few more missiles targeted on the United States. However, they can become a very, a rather important, adjunct and reinforcement to the strike capability of the Soviet Union. We have no idea how far they will go.

But, more than that, these are, to our nation, it means a great deal more. You all are aware of that, [the missiles] being in Cuba and not over in the Soviet Union.

Bundy: Well, I ask the question with an awareness of the political . . .

President Kennedy: I will say, my understanding's that . . . Let's just say that they get these in there. And then they get sufficient capacity, so we can't . . . with warheads. Then you don't want to knock them out because there's too much of a gamble.

Then they just begin to build up those air bases there, and then put more and more. I suppose they really . . . Then they start getting ready to squeeze us in Berlin. Doesn't that . . . ?

You may say it doesn't make any difference if you get blown up by an ICBM

---

tage" from deploying MRBMs and IRBMs in Cuba, but that such a development was incompatible with Soviet practice and policy because "it would indicate a far greater willingness to increase the level of risk in US-Soviet relations than the USSR has displayed thus far"; excerpt reprinted in McAuliffe, *CIA Documents,* p. 93.

7. Carter was partly in error. In fact, as indicated in the previous note, the estimators thought the deployment would improve the Soviet military position. This was a unanimous view in the intelligence community. Every lower-level expert, whether in State, the Office of the Secretary of Defense, the armed forces, or the CIA, believed (and separately wrote) that MRBMs and IRBMs in Cuba would materially improve the Soviet position in the strategic balance of power.

flying from the Soviet Union or one that was 90 miles away. Geography doesn't mean that much . . .

Taylor: We'd have to target them with our missiles and have th~ of pistol-pointed-at-the-head situation as they h~ present time.

Bundy: No ~

. . .ar plan over there for

. . .merican soldiers, Marines, and airmen

. . .aunched 1,800 Cubans against, a year and a half ago.

~ changed our evaluations. Well . . .

Robert Kennedy: Of course, the other problem is in South America a year from now. And the fact that you got these things in the hands of Cubans here, and then, say, some problem arises in Venezuela. You've got Castro saying: "You move troops down into that part of Venezuela, we're going to fire these missiles." I think that's the difficulty, rather than the [unclear]. I think it gives the [unclear] image.

President Kennedy: It makes them look like they're coequal with us. And that . . .

Dillon: We're scared of the Cubans.

Robert Kennedy: We let the . . . I mean, like, we'd hate to have it in the hands of the Chinese.

Dillon: I agree with that sort of thing very strongly.

Martin: It's a psychological factor. It won't reach as far as Venezuela is concerned.

Dillon: Well, that's—

McNamara: It'll reach the U.S., though. This is the point.

Dillon: Yeah. That is the point.

Martin: Yeah. The psychological factor of our having taken [accepted] it.

Dillon: Taken it. That's the best [way of putting it].

Robert Kennedy: Well, and the fact that if you go there, we're gonna fire it.

President Kennedy: What's that again, Ed? What are you saying?

Martin: Well, it's a psychological factor that we have sat back and let them do it to us. That is more important than the direct threat. It is a threat in the Caribbean . . .

President Kennedy: I said we weren't going to [allow it].

Bundy: That's something we could manage.

President Kennedy: Last month I said we weren't going to [allow it]. Last month I should have said that we don't care. But when we said we're *not* going to, and then they go ahead and do it, and then we do nothing, then I would think that our risks increase. I agree.

What difference does it make? They've got enough to blow us up now anyway. I think it's just a question of . . . After all, this is a political struggle as much as military.

Well, so where are we now? . . . Don't think the message to Castro's got much in it.

Let's just try to get an answer to this question: How much . . . It's quite obviously to our advantage to surface this thing to a degree before . . . First to inform these governments in Latin America, as the Secretary suggests. Secondly to the rest of NATO, people who have the right to some warning: [British Prime Minister Harold] Macmillan, de Gaulle. How much does this diminish . . . Not [telling them] that we're going to do anything, but the existence of them, without any say about what we're gonna do.

Let's say, 24 hours ahead of our doing something about it, we inform Macmillan. We make a public statement that these have been found on the island. That would be a notification, in a sense, of their existence, and everybody could draw whatever conclusion they wanted to.

Martin: I would say this, Mr. President. That I would . . . That if you've made a public statement, you've got to move immediately, or you're going to have a [unclear] in *this* country.

President Kennedy: Oh, I understand *that*. We'll be talking about . . . Say we're going to move on a Saturday. And we would say on a Friday that these MRBMs, that the existence of this, presents the gravest threat to our security and that appropriate action must be taken.

Robert Kennedy: Could you stick planes over them, until you made the announcement at 6:00, Saturday morning? And at the same time, or simultaneously, put planes over to make sure that they weren't taking any action or movement and that you could move in if they started moving the missiles in place or something. You would move in and knock . . . That would be the trigger that you would move your planes in and knock them out. Otherwise you'd wait until 6:00 or 5:00 that night. I don't . . . Is that . . .

Taylor: I don't think anything like that [would work]. I can't visualize doing it successfully that way. I think that anything that shows our intent to strike is going to place the airplanes and the missiles into . . . These are really mobile missiles. They can be pulled in under trees and forest and disappear almost at once, as I visualize [it].

McNamara: And they can also be readied, perhaps, between ~~...~~ in effect, say we're going to come in and the ~~...~~ very great danger to this coa~~st~~ ~~...~~ of the rea~~di~~

~~...~~ precede *any* public

~~...~~ ~~bel~~ieve so, yes. If you're going to strike. I think, before you ~~m~~ake any announcements, you should decide whether you're going to strike. If you are going to strike, you shouldn't make an announcement.

Bundy: That's right.

Dillon: What is the advantage of the announcement earlier? Because it's to build up sympathy, or something, for doing it. But you get the simultaneous announcement of what was there, and why you struck, with pictures and all—I believe would serve the same [purpose].

Ball: Well, the only advantage is, it's a kind of ultimatum. There is an opportunity of a response which would preclude it [the strike]. I mean, it's more for the appearance than for the reality. Because obviously you're not going to get that kind of response.

But I would suppose that there is a course which is a little different, which is a private message from the President to . . .

Martin: To Macmillan and de Gaulle.

Ball: That you're going to have to do this. You're compelled, and you've got to move quickly, and you want them to know it. Maybe 2 hours before the strike, something like that, even the night before.

Dillon: Well, that's different.

Ball: But it has to be kept on that basis of total secrecy. And then the question of what you do with these Latin American governments is another matter. I think if you notify them in advance, it may be all over.

President Kennedy: That's right. Then you just have to take Congress along . . .

Bundy: I think that's just not right.

President Kennedy: I'm not completely . . . I don't think we ought to abandon just knocking out these missile bases, as opposed to . . . That's a much more defensible, explicable, politically, or satisfactory in every way, action than the general strike, which takes us into the city of Havana, and it is plain to me, takes us into much more hazardous . . . shot down . . .

Now, I know the Chiefs say: "Well, that means their bombers can take off against us." But . . .

Bundy: Their bombers take off against us. Then *they* have made a general war against Cuba of it, which then becomes much more their decision.

We move this way [and] the political advantages are very strong, it seems to me, of the small strike. It corresponds to "the punishment fits the crime" in political terms. We are doing only what we warned repeatedly and publicly we would have to do. We are not generalizing the attack. The things that we've already recognized and said that we have not found it necessary to attack, and said we would not find it necessary to attack . . .

President Kennedy: Well, here's . . . Let's look, tonight. It seems to be we ought to go on the assumption that we're going to have the, course number two we've called it, which would be a general strike [and] that you ought to be in position to do that, then, if you decide you'd like to do number one.

Bundy: I agree.

Robert Kennedy: Does that encompass an invasion?

President Kennedy: No. I'd say that's the third course.

Let's first start with, I'd have to say first find out, the air, so that I would think that we ought to be in position to do one or two. One would be just taking out these missiles. If there were others we'd find in the next 24 hours . . . Number two would be to take out all the airplanes. And number three is invade.

Carter?: Well, they'd have to take out the SAM sites also, Mr. President.

President Kennedy: Okay, but that would be in two, included in number two.

[Several people start talking.]

Taylor: In order to get in to get the airfields, there's a good number we'd have to get.

Gilpatric: Well, isn't there a question whether any of the SAM sites are operational?

Taylor: We're not sure yet.

President Kennedy: Okay. Well, let's say we've decided we got to go in the whole way. So let's say that number two is the SAM sites plus the air.

Bundy: It's actually to clear the air, to win the air battle.

President Kennedy: Yeah, well, whatever it is. [Unclear.]

Now, it seems to me we ought to be preparing now, in the most covert way, to do one and two, with the freedom to make the choice about number one depending on what information we have on it—what kind of m~ requires, and how much is that gonna . . .

McNamara: Mr. President, it r~ started. And you ~ ~L

. . . ~j,

. . .~ re preparing. So , . .as given you the minimum time to . . we can brief the pilots and then crank in the new ~. . . .c. I would point out . . .

Bundy: To answer the question you asked: We don't have to decide how we're gonna do it. All we have to decide is if we want Sweeney[8] to be prepared to do it.

Taylor: That's correct.

McNamara: And Sweeney has said that he will take the tape that comes in tomorrow and process it Thursday and Friday [October 18 and 19] and prepare the mission folders for strikes on Saturday [October 20] or earlier, every day thereafter.

Taylor: Yes. The point is that we'll have to brief pilots. We're holding that back. And there'll be, I would say, 400 pilots will have to go to be briefed in the course of this. So I'm just saying this is widening the whole military scope of this thing very materially, if that's what we're supposed to do at this time.

President Kennedy: Well, now, when do we start briefing the pilots?

Taylor: They'll need at least 24 hours on that, when this new intelligence comes in.

President Kennedy: They will . . . In other words, then, until tomorrow. All I was thinking of—at least until . . .

Bundy: Can they be briefed in such a way that they're secure, [so] they have no access to—

McNamara: The President does not have to make any decision until 24 hours before the strike, except the decision to be prepared. And the process of

---

8. General Walter Sweeney, commander of the Tactical Air Command. Sweeney had earlier been placed in charge of all tactical strike planning under the relevant operational Commander-in-Chief, which was CINCLANT (Admiral Dennison).

preparation will not, in itself, run the risk of overt disclosure of the preparation.

Bundy: Doesn't [it] imply briefing, the preparation?

Taylor: It does, but—

McNamara: It implies the preparation of mission folders.

Taylor: Say, 24 hours before they go, they start a briefing.

I'd like to say this, Mr. President, the more time you can give, the better. Because they can then do a lot more rehearsing and checking out of all the pilots. So, while I accept the time cycle, I—

President Kennedy: Well, now, let's say you give a pilot . . . I mean, how does he find his way down to a SAM site off of one of those things?

Taylor: Well, they'll give him a target folder with all the possible guidance, and so on, to hit the target.

President Kennedy: They know how to do that, do they?

Taylor: Yes, sir. They're well trained in that procedure.

McNamara: Mission folders have already been prepared on all the known targets. The problem is that we don't have the unknown targets, specifically these missile launchers and the nuclear storage, and we won't have that until tomorrow night at the earliest. And it'll be processed photographically on Thursday, interpreted Thursday night, turned into target folders on Friday, and the mission could go Saturday. This is Sweeney's estimate of the earliest possible time for a spare strike against the missiles. Decision by the President on Friday, strike on Saturday.

As General Taylor pointed out, if we could have another day of preparation, which means no strike till Saturday, or alternatively more than 24 hours between the time of decision and the first strike, it will run more smoothly.

President Kennedy: Right. Well, now, what is it, in the next 24 hours, we need to do in order, if we're going to do, let's first say, one and two by Saturday or Sunday? You're doing everything that is . . .

McNamara: Mr. President, we need to do two things, it seems to me.

First, we need to develop a specific strike plan limited to the missiles and the nuclear storage sites, which we have not done. This would be a part of the broader plan, but I think we ought to estimate the minimum number of sorties. Since you have indicated some interest in that possibility, we ought to provide you that option. We haven't done this.

President Kennedy: Okay.

McNamara: But that's an easy job to do.

The second thing we ought to do, it seems to me, as a government, is to consider the consequences. I don't believe we have considered the consequences of any of these actions satisfactorily. And because we haven't considered the consequences, I'm not sure we're taking all the action we ought to take now to minimize those.

I don't know quite what kind of a world we live in ... and we've started it. We've put, let's ... illustration. I don't think ... Well, you ha...

...ight. Now, after we've launched ... world do we live in? How do we stop at that ... the answer to this. I think tonight State and we ought to ... on the consequences of any one of these courses of action, consequences which I don't believe are entirely clear to any of us.

Ball: At any place in the world.

McNamara: At any place in the world, George. That's right. I agree with you.

Taylor: Mr. President, I should say that the Chiefs and the commanders feel so strongly about the dangers inherent in the limited strike that they would prefer taking *no* military action rather than to take that limited strike. They feel that it's opening up the United States to attacks which they can't prevent, if we don't take advantage of . . .

President Kennedy: Yeah. But I think the only thing is, the chances of it becoming a much broader struggle are increased as you step up the . . . Talk about the dangers to the United States, once you get into beginning to shoot up those airports. Then you get a lot of antiaircraft. And you got a lot of . . . I mean, you're running a much more major operation, therefore the dangers of the worldwide effects are substantial to the United States, are increased. That's the only argument for it [the limited strike].

I quite agree that, if you're just thinking about Cuba, the best thing to do is to be bold, if you're thinking about trying to get this thing under some degree of control.

Sorensen: In that regard, Mr. President, there is a combination of the plans which might be considered, namely the limited strike and then, or simultaneously, the messages to Khrushchev and Castro which would indicate to them that this was none other than simply the fulfilling [of] the statements we have made all along.

President Kennedy: Well, I think we . . . In other words, that's a matter we've got to think about tonight. I don't . . .

Let's not let the Chiefs knock us out on this one, General, because I think that [what] we got to be thinking about is: If you go into Cuba in the way we're talking about, and taking out all the planes and all the rest, then you really haven't got much of an argument against invading it.

Ball: It seems to me a limited strike, plus planning for invasion 5 days afterwards to be taken unless something untoward occurs, makes much more sense.

Taylor: Well, I would be personally . . . Mr. President, my inclination is all against the invasion, but nonetheless trying to eliminate as effectively as possible every weapon that can strike the United States.

President Kennedy: But you're not for the invasion?

Taylor: I would not be, at this moment. No, sir.

We don't want to get committed to the degree that shackles us, with West Berlin.

McNamara: This is why I say I think we [have] to think of the consequences here. I would think a forced invasion, associated with assisting an uprising following an extensive air strike, is a highly probable set of circumstances. I don't know whether you could carry out an extensive air strike of, let's say, the kind we were talking about a moment ago, 700 sorties a day for 5 days, without an uprising in Cuba. I really . . .

Martin: In this morning's discussion we went into this, talked to some of your people, I believe, a little bit. And we felt an air strike, even of several days, against military targets primarily, would not result in any substantial unrest. People would just stay home and try to keep out of trouble.

McNamara: Well, when you're talking about military targets. We have 700 targets here we're talking about. This is a very damned extensive target system.

Taylor: That was in number [unclear], Mr. Secretary. But that's not the one I recommended.

McNamara: Well, neither is the one I'd recommend.

President Kennedy: What does that include? Every antiaircraft gun? What does that include?

Taylor: This includes related defenses, all sorts of things.

McNamara: Radar sites, SAM sites, and so on. But whether it's 700 or 200, and it's at least 200 I think . . .

Taylor: More in the order of 200, I'd say.

McNamara: It's at least 200. You can't carry that out without the danger of an uprising.

Robert Kennedy: Mr. President, while we're considering this problem to night, I think that we should also consider what Cuba's going to be a year now, or 2 years from now. Assume that we go in and knock these don't know what's gonna stop them from saying: "We're gon 6 months from now, bring them in [again]."

Taylor: Nothing permanent about it.

Robert Kennedy: Where are we 6 months f better position? Or aren't we in [a] worse out, and say: "Don't do it." I mean, c'

McNamara: You have to pu

Robert Kennedy: Then   n we're gonna have to sink P

Now, [think]   ou're going to get into it at a''   it over with, and take our l   . this . . .

                                          thing, or if he sticks those kinds
                                          gonna get into a war 6 months from

                         , this is why I think tonight we ought to put on
                      is and the probable, possible consequences thereof, in
                    Defense could agree on. Even if we disagree, then put in
                 cause the consequences of these actions have not been thought
              clearly. The one that the Attorney General just mentioned is illustrative
           hat.

President Kennedy: If it doesn't increase very much their strategic strength, why is it—can any Russian expert tell us—why they . . . ? After all, Khrushchev demonstrated a sense of caution over Berlin. He's been cautious. I mean, he hasn't been . . .

Ball: Several possibilities, Mr. President. One of them is that he has given us word now that he's coming over in November to the UN. He may be proceeding on the assumption, and this lack of a sense of apparent urgency would seem to support this, that this isn't going to be discovered at the moment and that, when he comes over, this is something he can do, a ploy—that here is Cuba armed against the United States. Or possibly use it to try to trade something in Berlin, saying he'll disarm Cuba if we'll yield some of our interests in Berlin and some arrangement for it. I mean that this is a trading ploy.

Bundy: I would think one thing that I would still cling to is that he's not likely to give Fidel Castro nuclear warheads. I don't believe that has happened or is likely to happen.

President Kennedy: Why does he put these in there, though?

Bundy: Soviet-controlled nuclear warheads.

President Kennedy: That's right. But what is the advantage of that? It's just as if we suddenly began to put a major number of MRBMs in Turkey. Now that'd be goddamn dangerous, I would think.

Bundy: Well, we did, Mr. President.

President Kennedy: Yeah, but that was 5 years ago.[9]

Alexis Johnson: We did it. We did it in England. That's when we were short. We gave England [unclear] when we were short of ICBMs.

President Kennedy: But that was during a different period then.

Alexis Johnson: But doesn't he realize he has a deficiency of ICBMs? [He] needs a PR [public-relations] capacity perhaps, in view of . . . He's got lots of MRBMs, and this is a way to balance it out a bit.

Bundy: I'm sure his generals have been telling him for a year and a half that he was missing a golden opportunity to add to his strategic capability.

Ball: Yes. I think you look at this possibility that this is an attempt to add to his strategic capabilities.

A second consideration is that it is simply a trading ploy, that he wants this in so that he could . . .

Unidentified: It means if he can't trade, he's still got the other.

[Various speakers begin talking simultaneously.]

Alexis Johnson: We are now considering these, then, Soviet missiles, a Soviet offensive capability.

Unidentified: You have to consider them Soviet missiles.

Alexis Johnson: It seems to me that if we go in there lock, stock, and barrel, we can consider them entirely Cuban.

Bundy: Ah, well, what we say for political purposes and what we think are not identical here.

Ball: But, I mean, any rational approach to this must be that they are Soviet missiles, because I think Khrushchev himself would never, would never, risk a major war on a fellow as obviously erratic and foolish as Castro.

Unidentified: A sublieutant.

Robert Kennedy: Let me say, of course, one other thing is whether we should also think of whether there is some other way we can get involved in this,

9. In late 1957, in the wake of fears arising from the Soviet Sputnik flight and concerns about Soviet missiles targeted at Europe, the United States had publicly offered to deploy intermediate-range ballistic missiles on the territory of its European allies. The Jupiters were not actually deployed to Turkey until 1961–62.

through Guantanamo Bay or something. Or whether there's some ship that . . . you know, sink the *Maine* again or something.[10]

Taylor: We think, Mr. President, that under any of these plans w~ ably get an attack on Guantanamo, at least by fire. They ~ mortars easily within range, and [with] any of these a~ to give air support to Guantanamo and probab~

President Kennedy: Well, that's why, it ~ we are going to be in a position to d~ Saturday or Sunday, then I wo~' depending on what ha~ tanamo, or some ~ ~n-

Taylor: M~ ~ set a schedule such ~

~uld be . . .

~ust wanted, I thought, we ought to be ~y time, though, if we decide that time is not ~ think we ought to be ready to do something, even ~o it. I'm not saying we should do it.

~f this is moving, short of the briefing. We've held back, we've ~ people . . .

President Kennedy: I understand.

What about, now, this invasion? If we were going to launch that, what do you have, what do we have to be doing now so that 10 days from now we're in a position to invade, if that was needed?

Taylor: I would say that my answer would be largely planning, particularly in the field of mobilization, just what we will want to recreate after we [unclear] these forces to Cuba.

I might say that air defense measures we're going to [take], we've started to take already. We moved more fighters into the southeastern United States and [are] gradually improving some of our patrol procedures, under the general guise of preparations for that part of the country. We don't think there'd be any leaks there that might react against our military plans. I repeat that our defenses have always been weak in that part of the country.

---

10. A reference to the mysterious explosion that sank the U.S.S. *Maine* while it was visiting Havana harbor during a period of tension between the United States and Spain over the conditions of Spanish rule in Cuba. The incident was widely believed to have precipitated the U.S. declaration of war that began the Spanish-American War in 1898.

President Kennedy: Mr. Secretary, is there anything that, or any of these contingencies, if we go ahead, that . . . the next 24 hours . . . We're going to meet again tomorrow on this in the afternoon. Is there anything . . .

McNamara: No, sir. I believe that the military planning has been carried on for a considerable period of time [and] is well under way. And I believe that all the preparations that we could take without the risk of preparations causing discussion and knowledge of this, either among our public or in Cuba, have been taken and are authorized. All the necessary reconnaissance measures are being taken and are authorized.

The only thing we haven't done, really, is to consider fully these alternatives.

Bundy: Our principal problem is to try and imaginatively to think what the world would be like if we do this, and what it will be like if we don't, if we fail in what we do.

McNamara: That's exactly right. We ought to work on that tonight.

Sorensen: This may be incidental, Mr. President, but if we're going to get the prisoners out, this would be a good time to get them out.[11]

President Kennedy: I guess they're not gonna get . . . Well . . .

Bundy: You mean, take them out.

Sorensen: No. What I meant was, if we're gonna trade them . . .

President Kennedy: They're on the Isle of Pines, these prisoners?

Robert Kennedy: No, some of them are. They're split up.

Bundy: If you can get them out alive, I'd make that choice.

President Kennedy: There's no sign of their getting out now, is there? The exchange?

Robert Kennedy: No, but they will take a few weeks.

President Kennedy: A few weeks.

Robert Kennedy: Yeah. You know they're having that struggle between the young Cuban leaders and the [unclear] . . .

Bundy: We have a list of sabotage options, Mr. President. It's not a very loud

---

11. There were long-standing negotiations between the Kennedy administration and Castro, carried on by intermediaries, to obtain the release of Cuban exiles who had been captured and imprisoned after the failure of the Bay of Pigs invasion in 1961. Castro had initially offered to exchange the prisoners for $28 million or 500 bulldozers. The administration had tried to raise the resources privately, but the effort became controversial, and negotiations were broken off. In 1962 Castro raised his price to $62 million. An American intermediary, lawyer and former World War II OSS chief James Donovan, persuaded Castro to accept some exchange of food and medicines instead of money. The negotiations involving Donovan were still under way at the time of the crisis, supervised for the administration principally by Robert Kennedy. The negotiations were concluded successfully after the crisis was over, and the released prisoners arrived in the United States at the end of 1962.

noise to raise at a meeting of this sort, but I think it would need your approval. I take [it] you are in favor of sabotage.

The one question which arises is whether we wish to do this in in waters or in positions which may—mining international Cuban waters may—hit . . . Mines are very indiscri…

President Kennedy: Is that what they're tal…

Bundy: That's one of the items. Mos…
and will simply be deniable, int…

The question that we r…
to authorize sabot…
ships.   …dy

P…

…ight now, do we?

…core any [unclear]?

…en in Cuba, the internal ones,

…esident, do you have any thoughts? Between
…wo?

…nson: I don't think I can add anything that is essential.

…**Kennedy:** Let's see, what time we gonna meet then, tomorrow?
… is it we want to have by tomorrow from the . . .

We want to have from the Department [of State] tomorrow, in a little bit more concise form, whether there is any kind of a statement we have to give. How much of a [unclear]?

And, number two, what do you think of these various alternatives we've been talking about, if you see there is any use bringing this to Khrushchev in the way of, for example . . . Do we want to, for example . . . Here is [Soviet Ambassador to the United States] Dobrynin now, he's repeatedly . . .

I've got to go to see Schroeder. Let's meet at 11:00 to 12:00. What time do I get back tomorrow night?[12]

Bundy: Reasonably early. Get back about 7:45.

President Kennedy: We meet here at 9:00?

Bundy: Mr. Secretary, some of the staff are in trouble with the dinner for Schroeder tomorrow night.

President Kennedy: Okay. Well, now, I don't think we'll have anything by noon tomorrow, do we?

---

12. President Kennedy was scheduled to see West German Foreign Minister Gerhard Schroeder on Wednesday morning, October 17, then to take a brief campaign trip after lunch and return late on Wednesday evening.

Bundy: Would you want to wait until Thursday morning [October 18], Mr. President?

President Kennedy: Looks to me like we might as well. Everybody else can meet if they want to, if they need to. The Secretary of State, the Secretary of Defense, can . . .

McNamara: I think it'd be very useful to meet, or else stay afterwards tonight for a while.

Bundy: It would be a great improvement not to have any more intense White House meetings. Trouble with all the comings and goings. If we could meet at the State Department tomorrow . . .

President Kennedy: All right. Then I could meet you, Mac, when I get back tomorrow and just as well, whatever the thing is. And then we can meet Thursday morning.

The question is whether . . . I'm going to see Gromyko Thursday,[13] and I think the question that I'd really like to have [answered] is some sort of a judgment on whether we ought to do anything with Gromyko, whether we ought to say anything to him, whether we ought to indirectly give him an ultimatum on this matter, or whether we just ought to go ahead without him.

It seems to me that he said we'd be . . . The ambassador [Dobrynin] told the Attorney General, as he told Bohlen the other day, that they were not going to put these weapons there. Now, either he's lying, or doesn't know. Whether the Attorney General saw [might see] Dobrynin, not acting as if we had any information about them, [and] say that, of course, they must realize that if this ever does happen that this is going to cause this . . . give a very clear indication of what's going to happen.

Now, I don't know what would come out of that. Possibly nothing. Possibly this'd alert them. Possibly they would reconsider their decision, but I don't think we've had any clear evidence of that, and it would give them . . . We'd lose a week.

Sorensen: You mean tell them that . . .

President Kennedy: Well, not tell them that we know that they've got it. But merely, in the course of a conversation, Dobrynin, having said that they would never do it . . . The Attorney General, who sees Dobrynin once in a while, would . . .

Sorensen: How would we lose a week?

President Kennedy: What?

---

13. Gromyko had just arrived in the United States for a series of meetings.

Sorensen: How would we lose a week?

President Kennedy: Oh, what we'd, Bobby, would be saying to them
short, is if these ever come up, that we're going to do . . . The pre
would have to take action. And this could cause the most fa
quences. On the possibility that that might cause t'
action.

I don't know whether he is, they are
their viewpoint, if they're awa
September 4 and 13]. A
of the Soviets e
blockade   ..in

                                                                ..this decision, in
                                                        .. is an important element

                                .. t change it. But they . . . It's quite a different
                        a contravenance on one . . .
                .. bet a *cookie* that Dobrynin doesn't know a bean about this.
        ..nt Kennedy: You think he *does* know.

Robert Kennedy: He didn't know. He didn't even know that [unclear], in
my judgment.

Taylor: There's evidence of sightings in late August, I think, and early
September, of some sort.

Sorensen: It seems to me, Mr. President, in your public presentation simultaneous or subsequent to an action, your hand is strengthened somewhat if
the Soviets have lied to you, either privately or in public.

Bundy: I'll agree to that.

Sorensen: And then if you, without knowing, ask Gromyko, or if Bobby asks
Dobrynin again, or if some other country could get the Soviets to say publicly
in the UN: "No, we have no offensive" . . .

Robert Kennedy: TASS, of course, said they wouldn't send offensive weapons
to Cuba.

President Kennedy: When did TASS say that?

Bundy: Yeah, the [September 11] TASS statement I read this morning . . .
No, the TASS statement. It's . . .

[Several speakers talk briefly at once; no clear statements.]

President Kennedy: Well, what about my question, for what I might say to
Gromyko about this matter. If you want me just [to] get in the record . . . like
asking him whether they plan to do it.

Bundy: Putting it the other way around, saying that we are putting great weight upon the assurance of his . . .

Ball: Well, I think what you get is to call their attention to the statement that you've made on this. [Someone agrees.] This is your public commitment, and you are going to have to abide by this, and you just want assurances from him that they're living up to what they've said, that they're not going to . . .

President Kennedy: Well, let's say he said: "Well, we're not planning to."

Bundy (reading from TASS statement of September 11): "The government of the Soviet Union also authorized TASS to state that there is no need for the Soviet Union to shift its weapons for the repulsion of aggression for a retaliatory blow to any other country, for instance, Cuba. Our nuclear weapons are so powerful in their explosive force, the Soviet Union has so powerful rockets to carry these nuclear warheads, that there is no need to search for sites for them beyond the boundaries of the Soviet Union."

President Kennedy: Well, what date was that?

Bundy: September 11th.

Dillon: When they were all there.

Taylor: Or certainly on the way.

President Kennedy: But isn't that . . . But, as I say, we have to . . . We never really ever had a case where it's been quite this . . . After all, they backed down in [supporting the] Chinese Communists in '58. They didn't go into Laos. Agreed to a ceasefire there.[14]

[Several speakers begin talking simultaneously.]

President Kennedy: What?

Bundy: I'm as puzzled as Bob is by the absence of a nuclear storage site.

Taylor: We don't know enough about it yet, and we [unclear] . . .

Bundy: I understand that. We may learn a lot overnight.

Martin: Isn't it puzzling, also, there are no evidence of any troops protecting the sites?

Taylor: Well there are troops there. At least there are tents; presumably they have some personnel.

Bundy: But they look like [unclear]. It's as if you could walk over the fields into those vans.

---

14. In the most recent of several confrontations in the Taiwan Straits, in 1958, China had shelled offshore islands under Taiwan's control and threatened to invade Taiwan, then linked by a mutual defense treaty with the United States. In Laos there had been a Communist insurgency against a pro-Western government that subsequently received significant U.S. aid. Heading off the threat of direct U.S. intervention, a negotiated ceasefire in Laos took effect in May 1961, followed by negotiations to render the country neutral.

President Kennedy: Well, it's a goddamn mystery to me. I don't know enough about the Soviet Union, but if anybody can tell me any other time since the Berlin blockade where the Russians have given so clear a provocati... know when it's been, because they've been awfully cautious sians . . . I never . . .

Now, maybe our mistake was in not saying that if they do this we're going to act. M

Robert Kennedy: Yeah, but th

President Kennedy: Th

Robert Kennedy

Preside

...at [nickname for Carter] ...nce. That means somebody in , take a look on the ground.

...ment] was 2 days before your statement [but ...ouse statement of September 4].

...try it. Your problems about exfiltration and your problems ...ng an individual as to what to look for are not handled in 24 hours.

McNamara: A better way would be to send in a low-flying airplane, and we have today put those on alert. But we would recommend against using the low-flying planes until shortly before the intention to strike.

Taylor: This was considered by the commanders today, and they're all of the opinion that the loss of surprise was more serious than the information we'd get from that.

Ball: I would think it would be very valuable to have them go in shortly before the strike, just to build the evidence. I mean, when you've got pictures that really show what was there . . .

President Kennedy: Now, with these great demonologists,[15] Bohlen and Thompson, did they have an explanation of why the Russians are sticking a [unclear] by itself?

[Several conversations go on at the same time. None of the intelligible fragments are of interest.]

President Kennedy: We're going to discuss the [unclear] budget [in a Cabinet meeting the next morning].

What about Schroeder? Do I have anything we want to say to Schroeder?

---

15. Kremlinologists, experts on the Soviet Union.

Bundy: We have a lot on that to discuss which was halfway in, early in the morning. I don't think it's very complicated. The big issue that has come up is Schroeder makes a very strong case for refusing visas on the ground that he thinks that that would undermine morale in Berlin in a very dangerous way. I think that's the principal issue that's between us.

President Kennedy: I wonder if we could get somebody to give me something about what our position should be on that.

Bundy: You want that? Yeah, very happy to. You want it tonight?

President Kennedy: No, no. Just in the morning.

[The meeting is breaking up. There are more fragments of simultaneous conversations.]

President Kennedy: That's very good, General. Thank you.

Carter: Mr. McCone is coming in tonight.

[Fragments of other discussions.]

Carter: I would suggest that we got into this hot water partly because of this.

President Kennedy: Yeah. I want to talk to him in the morning. I'd like to just be briefed [unclear].

Bundy: He won't be . . . Does he get back tonight?

Carter: Coming in tonight, yes, sir. I'm going to get [unclear].

Bundy: Then could he come in in the morning?

[Carter replies.]

Could he come in then at 9:30?

Carter: Sure.

[President Kennedy leaves the Cabinet Room. With the recording machine still running, McNamara, Bundy, Ball, and possibly others begin their own informal discussion of the crisis issues.]

McNamara: Could we agree to meet, midafternoon?

Ball: Any time you say, Bob.

McNamara: And then guide our work tonight and tomorrow on that schedule? Why don't we say 3:00? This'll give us some time to cover all we've done, and then do some more tomorrow night, if necessary tomorrow afternoon.

Bundy: Would it be disagreeable to make it a little earlier? I ought to get to a 4:00 meeting with Schroeder.

McNamara: I thought he said 2:00, I think, with Schroeder.

Unidentified: 2:00.

Bundy: Good.

McNamara: Really plenty of time between [unclear]. At 2:00 P.M. we'll do it at State.

Now, could we agree what we're gonna do? I would suggest that we divide the series of targets up by, in effect, numbers of DGZs[16] and numbers of sorties required to take those out, for a series of alternatives starting only with th missiles and working up through the nuclear storage sites and the M SAMs, and so on, so we can say: "This target system would t points, 80 points, and so many objects would take s out." Not because I think that there are reaso

Bundy: They're not really going t [unclear] . . .

McNamara: . . . but President, to get very easi

...e

...sal of the world

...s is something State would have to do, put it on paper. And we, I'll, be happy to stay in the morning, or something like that, in order that ...oagreement if we [unclear].

What I would suggest is that someone be deputied to do a piece of paper which really is: "What happens?"

I think the margin is between whether we [do the] take-out-the-missiles-only strike, or take a lot of air bases. This is tactical, within a decision to take military action. It may substantially, if it doesn't overwhelmingly, change the world. I think any military action does change the world. And I think not taking action changes the world. And I think these are the two worlds that we need to look at.

McNamara: I'm very much inclined to agree, but I think we have to make that point: within the military action [there is] a gradation.

Bundy: I agree, I agree. Oh, many gradations. And they have major effects. I don't need to exaggerate that now.

The question is: how to get ahead with that [other paper]. I would think, myself, that the appropriate place to make this preliminary analysis is at the Department of State. I think the rest of us ought to spend the evening, really, to some advantage separately, trying to have our own views of this. And I think we should meet in order, at least, to trade pieces of paper, before 2:00. Tomorrow morning, if that's agreeable.

16. Designated Ground Zeros, the precise aim points for explosives.

McNamara: Why don't we meet tomorrow morning. And with pieces of paper, from State, and—maybe you don't feel this is reasonable, but I would strongly urge that, tonight, State [unclear].

Bundy: Well, who is State's de facto [person in charge for this]? Are you all tied up tonight? Or what?

Ball: No, no. The situation is that the only [one] who's tied up tonight is the Secretary, and he is coming down at 11:00 from his dinner to look at what we will have done in the meantime.

Martin: Alex [Johnson] is back waiting for him.

Ball: Oh, good. We'll have Alex; we'll have Tommy [Llewellyn Thompson]. Well, we've kept this to our—this has been . . .

Bundy: But you have Tommy? I—

Ball: Talked to him this afternoon some.

Bundy: I'd be fascinated by this, the first sense of how he sees this.

Ball: Well, the argument was really between Hilsman's[17] demonologists, who were already cut in because they [unclear], who thought this was a low-risk operation. Tommy thought it was a high-risk operation by the Soviets—in other words, that they were taking real chances. Other people rather thought that they probably had miscalculated us and thought this wasn't a risky operation. You know, from the way they were going at it, either impatient, like the SAM sites hadn't been set up to protect it [the missile site]—the various factors which suggest to them that they didn't think anything was gonna happen. Tommy leaned the other way.

McNamara: Could I suggest that tonight we actually draft a paper, and it start this way:

Just a paragraph or two of the knowns. The knowns are that the SAMs are there. Let's say, the probable knowns, because we're not certain of any of them. The probabilities are the SAM system isn't working today. This is important. The probabilities are that these missiles are not operational today. The probabilities are that they won't be operational in less than x days, although we can't be certain. Pat said 2 weeks. I'm not so sure I'd put it that far. There's just two or three of the knowns.

I would put in there, by the way, the number of them [and] they're unprotected. Another known I'd put in is that they have about 50x MiG-15s, -17, and 19s. That they have certain crated, 10x crated MiG-21s, only one of which

---

17. Roger Hilsman, Assistant Secretary of State for Intelligence and Research.

we believe to have been assembled. They have *x* crated IL-28s, none of which we believe to have been assembled. This is, in a sense, the problem we face there.

Bundy: Do you believe State or the agencies should [unclear] knowns?

McNamara: Well [unclear]

[unclear] them in

[unclear] in that I do not think the Army and the Chiefs [n]ormally consider. And that is the possibility of genuinely making a quite large-scale strike, followed by a drop, followed by a recovery of the people dropped to get these things, and not simply to increase the chances that we've hit most of them. There's always incompleteness in a military, in an *air,* operation. But if these things are what the pictures show, you could drop a battalion of paratroopers and get them. Now what you do with a battalion, I grant you, is a hell of a problem.

I think there's an enormous political advantage, myself, within these options, granting that all the Chiefs didn't fully agree, [to] taking out the thing that gives the trouble, and not the thing that doesn't give the trouble.

McNamara: This, as opposed to an air attack on . . .

Bundy: Supplementary to an air attack. I mean, how're you gonna know that you've got them? And if you haven't got them, what've you done?

Ball: Well, this, of course, raises the question of: Having gotten this set, what happens to the set that arrives next week?

McNamara: Let me answer Mac's question first. How do we know we've got them? We will have photo recon, military, with the strike. Sweeney specifically plans this, and—

Bundy: Proving a negative is a hell of a job.

McNamara: Pardon me?

Bundy: Proving a negative is a hell of a job.

Carter: But Central's on the ground very well out of there, Mac.

Bundy: That's true.

McNamara: Terrible risk to put them [paratroopers] in there.

Bundy: I agree, I think the [unclear] is probably a bad idea, but it . . .

McNamara: I think the risk troubles me. It's too great in relation to the risk of not knowing whether we get them.

Bundy: Well . . .

McNamara: But, in any case, this is a small variant of one of the plans.

Bundy: That's right, it's a minor variant of one plan.

McNamara: It seems to me that there are some major alternatives here that I don't think we discussed fully enough today. And I'd like to see them laid out on the paper, if State agrees.

The first is what I still call the political approach. Let me say it's a nonmilitary action. It doesn't start with one, and it isn't gonna end with one. And I, for that reason, call it a political approach. And I say it isn't gonna end with one because, once you start this political approach, I don't think you're gonna *have* any opportunity for a military operation.

Ball: It becomes *very* difficult.

McNamara: But at least I think we ought to put it down there.

Unidentified: Right.

Bundy: And it should be worked out. I mean, what is the maximum—

Unidentified: Your ride is waiting downstairs.

Ball: Very good, thank you.

McNamara: Yeah, it should definitely be worked out. What, exactly, does it involve? And what are the chances of success of it? They're not zero. They're plus, I think.

Gilpatric: We did an outline this morning along these lines.

McNamara: All right. That's [unclear], anyway.

Bundy: But, do you see, it's not just the chances of success. It ought to be examined in terms of the pluses and minuses of nonsuccess, [McNamara agrees] because there is such a thing as making this thing pay off in ways that are of some significance, even though we don't act, or go with that.

McNamara: Yes, yes. I completely agree.

And this is my second alternative, in particular, and I want to come to that in a moment. But the first one, I completely agree it isn't . . . I phrased it improperly. Not the chances of success. It's the results that we're causing for mankind.

Bundy: Yep.

McNamara: Now, the second alternative, I'd like to discuss just a second because we haven't discussed it fully today, and I alluded to it a moment ago.

I'll be quite frank. I don't think there is a military problem here. This is my answer to Mac's question—

Bundy: That's my honest judgment.

McNamara: —and therefore, and I've gone through this today, and I asked myself: "Well, what is it then, if it isn't a military problem?"

Well, it's just exactly this problem: that if Cuba should possess a capacity to carry out offensive actions against the U.S., the U.S. would act.

Unidentified: That's right.

Unidentified: That's right. You can't get around that one.

McNamara: Now it's that problem. This is a domestic political problem. The announcement. We didn't say we'd go in or not, and kill th... we'd act. Well, how will we act? Well, we w—... it's really the act.

...ing in.

...*ara:* We search every ship.

Ball: There are two kinds of blockade: a blockade which stops ships from coming in, and simply a search.

McNamara: A search, that's right.

Ball: Yeah.

Well, it would be a search and removal, if found.

Bundy: You have to make the guy stop to search him. And if he won't stop, you have to shoot, right?

Ball: And you have to remove what you're looking for if you find it.

Unidentified: That's right.

McNamara: Absolutely. Absolutely. And then an ultimatum. I call it an ultimatum associated with these two actions, a statement to the world, particularly to Khrushchev, that we have located these offensive weapons. We're maintaining a constant surveillance over them. If there is ever any indication that they're to be launched against this country, we will respond not only against Cuba, but we will respond directly against the Soviet Union with a full nuclear strike.

Now, this alternative doesn't seem to be a very acceptable one. But wait until you work on the others.

Bundy: That's right.

McNamara: This is the problem, but I've thought something about the others this afternoon.

Ball: Bob, let me ask you one thing that seems slightly irrelevant. What real utility would there be in the United States if we ever actually captured one of these things and could examine it and take it apart?

McNamara: Not very much. No, no.

Ball: Would we learn anything about the technology that would be meaningful?

McNamara: No, no. I don't [unclear]. Pat may disagree with me . . .

Carter: I don't think so.

McNamara: Well, in any case, that's an alternative. I'd like to see it expressed and discussed.

Ball: Of course, if it takes 2 hours to screw a [war]head on, as a guy said this morning, 2 to 4 hours . . .

McNamara: Oh, by the way, that should be one of the knowns in this initial paragraph.

Ball: Yeah.

Bundy: That's right.

Ball: They've got all night. How're you gonna survey them during the night? I mean, it seems to me that they are some gaps in the surveillance.

McNamara: Oh, well, it really isn't the surveillance, it's the ultimatum that is the key part in this.

Ball: Yeah.

McNamara: And, really, what I tried to do was develop a little package that meets the action requirement of that paragraph I read. Because, as I suggested, I don't believe it's primarily a military problem. It's primarily a domestic political problem.

Ball: Yeah, well, as far as the American people are concerned, action means military action, period.

McNamara: Well, we have a blockade. Search and removal of offensive weapons entering Cuba.

I don't want to argue for this because I don't think it's a perfect solution by any means. I just want to . . .

Ball: No, no, I think it's an alternative.

Bundy: Which one are [we] still on, would you say?

McNamara: Still on the second one.

Ball: Now, one of the things we look at is whether the actual operation of a blockade isn't a greater involvement almost than a military action.

McNamara: Might well be, George.

Bundy: I think so.

McNamara: It's a search, not an embargo.

Ball: It's a series of single, unrelated acts, not by surprise. This coming in there, a Pearl Harbor, just frightens the hell out of me as to what goes beyond. The Board of National Estimates have been working on this ever since . . .

Bundy: What goes beyond what?

Ball: What happens beyond that. You go in there with a surprise attack. You put out all the missiles. This isn't the end. This is the *beginning*, I think. There's a whole hell of a lot of things . . .

Bundy: Are they all working on powerful reaction in your [. . .

Carter: Yes, sir.

Bundy: Good.

[Two . . .

. . . we . . . to divide category three . . . probable effect on the world thereafter. . . . is, at least in the sense of the Cuban uprising, which I happen to believe is a most important element of category three. It applies to some elements in category three, but not all.

But, in any event, what kind of a world do we live in? In Cuba what action do we take? What do we expect Castro will be doing after you attack these missiles? Does he survive as a political leader? Is he overthrown? Is he stronger, weaker? How will he react?

How will the Soviets react? What can . . . How could Khrushchev afford to accept this action without some kind of rebuttal? He can't accept it without some rebuttal. It may not be a substantial rebuttal, but it's gonna have to be some. Where?

How do we react in relation to it? What happens when we do mobilize? How does this affect our allies' support of us in relation to Berlin? Well, you know far better than I the problems. But it would seem to me if we could lay this out tonight, and then meet [at] a reasonable time in the morning to go over a tentative draft, discuss it, and then have another draft for some time in the afternoon . . .

Alexis Johnson: One kind of planning, Bob, that we didn't explicitly talk about today, is to look at the points of vulnerability around the world, not only in Berlin, not only in Turkey.

McNamara: Sure. Iran.

Alexis Johnson: Iran and all of them.

McNamara: And Korea.

Alexis Johnson: What precautionary measures ought to be taken?

McNamara: Yes, yes.

Alexis Johnson: Well these are both military and political.

McNamara: Exactly. And we call it a worldwide alert. Under that heading we've got a whole series of precautionary measures that we think should be taken. All of our forces should be put on alert. But, beyond that, mobilization, redeployment, movement, and so on.

Well, would it be feasible to meet at some time in the morning? Mac, what would you think?

Bundy: I ought to join the President for the meeting with Schroeder, and I'll be involved in getting started for that from about 9:30 on. I could meet any time before that.

Carter: Well, now, the President was going to see Mr. McCone at 9:30.

Bundy: That's right.

McNamara: Well, why don't we meet at 8:30?

Bundy: Fine.

McNamara: Let's try that.

Bundy: Okay.

McNamara: Now, there's not much we can do to help. I'd be happy to, though, if you think of anything we can do. We'll go to work tonight and get these numbers of sorties, by target systems, laid out. Riley's[18] up in Mac's office, and I'll go down there now and get them started on it.

Carter: I think Mr. McCone could be helpful to you all in the morning.

McNamara: Well, I think he should try to stay here at 8:30.

Carter: He's been worrying about this for a heck of a long time.

Bundy: Sure.

This small informal meeting then broke up. The recording picked up a few fragments of conversation. Bundy talked about eating supper with someone. Bundy and Ball apparently referred to the secretarial problems that arose from informing so few people about the crisis. Then there was silence. After a few minutes a man came in to clean the room. Evelyn Lincoln walked in, spoke briefly to him, and apparently she turned off the machine.

Everyone was still trying to conceal the existence of a crisis by appearing to maintain their known schedules. President Kennedy went to another farewell

---

18. We have not been able to identify Riley.

dinner for Bohlen. At the dinner he drew Bohlen aside and they had a long, animated, private conversation. Kennedy reportedly asked Bohlen if he could stay, but Bohlen feared that delaying his long-planned departure for Paris might arouse unwanted notice and comment.

Meetings resumed that evening at the State Department, winding up in Rusk's office at about 11:00. McNamara slept at the Pentagon that night. McCone returned to Washington.

THURSDAY, OCTOBER 18

11:00 A.M.

CABINET ROOM

As arranged on Tuesday, Kennedy's advisers met at 8:30 A.M. on Wednesday, October 17, in a conference room on the seventh floor of the State Department. McCone, now back in Washington, joined them. There Ball reiterated his opposition to any military action, expressing doubt that the Soviet leaders really understood what they had done. Thompson argued that Khrushchev knew what he was doing, wanted a showdown on Berlin, and believed that missiles in Cuba armed him for that confrontation. Taylor and McCone sided with Thompson. After less than an hour, McCone and Bundy left for the White House.

At 9:30 on Wednesday, McCone briefed President Kennedy. He came away with the impression that Kennedy, too, leaned toward prompt military action. Kennedy asked McCone to go to Gettysburg and give Eisenhower a full briefing, which McCone promptly did, bringing back a report that Eisenhower thought the situation intolerable and would support any decisive military action. Kennedy meanwhile proceeded to his meeting with the West German foreign minister, devoted to Berlin issues. Afterward the President attended another lunch for the visiting Libyan Crown Prince, then flew to Connecticut to campaign for a Democratic Senate candidate.

From Stevenson, Kennedy received a memo urging that he send personal emissaries to Khrushchev and Castro. Stevenson warned that any U.S. military action could lead to reprisals in Turkey or Berlin and could then escalate. "To start or risk starting a nuclear war is bound to be divisive at best," he wrote, "and the judgments of history seldom coincide with the tempers of the moment." While he said that he understood Kennedy's dilemma, he wrote with underscoring: "*the means adopted have such incalculable consequences that I feel you should have made it clear that the existence of nuclear missile bases anywhere is negotiable before we start anything.*"[1] Stevenson then returned to his duties at the UN in New York.

That same morning the Joint Chiefs of Staff reconvened. Their Joint Staff had worked through the night to come up with plans for air strikes against 5 different sets of targets. Identified by roman numerals I–V, these alternative plans would be frequently discussed in the days to come. They were as follows. with associated numbers of sorties. The estimated sortie n··· ' to climb as planning continued.[2] The ·-··· ·

2,002

_ ..ny strike limited only to the missile sites. They
..u..u also to view any blockade as merely a complement to, not an alternative for, an air strike. They assumed, in addition, that a blockade would require a formal declaration of war.

About 15 senior officials met again for several hours on the afternoon of October 17.[3] Almost all leaned toward taking some political action before launching an air strike. They reviewed a large number of possible courses of action and speculated about imaginable Soviet responses. McNamara and Taylor worried that any diplomatic efforts would alert the Soviets and thwart

1. Adlai Stevenson, letter to President Kennedy, October 17, 1962, reprinted in Laurence Chang and Peter Kornbluh, eds., *The Cuban Missile Crisis, 1962: A National Security Archive Documents Reader* (New York: New Press, 1992), pp. 119–120.

2. To derive sortie numbers, planners examined a target and determined how many individual aim points should be hit in order to ensure destruction of the target. Next they used training experience to judge how many bombs would need to be dropped on an aim point to be fairly sure that it was hit. Finally, planners incorporated attrition from enemy action or mechanical problems to calculate sortie numbers. These numbers first grew because new targets were identified. Later they grew because the staff began incorporating additional requirements for escort, air-defense suppression, and post-strike reconnaissance. A few days later, exasperated by the latest revision, Taylor exclaimed to his JCS colleagues: "What! These figures were reported to the White House. You are defeating yourselves with your own cleverness, gentlemen"; Notes taken from Transcripts of Meetings of the Joint Chiefs of Staff, p. 6, October–November 1962, National Security Archive, Washington, D.C.

3. These meetings were attended (though not everyone was there all of the time) by Robert Kennedy, Rusk, McNamara, Taylor, Bundy, McCone, Ball, Gilpatric, Alexis Johnson, Bohlen, Thompson, Sorensen, Martin, possibly Nitze, and (late in the day for a shorter time) Acheson.

an effective strike. McNamara and Gilpatric belittled the significance of the Soviet MRBM deployments for the overall strategic balance. McCone and Taylor argued that the MRBMs did, indeed, change the balance. But this difference of opinion did not prevent general agreement that the United States could not allow the Soviet deployment to stand. In this context, Kennedy's advisers for the first time discussed in detail the pros and cons of a blockade. Bohlen and Thompson continued to insist that Khrushchev's aim was to achieve something with regard to Berlin and that the U.S. government ought not to be diverted to concentrating exclusively on Cuba.

Kennedy had invited former Secretary of State Dean Acheson to join his circle of advisers. Formidably self-assured and gifted with cutting wit as well as great ability in advocacy, Acheson participated in these Wednesday meetings, weighing in in favor of a prompt air strike with no attempt at prior negotiation. Before adjourning for dinner, the conferees also reviewed the possibility of a blockade coupled with a declaration of war against Cuba.

During the break Robert Kennedy and Sorensen drove to the airport to meet the President on his return from Connecticut. Sorensen gave him a written summary of the day's discussions, emphasizing how fluid matters remained. (It included a list of around 20 questions as yet unresolved.) President Kennedy decided to stay out of the discussions until the next day. Robert Kennedy and Sorensen then returned to the State Department. The meeting resumed at 10:00, going until nearly midnight.

During this late-hour meeting, Rusk endorsed and elaborated on the alternative of a strike against the missile sites with no prior negotiation. Taylor and McCone supported him, with McCone mentioning Eisenhower's views. Bohlen still urged that an ultimatum be given before an attack. Thompson, Martin, and Gilpatric preferred a complete blockade with the declaration of war.

At the end of this meeting, Robert Kennedy summarized the major options that had been aired. They apparently were (a) an ultimatum to Khrushchev followed by a strike; (b) a limited strike without prior warning or negotiation, but notifying key allies; (c) political warning followed by a naval blockade and readiness for other actions; (d) a large-scale strike after some political preparation; (e) proceeding directly to an invasion. Sorensen's earlier note for Kennedy had a similar list. Various forms of political action and messages to Khrushchev were considered, as well as various kinds of strikes. Many questions were identified for further analysis, especially about likely Soviet responses.

On the night of October 17–18, a few officials wrote brief papers for the

President summarizing their personal beliefs. Dillon submitted a memo stating opposition to negotiations of any kind with Khrushchev. He recommended a blockade coupled with intensive surveillance of Cuba and a demand that Cuba begin removal of the weapons forthwith. If the Cubans refused, or if the military pronounced the blockade infeasible, Dillon favored an immediate air strike. He said that the Soviet Union had "initiated a test of our intentions that can determine the future course of world events for many years to come." He continued, "I . . . believe that the survival of our nation d⸻ elimination of the offensive wea⸻

Ball wro⸻

⸻g we have ⸻ condemn us as hypocrites in the ⸻. Ball recommended a blockade that might ultimately cripple and bring down the Castro government.[5]

Bohlen, preparing to depart for Paris, also wrote a memo for Rusk concisely explaining his preference for an ultimatum before a strike. Though he had taken a different view, Rusk was impressed with Bohlen's memo and decided to share it with his colleagues and President Kennedy when they next gathered at the White House.[6]

On the morning of October 18, Sorensen noted for Kennedy that "two big questions must be answered, and in conjunction with each other." One was which kind of military action to choose, and the other was whether political action, such as a letter to Khrushchev, should precede any military move. The

---

4. C. Douglas Dillon, "Memorandum for the President," October 17, 1962, in Chang and Kornbluh, *The Cuban Missile Crisis*, pp. 116–118.

5. "Position of George W. Ball," October 17, 1962, ibid., pp. 121–122.

6. In their conversation at dinner on Tuesday night, October 16, Kennedy had asked Bohlen to postpone his highly publicized departure for Paris and help with the crisis. Bohlen worried about the notice his change of plans would cause but said he would try to come up with a cover story. The next day Bohlen discussed the matter with Rusk, who thought Bohlen should proceed with his plans and that Thompson could provide the needed advice on the Soviet Union. Rusk called President Kennedy, and Kennedy called Bohlen and told him to go ahead with his departure.

On the morning of October 18 Kennedy changed his mind, possibly after reading Sorensen's note highlighting Bohlen's advocacy. Just before the 11:00 meeting transcribed here, Bohlen was summoned (from the airport) to come to the White House. On the phone, Bohlen convinced the President to let him go ahead with his travel, since he was now expected at a public event that day in New York. Robert Kennedy later voiced bewilderment and anger about Bohlen's decision.

"Rusk approach," he said, was for a strike without warning. The "Bohlen approach" would first approach Khrushchev.[7]

Meanwhile, intelligence analysts had pored over photos from the earlier U-2 flights. They found something new—evidence of fixed IRBM sites in addition to the MRBM sites that had already been identified. With twice the range of MRBMs (2,200 miles instead of 1,100) and warheads of roughly twice as much yield (up to 5 megatons), these missiles could menace all parts of the continental United States except the Pacific Northwest.

As officials received this new information on the morning of October 18, their attitudes hardened. McNamara called McCone to say that he now thought prompt and decisive action necessary. Taylor told the Joint Chiefs that the news tipped him toward supporting the maximum option—full invasion of Cuba. This then became the unanimous position of the JCS. These early-morning discussions of the new intelligence set the mood as President Kennedy again took the chair and his advisers filed into the Cabinet Room.

McCone: . . . based on photography from Sunday, October 14, and 2 [flights] from Monday, October 15. These are completely read out. We continued to run [flights] yesterday. We expect the initial readout to start later tonight and probably take 36 to 48 hours to complete the readout from the 6 [U-2] missions [flown on October 17].

President Kennedy: These missions [unclear]? They don't know what coverage they got, do they?

Lundahl: The total picture has not yet emerged yet, sir. We're flying in clouds, and we don't have the film yet in the National PI Center. It starts to come in this afternoon, shortly after lunch.

McCone: We think we got the entire island. But we didn't get the [unclear]. I think you should know that these 6 missions involve about 28,000 linear feet of film. When this is enlarged, it means the Center has to examine a strip of film 100 miles long, 20 feet wide. Quite a job.

Go ahead.

Lundahl: Yes, sir. Mr. President, gentlemen, the first and most important item I would seek to call to your attention is a new area hitherto never seen by us, some 21 miles to the southwest of Havana, which we have at the moment

---

7. Sorensen to Kennedy, October 18, 1962, National Security Files, Cuba—General: 10/15/62–10/23/62, JFKL. Dillon's approach—an ultimatum/blockade, then a strike—was thus close to Bohlen's. Ball's suggestion, for a blockade followed by political pressure, was different.

labeled a probable MRBM/IRBM launch complex. The name of the town nearest is this [Guanajay]. It is there.

The 2 sites, sir, numbers 1 and 2—are $2\frac{1}{2}$ miles apart. And enlarging this one, we look at it, and we see for the first time a pattern of medium/IRBM sites that looks like the things we have been seeing in the Soviet Union. There are 2 [launch] pads, here—and here. They are separated by 750 feet. There's a control bunker with cable scars [marks on the ground showing cable emplacements] going up into small buildings inboard of each of th

no equipment on the pads yet. The

has been

                                                                  there

                              [pad] up in here, but the spacing is

The orientation of the axis of the pads, 315 [degrees], will bring you into the central massif of the United States. We call it M/IRBM, sir. We have never identified, irrevocably, the signature of the Soviet intermediate-range ballistic missile, which is estimatedly a 2,000-mile missile. But the elongation of the pads and the location of the control bunkers, between each pair of pads, has been the thing that has suggested to our hearts, if not our minds, the kind of thing that might accompany an IRBM.

So we have at the moment labeled it as such and let the guided-missiles intelligence analysts come up, finally, with a true analysis of what the range of these missiles might be that are eventually accommodated on this set of pads.

If I may switch to the next one, sir.

President Kennedy: [Can I] go look?

Lundahl: Yes, sir. For comparison purposes, Mr. President, I showed the other day, when I was here [Tuesday, October 16], the sites that we had described to you the other day, the 3 that we showed you were [unclear] near San Cristóbal. The one with erectors and missiles. The one here, just with the missiles and no erectors. And this one here at an early stage of construction, with tenting and encamping materials, but neither missiles nor erectors. The date of that photography was 14 October, and the impression of this third site is contained in this illusion here, wherein I think you can see the equipment, the buildings and the housing, and so forth.

On the next day, and admittedly with better photographic cover, we see this same area that is shown in here with, now, missile erectors, probably off in here, vehicles, more vehicles, buildings, missile transporters, and a variety of equipment and additional things under construction. The impression one would gather is that there is some sense of speed with which they are proceeding in the construction on this particular base. May I pass that one over to you, sir?

Also, earlier, Mr. President, we reported to you a number of what we call cruise-missile sites, short-range coastal defense-type missiles starting out with the Banes site, with another one located at Santa Cruz del Norte, up here in the Havana area.[8] At the time of that reporting, there were 2 launchers at this position, here and here.

Since the coverage of that day, 2 more launching positions have been added outboard of those 2 positions. The launcher here is uncovered. You can actually see the launcher itself, and, down in this small revetment here, appears to be the winged kind of air-breathing missile which will go on it. It's a short, stubby-winged fellow which conforms with the cruise type of missile that we have seen before. So our opinion of this thing remains the same. We now just would report 2 additional launching positions at that complex.

Finally, Mr. President, at the very westernmost tip of Cuba, the island, we have San Julian airfield, 7,000 feet by 150 feet, which has hitherto been barricaded. Rows of stones and other kinds of materials preventing this [from being able] to be used by anybody. Now we see the barricades being removed from the 2 runways. And in this hardstand at the edge of the tarmac, enlarged up in here, we find 22 of those crates, some 60 feet long, which we have interpreted, from the deckside photography that the Navy had taken, to be, possibly, the crates that would accommodate the IL-28, or Beagle, types of aircraft. This field is long enough to accommodate those craft. I think they need something around 6,000 feet to take off. We have 7,000 feet. We definitely had not yet seen the Beagle IL-28. One fuselage had been taken from one of the boxes. It's up at this location. It's 58 feet long, which is about the length of the Beagle fuselage, and you can see the wing widths, but the actual wing tips have not yet been installed. We just caught them, apparently, at the start of the assembly operation. And it would appear that San Julian, this hitherto unused airfield, may be the locus for IL-28 activity.

That's all I have at the moment, Mr. President.

8. These briefings had been given on September 7. See page 53, note 10.

President Kennedy: What percentage of the island have we got covered up to here?

Lundahl: These separate missions, the one on Sunday, October the 14th, and 2 on Monday, October the 15th, represent a considerable percentage from north to south and from east to west. But the business of plotting the [areas obscured by] clouds has not been completely done, so I can't give you a good figure.

President Kennedy: But, in other words, from the informati͏ to the development of these new ꜰⁱˡ⸺ many differeⁿᵗ ⸺

⸺ₑd away, ⸻ ₜₕₑₛₑ things up and move them ₜₒ surface-to-air missile sites. We've seen 3 of these surface-to-surface cruise type of missiles sites at Banes and up here over at del Norte, and then down on the Isle of Pines.

We have one other type of missile site up here north of Havana which we haven't been able to identify yet, that's being either cruise or some other type of site, but which we're carrying [as] unknown.

And now we've added to this. In the briefings of the last couple of days we've added the field type of installation, this 650- or 1,100-mile missile, as it probably is, near San Cristóbal, with these 3 sites located here which we briefed on the other day [October 16]. And in the photography of Monday of this week, we've now added what looks like a more fixed type of site, conforming to a signature which we have seen—

President Kennedy: In other words, you have got 5 different missile sites?

Lundahl: Yes, sir.

President Kennedy: And how many pads on each site?

Lundahl: Well sir, at this location here we don't have pads, we have these erectors, these 60-foot-long objects that lay on the ground. There were 4 erectors there. We have found 3 erectors not yet in position but lying around indisposed here. And we have more erectors that are under the trees. We can't tell. But it would seem as though there's going to be 4 erectors at each of those locations, and it would appear that there's going to be 4 launch pads at each of those too. But these [new sites] will be [a] firmer type of launchings. And these will be the portable field type of launching equipment.

McCone: The GMAIC made an estimate that between 16 and 32 missiles would be operational within a week, or slightly more. This was an estimate made yesterday.

Taylor: Have any electronic emissions from the AA [antiaircraft radars for the SAMs] been picked up by the report that came in?

McCone: No. There are some SIGINT [Signals Intelligence] responses on Monday [October 15] that did not state conclusively that the radars were operational. However, we do estimate some of these SAM sites will be operational within a week's time.

President Kennedy: If an unsophisticated observer . . . If we wanted to ever release these pictures to demonstrate that there were missiles there, it might be possible to demonstrate this to the satisfaction of an untrained observer?

Lundahl: I think it would be difficult, sir. By some 8 years of experience in looking at the evolution in the Soviet Union, the signature emerges very clearly to us. I think the uninitiated would like to see the missile, in the tube.

President Kennedy: May I—

Bundy: If we go in by air [with a strike], we would have instantaneous low-level coverage.

President Kennedy: Go ahead.

McNamara: And there is a picture that is not here of what I call site number 1, by which I believe the uninitiated could be persuaded there were missiles.

Lundahl: I would concur on that, sir. The canvas coverings of all those missiles lying on trailers, in that low of a level, particularly as Mr. Bundy says, could, I think, very clearly impact on people.

President Kennedy: Thank you. When will we get the data, really, on the entire island, to the extent that we can?

Lundahl: Sir, there are 5 missions coming in today, as Mr. McCone says, some 28,000 feet [of film], the first 2 of which were inside [NPIC as of] this afternoon. We would seek to read them during the night. And then as the others come in, in the next 2 to 3 days, we will be going all out to read it on a 24-hour basis. But it is quite a volume of film to look at. We're trying to be accurate, as accurate as we possibly can. I would hope that, comes the weekend, we might have a fair grasp on all 5, plus whatever number of additional ones Mr. McNamara will run between yesterday and the end of the week.

Yes, sir. [He appears to collect his briefing materials.]

Rusk: Mr. President, it would seem that one of the first questions that we need to answer is: Is it necessary to take action? And I would suppose that there is plenty of reason to take action here. But, the more [Soviet] action that is taken . . . It looks now as though Cuba is not going to be an incidental base for a few of these things, but, basically [unclear] with MRBMs, and IRBMs, and that sort of thing, Cuba could become a powerful military problem in any contest we would have with the Soviet Union and a threat in any other part of the world. I think our colleagues in Defense will count on that very carefully, because that's a very important point. But we think that, when the full scope of this becomes known, that [taking] no action would undermine our alliances all over the world very promptly.

On September 4th you said: "There i~
force in Cuba f~

..... that

..........gs that were very unknown

.... as a clear warning to the Soviet Union that these were matters that we will take with the utmost seriousness. Then you talked about the various issues, generalizing, saying that would mean something very serious.

I think also we have to think of the effect on the Soviets if we were to do nothing. Now suppose that they were to consider this a major backdown, then this would free their hands for almost any kind of intervention that they might want to try in other parts of the world. If we are unable to face up to the situation in Cuba against this kind of threat, I think that they would be critically encouraged to go ahead and eventually feel like they've got it made as far as intimidating the United States is concerned.

I think also that we have an almost unmanageable problem in this country getting any support for a foreign policy that would assume we were going to sustain the cause of independence of states here and in all parts of the world. We have a million men in uniform outside the United States. We've got foreign-aid programs. We've got a major effort in the making in every continent. And it seems to me that inaction in this situation would undermine and undercut the long support that we need for the kind of foreign policy that will eventually ensure our survival.

Action involves very high risks indeed, and I think this additional information maybe even increases the risk because the challenge is much more serious and the kind of action, I would suppose, would have to be heavier than we have actually been talking about. But we can expect you would have to have in the back of your own mind, with whatever decision we take, the possibility and the likelihood of a Soviet reaction somewhere else running all the way from Berlin right around to Korea, and the possibility of a reaction against the United States itself. I don't think that you can make your decision under any assumption that this is a free ride, or easier in the U.S. orbit.

I would suppose that with those first missiles that we were talking about that we could strike with quick success in the matter of a couple hours' time [unclear] the 50 or 60 Soviet missile [unclear], where it's obvious that the matter is over and finished and that was the purpose of our engagement. That would have a much more reduced risk of a military response on the other side. But getting these other installations and getting involved in various parts of the island, I think, will increase the risk of a military response down there.

The action also has to be thought about in connection with alliance solidarity, and there we're faced with conflicting elements. That's a situation where it is clear that the alliance is with us and willing to understand the problem. Then an unannounced, unconsulted, quick action on our part could well lead to a kind of allied disunity that the Soviet attack will capitalize upon very strongly.

It's one thing for Britain and France to get themselves isolated within the alliance over Suez. But it's quite another thing for the alliance if the United States should get itself in the same position. Because we are the central bone structure of the alliance, I think this is a different kind of a problem that we have to think very hard about.

Now, I think that, as far as I'm concerned, all I have to say to you would be: If we enter upon this path of challenging the Soviets, the Soviets themselves embarking on this fantastically dangerous course, that no one can surely foresee the outcome. [Unclear.]

I was prepared to say, when I came over here, before I got this information [unclear] to support [unclear] the strike. [Now I'm] very clearly moved by the circumstances to escalate general action, at least as far as Cuba is concerned, and possibly in other situations.

Now, there's another part of this situation that bothers me considerably. I think the American people will willingly undertake great danger if necessary to go do something, if they have the deep feeling that we've done everything that was reasonably possible to determine whether this risk was necessary. Also that they have a clear conscience and a good theory of the case.

The first point is where history is necessary. We all, of course, remember the guns of August, where certain events brought about a general situation which at the time none of the governments involved could avoid.[9] And this first matter is something that is pretty important.

We had a clear conscience in World War II, the Pearl Harbor attack up against the background of Hitler's conduct [unclear]. In the case of Korea, we had an organized large-scale aggression from North Korea, and we were going in with United Nations blessing. Even with that start, the Korean aspect of it [several words unclear] the general support of the Ameri... was over.

Now, the...

... conflict.
...ongest legal basis for action we can ...sibility is a straight, straight declaration of war, which carries with it many legal privileges that are useful to have. But the Rio Pact, I would suppose Mr. Martin will have to comment on this. But I suppose the only way we have of [using that is] getting [a] two-thirds vote to take necessary action. But if we made an effort and failed to get the two-thirds vote [unclear], then at least we will have tried as far as the American people are concerned. We'll have done that.

Now, it seems to me, that the flow of information we have about the bases, all the bases all across the island of [unclear] Cuba, [unclear] declaration of a national emergency and necessary declaration of war on Cuba may not be the necessary step here. Now, rather than small single strikes here and there around the island, [unclear] put together [unclear] each strike becoming more difficult from a military point of view, and more difficult from a political point of view, it looks as though we have a larger problem to solve. And we may have to solve it in a larger way. Now, the alternative there is to go in with the short strikes, [unclear] strikes, and try and get them over with promptly, at least as far as these particular installations are concerned. But these other places, I think, will be larger problems, and [unclear]. I think that, considering the extent of all

9. Rusk is referring to events that preceded and immediately followed the outbreak of World War I in 1914, covered in a recently published well-known book, *The Guns of August*, by Barbara Tuchman.

this . . . whether the actions we take [unclear] are actually large enough to involve the greatest risks in any event. Therefore, we might as well solve the problem.

Mr. Bohlen left a note last night after our meeting, which broke up at about midnight, just before he left, and I would like to read just certain paragraphs of this. He said:

The existence of Soviet MRBM bases in Cuba cannot be tolerated. The objective therefore is their elimination by whatever means may be necessary.

There are two means in essence: by diplomatic action or by military action.

No one can guarantee that this can be achieved by diplomatic action, but it seems to me essential that this channel should be tested out before military action is employed. If our decision is firm (and it must be) I can see no danger in communication with Khrushchev privately, worded in such a way that he realizes that we mean business.

This I consider an essential first step no matter what military course we determine on if the reply is unsatisfactory. The tone and tenor of his reply will tell us something, but I don't believe that a threat of general nuclear war should deter us. If he means it, he would have so reacted even if the strike had come first.

My chief concern about a strike without any diplomatic effort is that it will immediately lead to war with Cuba and would not be the neat quick disposal of their bases, as was suggested. Furthermore, I am reasonably certain that the Allied reaction would be dead against us, especially if the Soviet retaliated locally (in Turkey or Italy or in Berlin).

A communication with Khrushchev would be very useful for the record in establishing our case for action.

In general I feel that a declaration of war would be valuable since it would open up every avenue of military action, air strikes, invasion or blockade. But we would have to make a case before our allies to justify such a declaration of war. If we acted first and sought to justify it later we would be in a spat of great consequence.

Finally, I feel very strongly that any belief in a limited quick action is an illusion and would lead us into a full war with Cuba on a step-by-step basis which would greatly increase the probability of general war.

That course would be, he says, a carefully worded and serious letter to Khrushchev, before we take the action. And then followed by a declaration of war. We were talking about this last night. I think it is in this range of problems that we need to concentrate our attention. Therefore, I suggest that is how we see the nature of this job. Our Defense colleagues may wish to talk more about the actual military aspect of the threat itself.

McNamara: Mr. President, may I suggest that there are a series of alternative planned arrangements. Roman numeral I was about 50 sorties, directed solely against the known MRBMs, known as of last night, to Roman numeral V, which covers an alternative invasion plan.

All of these plans are based on one very important assumption· we would attack, with conventional weapons, against an ene~ equipped with operational nuclear weapons. If there's ~ enemy is equipped with operational nuclear v· would have to be changed.

Last evening we were discuss~ action, assuming that a+ the view of the ~ was cert~
                                                    ..eral II,
                                          ..e inconclusive,
                                    , action prior to which
                              ..ie gains we had achieved.
                        ..uld certainly have recommended last
                  ..u more strongly today, that we not consider
            ..ian numeral I or Roman numeral II, so that we would
        ..g short of a full invasion as a military action. And this only on
    ..umption that we're operating against a force that does not possess
operational nuclear weapons.

President Kennedy: Why does this information change the recommendation?

McNamara: Last evening, it was my personal belief that there were more targets than we knew of, and it was probable there would be more targets than we could know of at the start of any one of these strikes. The information of this morning, I think, simply demonstrates the validity of that conclusion of last evening.

Secondly, when we're talking of Roman numeral I, it's a very limited strike against MRBMs only, and it leaves in existence IL-28s with nuclear weapon-carrying capability, and a number of other aircraft with nuclear weapon-carrying capability, and aircraft with strike capability that could be exercised during our attack, or immediately following our attack on the MRBMs, with great possible risk of loss to either Guantanamo and/or the eastern coast of the U.S.

I say great loss, I'm not thinking in terms of tens of thousands, but I'm thinking in terms of sporadic attacks against our civilian population, which would lead to losses I think we would find it hard to justify in relation to the alternative courses open to us, and in relation to the very limited accomplishment of our limited number of strikes.

Robert Kennedy: What about alternative number II, on the basis that you're going against offensive weapons. You're going to go against the missiles, and you're going to go against the planes. What's the argument against that? I mean that would prevent them from knocking our population base.

McNamara: It must be preferred over number I, in my opinion. It would have to be larger than is shown now because of the additional number of targets required, and it gets very close to alternative III, compared to the number of sorties. The number II [strike] was prepared before we had the additional information of last night's [photo] interpretation. We showed a hundred sorties. I think it more likely that number II, with the information of now, and the information we're likely to have today and tomorrow, will turn into number III, which is a 200-sortie strike. I doubt very much we could stop there.

Taylor: I would agree with that statement of the Secretary's. Really, II is hardly possible now. We're really talking about III, because we have to take the SAM sites out, if you want to go for [unclear] airfield strikes [unclear] targets related [unclear]. I think that's particularly true if we expect to have follow-up surveillance. SAM site facilities have become operational, and even though we take out [unclear] I and II, we [are] still going to have a requirement to know what's going on. [unclear] a long air war I would say, [unclear] under I, II, or III, actually.

President Kennedy: [With] number II, you don't need to take out the SAM sites before they become operational.

Taylor: They'll be operational at the same time.

McNamara: We have almost certainly added 2 more targets than are indicated here. Sixteen targets shown. We have at least 3 more targets from evidence since last night, and we will certainly have some more tonight and tomorrow. And, therefore, II merges very directly into III. If the SAM sites become operational, II becomes III because, in a very real sense, that's maybe the . . .

President Kennedy: Let me ask you this: If I remember, [we're] talking about III versus V, isn't it?

McNamara: Yes, sir.

President Kennedy: Well, now, the advantage of III is that you would hope to do it in a day.

McNamara: Yes. It could be done in a day.

President Kennedy: Invasion, that would be V, would be 7, 8, or 9 days, with all the consequences . . .

McNamara: That is correct.

President Kennedy: We would increase the tension.

Now, if we did III, we would assume that by the end of the day their ability to use planes against us—after all, we don't have that much range, so they'd have to come back to the field and [unclear]. You would say—

McNamara: You would assume, by the end of the day th~~~~ be nearly destroyed. I say nearly bec~~~~ ~~ around.

~~~~ ~~u ie going

~~~~ not certain they can stop it, this is why I emphasized ~~~ plan I did. I don't believe the Soviets would authorize their use against the U.S., but they might nonetheless be used, and, therefore, I underline this assumption, that all of these cases are premised on the assumption there are no operational nuclear weapons there.

If there's any possibility of that I would strongly recommend that these plans be modified substantially. Now, I evaded the question Secretary Rusk asked me, and I evaded it because I wanted this information. This stuff first. The question he asked me was: How does, in effect, how does the introduction of these weapons to Cuba change the military equation, the military position of the U.S. versus the U.S.S.R.?

And, speaking strictly in military terms, really in terms of weapons, it doesn't change it at all, in my personal opinion. My personal views are not shared by the Chiefs. They are not shared by many others in the Department. However, I feel very strongly on this point, and I think I could argue a case, a strong case, in defense of my position.

This doesn't really have any bearing on the issue, in my opinion, because it is not a military problem that we're facing. It's a political problem. It's a problem of holding the alliance together. It's a problem of properly conditioning Khrushchev for our future moves. And the problem of holding the alliance together, and the problem of conditioning Khrushchev for our future moves, the problem of dealing with our domestic public, all requires action that, in my opinion, the shift in military balance does not require.

President Kennedy: On holding the alliance. Which one would strain the alliance more: this attack by us on Cuba, which most allies regard as a fixation of the United States and not a serious military threat? And you'd have to outline a condition you have to go in, before they would accept, support our action against Cuba, because they think that we're slightly demented on this subject.

So there isn't any doubt that, whatever action we take against Cuba, no matter how good our films are, or what this is going to cause in Latin America, a lot of people would regard this as a mad act by the United States, which is due to a loss of nerve because they will argue that taken at its worst, the presence of these missiles really doesn't change the balance. We started to think the other way, I mean, the view in America. But what's everybody else going to think when it's done to this guy?

McNamara: Aren't the others going to think exactly as I do?

Taylor: May I comment, sir?

With regard to what we've just seen in intelligence, it seems to me three things stand out. The first is the very rapid energy with which they are developing the movement in the first 24 hours since Sunday [October 14]. They are moving very fast to make these weapons operational.

Whether they're operational today? I would agree with the Secretary that probably not, but I don't think anyone can assure you that at any time, that at least one or more of these missiles will not become operational.

Now, number two, the IL-28s. We've been expecting this. But now it turns up in a very powerful location, I would say, and [unclear] ideal place to take them out.

Third, the IRBMs. This really put a new perspective on the way I look at it [this problem]. Yesterday, when we only had a few of the mobile type, I was far from convinced that the big showdown would be required. And we're getting new pictures, and the vision of an island that's going to be a forward base of major importance to the Soviets.

All of the targets that we're seeing, however, are the kind that air attack [words unclear] we can't take this threat out by actions from here. So we had argued more and more that if, indeed, you're going to prevent that kind of thing . . .

Bundy: But you don't mean that you can't prevent it in the sense of stopping it from happening the next day. You mean that—

Taylor: For the long pull—

Bundy: —you're going to have to take the island?

Taylor: Yes, you can't destroy a hole in the ground. We can't prevent these constructions going ahead by any threat. Diplomatic action might stop it, but a totally diplomatic action [unclear] will not stop a threat of this kind from building up.

Now, if those statements are roughly correct, then what would it mean in terms of time? Well, it means that, insofar as getting the mobile missiles out, time is of the essence. But the faster the better, because it's not already too late. And I would say that, again, we're not sure that it is not too late to one or more of the missiles.

With resp---

... identified as a probable IRBM].

... unclear.]

McNamara: 2,000 miles [range]. An extra thousand miles [over the MRBMs].

Taylor: So there is no pressure of time from that point of view even though it's the more egregious danger you're talking about. So those are the problems that I have seen, and I think the, the Chiefs are going to agree on that.

There is one factor we talked about, at length, yesterday: the political action which Mr. Bohlen has recommended, and many others think must be done. Certainly militarily that is undesirable, if we really had in mind the urgency of taking out by surprise the missiles, and the IL-28s.

On the other hand, if we consider it politically necessary . . . We're quite sure it can be offset if we could be making military moves in readiness to reinforce the political action, or action to shorten the time of our reaction . . .

President Kennedy: Let me ask you this: If we gave, say, this 24-hour notice, getting in touch with Khrushchev, taking our action with our allies, I would assume that they would move these mobile missiles into the woods, wouldn't they?

Taylor: The danger is, Mr. President, if you're talking in terms of 24 hours—

McNamara: I would doubt it. Mr. President, I don't believe they're equipped to do that. I say that because if they were equipped to do that, they would have been equipped to erect them more quickly. I think that it's unlikely they would move them in 24 hours. If they were to move them in 24 hours, I think we could keep enough reconnaissance over the island during that period to have some idea of where they moved them. I have every reason to believe we'd know where they were.

McCone: It would take a little longer, though.

McNamara: What?

McCone: It would take a little longer to take very careful reconnaissance to know where they are.

Bundy: Why are you so confident that they couldn't hide them or get them into immediate range in 24 hours?

McNamara: Well, I didn't say they couldn't get them in immediate range in 24 hours. I don't believe that we would lose them with a 24-hour discussion with Khrushchev.

President Kennedy: If we have a communication with Moscow, say we sent somebody to see him, and he was there at the beginning of the 24-hour period, to see Mr. Khrushchev, how long would it be before Khrushchev's answer could get back to us, just by communication?

Thompson: It depends on totally what we . . . I would say 5 to 6 hours. Or you could telephone, of course.

President Kennedy: It wouldn't really have to be a call, would it?

Thompson: You can shorten the time a lot by using a highly confidential [unclear] machine.

President Kennedy: That would be a couple of hours?

Rusk: I think the quickest way might be to [unclear] delays on their end would be to bring them in an actual text, that was translated, and that would get to Khrushchev straight away, whereas somebody else might have a problem of making an appointment

[Several people talk at once.]

Alexis Johnson: But I think the one point on this that you have to bear in mind if you go [unclear] meeting this morning who, of course, believe that so far as we know, there is no stated relationship that makes these Soviet missiles or Soviet bases. The attempts that Castro made to ally himself with the Warsaw Pact, or to join the Warsaw Pact, or even to engage in a bilateral [defense treaty] with Moscow, apparently either were deferred or failed. He sent Raul [Castro] and Che Guevara to Moscow, a few months ago, apparently for that purpose, that and other purposes. Hence, if we were to take action with this present status, the Soviets would have some latitude as to how they might want to respond if they did at all.

On the other hand, if as a result of a warning, or of a communication with them, they declare these their bases, then we would have a different kind of problem because we have the problem of committing an action against a missile base that's theirs. And this might mean a war of different proportions.

President Kennedy: The question is really whether the Soviet reaction, and who knows this, would be measurably different if they were presented with an accomplished fact, the days or the one day [unclear] the invasion—the accomplished fact, whether their reaction would be different than it would be if they were given a chance to pull them out.

If we said to Khrushchev that "we would have to take actio... But if you begin to pull them out, we'll ... or whether he wo... ...

... ...ce is this blockade plan, this declaration of war and ...ose steps leading up to it. I think it's very highly doubtful that the Russians would resist a blockade against military weapons, particularly offensive ones, if that's the way we pitched it before the world.

President Kennedy: What do we do with the weapons already there?

Thompson: Demand they're dismantled, and say that we're going to maintain constant surveillance, and if they are armed, we would then take them out. And then maybe do it.

I think we should be under no illusions, this is probably in the end going to lead to the same thing. But we do it in an entirely different posture and background and much less danger of getting up into the big war.

The Russians have a curious faculty of wanting a legal basis despite all of the outrageous things they've done. There are some other points to this. The fact that you have a declaration of war, I think they would be running a military blockade legally established, and [this would] greatly deter them.

Robert Kennedy: In other words . . . Could you maybe run through [this idea] for [unclear] because he hasn't heard the explanation of the blockade.

Gilpatric: There is a paper there on that, course number two there [not referring to strike options], Mr. President. There was a concept for this.

President Kennedy: However, under this plan, we would not take these missiles that they now have out, or the planes they now have out.

Gilpatric: Not in the first stage, which is why I think it would be useful to say that if they were made operational we might, or would—

President Kennedy: Of course, then he would say that "if you do that, then we will" . . .

Thompson: As Chip [Bohlen] said, I agree with him, that if they're prepared to say: "All right, if you do this, then this is nuclear world war," then they would do that anyway. I think he would make a lot of threatening language and very big terms in keeping his—

President Kennedy: I think it is more likely he would just grab Berlin.

Thompson: I think if we just made the first strike, then I think his answer would be, very probably, to take out one of our bases in Turkey, and make it quick too and then say: "I want to talk." I think the whole purpose of this exercise is to build up to a talk with you, in which he tries to negotiate out the bases. There are a lot of things that point to that. One thing that struck me very much is, it's so easy to camouflage these things, or hide them in the woods. Why didn't they do it in the first place? They surely expected us to see them at some stage. The purpose was for preparation of negotiations.

Robert Kennedy: Maybe they have something.

Thompson: They may.

Taylor: May I ask whether military moves in these 5 to 8 days would be acceptable from the point of view of the State Department?

Ball: I think it would be helpful, certainly be helpful—

[Several sentences unclear.]

Thompson: Now, of course, Mr. President, there are obvious counters to the blockade. The obvious one being Berlin.

President Kennedy: Yes.

Robert Kennedy: Also the argument against the blockade is that it's a very slow death, and it builds up, and goes over a period of months, and during that period of time you've got all these people yelling and screaming about it, you've got the examination of Russian ships, shooting down the Russian planes that try to land there. You have to do all those things.

Alexis Johnson: On the Soviet reaction, it was Tommy and Chip that predicted the Soviets would not try to run the blockade, then they would have deserted their friends in Cuba. And I think there would be considerable political chaos in Cuba, if the Soviets deserted them . . .

Thompson: Also, I would assume you would be in negotiations with Chairman Khrushchev.

Taylor: [Unclear] in all logic he would have the blockade [unclear]. I guess that all of these military actions are viable for the blockade.

Bundy: I agree.

McCone: What would you do about a declaration of war as a military action?

Bundy: Simultaneously, it seems to me, you declare that a state of war exists, and you call the Congress.

Thompson: I think Khrushchev will deny that these are Soviet bases. I think that what he'd say is: "What are you getting so excited about? The Cubans asked us for some missiles to deal with these emigré bases which are threatening an attack." And that these are not missiles other than defensive. They're much less offensive than your weapons in Turkey. You've got these armed nuclear warheads. We haven't given any nuclear weapons to the simply to deal with the threat to Cuba.

Rusk: That would be taking their thoughts or weapons.

[Mixed voices.]

Bundy: If we act, th

Rusk: I thi

in th

. as possible for

. . . His answer would

to you about it." If he refused,

So I think you'd immediately assume

I think that the Attorney General's point is

is somewhat weakened in that during this period you

gotiating out this thing.

Rusk: But if he were to say: "Let's talk." Well, then you have to say to him: "Stop immediately all activities on such and such fields, sites, and so forth."

Thompson: I'd impose a blockade while you do it.

President Kennedy: The blockade would be sufficient if we go on about [unclear].

Alexis Johnson: Yeah, but if you impose the blockade on Cuba, then he imposes the blockade on Berlin. And then you start to talk. And he would be crazy to [unclear].

President Kennedy: That's what he would figure?

Unidentified: That's what he would figure, yes.

Thompson: Seems to me that one of the points of this—he's not a fool—I was always curious as to why he [Khrushchev] said he said he would defer this [a renewed confrontation over Berlin] until after the election. It seems to me it is all related to this.

Unidentified: Sure [unclear].

McCone: Mr. President, you might be interested in General Eisenhower's reaction to this after my talking with him.

I briefed him. I showed him the photography and all the rest of this, and he was careful, I think, not to take a position, because I have a position and I was very careful not to indicate to him your position. I will read my account of our conversation.

However, I should report that the thrust of his comments would indicate that he felt first that the existence of [Soviet bases] in Cuba was intolerable from the standpoint of this country.

Secondly, I think he felt that limited action such as waiting, or as anticipated in I, or II, or even III, according to this paper, would not be satisfactory. It would cause the greatest fear and concern with our allies and in all areas of the world where the Soviets might take similar action against installations—the United States installations—or put in jeopardy other installations in Turkey or Pakistan or elsewhere.

He felt really that if a move was made—I think if I were to pin him down he would recommend it—that it should be an all-out military action. He talked of conceiving it to go right to the jugular first, not landing on the beach and working slowly across the island. But concentrate the attack right on Havana first and taking the heart of the government out. And he thought, if this was done properly it would probably mean disarray, so it could be done with a minimum loss of life.

Now he said that without the benefit of specific knowledge of troop deployments, and equipment deployments, and so forth, of the Soviets, or of the Cubans, but I thought this would be of interest to you.

Rusk: So I think it should be considered that there would be a number of steps that you will have to take in which you would need to declare a national emergency or a declaration of war, [unclear] additional manpower, and there are other powers that in general could be important here.

Thompson: Another part of the Cuban dimension is that, since Castro's gone this far in denying it, I suppose, assuming that he didn't contest to putting these things in there, it seems to me in the end he [Castro] does, the fact is that Castro has to go.

But if we did this blockade, and any of these steps, and Castro attacked Guantanamo and so on, you've got a much better position in which then to go in and take him out than if it's started by some surprise attack by us. I gather it's fairly likely that Castro would do something.

Taylor: Certainly, if we take any of these military actions, I think we have to assume he will react against Guantanamo.

Dillon: Mr. President, what is the whole idea, I'm not quite clear, of talking to Khrushchev ahead of time? What could he do that would remove this danger that we have from these MRBMs that are presently already there? What could he do that would satisfy us? It seems to me very difficult to see any action you can take that he might say: "Sure, I'll take them out sometime," do the opposite the whole way . . .

I can't understand how we would achieve anything. We may achieve something in sort of a history in showing we've done something. But that's a different argument than the argument of really trying to achieve anything. I don't see how we would really achieve anything.

Rusk: [Unclear] In general, he might ~~~ ~

it up in his ~~~~ ~~~

... rest of the alliance is going to

... have given Khrushchev a chance to do some—

Bundy: It depends on what he says or he does, George, it seems to me.

Ball: However, if he makes a threat to go ahead—I mean, we can't stop him but that seems to me to be very much—

Bundy: We've got that speech all figured out. The one thing that he [Khrushchev] must know is that he's going to have to say something to us about this at some point. I think there's a reasonable chance Gromyko's going to make the speech [in his meeting with President Kennedy] this afternoon.

Thompson: Do you have some indication of it?

[Mixed voices.]

Taylor: Well, I presume that if there were any communication with Khrushchev it would be in such terms that it wouldn't really indicate the detail of our knowledge of these weapons, in other words, make him feel that the American eyes are right on it, right in our sight. Do you think we can convey that message without giving it away?

McCone: I don't think he believes that we don't know all about this. It's done in a semi-overt way. These convoys are moved; people have observed them; we've got refugee reports, gossip of all kinds. All that we know doesn't come from our aerial photography, by any manner or means.

I think the board studying this[10] would agree that, if Khrushchev would

---

10. The Board of National Estimates at the CIA was preparing a Special National Intelligence

engage us in some type of a negotiation, that we'd be locked into [it] and couldn't move. I don't think there would be an answer that would be so negative that it would give us freedom of action. Hence, it would be somewhat like the Geneva test convention business, where once we got into it, we couldn't get out of it.

President Kennedy: The only offer we would make, it seems to me, that would have any sense, the point being to give him some out, would be giving him some of our Turkey missiles.

Bundy: I believe, Mr. President, that is equally valid if we make the sudden strike. Now, I think it may well be important to have a message for Khrushchev's hands at that moment, saying, among other things, wicked things that led to this, but also that we understand this base problem. If they scrub them, then we do expect to dismantle our Turkish base. That has one small advantage, which is that if he strikes back, we will have at least given him a peaceful out.

I don't think we can keep that Turkish base.

Dillon: But you get to the same point by doing this thing simultaneously, than you do if you don't.

Rusk: [Unclear] seems to be a Cuba-Turkey exchange. It's quite serious. Now, it's true that we have talked with the Turks a year ago about getting those, taking the, Jupiters out of there for other reasons . . .

[Unclear brief exchange, in which someone refers to putting "a Polaris or two in those waters."][11]

Bundy: Which should make everyone feel better. We have [unclear] Soviet submarines are going to be in the Caribbean, and this is a political not a military problem.

McNamara: If there is a strike without a preliminary discussion with Khrushchev, how many Soviet citizens will be killed? I don't know.

McNamara: Maybe several hundred, perhaps minimal—

Bundy: Killed, as in casualties? Killed.

McNamara: Yeah, absolutely. We're using napalm, 750-pound bombs. This is an extensive strike we're talking about.

Bundy: Well, I hope it is.

Estimate, distributed the next day, on "Soviet Reactions to Certain U.S. Courses of Action on Cuba."

11. The principal idea then being considered for replacement of Turkish and other obsolescent land-based ballistic missiles deployed in Europe was to offer some sea-based substitute for them, possibly linked to the Polaris nuclear-missile submarines then entering service.

McNamara: I think we must assume we'll kill several hundred Soviet citizens. Having killed several hundred Soviet citizens, what kind of response does Khrushchev have open to him?

It seems to me that it must just be a strong response, and I think we should expect that. And, therefore, the question really is: Are we willing to pay some kind of a rather substantial price to eliminate these missiles? I think the price is going to be high. It may still be worth paying to eliminate the missiles. But I think we must assume it's going to be high. The very least it will
to remove the missiles in Italy and Tur

Dillon: Well, I

..... the
..... course of action where we strike
..... like Pearl Harbor. It's the kind of conduct that one might expect of the Soviet Union. It is not conduct that one expects of the United States. And I have a feeling that this 24 hours to Khrushchev is really indispensable.

President Kennedy: And then if he says: "If you are going to do that, we're going to grab Berlin." The point is, he's going to grab Berlin anyway. He's going to take Berlin anyway.

Bundy: We pay that price.

McNamara: I suspect the price we pay to Khrushchev will be about the same, whether we give him the advance warning or don't give him the advance warning. The advance warning has the advantage of possibly giving him an out that would reduce the requirement that we enter with military force. That's a fair possibility; not great. It has the advantage George has mentioned of causing less friction with the rest of the world.

It has some disadvantages, a reduction of military surprise, but the disadvantage of that is not very great. It carries with it, however, I believe, the great disadvantage that once you start down that course he outmaneuvers you.

Dillon: Well, the only advantage I see to it is the one you say, George, and that is that if you decide to do this, and you want to put yourself into the right position with the world, you [do this] as part of a [military] program that never stops. You have 24-hour notice. But you're under no illusion that anything he says is going to stop you [from proceeding with military action].

You go ahead and do it. You're not going for the purpose of getting him to come up and do something. What you're doing is to set the stage.

Alexis Johnson?: If you go the blockade route, you can take more time with these steps; on the other hand, you know the danger of these—

President Kennedy: He'll grab Berlin, of course. Then either way it would be we lost Berlin, because of these missiles, which, as I say, do not bother them [the European allies].

Thompson: My guess is that he would not immediately attack Berlin, but he would precipitate the real crisis, in order to try to [unclear] morale.

Dillon: The difference is that in Cuba we've shown that we will take action. At a point which nobody knows. That's the great danger now, is if they think we will never take action.

Bundy: . . . precipitate the Berlin crisis is just as bad, if we let this happen to us, against ourselves.

President Kennedy: You mean, in other words, in late November when he [Khrushchev] . . .

Robert Kennedy: [Unclear] moves into Berlin?

Bundy: If we could trade off Berlin, and not have it our fault . . .

Dillon: Well, that's the danger. The whole reaction in Cuba . . .

McNamara: Well, when we're talking about taking Berlin, what do we mean exactly? That they take it with Soviet troops?

President Kennedy?: That's what I would think.

McNamara: I think there's a real possibility there. We have U.S. troops there where they do.

I think it's perfectly clear. They get overrun. They get overrun.

Unidentified: [Unclear] then what do we do?

Taylor: Go to general war.

Bundy: It's then general war.

President Kennedy: You mean a nuclear exchange?

Unidentified: Mmm-hmm.

Unidentified: That's right.

Bundy: I guess the argument, if you go in, at the same time that you do this you say to him—

Unidentified: I doubt that will mean general war. I don't think he'd do it that way.

Rusk: But you have to start at least with tactical nuclear weapons [unclear] trying to attack—

Unidentified: I think you blockade, I don't—

Taylor: I think they'd use East German forces, rather than bring their own troops in.

President Kennedy: Let me ask you. It seems when you're talking about the alliance, you've got two problems. One would be the problem of the alliance when we say to them that the presence of these missiles requires a military action by us. There's no doubt that they will oppose that, because they'll feel that their risks increase, and this is a risk to us. They'll argue what is Secretary McNamara's point.

If we don't take any action, then ~~~ deterioration.~~~

~~~ ~~~ lessens
~~~ously is the prime failure—that's
~~~ the same time, maintain some degree of solidarity with our allies. Now, if you want that to be the course, then it would seem to me not to be too much different.

Dillon: But, from the point of view of our allies, they think, though, that certainly this strong setup in Cuba, just sort of weakens our ability to help them everywhere. So it is in the interest of the alliance to have this thing [unclear] even though it does create some dangers.

President Kennedy: Now, to declare a blockade on Cuba, do we have to declare war on Cuba?

[There is a chorus of answers. Several fragments can be heard. Someone says: "Yes, yes we do." Someone else says: "It is commonplace to make a declaration of war." Another says: "It makes it easier, and better." Another says: "Well, it makes it legal . . . but we have to consult with our allies." Someone else refers to "the Rio Pact and under the [September 20] resolution that was passed by Congress." The President then speaks over the hubbub.]

President Kennedy: I think we shouldn't assume we have to declare war. The declaration of a state of war is a . . . Because it seems to me if you're going to do that, you really—it doesn't make any sense—you have to invade. I think we ought to consider whether we do, at least let's just think. We do the message to Khrushchev and tell him that if work continues, et cetera, et cetera. At the same time, launch the blockade. If the work continues, that we go in and take them out.

We don't declare war. It seems to me that with a declaration of war our objective would be an invasion.

Ball: . . . great difficulty. A blockade without a declaration of war is an illegal blockade—

Bundy: And it would be a great act of aggression against everybody else.

Ball: —everybody. Including our allies.

Rusk: You could have a blockade imposed under Article 8 of the Rio Treaty. After all, this is within the territorial framework of the—

President Kennedy: There will be hardly anybody who gets excited because their ships are stopped under these conditions. They're not going to talk to us anyway. [Apparently examining a paper] Article 8 of the Rio Treaty [reads text inaudibly].

[Unclear exchange.]

Under what authority do we . . .

Rusk: Use of armed forces.

President Kennedy: Yes, but we can't unilaterally . . . [unclear reference to Organization of American States] maybe a week . . .

Martin: I think in 2 or 3 days it could be done. But I don't think . . .

President Kennedy: How many votes [in the OAS] do you have against it [a blockade]?

Martin: Probably 4 for sure.

President Kennedy: Mexico. Brazil. Chile.

Alexis Johnson?: Cuba and Bolivia.

President Kennedy: Yeah. Probably Ecuador.

Martin: No, Cuba's not in it. Ecuador I think we might get.

Rusk: Bolivia might not come.

Martin: Bolivia might well not attend. We're not completely sure.

Rusk: Because they're temporarily out of it.

President Kennedy: Well, obviously, knowing the Soviets and the way Khrushchev reacts always, I would think we can't assume that he'll stop working.

I'm not sure exactly what we get out of this particular course of action, except that it doesn't quite—it doesn't quite raise . . . immediately as high as it would under ordinary other conditions.

Ball: Mr. President, I would like to suggest that if we have a blockade, without some kind of ultimatum, work must stop on the missile sites or you take them out. But you'll have an impossible position with the country, because they will not sit still while work goes on, making these things operational. And

I think this is one of the real problems with the blockade, is that it's a rather slow agony and you build up all kinds of fears and doubts in the mind of people here.

Along the question of the blockade, I think it is Tommy's view that even the Soviet Union would be influenced by the question as to whether there was a declaration of war or not.

Thompson: So you might be able to frame it in such a way that if your world posture were: We're going to prevent this threat to ~~~~~ offensive weapons, and therefore ~~~~~ from getting ~~~~~

~~~~~sphere.

~~~~~ we're not concerned with what ~~~~~ of Cuba.

You will, in fact, get into the invasion before you're through.

Thompson: Well, I think you probably will the other way too, in the end.

Alexis Johnson?: On the other hand, if you do declare a blockade, and the Soviets do observe it, this could very quickly bring down Castro within Cuba, very quickly have the effect, have the effect of their appearing to be deserting him.

Ball: Khrushchev's ability to observe it would be greatly helped if there were a legal basis.

[Mixed voices.]

McCone: I don't think he will recognize a blockade. I think he will go right through.

Gilpatric: I don't think you have to have a blockade in any of these military persuasions. Certainly, if we invade, we've got to blockade.

McCone: Oh, I'm not talking about what we have to do, I realize that. I'm talking about his observance of it, or recognition of it, or respect, if we do that.

Thompson: I don't think they'd want to take any military action around Cuba, because they're at too much of a disadvantage there. That's why I think he might respect it, or take action in Berlin. It's a gamble which he's shown for years he's reluctant to take. I think he's building up now and probing to see whether or not he could do it. The strongest argument to me for a strike, is that that would be very convincing and dangerous to him.

Rusk: I think that this is the other part of the coin. He may feel he has to respond. But he knows he's dealing with people [the U.S. government] who are going to respond to him. Well, maybe he's just a little crazy and we can't trust him.

Taylor: I would think the credibility of our response in Berlin is enhanced by taking action in Cuba, rather than be[ing] diminished.

Bundy: I think you're right.

Taylor: If he's going to blockade Berlin, he'll do it regardless of . . .

President Kennedy: Say the situation was reversed, and he had made the statement about these missiles in Turkey similar to the ones I made about [Cuba], about operating missiles in Turkey. And he had made the statement saying that serious action could result if we put them in, and we went ahead and put them in. Then he took them out some day.

The thing is, the advantage of that is, it's all over. Hungary. It's over so quick, supposedly, that you know the next move is up to him [unclear] . . .

Thompson: I gather, from a military view, that this would lead, in the end, to an invasion. It wouldn't be over quickly. We'd have to have air cover over these people [unclear] . . .

Taylor: I think we'll get into this air damage regardless, Mr. President, because of Guantanamo, for example. And our surveillance requirements will result in dogfights over the island.

President Kennedy: We'll be taking out their planes.

Taylor: —I think sooner or later, we'll be—

President Kennedy: Well, that's what I meant. We go ahead. Let's just say this is a prospective course of action.

Tomorrow afternoon [Friday, October 19] I'll announce about the missiles, and say we're calling Congress back, and then we consider them Saturday morning, so everybody knows about it. It isn't Pearl Harbor in that sense. We've told everybody. Then we go ahead Saturday [October 20] and we take them out, and announce that they've been taken out. And if any more are put in, we're going to take those out.

Bundy: And the air force.

President Kennedy: And the air force. And we don't want any war, and so on and so forth, but we're not going to take the risk due to the fact that—

Ball: We would take the air force out tomorrow, too?

President Kennedy: Exactly.

Taylor: That's a little too fast for us. On the 21st [Sunday] we could get this out.

President Kennedy: Exactly.

[Mixed voices; unclear.]

President Kennedy: The race is against these missiles, but obviously Sunday or Monday. To announce, the day before, the existence of these . . . We ought to announce what we're going to do. We are going to call Congress back. We're gonna go ahead to do it the next morning.

Robert Kennedy: Even if you announce pretty much, you can almost hint that you're going to have to take some action.

President Kennedy: Well, we don't

Taylor:

. . . . . *. ..dy:* The advantage is of calling Congress back, I can see the only advantage, is that it gets the information that they are there before we attack. Whatever solidarity that that may induce. And in spite of the position of almost acting in a bad way.

Taylor: Would a few hours do rather than 24 hours, Mr. President?

Bundy: U.S. solidarity is the least of our problems.

President Kennedy: What did you say?

Bundy: U.S. solidarity—

President Kennedy: Oh, I meant the solidarity—

Unidentified: A simultaneous announcement would do that, Mr. President.

Robert Kennedy: I think George Ball has a hell of a good point.

President Kennedy: What?

Robert Kennedy: I think it's the whole question of, you know, assuming that you do survive all this, the fact that we're not . . . what kind of a country we are.

Rusk: This business of carrying the mark of Cain on your brow for the rest of your life is something . . .

Robert Kennedy: We did this against Cuba. We've fought for 15 years with Russia to prevent a first strike against us [unclear]. Now, in the interest of time, we do that to a small country. I think it's a hell of a burden to carry.

Thompson: Part of the strongest argument against this is that, killing the Russians, to my mind, means you are going to end up the whole way.

McNamara: Yes, well, I don't believe we can stop with a large air strike. If we kill Russians, we're going to have to go in. They can't stop [unclear] and have to go on.

President Kennedy: Let's just say we make this announcement. Say, the afternoon before we send a message to Khrushchev, saying that: "We said we'd have to do it. We're going to have to do it, and you ought to get those Russians out of there within the next twelve hours." And we lose a good deal of advantage as far as surprise. But what we, of course, are trying to do is get the missiles.

I'm not so worried about the air. But the atomic bombs, they can get a couple of them over on us anyway, but at least the [unclear]. Maintain their position over that island each time a plane takes off. There are not that many, after all.

Alexis Johnson: If you get a denial out of Gromyko this afternoon, saying they haven't any bases there, or that the Russians aren't establishing anything there . . .

[Unclear brief exchange.]

[Unclear] As far as these bases are concerned, then, you're striking against Castro. I don't think he'll be more surprised than we were to find Russians there, because we've been told there were none and then we found a Russian base.

Rusk: If the military situation doesn't require—if you took just a little more time before you actually hit, and you let several public opinions know about this in Cuba, as well as in the Soviet Union, it would be more difficult for the Soviet Union, because people realize that this is a major thing coming, and something may crack.

Thompson: There's one important related point, for which we have varied information. That is that Khrushchev got himself into this aggressive posture in Berlin and everything on his own. I mean, he's taken credit for it time and time again.

And the advantage that hasn't been mentioned about the notification to him is that he would have to show it to his colleagues, and there is a possibility that there'll be strength there. I think there was some indication that, in the abortive Paris summit meeting, he was under strict instructions to break that up because they were afraid to go down the course he was following.[12] There is some chance this could happen.

12. A planned Paris summit between Eisenhower and Khrushchev in May 1960 was cancelled after the shootdown of the American U-2 over Soviet airspace. At the time Thompson was the U.S. Ambassador in Moscow.

I mean, we haven't any solid information on this. But I can cite very minor things that happened at the time of the U-2 [shootdown] where the military, who normally would never talk to me, came over and tried to calm me down, that sort of thing, and showing they were concerned that Khrushchev was being impetuous and running risks. Although there are advantages and disadvantages about the response to some notifications.

President Kennedy: What do we ask him to do under that notification? Wⁿ is it we'd be trying to get out of him?

Alexis Johnson: I think you would have to say, ne representation, his instructions would be that could return with, or report to you. was going to begin immed

Rusk: We'd asʰ to tell C

ⱡnat any other ⱡnsatisfactory.

ⱡⱡⱡe bit of discussion if there is a with bases for Turkey. We substitute Polaris ⱡnere. It seems to me that negotiations would entirely negotiations would be part of this whole broad complex of ⱡⱡns. It doesn't have to be all-out war.

And there's some advantage even in our proposing it. And say: "This won't wait for your trip in November, come on over."

These other paths, it seems to me you're playing Russian roulette. You're flipping a coin as to whether you end up with world war or not.

President Kennedy: The only question is, whether you're going to get the time, whether he makes a guarantee. Now, as I say, he's not going to be any more happy about this than we are. He seems to be happier with the fact that he's taking much more of a risk than perhaps we would have taken.

But it seems if he responds, giving us an ultimatum in a sense, the question really is whether we're worse off then. There is an argument that we are worse off.

And [there is an argument] that he might accept something when it's accomplished just like we might. [As] in the case of Hungary. He wouldn't accept it perhaps so much in advance.

Thompson: I think McCone is right . . . If you approach him, you sure are almost certainly going to have to get into negotiations.

Rusk: Well, he might have a negotiation proposal; that doesn't mean that you have to get into it. Because the condition of it might be: You stop this work on these missiles—

Thompson: Accompanied with this notification that we are going to bomb Cuba if the work goes on with this. Accompanied with the blockade [words unclear] indicated a strong action.

President Kennedy: Well, I feel that there's a difference between our action, and therefore in their response, between our knocking out these missiles and planes, and invading Cuba.

Obviously, if he knocked out our missiles . . . If he had said that he was going to knock out our missile sites, and went and did it one afternoon in Turkey, it would be different than if the Russian army started invading Turkey. We'd be faced with a 10-day period of shootings.

And nobody knows what kind of success we're going to have with this invasion. Invasions are tough, hazardous. We've got a lot of equipment, a lot of—thousands of—Americans get killed in Cuba, and I think you're in much more of a mess than you are if you take out these . . .

I think this is all deduction, but if he invades Iran, it takes 10 days and a lot of fighting in Iran.

We're in a much tougher position [with an invasion] than if we take out those bases. It may be that his response would be the same, nobody can guess that, but by stretching it out you increase the . . .

Robert Kennedy: I don't think you have to make up your mind if you're going to invade. Even in the first 24 hours, 48 hours—

Taylor: We can't invade that fast, Mr. President. It will take at least 7 days, I think we have to make advance preparations—that we have to make now.

President Kennedy: You mean, getting these people in position?

Taylor: We're now not making any moves that give away our intentions.

Robert Kennedy: I think you can always hold that out.

President Kennedy: Guantanamo. I would think Castro's replies would be against Guantanamo.

Taylor: That's right. If we immediately jump in and defend Guantanamo.

Rusk: —it's quite clear, would it not be well to bring the dependents out? We have that—

Gilpatric?: That could be done very quickly. [4 seconds excised as classified information.] . . . be there, over this period, we'll keep shipping there.

Rusk: I think if we reinforce Guantanamo and simply explained at the moment, do this as quick as possible, that we are pulling the dependents out only to make room for the reinforcements.

Taylor: Well, if we could do that, that would be tough. We'd like to do that if that's acceptable.

President Kennedy: How many dependents are there?

Taylor: 2,200 plus.

President Kennedy: Now, what about holding Guantanamo itself? Shouldn't we worry, really, if we're considering taking some action on Sunday, we really be heading some ships and tro...

Taylor: We h...

...ng

...uld be against Guantanamo.

...namo, we're going to have to invade.

Taylor: He won't overrun Guantanamo or he'll have a good fight around the place. By the time we get the Marines in, with the carrier-based aviation, we'll hold Guantanamo.

President Kennedy: Now, there isn't anything we ought to be doing in the next 3 or 4 days, as far as the Navy?

Taylor: Many things, sir, but all of them have a certain visibility.

The great bottleneck in this invasion plan is the assembly of shipping. The shipping and moving of heavy equipment from the base down in Fort Hood. So that anything that we do not do will tend to impact the time. Thus if you do decide that you have to have a period of discussion, if we could be doing those things in that period of time, then we'd reduce the reaction [time] . . .

Dillon: Well, some of us say it wouldn't be bad if the plan went ahead. [Two people agree.]

McNamara: Mr. President, I would suggest that we not consider the actions we might take here which serve us, or in any way might serve us, until you've decided, one, when you want to make this information available to our public. Because we're sitting tight on all this at the present time, and any of these actions are likely to cause—

President Kennedy: Let's start going through now what your—

Robert Kennedy: Can I just ask you a question? How much time . . . ? If Mr. President goes on Sunday [October 21], or say we have the attack on

Monday [October 22], the air attack. How many days after that would you be prepared to invade?

Taylor: There are two ways to do it, Mr. President, while we're on the subject. One is quick-reaction planning, which gets to— [12 seconds excised as classified information.]

The second is certainly preferable militarily. On the other hand, if that length of time just doesn't fit into the overall plan, we'd deal with that.

Rusk: As far as the declaration of war point, or the invasion side of things. If you made the quick strike against these Cuban installations, you could at that point say that any reaction against the United States or Guantanamo would bring about a state of war with Cuba. Then you've got considerable pressure on them to stop it right there.

President Kennedy: Well, as I said, the advantage of giving Khrushchev notification—we might as well give Khrushchev the notification that we give everybody else—is that he can get his Russians out of there if we wants to, or to back down if he wants to.

Thompson: I think the first [advantage] is the point about our allies. If we have to face the crunch on Berlin, then we would have some of them still with us. Secondly, to give him a chance to back down or at least to . . . Thirdly, to get a negotiation [unclear].

President Kennedy: What is the suggested method if we are going to communicate with Khrushchev? Dobrynin? Or send somebody?

Thompson: We could telegraph something simultaneously.

Robert Kennedy: What do you think about a personal emissary, Mr. President? I think it could be somebody who could go in and just talk to them about it.

Rusk: The problem you've got is you almost have to announce at the same time what the situation is in Cuba [Robert Kennedy agrees] because . . . Unless you send someone that has low visibility.

Robert Kennedy: Well, I think you can get somebody on a plane.

[Unclear exchange.]

President Kennedy: So I take it [unclear] with Khrushchev—

Rusk: I think a written message through Dobrynin or somebody.

Thompson: A written message. So that he has to reply in writing. Otherwise you get a fuzzy conversation.

Robert Kennedy: How do you handle the evidence?

Thompson: He's pretty adept at these matters.

Rusk: Stevenson thinks a special emissary might be very advisable.

President Kennedy: Let's say we ask Mr. Robert Lovett to go over there. [Long pause.] You'd have to put him on a plane; you'd have to send him off there; you'd have to make an appointment with Khrushchev; all that would take . . .

[Mixed voices.]

Thompson: I wouldn't even suggest that you necessarily need to deliver it personally. Just send it. I would think just getting it to Khrushchev . . .

President Kennedy: What does that do for us? Do you think th . . . chance that he might—do what with th . . .

Thomp . . .

. . . , the military makes their moves in preparation for an invasion. This is a strong warning to them, in some ways.

President Kennedy: Well, if we get to a summit, then he's going to talk about Berlin.

[Several people speak, referring to the Gromyko meeting, to "the history of the world," to a number of ships turned around, and to "work stops, for one."]

Bundy: How much better are you off for history for asking 24 hours ahead of time, if he says: "I want a summit," and you say: "Nuts"?

Rusk: [Unclear] what has happened in Cuba. Before they can do something.

Bundy: You can have that in the first message. It's very likely that he would propose that we meet. But we can't meet unless we can have an agreement on these things.

Taylor: In the Gromyko call this afternoon, isn't there a possibility that we can get him to lie that he doesn't have . . .

Rusk: I was going to suggest that the President consider it, especially with Gromyko. [Unclear] in Cuba. Read to him from this paragraph of this statement of September 4th and see what Gromyko says. See if he will lie about it because [unclear] no offensive weapons there and so forth. But he really might not know. I don't think the President ought to disclose to Gromyko [unclear].

Robert Kennedy: What if he says you should be taking out what you've got in Turkey. Because they're no more offensive than your weapons in Turkey.

Rusk: We can certainly prepare some points to respond to that. Well, first the Rio Treaty.

Secondly, we have the earlier [unclear]. When they took strong action against Hungary, on the ground that this was on their side of that slate as well. This action in this hemisphere violates not only modern obligations but also the historic well-known foreign policies of the United States, in this hemisphere.

In any event NATO was successfully built as a direct response to Soviet aggression, and was fully registered under the UN. In 1946 we didn't have any allies. There was no Rio Pact or NATO or CENTO [Central Asia Treaty Organization] or SEATO [South East Asia Treaty Organization]. The only allies that we had were those that were the disappearing allies that fought together during World War II. Anything that came into being was as a result of Stalin's policies. It makes all the difference in the world.

President Kennedy: How many missiles do we have in Turkey?

Bundy: Fifteen.

[Pause.]

Plus nuclear-equipped aircraft.[13]

Robert Kennedy: Even if you went that far and decided to do that, perhaps the awful thing about Khrushchev, he'll say: "Well, this poses a problem for us. We're going to have to take whatever steps" . . .

Thompson: That's why I think you'd have to say this is totally unacceptable.

Robert Kennedy: If you get into it at all, if you went into it as blatantly as that. I suppose the other way is to do it rather subtly and say: "What are you doing in Cuba? What kind of missiles are you sticking in?"

Taylor: Well, if you admit that we have the advantage of indicating we suspect it without implicating our own knowledge of the situation. If he denies it, then you have something that you can use later. [Two people agree.]

Robert Kennedy: That's instead of the frontal approach, which indicates you have knowledge of it.

Rusk: I think you start off with talking about a general provocation in Cuba, as far as the American people are concerned.

Sorensen: Actually, I think the Attorney General's suggestion is a pretty good gambit, to say to them that Khrushchev was not going to do anything before our election, but look what he's doing in Cuba and so on.

13. U.S. nuclear bombs were also stockpiled in Turkey, under U.S. control, for possible use by Turkish (or U.S.) F-100 aircraft.

Taylor: Well, the accusations that are being made by Senator Keating and others is that there are missiles down there.

Sorensen: I wouldn't think that the President would disclose [it] this afternoon, though [with Gromyko].

[Mixed voices.]

Rusk: There would be some significance that Khrushchev [unclear] did not deny there were missiles there.

They must know now that we know.

Robert Kennedy: Well, if he said th-t-

a message to Kl

, for the

. that, as long you're thinking over this, tomorrow morning at this time we should have a quite a good deal more information, from the [unclear] we ran yesterday.

I'm worried about this getting out. I think it's remarkable that it's been held this week. For that reason I feel that we mustn't delay too long.

McNamara: Mr. President, I think we can hold it, however, until Monday [October 22]. I think the thing, the thing that is lacking is not more intelligence, although that will modify our position somewhat. What's lacking here is a real well-thought-out course of action, alternative courses of action.

I think we ought to go back this afternoon and split up into a couple of groups and assign one group one course of action, another group another course of action, and work them out in great detail. My guess is that both of these courses of action—really there are only two that we are talking about.

I would call one the rapid introduction to military action. The other is a slow introduction to military action. Those are really only the two courses of action that we are talking about.

The slow introduction is a political statement followed, or accompanied, by a blockade. The rapid introduction is a brief notice to Khrushchev followed by a strike. Now those are basically the only two alternatives we've discussed with you. We ought to take both of those and follow them through and find out what the prices are likely to be and how to minimize those prices.

President Kennedy: Well, let me you ask you this. Is there anyone here who doesn't think that we ought to do something about this?

[Pause.]

McNamara: Well, we're not clear, however, which of these versions to follow.

President Kennedy: Well, we've got so many different alternatives as far as military action. As I say, you have the blockade without a declaration of war. You've got a blockade with a declaration of war. We've got strikes I, II, and III. We've got invasion. We've got notification to Khrushchev and what that notification consists of.

Robert Kennedy: It's not really that bad, though. Because if you have the strike, you don't have to make up your mind about the invasion. That's not going to come for 3 or 4 days—

Bundy: In one sense you have to make up your mind because basically you have to . . .

Robert Kennedy: So all you have, really, as Bob says, are the two courses of action.

And I think that as long as it really has come down to this after talking about it for 48 hours . . . Because the idea of us going back and trying to put it down for you more definitively rather than you trying to discuss it . . .

Rusk: Well, I think the real issue is: What do you do, if anything, before you strike?

Dillon: When do you tell the press? Exactly what do you say to them?

Robert Kennedy: And when do you tell the American people. I think you should go back . . .

President Kennedy: Well, militarily you're not really in a position to do this strike until Monday, is that it?

Taylor: That is correct.

McNamara: May I suggest, Max, that we still keep open the possibility of [unclear]. I know that events have changed. We've got more targets and so on since then, Mr. President. But I don't think this is actually critical, and I don't think we need to decide this morning.

Taylor: Unless we really need it.

Unidentified: We need it. We need it.

President Kennedy: Well, now the only argument for going quicker than that, really, not only is the one that [the missiles] may leave [be moved] but also—

Bundy: Level of readiness.

President Kennedy: I don't know, if there are two of them ready, whether that makes a hell of a difference anyway. If they're going to fire nuclear missiles at us, then . . .

Taylor: All of this photography has been taken, Mr. President. I think we ought to take out everything that is visible at the time we hit them.

McNamara: It seems to me your instructions to us are our assumptions that we were going to be ready at the earliest possible moment regardless of whether you want us to go there or not. And that earliest possible moment for air strikes is Saturday morning [October 20]. That's the earliest possible moment.

Taylor: The strikes should be number III and number IV.

McNamara: And we're going to be ready for strikes III, IV ~~or V~~

And the second thing we ought to do is

interpret it

~Monday [October 22]. I would

~~October 20].

Robert Kennedy: Well, even though the missiles—

Taylor: The more time we've got, the better we can do it.

[Another unclear exchange, ending with Rusk apparently deferring to Taylor's judgment.]

Rusk: It's going to take some very careful work [unclear]. And if we overlook the steps that are necessary to give us the defense that we need against [unclear] and rush here, and if somebody really gets hurt . . .

Taylor: It's one thing for us to have time to get the work done but another thing to get the orders out and then have experienced men [unclear].

McNamara: I'm not suggesting a date. I'm simply suggesting that our action ought to be to plan for the earliest possible strike because there is one form of penalty we pay with untrained personnel. But with operational nuclear weapons we run great dangers. This is the thing that we must keep in our minds. I don't know when these weapons are going to be operational, but we may find some tonight that are, or tomorrow night, or Saturday night.

Dillon: But I don't think that we have to decide that now.

President Kennedy: We ought to be ready in case. [Unclear.]

Taylor: But may I assume that the categories I and II are out? That we are planning for III, IV, or V? If we do that, that will simplify our planning and arrangements.

Bundy: Did we raise the question of the President's going away?

President Kennedy: Yeah, I want to get an answer about that. I'm supposed to go start at 11:30 or 12:00 tomorrow [on a scheduled campaign trip]. If I cancel it, of course, it will leak.

[Pause.]

Well?

Dillon: It's very difficult to cancel it.

President Kennedy: I figure we'll be going on Friday. I can always come back late Friday night.

Now, the only thing is, we ought to have, probably, a meeting before I see Gromyko. I see him at 5:00.

McNamara: Mr. President, the only question is, if there should be a leak [unclear]?

Robert Kennedy: I'd just deny the leak.

Unidentified: Which leak? Of what?

[Mixed voices.]

McCone: I don't think you can deny the leak. I think that there's too much information on this through the refugee channels.

Robert Kennedy: Yeah, but nothing has come up in the last 3 days.

McNamara: Well, you don't deny the leak. What you say is: "There have been a number of rumors going around. I've asked the Central Intelligence Agency and the Defense Department to check this out. [Unclear.] We're investigating it; we're clearing refugees; we're taking every possible step to determine the condition."

[Mixed voices.]

Rusk: There is the other question, too, of what we are heading into here. The President hopes to unify the country by going on this trip this weekend [unclear].

President Kennedy: Unifying the country is not the purpose of the trip. [Laughter.]

The only problem is . . . Obviously the major story is why we called it off. Because unless we were about to proceed Saturday or Sunday, I'd better not call it off.

We are going over to Monday unless we get our sequences into a position where we can surface this thing by Friday afternoon. The minute I call it [this trip] off, this thing is going to break. Because every newspaperman will be around there, and somebody's going to get it. So I don't think I can call this off tomorrow without having this thing—unless we are ready to have it surface.

Dillon: I don't think there's any problem about unifying the country as long as you . . . You'll unify it just like that.

President Kennedy: What do you mean there's no problem?

[Several exchanges at once.]

McCone: The country will unanimously support [unclear].

Rusk: There may be some rumors about this meeting this morning.

Bundy: I still believe that our best cover is intensive review of the defense budget. Now we haven't had to use it yet. [Laughter.]

President Kennedy: That's all right because [unclear].

[Unclear discussion.]

Bundy: Martin isn't here, and I think it'

Rusk: Now I h

. . . . through a dinner. [Unclear.]

. . . . . on, with the interpretation coming out, this meeting [between President Kennedy and Gromyko] is apt to go beyond 7:30. We'll go for 3 or 4 hours.

President Kennedy: What, my meeting with him?

Rusk: Yes.

Dillon: Mr. President, I have one thing. As you know, I am supposed to be leaving Saturday afternoon to go down to Mexico City for this—the American conference opens Monday. I could leave Sunday if that made any difference. Now, there will be various things that we'll have to—

President Kennedy: Well, why don't we wait on that, because we'll all know better our schedule. Why don't you just call off the dinner on Sunday. I don't know what your pretext is going to be. [Unclear elaboration.]

Right, now. What did we . . . ? What is this you're going to do as far as meeting? Trying to get some more final judgments on all these questions which we turned around?

Sorensen: Well, can I make a suggestion there, Mr. President?

It seems to me that the various military courses have been outlined here as the Secretary says. They need to be developed in more detail, step by step and so on. But there has also been general but not unanimous agreement you are likely to need some kind of representation to Khrushchev ahead of time, maybe

---

14. Martin was there. Bundy meant that people should not reveal that Martin was there, since that would reveal that the meeting concerned Latin America, and their cover story would unravel.

very shortly ahead of time. And I think you ought to have, in great detail, drawn up what that representation would consist of. Whether it will be a letter. What will be a satisfactory answer.

President Kennedy: Yes. Well, we certainly have to do the Khrushchev. And decide how much time in advance we'd do it, or whether I would make a public statement that we really had talked about the afternoon before.

The question now is: How do we want to function?

Rusk: Well, I think we ought to draw the group together and set the military . . .

McNamara: I believe the military problem, the military plan, seems like [unclear]. But really what I was thinking of is this give-and-take here, which we haven't gone through. I think the price of any one of these actions is going to be very, very high. I think there are a whole series of actions that of course you can take. And it seems to me we have to narrow those down and then we ought to consider how can we reduce that price.

And I would suggest, therefore, that, under the guidance of State—this is primarily an international political problem. We develop two groups here, and then we have Defense and State people in those two groups and we take 2 or 3 hours this afternoon to let these two groups take these two basic alternatives. They can derive any number of variations they wish to.

But one is a minimum military action, a blockade approach, with a slow buildup to subsequent action. The other is a very forceful military action with a series of variances as to how you enter it. And consider how the Soviets are going to respond. This is what we haven't done.

Alexis Johnson: Well, not only the Soviet response, but what the response to the response will be.

McNamara: How we respond to these responses.

Alexis Johnson: We've done a good deal of work on that already.

McNamara: Well, I think it would be useful to pull it together.

President Kennedy: Well, let's see. Mr. Secretary, I will meet with you at 4:30 with Tommy before the Gromyko [meeting] to see where we are in this conversation. And at the end of the Gromyko conversation, we may want to have . . . I don't think we'll go 3 or 4 hours, but let's say we finish in 2 hours. I don't know how much it is. And then, whether we ought to, some time this evening, have another meeting based on what Gromyko said and see where we are.

Bundy: I hate to be worried about security all the time and I think evening meetings are very dangerous. I think they create a feeling around the town and almost inevitably people have to leave dinners. I think it's a very—

President Kennedy: Well, I'm going to leave right now, so why don't you, Mr. Secretary and Mr. McNamara, decide how we are going to proceed this afternoon. In any case, I will meet you [Rusk] at 4:30 and we will . . . Mr. Lovett is coming down here. He'll be here at 4:00 or 5:00. He can . . . Are you [speaking to Bundy] going to be in with me with Gromyko?

Bundy: Whatever you want.

President Kennedy: You don't need to be. Why don't you talk to Mr. Lovett and see whether he has any thoughts about it. And then we'll ~~tonight. Bundy will communicate~~ . . .

affecting . . .

. . . The

. . . ve catalogued Soviet reaction.

[Rusk appears to make arrangements for people to meet at his office at 2:30.]

Taylor: One of the things that has not been laid out for the President is mobilization requirements.

Rusk: Well, we can put some words on a piece of paper. We can't really say much about Soviet reaction. We can say what they may be.

Taylor: For that reason, though, I think we have to recognize that we will have to try to mobilize, if we make this strike. We've got to have the necessary alerts. [Unclear.] We've done a fair amount of work on it.

McNamara: I don't think we have had enough discussion among this group, enough serious discussion, of a blockade approach versus immediate strike approach. [Someone agrees.] So I'd at least like to get together to do that.

Dillon: I think you will think on the blockade approach, too, not just what it does to the Russians but what the effect is on the rest of our own people and on the rest of Latin America by allowing these things there. The [unclear] that they will under the blockade approach.

Thompson: If you announce at the same time that you are going to take them out if . . .

Alexis Johnson: As far as the blockade approach is concerned, the blockade is valuable if it has a chance of bringing down Castro. This will be much more satisfactory in Latin America than just taking out the missiles.

Robert Kennedy: Has a blockade ever brought anybody down?

Bundy: The missiles go [with] the blockade. I can't see that you do the missiles without . . .

Taylor: I think these things are unresolved.

Unidentified: But I think the blockade results in this.

Taylor: If you don't make them operational.

Rusk: I would think the blockade with at least [strikes] I or II would I guess be a pretty good-size war. But a blockade plus that would be a minimum in any event. Wouldn't it?

Taylor: The minimum in any event. That would make the only sense—

[Mixed voices.]

Thompson: A blockade on military weapons, plus getting the troops into position, plus the announcement that you're going to overfly it, and that you were going to strike if this thing went on. And all these other measures.

Dillon: That would mean overflying low-level [reconnaissance].

Unidentified: That's right.

Thompson: I would do all those things.

Bundy: The great advantage of that, of course, is you don't kill any Russians.

McNamara: This is the main theory.

Bundy: Or Cubans.

[Mixed voices.]

Dillon: . . . when they start shooting down your planes.

Rusk: Then they've escalated. Then they've escalated.

Taylor: Now the only military advantage is that you can be doing these things which you would like to do before we execute an invasion.

Alexis Johnson: Now, the blockade approach we contemplated here, though, has a considerable number of steps leading up to it. [Someone agrees.] There's not an immediate—

Ball: Political negotiations and military preparedness.

Gilpatric: If you announce a blockade, how long before it is actually imposed?

Thompson: Well, immediately. [Others agree.]

Alexis Johnson: . . . strike is over a period of hours, 48 hours . . .

You see, if you are going to do it within the framework, you have the two choices. You do it—well, three choices really. You do it unilaterally, without declaration of war. This is about the worst of all.

[Unclear exchange.]

Then you've got the OAS track that the Secretary was talking about. The way of getting in sanctions under the OAS support. And then you have getting a sanction under OAS plus declaration of war on our part are the three—

Ball: May I also point out that I think you can start the political discussions, and the military preparations, and have a blockade as part of these initial actions, without having decided whether your final action will stop with the blockade or will include military—

Bundy: Given a blockade or OAS consent or no?

Dillon: The whole purpose of a war is to destroy your enemy and that's the only purpose of it. And so, if you do declare war, you only justify the blockade on the basis of that is what it's going to do. You have to carry it through completely and totally, so it's not much difference.

Rusk: There's another disadvantage ʼ ˙ ˙
blockade and ˙ ˙

. ˙ˊˋˋˊˊˍ, in my judgment. At the

McNamara: This is something to think about. But, in any case, the minimum price you pay after the military course of action is missiles out of Turkey and Italy, and they may be out by physical means. Because of the Russians moving against them. And you have a serious potential division of the alliance. Now it seems to me that's the *best* possible situation you could be in as a result of the military course. I can visualize many worse situations.

Under the blockade, the best possible situation . . .

Bundy: I don't see what the blockade is going to solve.

McNamara: The best possible use of a blockade, it seems to me, is that the alliance is not divided. You have agreed to take your missiles out of Turkey and Italy, and the Soviets have agreed either to take them out of Cuba or impose some kind of control comparable to your control over the missiles in Turkey and Italy. Now, that's the best possible solution. There are many worse solutions.

Taylor: I thought last night we were hoping last night that we would get the collapse of Castro.

Bundy: I believe that Castro is not going to sit still for a blockade, and then that's to our advantage. I'm convinced myself that Castro has to go. It never occurred . . . His theme on his self-destruction. We have to help him with that.

McNamara: Well, maybe he's going to pay a bigger price.

Bundy: Later.

McNamara: Later. And I think that's a possibility. But the price is going to be larger. I really think that we've got to think these problems through more than we have.

At the moment I lean to the blockade because I think it reduces the very serious risk of large-scale military action from which this country cannot benefit under what I call program two [rapid introduction of military action]. Russian roulette and a broken alliance.

[Someone echoes: "Russian roulette."]

Robert Kennedy: What are the chances that you've got to say to him: "They can't continue to build these missiles. You're going to have to keep them flying over all the time." Well, at night it looks a little different than it did the next morning.

McNamara: Oh, he's not going to stop building. He's going to continue to build.

Robert Kennedy: [Unclear] though, Bob?

McNamara: This goes back to what you said—this type of blockade. I'm not sure you can say that.

Robert Kennedy: Are you going to let him continue to build the missiles?

McNamara: This goes back to what you begin to negotiate. He says: "I'm not going to stop building. You have them in Turkey. You've acted by putting the blockade on. That's done."

Robert Kennedy: Then you let them build the missiles?

McNamara: Then you talk.

Thompson?: Is this on the assumption that he would run the blockade?

McNamara: No, no. They have enough inside that they can continue the construction.

Robert Kennedy: We tell them they can build as many missiles as they want?

McNamara: Oh, no. What we say is: "We are going to blockade you. This is a danger to us. We insist that we talk this out and the danger be removed."

Robert Kennedy: Right. But now they just go ahead and build the missiles.

McNamara: [responding to an interjection] Overflights, definitely.

Robert Kennedy: They put the missiles in place, and then they announce that they've got atomic weapons.

McNamara: Sure. And we say we have them in Turkey. And we're not going to tolerate this.

Robert Kennedy: What is the relationship then between the blockade and the danger?

McNamara: Well, all this time Castro is being strangled.

Thompson: Why wouldn't you say that, if construction goes on, that you would—

McNamara: Well, I might, I might. But that is a more dangerous form of the blockade.

Taylor: What is your objection to taking out the missiles and the aircraft?

McNamara: My real objection to it is that it kills several hundred Russians, and I [unclear] . . .

[Mixed voices. Fragment: "all around the world." Someone else says: "Then you start killing people."]

Robert Kennedy: You put the blockade on, and then you tell . . . go ahead and construct the . . . Well

McNam

. . . in the

. . . a group and . . .

. . . [Sorensen] . . . Can't you and Tommy work on drafts?

[Nearly all but McNamara, Taylor, and Bundy then gather their papers and leave, talking on their way out.]

Taylor: We've got the President here, has said III, IV, V.

McNamara: In effect those cover I and II anyhow.

[Unclear exchanges.]

Bundy: Security, that's the problem.

Taylor: Well it's worth waiting, if that's the case.

Bundy: I wouldn't worry about the security. Not that much. We can hold this [secret].

Unidentified: I'm certain we can hold this.

Unidentified: Congress is not in town now. [Unclear.]

McNamara: We're advancing. We're further ahead now than we were yesterday at this time. If we put our heads on this tomorrow . . .

Bundy: I think everybody ought to give real attention to this paper [unclear].

[After another exchange, in which Taylor and Bundy appear to reiterate that security is vital, the room falls silent. The tape recorder continues running for more than 20 minutes until it runs out of tape or is turned off.]

THURSDAY, OCTOBER 18

NEAR MIDNIGHT

OVAL OFFICE

President Kennedy returned to his regular schedule, having lunch and a brief swim, then meeting with the Japanese minister of trade and industry. Acheson came to see him in person, and outlined his views in favor of an immediate air strike without prior warning to the Soviets.

At 3:30 Rusk and McNamara came back over to the White House from their resumed meetings at the State Department and briefly reported on progress. At 4:30 Rusk returned to the White House, this time with Thompson, and they prepared President Kennedy for his meeting with Gromyko. That meeting began at 5:00. Meanwhile Bundy, as planned, briefed and talked with Lovett. McNamara and McCone also spoke to Lovett.

The meeting with Gromyko lasted until about 7:15. Gromyko emphasized the need to settle the Berlin issue, indicating that the Soviets would do nothing before the U.S. elections in November. The Soviets would move on the Berlin issue later that month. If there was no understanding by that time, Gromyko said that "the Soviet government would be compelled, and Mr. Gromyko wished to emphasize the word 'compelled,'" to take steps to end the Western presence in Berlin. Gromyko described the Western military presence in Berlin as a "rotten tooth which must be pulled out."

Gromyko also complained about American threats against Cuba. The Soviet Union was only training Cubans in the use of defensive weapons. President Kennedy said that "there was no intention to invade Cuba" and that he would have been glad to give Khrushchev assurances to that effect, if asked. Yet Soviet shipments of arms to Cuba were an extremely serious matter, as a result of which the two countries faced "the most dangerous situation since the end of the war [World War II]." Gromyko referred to the Bay of Pigs attempted invasion in 1961. Kennedy cut in to say that he'd already admitted that this had been a mistake and that he "would have given assurances that there would be no further invasion, either by refugees or by U.S. forces." But since the Soviet shipments of arms had begun in July, the situation had changed.

Kennedy then read from his September 4 and 13 public statements, looking for a reaction. None was evident. The two leaders also discussed the ongoing negotiations to restrict nuclear testing, and Kennedy agreed to see Khrushchev when the Soviet leader came to the United States for the UN in November.[1]

When C

. . . avoid the press, . . . that section of the office building [the . . . of the West Wing of the White House]. I learned that the reason for this was that Gromyko had just left.

When I went into the President's office [the Oval Office], he was sitting in his rocking chair, with Rusk and Thompson on his left and the sofa, on his right, vacant. He motioned Bundy and me to it. He asked me if I had gotten the briefing and all the facts available, and I said that I had. He grinned and said, "I ought to finish the story by telling you about Gromyko, who, in this very room not over 10 minutes ago, told more barefaced lies than I have ever heard in so short a time. All during his denial that the Russians had any missiles or weapons, or anything else, in Cuba, I had the low-level pictures in the center drawer of my desk, and it was an enormous temptation to show them to him."[3]

The President then asked me what I thought of the situation, and I outlined briefly the philosophy which I felt would be appropriate here for the President to take, as well as the military steps which seemed to be called

---

1. Quotations are from the full State Department Memorandum of Conversation for the meeting (A. Akalovsky was the notetaker), Cuban Missile Crisis Files, 1992 Releases box, National Security Archive, Washington, D.C.

2. From an interview by Dorothy Fosdick for the John F. Kennedy Library Oral History Project, November 19, 1964. The interview took place only 2 years after the event, and Lovett had kept substantial notes of the session, which he had reexamined in preparing for this interview. Thus, the account provides an unusually detailed record of a crucial moment in the shaping of Kennedy's conclusions about how to proceed.

3. In fact they were not "low-level" pictures. Low-level reconnaissance of Cuba had not begun.

for. I urged the quarantine route [Lovett is using the term that later passed into common usage; it was then still called the blockade] as the first step, for reasons I have given above,[4] and the matter was discussed in some detail, with Rusk and Thompson joining in.

At about this stage of the discussion the door onto the Rose Garden opened, and the Attorney General came in and joined the discussion. The President asked me to repeat what I had previously said, and I did so. Robert Kennedy asked 2 or 3 very searching questions about the application of any blockade and indicated that he felt as I did about the necessity for taking a less violent step at the outset, because, as he said, we could always blow the place up if necessary, but that might be unnecessary, and then we would then be in the position of having used too much force. He did not support one of the arguments which I had made to the effect that it might be contended in the United Nations that we were guilty of an act of aggression if we ordered an air strike or an invasion, whereas the imposition of a quarantine could, I thought, be justified far more easily on the grounds that we were trying to prevent an aggression by removing the tools which might make it possible in the hands of the Cubans. I was, however, delighted to see that he was apparently of the same opinion that I was.

He also indicated that the President had received advice from another source that a full-stage invasion should be made and that still another adviser had strongly pled for an air strike. I remember commenting that the President would undoubtedly receive 2 or 3 more opinions, as I had observed it was a normal occupational hazard in dealing with military matters to get 3 men together and get at least 4 opinions.

A considerable amount of the discussion with the President centered on the possible reaction of the Russians, and Thompson talked on this point at some length. There seemed to be a consensus—by this time various members of his staff had come in on 3 or 4 occasions to tell the President that it was past dinnertime—that those were risks which had to be taken in the national interest and as a matter of national and world security. The whole subject of the protection of the Western Hemisphere was gone over at some length, and finally the Secretary of State and Ambassador Thompson withdrew [to go to the Gromyko dinner, which was beginning at 8:00], and the President

4. Lovett had explained earlier in this interview that he thought a tight blockade should precede air strikes and a possible invasion. The blockade would allow a demonstration of national will to persuade the Russians to withdraw their missiles without great bloodshed, without appearing "trigger-happy." His doubt, according to his notes of the time, "lay in the area of the willingness of the Administration to follow through on a course of action undertaken by it." This meant a full blockade, and not letting up until the objective was accomplished, and being ready to escalate if necessary.

went over again 3 or 4 elements in this picture. The Attorney General and I were asked to stay and join him for dinner.

As I had been through a rather rugged day, which started at 6:30 in the country, I asked the President's leave to return to New York at some reasonable hour, and he smilingly agreed. I caught the last shuttle out to LaGuardia [airport in New York City] and got home after midnight.

President Kennedy returned to his residential quarters for dinner at about 8:20. Meanwhile, at the State Department, meetings had ~~ ~~ coming and going. State's ~~~

~~~ ~~~ ~~~ Executive

~~~ not be tape recorded.

~~~ meeting there was continued agreement that the United States must act, though Bundy voiced a dissenting view. The group generally agreed that action should probably start with a blockade rather than an immediate attack. Kennedy discussed the timing of a possible announcement of the blockade and directed that detailed planning begin. The meeting broke up sometime around midnight.

After the others left, President Kennedy went to the Oval Office, possibly accompanied by his brother. Apparently aware that he had been unable to record the meeting, President Kennedy turned on the recording machine in the Oval Office and began to dictate.

President Kennedy: [Unclear] Secretary McNamara, Deputy Secretary Gilpatric, General Taylor, Attorney General, George Ball, Alexis Johnson, Ed Martin, McGeorge Bundy, Ted Sorensen.[5] During the course of the day, opinions had obviously switched from the advantages of a first strike on the missile sites and on Cuban aviation to a blockade.

Dean Acheson, with whom I talked this afternoon, stated that, while he was uncertain about any of the courses, he stated the first strike as being most likely

---

5. These were apparently the participants in the White House meeting that had just ended. Rusk and Thompson had stayed at the State Department attending the dinner for Gromyko, which dragged on until after midnight.

to achieve our result and less likely to cause an extreme Soviet reaction. That strike would take place just against the missile sites.

When I saw Robert Lovett later, after talking to Gromyko, he was not convinced that any action was desirable. He felt that the missile strike, the first strike, would be very destructive to our alliances. The Soviets would inevitably bring about a reprisal; that we would be blamed for it—particularly if the reprisal was to seize Berlin; and that we'd be regarded as having brought about the loss of Berlin with inadequate provocation, they having lived with these intermediate-range ballistic missiles for years.

Bundy continued to argue against any action, on the grounds that there would be, inevitably, a Soviet reprisal against Berlin and that this would divide our alliances and we would bear that responsibility. He felt we would be better off to merely take note of the existence of these missiles, and to wait until the crunch comes in Berlin, and not play what he thought might be the Soviet game.

Everyone else felt that for us to fail to respond would throw into question our willingness to respond over Berlin, [and] would divide our allies and our country. [They felt] that we would be faced with a crunch over Berlin in 2 or 3 months and that by that time the Soviets would have a large missile arsenal in the Western Hemisphere which would weaken our whole position in this hemisphere and cause, face us with the same problems we're going to have in Berlin anyway.

The consensus was that we should go ahead with the blockade beginning on Sunday night. Originally we should begin by blockading Soviets against the shipment of additional offensive capacity, [and] that we could tighten the blockade as the situation requires. I was most anxious that we not have to announce a state of war existing, because it would obviously be bad to have the word go out that we were having a war rather than that it was a limited blockade for a limited purpose.

It was determined that I should go ahead with my speeches so that we don't take the cover off this, and come back Saturday night [October 20].

President Kennedy then turned off the tape recorder.

9:45 A.M.

CABINET ROOM

.......d

......ing a regiment with 8 SS-4s

......ore at hand for a second salvo. They pronounced both sites already operational. They had found another regiment of SS-4s east of Havana near Sagua La Grande. They expected these 8 missiles to be operational within a week.

Although they had still spotted no actual IRBMs, the analysts were increasingly certain that the 2 sites near Guanajay were intended for 2,200-mile-range SS-5s. The photos showed permanent construction, for SS-5s were too big and heavy to be fired from mobile launchers. And it was the construction pattern that was the giveaway, for they had not only seen it in photographs of the Soviet Union; they had technical data supplied by the spy Penkovsky. Seeing new evidence of a nuclear warhead storage site in the area, the analysts predicted that the IRBMs would be operational in 6 to 8 weeks.[1]

The Joint Chiefs of Staff met at 9:00. Taylor told them about the previous night's meeting and the leaning toward a blockade of some kind. He said President Kennedy wanted to see them soon. The Chiefs agreed to recommend a massive air strike against Cuban military targets with no advance warning. They disagreed on the question of invasion, with Taylor again resisting this step. They then drove to the White House. McNamara joined them for their meeting with the President.

---

1. The estimates briefed on October 19 were written down in a joint estimate of GMAIC, JAEIC, and NPIC, "Joint Evaluation of Soviet Missile Threat in Cuba," 19 October 1962, in McAuliffe, *CIA Documents*, pp. 203–208.

President Kennedy's view of the Joint Chiefs was respectful but skeptical, with a touch of the former junior naval officer's attitude toward the top brass. His most recent experience with the military in a crisis had angered him. On September 30, only a few weeks earlier, at the peak of the crisis over the admission of a black student, James Meredith, to the University of Mississippi, Kennedy had called on troops to provide security amid violent chaos on the campus. He had felt the military had been unresponsive, remarking at one point to an aide (with the tape recorder running): "They always give you their bullshit about their instant reaction and their split-second timing, but it never works out. No wonder it's so hard to win a war."[2]

The Chiefs filed into the Cabinet room at 9:45. Taylor was accompanied by Air Force Chief of Staff LeMay. With them was Chief of Naval Operations George Anderson, a tall, handsome admiral who looked as if Hollywood had cast him for the part. Anderson was widely admired as a "sailor's sailor," Navy through and through, and his sermons on clean living had earned him the nickname "Straight Arrow." There was also Army Chief of Staff Earle Wheeler, whose reputation had been earned as a brilliant staff officer and Washington planner. Marine Corps Commandant David Shoup had the opposite reputation, having earned the Medal of Honor on the blood-soaked atoll of Tarawa in 1943 but known, by 1962, as uninformed or erratic in the paper battles of the Pentagon. President Kennedy turned on the recorder as the meeting began.

Taylor: Mr. President, as you know, we've been meeting on this subject ever since we discovered the presence of missiles in Cuba. And I would say the debates in our own midst have followed very closely in parallel with those that you've heard from your other advisers.

From the outset I would say that we found we were united on the military requirement: we could not accept Cuba as a missile base; that we should either eliminate or neutralize the missiles there and prevent any others coming in. From a military point of view that meant three things.

First, attack with the benefit of surprise those known missiles and offensive weapons that we knew about. Second, we continue surveillance then to see what the effect would be. And third, a blockade to prevent the others from coming in.

I would say, again, from a military point of view, that seemed clear. We were united on that.

2. Quoted in Richard Reeves, *President Kennedy: Profile of Power* (New York: Simon and Schuster, 1993), p. 363.

There has been one point, the importance of which we recognize, where we have never really firmed up our own position. Namely, the political requirements and the measures to offset the obvious political disabilities of this course of action. We know it's not an easy course of action, and it has at least two serious weaknesses.

The first is we're never sure of getting all the missiles and the offensive weapons if we fire a strike. Secondly, we see—all of us, all of your advisers—a very damaging effect of this on our alliances.

To offset that, I have reported back ...

ered. I think ...

... this morning, Mr. President, would be for you to hear the other Chiefs' comments, either on our basic, what I call the military, plan, or how they would see the blockade plan.

President Kennedy: Let me just say a little, first, about what the problem is, from my point of view.

First, I think we ought to think of why the Russians did this. Well, actually, it was a rather dangerous but rather useful play of theirs. We do nothing; they have a missile base there with all the pressure that brings to bear on the United States and damage to our prestige.

If we attack Cuban missiles, or Cuba, in any way, it gives them a clear line to take Berlin, as they were able to do in Hungary under the Anglo war in Egypt. We will have been regarded as [unclear]. We would be regarded as the trigger-happy Americans who lost Berlin. We would have no support among our allies. We would affect the West Germans' attitude toward us. And [people would believe] that we let Berlin go because we didn't have the guts to endure a situation in Cuba. After all, Cuba is 5 or 6,000 miles from them. They don't give a damn about Cuba. But they do care about Berlin and about their own security. So they would say that we endangered their interests and security.

---

3. Very late on October 18 Gilpatric, acting for McNamara, asked that the Chiefs work on how to help Latin American countries with their internal security, which of these countries could help the United States blockade Cuba, which offensive weapons should be included in a blockade, the possibility of blockading aircraft as well as ships, and related questions.

And the implication [would be] that all the rest [happened] because of the end reaction that we took in Cuba.

So I think they've got . . . I must say I think it's a very satisfactory position from their point of view. If you take the view that what really . . . And clearly, if we do nothing then they'll have these missiles and they'll be able to say any time we ever try to do anything about Cuba, they'll fire these missiles. So that I think it's dangerous, but rather satisfactory, from their point of view.

If you take the view, really, that what's basic to them is Berlin and . . . There isn't any doubt. In every conversation we've had with the Russians, that's what . . . Even last night we [Gromyko and I] talked about Cuba for a while, but Berlin—that's what Khrushchev's committed himself to personally. So, actually, it's a quite desirable situation [in Berlin] from their point of view.

Now, that's what makes our problem so difficult. If we go in and take them out on a quick air strike, we neutralize the chance of danger to the United States of these missiles being used, and we prevent a situation from arising, at least within Cuba, where the Cubans themselves have the means of exercising some degree of authority in this hemisphere.

On the other hand, we increase the chance greatly, as I think—there's bound to be a reprisal from the Soviet Union, there always is—[of] their just going in and taking Berlin by force. Which leaves me only one alternative, which is to fire nuclear weapons—which is a hell of an alternative—and begin a nuclear exchange, with all this happening.

On the other hand, if we begin the blockade that we're talking about, the chances are they will begin a blockade and say that we started it. And there'll be some question about the attitude of the Europeans. So that once again they will say that there will be this feeling in Europe that the Berlin blockade has been commenced by our blockade.

So I don't think we've got any satisfactory alternatives. Whether we balance off that, our problem is not merely Cuba but it is also Berlin. And when we recognize the importance of Berlin to Europe, and recognize the importance of our allies to us, that's what has made this thing be a dilemma for 3 days. Otherwise, our answer would be quite easy.

On the other hand, we've got to do something. Because if we do nothing, we're going to have the problem of Berlin anyway. That was made clear last night [in the meeting with Gromyko]. We're going to have this knife stuck right in our guts, in about 2 months [when the IRBMs are operational]. And so we've got to do something. Now, the question really is, what are we going to [unclear]?

It's safe to say 2 of these missiles [sites] are operational now; [they] can be launched 18 hours after the decision to fire has been reached. We've seen [unclear]. These missiles could be launched within 18 hours after the decision to fire. [Unclear recapitulation of the morning's intelligence briefings on the missile status.] They'd [the IRBMs] be ready in December of '62. It depends on [references to delivery systems and nuclear warheads] intermediate range. Communication, targeting, and an integrated air-defense system are now gaining operational status.

Taylor: That means that we're hearing electronic emissions now ~~~~~ that they have sectors for the air defen~~ ~~ ~~ intelligen~~ ~~

~~~~~~ certain conditions. And

~~ ~~~~ in Cuba, we think the credibility is sacrificed.

President Kennedy: That's right. That's right. So that's why we've got to respond. Now the question is: What is our response?

LeMay: Well, I certainly agree with everything General Taylor has said. I'd emphasize, a little strongly perhaps, that we don't have any choice except direct military action. If we do this blockade that's proposed, a political action, the first thing that's going to happen is your missiles are going to disappear into the woods, particularly your mobile ones. Now, we can't find them, regardless of what we do, and then we're going to take some damage if we try to do anything later on.

President Kennedy: Well, can't they [put] some of these undercover now [unclear], now that they've been alerted?

LeMay: There is a possibility of that. But the way they line these others up—I'll have to say it's a small possibility. If they were going to hide any of them, I would think they would have hid them all. I don't think there are any hid. So the only danger is that we haven't picked up some position in plain sight. This is possible. If we do low-altitude photography over them, this is going to be a tip-off too.

Now, as for the Berlin situation, I don't share your view that if we knock off Cuba, they're going to knock off Berlin. We've got the Berlin problem staring us in the face anyway. If we don't do anything to Cuba, then they're going to push on Berlin and push *real hard* because they've got us *on the run.* If we take military action against Cuba, then I think that the—

President Kennedy: What do you think their reply would be?

LeMay: I don't think they're going to make any reply if we tell them that the Berlin situation is just like it's always been. If they make a move, we're going to fight. I don't think it changes the Berlin situation at all, except you've got to make one more statement on it.

So I see no other solution. This blockade and political action, I see leading into war. I don't see any other solution. It will lead right into war. This is almost as bad as the appeasement at Munich.

[Pause.]

Because if this whole blockade comes along, MiGs are going to fly. The IL-28s are going to fly against them [U.S. ships]. And we're just going to gradually slip into a war under conditions that are at great disadvantage to us, with missiles staring us in the face, that can knock out our airfields in the southeastern portions [of the United States]. And if they use nuclear weapons, it's the population down there. We just slipped into a war under conditions that we don't like. I just don't see any other solution except direct military intervention *right now.*

Anderson: Well, Mr. President, I feel that the course of action recommended to you by the Chiefs from the military point of view is the right one. I think it's the best one from the political point of view.

I'll address myself to the alternative of the blockade. If we institute a blockade, from a military point of view, we can carry it out. It is easier for us and requires less forces if we institute a complete blockade rather than a partial blockade, because instituting a partial blockade involves visit and search of all of these neutral ships, and taking them in, perhaps, to ports, which will certainly cause a great deal of [unclear], than if we go ahead and institute a complete blockade.

If we institute a complete blockade, we are immediately having a confrontation with the Soviet Union, because it's the Soviet-bloc ships which are taking the material to Cuba.

The blockade will not affect the equipment that is already in Cuba, and will provide the Russians in Cuba time to assemble all of these missiles, to assemble the IL-28s, to get the MiGs in a contract-manner control system ready to go. And I feel that, as this goes on, I agree with General LeMay that this will escalate and then we will be required to take other military action at greater disadvantage to the United States, to our military forces, and probably would suffer far greater casualties within the United States if these fanatics do indeed intend to fire any missiles.

We certainly cannot guarantee under those circumstances that we could prevent damage and loss of life in the United States itself. I think we have a good chance of greatly minimizing any loss of life within the United States under the present conditions, if we act fairly soon, although we do recognize that will be very fast. I do not see that, as long as the Soviet Union is supporting Cuba, that there is any solution to the Cuban problem except a military solution.

On the other hand, we recognize fully the relationship to the Berlin situation. The Communists have got in this case a master situation from point of view, where every course of action unpleasantries

they u feel that we were weak.

the concept that [unclear].

President Kennedy: It seems to me that we have to assume that just in order to—military . . . When we grabbed their 2 UN people [as spies] and they threw 2 of ours out [of the Moscow embassy], we've got to assume that's going to be an [unclear]. They may not do it, any more than we can let these go on without doing something. They can't let us just take out, after all their statements, take out their missiles, kill a lot of Russians and not do anything.

It's quite obvious that what they think they can do is try to get Berlin. That may be a risk we have to take, but—

LeMay: Well, history has been, I think, the other way, Mr. President. Where we have taken a strong stand they have backed off. In Lebanon, for instance.[4]

Taylor: I would agree, Mr. President. I think from the point of view of face that they'll do something. But I think it will be considerably less, depending on the posture we show here. I can't really see them putting the screws in. The dangers of hitting Berlin are just as great or greater after our action down here, because we have our [unclear].

President Kennedy: They've got to wait for 3 months until they get these things all ready, and then squeeze us in Berlin. But I think at that point, for

4. A landing of thousands of U.S. Marines in Lebanon in 1958 was unopposed, and the bloodless action was believed to have prevented a takeover of Lebanon by anti-Western dissidents supported by the United Arab Republic and the Soviet Union.

what it is worth—it may not be worth much—but at least we have the support of Europe.

Taylor: That is true.

President Kennedy: This way we have to figure this [unclear] in Europe will regard this action . . . no matter what pictures we show afterwards of [missiles] having been . . .

Wheeler: Mr. President, in my judgment, from a military point of view, the lowest-risk course of action if you're thinking of protecting the people of the United States against a possible strike on us is to go ahead with a surprise air strike, the blockade, and an invasion, because these series of actions progressively will give us increasing assurance that we really have gone after the offensive capability of the Cuban/Soviets corner. Now, admittedly, we can never be absolutely sure until and unless we actually occupy the island.

Now, I've also taken into consideration a couple of other things at the present time. To date, Khrushchev has not really confronted us with Soviet power. In other words, he has not declared Cuba a part of the Warsaw Pact. Nor has he made an announcement that this is a Soviet base, although I think that there is a chance that he may do that any time, particularly later in November, when he comes to the United States. And this course of action would then immediately have us confronting the Soviets and not Cubans. And at that time Soviet prestige, world prestige, would be at stake, which it is not at the present time.

The effect of this base in Cuba, it seems to me, has at least two sizable advantages from his point of view and two sizable disadvantages from our point of view.

First, the announcement of a Soviet base in Cuba would immediately have a profound effect in all of Latin America at least and probably worldwide because the question would arise: Is the United States incapable of doing something about it or unwilling to do something about it? In other words, it would attack our prestige.

Not only that. Increasingly, they can achieve a sizable increase in offensive Soviet strike capabilities against the United States, which they do not now have. They do have ICBMs that are targeted at us, but they are in limited numbers. Their air force is not by any manner of means of the magnitude and capability that they probably would desire. And this short-range missile course gives them a sort of a quantum jump in their capability to inflict damage on the United States. And so as I say, from a military point of view, I feel that the lowest-risk course of action is the full gamut of military action by us. That's it.

President Kennedy: Thank you, General.

Shoup: Mr. President, there's a question in my mind. Under what circumstance would Cuba want to inflict damage on the United States? The placing of the kind of weapons and the bombers that can do that certainly demand a hell of a lot of attention. There's one feature of this that I've been unable to reconcile. And I wonder whether the American people and the other nations of the world can reconcile it, and that is that we are now so anxious or we're discussing the anxiety of eliminating the possibility of damage to America from the Cuban air raid, whereas for a good many months the wor~~ld~~ and we've known, that we have treme~~nd~~ in on us from ~~R~~

...wants

...qui~~re~~ment to eliminate this threat of damage, then it's going to take some forces, sizable forces, to do it. And as we wait and wait and wait, then it will take greater forces to do it.

And as long as it isn't done, then those forces will increasingly require a greater force. We'll be absolutely tied to that function. That means that they're going to have to stand by and take care of that function. And you will then have a considerable force of troops, ships, aircraft tied to this requirement that someday may happen.

I can't conceive that they [the Cubans] would attack us just for the fun of it. They might do it at the direction of Khrushchev. But I cannot see why they would attack us, because they couldn't invade to take us. So there's a question in my mind, in the political area and, as I say, the public and the people, what does this mean?

Does it mean they're [Cuba] getting ready to attack us, that little pipsqueak of a place? If so, Russia has a hell of a lot better way to attack us than to attack us from Cuba.

Then, in my mind, it all devolves upon the fact that they [the missiles] do matter. They can damage us increasingly every day. And each day that they increase, we have to have a more sizable force tied to this problem, and then they're not available in case something happens someplace else. And these guys either then have to take some action in Berlin, South Vietnam, Korea. You would be degrading. You'd have to degrade your capability against this ever-increasing force in Cuba.

So, in my opinion, if we want to eliminate this threat that is now closer, but it's not nearly the threat that we've experienced all these months and months, if we want to eliminate it, then we're going to have to go in there and do it as a full-time job to eliminate the threat against us. Then if you want to take over the place and really put in a new government that is non-Communist, then you'll have to invade the place. And if that decision is made, we must go in with plenty of insurance of a decisive success in as quick [a time] as possible.

President Kennedy: Well, it is a fact that the number of missiles there, I would say that no matter what they put in there, we could live today under. If they don't have enough ICBMs today, they're going to have them in a year. They obviously are putting in [unclear] missiles.

LeMay: Plus increase their accuracy against the 50 targets that we know that they could hit now.

But the big thing is, if we leave them there, it's a blackmail threat against not only us but the other South American countries that they may decide to operate against.

There's one other factor that I didn't mention that's not quite our field, [which] is the political factor. But you invited us to comment on this at one time. And that is, if we should talk about Cuba and the SAM sites down there. And we made pretty strong statements about the [unclear] Cuba, that we would take action against offensive weapons. I think that a blockade, and political talk, would be considered by a lot of our friends and neutrals as being a pretty weak response to this. And I'm sure a lot of our own citizens would feel that way, too. You're in a pretty bad fix, Mr. President.

President Kennedy: What did you say?

LeMay: You're in a pretty bad fix.

[Kennedy makes an unclear, joking, reply.]

Taylor: We've begun the blockade plan study, and we're studying its implications, but we really haven't gone into it deeply.

There are a few things that strike us from the outset. One is the difficulty of maintaining surveillance. We just don't see how they can do that without taking losses and getting into some form of air warfare [unclear].

Second, they're targeting Guantanamo, which is curious. [Unclear] obstacle to some degree. I might ask Admiral Anderson to comment on how we can protect our position in Guantanamo during a state of blockade.

Anderson: Well, our position in Guantanamo becomes increasingly vulnerable, because strictly the imposition of the blockade is going to infuriate the Cubans, and they have got a mass of militia, and they can come on around Guantanamo. And I don't know whether they would actually attack Guantanamo or not. But we would certainly have to provide increased forces around there to defend Guantanamo, which we're in the process of reinforcing right now. Also, they have these short-range cruise missiles. They have 3 groups of those primarily for coastal defense. Their MiGs, their aircraft all pose a threat to Guantanamo. So the threat is greatly increased and intensified during the course of a blockade.

Taylor: I think Guantanamo is going to cease to be a useful naval base, become more a fortress that's more or less in a permanent state of . . .

President Kennedy: If we were going to . . . deal of diff . . .

. . . were . . . . . . g our way across the island . . . . tion from taking out these offensive weapons.

LeMay: I think we have got to do more than take out the missiles, because if you don't take out the air at the same time you're vulnerable now in that section of the world for them to strike from their air. They could come in at low altitude and do it. Because we haven't got much of a low-altitude capability.

In addition, that air would be used against any other surveillance you have, too. So if you take out the missiles, I think you've got to take out their air with it, and their radar, communications, the whole works. It just doesn't make any sense to do anything but that.

President Kennedy: Well, I think that what we have—they're going to be here for some time. And what we've talked about is having ground-to-ground missiles.

You know, as I say, the problem is not really so much war against Cuba. But the problem is part of this worldwide struggle with the Soviet Communists, particularly, as I say, over Berlin. And with the loss of Berlin, the effect of that and the responsibility we would bear. As I say, I think the Egyptian and the Hungary thing and the obvious parallels are what I'm concerned about.

LeMay: If you lose in Cuba, you're going to get more and more pressure right on Berlin.

Taylor: The worldwide problem has certainly been before us, Mr. President. We haven't ignored it. We have been deterred, to my view, from getting ready to invade Cuba, as I think you know.

On the other hand, now that we see that it's not much going to be a place where they need a little supply of mobile missiles, as I thought perhaps earlier in the week, but really an organized base where the numbers of missile complexes are—

President Kennedy: Of course General Shoup's point, which he's offered for many years, is there isn't any doubt [that] if it isn't today, within a year they're going to have enough [unclear] stocked [unclear] the number of ICBMs they have. They may not be quite as accurate. But you get to put them on a city, whether it's 80 or 100, you're talking about the destruction of a country, so that our problem is that we begin to duplicate that here. And we're losing all our cities.

Taylor: And we can never talk about invading again, after they get these missiles, because they got the gun pointed at our head.

President Kennedy: Well, the logical argument is that we don't really have to invade Cuba. That it's just one of the difficulties that we live with in life, like you live with the Soviet Union and China.

That problem, however, is for us not to do anything, then wait until we finish up Berlin, and then we can't do anything about Cuba. But I do think we ought to be aware of the fact that the existence of these missiles does not add to the danger but does create a danger right there now. Right there [in the Soviet Union] now they've got enough to keep us, between submarines and ICBMs, whatever planes they do have, and now they discovered the [unclear] country [unclear], they pretty well got us here anyway.

Taylor: By logic we ought to be able to say we can deter these missiles as well as the Soviet missiles, the ones from the Soviet Union. I think the thing that worries us, however, is these being potentially under the control of Castro. Castro would be quite a different fellow to own missiles than Khrushchev. I don't think that's the case now, and perhaps Khrushchev would never willingly do so. But there's always the risk of their falling into Cuban hands.

Shoup: Mr. President, one other item about the Guantanamo thing. Any initiative on our part immediately gives them the, I don't know, not the authority but the right probably to let fly at Guantanamo Bay. And first, the weapons that they have, including now another SAM site or two to work on the place, plus surface-to-surface missiles . . . They have a considerable number of gun emplacements within range of Guantanamo. So unless something is done to also at the same time neutralize this ability to take on Guantanamo, well, Guantanamo is in one hell of a fix.

President Kennedy: [Unclear] General, what can we do about Guantanamo if we do this air strike and they retaliate?

Anderson: Mr. President, all our thinking on Guantanamo is this. We're reinforcing it right now, building up the strength for the defense of Guantanamo. We have air all earmarked to suppress the weapons which would be brought to bear immediately on Guantanamo. We would evacuate the dependents from Guantanamo immediately prior to the air strike; get them clear. I think that with the forces that we've put in there and the air that is available, we can handle the situation in Guantanamo.

LeMay: Most of the naval air is available to defend Guantanamo.

Taylor: This can go on indefinitely. This could become a Quemoy,[5] where the shelling g---

... [we destroy] the weapons, and that, ... includes the doggone airplanes that can bomb it. Unless the weapons that can cause trouble there are eliminated, all you have is a hunk of dirt that's taken a hell of a lot of people to hang on to.

President Kennedy: Well, let me ask you this. If we go ahead with this air strike, either on the missiles or the missiles and the planes, I understand your recommendations are to do both. When will that be ready?

LeMay: We can be ready for attack at dawn on the 21st [Sunday], I think it's the earliest possible date. The optimal date is maybe Tuesday morning [October 23].

President Kennedy: Tuesday is the optimal.

I suppose with this news now, to get 2 of them [MRBM sites] ready, we're running out of time, are we?

Taylor: This is the mobile missiles you're referring to now?

McNamara: Mr. President, I think it's highly questionable that they have 2 ready. It's best to assume they do, but such information we have indicates it's still not.

President Kennedy: Why is it Tuesday instead of Sunday, General? What's the argument for that?

LeMay: Well, we were told to get ready as fast as possible. We aren't recommending Sunday. We'd prefer Tuesday.

5. Taylor is suggesting an analogy between the potential Cuban harassment of Guantanamo and China's 1958 shelling of the offshore islands of Quemoy and Matsu, held by Taiwan, accompanied by China's threats to invade both these islands, and Taiwan itself.

President Kennedy: Well, the only problem I see is that it starts to break out in the papers.

LeMay: Well, we would prefer Tuesday. That was the only reason. We've had this planned for some time.

[Some outside noise affects the general sound quality. For several minutes, only fragments of conversations are audible. After an unclear brief exchange about intelligence on the mobile missiles, one exchange can be understood.]

President Kennedy: How effective is an air strike at this point, General, against the missile bases?

LeMay: Well, I think it would be guaranteed hitting.

[There is a discussion about mobile equipment, followed by an exchange about the timing of an invasion, and of U.S. air attacks continuing until an invasion might be launched.]

Wheeler?: Where is this—going back to the relationships between Cuba and Berlin. And I certainly feel that the Soviets are not [unclear].

There is no acceptable military solution to the Berlin problem. There is in Cuba. There's no acceptable political/economic solution to the Cuban problem. Conceivably, a solution to the Berlin problem lies in the diplomatic/economic/political field, if we put enough pressure on the Soviet bloc.

Now, if we act in Cuba and they respond by making immediately a deal with the East Germans and surrounding Berlin, denying our access to Berlin, there are some people in Berlin that can survive that for a long time, assuming that the Russians are not just overrunning the city with their own troops. Could we not apply sufficient diplomatic/economic/financial pressures to the entire Soviet bloc and gradually expand this so that, for a suitable period of time, we're progressively cutting the Soviet bloc off from their access to most of the countries in the free world? And at the same time have some sort of an acceptable, what would appear to be an acceptable long-range political solution to all of Berlin?

[48 seconds excised as classified information.]

President Kennedy: I appreciate your views. These are unsatisfactory alternatives. The obvious argument for the blockade was [that] what we want to do is to avoid, if we can, nuclear war by escalation or imbalance. Soviets increase their use; they blockade Berlin. We blockade for military purposes, which can be taken as an initial act to retain some degree of control. Those people last night were so remote from reality that there's no telling what the response.

Unidentified: Did they give any clue [during the Gromyko meeting], Mr. President?

President Kennedy: We talked about Berlin. They talked about the tension escalation. In Cuba they said these were defensive preparations. That's how they define these weapons, as defensive. [Unclear.]

Wheeler: Am I clear that today you are addressing yourself to whether anything at all should be done, but if military action is to be taken, you would favor . . . [unclear]

Taylor: The question of low-level [reconnaissance] flights to get evidence. We discussed that last night, and we're prepared to do them tomorrow. I'm a little concerned about doing that. If there's any likelihood of a ' attack . . .

President K

. . . with

. . . ments can be understood.]

. . . are two alternative courses. One is the blockade [unclear.] And how would you do it without a [unclear]. At the same time other people need to work in great detail on the air strike.

We've just talked to the President in very general terms. But every day the numbers [given] for airplanes we'll have in the air [unclear] is increasing. We should tell them exactly what we mean. What would we include? What sorties do we want?

Taylor: Those figures I showed you last night are the last ones in.

McNamara: What sorties does the Navy want if the Air Force carries out an air strike on missiles, SAM sites, airfields, and so on? [Unclear passage.] . . . same for the blockade.

Taylor: [Unclear] 125 a day is a rough guess. They don't have the surveillance requirements of the blockade either.

[Unclear; possible reference to low-level reconnaissance.]

McNamara: Can't we use these drones?

Taylor: If they're adequate. [Unclear.] Any other chores that, Bob, you want to tell?

McNamara: No, I think not.

Taylor: I will go with you.

Wheeler: I gather that, with the authorization of the movement of the reinforced battalion from the West Coast to Guantanamo, if we see fit to move an extra company in, that's perfectly okay.

Taylor: I saw that covert plan last night. You might want to look at that and decide if it looks alright. It seemed to me a little flat. I don't think the details matter. I don't think you need to say anything when we're coming in in this staggered way.

[The mostly inaudible discussion then turns to the organization and tasking of surveillance flights. There are references to the Joint Reconnaissance Group (JRG) and its relation to DIA or CIA.]

McNamara: The National Reconnaissance Office is involved in this. They're, in a sense, a third agency, responsible for the U-2s, responsible for the drones, anything relating to special reconnaissance for CIA, DIA. Carroll knows how to do this.

Taylor: I think the JRG has all they need. They're a real fine outfit.

Unidentified: They deal with DIA on a daily basis, so I'm sure we can pull it together really quickly.

[After more inaudible discussion the door closes and apparently only 2 or 3 people remain in the room.]

Shoup: You pulled the rug right out from under him. Goddamn.

LeMay: [with a chuckle] Jesus Christ. What the hell do you mean? [Unclear.]

Shoup: I agree with that answer, agree a hundred percent, a hundred percent.

He [President Kennedy] finally got around to the word "escalation." That's the only goddamn thing that's in the whole trick. Go in and out and get every goddamn one. Escalation, that's it.

Somebody's got to keep them from doing the goddamn thing piecemeal. That's our problem. Go in there and friggin' around with the missiles. You're screwed. You go in there and frig around with the lift. You're screwed.

LeMay: That's right.

Shoup: You're screwed, screwed, screwed. Some goddamn thing, some way, that they either do the son of a bitch and do it right, and quit friggin' around. That was my [unclear]. [Unclear] shot down, and then once you do it you can't fuck around and go take a missile out. If you want to do it, you can't fiddle around with taking out missiles. You can't fiddle around with the SAM sites. You got to go in and take out the goddamn thing that's going to stop you from doing your job.

Wheeler: It was very apparent to me, though, from his earlier remarks, that the political action of a blind strike is really what he's . . .

Shoup: His speech about Berlin was the real . . .

Wheeler: He gave a speech about Berlin, and he equates the two. If we smear Castro, if Khrushchev smears—will he run in?

[The remaining seconds of conversation are inaudible. The last participants leave, and the tape ends shortly afterward.]

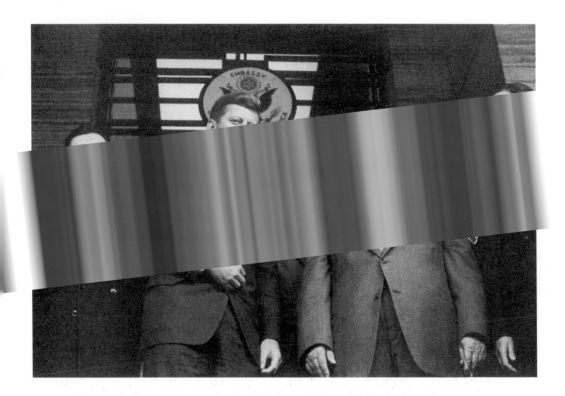

President John F. Kennedy and Soviet Chairman Nikita Khrushchev outside the U.S. embassy in Vienna, Austria, in June 1961. On Kennedy's right is Soviet Foreign Minister Andrei Gromyko, wearing what was for him a broad grin. Between Kennedy and Khrushchev is a U.S. translator; on Khrushchev's left is a Soviet translator.

Kennedy's "Executive Committee" for the missile crisis meeting in the Cabinet Room. The President is seated in front of the flag. To his right are Secretary of State Dean Rusk and Under Secretary of State George Ball. In front of the fireplace, with his face hidden, is Director of Central Intelligence John McCone. On McCone's right are Deputy Under Secretary of State for Political Affairs U. Alexis Johnson (chin in hand), Ambassador at Large Llewellyn Thompson (leaning forward), Attorney General Robert Kennedy (leaning back), Vice President Lyndon Johnson (leaning forward and almost hidden from view). Directly opposite the President is Secretary of the Treasury C. Douglas Dillon. On Dillon's right are three presidential assistants: McGeorge Bundy, Theodore Sorensen, and Kenneth O'Donnell. At the end of the table, leaning forward, is Assistant Secretary of Defense Paul H. Nitze. On Nitze's right, with his hand on his brow, is General Maxwell Taylor. Between Taylor and the President are Deputy Secretary of Defense Roswell Gilpatric and Secretary of Defense Robert S. McNamara.

Another view of Kennedy's "Executive Committee": the President is absent; Rusk is standing. Otherwise, the members are in the same positions.

Kennedy signing the quarantine proclamation on October 23. Rusk looks on.
McNamara is seated. Presidential press secretary Pierre Salinger stands behind Rusk.

Kennedy, McNamara, and Gilpatric.

Dillon (partly obscured), Lyndon Johnson, Robert Kennedy, and Llewellyn ("Tommy") Thompson.

Rusk, Kennedy, and McNamara.

The Kennedy brothers, standing just outside the Oval Office.

Kennedy and Ambassador to the UN Adlai E. Stevenson in the Oval Office.

Kennedy, retiring Director of Central Intelligence Allen Dulles, and his successor, John McCone.

Dillon and Kennedy.

The President at his desk in the Oval Office.

McGeorge Bundy, the President, Taylor, and McNamara on the south porch of the White House.

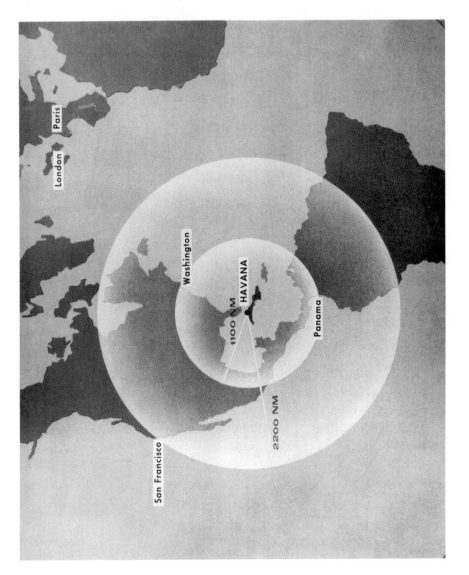

Target coverage by Soviet MRBMs and IRBMs based in Cuba. Variants of this map were widely published after President Kennedy's television address on October 22.

MRBM FIELD LAUNCH SITE
SAN CRISTOBAL NO 2
14 OCTOBER 1962

EQUIPME

CONVOY

6 MISSILE TRAIL

TENTS

One of the first U-2 photographs disclosing Soviet MRBM sites in

Inside the photograph:

SAN JULIAN AIRFIELD
CUBA
15 OCTOBER 1962

21 "CRATES" 60' X 8'

FUSELAGE 58' LONG

U-2 photograph of crated IL-28 bomber fuselages.

IRBM LAUNCH SITE
GUANAJAY NO.1
17 OCTOBER 1962

GUANAJAY IRBM LAUNCH SITE 1

VEHICLE REVETMENTS

CONTROL BUNKER

NUCLEA STO

CONTROL BUNKER

LAUNCH PADS

CO

One of the first U-2 photographs of an IRBM site.

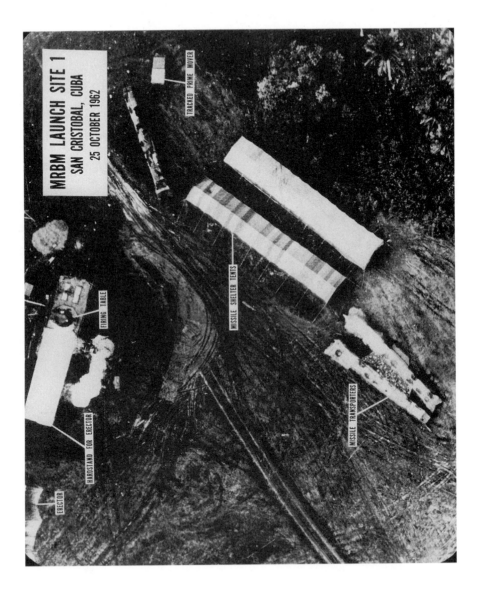

MRBM LAUNCH SITE 1
SAN CRISTOBAL, CUBA
25 OCTOBER 1962

TRACKED PRIME MOVER

FIRING TABLE

MISSILE SHELTER TENTS

HARDSTAND FOR ERECTOR

ERECTOR

MISSILE TRANSPORTERS

Photographic evidence of MRBM sites being rapidly completed an[ ]ese photos were taken by low-level reconnaissance aircraft; compare th[ ] understand the appeal of this risky method.

Evidence of IL-28 bombers being assembled, again from a low-level mission.

2:30 P.M.

OVAL ROOM OF THE EXECUTIVE MANSION

...ᴏᴜᴇᴅuled campaign trip, he
... ᴋᴇᴍᴍᴇuy and Sorensen "to pull the group together."[1] He wanted
to act soon, and his brother should call if and when he should cut short his
trip and return to Washington. At 10:35 the President left for visits that day
to Cleveland; Springfield, Illinois; and Chicago.

The meetings at the State Department ran all day and into the night. The
day started with advisers divided into two camps, one favoring a blockade and
the other favoring an air strike. Bundy said that, in the course of a sleepless
night, he had decided that an air strike was needed. Decisive action would
confront the world with a *fait accompli*. He said he had spoken with President
Kennedy and passed along this advice. Acheson, Dillon, McCone, and Taylor
agreed with Bundy. McNamara dissented. Ball said he was wavering. Robert
Kennedy then said, with a grin, that he too had spoken with the President, and
that a surprise attack like Pearl Harbor was "not in our traditions." He "favored
action," but action that gave the Soviets a chance to pull back.[2]

Rusk then suggested that the group divide into working groups to refine
the blockade and air-strike scenarios. It became plain to all, after hearing from
Justice Department and State Department lawyers, that a declaration of war
was not needed in order to impose a blockade and that an alternative, consis-

1. Theodore C. Sorensen, *Kennedy* (New York: Harper & Row, 1965), p. 692.
2. This account draws on several sources, but these and other quotations from the October
19 meetings are from minutes drafted by Deputy State Department Legal Adviser Ralph Meeker,
in *FRUS 1961–1963*, vol. 11: *Cuban Missile Crisis and Aftermath*, pp. 116–122.

tent with the UN Charter, was to obtain authorization from the OAS. Martin predicted that OAS approval could be obtained. Robert Kennedy stressed how crucial this judgment was, since a failed attempt to gain approval would be disastrous. Martin stood by his estimate.

After hours of discussion within and among the working groups, McNamara emerged as the chief advocate of an option that envisioned a blockade, then negotiations. McNamara thought that the United States would at least have to give up its missile bases in Italy and Turkey, probably more. During a sobering discussion of the danger of war, Robert Kennedy said that "in looking forward into the future it would be better for our children and grandchildren if we decided to face the Soviet threat, stand up to it, and eliminate it, now. The circumstances for doing so at some future time were bound to be more unfavorable, the risks would be greater, the chances of success less good."

As the afternoon waned, Rusk said there needed to be a planned action, then a pause to consider next steps. It was clear that advocates of a blockade could not support any military action that did not give the Soviets some chance to back out before they were attacked. It was also clear that advocates of a strike insisted on doing something about the missiles already in Cuba. Dillon had stressed that a blockade could be a first step, effectively conveying an ultimatum, with further pressure or military action following on.

So when McNamara and other military representatives commented that a strike could be made sometime after a blockade (though Taylor had his doubts), Robert Kennedy "took particular note of this shift" and, toward the end of the day, began portraying a blockade as only a first step that would not preclude other action. "He thought it was now pretty clear what the decision should be."

Sorensen had begun in the afternoon to draft a presidential speech. After reviewing the draft on Saturday morning, October 20, Robert Kennedy called his brother and asked him to come back to Washington.[3] Feigning a cold, President Kennedy left Chicago on Saturday morning and arrived back at the White House at about 1:30 P.M. He read the draft speech as his advisers sneaked by various routes into the Oval Room on the second floor of the Executive Mansion. Just as on the night of October 18, the meeting was held in the

---

3. The timing of the call is based on Sorensen. Much later, however, Lundahl told Brugioni that Robert Kennedy, worried about the tone of the meeting, called his brother on Friday, October 19, failed to reach him, then called him again on Saturday, got him, and urged him to return. Dino A. Brugioni, *Eyeball to Eyeball: The Inside Story of the Cuban Missile Crisis*, ed. Robert F. McCort (New York: Random House, 1991), pp. 303–304.

Mansion rather than in the West Wing business area of the White House. Therefore, the meeting could not be tape recorded.

Though the distinctions were blurred, four approaches had emerged by the time of the meeting. One was that of Taylor and Bundy, who wanted to start with an air strike. A second was that of Robert Kennedy, Dillon, and McCone, who preferred to start with a blockade but to treat it as a kind of ultimatum that might soon be followed by a strike. A third approach, advocated by Rusk, was to start with a blockade, try to freeze the Soviet action rather than ~~~ it, and then decide what to do. A fourth appr~~ ~ McNamara and Stevenson and an~~ a blockade but tr~ ~

~~~~pt, which was as

... we want to bring you up to date very briefly on the deployment of Soviet military weapons systems to Cuba. You have been briefed many times on the major buildup of equipment in Cuba prior to mid-October.

In the past week we have discovered unmistakable evidence of the deployment to Cuba of medium range ballistic missiles (i.e., 1020 NM range) and intermediate range ballistic missiles (i.e., 2200 NM range). These ranges imply coverage of targets from Dallas through Cincinnati and Washington, D.C. (by MRBMs) and practically all of the continental United States (by IRBMs).

There are 4 and possibly 5 MRBM sites deployed in field-type installations, 4 launchers at each site. Two of these sites are in a state of at least limited operational readiness at this time. All of the sites are in a state of continuous construction and improvement and we would expect the remaining MRBM sites to become operational in about one week's time.

In addition 2 fixed IRBM sites (with 4 launch pads at each site and permanent storage facilities) are being constructed near Havana. One of these sites appears to be in a stage of construction that leads to an estimate of operational readiness of 6 weeks from now, i.e. about 1 December, and

---

4. The briefing notes, with Cline's handwritten annotations, are reproduced in McAuliffe, *CIA Documents*, pp. 221–226.

the other in a stage indicating operational readiness between 15 December and the end of the year.

We have not seen nuclear warheads for any of these missiles, but we do not rely on ever seeing them in our photography. [Small excision of classified information.] We have found what appears to be a nuclear warhead storage facility at one of the IRBM sites at Guanajay, near Havana. It will probably be completed about 1 December along with the missile site itself.

Since the missile systems in question are relatively ineffective without them, we believe warheads either are or will be available. They could be in temporary storage prior to completion of the storage facility we have seen. The *Poltava*, a Soviet ship which we think is the most likely carrier of security-sensitive military cargoes into the tightly guarded port of Mariel, has made 2 trips to Cuba and is due back in about 10 days.

In summary, we believe the evidence indicates the probability that 8 MRBM missiles can be fired from Cuba today. Naturally operational readiness is likely to be degraded by many factors, but if all 8 missiles could be launched with nuclear warheads, they could deliver a total load of 16–24 megatons (2 to 3 MT per warhead). If able to refire, they could theoretically deliver the same load approximately 5 hours later.

When the full installation of missile sites we now see under construction is completed at the end of the year, the initial salvo capability if all missiles on launchers were to reach target would be 56–88 MT.

Lundahl then went through the photographs. When he had finished he turned to the President and said: "Mr. President, gentlemen, this summarizes the totality of the missile and other threats as we've been able to determine it from aerial photography. During the past week we were able to achieve coverage of over 95% of the island and we are convinced that because of the terrain in the remaining 5%, no additional threat will be found there."[5]

According to someone who talked to Lundahl, "The president was on his feet the moment Lundahl finished. He crossed the room directly toward Lundahl and said, 'I want to extend to your organization my gratitude for a job very well done.' Lundahl, rather embarrassed, hesitantly thanked the president."[6]

Nonverbatim minutes, presumably recorded by NSC Executive Secretary Bromley Smith, pick up at this point:[7]

5. Brugioni, *Eyeball to Eyeball*, p. 314.

6. Ibid. About 2 hours earlier Robert Kennedy and McNamara had visited NPIC, escorted by McCone, and reviewed its operations.

7. Minutes of the 505th Meeting of the National Security Council, October 20, 1962, 2:30–5:10 P.M., in *FRUS 1961–1963*, vol. 11: *Cuban Missile Crisis and Aftermath*, pp. 126–136.

The President summarized the discussion of the intelligence material as follows. There is something to destroy in Cuba now and, if it is destroyed, a strategic missile capability would be difficult to restore . . .

Secretary McNamara explained to the President that there were differences among his advisers which had resulted in the drafting of alternative courses of action. He added that the military planners are at work on measures to carry out all recommended courses of action in order that, following a Presidential decision, fast action could be taken.

Secretary McNamara described his view as the "block . . . route is aimed at preventing . . . depl . . .

. . . val of the strategic . . . . . and possibly agreement to limit our use of Guantanamo to a specified limited time. He added that we could obtain the removal of the missiles from Cuba only if we were prepared to offer something in return during negotiations. He opposed as too risky the suggestion that we should issue an ultimatum to the effect that we would order an air attack on Cuba if the missiles were not removed.[9] He said he was prepared to tell Khrushchev we consider the missiles in Cuba as Soviet missiles and that if they were used against us, we would retaliate by launching missiles against the USSR.

Secretary McNamara pointed out that SNIE 11-19-62, dated October 20, 1962, estimates that the Russians will not use force to push their ships through our blockade.[10] He cited Ambassador Bohlen's view that the USSR would not take military action, but would limit its reaction to political measures in the United Nations.

Secretary McNamara listed the disadvantages of the blockade route as follows:

8. No copy of this draft has been found: ibid., p. 128, n. 3.

9. Afterward, McNamara recalled in some detail the arguments that he had made at this meeting for and against a blockade, but he appeared to have no recollection of taking this Stevenson-like position with regard to possible negotiations with the Soviets. Interview with Robert McNamara conducted by Arthur M. Schlesinger Jr., John F. Kennedy Library Oral History Project, 1964, pp. 23–25.

10. "Major Consequences of Certain U.S. Courses of Action on Cuba," in McAuliffe, *CIA Documents*, pp. 211–220.

1. It would take a long time to achieve the objective of eliminating strategic missiles from Cuba.
2. It would result in serious political trouble in the United States.
3. The world position of the United States might appear to be weakening.

The advantages which Secretary McNamara cited are:

1. It would cause us the least trouble with our allies.
2. It avoids any surprise air attack on Cuba, which is contrary to our tradition.
3. It is the only military course of action compatible with our position as a leader of the free world.
4. It avoids a sudden military move which might provoke a response from the USSR which could result in escalating actions leading to general war.

The President pointed out that during a blockade, more missiles would become operational, and upon the completion of sites and launching pads, the threat would increase. He asked General Taylor how many missiles we could destroy by air action on Monday.

General Taylor reported that the Joint Chiefs of Staff favor an air strike on Tuesday when United States forces could be in a state of readiness. He said he did not share Secretary McNamara's fear that if we used nuclear weapons in Cuba, nuclear weapons would be used against us.

Secretary Rusk asked General Taylor whether we dared to attack operational missile sites in Cuba.

General Taylor responded that the risk of these missiles being used against us was less than if we permitted the missiles to remain there.

The President pointed out that on the basis of the intelligence estimate there would be some fifty strategic missiles operational in mid-December, if we went the blockade route and took no action to destroy the sites being developed.

General Taylor said that the principal argument he wished to make was that now was the time to act because this would be the last chance we would have to destroy these missiles. If we did not act now, the missiles would be camouflaged in such a way as to make it impossible for us to find them. Therefore, if they were not destroyed, we would have to live with them with all the consequent problems for the defense of the United States.

The President agreed that the missile threat became worse each day, adding that we might wish, looking back, that we had done earlier what we are now preparing to do.

Secretary Rusk said that a blockade would seriously affect the Cuban missile capability in that the Soviets would be unable to deploy to Cuba any missiles in addition to those now there.

Under Secretary Ball said that if an effective blockade was established, it was possible that our photographic intelligence would reveal that there were no nuclear warheads in Cuba; hence, none of the missiles now there would be made operational.

General Taylor indicated his doubt that it would be possible to prevent the Russians from deploying warheads to Cuba by means of a blockade because of the great difficulty of setting up an effective air blockade.

Secretary McNamara stated that if we knew that a plane was flying nuclear warheads to Cuba, we should immediately shoot it ... pointed out that the

[text obscured]

...... said he did not agree with the Attorney General or with General Taylor that this was our last chance. He said a missile buildup would end if, as everyone seemed to agree, the Russians would not use force to penetrate the United States blockade . . .

Mr. Bundy handed to the President the "air strike alternative," which the President read. It was also referred to as the Bundy plan.

The Attorney General told the President that this plan was supported by Mr. Bundy, General Taylor, the Joint Chiefs of Staff, and, with minor variations, by Secretary Dillon and Director McCone.

General Taylor emphasized the opportunity available now to take out not only all the missiles, but all the Soviet medium bombers (IL-28) which were neatly lined up in the open on airbases in Cuba.

Mr. McNamara cautioned that an air strike would not destroy all the missiles and launchers in Cuba, and, at best, we could knock out two-thirds of these missiles. Those missiles not destroyed could be fired from mobile launchers not destroyed. General Taylor said he was unable to explain why the IL-28 bombers had been left completely exposed on two airfields. The only way to explain this, he concluded, was on the ground that the Cubans and the Russians did not anticipate United States air strike.

Secretary Rusk said he hesitated to ask the question but he wondered whether these planes were decoys. He also wondered whether the Russians were trying to entice us into a trap. The Secretary stated his strong doubt that these planes were decoys. Director McCone added that the Russians would not have sent one hundred shiploads of equipment to Cuba solely to play a "trick." General Taylor returned to the point he had made earlier, namely, that if we do not destroy the missiles and the bombers, we will have to change our entire military way of dealing with external threats.

The President raised the question of advance warning prior to military action—whether we should give a minimum of two hours' notice of an air strike to permit Soviet personnel to leave the area to be attacked.

General Taylor said that the military would be prepared to live with a twenty-four-hour advance notice or grace period if such advance notice was worthwhile politically. The President expressed his doubt that any notice beyond seven hours had any political value.

There was a brief discussion of the usefulness of sending a draft message to Castro, and a copy of such a message was circulated.[11]

The President stated flatly that the Soviet planes in Cuba did not concern him particularly. He said we must be prepared to live with the Soviet threat as represented by Soviet bombers. However, the existence of strategic missiles in Cuba had an entirely different impact throughout Latin America. In his view the existence of fifty planes in Cuba did not affect the balance of power, but the missiles already in Cuba were an entirely different matter.

The Attorney General said that in his opinion a combination of the blockade route and the air strike route was very attractive to him. He felt that we should first institute the blockade. In the event that the Soviets continued to build up the missile capability in Cuba, then we should inform the Russians that we would destroy the missiles, the launchers, and the missile sites. He said he favored a short wait during which time the Russians could react to the blockade. If the Russians did not halt the development of the missile capability, then we would proceed to make an air strike. The advantage of proceeding in this way, he added, was that we would get away from the Pearl Harbor surprise attack aspect of the air strike route.

Mr. Bundy pointed out that there was a risk that we would act in such as way as to get Khrushchev to commit himself fully to the support of Castro.

Secretary Rusk doubted that a delay of twenty-four hours in initiating an air strike was of any value. He said he now favored proceeding on the blockade track.

Secretary Dillon mentioned seventy-two hours as the time between instituting the blockade and initiating an air strike in the event we receive no response to our initial action.

Director McCone stated his opposition to an air strike, but admitted that in his view a blockade was not enough. He argued that we should institute the blockade and tell the Russians that if the missiles were not dismantled within seventy-two hours, the United States would destroy the missiles by

11. Not found; *FRUS 1961–1963*, vol. 11, p. 131, n. 6.

air attack. He called attention to the risk involved in a long drawn-out period during which the Cubans could, at will, launch the missiles against the United States. Secretary Dillon said the existence of strategic missiles in Cuba was, in his opinion, not negotiable. He believed that any effort to negotiate the removal of the missiles would involve a price so high that the United States could not accept it. If the missiles are not removed or eliminated, he continued, the United States will lose all of its friends in Latin America, who will become convinced that our fear is such that we cannot act. He admitted that the limited use of force involved in a blockade ~~ ' '
task much harder and ~~ ' '

..........tes continue:

Deputy Secretary Gilpatric saw the choice as involving the use of limited force or of unlimited force. He was prepared to face the prospect of an air strike against Cuba later, but he opposed the initial use of all-out military force such as a surprise air attack. He defined a blockade as being the application of the limited use of force and doubted that such limited use could be combined with an air strike.

General Taylor argued that a blockade would not solve our problem or end the Cuban missile threat. He said that eventually we would have to use military force and, if we waited, the use of military force would be much more costly.

Secretary McNamara noted that the air strike planned by the Joint Chiefs involved 800 sorties. Such a strike would result in several thousand Russians being killed, chaos in Cuba, and efforts to overthrow the Castro government. In his view the probability was high that an air strike would lead inevitably to an invasion. He doubted that the Soviets would take an air strike on Cuba without resorting to a very major response. In such an event, the United States would lose control of the situation which could escalate to general war.

The President agreed that a United States air strike would lead to a major Soviet response, such as blockading Berlin. He agreed that at an appropriate time we would have to acknowledge that we were willing to take strategic

12. Sorensen, *Kennedy,* p. 694.

missiles out of Turkey and Italy if this issue was raised by the Russians. He felt that implementation of a blockade would also result in Soviet reprisals, possibly the blockade of Berlin. If we instituted a blockade on Sunday, then by Monday or Tuesday we would know whether the missile development had ceased or whether it was continuing. Thus, we would be in a better position to know what move to make next.

Secretary Dillon called attention to the fact that even if the Russians agreed to dismantle the missiles now in Cuba, continuing inspection would be required to ensure that the missiles were not again made ready.

The President said that if it was decided to go the Bundy route, he would favor an air strike which would destroy only missiles. He repeated this view that we would have to live with this threat arising out of the stationing in Cuba of Soviet bombers.

Secretary Rusk referred to an air strike as chapter two. He did not think we should initiate such a strike because of the risk of escalating actions leading to general war. He doubted that we should act without consultation of our allies. He said a sudden air strike had no support in law or morality, and, therefore, must be ruled out. Reading from notes, he urged that we start the blockade and only go on to an air attack when we knew the reaction of the Russians and of our allies.

At this point Director McCone acknowledged that we did not know positively that nuclear warheads for the missiles deployed had actually arrived in Cuba. Although we had evidence of the construction of storage places for nuclear weapons, such weapons may not yet have been sent to Cuba.

The President asked what we would say to those whose reaction to our instituting a blockade now would be to ask why we had not blockaded last July.

Both Mr. Sorensen and Mr. Ball made the point that we did not institute a blockade in July because we did not then know of the existence of strategic missiles in Cuba.

Secretary Rusk suggested that our objective was an immediate freeze of the strategic missile capability in Cuba to be inspected by United Nations observation teams stationed at the missile sites. He referred to our bases in Turkey, Spain, and Greece as being involved in any negotiation covering foreign bases. He said a United Nations group might be sent to Cuba to reassure those who might fear that the United States was planning an invasion.

Ambassador Stevenson stated his flat opposition to a surprise air strike, which he felt would ultimately lead to a United States invasion of Cuba. He supported the institution of the blockade and predicted that such action would reduce the chance of Soviet retaliation of a nature which would inevitably escalate. In his view our aim is to end the existing missile threat in Cuba without casualties and without escalation. He urged that we offer the Russians a settlement involving the withdrawal of our missiles from Turkey and our evacuation of Guantanamo base.

The President sharply rejected the thought of surrendering our base at Guantanamo in the present situation. He felt that such action would convey to the world that we had been frightened into abandoning our position. He was not opposed to discussing withdrawal of our missiles from Turkey and Greece [*sic*], but he was firm in saying we should on'~ ~ ' in the future.

...............ed.

... was ready to go ahead with the blockade and to take actions necessary to put us in a position to undertake an air strike on the missiles and missile sites by Monday or Tuesday.

General Taylor summarized the military actions already under way, including the quiet reinforcement of Guantanamo by infiltrating marines and the positioning of ships to take out United States dependents from Guantanamo on extremely short notice.

The Attorney General said we could implement a blockade very quickly and prepare for an air strike to be launched later if we so decided.

The President said he was prepared to authorize the military to take those preparatory actions which they would have to take in anticipation of the

---

13. To reassure the German allies but also to discourage any thoughts on their part of an independent nuclear deterrent, the United States in the late 1950s had begun to equip Luftwaffe aircraft with "tactical" nuclear bombs and missiles. The actual nuclear devices remained under U.S. control. The proposed multilateral nuclear force (MLF) was supposed to include Germans among the multinational crews whose ships would carry nuclear-armed missiles—with authority for actual release of the weapons to remain exclusively with the U.S. President. U.S. champions of the MLF, mostly in the State Department and sometimes referred to as "the cabal," hoped that it would not only dampen any German interest in nuclear weapons but would also lead the French and perhaps the British to abandon their own independent nuclear forces. See McGeorge Bundy, *Danger and Survival: Choices about the Bomb in the First Fifty Years* (New York: Random House, 1988), pp. 487–490. Some Western officials interpreted Khrushchev's position regarding Berlin as traceable chiefly to Soviet concern lest Germany acquire nuclear weapons. See Marc Trachtenberg, *History and Strategy* (Princeton: Princeton University Press, 1991), pp. 169–234. Robert Kennedy's suggestion here must have been startling to the State Department contingent, especially to Ball, who was active in "the cabal."

military invasion of Cuba. He suggested that we inform the Turks and the Italians that they should not fire the strategic missiles they have even if attacked. The warheads for missiles in Turkey and Italy could be dismantled. He agreed that we should move to institute a blockade as quickly as we possibly can.

In response to a question about further photographic surveillance of Cuba, Secretary McNamara recommended, and the President agreed, that no low level photographic reconnaissance should be undertaken now because we have decided to institute a blockade.

Secretary Rusk recommended that a blockade not be instituted before Monday in order to provide time required to consult our allies.

Mr. Bundy said the pressure from the press was becoming intense and suggested that one way of dealing with it was to announce shortly that we had obtained photographic evidence of the existence of strategic missiles in Cuba. The announcement would hold the press until the President made his television speech.

The President acknowledged that the domestic political heat following his television appearance would be terrific. He said he had opposed an invasion of Cuba but that now we were confronted with the possibility that by December there would be fifty strategic missiles deployed there. In explanation as to why we have not acted sooner to deal with the threat from Cuba, he pointed out that only now do we have the kind of evidence which we can make available to our allies in order to convince them of the necessity of acting. Only now do we have a way of avoiding a split with our allies.

It is possible that we may have to make an early strike with or without warning next week. He stressed again the difference between the conventional military buildup in Cuba and the psychological impact throughout the world of the Russian deployment of strategic missiles to Cuba. General Taylor repeated his recommendation that any air strike in Cuba include attacks on the MIGs and medium bombers.

The President repeated his view that our world position would be much better if we attack only the missiles. He directed that air strike plans include only missiles and missile sites, preparations to be ready three days from now.

Under Secretary Ball expressed his view that a blockade should include all shipments of POL to Cuba. Secretary Rusk thought that POL should not now be included because such a decision would break down the distinction which we want to make between elimination of strategic missiles and the downfall of the Castro government. Secretary Rusk repeated his view that our objective is to destroy the offensive capability of the missiles in Cuba, not, at this time, seeking to overthrow Castro!

The President acknowledged that the issue was whether POL should be included from the beginning or added at a later time. He preferred to delay possibly as long as a week.

Secretary Rusk called attention to the problem involved in referring to our action as a blockade. He preferred the use of the word "quarantine."

Parenthetically, the President asked Secretary Rusk to reconsider the present policy of refusing to give nuclear weapons assistance to France. He expressed the view that in light of present circumstances a refusal to help the French was not worthwhile. He thought that in the days ahead we might be able to gain the needed support of France if we st~~~ ᵗ them with their nuclear ᵂᵉᵃ

... Cuba. Only if we were ... that we were prepared to talk about the withdrawal of missiles from Italy and Turkey. In such an eventuality, the President pointed out that we would have to make clear to the Italians and the Turks that withdrawing strategic missiles was not a retreat and that we would be prepared to replace these missiles by providing a more effective deterrent, such as the assignment of Polaris submarines. The President asked Mr. Nitze to study the problems arising out of the withdrawal of missiles from Italy and Turkey, with particular reference to complications which would arise in NATO. The President made clear that our emphasis should be on the missile threat from Cuba.

Ambassador Stevenson reiterated his belief that we must be more forthcoming about giving up our missile bases in Turkey and Italy. He stated again his belief that the present situation required that we offer to give up such bases in order to induce the Russians to remove the strategic missiles from Cuba.

Mr. Nitze flatly opposed making any such offer, but said he would not

14. Like Eisenhower before him, Kennedy had never been an all-out opponent of France's having independent nuclear forces. He had gone along, however, with the MLF scheme and had approved public statements by McNamara that described such forces as "dangerous, expensive, prone to obsolescence, and lacking in credibility as a deterrent." He had also drawn upon himself strong French criticism because of a loosely worded press conference remark that seemed to single out French nuclear forces, but not British, as "inimical to the community interest of the Atlantic alliance." See Bundy, *Danger and Survival*, pp. 484–486.

object to discussing this question in the event that negotiations developed from our institution of a blockade.

The President concluded the meeting by stating that we should be ready to meet criticism of our deployment of missiles abroad but we should not initiate negotiations with a base withdrawal proposal.

During the 2 hours and 40 minutes of this meeting, lines had been clearly drawn between the groups that would later be labeled "doves" and "hawks."[15] It is a pity that Kennedy held the meeting outside the reach of his microphones, for not even the anodyne vocabulary of an official notetaker conceals the intensity of the exchanges. McNamara seems even more emphatic than usual in describing the possible consequences of not following a "blockade and negotiate" strategy. Stevenson pleads for such a strategy even after the President has "sharply rejected" negotiations about Guantanamo and has declared that the United States will not initiate talks about trading away the IRBMs in Turkey and Italy. Nitze has "flatly opposed" Stevenson. Dillon has come down hard in saying that the missiles in Cuba are "not negotiable." Taylor has intervened time and again to argue for an air strike and against a blockade, while Rusk has said categorically that "a sudden air strike had no support in law or morality, and, therefore, must be ruled out."

President Kennedy has emerged from the meeting midway between the "hawks" and the "doves." He has rejected making any offer to negotiate, at least for the time being. He has come down in favor of a blockade, now to be labeled a quarantine. The blockade is to be coupled with a demand that Khrushchev remove the missiles, with at least an air strike (a narrow one, President Kennedy hopes) readied if Khrushchev does not comply. This was closest to the option pressed by Dillon and McCone, with backing from Robert Kennedy. After the meeting McCone followed up with Robert to nail down this outcome. Later, in the evening, McCone spoke directly with President Kennedy; McCone noted then that the President "said he had made up his mind to pursue the course which I had recommended and he agreed with the views I expressed in the afternoon meeting."[16]

After the meeting President Kennedy wandered out onto the "Truman" balcony outside the Mansion's Oval Room with his brother, Sorensen, and

15. The terminology may have been Kennedy's own. It achieved popularity through a postmortem on the crisis: Stewart Alsop and Charles Bartlett, "In Time of Crisis," *Saturday Evening Post*, December 8, 1962, for which Kennedy was a source. See Michael Beschloss, *The Crisis Years: Kennedy and Khrushchev, 1960–1963* (New York: HarperCollins, 1991), p. 569.

16. McCone to File, October 20, 1962, in *FRUS 1961–1963*, vol. 11, pp. 137–138.

perhaps one or two others. Reflecting momentarily on domestic politics, he predicted that the crisis would damage the Democratic party in the upcoming congressional elections. Some Democratic supporters might feel (like Stevenson) that they were being too warlike, while many voters would feel that Republican warnings about Cuba had been proved right. "Well," Sorensen clearly remembered him commenting ruefully (and perhaps sardonically), "I guess Homer Capehart is the Winston Churchill of our generation."[17]

When Taylor returned to the Pentagon he told the Chiefs: "Th:. one of our better days." He a...

...y Library Oral
... Republican senator from Indiana who, with Keating,
... the key spokesman throughout the summer for taking some military action (including a blockade) against Cuba. In fact when the blockade idea first came up as a response to the missiles it met with some skepticism because it "had a certain Capehartian ring to it"; ibid., p. 52.

18. Notes Taken from Transcripts of Meetings of the Joint Chiefs of Staff, October–November 1962, p. 13, National Security Archive, Washington, D.C. These notes must be used with some care, but we rely on passages that the original notetaker marked as direct quotations.

MONDAY, OCTOBER 22

11:30 A.M.

CABINET ROOM

Though the administration's efforts to preserve secrecy had been remarkably successful, the cover was beginning to crack. The major Sunday papers had headlined a massive surprise attack by China against India, with Chinese armies pouring across the Indian border on two widely separated fronts. The *Washington Post,* however, confined this story to the left side of its front page and on the right side ran a 5-column headline: "MARINE MOVES IN SOUTH LINKED TO CUBAN CRISIS." Although the piece contained few specifics, it cited the mobilization of troops, planes, and ships in and around Key West, allegedly for a training exercise in waters around Puerto Rico, as one of "numerous indications . . . that a major international development was in the making."

Well-connected Washington columnists such as Walter Lippmann and Joseph Alsop already knew that the focus of the coming crisis would be Soviet offensive forces in Cuba. So did *Post* reporters. Kennedy, told by White House Press Secretary Pierre Salinger that the whole press corps would soon have the details, called friends at the *Times* and *Post* to ask that they hold off through Monday. (The *Times* actually learned of the story through this phone call.)[1] Clearly, the President was going to have to make a public statement no later than Monday evening.

The one missing piece in settling President Kennedy's decision was a last check on the viability of an air strike. At midday on Sunday, October 21, he met with General Walter C. Sweeney, who was responsible for planning possible

---

1. See Montague Kern, Patricia W. Levering, and Ralph B. Levering, *The Kennedy Crises: The Press, the Presidency, and Foreign Policy* (Chapel Hill: University of North Carolina Press, 1983), pp. 123–127.

air operations against Cuba. Also present were Robert Kennedy, McNamara, Taylor, and McCone. Again they met in the Oval Room of the Executive Mansion to avoid a curious press, so, again, this session was not recorded. McNamara, however, prepared a detailed record of this meeting later that day.[2]

The Secretary of Defense [McNamara] stated that following the start of an air strike, the initial units of the landing force could invade Cuba within 7 days. The movement of troops in preparation for such an invasion will start at the time of the President's speech. No mobili~~~~ ~~

required for ~~~~ ~~~

... ... discussion, confirmed this

~~~ ... location of the sites for 36 of these launchers is known. 32 of the 36 known sites appear to have sufficient equipment on them to be included in any air strike directed against Cuba's missile capability.

We believe that 40 launchers would normally be equipped with 80 missiles. John McCone reported yesterday that a Soviet ship believed to be the vessel in which the Soviets have been sending missiles to Cuba has made a sufficient number of trips to that island within recent weeks, to offload approximately 48 missiles. Therefore, we assume there are approximately that number on the island today, although we have only located approximately 30 of these.

General Sweeney outlined the following plan of air attack, the object of which would be the destruction of the known Cuban missile capability.

a. The 5 surface-to-air missile installations in the vicinity of the known missile sites would each be attacked by approximately 8 aircraft; the 3 MiG airfields defending the missile sites would be covered by 12 U.S. aircraft per field. In total, the defense suppression operations, including the necessary replacement aircraft, would require approximately 100 sorties.
b. Each of the launchers at the 8 or 9 known sites (a total of approximately 32 to 36 launchers) would be attacked by 6 aircraft. For the purpose, a total of approximately 250 sorties would be flown.

2. Robert McNamara, "Notes of October 21, 1962, Meeting with the President," reprinted in Laurence Chang and Peter Kornbluh, eds., *The Cuban Missile Crisis, 1962: A National Security Archive Documents Reader* (New York: New Press, 1992), pp. 144–145.

c. The U.S. aircraft covering the 3 MiG airfields would attack the MiGs if they became airborne. General Sweeney strongly recommended attacks on each of the airfields to destroy the MiG aircraft.

General Sweeney stated that he was certain the air strike would be "successful"; however, even under optimum conditions, it was not likely that all of the known missiles would be destroyed. (As noted . . . above, the known missiles are probably no more than 60% of the total missiles on the Island.) General Taylor stated, "The best we can offer you is to destroy 90% of the known missiles." General Taylor, General Sweeney and [McNamara] all strongly emphasized that in their opinion the initial air strike must be followed by strikes on subsequent days and that these in turn would lead inevitably to an invasion.

CIA representatives, who joined the discussion at this point, stated that it is probable the missiles which are operational (it is estimated there are now between 8 and 12 operational missiles on the Island) can hold indefinitely a capability for firing with from $2\frac{1}{2}$ to 4 hours notice. Included in the notice period is a countdown requiring 20 to 40 minutes. In relation to the countdown period, the first wave of our attacking aircraft would give 10 minutes of warning; the second wave, 40 minutes of warning; and the third wave a proportionately greater warning.

As noted above, General Sweeney strongly recommended that any air strike include attacks on the MiG aircraft and, in addition, the IL-28s. To accomplish the destruction of these aircraft, the total number of sorties of such an air strike should be increased to 500. The President agreed that if an air strike is ordered, it should probably include in its objective the destruction of the MiG aircraft and the IL-28s.[3]

The President directed that we be prepared to carry out the air strike Monday morning or any time thereafter during the remainder of the week. The President recognized that [McNamara] was opposed to the air strike Monday morning, and that General Sweeney favored it. He asked the Attorney General [Robert Kennedy] and Mr. McCone for their opinions:

---

3. McCone's notes (also prepared that day) added: "There was complete agreement that military action must include an invasion and occupation of Cuba." McCone also remembered that: "McNamara and General Taylor . . . also stated that any warning would very possibly cause the movement of missiles to obscure unknown locations from which they could become operational. General Taylor therefore recommended, on the basis of military grounds, that the air strike be conducted immediately, suggesting tomorrow morning, and that it be without warning. Secretary McNamara confirmed the military appraisal expressed above but made no recommendation as to policy"; John C. McCone, "Memorandum of Meeting . . . 21 October 1962," in McAuliffe, *CIA Documents*, p. 241.

a. [Robert Kennedy] stated he was opposed to such a strike because:
   (1) "It would be a Pearl Harbor type of attack."
   (2) It would lead to unpredictable military responses by the Soviet Union which could be so serious as to lead to general nuclear war.
   He stated we should start with the initiation of the blockade and thereafter "play for the breaks."
b. Mr. McCone agreed with [Robert Kennedy], but emphasized he believed we should be prepared for an air strike and thereafter an invasion.

After this meeting Pr... ...help admiring ... this deliberate and provocative challenge to ... United States in the knowledge that if the Americans reacted violently to it, the Russians would be given an ideal opportunity to move against West Berlin. If, on the other hand, he did nothing, the Latin Americans and the United States' other Allies would feel that the Americans had no real will to resist the encroachments of Communism and would hedge their bets accordingly."

Musing more broadly, Kennedy remarked that he doubted whether he would ever again have an equally good excuse to invade Cuba. "He, therefore, did his devil's advocate act even at that stage," Ormsby-Gore wryly recalled.[4] Kennedy commented that the existence of nuclear weapons was making a secure and rational world impossible. The IRBM bases in Turkey and elsewhere were more or less worthless, and probably had not been a good idea in the first place. He also worried that the West Germans were refusing to face up to the realities of the situation surrounding Berlin. President Kennedy arranged for a message to be delivered in London a few hours later for Macmillan, giving him early warning of the breaking crisis and the impending U.S. moves.[5]

4. Interview with Lord Harlech (Ormsby-Gore) conducted by Richard Neustadt, transcript approved March 12, 1965, John F. Kennedy Library Oral History Project, p. 15.

5. For Ormsby-Gore's reports of the conversation to London, see Washington no. 2636, "Cuba," 22 October 1962; and Washington no. 2650, 23 October 1962, both in Public Record Office (hereafter PRO), PREM 11/3689, 24020. On the advance message to Macmillan see Washington no. 2630, 21 October 1962, and the October 21 message from Kennedy to Macmillan, T488/62, both in ibid.

Shortly after seeing Ormsby-Gore, President Kennedy held another meeting at the White House, again convened as a meeting of the National Security Council, at 2:30 P.M. Again, to avoid press questions about the after-hours gathering, he held the meeting in the Oval Room of the Executive Mansion. It was therefore not taped.

We pick up our account with a portion of the meeting minutes prepared by the NSC staff.[6] Taylor brought Admiral Anderson with him to the meeting. Stevenson was there too. The starting point for discussion is a new Sorensen draft (the third) for President Kennedy's speech. Much of the discussion centers on efforts, led by Dillon and McCone, to toughen key passages describing the President's goals and diplomatic strategy, with Stevenson rising to defend Sorensen's draft.

> . . . The question was raised as to whether the speech should emphasize Soviet responsibility for the missile deployment or Castro's irresponsibility in accepting them. Secretary Rusk argued that we must hold the USSR responsible because it is important to emphasize the extrahemispheric aspect of the missile deployment in order to increase support for our contemplated action.
>
> The President referred to the sentence mentioning the deployment of missiles by the Soviet Union and called attention to our deployment of missiles to Italy. Secretary Rusk pointed out that our missiles were deployed to NATO countries only after those countries were threatened by deployed Soviet missiles. Hence, our deployment was part of the confrontation of Soviet power, and, therefore, unrelated to the Cuban deployment by the USSR.
>
> The President pointed out that Soviet missiles were in place, aimed at European countries, before we deployed United States missiles to Europe.
>
> Secretary Dillon recalled that we sent United States missiles to Europe because we had so many of them we did not know where to put them.[7]

---

6. Minutes of the 506th Meeting of the National Security Council, October 21, 1962, in *FRUS 1961–1963*, vol. 11: *Cuban Missile Crisis and Aftermath*, pp. 141–149.

7. President Kennedy was struck by this comment, which he remembered somewhat differently. He jotted down on a notepad later, as we interpret his handwriting: "Sunday afternoon— In course of discussion, on missiles in Turkey & Italy—Douglas Dillon stated that the reason Jupiters were sent was they were flops & this would have been proved if they had not been sent." Kennedy added: "Rusk rather quiet & somewhat fatigued during discussion." President's Of-

The President referred to the sentence in the draft speech which states that the USSR secretly transferred weapons to Cuba. He said we should emphasize the clandestine manner in which the USSR had acted in Cuba.

The Attorney General wanted to be certain that the text as drafted did not preclude us from giving nuclear weapons to Western Germany, West Berlin, and France in the event we decided to do so.

It was agreed that no message [a direct ultimatum] would be sent to President Dorticos of Cuba at the present time and the draft speech was so revised.

The question of what

returned to a sentence in the earlier part of the draft . . . and asked whether we were firm on the phrase "whatever steps are necessary." The President agreed that these words should remain so that he would not be hindered from taking additional measures if we so decide at a later date . . .

Secretary Rusk commented that our objective was to "put out the fire" in Cuba and get United Nations teams to inspect all missile activity in Cuba. The President felt that a better tactic was for us initially to frighten the United Nations representatives with the prospect of all kinds of actions and then, when a resolution calling for the withdrawal of missiles from Cuba, Turkey, and Italy was proposed, we could consider supporting such a resolution.

Ambassador Stevenson said we should take the initiative by calling a U.N. Security Council meeting to demand an immediate missile standstill in Cuba . . .

Secretary Rusk raised the question of whether we should move first in the United Nations or first in the OAS. He said our United Nations action should be aimed at removing the missile threat while our objective on the OAS would be to persuade other Latin American countries to act with us under the Rio Treaty.

In response to the President's question, Assistant Secretary Martin said

fice Files, Correspondence—Cuba—Conference Notes and Doodles, JFKL (in slip for Notes, 10/23/62).

that if there were a United Nations action before the OAS acted, the usefulness of the OAS would be seriously affected. Secretary Rusk felt we should act first in the OAS, then in the United Nations where our action program could be more flexible.

The President agreed that a reference in the draft speech to a Caribbean security force should be dropped.

The President said we should pin the responsibility for the developments in Cuba directly on Khrushchev. In response to the President's question, Ambassador Thompson agreed—naming Khrushchev would make it harder for him to reverse his actions in Cuba, but such reference to him would be more effective in producing favorable actions.

The President asked that the phrases [in the speech] describing the horrors of war should be deleted . . .

The President agreed that the invitation to a summit meeting should be deleted.

Ambassador Stevenson repeated that he favored an early conference with the Russians on terms acceptable to us, to be held in an atmosphere free of threat. The President responded that he did not want to appear to be seeking a summit meeting as a result of Khrushchev's actions. Ambassador Thompson agreed. The President added that we should not look toward holding a meeting until it is clear to us what Khrushchev really thinks he will obtain worldwide as a result of his actions in Cuba.

Secretary Rusk said our first objective was to get a fully inspected missile standstill in Cuba before we sit down to talk with the Russians. Mr. McCone was concerned that if we let it be known that we are prepared to talk with the Russians now, it would appear to outsiders that our only response to Khrushchev's challenge was to negotiate.

The Attorney General said that in his view we should anticipate a Soviet reaction involving a movement in Berlin. Secretary Dillon felt that the Soviet reaction in Berlin would be governed by the actions we would take in response to the Russian missile deployment in Cuba.

Following a discussion of ways in which we could reach the Cuban people through television despite Cuban jamming efforts, the President told [acting USIA Director Donald] Wilson that we should go ahead with the television project involving the relay of signals via instruments aboard a ship at sea for use anywhere.

The Attorney General felt that the paragraphs in the President's draft speech addressed to the Cuban people were not personal enough. The President asked that these paragraphs be rewritten . . .

In response to a Presidential question, General Taylor said an invasion of Cuba could be carried out seven days after the decision to invade had been taken. Secretary McNamara . . . promised the President a breakdown of the decisions which he would have to take immediately in order to reduce the seven-day period.

The President said that in three or four days we might have to decide to act in order that we would not have to wait so long prior to the landing of our forces. As he understood the situation, a decision taken today would mean that an air strike could not be undertaken before seven days, and then seven days later the first forces could be ashore.

General Taylor explained that air action would be necess~~ary~~
situation under control prior to the dropp~~ing~~ ~~of~~
90,000 men could be la~~nded.~~
The P~~resident~~

~~in~~ Cuba, Soviet
~~mo~~ve to squeeze us out of Berlin.
~~th~~at in his view a blockade would either inevitably
~~an~~ invasion of Cuba or would result in negotiations, which he believes the Soviets would want very much. To agree to negotiations now would be a disaster for us. We would break up our alliances and convey to the world that we were impotent in the face of a Soviet challenge. Unless the Russians stop their missile buildup at once, we will have to invade Cuba in the next week, no matter what they say, if we are to save our world position. We cannot convey firm intentions to the Russians otherwise and we must not look to the world as if we were backing down.

Secretary McNamara expressed his doubt that an air strike would be necessary within the next week.

Admiral Anderson described, in response to the President's question, the way the blockade would be instituted . . . He favored a twenty-four-hour grace period, beginning with the President's speech, during which the Russians could communicate with their ships, giving them instructions as to what to do in the event they were stopped by United States ships . . .

Admiral Anderson said we had a capability to protect United States ships in the Caribbean. If the Komar ships [missile-carrying patrol boats] took any hostile action, they could be destroyed, thereby creating a new situation. If a MiG plane takes hostile action, he would like to be in a position to shoot it down, thereby creating again a new situation. He estimated that the Soviets could not get naval surface ships to the area in less than ten days and Soviet submarines could not get to the area in less than ten to fourteen days.

In response to a question, Admiral Anderson said that if the Navy received information that a Soviet submarine was en route to Havana, he would ask higher authority for permission to attack it.

Secretary McNamara said he favored rules of engagement which would permit responses to hostile actions, including attacks to destroy the source of the hostile action.

The President answered a question as to whether we were to stop all ships, including allied ships, by saying that he favored stopping all ships in the expectation that allied ships would soon become discouraged and drop out of the Cuban trade . . .

[Turning to diplomatic measures] The President said we must assume that Khrushchev knows that we know of his missile deployments, and, therefore, he will be ready with a planned response. He asked that the draft speech emphasize his belief that the greatest danger to the United States in the present situation is doing nothing but acknowledging that in days to come we would be seriously threatened.

Ambassador Stevenson read from a list of problems which he foresaw in the United Nations. Secretary Rusk . . . repeated his view that the aim of all our actions is to get a standstill of the missile development in Cuba to be inspected by United Nations observers and then be prepared to negotiate other issues.

The President asked Assistant Secretary of Defense Nitze to study the problem of withdrawing United States missiles from Turkey and Italy. Mr. Nitze said that such a withdrawal was complicated because we must avoid giving the Europeans the impression that we are prepared to take nuclear weapons of all kinds out of Europe . . .

The President asked why we could not start with a demand for the removal or the withdrawal of the missiles and if at a later time we wanted to negotiate for a less favorable settlement, we could then decide to do so. The Attorney General said we should take the offensive in our presentation to the United Nations. Our attitude should not be defensive, especially in view of the fact that Soviet leaders had lied to us about the deployment of strategic missiles to Cuba.

The President interjected a directive that we reverse our policy on nuclear assistance to France in the light of the present situation.[8]

8. When Nitze pursued this presidential directive on October 24, State officials supporting the NATO multilateral-force idea combined to block the move. Nitze was already too late. No one attempted to get Kennedy's offer into the talking points that Dean Acheson, Kennedy's emissary, took with him to Paris. Once de Gaulle had given his strong support without this offer, as he did on October 22, the original presidential impetus behind the idea evaporated.

Ambassador Stevenson repeated his view that the United States would be forced into a summit meeting and preferred to propose such a meeting.

The President disagreed, saying that we could not accept a neutral Cuba and the withdrawal from Guantanamo without indicating to Khrushchev that we were in a state of panic. An offer to accept Castro and give up Guantanamo must not be made because it would appear to be completely defensive. He said we should be clear that we would accept nothing less than the ending of the missile capability now in Cuba, no reinforcement of that capability, and no further construction of missile sites.

Secretary McNamara stated his view that ... we would have to invade C...

The Pre...

... primarily on

... need for further discussion of this matter and ... that Secretary Rusk speak to him later about it.

As the meeting concluded, the President asked that the word "miscalculate" be taken out of the draft letter prepared for him to send to Khrushchev. He recalled that in Vienna Khrushchev had revealed a misunderstanding of this word when translated into Russian. He also requested that reference to a meeting with Khrushchev be deleted from the draft letter.

After the meeting, President Kennedy passed along a request that special precautions be taken to be sure that, if the Soviets launched a reprisal strike at any point, the Jupiter missiles in Turkey and Italy would not be fired without express presidential authorization. The Chiefs took umbrage at this request and sent back word that they opposed issuing any such special instructions, since doing so would imply lack of confidence in the effectiveness of standing orders.

The entire apparatus of the U.S. government was now moving into action. An immensely complicated program was under way. A State Department chronicler of the crisis offers this glimpse of the frenzy[9]

9. Frank Sieverts, "The Cuban Crisis, 1962," internal State Department history, August 1963, transmitted to the White House in Robert Manning to McGeorge Bundy, "History of the Cuban Crisis," August 22, 1963; copy obtained at National Security Archive, Washington, D.C.

SUMMARY OF ACTIVITIES

Midnight October 20 to midnight October 22, 1962

In the 48 hours from midnight Saturday, October 20 to midnight Monday, October 22, the State Department, working in augmented shifts around the clock, accomplished the following tasks:

1. *Informed 21 Embassies in Latin America* of the up-coming President's speech and instructed them on approaches to the various governments;
2. Dispatched *special briefing officers* to London, Paris, Bonn;
3. Sent the text of the *President's speech and a letter from the President to Khrushchev* to Embassy Moscow and handed the *same documents to the Soviet Ambassador* in Washington;
4. Dispatched individual *letters from the President* to:

   Prime Minister Macmillan
   General de Gaulle
   Prime Minister [Jawaharlal] Nehru
   Chancellor Adenauer
   Prime Minister [John] Diefenbaker [of Canada]
   Prime Minister Fanfani
   Mayor [Willy] Brandt [of West Berlin]

5. Sent instructions to *60 U.S. Embassies* in all parts of the world regarding delivery of the President's speech, and a letter in some cases, to the Head of Government;
6. Dispatched a *letter from the President to the Chief of State of 21 Latin American countries;*
7. Dispatched a *letter from the President to the Heads of Government in 18 countries* with which we have alliances or who are represented on the Security Council;
8. *Warned 134 Embassies and Consulates* to take precautions against hostile demonstrations;
9. Sent *text of President's speech to 129 Embassies and Consulates;*
10. *Informed 21 Embassies in Latin American countries of our call for an OAS meeting* for October 23 and *furnished them the text of a proposed OAS resolution;*
11. Sent text of *draft Security Council resolution to 21 Latin American countries and 7 countries which are members of the Security Council;*
12. Provided an *oral briefing on the situation to 95 foreign Ambassadors* by top State Department officials;

13. Delivered a *letter to the Security Council President calling for an urgent SC meeting* and enclosing a draft resolution;
14. Provided a *background briefing to the press* by High State Department officials.

Summary:

Transmitted *15 separate Presidential letters or other documents* to total of *441 recipients,* with appropriate instructions. Provided *oral briefings to 95 foreign Ambassadors* and an unknown *number of American newsmen.*

McCone again briefed former Presi~~dent Ei~~
home in Washingto~~n. Ei~~
mili~~t~~

~~...~~onal lead-
~~...~~ously fetched by soldiers and
~~g...~~ for a meeting the next day with the President.
~~...y~~ morning, October 22, Kennedy convened his advisers, now during normal business hours, in the Cabinet Room. One of those who had probably attended earlier meetings but who spoke for the first time at this meeting was Kenneth O'Donnell. A Harvard classmate of Robert Kennedy and an aide to John Kennedy since the senatorial campaign of 1952, O'Donnell was Special Assistant to the President, charged especially with managing the President's time. Others called in this morning, who had not been at previous meetings, were Henry H. "Joe" Fowler, the Under Secretary of the Treasury (eventually Dillon's successor as Secretary); Roger Hilsman, formerly a Columbia professor of political science, now Assistant Secretary of State for Intelligence and Research and thus, in effect, chief of intelligence analysis for the State Department; and Iowa lawyer Edward A. McDermott, Director of the Office of Emergency Preparedness, who was responsible for planning civil defense and other measures for emergencies or even nuclear attack.

---

10. McCone also briefed Vice President Johnson on Sunday evening. Johnson favored the surprise strike, complaining that "we are telegraphing our punch" and "locking the barn after the horse was gone." Johnson finally agreed reluctantly with the blockade plan, "but only after learning among other things the support indicated by General Eisenhower"; McCone to File, "Meeting with the Vice President on 21 October 1962," in McAuliffe, *CIA Documents,* p. 245.

Shortly before the meeting began, President Kennedy turned on the tape recorder. At first the sound quality is poor.

[Rusk and President Kennedy discuss proposals for negotiated removal of Soviet missiles from Cuba and American missiles from countries that are not nuclear-weapon states.]

President Kennedy: Removal on a bilateral basis. Not just theirs, but both sides.

Rusk: Removal may take more time. I'm thinking about . . .

Unidentified: The presence of inspection teams?

Rusk: The presence of UN observer forces at all such times, to see that they [the missiles] are not operational and all work on such matters has stopped.

President Kennedy: Well, maybe that's the first stage. But I think we ought to have . . .

Rusk: Removal [unclear].

President Kennedy: Now, we don't stop the quarantine when this happens, do we? We have to decide that. [Unclear.] We have to see how it looks before . . .

Rusk: Removal of the quarantine would be for the United Nations to determine.

President Kennedy: Okay. But we don't have to commit ourselves to remove the quarantine in our proposal. Yeah.

But I think we've got to always keep on this pressure on the removal, because I don't think we're gonna be a hell of a lot better off if they're just sitting there, to be honest with you. We're not gonna be better off.

[Unclear exchange.]

[Unclear] not going to fire them anyway. I agree we're somewhat better off, even psychologically. They cease to become quite the factor they were. We are better off.

Maybe this is just a political problem. But I think we ought to be looking forward to the day when they are removed from Cuba, Italy, and Turkey.

Bundy: I don't think there's any harm in having a neutral nation for immediate inspection and sort of sanitization. The rest will follow. You can't have everything in one bite.

President Kennedy: Okay. All right, where were we?

Rusk: Bob McNamara does not want to see this quarantine lifted anywhere until it is absolutely certain that this is under control.

President Kennedy: Well, let's work that one through. What we'll have to do is say: There'll have to be some assurances that there won't be additional ones shipped in. We can't just let [unclear] shipments go in. There'll have to be some mechanism for inspection of every ship that comes in. And any [ship] that then goes into Turkey and Italy.

[Unclear exchange, with references to the OAS. Then the participants turn to another review of the draft speech President Kennedy is scheduled to deliver that evening. The President's message to Prime Minister Macmillan in London is also discussed. Then back to the speech. There are brief interjections then the tape picks up the sound of Dulles

question—you—that a number of

[men held prisoner in Cuba] are in jail.

President Kennedy: Jobs they held. [Unclear.] Where are they now? [Unclear.]

One thing I thought we ought to think about is the government-in-exile for Cuba. Or the possible reputation of it. Is there somebody who can . . . take on that?

Rusk: Yes, we're working on that, Mr. President. At the moment we're trying to keep [unclear].

[President Kennedy reads a passage referring to the failed invasion of the spring of 1961; his comment on it is unclear. There are then a few inaudible exchanges.]

President Kennedy: Did Castro's persistence in his campaign against the democratic [unclear] ever prevail? Page 13. "Prevail"? [Unclear] reaction.

[Inaudible discussions with references to "Hungary 1956."]

Twenty-two. "Success." Let's not say that. [Unclear] greatly. [Marks up draft. Inaudible comment.] Then go on: "We cannot believe . . ."

[We] ought to let Nitze see it. [Unclear.] Berlin—Berlin . . . Resolve, our resolve, would be vetoed by the Russians.

[Pause as the speech review is completed.]

Very good. First class.

Robert Kennedy: May I just say one question? When you're tracing the history, in view of the fact that they're going to come back on Turkey and Italy, whether it would be well if Dean Rusk tries the argument that was so effective about why we started to build these alliances around the world. To meet the argument that George made [unclear].[11]

[Unclear reply by Rusk.]

President Kennedy: We've kept adding there. But, we've got a memorandum being prepared, George [Ball] is [unclear].

[Someone refers to "working on it by noon."]

Bundy: That's what they're getting. They're getting that together. We're getting all the facts on what we can use.

Robert Kennedy: Contrasted with this [in Cuba].

McCone: Arthur [Lundahl suggests], on page 21 we'd better take out the references to the 32 missiles with atomic warheads being in the press. [Unclear] cannot be compromising our intelligence.

[Pause.]

President Kennedy: Okay. What do we do now?

Alexis Johnson?: OAS resolution at the bottom of the page there.

President Kennedy: This'll be tomorrow night?

[Unclear exchange.]

Okay. Fine.

I spoke to someone this morning about the desirability of getting some Latin American ships on this quarantine.

Ball: Our message to them is that we'll be in touch with them on that.

[Unclear exchange.]

Rusk: Our armed forces never allow any foreign forces [unclear].

President Kennedy: That's all right. But I think it would be good to have a . . .

Ball: We've made that offer in your letters, the instructions to the [ambassadors conveying the President's message to Latin American leaders] . . .

[Unclear reference to Berlin.]

President Kennedy: The Berlin group.

[Aside to someone else] You want to go see what's in there?

Nitze: You want to just glance over the . . . ?

[Unclear.]

There are a couple of issues.

[Unclear.]

11. An exchange during the 11:00 A.M. meeting on October 18.

Martin: An hour before you speak, sir, we'll talk to the OAS and NATO ambassadors at the [State Department] Operations Center.

President Kennedy: Who'll make the speech?

Martin: I will, sir. A couple of issues are: I think that the Secretary of State should not give numbers of missiles, or show the map that shows the IRBM sites. The issues are that the photo [unclear]. I have slides, which are just illustrative. They are actual pictures of missiles. They're actual photographs. And I will pass out photographs of the sites.

President Kennedy: Got that?

President Kennedy: [Unclear.] Adlai [Stevenson] can have them available for background briefings, but not to show them up there. [Unclear.]

Now, with the press briefings of the various kinds. I don't suppose we have to have a formal press conference [unclear]. There'll be a lot of things we won't want to discuss. So . . . background.[12]

Unidentified: [Unclear] it would be on background. But on Tuesday [October 23] or Monday night, after . . .

President Kennedy: The first story, I think, would be my speech.

Ball: The idea was that McNamara would give one [background briefing], and then I would, possibly with Martin.

President Kennedy: McNamara would give one at 8:00. And then they'd come over and get one from . . .

Ball: No, no. The McNamara one would be solely on the military aspect. We've got a lot of questions to answer on the other moves. But on background.

President Kennedy: Do we show the press the pictures?

Martin: Two backgrounders. One is—let's call it the intelligence backgrounder. Give them the facts. The other is the policy one.

---

12. A "background" press briefing. The ground rule for a background briefing is that the briefer may be quoted not by name, on the record, but instead by more general references, such as to a "senior administration official." An "off the record" briefing is one in which the official may not be quoted at all.

[Unclear.]

Ball: We've been talking to Pierre [Salinger]. We're going to do a backgrounder to answer questions on policy, and so on. They [the press] have got a lot of problems with understanding the OAS, and the relationship, and so on.

President Kennedy: What time will we go with this?

Bundy: It'll be the same time as McNamara. Three-quarters will be different.

President Kennedy: What'll you do about the [unclear] and all those. Which one do they go to?

[Unclear reply.]

You work that out. Get Pierre. We'll talk about that at 3:00 this afternoon.

The preliminary judgment is, therefore, to show these pictures to the press on a background basis, but we don't release them.

[Unclear.]

Carter: I'd rather not have anything handed out, because somebody will swipe one. Sure as hell. [Laughter.]

[Someone refers to a "transparency" that could be passed around. More unclear discussion.]

President Kennedy: Now, the point of the matter is, these things [missiles] are so mobile that it doesn't require a hell of a lot of work just to make it look like they've been [unclear] working too much here. The other ones are not ready, and they're the ones that are [unclear] more. The other ones are mobile and can move rather quickly. So . . . We ought to take the blockhouses and so on, and make sure . . .

Unidentified: Do you realize how long ago you spotted [the missiles] . . .

Carter: Well, the fact of the matter is that it was only a week ago, last Thursday or Friday, that we got the [authorization].[13]

Ball: Well, we want to be careful, because Ken Keating claims they had them before that.

Robert Kennedy: That's the point. Why didn't we detect them a month ago?

Carter: [Unclear.] There weren't any descriptions of that kind. There were—

President Kennedy: This is an important point. You better be at that 3:00 meeting.

Carter: Yes, sir.

13. The October 11 authorization for a U-2 flight directly over Cuban territory, rather than along the periphery of the country.

President Kennedy: That's the important point. What the refugee [reports said] . . . Keating just had it right, but had it for the wrong reasons. That frequently happens. But that is the point, what they [refugees] really were describing were SAM missiles.

Carter: The first refugee reports we got that were really hard—and believe me we've looked at everything there was and we flew to the places to make sure. But the first ones we got—

President Kennedy: You better be on that at 3:00.

Robert Kennedy: The other point . . .

. . . *President Kennedy:* I'd sure have that for the press. We gotta have Mc-Namara. Just for example. The question has got to be very important. And as a matter of fact we ought to have it for the [congressional] leadership. We can show . . .

Bundy?: Do this for the embassies too.

[Unclear comment by Robert Kennedy.]

President Kennedy: The 3:00 is where we hope to go over the press part. I think we ought to be thinking of all the unpleasant questions they could ask me.

[Unclear discussion of the speech.]

Because it's very good now, and the . . .

Unidentified: I think we ought to get Jim Greenfield[14] in there and sit down and think of all the [unclear].

President Kennedy: You're supposed to be there at 3:00. Make sure that the press men are there, anybody else, so we can go through all these things.

Let's finish this. [Writes.] May want to do that thing.

Is there 100 fighters on that [Cuba]?

Unidentified: Total. That counts the MiG 15s.

14. James Greenfield, Deputy Assistant Secretary of State for Public Affairs, previously a *Time* correspondent.

President Kennedy: 2,000 Soviet military personnel. We've been sort of using that different word. Shouldn't we better say "technicians"?

[Unclear exchange.]

Why don't you say "military technicians."

Unidentified: Why not just "personnel"?

President Kennedy: Okay. This is all right.

All right, now the question is—yeah?

Martin: The scenario calls for me to brief the OAS and NATO ambassadors prior to your televised speech. Later that evening, P+1 hour,[15] the nucleus of this should be offered [unclear].

[Unclear. As the audio quality of the recording begins to improve, President Kennedy interrupts Nitze's briefing on Berlin planning to question him about the status of the president's request, the previous day, to have the Chiefs issue special instructions to restrain possible use of the Jupiter missiles in Turkey pending specific presidential authorization.]

President Kennedy: [Unclear] nuclear weapons there, and if they're attacked. Not to fire their weapons after that.

Nitze: That's a question mark, and I haven't got the answer.

Alexis Johnson?: You raised that with Defense?

Gilpatric: McNamara and I wrote out a suggested instruction from him [President Kennedy] to the Chiefs, and we took it up with the Chiefs. The Chiefs came back with a paper saying that those instructions are already out.

President Kennedy: Well, why don't we reinforce them because, as I say, we may be attacking the Cubans, and a reprisal may come. We don't want these nuclear warheads firing without our knowing about it.

Rusk: The ones in Turkey are not operational yet?

Nitze: Yes, they are.

Gilpatric: Fifteen of them are on alert right now.

President Kennedy: Can we take care of that then, Paul? We need a new instruction out.

Nitze: All right. I'll go back and tell them.

President Kennedy: They object to sending a new one out?

Nitze: They object to sending it out because it, to their view, compromises their standing instructions. You can reinforce one standing instruction . . .

Bundy: Let's have a look at the existing order and see how definite it is, and

15. P hour was the time of the President's address, 7:00 P.M. that day.

then simply say: "The President directs your attention again to umptyump section" . . .

Rusk: You can send a personal message to the commander saying: "Be sure you can fully understand paragraph so-and-so of your orders."

Nitze: They did come back with another point, and that is: NATO strategic contact [Soviet nuclear attack] requires the immediate execution of EDP in such events.

President Kennedy: What's EDP?

Nitze: The European Defense Pl~~~ ~ ~ ~ ~ ~

~~~ ~~~~~ws *do* know, so that they ~~~ ~~~ and put the United States under attack. I don't think we ought to accept the Chiefs' word on that one, Paul.

Nitze: All right.

President Kennedy: I understand why they did that. These fellows think everybody knows as much as we know. And they don't.

Rusk: They might think a nuclear war is already on.

Nitze: I'm sure that these fellows are . . . Surely they're indoctrinated not to fire. This is what Secretary McNamara and I went over, looked into, and they really are—

President Kennedy: Well, let's do it again, Paul.

Nitze: I've got your point and we're going to get that. [Laughter, probably at Kennedy's insistent refusal to take it on faith that military standing orders would be observed, and Nitze's discomfort at giving in to him.]

Bundy: Send me the documents, and I will show them to a doubting master [presumably Kennedy].[16] [Laughter.]

President Kennedy: You were [unclear]?

---

16. About an hour later Taylor sent a message (JCS 6866) to the Commander-in-Chief of U.S. Forces in Europe (and the Supreme Allied Commander for NATO), General Norstad, which stated: "Make certain that the Jupiters in Turkey and Italy will not be fired without specific authorization from the President. In the event of an attack, either nuclear or non-nuclear . . . US custodians are to destroy or make inoperable the weapons if any attempt is made to fire them." Norstad was further instructed to keep this order secret from the Turks and Italians.

Bundy: Yes, may I? Therefore, many things may need to be done after a Berlin tension is initiated on the Soviet side that we would not want to make too much noise about now.

A quite different thing is the immediate process, which is that we must and will have to find all the ways we can of continuing our regular business on Berlin, and of getting it clear to our allies the context, in which this Cuban action is a reinforcement of their position rather than an extraordinary [unclear].

President Kennedy: Very good point. Otherwise, the credibility on Berlin . . . in view of my statement.

Bundy: Well, there are two points. There's credibility and there is the fact that, if this buildup [in Cuba] continues, their fundamental guarantee [of American nuclear protection] might be endangered.

President Kennedy: Those are good points. I don't think we've thought enough about them in our communications to these heads of state. We ought to. We ought to remind Acheson of that.

[Bundy agrees.]

When does he [Acheson] make his thing [briefing to the North Atlantic Council]?[17]

Bundy: Tomorrow.

Unidentified: Today.

Bundy: Today's the NAC? Oh, I thought it was tomorrow.

[Mixed voices.]

Unidentified: At 5:00 [Eastern Daylight Time].

Unidentified: P minus 2.

Unidentified: P minus 2, 5:00.

Bundy: How about getting on the phone to him [Acheson]?

President Kennedy: All right.

Ball: I think he has it. He has his own [take on] Berlin. [Unclear.] This is one of the points he was making.

President Kennedy: The only other thing is our letters to any heads of state. What about [Italian Prime Minister Amintore] Fanfani? Did you write him a letter?

Unidentified: That's fine [unclear], yes.

President Kennedy: That's gone, then.

---

17. The North Atlantic Council (NAC) is the governing body of the NATO alliance, then headquartered in Paris. Acheson was being dispatched to brief first de Gaulle and then the North Atlantic Council, which usually meets at the level of each member country's permanent representative (ambassador).

Bundy: We've written more letters that you haven't seen.

President Kennedy: That's all right. But I think what we ought to do is to have a background for our ambassadors, sort of instructions, and these two points [about Berlin] are very good points that ought to be in that thing for their conversations with the people over there.

Gilpatric: I thought I'd make these points this afternoon when I meet with the military subcommittee just before your speech.

President Kennedy: Fine.

Bundy: So, the basic tie-in here is th~

undermin~

~ ~onecтion—assurance of full
~~ consultation.

President Kennedy: [Has just been passed a note.] The Russians are going to make a major announcement in 2 hours?[18] [Speaking to group] They're going to announce it, he said.

Bundy: You want to get on the air quicker?

President Kennedy: No. Let's just get it on the air. I think that what we will do—

Ball: I wouldn't get on the air quicker.

Sorensen: Let me, Mr. President, make some other attempts to check it out.

President Kennedy: I think you ought to announce that I'm going on the air at 7:00.

Sorensen: We just have the time.

President Kennedy: Well, when are you going to announce it?

Salinger: We're going to announce it as soon as I can get the time back guaranteed.

President Kennedy: [We've got it] already. Well, why don't you announce that and at 7:00, so at least we're not going on the air after the Russians are.

Sorensen: We may not be able to make it in 15 or 20 minutes, Mr. President.

---

18. This was news that Soviet Foreign Minister Gromyko would be making a statement at 2:00 P.M. Washington time, upon departing from the United States.

President Kennedy: Well, wait a minute, the quicker the better on that. Because what we don't want to do is have the Russians announce this thing.

Unidentified: Right. So announce to the press we request 7:00 [unclear].

President Kennedy: We're going to *get* 7:00. We request this time for 7:00. Have you announced the [congressional] leadership meetings?

O'Donnell?: Not all that.

President Kennedy: Right now. Right now.

The announcement of the President's forthcoming address was then made, at about noon.

President Kennedy: All I can think is that they [the Soviets] are going to announce that the missiles are for defensive purposes.

Bundy: Well, we don't know what they're going to do.

Nitze: They're certainly going to defend it. A great big announcement defending them.

Rusk: Those attack [unclear] scenarios last night pointing to the Turkish missiles.

Robert Kennedy: I think if you find that they're going to announce it, what you can do is to put out the statement in an hour.

President Kennedy: Put out the statement?

Robert Kennedy: Yes. Just put out a statement of what we've found and that you're going to go talk to the American people at 7:00 tonight.

President Kennedy: If we hear they, in 2 hours they're going to have a statement, then we'll announce it.

Robert Kennedy: Something certain.

President Kennedy: So it doesn't look like the Russians first announced this thing.

Ball: I think it's awfully important to get ahead of the Russians.

Unidentified: Yeah, like we discussed.

Rusk: [Unclear] "the President will confirm to the nation this evening that," what I want—

President Kennedy: Just say: "The President today announced that Soviet missile bases have been discovered and he will discuss the American actions to be taken or something at 7:00 tonight on TV." Then it isn't a whirl or flash go around that the Russians have announced it.

[Unclear.]

Mac, you are prepared to announce it right now, though?

What else do we have to worry about in Berlin? [Nervous laughter.]

Rusk: Well we've really got to get something to say fast because there may be material in this—

President Kennedy: Well, if they're going to do that in 2 hours, the question is whether we ought to announce what action we're going to take at the time we announce it. Additional, more details.

Sorensen: We could distribute your speech right away.

President Kennedy: But—

Ball: Well, the trouble is you may want to revise the ~~~~ ' order to hit [unclear]

... ~~~ papers

... not the Russians announce it.

And then, secondly, whether—probably with the other question—we ought to put any more action with these details.

Rusk: I think we'll have all the action you have taken [unclear].

President Kennedy: What they're going to do. I don't think they think we're going to invade. I [don't] think they think we're going to invade Cuba. That's not the way the buildup has been.

Robert Kennedy: I think that would be bad to have them say: "Don't invade Cuba or we're going to knock your block off." And then we go on television tonight and announce our plans. So, I mean, I don't think you lost anything—

President Kennedy: By announcing the fact.

Robert Kennedy: —by announcing the fact that you've ordered a—

President Kennedy: Unless we get any particulars, I think we ought to get to work on this. We don't have much time.

President Kennedy then rose from the table and the meeting broke up. The tape recorder was turned off.

MONDAY, OCTOBER 22

3:00 P.M.

CABINET ROOM

No premature announcements were needed. Gromyko simply gave a brief departure statement at 2:00 P.M.

At 3:00 P.M. Kennedy again gathered his chief advisers in a final preparatory session before he began announcing the policy, a process that would begin with his briefing of congressional leaders 2 hours later. The discussion was convened as a meeting of the National Security Council and included all the Joint Chiefs of Staff, O'Donnell, Fowler from Treasury, Hilsman from State, McDermott from the Office of Emergency Preparedness, and possibly a few other officials who had not been included before. (We cannot identify all the voices.) President Kennedy did not immediately turn on the tape recorder, but the minutes summarize the opening exchanges.[1]

> The President opened the meeting by asking Secretary Rusk to read the . . . message from Prime Minister Macmillan which had just been received. [The message was read again, on tape, in the next session and is not repeated here.] Secretary Rusk observed that for a first reaction to information of our proposed blockade it was not bad. He added that it was comforting to learn that the British Prime Minister had not thought of anything we hadn't thought of.
>
> The President commented that the Prime Minister's message contained the best argument for taking no action. What we now need are strong arguments to explain why we have to act as we are acting.
>
> Secretary Rusk stated that the best legal basis for our blockade action was

---

1. Minutes of the 507th Meeting of the National Security Council, October 22, 1962, in *FRUS 1961–1963*, vol. 11: *Cuban Missile Crisis and Aftermath*, pp. 152–153.

the Rio Treaty . . . The Attorney General said that in his opinion our blockade action would be illegal if it were not supported by the OAS. In his view the greatest importance is attached to our obtaining the necessary fourteen favorable votes in the OAS. Secretary Rusk commented that if we do not win the support of the OAS, we are not necessarily acting illegally. He referred to the new situation created by modern weapons and he thought that rules of international law should not be taken as applying literally to a completely new situation. He said we need not abandon hope so early . . .

Director . . .

. . . . out the importance of fully supporting the course of action chosen which, in his view, represented a reasonable consensus. Any course is extremely troublesome and, as in the case of the Berlin wall, we are once again confronted with a difficult choice. If we undertake a tricky and unsatisfactory course, we do not even have the satisfaction of knowing what would have happened if we had acted differently. He mentioned that former Presidents Eisenhower, Truman, and Hoover had supported his decision during telephone conversations with each of them earlier in the day.

The President then summarized the arguments as to why we must act. We must reply to those whose reaction to the blockade would be to ask what had changed in view of the fact that we had been living in the past years under a threat of a missile nuclear attack by the USSR.

A. In September we had said we would react if certain actions were taken in Cuba. We have to carry out commitments which we had made publicly at that time.

B. The secret deployment by the Russians of strategic missiles to Cuba was such a complete change in their previous policy of not deploying such missiles outside the USSR that if we took no action in this case, we would convey to the Russians an impression that we would never act, no matter what they did anywhere.

C. Gromyko had left the impression that the Soviets were going to act in Berlin in the next few months. Therefore, if they acted now in response to our blockade action, we would only have brought on their Berlin squeeze earlier than expected.

At this point in his explanation, President Kennedy turned on the tape recorder.

President Kennedy: . . . Khrushchev if we completely failed to react in the case of Cuba.

In addition, seeing that we failed to react, the effect in Latin America would be perhaps the balance of power really had shifted and that it's just a question of time. There was a feeling of inevitability, that the Soviet advance would have been marked. So we decided to do something. And then we start here.

Now, it may end up with our having to invade Cuba. We should be in a position to do so. There obviously is going to . . . Khrushchev will not complete this without a response, maybe in Berlin or maybe here. But we have done—I think, the choices being all second best—I think we've done the best thing, at least as far as we can tell in advance.

We haven't settled two or three matters which are going to have to be settled in the coming days. What are we going to do when one of our U-2s are shot down, which we have to anticipate maybe in the next few days, over a SAM site? What will be our response there? Number one.

And, secondly, what will we do if the work continues on these sites, which we assume it will. I think we've got to begin to meet tomorrow and begin to consider what action we take in those cases. Do we attempt to start a blockade? Or do we begin . . . If they shoot down one of our U-2s, do we attack that SAM site or all the SAM sites? These are matters I think we ought to be all thinking about in the next 24 hours and, beginning tomorrow, begin to decide exactly what we will do in that case.

But I think that, as I said, for the press, those who are abroad, and others, those arguments about doing nothing, I think the reasons why we have to do something are quite clear. I don't think there was anybody ever who didn't think we shouldn't respond.

But why the different actions? At least I've attempted to communicate why we took the course we did, even though, as I've said from the beginning, the idea of a quick strike was very tempting, and I really didn't give up on that until yesterday morning. So I may . . . After talking to General Sweeney and then after talking to others, it looked like we would have all of the difficulties of Pearl Harbor and not have finished the job. The job can only be finished by an invasion.

As I understand, we are moving those forces which will be necessary in case, at the end of the week, it looks like that would be the only course left to us, even though I recognize we have to do the air strikes with all the disadvantages we'll now have. I want to say very clearly to the military that I recognize the appreciable problems in any military action we have to take in Cuba by the warning we're now giving.

But I did want you to know that the reason we followed the course we have was because, while we would have been able to take out more planes and missiles without warning, as we *are* involved all around the world and not just in Cuba, I think we get shocked, and the [damage to the] alliance been nearly fatal. Particularly [since] I think

drastic action by Khrushch

But

can be

ing crisis on our hands.

possibly very fast.

. . . ncy: Mr. President, did you want to go in at all into the questions that are bound to arise and what the answers are to those? For instance, why we didn't put a blockade in a month ago? Why we just detected it a week ago? Or why we didn't—of course, we handled [that]—why we didn't take more forceful action.

President Kennedy: Oh yeah, we've got some of these questions which, as I say, we have around the government.

The first question [Rusk raised, whether the action was strong enough], as I say, everybody has to follow their own judgment in these matters. It just seems to me to be the appropriate answer.

But I'm not . . . Everybody has to decide for themselves the question.

The first question [Robert Kennedy raised], why was action not taken earlier? Well, we still are not sure we're going to get the 14 votes in the OAS. We'd begun the quarantine 6 months ago . . . Let's say we'd begun it in August, when there was no evidence that the Soviet military buildup was going to be offensive. We obviously would have had difficulty getting 14 votes for a blockade. We wouldn't have had any support by any of the countries, really, of Western Europe as the . . . Had it then begun on Berlin, which it inevitably would have, it would have appeared that we had thrown Berlin into jeopardy, and perhaps lost it because of, rather almost, a fixation on the subject of Cuba, which up to quite recently most of us never, did not, assume would be turned into an offensive base. So we would have to probably . . . If we didn't get an OAS resolution it would have had to lead to a declaration of war. And a declaration of war on Cuba at that point would have placed us in an isolated position.

The whole foreign policy of the United States since 1947 has been to develop and maintain alliances within this hemisphere as well as around the world. It would have done for Castro a good deal, rebuilding a very faded prestige in Latin America. And that point of view would have also endangered our interests.

And, of course, no one at that time was certain that Khrushchev would make such a far-reaching step, which is wholly a departure from Soviet foreign policy, really since, I would say, the Berlin blockade. And, as I say, we might have more responsibility for [the] loss of Berlin, without having any justification for our action.

Now, (b) [Robert Kennedy's second question]: The surveillance of the island did not disclose any buildup of offensive capabilities at least until Tuesday [October 16]. We heard rumors of the—from refugees. But when those were borne out, Mr. Hilsman, who's in charge of that [intelligence for the State Department], says that most of them were . . . They were all talking about the SAM sites, the ground/air missiles. Is that correct?

Hilsman: I wouldn't say I was in charge of the whole thing.

President Kennedy: Well, whoever. At least from the refugee interrogation. What about the refugee interrogation?

Hilsman: Well, yes, well, the situation here is that Mr. McCone will have to speak to it.

Actually, this particular site is the first one [that] was covered by Air Force photography on August 29th and there was nothing there. When we rechecked again there was nothing there, August 29th.

We began to be more, began to be suspicious in general as the ships kept coming in, big crates there, and sharply suspicious when, on the 28th of September, we saw the IL-28 crates. We then began to get a few reports, collateral reports, about this particular site.

We were precluded from flying over that particular site by a cloud cover for a long period of time there, days on end, but I'll let Mr. McCone correct me on that. Then, when finally the weather broke, it was a Sunday [October 14], we got a flight over it, and we then saw the beginnings of the deployment there. And you can be sure I have photographs, between Sunday and Monday, to show the dramatic progress in only 24 hours.

President Kennedy: Well, I want to have those available.

McCone: I think we have to be careful at this point, because there were some refugee reports. I think this is what Keating has been basing his position on. I wouldn't be too categoric that we had no information, because, as a matter of fact, there were some 15, I think, various refugee reports which circulated around that were indicative that something was going on.

But we had no surveillance, I think, from August the 29th till the 14th of October, that gave us positive information. Therefore we were dealing during that period with conjecture and assumptions, rather than hard int...

But I would be a little bit ...

... you ... photography, it would be difficult on ... nonpermanent sites to tell, up until a week or 10 days ago, even if we had a flight across there. So I don't think we have to say that it goes back into September, the middle of September or early September, or the end of August. Even if we had a flight in the middle of September, the chances are we wouldn't have been able to tell up until the last 10 days or 2 weeks.

President Kennedy: There is, of course . . . I don't think any Soviet experts assumed that they would engage in this radical alteration, in view of the fact that no Eastern European satellite, for example, has such [nuclear] weapons on their territory. This would be the first time the Soviet Union has moved these weapons outside their own backyard.

Robert Kennedy: The other thing, of course, is that the Russian ambassador [Dobrynin] has told officials within our government, continuously up until just last week, as well as Gromyko's conversation with you, that this would not be done.

President Kennedy: It should be understood that the media . . . Then, of course, we issued our statements on September 4th and 13th and secured OAS approval of stepped-up surveillance.

We understood that the medium-range missiles are a field type that can be moved in an hour. The intermediate-range missile sites are excavations, so they're going to be developing.

Now, the second question [actually Robert Kennedy's third question] I've already referred to: Why not take stronger action now, such as an air strike or an invasion. I think I've already answered that.

Bundy: Mr. President, I think it may be quite important not to get into too much public discussion into the difficulty of hitting these targets. I was out of the room when you discussed this, but I don't think we want to . . . We may be doing this in a few days [unclear].

President Kennedy: All right.

Unidentified: To say we can't do it, is not the perfect prelude to that.

President Kennedy: No.

Robert Kennedy: It's a Pearl Harbor thing.

Rusk: What [do] we say about it to those who want to tie our hands for the future at this time? I think we say we have obligations to bring such threats to the OAS, to the United Nations. We can be sure our own people fully understand, and give the other side a chance to rethink what it's doing and to take another course.

Bundy: That's why the position of the government is to deal with this matter firmly and resolutely with the minimum necessary force to make the result.

President Kennedy: But it is a fact that even with the air strike we didn't, we couldn't, have gotten . . . We couldn't, perhaps, get all the missiles that are in sight.

Bundy: Entirely true, Mr. President. But I don't think the next few days is the time to talk about it.

President Kennedy: I know, but I want everybody to understand it, Mac. The fact of the matter is there are missiles on the island which are not in sight.

Now, Bobby mentioned Pearl Harbor. Is this action justified, what we're now doing? This is one of the problems which are going to be most troublesome in our discussions with our allies. Inasmuch as the Soviet missiles are already pointed at the U.S., and U.S. missiles are [pointed] at the U.S.S.R., particularly those—the most obvious example is in Turkey and Italy. In other words, what is the distinction between these missiles and the missiles which we sent to Turkey and Italy, which the Soviets put up with, which are operational, and have been for 2 to 3 years. My understanding is that the State Department is preparing a brief on that matter.

Ball: We have prepared that, Mr. President. We've prepared the factual statement.

Rusk: A week ago. On that, in 1957 there was the decision by NATO [that] it's fairly certain that these weapons are imminently in Europe. This was in the face of an announcement by the Soviet Union that they were equipping their armed forces with nuclear missiles. In the face of a demand on their part that all forces, all NATO forces in Europe, renounce the use of such weapons. Therefore, in the great Soviet-NATO confrontation, the Soviets were insisting upon having hundreds of these weapons aimed at Europe and none of these weapons pointed the other way. That is the NATO . . . That's the Turkey/Italy situation.

President Kennedy: At the time we sent these missiles to Turkey and to Italy, did we have intercontinental ballistic missiles ourselves? Or did the Soviets—

Rusk: Well, we sent them only in '59, sir. So I doubt—

Taylor: That was just at the start of our [ICBM] program. [Aside to someone else:] Did they have any operational?

President Kennedy: We ....

.... take a

.... go over.

.... case, the Soviet move was undertaken secretly, accompanied by false Soviet statements in public and private. The departure from the Soviet position that it has no need or desire to station strategic weapons off the Soviet territory; their statement in TASS in mid-September said that they had rockets and that therefore there was no need to do this.

Our bases abroad are by published agreement to help local people maintain their independence against a threat from abroad. Soviet history is exactly the opposite. Offensive missiles in Cuba have a very different psychological and political effect in this hemisphere than missiles in the U.S.S.R. pointed to us. And had we done nothing, Communism and Castroism are going to be spread through the hemisphere as governments frightened by this new evidence of power have toppled.

(B): All this represents a provocative change in the delicate status quo both countries have maintained. He [Khrushchev] accepted this one [provocative action], and he may, anyway, even try more. In this sense this is a probing action preceding [renewed confrontation over] Berlin, to see whether we accept it or not.

In another sense, Khrushchev was desperate enough to change his missile policy and take this step for the very reason that we have so long frustrated his design in Berlin. And that's . . . Is Thompson here?

Bundy: Yes.

President Kennedy: I think that, in talking the other day [October 18], he [Thompson] made this point, that [seeing Thompson] you thought that part of this may be due to the point that he [Khrushchev] has a sense of frustration about Berlin and not a very clear way of getting control of it.

Thompson: Mr. President, he made it quite clear in my last talk with him, that he was squirming under the problems that he was . . . That he felt he couldn't back down from the position he'd taken. He'd come so far. At the same time he was worried about the fact that he was going forward to it [confrontation over Berlin] and going to lose, and then would have to go on and flip the coin as to whether or not we reacted.

Rusk: Sir, I know we talked about this point too. And I wonder what your judgment would be about using it with some of our background that I have. That is, that these missiles do create a special threat for the United States quite apart from the fact that we have been living, we know, under the threat of certain Soviet missiles, because these increase the threat to a country [the United States] which is a principal nuclear support of 41 allies all over the world.

It really comes back a little bit to the military argument we had the other day. It seems to me that it ought to be pointed out that missiles of this magnitude is not something that we can brush aside, simply because the Soviets have some other missiles that can also reach the United States.

The fact is that, [just among us] here in this room, the number of missiles that launch in these sites would double the known missile strength the Soviet Union has to reach this country.[2] And that, since we are the basic nuclear strength of all these alliances, it is the United States [that matters], and this is a matter we can't ignore.

Thompson?: [Unclear.] You might not want to use this. But it seems clear now that Khrushchev's statement about putting all Berlin off until after the [U.S. congressional] election was tied to all the plans for this.

President Kennedy: Does the position by Khrushchev justify trading off Berlin for Cuba? First, the island is not comparable. We have no strategic weapons moving into Berlin and have offered internationally supervised free

2. The kind of estimate on which Rusk based this assertion was: "Sites now identified will, when completed, give Soviets total of 36 launchers and 72 missiles. This compares with 60–65 ICBM launchers we now estimate to be operational in the USSR"; CIA, "Soviet Military Buildup in Cuba," 21 October 1962, in McAuliffe, *CIA Documents,* p. 259. The intelligence community also reported, late in the evening of October 21, that Soviet deployments would result in a "first salvo potential of 40 missiles with a refire capability of an additional 40 missiles . . . this threat against the U.S. is approximately one-half the currently estimated ICBM missile threat from the USSR"; GMAIC, JAEIC, and NPIC, "Supplement 2 to Joint Evaluation of Soviet Missile Threat in Cuba," 21 October 1962, ibid., p. 262. Rusk was actually more accurate than he knew, because these estimates had significantly overstated the number of ICBMs in the Soviet Union.

plebiscites by people, to determine whether they wanted us there. If the Cuban people had that same opportunity, that could produce a different situation.

(B): Gromyko made it very clear last week, as they have in all their conversations, [that] they're getting ready to move on Berlin anyway. This does not increase their determination to move on Berlin, no matter what we do, because he said they're going to do it anyway. This may give them a different way of doing it, but they're going to do it anyway.

(C): Our quarantine will not keep out food or m~~~~~~ endanger war. In other ~~~~

~~~~point, and they watch. They know that ~~~~ are no offensive weapons in Berlin. They have plenty of ways of knowing that.

Taylor: Sometimes they get out; sometimes they don't. And they do let these people look through the tailgates in the trucks.

Rusk: But the central point here is that we're in Berlin by right as well as by the acknowledgment and agreement of the Soviet Union. They're bringing these things into Cuba contrary to the Rio Pact. So there's all the difference in the world.

President Kennedy: Yes. So I think we want to make . . . What we're trying to do is make a distinction between our actions and a Soviet blockade of Berlin, or the [Soviet] blockade of '47–'48. The 3-year surveillance and inspection which they had over the movement of troops and personnel [into Berlin]. The fact that no weapons, no strategic weapons, were placed there. And the fact that we're permitting goods to move into Cuba at this point, food and all the rest. This is not a blockade in that sense. It's merely an attempt to prevent the shipment of weapons.

Khrushchev's conclusion, his purpose apparently, was to force us into, add to his strategic nuclear power, force us into a choice of initiating an attack on Cuba, which would free his hand, et cetera, and/or appearing to be a resolute ally. So it's time we chose to get on the road.

I want to go back to saying: I think that the talk that we considered [at] any time an air attack. I want to restate that now, and that is a matter which I don't think we ought to discuss under these conditions. We may have to do it. In any case, we don't want to look like we were considering it. So I think we ought to just scratch that from all our conversations, and not ever indicate that that was a course of action open to us. I can't say that strongly enough. We don't want to ever have it around that this was one of the alternatives that we considered this week. I think it will be very difficult to keep that quiet. But I think we ought to. We might have to do it in the future. And, in addition, it will become a propaganda matter, that this was a matter seriously considered by the U.S. government. So let's not consider that as one of the alternatives in any discussion.

Anybody else have any thoughts about this?

Sorensen: [Unclear] some more questions, Mr. President.

Robert Kennedy: I think probably the reason, when you compare—when he—brings up why you didn't have an attack or why you didn't have an air strike, to say that it was just not considered on the basis of the fact that we couldn't have the Pearl Harbor kind of operation, rather than go into all the detail of why it would not . . .

Rusk: It was not done because it was not considered.

Robert Kennedy: Yeah. Rather than go into all the details, the military reasons we didn't.

President Kennedy: All right. Well, I think that's fair enough.

Taylor: Mr. President, I should call attention to the fact we're starting moves now which are overt, and will be seen and reported on and commented on. So that movement tomorrow, for example, the East Coast. We'll start moving some shipping and start loading some Marines on the West Coast. You'll be faced with the question: "Are you preparing to invade?" We'll be faced with that question.

President Kennedy: What do you suggest saying on that?

Rusk: Mr. President, I would suggest that we urge the press not to come back on each one of these things. We say that, obviously, precautionary moves are going to be taken. That it does not serve the public interest to call attention to each and all of them. We are in a very critical situation, and that we cannot be forced to relate each of these moves. That naturally, with tensions as high as they are at the present time, the President's going to be disposing forces, but it's not in the public interest to try to explain each one of the moves.

Bundy: One slightly supplementary point. We don't want to look as if we got scared off from anything. There is no current order for invasion. I think that's very important.

Rusk: Well, if the President's speech talks about what he's going to do, therefore there are a lot of things that you could do that he's not doing at the moment. I wouldn't, at this moment, deny any particular line of action too categorically.

Robert Kennedy: Keep it ambiguous.

President Kennedy: In other words, though, I think we shouldn't have it hanging over us that we're preparing invasion. That isn't strategically or politically useful.

Bundy: We've told the Department of Defense to be ready for any eventuality.

President Kennedy: The [unclear]

[unclear] always said about the military that it's their business to have plans for any contingency."

President Kennedy: My plans . . . I don't think we need to say more. Not in a military sense.

Rusk: If we were invading Cuba the President would have [unclear].

Bundy: The policy is, goes, only as far as this speech. I think it's one way of saying it. But they'll work it out. [Unclear.]

President Kennedy: What did we do in the Korean War about the movement of troops? What kind of a limitation was placed on the—what sort of censorship, if any? Does anybody remember that?

Taylor: I was in Korea, but I'm not sure.

President Kennedy: No, within the United States.

Hilsman: In the United States no troop movements were reported. Two or three newspapers who did, because they reported the ships' movements, were severely censored.

President Kennedy: Well, now, we weren't at war there. I think I'd like to have the press people, Arthur Sylvester,[3] et cetera, and Pierre [Salinger], find out what they did in the first days of Korea in regard to putting holds on the press, if any. Or whether, what the technique was, whether it was done voluntarily, or what they did. Because I think we might have to think about the same sort of—

---

3. The press spokesman for the Department of Defense.

McNamara: Mr. President, I have a group working on that, because we just have to tighten up on security throughout the Defense Department. This group, of which Arthur [Sylvester] is a member working on it, will report to me today [unclear]. Specifically, I've asked them to go back and get out the procedures and rules and the experience [unclear].

Rusk: We were not in a state of war with Korea. We relied upon self-imposed, voluntary censorship at the request of the government.

President Kennedy: Well, we may have to send some sort of request out to every newspaper in the country. And Secretary McNamara is of course going to give us a report on that.

O'Donnell?: Mr. President, that voluntary censorship code has been brought up to date and is being considered by this group, and Pierre.

Rusk: Do we intend to extend our stop-and-search program to aircraft, to determine whether nuclear weapons are being sent to Cuba by air?

President Kennedy: I don't think we ought to do it on the aircraft just yet. Because if we get them on Berlin, we may have to rely on aircraft, and I don't think we ought to initiate that.

Robert Kennedy: What answer do you give to the press?

Rusk: The press on that, and the future shipment to Cuba of petroleum and military products, is: "These are matters on which it would not be wise to commit at this time."

President Kennedy: What sort of progress have we made with Dakar?[4] What are we doing about that?

McCone: We will have a plan, partly in execution, by the latter part of this afternoon. I'm waiting for you to see the documents. As soon as I get that—

President Kennedy: We're getting all [words excised as classified information] in there to help us?

[2-second reply excised as classified information.]

Bundy: I believe, myself, Mr. President, we ought to ask that the Defense Department review intensively this question of possible nuclear warheads by air and all the alternative methods that we might . . .

McNamara: We have, Mac. We've asked Admiral Dennison to lay out the

---

4. Because of the more limited range of aircraft at that time, Dakar and Conakry, in West Africa, were principal way stations and refueling points for flights across the Atlantic into the Caribbean, i. e., Soviet flights into Cuba. The United States worked quietly with France and the local governments to restrict and monitor these flights during the crisis.

plans for it. I was proposing we answer that question by saying that we're prepared to quarantine movement of weapons by whatever means, period.

Sorensen: Once again, you can refer to the words in the President's speech.

President Kennedy: The speech wasn't quite clear on that.

Sorensen: Yes indeed it was. It said "cargo and carriers."

Robert Kennedy: There's no intention of air at the present time.

Unidentified: No, that isn't.

Unidentified: There is a related but more limited question do we do—

capabilities, particularly if they were to use a bomber. Even in the TU-114 they can probably fly direct.[5]

Unidentified: Without all the flight coverages.

McNamara: Oh, probably. Depending on how they refuel and so on. A light load. It appears that they can.

Therefore, what I've instructed is that we will be informed of any airplane that appears to be moving from the Soviet Union to Cuba. And we'll have to watch this carefully and decide what to do at that time. Admiral Dennison, in the meantime, will be prepared with plans to put into effect should he be ordered to do so.

Bundy: It becomes all the more important to be vague on this one.

[25 seconds excised as classified information.]

President Kennedy: Seems like we'll have to make a decision by tomorrow, along with these other matters.

McCone?: There's a question of whether these [offensive weapons] might be loaded in the ships, below the water line. Probably.

Rusk: Mr. President, are you effectively contemplating a call-up of the National Guard or Reserve units and in the present context declaring a national emergency? I would say not, at this time, but we've got to be able to change in an hour's time.

---

5. The Tupolev 114 was a transport aircraft.

President Kennedy: As I understand, Admiral Anderson may be calling up some last [unclear].

Anderson: We're going to hold off for the time being, keep it under review from day to day.

President Kennedy: That's true also, I guess, of the Air Force and . . .

Taylor: All the services have possible requirements in that region.

President Kennedy: What about the Treasury, in regard to the state of gold and all the rest?

Fowler: Well, first, a related question, what's been coming under discussion here, perhaps could come up tomorrow in connection with these other things, is whether the present trade embargo, which does have some exceptions and limitations, will be brought about to be . . . ? What are all the loose ends that are not now covered?

Then there are a series of questions which all are conditioned on the when-circumstances-warrant consideration, such as closing stock and commodity exchanges, additional foreign-asset controls, general credit controls. And of course, most important, the question of imposing foreignexchange and gold controls when circumstances warrant.

We want to particularly impress the point that this should not be mentioned in any listing or consideration of possible measures before imposition. In other words, it should only be mentioned, in any context, at the point when we're about to move. Because—

President Kennedy: Well, let me ask you, if you [unclear], within an hour or so could you just prevent the transfer of gold to the account of anyone who has dollars abroad?

Fowler: Yes, sir. Our view is [that] proper procedure in this particular connection would be, however, to utilize the existing arrangements, swap arrangements, to soak up any flight of capital, initial flight of capital, and only invoke foreign-exchange restrictions when it appears that the existing arrangement for swaps was inadequate to deal with the situation because of increased flight.

And similarly, on gold movements, we always know in advance when there would be any transfer, and we can deal with the gold-transfer problem on an ad hoc basis as particular situations develop and are important.

So, insofar as both of those sectors are concerned, foreign exchange and gold control, we would advise a waiting procedure, having the arrangements all in the standby form to be utilized as necessary.

President Kennedy: The stock market we [unclear] and see what happens tomorrow.

Fowler: Yes. I'd be . . . On this range of questions that I've just mentioned, perhaps Mr. McDermott would want to speak to this, that there is a question of where responsibility would be placed to take the actual decisions. You yourself would be occupied with a number of other matters and . . . Various independent actions being taken through various existing authority without consultation with OEP [Office of Emergency Preparedness] or some other coordinating point that you designate, that might be quite unwise, and so we do raise the question of: To whom we should consult on such a ~ the closing of the Exchange should any situation or ~

President Kennedy: Well, [unclear]—

Bundy: We're reviewin~ '' involve the ~

. . . do?

. . . is an act of war. Insofar as the user, of . . ., whether it's war or not is a matter of intention. We are . . . orce here for other purposes. There is an actual exercise of force in relation to obligations of the United States under the Rio Pact and otherwise. I thought that this in itself is not, from our point of view, an act of war.

President Kennedy: Let me ask, are we going to stop ships that come from friendly countries which obviously wouldn't be carrying strategic weapons, or when we get certification from those countries that these ships do not carry them? Whether we want to start stopping right at the beginning, so that we get the precedent established, in case we want to extend this to oil and petroleum.

McNamara: Mr. President, Admiral Anderson and I were discussing this. George, perhaps you should answer.

Anderson: Well, I think that we should stop and visit and search and play this thing straight. Actually, we have pretty good information as to which ships are carrying offensive-type equipment. All Soviet bloc.

Rusk: Sir, I think it's important to stop all shipping, because the positions are: It's lawful to do this. So that it has to be effective, and to make it effective you stop all ships.

---

6. Edward McChesney Martin, Chairman of the Federal Reserve Board.

McNamara: The specific instructions [that] were given Admiral Dennison are: ships, including submarines, Soviet and non-Soviet, would be intercepted.

President Kennedy: Let me just go back once more with this about any action, direct action. The invasion. I think we've got an agreement about what our status is *re* invasion, no other status is given. I've only said be prepared for eventuality.

The question of air action, I think we'll stick just with: It comes to be a question of the Pearl Harbor thing, and not go into any military details. It's just very important, and security's been so well held with this group, that I don't have any problem with that. But I do think it's highly important that we not discuss the tactical nature or the strategic nature of it, this particular Pearl Harbor recommendation.

Bundy: I think that "No orders have been given" is the perfect phrase.

President Kennedy: Thank you very much.

[The meeting then ends, and after a few minutes the participants are urged to leave by a staff person who explains that the room is needed for another meeting (with a visiting African leader). McCone and Bundy have lingered in a discussion of past intelligence-gathering on possible missiles in Cuba, a matter on which they clashed in September. Bundy can be heard saying: "The last thing that's useful is post-mortems here." Then silence, and the recording ends.]

MONDAY, OCTOBER 22

5:00 P.M.

CABINET ROOM

_... _ _ost_ and other dailies had had _..._ _that_ morning about an impending crisis. Less friendly papers such as the *Chicago Tribune* were speculating that Senators Keating and Capehart and other administration critics might be about to be proved right in their charges that the Soviets were turning Cuba into an offensive military base. Though at that point the President had not yet asked for air time, he was expected to address the nation Monday night.

Kennedy had the satisfaction of seeing Monday morning stories reporting that he had Eisenhower's backing. After receiving McCone's briefing, Eisenhower appeared on an ABC television news program. Reversing the position he had taken in Boston a week earlier, Eisenhower said Republicans might criticize past administration policies, but "the President's immediate handling of foreign affairs was not a legitimate topic."[1]

Now he needed to brief Democratic and Republican leaders of Congress. Then he would deliver his nationally televised address to tens of millions of anxious viewers across the country, a speech that would be rebroadcast and distributed in many languages around the world.

Congress had not been in session. The 20 members who filed into the Cabinet Room had been gathered from all over the country, usually by military officers calling or arriving with an urgent message and offering military trans-

---

1. *New York Times,* October 22, 1962, p. 1.

port to bring them back to Washington. The Senators included, in alphabetical order, Everett McKinley Dirksen (R., Ill.), the minority leader; J. William Fulbright (D., Ark.), Chairman of the Foreign Relations Committee; Bourke B. Hickenlooper (R., Iowa), Chairman of the Republican Policy Committee; Hubert H. Humphrey (D., Minn.), the majority whip; Thomas Kuchel (R., Calif.), the minority whip; Michael J. "Mike" Mansfield (D., Mont.), the majority leader; Richard Russell (D., Ga.), Chairman of the Armed Services Committee; Leverett Saltonstall (R., Mass.), the ranking minority member of the Armed Services Committee; and George A. Smathers (D., Fla.), a good friend of Kennedy's and a person, obviously, with strong interest in Cuba. Members of the House included Hale Boggs (D., La.), the Democratic whip; Charles A. Halleck (R., Ind.), the minority leader; John Taber (R., N.Y.), the ranking minority member of the Appropriations Committee; and Carl Vinson (D., Ga.), Chairman of the Armed Services Committee. John McCormack (D., Mass.), who had become Speaker of the House in November 1961, following the death of Sam Rayburn, was listed as among those present but said nothing.

Those to whom Kennedy would listen most intently were Russell, Mansfield, Fulbright, Vinson, Dirksen, and perhaps Halleck. Though Russell's power was waning, largely because of his adamant opposition to almost any civil rights legislation, he remained the single most influential member of the Senate. His judgment carried great weight with the whole bloc of Southern Democrats and with Republicans as well. Mansfield was also respected by a large number of fellow Senators. On foreign policy issues, Fulbright's voice in the Senate was second only to Russell's. Only later would he acquire a reputation as a maverick, and Kennedy had wanted him as Secretary of State but had passed him by because of his open support for racial segregation. "Uncle Carl" Vinson had the dominant voice in the House on defense programs. Also, he and Russell worked closely together. Dirksen and Halleck not only enjoyed influence with fellow Republicans in Congress but regularly appeared on television to state party policy. Because of Dirksen's distinctive bass voice, delivery in the manner of a Shakespearean actor, and talent for producing quotable comments, this so-called "Ev and Charlie" show drew a large audience.

All these Senators and members of the House knew that something grave was happening. They also knew the President was scheduled to give a nationally televised speech. But beyond that, they had been left, until this moment, with rumors or more or less educated guesses.

Though Kennedy knew precisely what he intended to say to the nation, he needed to approach the congressional leaders as if seeking their wisdom, not just reading them a lesson. This was not easy to manage, and the session turned out to be at least as difficult as the one 3 days earlier with the Joint Chiefs.

President Kennedy turned on the tape recorder as the intelligence briefing got underway.

McCone: . . . carrying military personnel not in uniform as well as civilian technicians and military equipment.

At first it was impossible to tell the nature of the military material transported in this unprecedented Soviet supported

. . . . aerial reconnaissance, on . . . , indicated no offensive weapons. And flights scheduled for September the 17th and September the 22nd aborted because of weather. Flights in late September and early October gave us added information on the surface-to-air defense installations but did not reveal the offensive missiles or sites.

On October the 14th, we received unmistakable proof of the beginning of the installation of offensive missile sites, that is, a flight on October the 14th, the results of which were obtained a day or so later. Since then, during the past week, the deployment of missiles and missile equipment has continued, and the construction of missile base complexes has proceeded in an urgent, highly secretive manner.

The deployment is continuing. There are now 25 Soviet-bloc ships on their way to Cuba. There are 18 Soviet-bloc ships in Cuban ports. There are 15 on their return voyage. Some ships have made 2 or 3 shuttle trips back and forth. About 175 Soviet-bloc shipments to Cuba have been made since mid-July.

What we have seen to date, either completed or under construction in Cuba, are 24 missile-launcher positions for medium-range ballistic missiles of a range of 1,020 miles located at 6 base complexes, and 12 launch pads for intermediate-range ballistic missiles of 2,200 miles located at 3 bases. A total of 36 launchers at 9 separate bases. Missiles in these categories are capable of delivering warheads in the megaton range [of explosive yield]. We expect deployment of 2 missiles per launch position, although to date we have actually seen about 30 medium-range missiles. We have not yet seen any intermediate-range missiles, although they may be in Cuba under cover, or on the ship *Poltava,* which is due to arrive in Cuba in about 5 days and is peculiarly arranged for the carrying of long cylindrical items and cargo.

The sites are in varying degrees of operational readiness. On the basis of latest evidence, we now believe 4 MRBM sites containing 16 launchers are in full operational readiness as of October the 22nd. We now estimate the remaining 2 MRBM sites containing 8 additional launchers will come into full operational readiness on the 25th and 29th of October, respectively.

Dirksen: Eight?

McCone: Eight more, yeah.

The building of these MRBM sites is a rather simple operation and is accomplished in a week to 10 days' time. These MRBMs are considered mobile. They are fired from a trailer-bed type launcher, and their location as now established might suddenly shift to a new location difficult to determine by surveillance methods.

The 3 IRBM sites containing 12 launch pads still seem likely not to reach full operational readiness until December. However, emergency operational readiness for firing some of the IRBM missiles might be reached somewhat earlier.

In addition, there are 24 primary surface-to-air missile sites in Cuba, of which we believe 22 are now operational. There are also, we believe, 3 coastal-defense missile installations with surface-to-surface cruise missiles of about 40-mile range, and 12 missile-launching patrol craft, each craft capable of carrying 2 surface-to-surface missiles with an effective range of 10 to 15 miles.

Finally, we know that about 40 MiG-21s, an advanced-model Soviet supersonic interceptor aircraft, and 20 IL-28s, a Soviet jet bomber with a range of about 1,500 miles, have been delivered to Cuba.

Amid all of this buildup of military strength, evidence of the presence of nuclear warheads has been carefully sought, needless to say. We have found 1 and possibly 3 of what appear to be nuclear-weapon storage sites. We cannot produce evidence to show that nuclear warheads for these missiles are in Cuba, but we are afraid firm evidence on this point may never become available from intelligence resources at our command. The warheads could be in Cuba, in concealment or temporary storage, without our discovering them. Nevertheless, since the medium-range and intermediate-range ballistic missiles are relatively ineffective weapons without nuclear warheads, we think it prudent to assume that nuclear weapons are now or shortly will be available in Cuba.

Mr. Lundahl is here, and he has some of these photographs, and, with your permission, Mr. President, I'd like to display them.

Lundahl: Mr. President, gentlemen, I would seek to very briefly summarize in graphic form the statistics which Mr. McCone has shown to you.

Starting from the west end of the Cuban island the medium-range ballistic-missile launching sites are at the following positions: MR-1, MR-2, MR-3, MR-6, which was discovered later, MR-4, and MR-5. These missiles shoot over a thousand miles, are mobile, rapidly put into position and fired from launch erectors. After we've summarized the graphic [...] show you

[...] to radii circles drawn over [United States].

In addition, there is sited for you surface-to-air missiles, which were the first of the defensive forces being built up in Cuba. These are symbolized by the black dots that go completely around the perimeter of Cuba at these locations shown, a total of 24 of them at the present time, 6 missiles in each position, high-altitude firing. Of these 24, 22 are operational right now. In addition, we found at this point on the coast at Banes, where the red triangle is shown, and then again at Santa Cruz del Norte, and here, and then again at the Island of Pines, cruise missiles, short and stubby-winged missiles which are primarily used in attacks against shipping, short-range, 30-odd-mile type of affair.

In addition to that, in the center of the island, at Santa Clara airfield, we have found approximately—exactly—so far 39 MiG-21s, which are the equivalent of our F-106s. We call them "Fishbeds," or delta-winged fighters. Very, very high-performing aircraft.

In addition to that, at the far end of the island, at San Julian airfield we have found unloading, at the present time, IL-28 aircraft, Soviet designated "Beagle," jetlike bombers. We, I think, must assume that all 21 of those crates is going to divulge one of these craft, but as of the last date of our coverage a few days ago, just one of them had been assembled. The fuselages for 3 or 4 were being put together and the other crates were being emptied at that time.

We have also found at the locations where the arrows are shown, the red arrow here, and the red arrow here, what look like good possibilities for nuclear weapons type of storage sites. And I will seek to show you, in the few minutes that we have, some of the buildup at least as is supported by the photographic evidence at hand.

If I may drop this one down—may I make one more remark, Mr. McCone? I forgot it—Mariel port here. We have found something new: guided-missile-configured PT boats with 2 launchers on the aft end of each of these craft, firing forward. This is an antishipping type of device. A total of 12 of these KOMAR class guided-missile-configured PT boats.[2]

If I drop these down, I will seek now to show you, in briefest of terms here, what these things look like, starting first off with the most significant items: intermediate-range ballistic missiles. This is one—the IR-1 site over here. These are the pads. They are elongated scraped-out areas with control bunkers between each. The cables go from the control bunkers to the edges of the pads, where there are small buildings on the inboard side. Another pair of pads over here, with the control bunker between them and the cables going to the inboard side. These are 750 feet apart [8 seconds excised as classified information]. Most significantly, the axis of these long pads is on a bearing of 3-1-5 [315 degrees], which brings you from this area straight up the middle part of the United States.

Right at the eastern part of this particular area, I would cite for your attention a security-fence arrangement where we think one of the possible nuclear-storage sites exist. They are producing concrete in arches for mounding of structures probably to go underground. We have one good-sized building partially mounded already, 114 by 60 feet, at this location here. The security fencing comes around on this side, work is going on, lots of construction material and mobile [vehicles] here and there. A good possibility right next to an IRBM launching site.

If I drop this one down, I would like to show you one of the—this is the second IRBM site. This first one was in the mid-stage of construction, this second one is slightly slower. You can see the long bearings to the scratches, three of them clearly here, the fourth one coming in, the control bunker between the two of them and the bearing, again, 3-1-5. The second site is 2½ miles away from the first site. This is in the early stage of construction. The other one I showed you was in the mid-stage of construction.

2. The KOMARs were 83-foot-long patrol boats, each with 2 canisters firing 15-mile-range radar-guided SS-N-2 (STYX) cruise missiles. See Dino A. Brugioni, *Eyeball to Eyeball: The Inside Story of the Cuban Missile Crisis*, ed. Robert F. McCort (New York: Random House, 1991), p. 388.

Next, if I might, Mr. President, I would seek to show an example of what the third IRBM site looks like, which was farther down the coast at a place called Remedios. This is, again, in an early stage of construction. But the launch pads are here and here and here and here, the control bunkers between each, the cables going out to each and, again, the bearing of the long axis 3-1-5. Arched-roof buildings going in close by, possibly additional storage, tents where Soviet-type troops live, vehicles, and another concrete-batch plant to make the arches and construction materials to support this particular b...

Coming on down to our next...

...feet. There are guard tents around ...ere and additional mobile equipment. A strong suggestion as a possible nuclear-storage site.

I would like to show you an example or two of the medium-range ballistic-missile launching sites—if you could get one for me, Ray [Cline]. First off, while we're getting that out, I would like to show you the MiG-21 buildup. This is shown here at the center at Santa Clara airfield, which is 10,400 feet long and here 16 "Fishbeds" in this locale, 12 "Fishbeds" in here. Those are the MiG-21s, 11 more over here, a total of 39, and some 15 MiG-15 [and] -17s as well. The field is well developed, and the craft are flying. We have seen some in operation taking off of the field during the course of our operation.

We have also gathered information about the jetlike bombers to which Mr. McCone referred. This is at the westernmost tip of the island, at a place called San Julian. This field has been not used for over a year. It has been barricaded with rock piles stretching across. These have been cleared away and at this edge of the tarmac—enlarged for your attention down here—are these crates which are being unloaded. There are 17 crates in here standing side by side and 4 that are starting to be unloaded, and one of the aircraft has come into full form, and it is indeed an IL-28 jetlike bomber.

We have several MRBM sites which I think would be interesting to show you. This is MR-3, which is one of the 3 at the western end of the island. These are slightly different from the ones we have shown you before. We have missile erectors, vehicles, buildings, missile erectors over in here, new buildings under construction, concrete arches. The whole place in a few days has seen the extensions of the military personnel, vehicles, and construction equipment and leaves little doubt in our mind to the fact that this is what we feel conforms to the MRBM launching site.

We have, in addition, enlarged for you, at MR site number 1 at 3 different scales of enlargement—10 times, 20 times, and 30 times—the missiles themselves. There are 7 missiles aligned side by side this carrier here. I think you can see the missiles. They are cylindrical. They are approximately 65 feet long. They are blunt-ended because the canvas hangs over them, which implies that the conical-shape warhead, the nose cone, when put on to the front would add another 6 or 7 feet to bring it up to some 72 feet, which conforms to the SS-4 "Sandal," which is the 1,000-mile missile. We've seen this kind of missile carried through the streets of Moscow on the May Day parade. We have said, as Mr. McCone pointed out to you, there are something in the vicinity of 24 of these missiles lying around at separate MR bases to which we have referred.

Here is the case, down the point, at MR-2, a few miles away again, we have 6 missiles. They have canvas or netting stretched over the top of them and missile erectors beside them. These missiles are carried into position. The erector launches it directly at the point where the vehicle stops, and it is prepared to fire right then at that point. Little preparation, just hard ground, flat and clear. They are wheeled into position, and they are ready to fire within 6 to 8 hours.

We have dozens and dozens of other examples. But if I've made the point with you that the facts that have been drawn on this chart are backed up by photographic data, that there is no doubt in our mind of our identification, I think I will have accomplished my point, Mr. President.

President Kennedy: Are there any questions?

Fulbright?: What's the radius of the IL-28?

Lundahl: 1,500 miles, sir.

McCone: That's range, sir.

Lundahl: Range. Radius is 750.

Fulbright?: Do they carry atomic weapons, bombs?

Lundahl: They certainly can.

McCone: Yes, they can carry them—atomic bombs. About 4,000 kilotons [yield].

Russell: I understood there was some discussion about that intermediate missile. Some of our people think that missile can shoot 1,700 miles, don't they?

McCone: 2,200, the IR—the intermediate—

Russell: When you're talking about 1,000, I thought the minimum that we put them, that missile, back when you was putting it in Russia was 1,100, and some people thought it was good to have a range of 1,700. This is the one that's wheeled up on the truck.

Cline: I have an intelligence report that puts it at 1,020 miles, nautical miles.

Russell: I beg your pardon?

Cline: 1,020 nautical miles is what the general agreement—

Russell: Oh, that. Nautical miles. That's considerable [unclear]. 1,100 is statute miles.

Unidentified: Yes.

. . . . missile parade. This is the . . . . . which has been identified on the ground in Cuba.

McCone: I have only one thing to add, Mr. President. And that is from a variety of intelligence sources we have concluded that these bases, both the ground-to-air SAM sites as well as the missile sites, are manned by Soviets and, for the most part, put the Soviet guards to keep the Cubans out. We don't think that there are very many Cubans on these things.

Russell: Mr. McCone, one question. I am sure you are monitoring this. Do you think that they have in their complex any electronics installed yet?

McCone: We do on the MRBMs, the more advanced. We do, yes.

Russell: Is that true as to the surface-to-air sites?

McCone: Yes. On the surface-to-air we have found that their radar have been latching on to our U-2s the last couple of days, and, while they have not fired a missile at us, we think that they will within a short time.

Kushel: My God. Are those pictures taken with a U-2?

McCone: They are taken with a U-2. And, Mr. President, I would just like to say for the advantage of . . . Everybody here knows we have briefed a number of people. We're just referring these to pictures taken from military reconnaissance planes. We're making no reference to the U-2s involved.

President Kennedy: Another thing is the numbers. We're not using the precise numbers.

McCone: Yeah, we're not using the precise numbers publicly, nor are we making any reference to the U-2s' military reconnaissance.

That's all I have.

Kuchel: May I ask, Mr. President, as to the timetable of your estimates, now, when they could really mount an extensive attack against the United States. I mean, I know some of the missiles are ready to go—

President Kennedy: Mr. McCone will respond to that.

Kuchel: —6 weeks, 5 weeks, 3 months, 2 months, one month?

McCone: Yes, sir. We think at the present time they have 2 [to] 3 of their MRBMs in place, which would mean 16 launchers ready to go at the present time. We think that 2 more will be operational by the end of this month. So that you could say, by October 30th there'll be 5, and 4 will be 20 launchers in place. We think the 8—or 12, rather—IRBMs will come into operational status in December with the possibility that some of the pads might be operational a couple of weeks in advance of that.

Now, we do not know the condition of the warheads, because we are unable to detect that with photography. We have no clandestine sources on the warheads.

Kuchel: Wouldn't that be suicide if they did that?

McCone: Yes, it would be suicide, but—

Kuchel: All right—because we could try to respond.

Rusk: As part of the general nuclear exchange. That would be in part of the general nuclear exchange.

Kuchel: Is there any intelligence tie-up or information that indicate that this particular culmination in Cuba is associated with the Chinese operation against India as a basic worldwide movement?

McCone: No, we have no information whatsoever with respect to that at all.

President Kennedy: Perhaps a word from Ambassador Thompson. He has had a lot of conversations with Khrushchev. Perhaps you might wish to say something about evaluation of his purposes.

Thompson: Mr. President, I had a talk with Khrushchev at the end of July. He made very clear that he was . . . He gave an indication that time was running out on his going any further on the Berlin issue. And that at the same time he felt that he had gone too far in to go back, and he was concerned that if he went forward, he would either lose or start a war.

It also seems subsequently that his timing—his indication was that he didn't want to talk until the end of November—was related to this buildup. Of course, the concern is then that—what would you do about it is to . . . The effect on our lives is that if, in fact, one of his purposes, or a main one, was the showdown on Berlin. In my view that's the main thing that he had in mind.

Russell: I'm sorry, I didn't get that last.

Thompson: That that was the main thing he had in mind. The purpose was to have a showdown on Berlin and he thought this would help him in that.

Russell: You mean the buildup in Cuba?

Thompson: Mm-hmm [agreeing].

Saltonstall: Mr. President, Mr. Thompson, then you tie this, what we've just heard, into Berlin?

Thompson: That's correct.

Rusk: Mr. President, I would like to make one or two comments if I because I think that this does mean a major and and Soviet action. This is the f outside of th

ished with Soviet

ize that this is the most major development from the Soviet point of view since the Berlin blockade of 1947 and '48 [actually 1948–49]. Why they choose to pursue such a reckless and hazardous approach to this client is just speculation. This has both military and, of course, political ramifications.

But I think we ought not, in any sense, to underestimate the gravity of this development in terms of what it means to the Soviet point of view. They are taking risks here which are very heavy indeed and—

Russell: Very heavy what?

Rusk: Risks which are very heavy indeed.

I think, I think, there is real reason to think there has been quite a debate going on in the Soviet Union about the course of action. The peaceful-coexistence theme was not getting them very far, and maybe—it seems clear now that the hard-line boys have moved into the ascendancy. So one of the things that we have to be concerned about is not just the missiles, but the entire development of Soviet policy as it affects our situation around the globe.

Russell: Mr. Secretary, do you see any off chance that it'll get any better? That they'll keep on establishing new bases and dividing our space. How can we gain by waiting?

Rusk: I'm not suggesting that it'll get any better.

President Kennedy: As I say, this information became available Tuesday morning. Mobile bases can be moved very quickly, so we don't know, [but] we assume we have all the ones that are there now. But the CIA thinks there may be a number of others that are there on the island and have not been set up which can be set up quite quickly because of the mobility.

Intermediate-range ballistic missiles, of course, because of its nature, can take a longer time. We'll be able to spot those. The others might be set up in the space of a very few days.

Beginning Tuesday morning after we saw these first ones, we ordered intensive surveillance of the island, a number of U-2 flights until Wednesday and Thursday. I talked with—asked Mr. McCone to go up and brief General Eisenhower on Wednesday [October 17].

We decided, the Vice President and I, to continue our travels around the country in order not to alert this—until we had gotten all the available information we could. The last information came in on Sunday morning giving us this last site [Remedios IRBM site] which we mentioned.

We are presented with a very, very difficult problem because of Berlin as well as other reasons, but mostly because of Berlin, which is rather . . . The advantage is, from Khrushchev's point of view, he takes a great chance but there are quite some rewards to it. If we move into Cuba, he sees the difficulty I think we face. If we invade Cuba, we have a chance that these missiles will be fired on us.

In addition, Khrushchev will seize Berlin and that Europe will regard Berlin's loss, which attaches such symbolic importance to Berlin, as having been the fault of the United States by acting in a precipitous way. After all, they are 5 or 6,000 miles from Cuba and much closer to the Soviet Union. So these missiles don't bother them, and maybe they should think they should not bother us.

So that whatever we do in regard to Cuba, it gives him the chance to do the same with regard to Berlin. On the other hand, to not do anything but argue that these missile bases really extend only what we had to live under for a number of years—from submarines which are getting more and more intense, from the Soviet intercontinental ballistic missile system, which is in a rapid buildup [and] has a good deal of destruction which it could bring on us, as well as their bombers—that this adds to our hazards but does not create a new military hazard. And that we should keep our eye on the main site, which would be Berlin.

Our feeling, however, is that that would be a mistake. So that, beginning tonight, we're going to blockade Cuba, carrying out the [action] under the Rio Treaty. We called for a meeting of the Rio Pact countries and hope to get a two-thirds vote from them to give the blockade legality. If we don't get it, then we'll have to carry it out illegally or under declaration of war, which is not as advantageous to us.

Dirksen: Now, we don't know if Khrushchev would respond to a complete blockade?

President Kennedy: A blockade as it will be announced will be for the movement of weapons into Cuba. But we don't know what the [Soviet-]bloc ships will do. In order not to give Khrushchev the justification for imp... complete blockade on Berlin ...

... the days go on to other—petroleum, ..., lubricants and other matters, except food and medicine. These are matters we will reach a judgment on as the days go on.

Now, in the meanwhile, we are making the military preparations with regard to Cuba so that if the situation deteriorates further, we will have the flexibility. Though the invasion is—the only way to get rid of these weapons is—the only other way to get rid of them is if they're fired, so that we're going to have to, it seems to me, watch with great care.

I say if we invade Cuba, there's a chance that these weapons will be fired at the United States. If we attempt to strike them from the air, then we will try to get them all, because they're mobile. And we know where the sites are, inasmuch as we can destroy the sites. But they can move them and set them up in another 3 days someplace else, so that we have not got a very easy situation.

There's a choice between doing nothing if we felt that that would compel Berlin rather than help [unclear] compel Latin America. So after a good deal of searching we decided this was the place to start. I don't know what their response would be. We've got two, three, four problems. One will be if we continue to surveil them and they shoot down one of our planes. We then have the problem of taking action against part of Cuba.

So I think that—I'm going to ask Secretary McNamara to detail what we're doing militarily—if there's any strong disagreement in what at least we set out to do, I want to hear it. Otherwise, I think what we ought to do is try to keep in very close contact before anything gets done of a major kind differently, and it may have to be done in the next 24 to 48 hours, because I assume the Soviet response will be very strong and we'll all meet again. Needless to say, the Vice President and I have concluded our campaigning.

Fulbright?: Mr. President, do I understand that you have decided, and will announce tonight, the blockade?

President Kennedy: That's right. The quarantine.

Rusk: Mr. President, may I add one point to what you just said on these matters?

We do think this first step provides a brief pause for the people on the other side to have another thought before we get into an utterly crashing crisis, because the prospects ahead of us at this moment are very serious. Now, if the Soviets have underestimated what the United States is likely to do here, then they've got to consider whether they revise their judgment quick and fast.

The same thing with respect to the Cubans. Quite apart from the OAS and the UN aspects of it, a brief pause here is very important in order to give the Soviets a chance to pull back from the frontier. I do want to say, Mr. President, I think the prospects here for a rapid development of the situation can be a very grave matter indeed.

Russell: Mr. President, I could not space out under these circumstances and live with myself. I think that our responsibilities are quite immense, and stronger steps than that in view of this buildup there, and I must say that in all honesty to myself.

I don't see how we are going to get any stronger or get in any better position to meet this threat. It seems to me that we are at a crossroads. We're either a first-class power or we're not. You have warned these people time and again, in the most eloquent speeches I have read since Woodrow Wilson, that's what would happen if there was an offensive capability created in Cuba. They can't say they're not on notice.

The Secretary of State says: "Give them time to pause and think." They'll use that time to pause and think, to get better prepared. And if we temporize with this situation, I don't see how we can ever hope to find a place where . . .

Why, we have a complete justification by law for carrying out the announced foreign policy of the United States that you have announced time—that if there was an offensive capability there, that we would take any steps necessary to see that certain things should stop transit. They can stop transit, for example, though, in the Windward Passage and the Leeward Passage, easily with the nuclear missiles and with these ships. They could blow Guantanamo off the map. And you have told them not to do this thing. They've done it. And I think that we should assemble as speedily as possible an adequate force and clean out that situation.

The time is going to come, Mr. President, when we're going to have to take this step in Berlin and Korea and Washington, D.C., and Winder, Georgia, for the nuclear war. I don't know whether Khrushchev will launch a nuclear war over Cuba or not. I don't believe he will. But I think that the more that we temporize, the more surely he is to convince himself that we are afraid to make any real movement and to really fight.

President Kennedy: ...

... to start those operations. They'll become effective as promptly as the initial political moves are completed. Sometime tomorrow or the next day.

Our orders are to hail the incoming vessels, both Soviet and non-Soviet, surface and submerged, to stop them, to search them, to divert those carrying designated goods, offensive weapons initially, to ports of their choosing. If they refuse to stop, to disable them and then to take them in as prizes.

This operation, obviously, is going to lead to the application of military force. It is entirely probable that the first ship, first Soviet ship hailed, will attempt to penetrate the quarantine, in which case Admiral Dennison has orders to disable the ship, reducing the damage to the minimum for that purpose, but sinking it if necessary.

Halleck?: Mr. Secretary, may I just interrupt to ask if taking a ship into custody, would that include the seizure or the destruction of offensive weapons found on board the ship? Or would the weapons on board the ship accompany the ship into quarantine?

McNamara: It depends on the character of the weapon. If there is any danger associated with moving the weapon in a prize to port, it would be destroyed at sea.

During this period, we will provide air cover over the sea-lanes used by U.S. merchant ships in and around Cuba. It's entirely possible that during this period the MiG-15s, -17s, and -19s, which weren't discussed today but of which there are substantial numbers in Cuba, or the MiG-21s, will attack certain U.S.

merchant ships. Admiral Dennison has been instructed to provide cover to our ships; in the event attacks take place, to destroy the attacking aircraft.

Further, we will continue air surveillance over the island of Cuba. As Mr. McCone pointed out, approximately 22 of the 24 surface-to-air missiles sites appear to be operational. They have launched aircraft, by direction of those sites, against the U-2s in the last 2 or 3 days. None have successfully conducted an attack on the U-2s. Undoubtedly a successful attack will take place in the future. When that does, our aircraft are instructed to attack the attacking aircraft with a strike.

We will redeploy our air-defense forces within this country to better protect the southeastern coast of the country. We have reinforced Guantanamo with several additional units of Marines; about 7,000 additional men have been placed in there in the last several days. We have today evacuated the dependents from Guantanamo.

We have placed SAC on a one-eighth airborne alert starting this morning that will be completed, and we will have one-eighth of SAC on an airborne alert 24 hours a day within about 28 hours from early this morning.[3]

We have been asked by the President to be prepared for any eventuality, and for that purpose we are moving troops and aircraft to positions from which further deployments can be made in the future.

Mr. President, I have summarized the moves we have made.

Russell: Mr. President, I don't want to make a nuisance of myself, but I would like to complete my statement.

My position is that these people have been warned. They've had all the warning they could expect, and our Secretary of State speaks about the pause. When you enforce this blockade, Khrushchev's never said up until now that he would fight over Cuba. He even goes as far as rattling his missiles, and making firmer and firmer and firmer statements about what he's going to do about Cuba. And you are only making sure that when that day comes, when if they do use these MiGs to attack our shipping or drop a few bombs around Miami or some other place, and we do go in there, that we'll lose a great many more men than we would right now and—

President Kennedy: But, Senator, we can't invade Cuba versus . . . The case was somehow to assemble our force to invade Cuba. That's one of the problems we've got, we have, in order to surface the movement of troops beyond what

---

3. This meant that one-eighth of all U.S. strategic nuclear bombers would be in the air at any given moment, immune from an attack against their airfields, loaded with nuclear weapons, and able to move against their targets in the Soviet bloc.

has been surfaced in the last 48 hours. But we have to bring some troops from the West Coast, and to assemble the force which would give us the 90,000-odd men who might participate in an invasion will take some days. That's why I wanted Secretary McNamara . . . We are now assembling that force, but it is not in a position to invade Cuba in the next 24 to 48 hours.

Now, I think it may very well come to that before the end of the week. But we are moving all of the forces that we have, that will be necessary for an invasion, to the area around Cuba as quickly as we possibly can—

Russell: I think if it . . .

President Kennedy: But Secretary McNamara can say we just don't have forces ready.

Russell: This blockade is going to put them on the alert. It's going to give the Russians . . . Khrushchev will be making incendiary statements, and he'll get worse everywhere he goes and making more and more sure that, when we are forced to take action in Cuba, that we will still have to further divide our forces and be weaker at every point around the whole periphery of the free world.

President Kennedy: Well, Senator, Secretary McNamara described our military problem, and maybe we can see what—

Halleck?: I just want to reminisce just a little bit. We were here in April. We were told by somebody in the Pentagon sitting right over there that it would take us 3 months to take Cuba. Am I right about that?

President Kennedy: Mr. McNamara, why don't you make a statement.

McNamara: Let me make a statement and perhaps I can throw some light on that.

To carry out an invasion against the substantial buildup that has taken place in Cuba would require use of about 250,000 U.S. military personnel. That figure includes air, sea, and ground personnel. The invasion force itself, excluding reserve forces that would have to be available, would be on the order of 90,000, depending upon exactly how it was done, what portion would be airborne, air-dropped, and what portion would be sea-landed. The force would require the gathering together of over 100 merchant ships. It requires the call-up from the reserves of C-119 squadrons. Several hundred aircraft must be assembled for that purpose, in addition to the aircraft on active duty. It requires the movement into the ports, as the President indicated, of units of the West Coast, both Army units which will move across the country with their equipment by rail and Marine units which will move by sea from [Camp] Pendleton and which will be part of the potential invasion force. These movements have started, will essentially not be started, however, prior to a certain point ahead of the time that it became possible to surface this operation.

We can be prepared within 7 days to start an invasion. It's quite clear that that invasion must be preceded by a substantial air attack. I'll mention the figure, I know that I can count on you to keep it in confidence. At least 2,000 bombing sorties must take place prior to the invasion. There are about 8 to 10,000 Soviet personnel, probably military personnel, known as technicians but undoubtedly military personnel, on the island at the present time maintaining the missile bases that were discussed and the surface-to-air missile sites.

Vinson?: Bombing sorties with what kind of bombs?

McNamara: Initially iron bombs.

The plans for invasion have been laid out in great detail. The movements preparatory thereto have been started with the direction of the President, and, as I said, it will take at least 7 days to carry out the air strikes necessary to introduce these things.

Russell: Do you see from your position in the Pentagon where we're getting better prepared militarily vis-à-vis the Soviet forces by delaying and waiting—putting this thing over till next year?

You put these tired old B-45s, -47s, or B-49s, whatever they are—

McNamara: -47s.

Russell: -47s—all of them already wore out, now, you put them on 24-hour alert, and that's most of our force. That's three-fourths of it, remember. Over two-thirds.[4] You have [unclear]; you don't have anything. And you just can't depend on these missiles, our missiles. Our intermediate missiles won't intercept. But you think they're running in our favor?

McNamara: I do.

Russell: What do you base that on?

McNamara: The B-47s and B-52s we have prepared for airborne alert by procuring, as you know, the additional spares necessary to support an airborne alert. I have no doubt whatsoever that we can maintain an airborne alert

---

4. The aging medium-range B-47 bombers still made up the bulk of the aircraft in Strategic Air Command. They were being replaced by the newer intercontinental-range B-52.

indefinitely without degrading our force. And this opinion is shared by General LeMay.

I have no question but what with a blockade we can not only stop but eventually attrit, stop the buildup but also attrit the Cuban force, and do this as the President directs. Moreover, we must have the 7-day period of preparation for an invasion.

Russell: Well, can you tell me when you first got these notifications [about the missiles]—first got them out? You said over 7 days.

McNamara: First notification came in T····· been intensive review d···· far f·

·_·. ιι s

·· ..ιucn as we have without

·· ινιι. Secretary, do the Joint Chiefs of Staff approve of all the plans with reference to the invasion, if it gets—

McNamara: Yes, sir. The President ordered us to prepare an invasion of Cuba months ago. I think it was—Mr. President, perhaps you recall better than I, but I believe it was November of last year. And we have developed plans in great detail. We've developed a series of alternative plans, several of them. We've reviewed them with the President over the past 10 months on 5 different occasions. We're well prepared for an invasion—as well prepared as we could possibly be, facing the situation we do.

I think it's quite remarkable, startlingly so, as a matter of fact, that we can consider an invasion with 7 days' preparation. No invasion of this size, that any of my military staff can recall, has ever been prepared with no more than a 7-day lead time.

Dirksen: Does this have the approval of the National Security Council?

McNamara: Yes. The plans? Yes.

Dirksen: Were they unanimous?

President Kennedy: We met yesterday . . . Let me just say, Senator [Russell], I understand your . . . There's two or three points.

In the first place, in order to invade Cuba as we attempt this buildup of force, one of the reasons why we've been concerned this week is we wanted to know all the sites. We wanted to know the firing position of these missiles.

If we go into Cuba we have to all realize that we are taking a chance that these missiles, which are ready to fire, won't be fired. So that's a gamble we should take. In any case we are prepared to take it. The fact is that that is one hell of a gamble, but I think that we're going to have to assume that. Because we've finally decided that [if] we're going to do it, we want to have everybody in this room in here with us so we all decide this thing together. But that's going to have to be the judgment.

In the meanwhile, we are going to move all of the available forces that we have to be in a position to carry out this invasion as quickly as we possibly can. But the key question is going to be, and we all ought to be thinking about it in the next 48 hours, is two or three key questions. In the first place, if the Russians as a response . . .

We just have this report.[5] "[9 seconds excised as classified information.] The Soviets expect to call a certain [United Nations] Security Council meeting for the 23rd or -4th of October and expect the President to announce tonight a blockade of Cuba. [1 second excised as classified information] They do not expect this blockade to include Russian ships, because this would mean war. There has been unusual activity all day long on the part of the Russian and Cuban delegations and the rest of the Soviet"—et cetera, et cetera . . .

So, we may have the war in the next 24 hours.

What I want to say is we are going to move, with maximum speed, all of our forces to be in a position to invade Cuba within the 7-day period. Number One.

Number Two. This group will meet in the next 48 hours, probably ought to come back again to see where we stand 2 days from now and make a judgment as to whether we should take that risk of going in there, under the conditions we have described.

Number Three. We have the prospect, if the Soviet Union, as a reprisal, should grab Berlin in the morning, which they could do within a couple of hours. Our war plan at that point has been to fire our nuclear weapons at them. But these are all the matters which are—which we have to think about.

Russell: Excuse me again, but do you see a time ever in the future when Berlin will not be hostage to this?

President Kennedy: No, I think Berlin is—

Russell: Depending on what they do down there, whether they fire on us or not. Berlin will be hostage to these same circumstances.

---

5. McCone's notes from this meeting mention that President Kennedy "read an intelligence note from a United Nations source"; McCone to File, "Leadership Meeting on October 22nd at 5:00 P.M.," 24 October 1962, in McAuliffe, *CIA Documents,* p. 277.

President Kennedy: No doubt. There is no doubt.

Russell: And if we're going to back up on that, we might as well pull our armies in from Europe and save 15 to 25 billion dollars a year and just defend this continent. We've got to take a chance somewhere, sometime, if we're going to retain our position as a great world power and . . .

You know, General LeMay sat right here the last time we met here—I notice he's not here today, I don't believe he is—and said that he could get in under this radar and knock out all these installations. I didn't hardly think he could at that time, but he said . . .

. . . the reasons why this matter has been held up.

The difficulty with that is, we're not sure of getting them all. We don't know what the orders are. If there was a second strike on Turkey or Italy, where we've got missile bases, the commanders might fire. They might think that it was part of a general attack. We're not sure of getting them all.

In addition, there are at least as many which are still probably in trailers, we figure, and not at the site. So that you would do the Pearl Harbor attack and you'd only get half . . . [tape interrupted] . . . hasn't had at all, the chance somebody's going to blow that button.

Russell: You said after the Cuban on October—I recall it very well because I heard it over the radio—that you hoped that the Organization of American States would stand up with us to meet this finish but that, if it didn't, that we would undertake it alone. Now I understand that we [are] still waiting while the Secretary of State tries to get them to agree to it.

President Kennedy: I'm not waiting.

Russell: I think we can [unclear] from here. I'm through. Excuse me. I would have been arguing with myself . . . So I hope you forgive me, but you asked for opinion—

President Kennedy: No, I did ask for opinions. But it's a very difficult problem that we're faced with. I'll just tell you that. It's a very difficult choice that we're faced with together. Now, the—

Russell: Oh, my God, I know that. A war, our destiny, will hinge on it. But it's coming someday, Mr. President. Will it ever be under more auspicious circumstances? We've got this little war over here now between China and India that they may clean up tomorrow except . . . Now, that will make a great deal of difference if we moved in down there to clean up Cuba, that war there as far as India and China concerns me, all over the world. I mean, what Russia would do because they are occupied with fighting each other there.

Now, I don't see how we are going to be better off next year, including with the Organization of American States. I assume this blockade will be effective for a while till they make up their minds to try to force their way through.

President Kennedy: Well now, the Organization of American States, quite obviously we'd do better if we'd gotten the other Latin American countries tied in. It's foolish to kick the whole Rio Treaty out the window.

Russell: Well, I don't want to do that.

President Kennedy: We're going to do the blockade in any case, Senator. The legality of the blockade depends—it's a peacetime blockade—upon the endorsement, under the Rio Treaty, of the OAS, which meets tomorrow morning. If they don't give us the 14 votes, the two-thirds vote, then we're going to do it anyway. But in that case we are going to have to have what's legally an illegal blockade or a declaration of war.

Now, we will carry a blockade on in any case. We hope with the endorsement—this will make it in a much more satisfactory position if we had that endorsement. But we're going to do it anyway.

In the meanwhile, we've prepared these troops, and then we'll have to just make the judgment later in the week about what we're going to do about it. I understand the force of your arguments. The only point we all have to consider is, if we invade, we take the risk, which we have to contemplate, that these weapons will be fired.

Humphrey: President, have the—anybody in NATO been—

President Kennedy: Yes, this afternoon have been informed what we are going to do. Mr. Macmillan, of course, they are not very happy. We told General de Gaulle today, the NATO Council, and these will all be done this afternoon. And the Secretary, Mr. Adenauer, was informed about an hour ago. The only one we've heard from is Macmillan.

Fulbright: President, could I ask a question? What was their reaction?

President Kennedy: Well, Macmillan, I don't know whether we've got the cable. I suppose we can get the cable from Mr. Macmillan.

Halleck: Mr. President, when we were here before, I had raised the question about whether this buildup in Cuba was defensive or offensive. At that time it was said it is defensive.

President Kennedy: That's correct.

Halleck: I think Mr. McCone and General Carter [unclear]. Are we absolutely positive from these photos that they're building up now an offensive operation?

President Kennedy: Yes.

Halleck: We're sure of that?

President Kennedy: That's correct.

McNamara: May I say this? You might question the missiles, but you can't question the IL-28s. They have—

Halleck: What are they? What's an IL-28?

McN...

...is certainly offensive. It certainly is, but we can't—we haven't seen it with the warhead actually in place, and you might possibly have some question in your mind about it. But you can't have any question in your mind about the IL-28 bombers. These without any doubt whatsoever are offensive weapons.

McCone: I think the evidence that these are offensive weapons is conclusive, except for the fact that we do not have, which I said, positive knowledge that the warhead is actually there.

Unidentified: Do you have any on-the-ground—

Russell: Is there any missile of that type that used a conventional warhead?

McCone: No. No. None that uses—

[Unclear group conversation.]

Russell: —atomic, wouldn't that be the most difficult thing? You think you could find an atomic warhead from a U-2 even if you could get out to 12–15,000 feet? It wouldn't be very likely, to leave that out exposed in some open place where you could pick up the picture of it.

Fulbright: Mr. President, do you interpret the blockade will be considered by Russia as an act of war?

President Kennedy: Well, that's only this report, they may or may not.

Fulbright: Of course, it takes two parties to determine that. They might say it's not an act of war. But you're basing your whole—

President Kennedy: No. But they may or they may not, or they may then put a blockade on Berlin. That would be—I don't think there is any doubt that they are going to threaten us.

Fulbright: Mr. President.

[Pause.]

President Kennedy: I just, as I say . . .

Gentlemen, this is from the Prime Minister [Macmillan] now. We let him know more in advance because of the security [unclear] they have, sort of. I let him know last night what our information was, and then I sent him over this afternoon the speech. He said there's just—at least he indicated [unclear]. [He begins reading Macmillan's letter.]

Dear Mr. President,

I first want to say I am sorry about the proposed [unclear]. Ambassador [David] Bruce called to see me this morning and gave me evidence of the Soviet buildup in Cuba. I quite understand how fiercely American public opinion will react when it knows these facts. I have, at this moment, received through our teleprinter the text of your proposed declaration tonight. Let me say, first, that we shall of course give all the support we can in the Security Council. I hope that you will provide us immediately with the best legal case that can be made in support of the broad moral position so that our representative can weigh in effectively. Of course the international lawyers will take the point that a blockade which involves the searching of ships of all countries is difficult to defend in peacetime. Indeed quite a lot of controversy has gone on in the past about its use in wartime. However, we must rest not so much on precedent as on the unprecedented condition of the modern world in a nuclear age.

If, as I assume, the Security Council resolution is vetoed the only appeal is to the [General] Assembly. What the result will be there, no one can tell but I doubt whether they will be in favor of any conclusive action or even if they are I do not see how they will enforce it. What I think we must now consider is Khrushchev's likely reaction. He may reply either in words or in kind or both. If he contents himself with the first, he may demand the removal of all American bases in Europe. If he decides to act, he may do so either in the Caribbean or elsewhere. If he reacts in the Caribbean his obvious method would be to escort his ships and force you into the position of attacking them. This fire-first dilemma has always worried us and we have always hoped to impale the Russians on this horn.

President Kennedy: This is in regard to Berlin. [Returning to the letter:]

No doubt you have thought of this but I would be glad to know how you feel it can be handled. Alternatively, he may bring some pressure on the weaker parts of the free world defense system. This may be in Southeast Asia, in Iran, possibly in Turkey, but more likely in Berlin. If he reacts outside the Caribbean—as I fear he may—it will be tempting for him to answer one blockade by declaring another. We must therefore be ready. Any retaliatory action on Berlin as envisaged in the various contingency plans will lead us either to an escalation to world war or to the holding of a conference. What seems to be essential is that you and I should think over and decide in what direction we want to steer things within the Alliance and elsewhere. We should take counsel

. . . conference he will of course try to trade his Cuba position against his ambitions in Berlin and elsewhere. This we must avoid at all costs, as it will endanger the unity of the Alliance.

With warm regard, Harold Macmillan.[6]

Saltonstall: Mr. President, you've twice said that a blockade would be illegal unless the OAS gave us 14 votes. Why is it? My only thought is, why emphasize at all any question of illegality?

President Kennedy: We're not. We can always make it legal, as I say, by declaration of war and, in addition, we will do it anyway. But it would give it a particular sanction if we have the OAS endorsement in the morning. If we don't get it, we'll continue it anyway.

Saltonstall: Well, will they give you—do you think—if they give you the endorsement, we'll have any even nominal assistance from them?

President Kennedy: Well, we're going to try to see if we can get some ships from them. At least joining them.

Saltonstall: My only point—

[Unclear group conversation.]

—Mr. President, whether or not we get the endorsement—

President Kennedy: We have to—well, I've announced the imposition of that. In the speech I'm going to say we're putting in this quarantine and we're

---

6. President Kennedy read the letter without omissions. For a copy of the letter, without the apology in the first line, see London 7396, 22 October 1962, PRO, PREM 11/3689, 24020.

going to say we're going to do it. But we're saying we're also calling them in. Not so that we—

Russell: When will you make this speech, Mr. President?

President Kennedy: 7:00 tonight.

Russell: Oh, tonight.

President Kennedy: Yes.

Dirksen: Generally speaking, Mr. President, what will you cover in the speech?

President Kennedy: I'll cover the description, generally, of this missile buildup.

Dirksen: In detail?

President Kennedy: That's right. Well, not the figures.

I'll discuss the double-dealing of the Russian statements in the past about not moving weapons in there, including Gromyko's statement last Thursday [October 18] to me that they were only defensive. I'll indicate that this is a basic change in Soviet strategy and therefore of very grave importance, and thus the calling of the Rio countries tomorrow morning.

Announce that—what our position's going to be in demanding the removal of these at the UN and telling the Cubans that they've been sold out. And announce that we're going to take other action with regard—to take all other steps to be in position.

We're not going to say anything about invasion. I think it would be a great mistake to talk about invasion, bombers, et cetera. We ought to be assembling. The instructions I've given to Secretary McNamara are to assemble the forces which would be needed in any contingency. I do want to be in a position to do what we have to do, if that's what we do. It seems to me we are better off not to talk about it because we have to have this delay of time. But, as I say, I appreciate the vigor and the strength of what Senator Russell feels and says, and we're going to be all back in this room this week to discuss—

[Unclear group conversation.]

Russell: Mr. President, but I think if Khrushchev ever starts talking around like before he moved in Hungary, that that would start World War III. And I think if we delay here and let him make a great many statements about what he's going to do, and get up a tremendous row in this hemisphere between the nations here, that we'd be much more likely to have to abandon the venture completely, which I greatly fear we will before we're through. Or else we will start a much greater war over the world than we would—

President Kennedy: I understand.

Russell: You know, the right of self-defense is pretty elemental, and you relied on that in that very telling statement you made. You relied on that, the right of self-defense, and that's what we'd be doing.

Smathers?: Senator, if it becomes necessary, in my judgment, to have an invasion, and you have a superior force, then you should apprise the Cuban people, because then they would be anxious to be on the winning side. If they are convinced that you are going to have a speedy victory then they'll lend their support. If they think it's going to be a long-drawn-out fight, you are liable to have many of the people supporting Castro.

Fulbright: Mr. President, one thing . . .

to me . . .

. . . statements they've made . . . I think . . . assume they would not let us build up over a 6-, 7-, or 8-day period an invasion force without making these statements.

In addition, I think the inevitable result would be the immediate seizure of Berlin. It may be anyway.

Fulbright: I don't see a blockade as being . . . It seems to me the alternative is either just to go to the UN and solve without this, or an invasion. A blockade seems to me the worst alternative.

McNamara: Mr. President, may I mention that whether an invasion is a confrontation with the Soviets needs to be considered in light of the fact that it would immediately be preceded by over 2,000 bombing sorties directly against the locations occupied by something on the order of 8,000 Soviet military personnel.

Fulbright: But that's quite different. They're in Cuba. Cuba still is supposed to be a sovereign country. It isn't a member of the Warsaw Pact. It's not even a satellite. It's considered just a Communist country.

Russell: Do you think the number of sorties is going to get lower, or the number of Russians gets fewer?

Fulbright: I don't like the idea of a blockade at all. It seems to me that it complicates the whole thing.

President Kennedy: What are you in favor of, Bill?

Fulbright: I'm in favor, on the basis of this information, of an invasion, and an all-out one, and as quickly as possible.

President Kennedy: Well, now, we've got the 7-day period, as I say.

Fulbright: Well, I just say, I would do nothing until you're ready to invade. A blockade leads into quibbling and delays among our own people, and especially the probability, certainly, of a confrontation with Russia itself. It will give them a better excuse for retaliation than our attack on Cuba.

President Kennedy: The fact is you're not—more confrontation [with] an invasion of Cuba? An attack on these sites with all—

Fulbright: But they're Cuban sites. They're not Russian sites, and a Russian ship is a Russian ship. I mean, if they can save face, they can just forget it. They're over there, I guess, in whatever their capacity is, not part of Russia.

I don't know about a blockade, it's . . . It really leads to a real confrontation with Russian ships and you have to sink a Russian ship. This is a real first shot. You're saying you're evading, under Macmillan's theory. You know, this first-firing point of view with Russia. And you don't do that when you fire on a Russian ship. And you have to do it if you put a blockade in. Then you'll fire the first shot.

But firing against Cuba is not the same as firing against Russia. I don't think a blockade is the right way at all if it's as serious as—and I accept the evidence, I don't question that. It seems to me that the time has now come, under your statement of the 13th of September, for an invasion. You said, if it changes and it's offensive, we'll take what's necessary for our defense. And if I understand it correctly, that means nothing but an invasion. Now, how quick you can do it. Seven days is not too long.

But a blockade seems to me the worst alternative. But I don't see why you can avoid saying an attack on a Russian ship is really an act of war against Russia. It is not an act of war against Russia to attack Cuba.

President Kennedy: Oh, no. If we have the [OAS] endorsement, just to talk about the legalities of it, it isn't an act of war.

Fulbright: It won't be legal—I'm not making the arguments for legal. This is self-defense.

President Kennedy: Let's say we get it legal under the Rio Treaty, and I think we've got a legal right to take the action we have in regard to the shipment of offensive weapons in there.

Now, when you talk about the invasion, the first [point], excluding the risk that these missiles will be fired, we do have the 7 or 8,000 Russians there. We are going to have to shoot them up. And I think that it would be foolish to expect that the Russians would not regard that as a far more direct thrust than they're going to regard on the ships. And I think that the inevitable end result will be the seizure of Berlin.

Now, as I say, we may have to put up with all that and . . . But, I think, if we're talking about nuclear war, the escalation ought to be at least with some degree of control. In addition, we've got this 7-day period. But you can't . . . I don't think in stopping Russian ships—I know that's offensive to the Russians. When you start talking about the invasion it's infinitely more offensive.

Fulbright: But not to the Russians, it seems to me. They have no right to say that. We're [not] going to attack on Russia. I don't think that they have.

Mansfield: I can't quite agree, Bill.

Dirksen: Mr. President, as this thing moves on, and it will take ~~tion, do you contemplate~~

. . . that we ought to go on the assumption that we might meet definitely Thursday, but maybe before if events require it. It's going to take some time to carry out this invasion before the next meeting, and at that time we may want to reach a judgment on that. In the meanwhile, we ought to be assembling all our forces.

Dirksen: Mr. Secretary, how are we equipped with amphibious craft?

Russell: These people are a lot—some of—

Dirksen: How are we equipped with amphibious craft?

McNamara: We increased our amphibious craft by about a third approximately 10 months ago, and we have adequate numbers of amphibious craft for this purpose. We do have to, as I suggested, either charter or requisition over 100 merchantmen. In fact, 70 percent of all the merchantmen in U.S. ports today.

Vinson: Secretary, how long will it take to bring the Marines from Pendleton to the Canal? If you want to talk to that.

McNamara: We're loading the Marines today. It will take about 11 days between the time they leave Pendleton and the time they land in Cuba. They are not in the first wave. We have alternatives—Mr. Chairman, we have alternative plans. Under one plan we go in with a lighter force, a higher percentage airborne. The other plan we go in with a higher percentage seaborne. It's the second plan that uses those Marines. They come in subsequently in the first plan.

Vinson: Don't you think, when the time comes, that you should strike with all the force and power and try to get it over with as quickly as possible, instead of prolonging it, and settle your force? You have two in the Marines now, one on the East Coast, one in the Atlantic and the Pacific. Don't you think, if you strengthen the forces, that you carry enough strength there to win this fight quickly?

McNamara: Either plan, we believe, will lead to a—to victory.

Vinson: I know that—have to wind it up quick.

McNamara: Well, the Chiefs have organized these two in such a way that it's simply a matter of days difference between the two. One provides for a 7-day lead time; the other provides for a somewhat longer lead time. And the choice between the two plans is associated with a requirement for invasion by a particular date following the decision.

Vinson: Your decision, Mr. President, is based on the fact that it's a risk whatever we do, and that you hope, with the risk of a blockade, it's less of a risk than actually an invasion now. And—

President Kennedy: Two things. First, we have to assemble the forces, being an open society, unlike what the Hungarians had [in 1956]. But quite obviously, if we could throw the force to the shore tonight, that would be a different situation. We're going to have the 7 days now to move these forces, and the question of whether we are going to invade is going to be in public speculation. But before we reach the point where we are physically able to do it, we are going to take *this* action.

Now, this action is not quite as hopeless a . . . It provides for the beginning of an escalation. I don't know where Khrushchev wants to take us. We've got this obligation on Berlin, which is a very difficult place for us to defend. He may put in a blockade in Berlin and may grab it, in which case we will be taking action there and also in Cuba.

This is only . . . Let me just say that I said at the beginning that the person whose course of action is not adopted is the best off. Because no matter what you do, we can go in there with an air strike and you can have the United States . . . Some people would say, well, let's go in there with an air strike. You'd have those bombs go off and blow up 15 cities in the United States. And they would have been wrong. We would have—you can go in there and you can not invade and have a worse situation and encourage Khrushchev. You can invade and have those bombs go off and have him also seize Berlin. We have not got . . . The people who are the best off are the people whose advice is not taken because whatever we do is filled with hazards.

Now, the reason we've embarked on the course we have—I'll say this to Senator Fulbright—is because we don't know where we're going to end up on this matter. Ambassador Thompson has felt very strongly that the Soviet Union would regard, will regard the attack on these SAM sites and missile bases with the killing of 4 or 5,000 Russians as a greater provocation than the stopping of their ships. Now, who knows that? We talked to Ambassador Bohlen. We've talked to Ambassador Thompson. We just tried to make a judgment on a matter about which everyone is uncertain. But at least that—at least it's the best advice we could get.

So we start here, we don't know where he's going to take us or wh~~ ~~ going to take ourselves. But Cuba i~ ~~

~~...~~ ~~...~~ at least we start here, then ~~...~~ we go. And I'll tell you that every opportunity is full . . .

I better go and make this speech [on television to the country].

Humphrey: Mr. President, what happens if the UN demands that we come before the UN, and there's a demand for a conference between yourself and Premier Khrushchev, which I think is [unclear] takes place. I think these are the inevitabilities.

President Kennedy: We are asking at the UN for withdrawal of these missiles. Now one point that has made our problem somewhat more complicated is the fact that we sent these missiles over to Turkey and Italy in 1959. So this is going to complicate our posture to the world. It's going to make it more difficult.

Halleck: Mr. President, if I may talk, just one . . .

I didn't know what I was called in for. Happy to come. I'm glad you asked me. I don't have the background information to make these decisions. You do. And I've been glad to speak a piece or two here, but whatever you decide to do . . .

President Kennedy: I appreciate that.

Unidentified: Well, we passed a resolution which shows the position of . . .

President Kennedy then turned off the tape recorder and left the Cabinet Room to prepare to deliver his televised speech, in less than half an hour.

Around the world, all U.S. military forces began executing orders to come to Defense Condition 3. Defense Condition 5 was normal peacetime readiness. Defense Condition 1 was general war. Nuclear submarines began leaving ports; aircraft and troops were on alert around the world.

At 7:00 P.M. Eastern Daylight Time all normal television programming was preempted, and President Kennedy delivered his address to the nation:[7]

Good evening, my fellow citizens. This Government, as promised, has maintained the closest surveillance of the Soviet military build-up on the island of Cuba. Within the past week unmistakable evidence has established the fact that a series of offensive missile sites is now in preparation on that imprisoned island. The purposes of these bases can be none other than to provide a nuclear strike capability against the Western Hemisphere.

Upon receiving the first preliminary hard information of this nature last Tuesday morning (October 16) at 9:00 A.M., I directed that our surveillance be stepped up. And having now confirmed and completed our evaluation of the evidence and our decision on a course of action, this Government feels obliged to report this new crisis to you in fullest detail.

The characteristics of these new missile sites indicate two distinct types of installations. Several of them include medium-range ballistic missiles capable of carrying a nuclear warhead for a distance of more than 1,000 nautical miles. Each of these missiles, in short, is capable of striking Washington, D.C., the Panama Canal, Cape Canaveral, Mexico City, or any other city in the southeastern part of the United States, in Central America, or in the Caribbean area.

Additional sites not yet completed appear to be designed for intermediate-range ballistic missiles capable of traveling more than twice as far—and thus capable of striking most of the major cities in the Western Hemisphere, ranging as far north as Hudson Bay, Canada, and as far south as Lima, Peru. In addition, jet bombers, capable of carrying nuclear weapons, are now being uncrated and assembled in Cuba, while the necessary air bases are being prepared.

This urgent transformation of Cuba into an important strategic base—by the presence of these large, long-range, and clearly offensive weapons of sudden mass destruction—constitutes an explicit threat to the peace and security of all the Americas, in flagrant and deliberate defiance of the Rio Pact of 1947, the traditions of this nation and Hemisphere, the Joint Resolution of the 87th Congress, the Charter of the United Nations, and my own public warnings to the Soviets on September 4 and 13.

7. *Public Papers of President John F. Kennedy, 1962* (Washington, D.C.: Government Printing Office, 1964), pp. 806–809.

This action also contradicts the repeated assurances of Soviet spokesmen, both publicly and privately delivered, that the arms build-up in Cuba would retain its original defensive character and that the Soviet Union had no need or desire to station strategic missiles on the territory of any other nation.

The size of this undertaking makes clear that it has been planned for some months. Yet only last month, after I had made clear the distinction between any introduction of ground-to-ground missiles and the existence of defensive antiaircraft missiles, the Soviet Government publicly stated on September 11 that, and I quote, "The armaments and military equipment sent to Cuba are designed exclusively for defensive purposes," and, and I quote the Soviet Government, "There is no need for the Soviet Government to shift

had already done, that Soviet assistance to Cuba, and I quote, "pursued solely the purpose of contributing to the defense capabilities of Cuba," that, and I quote him, "training by Soviet specialists of Cuban nationals in handling defensive armaments was by no means offensive," and that "if it were otherwise," Mr. Gromyko went on, "the Soviet Government would never become involved in rendering such assistance." That statement also was false.

Neither the United States of America nor the world community of nations can tolerate deliberate deception and offensive threats on the part of any nation, large or small. We no longer live in a world where only the actual firing of weapons represents a sufficient challenge to a nation's security to constitute maximum peril. Nuclear weapons are so destructive and ballistic missiles are so swift that any substantially increased possibility of their use or any sudden change in their deployment may well be regarded as a definite threat to peace.

For many years both the Soviet Union and the United States, recognizing this fact, have deployed strategic nuclear weapons with great care, never upsetting the precarious status quo which insured that these weapons would not be used in the absence of some vital challenge. Our own strategic missiles have never been transferred to the territory of any other nation under a cloak of secrecy and deception; and our history, unlike that of the Soviets since the end of World War II, demonstrates that we have no desire to dominate or conquer any other nation or impose our system upon its people.

Nevertheless, American citizens have become adjusted to living daily on the bull's eye of Soviet missiles located inside the U.S.S.R. or in submarines.

In that sense missiles in Cuba add to an already clear and present danger—although it should be noted the nations of Latin America have never previously been subjected to a potential nuclear threat.

But this secret, swift, and extraordinary build-up of Communist missiles—in an area well known to have a special and historical relationship to the United States and the nations of the Western Hemisphere, in violation of Soviet assurances, and in defiance of American and hemispheric policy—this sudden, clandestine decision to station strategic weapons for the first time outside of Soviet soil—is a deliberately provocative and unjustified change in the status quo which cannot be accepted by this country if our courage and our commitments are ever to be trusted again by either friend or foe.

The 1930's taught us a clear lesson: Aggressive conduct, if allowed to grow unchecked and unchallenged, ultimately leads to war. This nation is opposed to war. We are also true to our word. Our unswerving objective, therefore, must be to prevent the use of these missiles against this or any other country and to secure their withdrawal or elimination from the Western Hemisphere.

Our policy has been one of patience and restraint, as befits a peaceful and powerful nation, which leads a worldwide alliance. We have been determined not to be diverted from our central concerns by mere irritants and fanatics. But now further action is required—and it is underway; and these actions may only be the beginning. We will not prematurely or unnecessarily risk the costs of worldwide nuclear war in which even the fruits of victory would be ashes in our mouth—but neither will we shrink from that risk at any time it must be faced.

Acting, therefore, in the defense of our own security and of the entire Western Hemisphere, and under the authority entrusted to me by the Constitution as endorsed by the resolution of the Congress, I have directed that the following initial steps be taken immediately:

First: To halt this offensive build-up, a strict quarantine on all offensive military equipment under shipment to Cuba is being initiated. All ships of any kind bound for Cuba from whatever nation or port will, if found to contain cargoes of offensive weapons, be turned back. This quarantine will be extended, if needed, to other types of cargo and carriers. We are not at this time, however, denying the necessities of life as the Soviets attempted to do in their Berlin blockade of 1948.

Second: I have directed the continued and increased close surveillance of Cuba and its military build-up. The Foreign Ministers of the Organization of American States in their communiqué of October 3 rejected secrecy on such matters in this Hemisphere. Should these offensive military preparations continue, thus increasing the threat to the Hemisphere, further action will be justified. I have directed the Armed Forces to prepare for any eventualities; and I trust that in the interests of both the Cuban people and the Soviet technicians at the sites, the hazards to all concerned of continuing this threat will be recognized.

Third: It shall be the policy of this nation to regard any nuclear missile launched from Cuba against any nation in the Western Hemisphere as an attack by the Soviet Union on the United States, requiring a full retaliatory response upon the Soviet Union.

Fourth: As a necessary military precaution I have
Guantanamo

sphere

, presence of outside powers. Our other

around the world have also been alerted.

Sixth: Under the Charter of the United Nations, we are asking tonight that an emergency meeting of the Security Council be convoked without delay to take action against this latest Soviet threat to world peace. Our resolution will call for the prompt dismantling and withdrawal of all offensive weapons in Cuba, under the supervision of United Nations observers, before the quarantine can be lifted.

Seventh and finally: I call upon Chairman Khrushchev to halt and eliminate this clandestine, reckless, and provocative threat to world peace and to stable relations between our two nations. I call upon him further to abandon this course of world domination and to join in an historic effort to end the perilous arms race and transform the history of man. He has an opportunity now to move the world back from the abyss of destruction—by returning to his Government's own words that it had no need to station missiles outside its own territory, and withdrawing these weapons from Cuba—by refraining from any action which will widen or deepen the present crisis—and then by participating in a search for peaceful and permanent solutions.

This nation is prepared to present its case against the Soviet threat to peace, and our own proposals for a peaceful world, at any time and in any forum in the Organization of American States, in the United Nations, or in any other meeting that could be useful—without limiting our freedom of action.

We have in the past made strenuous efforts to limit the spread of nuclear weapons. We have proposed the limitation of all arms and military bases in a fair and effective disarmament treaty. We are prepared to discuss new proposals for the removal of tensions on both sides—including the possibilities of a genuinely independent Cuba, free to determine its own destiny. We have no wish to war with the Soviet Union, for we are a peaceful people who desire to live in peace with all other peoples.

But it is difficult to settle or even discuss these problems in an atmosphere of intimidation. That is why this latest Soviet threat—or any other threat which is made either independently or in response to our actions this week—must and will be met with determination. Any hostile move anywhere in the world against the safety and freedom of peoples to whom we are committed—including in particular the brave people of West Berlin—will be met by whatever action is needed.

Finally, I want to say a few words to the captive people of Cuba, to whom this speech is being directly carried by special radio facilities. I speak to you as a friend, as one who knows of your deep attachment to your fatherland, as one who shares your aspirations for liberty and justice for all. And I have watched and the American people have watched with deep sorrow how your nationalist revolution was betrayed and how your fatherland fell under foreign domination. Now your leaders are no longer Cuban leaders inspired by Cuban ideals. They are puppets and agents of an international conspiracy which has turned Cuba against your friends and neighbors in the Americas—and turned it into the first Latin American country to become a target for nuclear war, the first Latin American country to have these weapons on its soil.

These new weapons are not in your interest. They contribute nothing to your peace and well being. They can only undermine it. But this country has no wish to cause you to suffer or to impose any system upon you. We know that your lives and land are being used as pawns by those who deny you freedom.

Many times in the past Cuban people have risen to throw out tyrants who destroyed their liberty. And I have no doubt that most Cubans today look forward to the time when they will be truly free—free from foreign domination, free to chose their own leaders, free to select their own system, free to own their own land, free to speak and write and worship without fear or degradation. And then shall Cuba be welcomed back to the society of free nations and to the associations of this Hemisphere.

My fellow citizens, let no one doubt that this is a difficult and dangerous effort on which we have set out. No one can foresee precisely what course it will take or what costs or casualties will be incurred. Many months of sacrifice and self-discipline lie ahead—months in which both our patience and our will will be tested, months in which many threats and denunciations will keep us aware of our dangers. But the greatest danger of all would be to do nothing.

The path we have chosen for the present is full of hazards, as all paths are; but it is the one most consistent with our character and courage as a nation and our commitments around the world. The cost of freedom is always high—but Americans have always paid it. And one path we shall never choose, and that is the path of surrender or submission.

Our goal is not the victory of might but the vindication of right—not peace at the expense of freedom, but both peace and freedom. here in thi Hemisphere and, we hope, around the

achiev

thereto has been handed to

ador in Washington. In view of the gravity of the developments to which I refer, I want you to know immediately and accurately the position of my Government in this matter.

In our discussions and exchanges on Berlin and other international questions, the one thing that has most concerned me has been the possibility that your Government would not correctly understand the will and determination of the United States in any given situation, since I have not assumed that you or any other sane man would, in this nuclear age, deliberately plunge the world into war which it is crystal clear no country could win and which could only result in catastrophic consequences to the whole world, including the aggressor.

At our meeting in Vienna and subsequently, I expressed our readiness and desire to find, through peaceful negotiation, a solution to any and all problems that divide us. At the same time, I made clear that in view of the objectives of the ideology to which you adhere, the United States could not tolerate any action on your part which in a major way disturbed the existing overall balance of power in the world. I stated that an attempt to force abandonment of our responsibilities and commitments in Berlin would constitute such an action and that the United States would resist with all the power at its command.

It was in order to avoid any incorrect assessment on the part of your Government with respect to Cuba that I publicly stated that if certain

8. *FRUS, 1961–1963*, vol. 6: *Kennedy-Khrushchev Exchanges*, pp. 165–166.

developments in Cuba took place, the United States would do whatever must be done to protect its own security and that of its allies.

Moreover, the Congress adopted a resolution expressing its support of this declared policy. Despite this, the rapid development of long-range missile bases and other offensive weapons systems in Cuba has proceeded. I must tell you that the United States is determined that this threat to the security of this hemisphere be removed. At the same time, I wish to point out that the action we are taking is the minimum necessary to remove the threat to the security of the nations of this hemisphere. The fact of this minimum response should not be taken as a basis, however, for any misjudgment on your part.

I hope that your Government will refrain from any action which would widen or deepen this already grave crisis and that we can agree to resume the path of peaceful negotiation.

Sincerely, John F. Kennedy

Shortly after delivering his televised speech, President Kennedy had a phone call placed to Prime Minister Macmillan. During the afternoon he had approved dispatch of a reply to Macmillan's letter (the one he had read to the congressional leadership). The reply read as follows:[9]

Dear Friend,

First let me say how sorry I am that the proposed text of my statement has been so slow to get to you. We must use our own machine in such cases.

I am instructing our experts to confer at once with yours to provide the best possible legal case, which will rest in the first instance on the Rio Treaty. But you are certainly right about the wider issues which arise in the nuclear age, and our people feel a strong case can be built on them.

It is this whole series of wider issues that has governed my initial decision. I fully recognize the hazards which you rightly point out, but I have had to take account also of the effect of inaction in the face of so obvious and deep a Soviet challenge. This is not simply or mainly a matter of American public opinion, and as for living under a missile threat, we too have been doing that for some time. But this is so deep a breach in the conventions of the international stalemate that if unchallenged it would deeply shake confidence in the United States, especially in the light of my repeated warnings. It would persuade Khrushchev and others that our determination is low, that we are unable to meet our commitments, and it would invite further and still more dangerous moves.

9. PRO, PREM 11/3689, 24020.

I recognize the particular hazard of a riposte in Berlin, but in the wider sense I believe that inaction would be still more dangerous to our position in that outpost.

I assure you most solemnly that this is not simply a matter of aroused public opinion or of private passion against Cuba. As I am sure you know, I have regularly resisted pressure for unreasonable or excessive action, and I am not interested in a squabble with Castro. But this is something different: the first step in a major showdown with Khrushchev, whose action in this case is so at variance with what all the Soviet experts h----

is necessary to r----

.... minimum of force,
.. ... sure escape from the problem of the first shot. Our best basic course is firmness, now. I look forward to our talk.

Sincerely, John F. Kennedy

President Kennedy and Prime Minister Macmillan began their conversation about 7:30 P.M. Washington time; it was 12:30 A.M. in London.

President Kennedy: Prime Minister?

Macmillan: Yes, I can hear you well.

President Kennedy: Prime Minister, I'm glad to talk to you, and I appreciate your messages today. I've just finished giving my speech. I'm sorry to confront you with all the problems that are going to come out of it, but our strong feeling was that after my statements to them against bringing missiles in, after their frequent statements that they weren't, the fact that this was done in a wholly clandestine way would have left us in November, when Mr. Khrushchev was planning to come over . . . He kept saying that he was waiting till after the elections, but obviously he was waiting to so substantially increase his military power that it would have, we think, just unhinged all of Latin America and thrown into question any of our statements about Berlin.

Macmillan: Yes, I quite see that. What's worrying me is how do you see the way out of this? What are you going to do with the blockade? Are you going to occupy Cuba and have done with it or is it going to just drag on?

President Kennedy: We could not occupy Cuba for some days, and we are preparing a potential for that kind of action if it's necessary. But we didn't start off with that action for two reasons. First, because there has to be a gap of some days to assemble the forces, which of course will always be public information. And, secondly, because we want to see a little where we begin to go on this road. We don't know what's going to happen in Berlin. We don't know what's going to happen any place else. This seemed to be the action we could take which would lessen the chance of an immediate escalation into war, though of course it could bring that result.

Macmillan: Yes, that's quite true.

Is your blockade going to extend beyond the military and arms into things like oil and all the rest of it in order to bring down the Castro government?

President Kennedy: At the beginning we're going to confine ourselves to offensive weapons of war in order not to give him a complete justification for Berlin. In other words, we're not shipping offensive weapons of war into Berlin, so we're just confining it [the blockade of Cuba] to that. But it may be that within the next few days we may need to move it to petroleum, oils, lubricants, and other things. But we don't want to do that just now, because it gives him an obvious tit for tat in Berlin.

Macmillan: What do you think Khrushchev's action will be? In the United Nations to start with or some action of a positive kind?

President Kennedy: He may do what you suggest [in Macmillan's letter] and make us stop one of his ships by force and then take some action in Berlin. He could seize Berlin, or he could put on a blockade there, and there are any number of things he could do. We just have to expect that whatever it's going to be, it's going to be unpleasant. But I don't think anybody is able to predict with certainty what he will do right now. But I would suspect that he will do something unpleasant to us in Berlin, which I think he is going to do anyway.

Macmillan: Well, then what do you think the next step will have to be? To have some kind of conference with him or not?

President Kennedy: What we want to do is get these weapons out of Cuba. The Castro regime is not the issue, or the Communists. We have had no plans to invade Cuba. In fact, as you know, I have taken the position that we should not, but we want to get these missiles out of Cuba. Now, I don't know what kind of a negotiation we could go on, which would permit some exchange on that, but that of course should be the object of our policy.

Macmillan: Yes.

What worries me, I'll be quite frank with you, [is] having a sort of dragging-on position. If you occupied Cuba, that's one thing. In my long experience we've always found that our weakness has been when we've not acted with sufficient strength to start with.

However, we've got to wait now and see what the Russian reactions are. Then we must get into very close touch. They may react in words, by arguing at the United Nations and all the points that I made in my message to you. Or they may react in deeds, either in the Caribbean area or in Berlin, or elsewhere. But we must be ready to decide whether we're going to meet that by demanding a conference and settle the whole thing up, or wheth... going to force the issue by warlike m...

very ...

..... reluctant to do that unless

..., particularly when we can't do it for at least a week because we have to assemble our vessels. So that if we obviously had a sufficient force on hand and could take Cuba tonight that would be very nice, but we don't have that force.

Now, we may come to this invasion by the end of the week, but we are assembling our forces in preparation for it. But what we're attempting to do is to begin this escalation in a way that lessens the chance of a seizure of Berlin, or World War III. Now, we may not be able to prevent either, but at least we have served notice on him that we cannot accept the procedure and the actions which he carried out.

Macmillan: Yes, I very much appreciate that, and I have just got a message from David [Ormsby-Gore], who has explained to me his talk with you, and this is very valuable.

I think all we can do now is just to wait for the reactions. And if you would get in direct touch with me or through David Gore so that we are actually working together all the time, it's very important.

Meanwhile, may I ask you? Have you been in direct touch with Khrushchev? Have you had a telephone talk with him or anything like that?

President Kennedy: No, I haven't. I sent him a letter about an hour ago telling him what we were going to do.

As I said in my speech about his assurances, he played a double game. You remember that he kept saying he was coming over here after the election and would do nothing to disturb the situation until after the election. He said that the weapons were defensive, that they weren't moving any missiles there and all the rest. And obviously he has been building this up in order to face us with a bad situation in November at the time he was going to squeeze us on Berlin. So I didn't feel there was much point in phoning him up, so I just sent him a letter telling him what we're going to do.

Macmillan: Yes. Well, I think that's all that we can do for the moment.

As soon as we've seen the world's reactions . . . What I'm only anxious [about] is, you know how much I feel for you and sympathize. We've been all through these sort of things ourselves. We know the difficulties and I think, if we can keep in the very closest touch . . .

I haven't yet heard from de Gaulle and Adenauer; have you?

President Kennedy: No, I haven't heard from either one of them. We didn't get in touch with them until this afternoon, so they haven't had much chance to get back to me.

One of the points which I think is important about this buildup here is that this buildup, if completed or when completed, will double the number of missiles which the Soviet Union could bring to bear upon the United States.[10] It would also overcome our warning systems because they come from the south, and we don't have an adequate warning. And it comes from so close by that there's always a temptation for them to engage in a first strike or to face us with such a dangerous situation over Berlin that we would have had to quit. That's obviously his purpose. And that's why we feel that we have to take some action.

Now, our action is obviously moderated by the realization that we could move very quickly into a world war over this, or to a nuclear war, or to lose Berlin, and that's why we've taken the course we've taken. Even though, as I say, it doesn't represent any final answer.

The invasion itself, as I said, requires 7 days for us to mobilize our forces, which we cannot do under any cloak of secrecy. We may find we have to come to that. But we are preparing for that in the meanwhile. But I won't do anything about that until I've discussed this with you again. But what we're attempting to do is to warn Khrushchev that this action he's taken constitutes a very

10. Rusk had made this assertion in the midday meeting. Records at the JFKL also indicate that Bundy was sitting in during this conversation with Macmillan and passed Kennedy a note suggesting these arguments about the military significance of the missiles in Cuba. Memorandum of Conversation, The President and Prime Minister Macmillan, October 22, 1962, National Security Files, box 37, Cuba—General—Macmillan Telephone Conversations, 10/62–11/62, JFKL.

hazardous threat, which may lead to a great number of courses which would be unpleasant for us, but awful unpleasant for him.

Macmillan: Well, I quite understand that, and, as you know, we'll do all we can to help in the United Nations and all that. But the actual realities are quite serious and you quite understand them.

What worries me is, again I say, that if we are forced to a conference all the cards are in this man's hand. But, however, you explained to me what are the possible developments you may have to take. And if we do have to tell . . . . . and meet him, in the last resort the m . . . . view. You . . .

. . . . y want to tell you how much . . . . But if you'll keep in touch with David and me, the best we can do now is just to see what happens next.

President Kennedy: Yes, I will, Prime Minister. Many thanks for your thoughts, and I'll be talking to you within the next day or so.[11]

---

11. "Record of a Conversation between the Prime Minister and President Kennedy at 12:30 A.M. on Tuesday, October 23, 1962," PRO, PREM 11/3689, 24020. We have modified the punctuation from the original, but not the text.

TUESDAY, OCTOBER 23

10:00 A.M.

CABINET ROOM

Having lived so long with knowledge of nuclear peril, Americans reacted to Kennedy's speech with alarm but not panic. Everywhere, families stocked up on food, gasoline, and other emergency supplies. Reservists prepared for a callup. In homes and in bars, television watchers saw footage of airplanes taking off and troop trains moving tanks and soldiers. An atmosphere of tension was pervasive. Kennedy's transition adviser, Richard Neustadt, a professor at Columbia University, wrote Sorensen: "The reaction among students here was *qualitatively* different from anything I've ever witnessed . . . these kids were literally scared for their lives."[1]

All through the night, lights had burned in Washington. At NPIC and elsewhere in the intelligence community, analysts anxiously scrutinized every intelligence indicator of any Soviet military activity. Although they saw Soviet (and Cuban) forces being brought to a higher state of readiness, they detected no evident deployments of field units for action against Berlin or Turkey.

At 9:00 A.M. the representatives of the Organization of American States began meeting to consider the American proposal for endorsement of U.S. goals and U.S. actions against Cuba and the Soviet Union, presented by Rusk. The United Nations Security Council would begin its meeting later in the day.

At 10:00 A.M. President Kennedy gathered his chosen advisers, now con-

---

1. Montague Kern, Patricia W. Levering, and Ralph B. Levering, *The Kennedy Crises: The Press, the Presidency, and Foreign Policy* (Chapel Hill: University of North Carolina Press, 1983), p. 126.

vened as the Executive Committee of the National Security Council. He turned on the tape recorder as the intelligence briefing began.

[The initial 5 minutes of the recording have been excised as classified information. Declassified summaries indicate that this portion of the briefing presented evidence about Soviet military activity and the exclusive involvement of Soviet personnel in manning missile sites, as well as some discussion of the nationality of the pilots flying the aircraft in Cuba. McCone may have been reporting that about half of the MiG aircraft were being flown by pilots, one Czech flier had

where they are from yesterday's photography. Also, at other sites, there's evidence of extensive camouflage. [To an aide] I'd like to see those pictures.

Robert Kennedy: The question that I've heard raised rather extensively is why this was not uncovered until now, when there were some reports started as to why we did know about it, and therefore why a blockade of some kind was not instituted earlier. And so that this is the second question. What we are doing now is, in fact, closing the barn door after the horse is gone. And those questions that will be raised . . .

President Kennedy: I think that ties into Senator Keating's frequent statements. I'm having Senator Keating's statements analyzed. Actually they are quite inaccurate. He made a statement 2 days ago that it was being built there, these pads, which would be ready for fire at the United States in 6 months. So this information was . . . He had a piece of it, but it was not precise. In other words, that is what is going on now.

It seems to me that somebody in a responsible position ought to take up this question. I don't think that it's realized how quickly these mobile bases can be set up and how quickly they can be moved. So that I'm just wondering now what his judgment is of the best way of getting this point over in the view of the next 24 hours . . . There will be some spraying all around about the crisis' beginnings, and we just have that problem of . . .

McNamara: Mr. President, later today, as we will see, I believe I should have an on-the-record press conference. I had an off-the-record for a very brief background briefing for one hour last night with about 125 newsmen, and I covered this point exactly on that. However, I think that we need more than that.

I think we need briefings of congressional personnel. Four of them were here last night. If necessary, we ought to send some people out, particularly to Jerry Ford,[2] for example, and certain other congressional leaders who will be asking this kind of a question. And there are many other individuals in the city who ought to be briefed apart from those that I will see tonight. The Scotty Restons[3] and that.

President Kennedy: Will you see—

McNamara: Well, I will probably not see Scotty.

Ball: I had a private talk with Scotty and went over this on the phone.

President Kennedy: —any of these people that John [McCone] ought to see?

Vice President Johnson: Yes. He ought to see Senators Russell and Fulbright as soon as he can today. I saw your speech with them last night and I think that the attitude was much better than was indicated here. And particularly, some of the statements that you made that you were going to prevent the use of these missiles, and against us, and that explains a little better. That's better. We didn't quite say that in the meeting yesterday. They didn't get everything in the meeting they got from your speech, and McCone can give them a good deal more. I tried to give them a little bit myself, later, after the speech.

President Kennedy: Well, actually—

Vice President Johnson: I've seen Mr. McCone this morning and I told him that I thought he'd clear up . . .

President Kennedy: Well, why don't you see.

McCone: I'll do that.

President Kennedy: It seems to me, you may want to send for your committee, I mean the group of people that you deal with, just to get the . . . But I think—why don't you—people that you know . . . And I think it should be on a completely off-the-record basis.

McCone: Well, I'll talk with Russell and Vinson. They are the fellows that run the two committees that I deal with.

President Kennedy: You may want to get Ford in.

McCone: Well, that brings in Cannon.[4]

---

2. Gerald Ford, later President of the United States, was then a Republican member of the House of Representatives from Michigan.

3. James "Scotty" Reston, a prominent reporter and columnist for the *New York Times.*

4. Clarence Cannon (D., Mo.), Chairman of the House Appropriations Committee.

McNamara: I can take care of Ford.

McCone: I had a long, long meeting with Cannon, [Gerald] Ford, [John] Taber, and Mahon[5] the day they left [after Congress recessed in mid-September]. Now, this was before we had the evidence, but there were enough shreds of things coming through so this will not . . . that I predicted this is what we were going to do. But I told them we had no positive evidence. So, I think we've handled Ford all right.

McNamara: . . . pick up Mahon too.

President Kennedy: What . . .

. . . might want to talk to.

McNamara: I think someone ought to catch [columnist Stewart] Alsop.

Ball: I saw Reston. I saw Alsop with Reston and I had about an hour with them.

McNamara: On this particular point?

Ball: Well, we went over this point among others. And I think they were pretty well set.

President Kennedy: Well, why doesn't John McCone use his judgment. [Unclear exchange.] Why don't you [do] Alsop and—

Bundy: Arthur Krock.[6]

President Kennedy: —well, Arthur. I wouldn't have said Arthur. Tell them to come down and [unclear] Arthur, but you're a friend of his, maybe. You use your judgment on that.

Ball: The three I saw yesterday were—

President Kennedy: [Unclear] suggesting it's part of the political campaign.

Ball: —were Alsop, Reston, Al Friendly,[7] and Walter Lippmann is coming in to see me this morning.

President Kennedy: I think Bill White.[8] Who wants to talk to Bill White?

---

5. Congressman George H. Mahon (D., Tex.)

6. A member of the editorial board of the *New York Times*.

7. Alfred Friendly, a reporter for the *Washington Post*.

8. William S. White, a columnist for the Hearst newspapers.

Unidentified: The Vice President would like to.

President Kennedy: Him and . . .

Thompson: Phil Graham[9] called me last night. He was all right.

President Kennedy: —Ben McKelway. I guess I could tell him. Well, I'll tell you what, Lloyd [?], after this meeting, I'll have some suggestions to you to State about some of these special people that we think ought to get some special time today.

McCone: I think I'll call up Eisenhower and get permission from him to use his name in talking with these congressional people. [Unclear] his view of this thing, as a facilitator. I wanted to bring it up last night [in the meeting with the congressional leadership], but I was afraid that it would be a violation of confidence.

President Kennedy: [Unclear] and doesn't have it come from him.

I think the point is, this mobile business isn't quite clear. Everybody thinks this military base takes a long time to construct, and I think that that's—

Bundy: The man that's very important from that point of view is Hanson Baldwin.[10] His article this morning is the perfect problem on this.

President Kennedy: We can get him [unclear].

Bundy: If you can get past him. [Laughter.]

McNamara: We can get through to him through the Navy.

President Kennedy: All right. Well, anyway, we'll . . . We got that.

Robert Kennedy: What about the answer to the question of what we're going to do about them [the missiles already in Cuba]?

President Kennedy: I don't think we probably ought to answer that. You just better wait for the next hour.

Robert Kennedy: Well, I think that they're going to ask Bob at the press conference, and the status.

President Kennedy: Whether we're going to go invade or—

Robert Kennedy: Well, no. I suppose you say we're going to try and make efforts through diplomatic—

McNamara: Well, I would suggest not saying that. Last night they asked me that 5 times, and I repeated every time the words the President used: We will take such further action as is required to accomplish our objective.[11]

---

9. Philip Graham, publisher of the *Washington Post.*

10. A reporter on military affairs for the *New York Times.*

11. President Kennedy's exact words were: "Should these offensive military preparations continue, thus increasing the threat to the Hemisphere, further action will be justified. I have directed the Armed Forces to prepare for any eventualities."

Ball: That's exactly what we've stuck to.

McNamara: And they said: "Does this mean military action?"

Bundy: It is of great importance in this that, unless we get a clear-cut decision around this table to change, we stay right with the President's speech. We're just getting, [U.S. Ambassador Foy] Kohler has reported that he was handed 2 documents, the Soviet statement that's just coming over the ticker—we have only an incomplete version—and another thing, which he sent telegraphically but he didn't say what it was.

President Kennedy: W...

...are a

...ore.

President Kennedy: What's your second point, Bobby?

Robert Kennedy: Just this. Second, the fact that we're doing this, the fact that they've got these missiles already there. I suppose I could probably get by with this answer for about 24 hours. But we're going to have difficulty after that.

Bundy: In a broader sense, I don't think the country's reaction is that we've done too little.

Robert Kennedy: The people are going to start thinking today about the fact that they're there. It must be—

President Kennedy: Well, what I was going to say, I think we ought to get an analysis from CIA or from someone as to what the effects of the blockade of everything but food and medicine would be on Cuba, given their known supplies and what it would do to the country's economy, what the political effects would be, in Cuba as well as outside. We should certainly have to have that as one of our possible courses of action.

Robert Kennedy: On Berlin too?

President Kennedy: The idea is probably that, what the effect of a blockade in Berlin would be by then.

Unidentified: There's much work that has already been done.

[Unclear group discussion.]

Lundahl: Missiles up there, the MRBMs. You'll recall 4 of them were here.

President Kennedy: What was that photograph? Yesterday?

Lundahl: Yes. So the 4 of them were here in the forward position, so 2 of them have gone. And where they might have gone, we don't know at the present time. They could be back in the trees? Another locale?

President Kennedy: I think that you, Bob, ought to have this point of this, emphasizing the mobility of these and the way they can be flown in by air or taken in by submarine.

McNamara: Mr. President, I reviewed this particular picture last night with the press. I showed it to them. I pointed out the mobility. I told them of the convoys coming in here, our watch of those. And that between Sunday and Monday, in one 24-hour period, I didn't identify the day, I stated the number of buildings that have been added, and the change in the site situation.

And to emphasize, I showed them also a picture of an IRBM site and emphasized the difference between MRBMs and IRBMs. The MRBMs are mobile and we estimated that they could be set up, torn down, moved, and set up again in a 6-day period. And this was why it was only this week that this information became available.

President Kennedy: Let's get that on the record.

McNamara: Yeah, I have a transcript of that.

May I also say that those pictures were in the hands of the Tactical Air Command, in target folders, at 10:00 P.M. last night. We sent down almost 25 sets of them. So we were taking U-2 photographs one day and targeting them the next. Based on them.

President Kennedy: Okay. Do you mind if I have these?

McCone: So we're showing this coverage now. Everything in the island is covered except the—

Lundahl: 97 percent.

Unidentified: They were covered 97 percent. [Unclear.] We have, there are 3 [low-level reconnaissance] missions out today.

McNamara: Mr. President, the third action we need to take is a determination of when the proclamation will be effective, the proclamation of the quarantine, the time it will be issued, the time it will become effective, and the time for the first intercept of a ship under the terms of that proclamation. We would propose that it be issued as soon as possible on the day following OAS action. We hope that that would be before 6:00 tonight. If it is issued before 6:00 tonight, we propose that the quarantine be effective at dawn tomorrow. This is a lesser grace period of—approximately 12-hour grace period, instead of the 24 hours that we discussed previously. [11 seconds excised as classified information.]

Furthermore, it will be to our advantage to make the quarantine effective at dawn, because this will allow the day of naval activity tomorrow, which would not be possible were the quarantine to be effective 24 hours after this evening. We'd have to wait until the following day.

We'd like the day of naval activity tomorrow because there is one particular ship we're interested in. The *Poltava* is way out here on the 22nd, and tomorrow morning it will be someplace in this area, which is still on the order of, perhaps, 1,200 miles from Cuba, and we can't get a cruiser out there with any certainty by tomorrow morning with the necessary submarine escort.

So we would propose to go after this ship, which we believe hatches, which are large enough

... would like to have the first ship either ...around or stopped if it has offensive weapons, one or the other.

President Kennedy: We'd like to grab this anyway, but since they turned around last night, they're back—

McNamara: Well, I doubt that they've turned around yet. We have no indication they have, which will be checked today. But it would seem to me it's likely they'll turn around when they're halted—requested to halt—in which case our first intercept has been successful. If they don't turn around, and we search and find offensive weapons on board, it's successful. What we wish to avoid is intercepting one of the other ships that may not have offensive weapons on it.

President Kennedy: In my eyes, we just have to assume that any ship, in view of my statement, that has offensive weapons will be turned around now, before they get within the range . . .

McNamara: I think our plan ought to be designed to try to catch an offensive-weapons ship. That's the objective, and to do it as promptly as possible after the effective time of the quarantine. And for that purpose, we'd like the quarantine made effective tomorrow and go after that ship.

Alexis Johnson: Would you declare a zone, Bob, where you would intercept? You would declare a zone?

McNamara: No, we don't propose to declare a zone.

Alexis Johnson: You intercept anyplace?

McNamara: We intercept anyplace where it appears that the ship is moving towards Cuba.

Robert Kennedy: What about other ships?

McNamara: We'll wait until we get the first one before we choose the second one.

President Kennedy: Do you think we ought to stop these now?

McNamara: I don't believe so, Mr. President, until we have this first intercept. I think it's extremely important to try to pick a ship that has offensive weapons on it. It would be an unfortunate incident if we hailed a ship that refused to stop; we then disable it and found it didn't have offensive weapons on it. That would be a poor way to start.

So what we're trying to do is find one that has offensive weapons. Hail it. Either have it turned around, in which case we've got a success; or, alternatively, disable it and find the offensive weapons.

President Kennedy: Well, what I think we ought to do is try to keep this as private . . . My guess is that anything that has offensive weapons, particularly missiles or missile support, will be turned around by them so that we don't grab it. And therefore, we ought to be able to announce in a day or two which ships were turned around and which came out.

McCone: You've got them all under surveillance, don't you?

McNamara: Yes.

McCone: That *Kimovsk* is a good prospect, however. It's the type of ship that's used for the transportation of heavy construction equipment. This might be the purpose of that voyage.

President Kennedy: May I just say that one of the answers to this problem that Bobby raised, which you may not want to put on the record, but off the record, is that we're not saying that there's any action we're actually taking, this action alone, because the blockade results in the elimination of these, because quite obviously, they're already there. There's no action we ever could have taken, unless we invaded Cuba a year ago, to prevent them being there, because the missiles themselves could have come in by submarines and personnel in separately; particularly the mobile kind that they could set up in a week. And there's just no way, unless you were going to invade Cuba 6 months ago, really. You might say, no, we might have found them 2 weeks before, but you still wouldn't have found that they were there.

So there's no answer to this unless you were going to invade Cuba 6 months ago, or a year ago, or 2 years ago, or 3 years ago. That's the—the fact of the matter is there wasn't anybody suggesting an invasion of Cuba at a time when they necessarily could have stopped these things coming onto the island. It's possible they could have come on in July on the first ship, before the other technicians came on. It could be the mobile kind. So that what we are doing is throwing down a card on the table in a game which we don't know the ending of. But it's not, at least, at the beginning.

We recognize that the missiles are already there. But we also recognize there's not a damn thing anybody can do about the missiles being there unless we had invaded Cuba at the time of the Bay of Pigs or a previous Cuban invasion the year before. That's part of the problem. Some of that you can't put on the record, but it's a very legitimate point. There's no way we can stop this happening now. We could have stopped it 4 months ago, but the SAM and all the rest, mobile missil...

... ...chester *Guardian* saying we're wrong.

McNamara: Mr. President, based on the assumption the proclamation would be issued this evening, we would also like to issue the notice this evening that we are extending the tours of duty of all Navy personnel now on active duty and all Marine personnel on active duty, the reason being that we are entering the period of high activity for the Navy and we are utilizing the Marines to reinforce Guantanamo.

This will require, or I think can best be done by, an executive order signed by you. I have such an executive order here. I will leave it with Ted Sorensen to bring to your attention today. We should have it signed today and we will issue that.

Bundy: May I take you back one second?

President Kennedy: Yes.

Bundy: There is no question of international law with respect to the amount of notice on a blockade?

McNamara: No, we believe not. Our lawyers examined that, Mac, and tell us that if the proclamation is made effective tonight, we can make the quarantine effective tomorrow.

Alexis Johnson: Is that approved, Mr. President?

President Kennedy: Yes, yes.

McNamara: Then I will need this executive order from you sometime today.

President Kennedy: All right.

McNamara: Now, you asked me yesterday to consider reaction to a U-2 accident, and we would recommend this: That SAC be instructed to immediately inform the Joint Chiefs, as far as myself and yourself, upon any deviation from course of U-2 aircraft that is unexplained.[12] They maintain a minute-by-minute check on the U-2s as they proceed through their flight pattern. They will be able to tell us when the U-2 moves off course and, we believe, why, particularly if it's shot down. That information can be in here in a matter of minutes, literally 15 minutes after the incident.

We are maintaining aircraft on alert that have the capability, if you decide to instruct to do so, to go in and shoot the SAM site that shot down the U-2. It would be approximately 8 aircraft required to destroy the SAM site. We would recommend the information on the U-2 action to come in here so that we can present recommendations to you at the time that the action is required. I believe we would recommend that we send the 8 aircraft out to destroy the SAM site. If that is your decision, those aircraft can move out, destroy the SAM site, and have it destroyed within 2 hours of the time the U-2 itself was struck, so that we could announce almost simultaneously the loss of a U-2 and the destruction of the SAM site that allegedly destroyed it.

President Kennedy: Well, I have two questions. First, is it possible to send— so that we assure the cause of the action—is it possible to send an accompanying plane outside the 3-mile limit [on Cuba's national airspace], or is that too burdensome [unclear]?

McNamara: Well, it's not so much that it's burdensome as that it's uncertain. And we think that the best way to handle it is through the SAC report.

President Kennedy: Is somebody flying along? Is there some way, if they do get hit, that they can get into the ocean and get picked up?

McNamara: Yes, yes. We do have air-sea rescue aircraft associated with them.

President Kennedy: Now, two things. First, do we want to indicate that in advance, number one? Or, number two, if we lose one of our officers in the planes, then the next fellow we send out . . . I suppose what we do is, when we take out that SAM site, we announce that if any U-2 is shot down, we'll take out every SAM site.

Bundy: Is surveillance being reaffirmed in the OAS, George?

Ball: No, it is not.

Bundy: We think we have enough?

---

12. At that time the Strategic Air Command (in cooperation with the then-secret National Reconnaissance Office of the U.S. Air Force), not the CIA, was operating the U-2s flying over Cuba. SAC would later draw on CIA pilots in support of its effort.

Ball: We have enough.

President Kennedy: Then I would think what we would do is, if the first one we had taken out, then announce what's happened. And then we would announce that any further reconnaissance planes which are authorized by the OAS are done, then all these SAM sites . . . SAM site and a U-2 today.

Taylor: One point I might make, Mr. President, I think it's highly unlikely we can really identify the guilty SAM site. That doesn't really matter, I don't think.

And secondly, with these pl~~~~ ~~~~

~~~~~~ . . . ormation received from the airplane.

Bunay: Wouldn't it depend, how much information?

President Kennedy: Well, I think we can make the . . . We're going to have the chance to . . .

Bundy: Well, Mr. President, I think the next question I was going to ask is, if you were unavailable, which with a 15-minute thing of this kind we can't ever be certain of, in terms of the detail of the information . . . Do you want to delegate that authority now to the Secretary of Defense or do you want to—or what's your—?

President Kennedy: Well, what we want to do is, I will delegate to the Secretary of Defense on the understanding that the information would be very clear, that the accident that happened was not—

Bundy: That it was in fact a matter of military action.

President Kennedy: Exactly.

McNamara: Only if you're unavailable and only if it's clear.

President Kennedy: Now, the only other question is whether we ought to at some point, in the day after the OAS acts, that we reaffirm just unilaterally the OAS implementing the decision of October 6th on surveillance so that there is some warning.

McNamara: I have told the press. I read the statement before, in a press conference last night, and it's very clear. And I told the press some background, that that was what we're going to do. And I think tonight I can say it after the OAS meeting, whether it reaffirms or doesn't reaffirm.

President Kennedy: We won't state what our action will be.

McNamara: No, we will certainly say that we are continuing surveillance as, in effect, directed by the OAS.

Alexis Johnson: Let me tell you, the OAS resolution as presently drafted is very broad. While not specifically mentioning surveillance as such, surveillance would be encompassed, including the use of arms. The resolution, proposed resolution, is, recommends, that member states, in accordance with Article 6 in the Rio Treaty, "take all measures, individually and collectively, including the use of armed force"—well, this certainly includes reconnaissance—"which they may deem necessary to ensure that the government of Cuba cannot continue to receive from a Sino-Soviet power military material."

President Kennedy: Does that resolution not give us the authority for an invasion with it, if it continued to receive?

Alexis Johnson: Yes, it—I wouldn't . . . I'd like to have the Under Secretary answer that, but I should think that—

Ball: This is being submitted this morning. But it's further to that [reading again from the draft OAS resolution]: "to ensure the government of Cuba cannot continue to receive from the Sino-Soviet powers military material and related supplies which may threaten the peace and security of the Continent and to prevent missiles in Cuba with offensive capability from ever becoming an active threat to the peace and security of the Continent." Practically every-thing is—

[Unclear exchange.]

President Kennedy: Okay. Continue, Mr. Secretary.

McNamara: The next contingency is an air intercept. We don't know and we're not prepared to recommend to you action relating to air intercept. We will maintain, with the help of CIA and our own resources, the careful watch on the movement of Soviet aircraft to Cuba. We'll inform you immediately upon receiving any information indicating that such aircraft is moving in there. The Navy and the Joint Chiefs are considering how we might intercept and what the rules of engagement will be, and we will be prepared to talk about that later.

You asked about the aircraft on alert against the 9 missile sites. They are on alert. They will be prepared to move against those sites. We do believe we should have warning the night before, in preparation for a dawn strike, however. In an emergency, it could be done with less warning, but we would recommend against it, except in emergency.

Taylor: This is a part of the overall strike plan. We'd have to pull out that portion and execute it.

McNamara: The next subject: invasion preparation and the action we're taking to be prepared for an invasion.

The most important single action we need to take, and the one with the longest lead time, is the chartering of merchant vessels, cargo vessels in particular. We need about 134 ships. Of the 134, about 20 are military vessels. We are diverting those from their other activities and assembling them now. Of the remaining 114 we started yesterday to charter, we chartered 4 yesterday. There are 9 others we could have chartered that we turned down b━━━━ ━━━━ were either unsuitable ━━ ━┴━━━━

━━ ━━━━━━━━ to recommend such requisitioning to you this morning. We do believe we should proceed to charter today, and the Chiefs are working out a very careful analysis of when these additional ships are required in relation to the early days of an invasion. We think that the action we're proposing is satisfactory for today.

We do not propose to call up today the transport aircraft, 21 squadrons—16 aircraft apiece, some 300 transport aircraft—that would come from the Air Reserve and Guard that are essential for the invasion forces. This can be done at the start of the preparations for the invasion, either simultaneous with the air strike or shortly before, giving a lead time of something on the order of 5 to 7 days for those air squadrons. So we don't believe that today we should take that action.

McCone: I'd like to bring up the shipping again. This concerns me because it not only preempts the large percentage of the ships, but you also affect industry in a great many areas. For instance, the lumber industry in the entire Northwest is dependent upon American-flag ships coming around. And these come from Japan, Honolulu, and elsewhere, and pick up cargo and come around.

What you do by preempting these ships is you turn the entire East Coast lumber business up to Canada. Now, practically all industry that ships by water is affected, whether they ship coastwise or intercoastal. I wonder if we shouldn't consider using flags of, ships of, friendly nations. There's great numbers of ships laying around, and the entire requirement could be served by a fraction of the cost. If this could be done, as a matter of politics, whether there is legal restriction or whether it would be impossible to arrange diplomatically . . . But I would think the Germans, for instance, might go along. There are a hell of a lot of German ships around, British ships.

Gilpatric?: I would think the risk involved, Mr. President, would preclude any offering of foreign bottoms that might get involved in an invasion of Cuba.

[Unclear exchange.]

McNamara: The question of what to do on shipping is a very complicated one. All I'm prepared to recommend now is that we go ahead with chartering on the commercial basis, voluntary basis. And tomorrow we'll be prepared to raise it again. We have Admiral Sylvester of the Navy in charge of this. He's examining all alternatives, and we just don't know what course we should follow.

McCone: I think, in addition to the problem of the ships themselves, we ought to look at the effect on the economy. This is very, very serious.

McNamara: Yes. This is the primary reason why we're not recommending requisitioning. It will disturb the whole export flow of goods.

McCone: Well, it won't disturb the export because most of your export is arranged—part of your export goes in foreign bottoms.

McNamara: Well, part of it goes into American bottoms. It disturbs the trade in any case, we agree.

McCone: What's going to be affected is your coastal lines and intercoastal operations, which can't go under foreign bottoms. It's against the law. This is what's going to be affected.

President Kennedy: Well now, can we—there's no way—I know what the law says but is there any power we've got that can get, exempt them from that law during this period? We shouldn't be that hamstrung. Are there emergency powers or anything?

McCone: I don't know whether there is or not.

President Kennedy: If we could ship by foreign bottoms, that would . . . We'll do that.

Who's working with you on the shipping over in your shop?

Gilpatric: I'm working on that with Admiral Sylvester.

President Kennedy: Okay.

Gilpatric?: Next part is to confirm again, Mr. President, we proposed to exclude petroleum, oil, and lubricants from the initial list of the prohibited goods.

The final point relates to low-level reconnaissance. I believe it's John McCone's recommendation, if it isn't that of the Chiefs, that we undertake a series of low-level flights today to establish details of these missiles and to obtain the evidence to prove to a layman the existence of missiles in Cuba.

McCone: May I raise the question please, sir, on the matter of exempting POL. One of these things which we might think about is, there is some action to be taken on the loss of a U-2 would be a tightening of the embargo, and the next obvious step is to POL. You may not want to take it at this point. But I think this is something we should at least give some consideration to.

Bundy: Needs to be looked at every day.

President Kennedy: Well,

[obscured text]

... importance of proof at the UN.

[Unclear question about low-level reconnaissance.]

McNamara: This is [at an altitude of] approximately 200 feet, we think, moving across here [indicating on a map].

President Kennedy: So, in other words, then, we'd do that today?

McNamara: That would be our recommendation.

President Kennedy: There is a question about whether these things really exist?

Bundy: No, Mr. President, we have an immediate question as to what to say about what we now know. For example, our position currently has been that we will show pictures without leaving them in people's hands and not making them available for publication. We showed them to friends and to newspapermen, but not in the Security Council.

I, myself, think we are now ready to take the view that the pictures can be shown in the Security Council, if I understood the directive this morning. The second question is whether locations can be mentioned.

There is some feeling in New York that if we say we ought to go and look at the town of umptyump, that this will carry conviction. The question that I would put is, which towns, whether to do this and, if so, which towns. We obviously must not do it in a way which indicates that we only know about some of these, because that will show what, if anything, we're missing. But it may be that the best thing to do is [unclear] it for 24 hours.

President Kennedy: Well, I don't think we ought to give them the towns until we've got some agreement as to whether we're going to go there. We'd give away quite a lot, a hell of a lot.

Bundy: We pick the sites, the ones that one might suggest.

[Unclear group discussion.]

President Kennedy: Well then, why don't we do this film thing then anyway, because we've . . . You're going to start moving these . . .

Robert Kennedy: I have a question. When we were over at the laboratory the other day[13] the indication was that the low—

McNamara: I think they were wrong, Bobby. This is a strip [of film] taken to show the benefits of low-level.

McCone: Went into that. [10 seconds excised as classified information.] This is new film, a new camera, and it's very, very much better.

The reason I feel this, Mr. President, is that initial comment in the European press has been a bit skeptical in both Britain and in France. Most particularly, Mateos made some statements in the Philippines that, if the evidence was conclusive, the attitude of Mexico toward Castro and Cuba would change.[14]

I think we ought to get the "conclusive." I think this is the way to go.

President Kennedy: Okay. [Unclear.]

Sorensen: Do you want to put those [flights] on right now?

McCone: Yes.

McNamara: They're on alert now.

President Kennedy: Well, General, they go in under the radar relay? This does not give away . . . If we're going to have to do that technique again [for an air strike], you can't give away . . .

Taylor: No, sir, we don't think so. We don't think there's any real danger. There's always a certain amount of danger in doing it. [Unclear.]

Robert Kennedy: Will that give away exactly where we know that the—

Bundy: Are you going to do everything? You think that we want to leave one out or put some others in?

McNamara: No, I think we ought to do all 9 [missile sites].

Robert Kennedy: Yeah, but do you think it would be worthwhile?

---

13. Robert Kennedy's visit, with McNamara, to the NPIC on Saturday morning, October 20.

14. Mexico's President Adolfo Lopez Mateos was visiting Manila when the crisis broke. His plane was met by Americans bearing evidence about the missile deployment when it refueled in Honolulu en route back home.

Bundy: How about with respect to the tenth [missile site] that was in the papers this morning?

McNamara: Well, we don't know where the tenth is. We looked very carefully last night for it.

McCone: We have only collateral information about it. [Unclear.]

McNamara: This is the part we have to handle very precisely. It is very dangerous, and I don't think that we ought to stay over that territory any longer than . . .

Robert Kennedy:

McNamara: Well, the one we don't know about is—at the moment, we think, it's not started. It looks as though the crew that will construct a tenth site is working on the ninth.

McCone: Why don't we take one flight over to view over Havana harbor or Mariel and stay away from . . .

McNamara: No. It's terribly dangerous. These are low-level flights.

Bundy: We can't all run the flights.

[Brief, unclear discussion about consistent policy and Korean experience.]

McNamara: We propose no further action on the Reserve and Guard today, Mr. President, other than to extend the tours of the Navy and Marine personnel.

We may wish to call up about 10,000 Navy men to man the 40 destroyers and about 12 antisubmarine squadrons tomorrow or the next day. There is not the need for that as yet. We'd like to postpone it. It's an action that's difficult to reverse. The extension of tours that we will propose tonight can be reversed very easily.

President Kennedy: The question is, though, if we're leading up to an invasion, are we doing all the things that we would have to do?

McNamara: We believe so. The Reserves would not be used in the invasion, exclusive of the transport aircraft that would be required.

President Kennedy: What about the movement of the 101st [Airborne Division], 82nd [Airborne Division], and all the rest?

Gilpatric: They're all moving.

The 5th Infantry Division[15] of the Marines is moving from the West Coast, and the 1st Armored Division from Fort Hood is moving from its post.

President Kennedy: The other question is the airfields down in Florida. Everybody's lived in peace so long that . . . Is everything going to be lined up on those 3 airports in Florida in a way which they come in if they—obvious they will take a reprisal. I should think one of their planes would strafe us.

Taylor: We're aware of that, Mr. President. It's true, these fields are congested. Unfortunately, a lot of the congestion is necessary. We are dispersing the planes as well as they can on Key West. We've reinforced the air defenses to the extent we're capable of.

We have our own—General LeMay has been put in charge of representing the Chiefs on the air defense, as the air-defense arrangements [stand] down there. He is sending one of his most experienced officers down today on the ground to take a look at the situation.

We have talked to Admiral Dennison about these fields. He knows the situation, but he feels that he prefers it to stay that way because it will help him to increase readiness.

President Kennedy: Well, what I'd like to do is, are we going to have somebody take photographs of those fields about 5:00 this afternoon or 4:00 this afternoon, and just get an idea what our . . . ? Because if there's any doubt . . .

Because these people don't know that we're maybe going to hit a SAM site tomorrow and their reprisal would be to strafe an airfield. And it would be nice to know what our targets are.

Taylor: That's quite true. These are very light targets; there's no doubt about it. Unfortunately, our fields are so limited, and our requirements are so great, we really can't . . .

President Kennedy: Well, for example, they're using the West Palm Beach airport? That's a hell of a military airport. It hasn't been used.

Taylor: I don't know.

President Kennedy: You see, you could close that off because there's not much travel that goes through there. They could get out of Miami and go and then take off over that field. And there's a lot of barracks there, too. Go check on that.

Taylor: They're using Opa Locka.

---

15. Actually the 5th Marine Expeditionary Brigade.

President Kennedy: West Palm is a pretty good field, and it was a good base in the war, and it would be good use to us now.

Taylor: We just haven't got enough fields in this area to support . . .

President Kennedy: No, but I do think that the better . . . We have to figure that if we do execute this plan we just agreed on this morning [for retaliation if a U-2 was shot down] that they're going to strafe our fields, and we don't want them to shoot up 100 planes. We've just got to figure out some other device.

[Unclear exchange.]

Taylor: This is one of th- ~

catio~ ~

[. . . ~~~~~~y turned off the tape recorder during a ~~~~~ or communications difficulties, particularly with Latin America. "After a brief discussion of communications Bundy stated that subject under study by Dr. Wiesner, and urged State, Defense, and CIA communications specialists to contact Wiesner."[16] President Kennedy may have left the room during this exchange. The recording resumed with the State Department's report on its activities.]

Ball: [Explaining the need to display photographs in presentations later that day at the United Nations] The point is that they need these things they probably can't have, but anyway, I'll read them [the list of requests from Stevenson and McCloy in New York].

A large map marked in color showing at least some of the sites. I mean, they don't insist upon showing all the sites, and they would make it very clear that there are other sites which they know about which they are not disclosing.

An indication of the rough orders of magnitude of sites—of each site and the number of missiles accommodated at those sites. The photographs showing locations and dates and not merely anonymous photographs. They would also have thought they would like, but I told them I thought this was out of the

16. McCone to File, "Memorandum of Meeting of the Executive Committee of the NSC, 10:00 A.M., October 23, 1962," in McAuliffe, *CIA Documents*, p. 285. Jerome B. Wiesner, a professor of electrical engineering at the Massachusetts Institute of Technology, served as President Kennedy's Special Assistant for Science and Technology.

question, photographs similar in places in the U.S.S.R. They then came back and said couldn't they have them pre-May 1960 because it was clear we were flying U-2s before that time. I told them I thought that this was quite unlikely. They are very concerned about having this evidence, and—

Bundy: Mr. President, I suggest that we proceed on a two-stage basis. Your operation you just ordered will produce much more interesting and effective evidence tomorrow.

President Kennedy: Yes.

Bundy: Say ample evidence is available and will be presented if the question is challenged. We doubt if the opposition dares to challenge it. But it is perfectly natural to take the tactical position for 24 hours.

Ball: Excuse me, I'm sorry. It will be more than 24 hours, wouldn't it? You fly these—

McNamara: No, no. Wait a minute. That's the tactical intelligence to be done in 2 or 3 hours after they've landed.

President Kennedy: If that is challenged, if these pictures we're now getting don't come out, then we can release at least a couple of these [U-2 photos], enough to sustain them. I invite them to challenge it.

McCone: I think, from an intelligence point of view, we can meet most of these requirements. I'd like to think about that pre-1960 flight. There's a question of the effect on you, Bob, from a military point of view.

McNamara: I think that the way to meet that is to take a picture of a May Day [Moscow military] parade. Nuclear weapons. Take that.

McCone: We have that.

President Kennedy: Actually, John, if you don't say at what altitude these were taken or the date, then . . . If you don't say what altitude, you're not giving much away, are you, of these pictures?

McCone: It indicates the number—

President Kennedy: I'll tell you what we'll do. Let's let Mr. McCone and Mr. Lundahl settle as to what we ought to give to them and then under what condition.

Ball: I have nothing more.

President Kennedy: Well, the only thing, as I say, is, Mac, once again, is that if the Russians respond with actions which make an invasion desirable or inevitable, I want to be able to—people to feel that we haven't wasted any days to get going.

Taylor: The real problem is the shipping problem, Mr. President.

President Kennedy: I think we ought to have Bob look at that, and I think we probably ought to be [ready] for the next week, talking to lumber and everybody else that we need to be . . . if that's the only way we can do it. And then it may be that other . . . There may be some emergency powers which will exempt them from the Jones Act,[17] and they can go on foreign bottoms for this 2-week period. And let them do it, and who's going to challenge it? Necessity?

Thompson: Mr. President, there are two questions I'd like to raise. One is, if we don't get OAS action today for this period, it appears we're going to get it the next day. Do you want, in effect, to actually stop Soviet ships _____ tomorrow? The ____ _____

_____ than they do now.

President Kennedy: I think we ought to accept that. That's my quick reaction, unless somebody else says . . . But I don't think we're in very good shape to have a big fight about whether they inspect our trucks or something else. We ought to—

Taylor: We're going to take time out, Mr. President, and not go through until we look it over very hard.

Thompson: Wouldn't it be any better to stop these convoys [into Berlin] in the next day or so?

President Kennedy: And then we'd be getting in the pattern where it's tough to begin again. I would rather have them inspecting them.

Bundy: Mr. President, my suggestion is that we ought to have the second meeting with this committee in the afternoon. We will know about the OAS. We will know about the initial reaction of the ambassadorial group. We will know if the [low-level reconnaissance] pictures came through. We will know about what Kohler's message is [from Moscow].

President Kennedy: Right. Try to keep these meetings as brief as possible.

[The meeting starts to break up. Some fragments of conversations are audible.]

Bundy: I'll set an hour [for the next meeting] when I know a little more, probably about 5:00.

17. The Jones Act of 1928 required certain exporters to use American ships except in emergencies.

President Kennedy: You can make it a little later.

Unidentified: 6:00 is more likely.

Bundy: 6:00 unless you get further notice.

[Several conversations at once.]

President Kennedy: As I say, the press thing, everybody will be available today, and Ken [O'Donnell] will be able to talk in the next few minutes.

[People are leaving. Bundy calls to McNamara and a few others.]

Bundy: Could I have your attention for one more moment? There's something I know the Attorney General's interested in. We need to get a working party that will be concerned not with today or tomorrow, but with processes of this through time. Would you all consider whom you might want to have in your department, and I'll ask Ken for names at the end of the day.

Taylor: Now, this is to do what kind of work, Mac?

Bundy: To think ahead.

[Unclear exchange.]

I'm really thinking in the range of things that this group isn't going to pay much attention to.

McNamara: Yeah, I think we need one [unclear].

Bundy: That would be ideal. That would be ideal.

McNamara: You can count on us on that. [Unclear.]

Bundy: I also think that without regard to departments, there's the problem of temperament and style as to who should run this. I have not hit upon the right person yet. I'm not sure that Paul [Nitze] might not be the man to beat. Well, if you give me individual suggestions on that, I'll try and have it worked out.

Unidentified: All right, but not until tomorrow. Because if we can get it organized in the course of the day, we'll have done a good job.

Ball: [to McCone] Now, this business of getting back to showing some way [unclear].

Thompson: Well, it really doesn't matter [unclear] . . . the pictures you show.

[Unclear exchange.]

McCone: My thought is this: To select two of the best [intelligence] people [to be sent to New York to explain photos] that . . . [unclear].

[Unclear exchange.]

McNamara: That was [unclear] TASS, transmitting a Soviet defense ministry order stating that there would be no demobilization of forces. [Laughter.]

[Mixed conversations.]

Unidentified: I asked this yesterday. It gave me real pleasure to get out a memorandum which, if you say you will be ambassador [unclear], as appointed [unclear], and following protocol, there is only one. Let's see who it is. [Laughter.]

[Mixed conversations. Most leave. Ball, McCone, and a few others remain.]

McCone: Now the thing is, do you release this to the press?

Ball: If you show it [the intelligence on the missiles] to the Security Council, [unclear].

Thompson: This is all I'm thinking of. You've got two choices. You can show the individuals, friendly members in the Security Council, or you ~~ it in a Security Council meeting. If you prod~ meeting, it seems to me th~ giving ~~

~~ u y, and I think this is ~~ first instance. Now, whether the question's ~~ of presenting it formally in the Security Council, it seems to me you're in an impossible position in showing it to anyone. [Unclear] Soviet member of the Security Council.

McCone: Why don't we get hold of Stevenson right now and tell him right now, before, what we talked about.

Ball: Yes, yes. I think you can get ahold of him.

Alexis Johnson: Are we going to have somewhere where both Mr. McCone and I can [unclear]?

[Unclear exchanges continue. A phone call is being placed to Ambassador Stevenson at the American mission to the UN in New York. Meanwhile Rusk arrives, fresh from the OAS session.]

Unidentified: 3:00. We'll meet right here. That's all I'm saying. [Unclear.]

Rusk: There are several instructions. So they're [OAS ministers] meeting again at 3:00. It looks like we'll have everybody but the abstention with Mexico on one paragraph, and that's going to be straightened out before 3:00. Word is Mateos is on a plane.[18] But we'll have the resolution, with a large majority, shortly after 3:00. They're really running around. Bolivia, who had withdrawn from the OAS pending their settlement with Chile, turned up this morning.

---

18. Because Lopez Mateos was on a plane returning from his visit to the Philippines, he was unable to approve revised instructions for Mexico's representative at the OAS meeting.

[Several voices: "Terrific. Terrific."]

Alexis Johnson: Now, we can put the question of the timing of the [quarantine] proclamation. I should think that we should be ready at 4:00.

McNamara: I have it right here. It's all cleared by our lawyers. I believe your lawyers were putting—

Rusk: Now, what is the . . .? Privately I've been talking to the two or three of these fellows that could be contacted this afternoon. Therefore it's very important that we have this resolution passed.

[Unclear exchange.]

Alexis Johnson: The meeting of the Security Council is set for 4:00 this afternoon.

Rusk: I understand the long TASS statement is on the wire. Have you been getting that in here?

Unidentified: Not yet.

Rusk: Let's don't howl too soon here, boys.

Alexis Johnson?: If the OAS has acted before the Security Council, oh that's going to be a big help. Mmmm.

Rusk: [reading report on TASS statement] No demobilization. Meeting of forces of the Warsaw Pact. Well, my God.

Well, as a matter of fact, I don't know what John McCone thinks of this, [but] I think it was very significant that we were here this morning. We've passed the one contingency: an immediate, sudden, irrational strike.

Unidentified: Yeah, yeah.

Rusk: Further news from the UN is . . .

When I say that we're here, that they're here either [chuckle]. I'll say, we're here today.

When we asked for a Security Council meeting at 3:00 this afternoon, Zorin[19] was dragging his feet.

Ball: Well, I just talked to Stevenson, and he says, and Stevenson says, he [Zorin] is dragging his feet because the Russians are getting up a request for a resolution of their own. And there's going to be the countercomplaint filed. And this is what they're dragging their feet for. So they're meeting at 4:00.

Thompson: That's significant, because they let the Cubans bring the first one [proposal in the UN].

Alexis Johnson: Well, we caught them [the Soviets]. We caught them without their contingency [plan].

---

19. Soviet Ambassador to the UN Valerian Zorin.

Unidentified: Well, the Security Council will be happy to evacuate them. [Laughter.][20]

Rusk: I'll go on back at 4:00. [Unclear.]

Alexis Johnson: We really caught them with their contingencies down.

[Unclear group discussion. Rusk has apparently left, and the informal gatherings are breaking up. Someone can be heard saying: "Great news." A few advisers remain.]

Alexis Johnson: Well, they're doing so at Honolulu [briefing Mateos and his refueling stop]. [Unclear.]

...... it by the time he got to Honolulu, and hopefully he, as we will arrange with . . . The Mexico embassy was arranging for the Mexican government to contact him at Honolulu.

[Unclear reply.]

Alexis Johnson: Yes, it should be about now. It was—at 8:00 it was about 3 hours. But the embassy down there was on it and making telephone contact with Honolulu.

Ball: Your meeting with the ambassador [unclear]?

Unidentified: All ears, splendid. Just splendid. The Secretary [Rusk] handled the neutrals, and apparently he did a superb job. I talked to a few of them afterwards.

Ball: And the first reactions from all the other ambassadors, the NATO ambassadors, was very good.

Alexis Johnson?: The briefing, being able to give them this briefing, this is what counts.

Ball: I'll tell you what the problem with Stevenson is. What's the most [effective] was actually seeing pictures, while—

Unidentified: Seeing the pictures.

Bundy: [to someone entering the room] Did Dean tell you how he made out?

---

20. The context of this bit of gallows humor is that most of these officials had, in recent days or hours, been obliged to review plans for the evacuation of themselves or family members in case of a Soviet nuclear attack.

[Unclear group discussion.]

Bundy: Let me tell you one more thing. In order to get Berlin's contingency planning forward, and to have it centralized under our authority, it has just been agreed by the two, by Secretary Rusk and the President, that Paul Nitze will become the chairman of the special working group of this committee for Berlin. Now, if Berlin gets hot, it will come right into the whole [Executive] Committee. But we've got to have some group doing this while the rest of us are doing all these other things.

Unidentified: Okay.

Bundy: I haven't notified Paul yet, but he's senior man in the government [unclear] on this.

[Mixed voices. The call to Stevenson has come through.]

Ball?: [talking on phone to Stevenson] I'll put John McCone on. I think we can work this out some way. And I'm going to get on the other phone. I think we can work this out some way, and I'm going to get on the phone.

[Unclear discussion.]

McCone: [talking to Stevenson] Now, we want to do everything we can to meet your requirement and to be as very forward as possible. There are two problems, of course. One is revealing too much that must affect any future undertaking that we might be obliged to go forward with.

And second is, we're revealing too much about our means. With regard to the latter, I'm not concerned about that if we keep this on the basis of military reconnaissance, which it is. But not identifying the kind of equipment. [Pause as Stevenson replies.]

But now the question is whether this has to be made public. Your meeting of the Security Council is probably going to be televised, I understand. And again, whatever information is released cannot be given to the members, individually or collectively, to inform them? Or does it have to be presented formally? [Pause as Stevenson replies.] I see. [Pause.] Mm-hmm. [Pause.] Mm-hmm. [Pause.] Yeah. [Pause.]

Well, you're answering the question now, and that is this: Your case must be made in the open forum, if it has to be made at all. So, therefore, any decision, that releases that into the public domain. [Pause.] Pictures of what? [Pause.] Yeah. [Pause.] Yeah. [Pause.] Mm-hmm. [Pause.]

In other words, if you have the map—a couple of locations and then say there are more. [Pause.] Yeah. [Pause.] Mm-hmm. [Pause.]

Well, all right. Let me go over this, and I'll tell you what I'll do. I don't want to— [Pause.] You do?

The problem of these pictures is this. When you release them—if you're going to give anything to any foreign delegate, you have to give it to the press. Now, these pictures, blown up as they are, are, under study, are convincing to you and to me. You reproduce those in the newspaper, and they're totally unconvincing, you see? [Pause.] That's right. [Pause.] Yeah. [Pause.] Mm-hmm. [Pause.] Yeah. [Pause.] Mm-hmm. [Pause.] Yeah. [Pause.]

Well, for now, I'll tell you what I'll do. Let me go into this and I'll send a couple of fellows up there right away. [Pause.]

Well, I don't like surfacing things. Th...

...man. B...

...u.uu, 7:00. Well, this might ...more distinctive pictures than what we have. This would be [photos taken] at 2–300 feet, you see? [Pause.]

Yeah, but we won't get that—we couldn't get it into your hands until late this evening. [Pause.] I see. [Pause.] Yeah. [Pause.] I could do that. [Pause.] Yeah.

Well, that's why we're taking this [low-level photography]. Now, of course, we'll have to see what the results are. If we just release them . . . We just released the [low-level] flight a half-hour ago, so they won't be back for another couple of hours. [Pause.]

Well, then we'll have to go home. But we'll have to see. In any event, I'll do two things. I'll have one more come up there to work with you in the preparation of the scenario of what we've got. Then I'll be prepared to get this other stuff up to you just as quick as available. [Pause.] Yeah. [Pause.] Yeah. [Pause.] Yeah.

All right, fine. Now, just a minute. Tommy Thompson has something he wants to mention.

Thompson: Would it be feasible for him to say that these pictures have been shown to every non-Communist delegate and ambassador to Washington? Any delegates who want to see them can see them at the American delegation.

Ball: [on other line] If any what?

Thompson: If any delegate wants to see them, he can see them at the American delegation.

[Pause.]

McCone: There were messages of one of the 7 ships this morning at 1:00, but we couldn't read them out. So I don't think anybody knows what's going on.

Now, Tommy Thompson's question suggested one approach that you might consider, Governor. And that is that you tell your members of your committee that these pictures have been shown to all non-Communist ambassadors and they invite them to come to your office to see them, as a means of getting around presenting them in public. Now, I don't know whether that—[Pause.] Yeah. [Pause.] That's fine. [Pause.] That's correct.

Yeah, [unclear] if necessary, and we'll throw them into the public domain, which we don't want to do. Well, but you think it over, and I'll have Lundahl up there. [Pause.] Mm-hmm. [Pause.] Yeah. [Pause.] Yeah. [Pause.]

Well, you think it over, and I'll let you know when he calls again. And Lundahl and one man will come with him. [Pause.]

Well, he'll probably get away from here at 12:30, take an hour on the plane, so he'd be in your office at a quarter past 2:00. [Pause.] Real good. [Pause.] All right.

[Ball hangs up.]

Thompson: Does he like that idea?

McCone: Yes, he thought it was good. He was going to go ahead with it with a friendly ambassador. He's going to think about the UAR [United Arab Republic: Egypt and Syria] and Romania.

Thompson: Well, I wouldn't think about the UAR.

McCone: [on the phone to someone else] Listen, it's Mr. McCone. Would you get Mr. Ray Cline for me? Dr. Cline at the CIA. And put the call in here? Thank you.

Ball: Maybe I should get Roger [Hilsman], too, so we don't cross things. [Unclear.] Roger worked with this.

Unidentified: I've talked to Roger. Roger was going up [to New York], and I talked to him.

McCone: I'll send Ray, Ray Cline and Lundahl, up there.

Ball: Yeah, yeah. And have him get in touch with Roger so that we—

Unidentified: Oh, yeah. OK, gentlemen.

McCone: George, if it's this hard to start a blockade around Cuba, how are they ever going to be able to start World War III? [Laughter.]

Unidentified: Ray Cline.

McCone: Oh, thanks.

Hello? Say, Ray, Governor Stevenson and Jack McCloy are having some difficulty on putting together a convincing case to the Security Council. In the event they're challenged, you see. I told them that we could not surface Lundahl, but I have Lundahl going up there to help him with his scenario. Actually, Lundahl probably couldn't get in the place if they wanted him to, see?

Now, what I'd like to do is to have Lundahl and you, if you could, or if you can pick the best man you can to work with Lundahl. This is a matter of helping Stevenson, McCloy, and Lovett, you see.[21] That's a pretty senior group of people. And you know them all.

[Aside to Jerome Wiesner] Jerry, just a minute.

Now, what they were going to

.... the low-level flights, and they're .... And we'll get those pictures back early this afternoon. And that will do us a lot of good. [Pause.]

No, because he's got to be prepared at 4:00. So you get Lundahl and get what's-his-name on his plane and then go on up. You'll need some security men. And they can meet you there and all the rest. [Pause.]

Yeah, Lundahl knows how to do all that. [Pause.] Yeah, and if that plane is not available, get a MATS [Military Air Transportation System] plane. [Pause.] Yeah. [Pause.] Yeah. [Pause.] Yeah. [Pause.] All right. [Pause.] Yeah, do that.

Now, they're pulling Roger [Hilsman] out of this UN operation, and we're going to take that, see? [Pause.]

Yeah, I told Stevenson you'd be in his office at a quarter past 2:00. [Pause.] Well, you better find out exactly. They'll know in New York. The thing for you to do is to get going—okay.

[McCone hangs up.]

Mr. Wiesner?

Wiesner: You started to talk about something yesterday that I didn't pick up enough on, and then I had a second question for you. We had talked about possible neutron detectors.

Unidentified: About what?

---

21. President Kennedy had asked Lovett and McCloy to aid Stevenson in presenting and supporting the American position at the UN. Arthur Schlesinger Jr. was also in New York helping Stevenson.

Wiesner: Neutron detectors for nuclear-weapons detection.[22] Last time I looked at this there was nothing really sensible kicking around. You implied that there was some work going on that maybe I should take a look at.

McCone: Well, there was, and there was a black box, and our fellows thought it was working good enough.

Wiesner: Who in your place should I talk with?

McCone: Pete Scoville.[23]

[6 minutes excised as national security information. When the recording resumes, McCone is with Sheffield Edwards, CIA's Chief of Security; and a Mr. Smith, identified later on the tape as area manager for North American communications. They talk with Wiesner about the status of communications between Washington and various locations in Latin America.]

Wiesner: . . . We would have to have [Osprey?] use their equipment. Normally they, except for the outstations of the various oil companies and mining companies, they would be located in the capital cities also, as we are.

McCone: The radios? Let me see that.

Wiesner: There is a very elaborate American-owned commercial network into the Central American area that is associated with United Fruit.

Unidentified: United Fruit Company. They are not necessarily in cities. Plantation areas.

McCone: Have you got that personnel?

Unidentified: Yes, sir. We made a study of it rather quickly, and it indicates that we will need 43 people to put these stations on the air 24 hours a day.

McCone: How many do you got on now?

Unidentified: 29.

McCone: You've got 29.

Wiesner: So you're going to need 43 more if you want to keep it going 24 hours a day, 7 days a week.

McCone: This is the most complete system, and the government has none. You see, State has none and the military has very little.

Unidentified: And I doubt whether you could augment it very rapidly. You couldn't make a strike rapidly.

McCone: Well, we have the most rapid. The quickest thing you can do is to

---

22. Technology to detect the possible presence of nuclear weapons would be useful in any inspection of Soviet ships or aircraft en route to Cuba, either overtly through the official quarantine or covertly. The technology, referred to as "black boxes," might also be useful if the crisis was settled by some international inspection of sites in Cuba to verify the withdrawal of Soviet weapons.

23. Herbert "Pete" Scoville, the CIA's Deputy Director of Research.

get technicians of one sort or another to operate it and put this on a 24-hour-a-day basis and then get additional backup on moves and backup—carefully selected, remote and secure places.

Unidentified: You ought to get together with State and see what additional arrangements they have made with the commercial operators. I know they have some. See whether this does give us additional [links] with the Soviets. And then see whether the political people plus your people can put these things where we are most likely to have trouble, and therefore where we ought our efforts to increase communication

McCone: The

was an alerting system?

Smith or Edwards: There is at 9 [embassies], where if you try to call them up you get the Marine guard.

Wiesner: But this exists only at 9?

Smith or Edwards: Nine of these stations. Might this be easier to do than . . .

Wiesner: The problem I wanted to touch base with you on is to make sure that I was not going in a direction contrary to yours.

McCone: No, we're just—I think that we've got this on 24 hours. But of course this lasted last night, but it can't be maintained.

Wiesner: Why don't we get together with these people to see what additional things there are and see whether they feel there is a need.

McCone: You go right ahead, and I'll work closely with State.

[To others] Dr. Wiesner has given us permission to attend to this. We want to support both State and Defense in every way possible and, except emergency measures that are necessary, find the operators, needing a few from overseas stations of our own, and we'll take the measures necessary. And we're employing the military, and if we have to do a recruiting job for outsiders, we'll do that.

Wiesner: . . . number is necessary to bring the whole network up to 24 hours. That may be selected first that—

Smith or Edwards: Of the 43, we can find 20 within our own organization.

Wiesner: Wow. But there's one thing that's worrying me. One real concern in a crisis [unclear]. We need to keep that in mind. Let's not get ourselves—

Unidentified: If you bring in those 20, will you impair [communications in] Frankfurt?

Unidentified: We'll begin to. We're talking about replacements who are home on home leave, or scheduled to go out again. And we're going to pull them in and send them to Latin America, which means other places—

McCone: At what rate can you track down on this system?

Unidentified: Sixty words a minute. [Unclear.]

[McCone leaves the room.]

Wiesner: Well, look. We're still going to get the President's directive. I think it should straighten this out by the end of the day. Why don't we get together with you and try to get State people over too?

Unidentified: [Unclear] purposes of something like the meeting you had last night.

Unidentified: But I think it will be a smaller group, and probably tomorrow morning.

Unidentified: All right. That's a good idea.

Edwards?: Let me explain something. Mr. Smith is our area manager for the American communications. Mr. Bloom [?], he was out of town yesterday, down at Norfolk working with CINCLANT on another problem which is going to require about 20 people.

Unidentified: What is that?

Unidentified: This is a contingency operation of the military.

Unidentified: He didn't tell me he will be able to come [unclear].

Unidentified: I know Jim [?] is dying to get this out, and he [unclear]. When he says 43 more people, that means 3 men in addition instead of the one or 2. This still means for the early, brief period of time, and the brief now being in the order of a magnitude of weeks, you now have continuous coverage. But if you're going in to sustain operations, I would think in terms of plus.

Unidentified: But really, I don't think . . . It [the crisis] will not be much more now, or it will be for a relatively brief time in the future.

Unidentified: I like to hear you say that.

Unidentified: Well, I'm just guessing.

Unidentified: That's correct.

[Everyone leaves, the room falls silent, and the tape recording ends.]

TUESDAY, OCTOBER 23

6:00 P.M.

CABINET ROOM AND OVAL OFFICE

.......y. The version of Khrushchev's letter received by the White House, as translated by the embassy and sent in the telegraphic style then used in most cables, was as follows:[1]

Mr. President:

I have just received your letter, and have also acquainted myself with text of your speech of October 22 regarding Cuba.

I should say frankly that measures outlined in your statement represent serious threat to peace and security of peoples. United States has openly taken path of gross violation of Charter of United Nations, path of violation of international norms of freedom of navigation on high seas, path of aggressive actions both against Cuba and against Soviet Union.

Statement of Government of United States America cannot be evaluated in any other way than as naked interference in domestic affairs of Cuban Republic, Soviet Union, and other states. Charter of United Nations and international norms do not give right to any state whatsoever to establish in international waters control of vessels bound for shores of Cuban Republic.

It is self-understood that we also cannot recognize right of United States to establish control over armaments essential to Republic of Cuba for strengthening of its defensive capacity.

We confirm that armaments now on Cuba, regardless of classification to which they belong, are destined exclusively for defensive purposes, in order to secure Cuban Republic from attack of aggressor.

---

1. *FRUS, 1961–1963*, vol. 6: *Kennedy-Khrushchev Exchanges*, pp. 166–167.

I hope that Government of United States will show prudence and re-nounce actions pursued by you, which could lead to catastrophic conse-quences for peace throughout world.

Viewpoint of Soviet Government with regard to your statement of Oc-tober 22 is set forth in statement of Soviet Government, which is being conveyed to you through your ambassador in Moscow.

N. Khrushchev

At the OAS the U.S. resolution passed without any "no" votes and with only 2 abstentions, and those were soon changed to make the support unanimous. At the United Nations Stevenson led a heated attack on Soviet policy in the Security Council and effectively used the photos and other intelligence sup-plied by CIA in briefings for the delegates. The Soviet ambassador said the American charges were false and argued that only defensive weapons had been supplied to Cuba. He neither confirmed nor denied the presence of ballistic missiles.

The F8U Crusader aircraft conducting low-level reconnaissance flashed across Cuba, a few hundred feet above the ground, high-speed cameras run-ning. They encountered no enemy fire.

The Executive Committee of the National Security Council reconvened at 6:00 P.M. to review developments and plan for the next day, when they actually expected to confront Soviet ships on the high seas.

President Kennedy turned on the tape recorder as his advisers took their seats in the Cabinet Room.

Bundy: Mr. President, the first thing we ought to do is to get this [quaran-tine] proclamation approved, because it needs to be on its way just as soon as possible for the convenience of the Naval forces. I think the Secretary of Defense and the Secretary of State have had their joint legal experts working on it.

Are there some particular comments Mr. Ball or Mr. McNamara would like to make, or the Secretary? This is the proclamation which we ought to formally review in the presence of the President before it is in fact sent on its way.

President Kennedy: Sino-Soviet. Would it be proper to put the Chinese in?[2] Is that necessary, and why? What do you say is—well, why don't we . . .

---

2. The quarantine proclamation began with a reference to the "establishment by the Sino-Soviet powers of an offensive military capability in Cuba." The term "Sino-Soviet powers" had also been used earlier in the day in the resolution that had been adopted by the OAS and submitted to the UN Security Council.

Rusk: That language has been used in the resolutions now, of the "Sino-Soviet powers," although the actual [unclear] is the Soviet Union.

President Kennedy: Sino . . . Soviet Union? Well, the actual effect of this is going to be to [unclear] in Asia.

Rusk: [reading] Sino-Soviet.

President Kennedy: 2:00 P.M.?[3]

McNamara: 2:00 P.M. Greenwich Time is 10:00 in the morning, Eastern Daylight Time. It's probably 11:00 in the morning, Daylight Tim—

Gilpatric: [Unclear] the patrol path ~f ~~

divisions. Land-based

—, is, the proclamation is the
. . .uionally when you have, the nature of this kind
. . .uuc, this is the act which says this is an illegal thing. If we don't give them notice, [unclear].

President Kennedy: Well, what about all the patrol craft?

McDonald: Now, that's a separate question. That can be solved by putting that item last or by deleting it.

Robert Kennedy: Mr. President, really, you can put any items that you want because, as you see, the paragraph afterwards—

[Unclear group discussion.]

Unidentified: The words "surface-to-surface missiles" should be the very first words.

President Kennedy: Right, I think that would be fine.

Gilpatric: You either do or do not include MTBs [motor torpedo boats]? You put it down just before the final clause.

President Kennedy: I think now, at this point, we can stop them anyway, can't we? The instructions to . . .

3. The proclamation stated that the quarantine would begin at 2:00 P.M. Greenwich Time, October 24, 1962.

4. The adviser is listing the items authorized for interdiction by the quarantine proclamation. Patrol boats were being constrained in order to keep them from being in a position to attack transports that could be carrying American divisions.

McNamara: Well, I can issue instructions tonight, whether or not we put them in here. I think I should.

Robert Kennedy: You see the paragraph on page 3: "The Secretary of Defense shall take appropriate measures to prevent the delivery of prohibited material to Cuba" . . . Then "The Secretary of Defense may make such regulations and issue such directives as he deems necessary" . . .

President Kennedy: That's been designated, [unclear] the offensive.

Robert Kennedy: "Make such regulations" . . . So he can do whatever he wants.

President Kennedy: Right.

Bundy: Let's just say "surface-to-surface missiles," [unclear] "bombers"—

President Kennedy: Fighter-bomber aircraft? Why don't we say bomber aircraft? [Reading again] "Air-to-surface rockets and guided missiles, warheads for any of the above weapons; mechanical or electronic equipment to support or operate . . . any other classes" . . . Okay.

Bundy: We start, in other words, with the language at the top of page 3, last 3 lines of page 2.

Ball: The word "land-based," Mac.

Bundy: What?

Ball: You do not want to keep the word "land-based" in.

Bundy: No. Cut "land-based" and begin "surface-to-surface missiles."

President Kennedy: You do not want to keep the words "land-based"?

Unidentified: No.

Taylor: In other words, if we wanted that, the Secretary of Defense can do that.

President Kennedy: He'll do that, yeah. We'll have him, yeah.

McNamara: I believe the order includes the original language.

Bundy: I do raise the question. I see no other way of doing it. But I think it's important to observe that we do now designate, delegate, to the Secretary of Defense, the breadth of the blockade. Is that necessary, legally?

Robert Kennedy: I think that going to change the existing blockade every time—you want to be able to change it. It's not really just on the subject of change. I think there's a difference.

McNamara: Do we change "fighter-bomber" or not? [Unclear.] No. We keep bomber aircraft.

President Kennedy: [reading the proclamation] . . . "another destination of its own choice" . . . Oh, I see. In other words, if we knew they are on there, we can just tell them to go home.[5] If they did.

---

5. This portion of the proclamation provided that a proscribed vessel "shall, wherever possible,

Robert Kennedy: Bob McNamara and I [unclear].

McNamara: Can we search a vessel which was proceeding toward Cuba that was hailed, requested to stop, did not do so, but turned around and proceeded to reverse direction away from Cuba? It's both a legal question and a practical question. The legal foundation is, such an act can be confused [with evasive action]. But as a practical matter, I don't believe we should undertake such an operation immediately.

President Kennedy: That's right.

The way you can do it is to set out a zone, and then pick up any vessels within that zone and say you don't know whether, when they turned around, whether they're going to try to come into Cuba in a different fashion. Maybe you don't want to do it in the first 48 hours.

President Kennedy: I think if we got a vessel that was suspicious, that we ought to try and grab it. But my guess is that anything that's really that suspicious at this point, they're not going to choose this to have the test case. They're going to turn that thing around.

Bundy: Well, we'd get an exception, if we get one that's hot.

McNamara: Well, this particular vessel is 1,800 miles out [from Cuba]. That's one of our major problems.

President Kennedy: We'd have to grab it there.

McNamara: We'd have to grab it there, which—

President Kennedy: . . . turn it around. Do we want to grab it if they turn it around at 1,800 miles away?

Robert Kennedy: I think that's too far. If it keeps coming . . . Do we know whether it's still coming?

McNamara: It's still coming. It has not yet turned around. [Pause.] No. [34 seconds excised as classified information.][6]

---

be directed to proceed to another destination of its own choice and shall be taken into custody if it fails or refuses to obey such directions."

6. In his recollection of this meeting, which contains certain details indicating that he refreshed

I recommend that we not, tonight, decide this issue on that particular ship that's 1,800 miles out. We ought to follow it tonight and see what happens.

Robert Kennedy: I think it would be damn helpful to come in with that kind of evidence.

McNamara: This ought to be our primary objective, early after the effective date of the blockade, to grab a vessel obviously loaded with offensive weapons.

Robert Kennedy: It would be a hell of a lot of help.

McNamara: Our prime target at the moment is the *Kimovsk,* which is within our range tomorrow, and which we hope we can get around 11:00 or 12:00 tomorrow morning. But we haven't yet pinpointed it this afternoon. They're still searching for it.

[Unclear reply by President Kennedy.]

McNamara: No. They know approximately what area of the ocean it's in.

Rusk: Mr. Secretary, the direction of the ship is pretty important, particularly if it's gonna be a ship with missiles and warheads and things like that on it. I don't know whether the Navy have the capability of giving surveillance or tailing such a ship. But how do you distinguish between a ship that, in fact, is turning around from one that is going to play cat-and-mice with you?

McNamara: Oh, we have ample ability to tail them. As a matter of fact—

Rusk: I would think that if you could get them in as far as possible, initially, and then, if they do seem to be turning around, give them the chance to turn around and get on their way.

McNamara: Oh, any ship that we stop or hail and request to stop, which then deviates from course, we will follow. This is in the instructions.

But the suggestion of the Attorney General, and I think it's an excellent suggestion, but not to apply the first day, is that even if it's turned around and proceeds indefinitely away from Cuba, we would nonetheless stop it and search it, because it very probably would have offensive weapons on board. And I think that's very likely the case.

Rusk: So if it's going away from Cuba with offensive weapons on board, what is your plan?

---

his memory either by checking his notes or by listening to this recording, Robert Kennedy wrote: "During the course of this meeting, we learned that an extraordinary number of coded messages had been sent to all the Russian ships on their way to Cuba. What they said we did not know then, nor do we know now, but it was clear that the ships as of that moment were still straight on course"; Robert F. Kennedy, *Thirteen Days: A Memoir of the Cuban Missile Crisis* (New York: W. W. Norton, 1969), p. 60.

McNamara: Well, the suggestion was that we stop it, search it, and if it has—

Robert Kennedy: Our argument is that this particular ship is—has been—has made trips to Cuba, it's been destined to Cuba. You don't know when it turns around what direction it's actually going.

I think that the hullabaloo that would be created by the fact that if it deviated from our course . . . We can always say we didn't know where it was going to go, and the advantage—

McNamara: Evasive action.

Robert Kennedy: Yes. And the advantage of h . . .
with the pictures and the . . .
plaints

. . . Cuba.

. . . a matter that we're going to know in the . . . . . . ould think that if they just keep coming into Cuba, obviously, probably tomorrow morning is going to be when they'll refuse to haul to, and we'll have to shoot at it. So that's really our problem tomorrow. Then, it seems to me, later we can decide, when we know what they're going to do, whether we start grabbing them as they leave. So I think we're going to have all our troubles tomorrow morning.

McNamara: I think so too. I've tried to simplify tomorrow as much as we can.

President Kennedy: They're actually faced with the same problem we were faced with in the Berlin blockade [of 1948–49]. Whether to fire and feel afterwards that they really pushed it. Now, that's the problem. We've given them as clear notice as they gave us. Even in '47 and '8, when we had the atomic monopoly, we didn't push it.

But they're going to.

Well, what is it we have to . . . What are the other policy questions? [Reading] "Any vessel or craft which may be proceeding toward Cuba may be intercepted and may be directed to identify itself, its cargo, equipment and stores and its ports of call, to stop, lie to, submit to visit and search, or to proceed as directed . . ." Now, we don't say any vessel within the vicinity of Cuba, which is proceeding towards Cuba, do we?

[Unclear reply.]

President Kennedy: And "proceed to another destination of its own choice . . ."

Ball: I'd like to raise the question as to whether we shouldn't have some [unclear] limits, however. It seems to me that the idea that we're picking up Soviet ships anywhere, just on the prima facie supposition . . . That gets into difficulty.

McNamara: We have two problems. One is the proclamation. We certainly wouldn't want to put out a limit in the proclamation. I think that first we should get this out of the way, and then consider the practical problem of how we apply this.

President Kennedy: How far out would the ship be?

McNamara: Something on the order of 800 miles, perhaps. We want to be outside of the IL-28 range, which is estimated to be 740 miles. I don't believe any IL-28s are operative today, but they may well be in the future. In any case, we want to be, during the first day, out of danger.

Nitze: The really [unclear] point is how far out we are going to operate. Tommy and I said we recognize the advantage of something close to [Cuba]. But the more important thing is to have it far enough away, so that we didn't have to increase the risk of having to shoot a plane, at least at that time. Therefore, the decision to do it quite far out.

McNamara: I think, in the first day, there are two primary requirements. The first is to avoid an attack from Cuba, if we possibly can. That means to be at least outside the MiG-21 range and the MiG-19 range. The MiG-19 range with external fuel tanks is around 450 nautical miles.

The second requirement is to choose a ship that has offensive weapons on it and stop it, and search it, and get the evidence.

Now, those two requirements dictate the choice of *Kimovsk* for tomorrow, if we can find it and if we can stop it. That's the way we have laid out tomorrow's operation.

President Kennedy: Is there a chance that vessels will arrive [in Cuba] on Friday [October 26] or Thursday [October 25]? I don't know whether this is a problem, if that's important, but [ships] having beat the blockade. I suppose you can't pick them all up.

McNamara: Well, we're not certain, Mr. President.

President Kennedy: Well, in any case—

Bundy: We do not know of anything that gives us particular concern, that we're not planning to stop.

President Kennedy: All right. I think we're all set to sign this thing [the quarantine proclamation].

Sorensen: It's a minor problem I'd like to raise. We do have a minor drafting problem. It seems to me that the order ought to specify when ships are taken into custody. I suggest, towards the top of page 4, in the third line, strike the word "not" and change the word "unless" to "if."

President Kennedy: Now, where is that again? Wait a second. Top—

Sorensen: Top of page 4, line 3: "Shall be taken into custody." Otherwise there's no order to give that these ships with material shall be taken into custody.

Gilpatric: Excuse me. T... th...

Rusk: Well, this would completely change the foundation on that.

Bundy: Now, the reason for custody is failing, to refuse, to respond or comply. That's the legal position in this paragraph as it now stands. Do you want to change that?

Sorensen: I think that, well, it's a minor technical point, but the first point you're talking about is that there are those that, you hail the ship, and they refuse to comply. The second is where they actually have the material on board.

President Kennedy: Is there any objection to the change?

[Brief pause.]

Well, let's change it then.[7]

Now, the only question I come back to again is whether in a proclamation of this kind, whether we want to name . . . What we're going to do is stop and take possession of offensive military weapons into Cuba. Because, it's important whether we leave in or out [naming] the Sino-Soviets anywhere. To put it in somewhat, saying that if they do this, we're just going to stop the possession of weapons, or do they come from . . . We know they're coming,

---

7. With the change, this portion of the proclamation read: "Any vessel or craft which fails or refuses to respond to or comply with directions shall be subject to being taken into custody. Any vessel or craft which it is believed is en route to Cuba and may be carrying prohibited materiel . . . shall, wherever possible, be directed to proceed to another destination of its own choice and shall be taken into custody if it fails or refuses to obey such direction."

but is it more—is it then harder to name them in a way which may not be desirable? More challenging?[8]

Rusk: Mr. President, these [advanced weapons] are spread all over the world now. And these other weapons, a cruiser for Chile, for example, couldn't be thought of as offensive weapons.

President Kennedy: I'm ready.

[Bundy appears to collect the proclamation. There is the sound of writing.]

Unidentified: It's on [news ticker] tape ready to go out now. We want to get this out just as fast as we can.

[Unclear exchange.]

Bundy: But the president will actually sign at 7:00.

President Kennedy: It's available for immediate distribution.

Unidentified: We can put it on the tape—on the wire right now. Have your people made the corrections?

Bundy: There are these corrections.

Unidentified: Oh, I agree. Can we send it out, clear it out now?

President Kennedy: Everybody. And the wording will be, this is a proclamation the president will sign at 7:00. Yeah, 7:00, I guess, to the press.

Bundy: I think that's [unclear]. If you stand on this point about the Sino-Soviet . . . raise it again . . . But, it reads "the establishment by" . . . Is the "Soviet power" enough, Mr. Secretary, or does it really need the double ["Sino-Soviet"]?

Rusk: See the OAS resolution; stick with it. In the first paragraph, we could say "extra-hemispheric powers with offensive nuclear capability." In the first paragraph. When we get down to the order of consultation with the OAS.

President Kennedy: But you've got to use the Sino-Soviet [unclear]. Okay. Well, somebody get Pierre [Salinger] then, and get what he needs.

Okay. Now let's get to the . . .

Bundy: Mr. President, one other item that I think is [unclear]. There is a proposal which has been prepositioned without an approval, as you were not enthusiastic about it earlier in the day, for sending an additional message to Chairman Khrushchev.

President Kennedy: What does Tommy say?

---

8. President Kennedy was trying to decide whether it was necessary to specify a national origin of the prohibited weapons. In other words, was it too confrontational, or necessary, to specify that Sino-Soviet weapons were prohibited, or could weapons just be identified by type or category?

Thompson: I think it would be useful if . . . We kicked this off a little earlier.

The idea was that they will, tonight, be deciding on what instructions are going to go to these ships. I wouldn't be surprised if there is, if there was, a debate. They can tell there is an alternative to going ahead with forcing this thing. That means we fire on them, and therefore kicks off probably the retaliation in Berlin.

The second point, which you already . . . You have a letter [now in from Khrushchev] to answer. This is an answer to put the ball in his court

President Kennedy: [addr—

. . .eps which started the current chain of events was the action of your government in secretly furnishing offensive weapons to Cuba. We will be discussing (we are discussing) this matter in the Security Council. In the meantime I am concerned that we both show prudence and do nothing to allow events to make the situation more difficult to control than it already is.

"I hope that you will issue immediately the necessary instructions to your ships to observe the quarantine, the basis of which was established by the Organization of American States this afternoon. You may or may not have sent this. We have no desire to fire upon your vessels."

Now, this depends a good deal on intelligence. And we've had no indication of any Soviet instructions or reactions in any way to pull away, or narrow, or widen the gap.

McCone: None at all.

Rusk: Just the converse.

McCone: Intelligence might indicate the contrary. Gossip at the United Nations so far has indicated the contrary—that the instructions are to go through. But we have nothing very hard.

Thompson: The Soviet embassy this afternoon gave a copy of Khrushchev's letter to you to the Soviet affairs section [of the State Department]. That indicates they will rely on this exchange, rely on the record.

Nitze?: We still have one problem in this, and that is that they might come back and reply, saying: "We will not send our ships in. But we would expect from you comparable observance in the criterion you've set, and you won't attack anything in Cuba or extend the blockade." In other words, set up a situation in which they freeze the status quo with the missiles there.

Bundy: Very unlikely, but possible.

President Kennedy: Well, we can always come back and say that's unacceptable.

This is just probably one last effort before what's going to happen tomorrow morning. Anybody have any objection to sending this? [To Thompson] You think it's a good thing to do?

Thompson: No, I don't feel strongly about it. I think it could be helpful in their last-minute decision.

President Kennedy: Okay. Well, let's send it, then. I don't think we're giving away much.

I don't think we want that last sentence in there, do we?

Okay. Well, let's send that, then.

Bundy: Will you do that, George, or—

Ball: It's this draft we're agreed upon then, without the last sentence.

President Kennedy: Are we telling the Soviet embassy this begins tomorrow morning?

Ball: Well, we legally established this afternoon. Now, this was the basis for which it was legally established.

President Kennedy: Do they know we're saying this commences tomorrow morning [Washington time]?

Ball: It [the last sentence of the letter] really ought to be: "the basis for which was legally established this afternoon."

President Kennedy: "Which commences" . . . Have you told them it's going to commence tomorrow morning?

Ball: Well, that's what this present proclamation [says], which will be delivered to them by our embassy.

Unidentified: I think it might be well . . . You know, that's going to be a little time getting to them.

President Kennedy: This letter may have a little priority.

Bundy: [redrafting last sentence of letter] "and which will go into effect at 1400 hours Greenwich time, October 24."

Within an hour the letter was sent to the U.S. embassy in Moscow for delivery to Khrushchev. Its text was as agreed, ending with: "I hope that you will issue immediately the necessary instructions to your ships to observe the terms of the quarantine, the basis of which was established by the vote of the Organization of American States this afternoon, and which will go into effect at 1400 hours Greenwich time October 24."

Rusk: The mobs [of protesters] that we stimulated turned up in London instead of Havana. 2,000 people.

President Kennedy: Surrounding the American embassy?

Rusk: Bertrand Russell's [British peace movement] people stormed the embassy there. We haven't had any reports of them disarming Cul

Bundy: South America?

. . . . ing to say exactly what instructions we'll give to Dennison. We ought to try to avoid shooting a ship, a Soviet ship carrying wheat to Cuba or medicine or something of that kind of item. And therefore, I would propose to try to pick a ship which almost certainly carries offensive weapons as the first ship. And not allow any other Soviet ship to be hailed until that particular ship has been hailed. Now, this is going to be difficult because it means we have to try to see in advance what the ships . . .

President Kennedy: Does it mean, though, that by the end of the day, Thursday [October 25], there will be ships arriving in Cuba which will make it, clear, from before the blockade?

McNamara: Oh yes.

President Kennedy: The only problem I see, Bob, I would think that the Soviets, if there is a vessel among them [carrying offensive weapons], that's the one vessel I would think they would turn around.

[22 seconds excised as classified information.]

McNamara: . . . There's been no change in course that we have as yet detected.

Rusk: Well, that could well be the biggest of the ships.

Bundy: They're all going on course, aren't they?

McNamara: They're all going on course. That's right. As best we can tell.

[8 seconds excised as classified information.]

Rusk: I would think that there would be some advantage in testing out on any other kind of ship.

McNamara: You mean a British ship and so on?

Rusk: No. I mean a Soviet ship that didn't have food and medical provisions.

McNamara: But the instruction from Khrushchev is very likely to be: "Don't stop under any circumstances." So the baby-food ship comes out and we hail it. I think we shoot it. We shoot . . .

President Kennedy: That's what could happen. They're gonna keep going. And we're gonna try to shoot the rudder off or the boiler. And then we're going to try to board it. And they're going to fire guns, machine guns. And we're going to have one hell of a time trying to get aboard that thing and getting control of it, because they're pretty tough, and I suppose they may have soldiers or marines aboard their ships. They have technicians who are in the military. So I would think that the taking of those ships is going to be a major operation. We may have to sink it rather than just take it.

Bundy: Or to get aboard it, and blow it up?

President Kennedy: I think that's less likely than having a real fight in trying to board it, because they may have 5, 6, or 700 people aboard there with guns. A destroyer . . .

McNamara: Most of these [Soviet] ships, Mr. President, are not likely to have that kind of a crew on board. The crews are relatively small in the type of ships that we wish to stop.

Rusk: What would we do now about a ship that has been disabled, and it's not going to sink? It just can't go anywhere?

McNamara: We have tows.

Rusk: Dakar?

McNamara: We tow it to a prize port.

Ball: I see, which means a United States port.

McNamara: Yes. Charleston. Jacksonville.

President Kennedy: Well, then we take it back to port and we find out it's got baby food on it.

McNamara: Well, we inspect it before we take it into port to try to—if it's baby food being shipped, we're in . . .

[Unclear brief exchange, culminating in laughter].

President Kennedy: Well, that's what we're going to have to do.

Now, the only thing is, these fellows need as detailed instructions as possible, from those who are knowledgeable about the sea and know just how to proceed on this.

Let's say they shoot, and the boat stops. Then they try a signal for a boarding party, and they say they're not going to permit a boarding party aboard. The ship is drifting. Then I don't think we can probably get aboard, unless we want to go through a machine-gun operation. The destroyers aren't equipped. Now, the ship may be tough to get aboard. You have a real fight aboard there.

Gilpatric: Well, the cruisers have helicopters.

McNamara: Unless these freighters are carrying substantial security guards—I don't believe we have evidence they are—it shouldn't be too difficult. In a search there may be a firefight, but it ought to be a small one. The normal—

[Unclear interjections.]

McCone: It won't be easy.

Rusk: [Unclear] Kh~ ~

. . . . . .boats have cameras.

. . . . . .that they are to understand what's allowed to be

. . . . ponse, first to stop, or not to stop. Secondly, when they do the action as they do, they're liable not to permit you to board.

Now, what do we say if there is machine-gun fire, et cetera—our vessel trying to board. Now, what do we say to them then? Do we let them drift around?

McNamara: I think at that point, Mr. President, we have to leave it to the local commander. Depending on the seas, and whether there is a submarine in the area, there are just a host of circumstances we've thought of. We don't believe we should try to give orders from here in relation to—

President Kennedy: We don't want to tell them necessarily to go aboard there. If we disable it and they should refuse to let us aboard, I think you stay with it, certainly for a day or so, and not boarding. Just let it drift.

Taylor: I think we just have to say, Mr. President, to use a mission type of order: To use the minimum force required to—

President Kennedy: That doesn't give them quite . . . I think it misses the point. If we disabled the ship and they're 800 miles out and they refuse to let us aboard, I don't think that we ought, he ought, to feel that he has to board that thing in order to carry out our orders.

Taylor: Well, he . . . To keep ships from going to Cuba, that's his basic mission now.

President Kennedy: I think in the beginning it would be better, if this situation happened, to let that boat lie there disabled for a day or so, not to try to board it and have them reopen machine guns and have 30–40 people killed on each side. That would be . . .

McNamara: I think there's some problem, Mr. President. If for some reason they are moving in the area, we ought to board it, and inspect it, and get out of there if necessary, towing the ship or leaving the ship there. This [Soviet] sub, moving in, we have some serious problems. This is one of the difficulties we face. Admiral Anderson is somewhat concerned about the possibility that they'll try to sink one of our major vessels, such as a [aircraft] carrier.

Gilpatric: The submarine just fueled yesterday in the Azores and is moving west.[9]

McNamara: They sent a ship under high speed to fuel a submarine yesterday, which did fuel and was observed fueling. And the sub was obviously going to move into a Cuban area. There may well be others that we're not aware of. I think we have to allow the commander on the scene a certain amount of latitude to—

Bundy: Do you have the [aircraft carrier U.S.S.] *Enterprise* in the area?

McNamara: We have the *Enterprise* in the area, yes. And [the aircraft carrier U.S.S.] *Independence.*

President Kennedy: Do we want to keep the *Enterprise* there?

McNamara: Well, the *Enterprise* is not at this moment anywhere close to the area of the *Kimovsk.*[10]

McCone: We need aircraft surveillance of the area.

President Kennedy: A submarine could really do these aircraft carriers— could do a lot of damage.

Bundy: Well, we expect to know reasonably well where the submarines are. Am I not right? [Others agree.]

President Kennedy: All right. Mr. Secretary, well, I think I'd make sure that you have reviewed these instructions that go out to him.

McNamara: I have, and I will do so by the end of the night, sir.

Bundy: Well, we have some decisions coming out of this morning['s meet-

9. Several Soviet F-class (termed "Foxtrot") attack submarines, then the most modern such vessels in their navy, had left Murmansk at the end of September and had moved into the open Atlantic, the first time such submarines had ventured so close to American waters. There they were apparently to rendezvous with a Soviet oiler, the *Terek,* and a supply ship that had been deployed to the same area of the Atlantic. The U.S. Navy endeavored to monitor these movements as closely as possible. See Dino A. Brugioni, *Eyeball to Eyeball: The Inside Story of the Cuban Missile Crisis,* ed. Robert F. McCort (New York: Random House, 1991), pp. 385–386.

10. The military experts expected the Soviet submarines to provide an undersea escort for the most important vessels heading toward Cuba, such as the *Kimovsk.*

ing]. The Attorney General has one, which is the problem of foreign bottoms on coastwise shipping.

Gilpatric: May I first say that we found this is not the problem that we thought. There are only 18 American-flag ships now engaged in coastal trade or any coastal trade on the Atlantic, and they're all specialized types of design, John, and they would not be the type that we would take. The ships that we would requisition or charter are all engaged in the export/import, foreign trade. They represent about 10 percent of the total foreign trade on the Atlantic. Our take would be . . . John, with

McCone: Intercoastal too? I'm sure offshore ships are coming back—Japan, Honolulu. And lumber and all that.

Gilpatric: We're not going to take those.

Rusk: Maybe we should pick up some ships under charter with the Soviet Union.

Gilpatric: Well, we want [American-]flag ships.

President Kennedy: They may attempt to stop one of our ships. Might not sink 'em.

McNamara: I think it's particularly possible that the Cubans will try to stop or sink some of our ships in the Passages [unclear].

President Kennedy: Are we sending out some warning to our merchant ships?

McNamara: We are sending warnings out to them, and we are also providing air cover of a sort. We can't provide constant cover over every merchant in that area, but we do have air cover over the area, and we will be prepared to attack their attackers. So I think this is a real possibility. We could lose a merchant ship in and around Cuba, quickly.

President Kennedy: Okay.

Bundy: Is there anything you want to add on the foreign bottoms?

Robert Kennedy: It's not a problem. It's academic. The answer to the question is [unclear].

McCone: Very quickly, Mr. President, do you have the report of the low-level flights we were doing today? Well, we just got the photographs and they're not very [unclear]. They don't give you very much [unclear].

[The voices fade as the reel of tape apparently comes to an end. During the interval while the tape is being replaced, President Kennedy apparently urges that General Norstad be retained as NATO Supreme Commander in Europe during the crisis, putting off the scheduled transfer of command to General Lyman Lemnitzer. Kennedy has been particularly impressed by a cable from Norstad, received earlier that day, describing how he has tempered the possible alert of NATO defense forces in order to keep from inflaming international sensitivities.[11]

Then Assistant Secretary of Defense for Civil Defense Steuart Pittman begins a briefing on U.S. readiness to withstand a Soviet nuclear attack. The tape recording resumes at this point, but the audio quality is poor.]

Pittman: . . . from Cuba, or the possibility of the use of nuclear weapons. So that in the [unclear] from Cuba there is a somewhat limited extent of weapons [unclear].

Local civil-defense organizations have been preparing for that kind of event through the years. Most of our efforts in the last years have been to redirect their attention to the subject of nuclear warfare and for a particularly strong civil defense, and to aid the military [unclear] organization—exactly what kind of police and firefighting, mass casualty care, and so on. They're imperfect, but there's something there in the cities and the rural areas.

If nuclear weapons are used, we can draw an arc and try to assess the civil-defense capabilities at [a possible missile strike radius of] around 1,100 nautical miles [from Cuba], and make a little allowance for [radioactive] fallout on the outer fringe. That takes in 92 million people [in the United States], 58 cities of over 100,000 population. For a light, relatively light, nuclear attack of this type, we would lower the protection factors we use in deciding what existing buildings would serve as adequate protection [against blast, heat, and direct exposure to radiation from the nuclear detonation]. We'd be up against going down to a 40-protection factor. We now set a limit of a 100-protection factor. That would be [buildings that are] cutting the radiation by 40 times instead of 100 times.

11. See McCone to File, "Executive Committee Meeting on 23 October 1962, 6:00 P.M.," in McAuliffe, *CIA Documents,* p. 291. Norstad's cable, which so impressed President Kennedy, had explained that he was not putting U.S. forces in Europe into the highest state of preparedness for war but was merely recommending to commanders that "certain precautionary military measures should be taken of a non-provocative and non-public nature"; Paris 1907, 22 October 1962, Record Group 59, National Archives, Washington, D.C.

To do this, we'd have the information in hand, and in the hands of the local civil-defense directors of states, on buildings that will take care of 40 million people of the 92 million in this area. The spaces are stocked, and in the process of being stocked, for the 100-protection factor or above. But sometimes it's got to be a lower-protection-factor space. The [unclear] spaces had intended to be stocked by now. We can do a little acceleration [unclear].[12]

President Kennedy: Okay. Well, let me just ask you this. It seems to me the most likely problem you're going to have in the next 10 days is if we decide to invade Cuba. We need to [consider that they] fire these weapons. Or at least we've got to go un...

... fallout, the only protection that exists today is in the cities, and there's little or no protection in the rural areas.

President Kennedy: Well, we have to assume that there isn't going to be very much, and on the assumption of that, we're not going to have an all-out nuclear exchange. If we were going to have an all-out nuclear exchange, then we'd have a different problem.

Let's say we're going into Cuba, and there's maybe, involved, 5 or 10 or 15 [missiles launched against the United States]. That kind of fallout. Not the usual—I don't know how many megatons. What is it we do, before we go in, by the time we say we're going to invade Cuba, if we give you, say, 5 or 6 or 7 days' notice? What can we do during this period of a week in which this risk will be with us, for 3 or 4 days? What is it that we ought to do for the population in affected areas, in case the bombs go off? Is there something we can do?

[At this point the recording becomes practically inaudible for about 11 minutes. McCone summarized the ensuing discussion as follows: "The President asked what emergency steps could be taken. Replied that many arrangements could be made without too much publicity, such as repositioning food, actually obtaining space, putting up shelter signs, etc. I got the conclusion that

---

12. Pittman is referring to stocking with survival supplies civil-defense, or fallout, shelters where people would take refuge in order to try to survive a nuclear attack and its aftermath.

not very much could or would be done; that whatever was done would involve a great deal of publicity and public alarm."[13]

The recording then becomes slightly more audible, with fragments of conversation referring to SAM sites and to Nitze's assignment as chairman of a subcommittee to examine Berlin issues. In this capacity Nitze was invited to sit in regularly on Executive Committee meetings. The meeting can be heard breaking up, with people leaving. Several conversations are going on at once. Bundy can be heard making another suggestion.]

Bundy: . . . and, second, we need to have a group concerned with a little further down the road than we're able to get at meetings like this. I think it would be useful if we could preempt Walt Rostow,[14] and provide an executive secretary for the White House, and swing that into another subcommittee of this enterprise with some of the people who have already begun working on that. It's a little different than what we've got today.

Unidentified: We talked about it today at lunch and liked it.

[Unclear group discussion.]

Bundy: Department of State [unclear] responsibility to this committee, too, and rather than have two bodies, it would be best to have one.

[Mostly inaudible group discussion continues for a few more minutes. Concern is expressed that some action under consideration might prompt a Soviet response affecting Berlin. Taylor can be heard agreeing that the few people remaining should "wait until the President comes back, and see what his reaction is."]

President Kennedy publicly signed the quarantine proclamation shortly after 7:00 P.M.

During the day, with support from U.S. ambassador David Bruce, Macmillan had been pressing hard for U.S. permission to display photographs of the missile sites to the mass media in order to pacify domestic protests about the American action. Possibly as a result of some misunderstanding in communications between the Prime Minister's office and the White House, Macmillan told Bruce that the White House had granted permission for the photos to be shown on TV. A CIA briefer then gave a background briefing to waiting reporters, who filmed his displays. News of the televised photographs broke that evening in Washington, arousing press anger (since the British journalists had "scooped" their Washington counterparts) and official consternation.

---

13. McCone to File, "Executive Committee Meeting," p. 291.
14. Counselor of the Department of State and Chairman of the Policy Planning Council.

President Kennedy joined his advisers shortly after signing the quarantine proclamation. As audible recording resumes, there seem to be only a few people in the room, and the atmosphere is informal. President Kennedy first reacts to the news of the British broadcast of the missile photographs.

[Unclear group discussion.]
President Kennedy: Bobby?
Robert Kennedy: Yeah?
President Kennedy: I don't ~

President Kennedy: Get somebody to call up [Ambassador] Bruce.[15]
[Unclear discussion.]
Thompson: No. In fact, that's an act of war. I think that the danger . . .
Robert Kennedy: General Clay indicated that he would go to Berlin, and that he would be glad to go in an official capacity.[16] I guess the general agreement is that there would be, that it would focus attention on Berlin right at the moment by him going there.

Perhaps General Taylor could tell him that we appreciate the offer and that [unclear].

[Unclear exchange.]
Taylor: Mr. President, this was at 5:55, he [Clay] tried to get me.
President Kennedy: You can call, General. Just say, we don't want Berlin squeezed. And we may be getting you to go [there] over the next 2 or 3 days . . .
Bundy: I want him on standby. [President Kennedy agrees.]
[Unclear group discussion.]

15. The White House later put out the explanation that it had intended to release the pictures anyway but that an errant embassy official in London had jumped the gun. McCone supervised the reproduction of photos, identical with those made available in England, which were distributed late that night to the Washington press corps.

16. General Lucius Clay had been the head of the U.S. military government in Germany after World War II and before the creation of the Federal Republic. A well-known and well-regarded figure in Germany, Clay had been President Kennedy's special representative to Berlin until the spring of 1962. He was still a consultant to the Joint Chiefs of Staff.

Robert Kennedy: Hey, General?

Taylor: Yeah?

Unidentified: Now, what do I say with [unclear]?

President Kennedy: Should I say I want to review our whole military strategy? [Laughter.]

Robert Kennedy: I've got a feeling I don't like to see you people go. You've got all the answers!

[The room falls silent as people leave. Robert Kennedy and the President are apparently alone, with the tape recorder still running.]

Robert Kennedy: What was that?

President Kennedy: Christ, I've got a dinner tonight.

Robert Kennedy: What?

President Kennedy: I've got a dinner tonight. [Unclear] invited somebody along and [unclear].[17]

Robert Kennedy: [Unclear], doesn't it?

President Kennedy: It looks really mean, doesn't it?

But, on the other hand, there wasn't any other choice. If he's going to get this mean on this one, in our part of the world [unclear], no choice. I don't think there was a choice.

Robert Kennedy: Well, there isn't any choice. I mean, you would have been, you would have been impeached.

President Kennedy: Well, I think I would have been impeached.[18]

[Unclear brief exchange.]

---

17. Returning a favor of hospitality shown when Jacqueline Kennedy had visited India, President Kennedy had agreed before the crisis to host a dinner on October 23 for the Maharajah and Maharani of Jaipur, staying at the White House guest quarters in Blair House.

18. Robert Kennedy recalled a part of this exchange in his memoir. In his account President Kennedy said: "'It looks really mean, doesn't it? But then, really there was no other choice. If they get this mean on this one in our part of the world, what will they do on the next?' 'I just don't think there was any choice,' I said, 'and not only that, if you hadn't acted, you would have been impeached.' The President thought for a moment and said, 'That's what I think—I would have been impeached'"; *Thirteen Days*, p. 67. Robert Kennedy placed this conversation the next morning, October 24. However, from both the tape itself and various small clues in the conversation (such as the discussion about the release of photos in Britain, the brief exchange with Taylor at the start, and the references to the dinner), we think it more likely that the conversation occurred at about 7:30 P.M. on October 23. Robert Kennedy did recall in his memoir that after that evening's group meeting, and a smaller informal gathering after the proclamation signing, "the President and I talked for a little while alone. He suggested that I might visit Ambassador Dobrynin and personally relate to him the serious implications of the Russians' duplicity"; ibid., p. 63. The germination of this suggestion is apparent later in this taped conversation.

If there had been a move to impeach, I would have been [unclear], on the grounds that I said they wouldn't do it, and . . .

Robert Kennedy: [Unclear] something else. They'd think up some other step that wasn't necessary. You'd be . . . But now, the fact is, you couldn't have done any less.

The fact is, you got all the South American countries to vote unanimously in the OAS. After 2 years [in office], they have unanimously voted for this, and then get the reaction from the rest of the allies like General de Gaulle and . . . had to do it. You can't be all . . . I mean, if it's

Robert Kennedy:

President Kennedy: The ships are going to go?

Robert Kennedy: He said this is [chuckles slightly], this is a defensive base for the Russians. It's got nothing to do with the Cubans.

President Kennedy: Why are . . . They're lying [unclear] that. Khrushchev's horseshit about the election. Anyway, the sickening thing that's so very bad is what this revealed about . . . [sarcastically] This horror about embarrassing me in the election. Who said [unclear]?

Robert Kennedy: Well, you know, he [Georgi Bolshakov] probably heard it.

I hadn't seen him. Then he came back to see me, and he said Khrushchev had a message for you. And I followed it up. The ambassador [Dobrynin] kept telling me: "Don't pay attention to Georgi."

President Kennedy: But they didn't tell you that there were missiles there.

Robert Kennedy: No. Remember, I told you that.

I said to—tell Charlie Bartlett to get hold of Georgi.[20]

---

19. Georgi Bolshakov, a military attaché at the Soviet embassy, who was presumed to be affiliated with Soviet military intelligence or the KGB. Until the summer of 1962, Bolshakov had been the principal channel for special private communications between the White House and the Kremlin. The channel ran through Robert Kennedy, and the two men had become close friends. The 1962 arrival of the new Soviet ambassador, a talented and seasoned diplomat, Anatoly Dobrynin, displaced Bolshakov as Dobrynin sought successfully to make himself the principal contact in this special channel.

20. Charles Bartlett, a journalist and a friend of the Kennedys. There are varying accounts

President Kennedy: What did he say?

Robert Kennedy: Let's just say that it was based a good deal [by Bartlett] on: President had great confidence in the ambassador [Dobrynin]. We had this exchange. The ambassador said that they weren't going to put the missiles in there. The President went on television [on September 13], took his position based on a lot of these personal assurances because he thought that he could believe them.

President Kennedy: The ambassador and all the rest.

You said that to [unclear] Georgi.

Robert Kennedy: I told him so.

[Unclear exchange; reference to Bartlett.]

Robert Kennedy: I think they're pretty good. You know, the press reaction.

President Kennedy: Until tomorrow morning.

Robert Kennedy: We all recognize it's going to get unpleasant.

President Kennedy: [Unclear] I mean, if we get it . . .

Robert Kennedy: That's the thing. Luckiest thing in the world [that news of the missiles in Cuba did not leak earlier]. Number one, [unclear] want or [unclear] want out. You really had to make up your mind on Thursday [October 18]. I mean, if the facts got out, you'd have had to make up your mind, and forced to move, and couldn't get hold of the South American countries and Central America, and get this thing set up. That would've been awful tough. I think we would have just . . .

President Kennedy: [Unclear] air strike?

Robert Kennedy: Yeah.

President Kennedy: I mean, you look at the status. You see a mess over there. Go in there and shootin' up, everything up. Then the Russians would really be tense. This way they have to . . . We have the united thing with the whole hemisphere, and go in and we know [unclear].

Robert Kennedy: I don't know whether you could get . . . You know, talking about the ships, I don't know whether we could pursue that with them. But if you get the group from the OAS, they disable the ship, or stay with the ship. Then they fire guns or things across the bow. Then they send for representatives from OAS or something. It's not just the United States doing this. And then

---

about interactions between Bolshakov, Robert Kennedy, and Bartlett during the crisis. See Michael R. Beschloss, *The Crisis Years: Kennedy and Khrushchev, 1960–1963* (New York: HarperCollins, 1991), pp. 500–501.

they come out. I don't know what they do when they get there, but they request to board or request the ship to stop. And they name the OAS.

President Kennedy: Take [unclear] the United States. [Unclear] have a committee to oversee. Not the blockade.

Robert Kennedy: Yeah, not have the United States be doing it.

President Kennedy: The OAS is a better type of exposure.

Robert Kennedy: Let's say, once they locate the ship, have the OAS [unclear]. Have the OAS fly, to move out, to board our ship.

President Kennedy: How would they land?

embassy. Robert Kennedy confronted Dobrynin with accusations of deceit. Dobrynin said he had known only what his government had told him. Asked if Soviet ships would challenge the quarantine, Dobrynin said that those were their instructions, and he knew of no changes.

Meanwhile, after a private dinner, President Kennedy discussed the crisis and the day's diplomatic activities at length with Ormsby-Gore. Robert Kennedy joined them at the White House and reported on his meeting with Dobrynin. Both Americans asked Ormsby-Gore how he thought the matter would end. He thought there would either be war or a negotiated settlement, and that everyone in their right mind would prefer the latter alternative. However, before Kennedy met Khrushchev the Soviet leader should have no doubt about America's resolution and that the United States would make no unilateral concessions. Otherwise the results would be disastrous. Ormsby-Gore reported that both Kennedys agreed "with this summing up."

President Kennedy had also reviewed with Ormsby-Gore the ideas discussed earlier in the evening for intercepting the first Soviet ships. Ormsby-Gore urged that instead of attempting an interception 800 miles from Cuba, as McNamara had recommended at the meeting, the Americans shorten the radius to 500 miles and thus give the Russians more time to consider their options. Kennedy promptly phoned McNamara and passed along this suggestion. Again McNamara urged the need to stay out of range of Cuban aircraft. President Kennedy was unimpressed by this argument, and they agreed that a line 500 miles out made more sense, though the actual application might vary and would depend on the circumstances of the interception.[21]

As the day ended, military forces around the world moved into states of higher readiness. That evening Castro delivered a televised address ordering a full mobilization and placing Cuban armed forces on the highest stage of alert.

21. On Robert Kennedy's meeting with Dobrynin see Robert Kennedy to President Kennedy, October 24, 1962, in *FRUS 1961–1963,* vol. 11: *Cuban Missile Crisis and Aftermath,* pp. 175–177. The general content of the meeting with Ormsby-Gore is confirmed in Kennedy, *Thirteen Days,* pp. 66–67; but for details we relied on the ambassador's reports of his talks, both titled "Cuba," Washington 2662 and Washington 2664, and both sent on October 24, 1962, PRO, PREM 11/3690, 24020.

Though the earlier White House discussions on October 23 might have given the Kennedys the impression that there was a quarantine "line" fixed at a given radius from Cuba, there is little evidence that such a formal line was actually contemplated by the relevant military planners. Interceptions were being contemplated in a more flexible way, with attention to danger both from aircraft in Cuba (almost all of which were the shorter-range MiGs) and from Soviet submarines, as well as concentration on the specific ships that would be intercepted.

WEDNESDAY, OCTOBER 24

10:00 A.M.

CABINET ROOM

‑‑‑, on a
‑‑‑y convened, the quarantine
‑ ‑‑‑ legal effect.

‑‑ ‑‑‑ same time the quarantine became effective, the Strategic Air Command moved from the general Defense Condition 3 that applied to all U.S. armed forces to the higher Defense Condition 2, the level just below general war. In addition to ICBMs and submarine-based ballistic missiles, every available bomber—more than 1,400 aircraft—went on alert. Scores of bombers, each loaded with several nuclear weapons and carrying folders for preassigned targets in the Soviet Union, were kept continuously in the air around the clock, with shifts, refueled by aerial tankers, taking turns hovering over northern Canada, Greenland, and the Mediterranean Sea. The Soviet government was presumed to be aware of these movements.[1]

President Kennedy turned on the tape recorder as McCone presented his briefing on the intelligence that had come in through the night.

McCone: . . . We do not believe the measures to achieve a higher degree of action readiness for Soviet and Soviet-bloc forces are being taken on a crash basis.

1. The enhanced readiness and deployment of SAC forces were ordered, with McNamara's approval, in JCS 6917 to CINCSAC [Commander-in-Chief, Strategic Air Command], 23 October 1962; Notes Taken from Transcripts of Meetings of the Joint Chiefs of Staff, October–November 1962, p. 17, National Security Archive, Washington, D.C. See also Scott D. Sagan, *The Limits of Safety: Organizations, Accidents, and Nuclear Weapons* (Princeton: Princeton University Press, 1993), pp. 62–67.

Communist reaction to the U.S. quarantine action against Cuba has not gone beyond the highly critical but uncommitting statement issued yesterday by the Soviet government.

Surveillance of Cuba indicates the continued rapid progress in completion of the IRBMs and MRBMs. No new sites have been discovered. We had these two [low-level reconnaissance] flights yesterday, but one of them had 40 percent cloud coverage. Another one had 15 percent [unclear]. Buildings believed to afford nuclear storage are being assembled with great rapidity. Cuban naval vessels have been ordered to blocking positions at Banes and Santiago Bays.

Survey of Soviet shipping shows 16 dry-cargo and 6 tanker ships en route to arrive in Cuba. Of these 22, 9 are in position to begin arriving by the end of October. Three ships have hatches suitable for carrying missiles, and 2 of these are among the ships that have received urgent coded traffic from Moscow. [Unclear.] At 1:00 A.M. yesterday, there were 7 ships, including the *Poltava* but not the *Kimovsk*. At 2:30 A.M. this morning, all ships, including the *Kimovsk*, were contacted. [Unclear] then, shortly afterwards, that both [messages to the ships] came out of Odessa control [station for Soviet shipping]. Shortly after that, the Odessa control station notified all ships that, hereafter, all orders would come from Moscow.

The official world reaction showed generally favorable response to the U.S. action, particularly in Latin America.

There are no indications of any Soviet aircraft approaching Cuba. Additional information reported a [Soviet] submarine is tracking the *Kimovsk*. However, the latest position report indicates they're about 200 miles from [unclear]. There are 3, or possibly 4, submarines in the Atlantic.

A Cuban airliner left Goose Bay this morning, from Dakar, bound for Havana, and had aboard 75 people and [unclear] thousand pounds of cargo.

[24 seconds excised as classified information. After the excision there are references to "black boxes," "detection," "aircraft," and "ships."]

I have ordered the [interagency intelligence] Watch Committee to meet every morning at 8:00. Today they reported [unclear]. They concluded that the Soviet Union, for the past several days, has taken steps to bring its military forces into a complete state of readiness. There are indications of preparations for the deployment of long-range aircraft to Arctic bases. We have so far noted no major redeployment of other Soviet-bloc forces. However, there are tentative indications [unclear] in the European area. Bloc military forces [unclear] higher state of readiness.

I think that's all of the . . .

Dillon: A practical thing. Coast Guard and Treasury have lifted up 6 of these "black boxes" for CIA's use. As a result, we're out of them, and we're not in a position to carry out our port security, as far as . . .

President Kennedy: Who would have the responsibility for replacing them? The CIA?

McCone: I don't know. We'll get some more. We ordered . . . It'll take a little while to get any.

President Kennedy: I would think we'd need enough f~~~ ~ ~ ~ ~ ~ sibility to the agency [CIA] ~~ ~~

~~~~~ low-level

~~ ~~~ new flight, this is an MRBM launch ~~~~~~~ 5, and right back to accompany it is the low-level flight which was consummated yesterday.

Down around the south you see the architecture. The missile bay buildings are here. That is a missile on a trailer that is probably battened down with canvas, as you can see. The erector and launch pad is also covered.

President Kennedy: Camouflaged?

Lundahl: Yes, sir. They've got some kind of markings on the top of it. In some instances, you can see it better than others. This is the hydrogen peroxide. The auxiliary vehicles are over in here. This is another erector and launch pad, again battened down with canvas and various kinds of materials to make it harder to see. This is the missile ready building. These are fueling vehicles, and I think it fits very closely [unclear].

There is one pad here, sir, with the erector on it, and the secondary is over at this area here. And these are the missiles already shown. We don't get a clear, unobstructed look at a missile because they're all covered over.

I have a couple [of] others that relate to the same story. Here is a high-level—a high-speed aircraft is going by one of the erectors. Sir, you can see the kind of camouflage netting over the top of it. I think you can see the large cable that goes back into the power system that erects that thing. You see the supporting vehicles, at the base of that cliff. This is again on that same MR-5 rig.

I have another one here, sir. This is again at MR-5. This is another look at one of these launcher-erectors. See, it's covered over with canvas netting.

President Kennedy: It would be awfully difficult. If they could get the ground cover down, they'd be awfully difficult to find.

Lundahl: It never was successful in World War II, sir. We always managed to get through the camouflage. It was successful best against high-level bombers who were trying to pick their aiming points. But the PI [National Photographic Interpretation Center] uses camouflage detection, and a lot of other things that haven't been brought into this meeting here. I think we'll find them once we know what they are.

[Unclear brief exchange.]

There are 5 missiles there, sir, lying side by side right along the road.

[Mixed voices.]

This is [unclear], sir. There's nothing but light framing, and canvas stretched over these missiles. They're all covered over, as you can see. Support personnel walking around on the ground down there on the parking lot. This is the old [unclear], the MR-4 site, and actually I can show you one of the low-level shots which ties to that one.

This is an IRBM site with fairly extensive construction. You can see the troops standing around. That is one launch pad there with a kind of a pup tent over the hole in the ground. The conduiting goes back to this black wall here. Here are the cables that come out of the control bunker in here. This is the cable track that goes into the specific vehicle positioned here. This is the other launch pad over here. There is generally no concrete bunker or bearing structures in here. This is what we think is probably one of the nuclear storage bunkers. It's the [unclear].

[Unclear exchange.]

McCone: I would like to have more of these [unclear] low-level [unclear]. This is the complete readout. I would like extend the [unclear] . . . send them up between 11:00 and 12:00 this morning.

President Kennedy: Actually, these are not particularly, not as dramatic as those earlier ones which had the active missiles early on.

McCone: Well, he used camouflage.

[Unclear exchange.]

Rusk: . . . indications that the Cuban armed forces have been given their instructions not to shoot at overflying aircraft, except in self-defense.

[Unclear exchange in which Rusk discusses the source of the information] . . . got that from a naval communications ship.[2]

---

2. A U.S. Navy electronic intelligence ship, the U.S.S. *Oxford,* was then deployed in international waters just off the coast of Cuba.

Mr. President, I would like [unclear] hostile reaction. And there has been, all the way through, an element of caution and [no] freedom of action from Moscow [unclear]. His [Khrushchev's] public line seems designed to leave him with some option to back off, if he chooses. The impression of a pure U.S.-Cuban fracas will be hard to maintain once we're in a U.S.-Soviet incident at sea.

On balance we think the probable Soviet [unclear] is to provoke such an incident, in the expectation that the result [unclear] will stim... on the U.S. to end the quar.......

...... this

...... our other operational matters first.

... is the communication problem. Dr. Wiesner and an interdepartmental team is standing by. But perhaps first you want to hear from the Secretary of Defense on the current military situation.

McNamara: Mr. President, first [unclear mention of the vulnerability of U.S. aircraft on crowded airfields in Florida; photos of the U.S. aircraft on these fields are being displayed]. These are our own aircraft, about 150 of them in position. [Unclear; reference to Homestead Air Force Base.]

Taylor: [Unclear] . . . What we have done is to put them in a very high state of readiness, beyond, I would say, the level which is now necessary.[3]

The question then is if we backtrack somewhat, and we at least move the planes out, perhaps leaving the logistical support in place while moving onto . . . [Unclear] . . . below the level [of readiness] which we now maintain, which is [being able to launch strike aircraft within] 4 hours.

President Kennedy: Where are you dispersing these planes [unclear]? [Unclear reply by Taylor.]

[Unclear] . . . the site, 50 to 60 MiGs that come over, they'll shoot up, they'll take out a lot of our men.

Taylor: We're making every preparation against that that we can, and that

---

3. The Joint Chiefs of Staff had met earlier that morning. Taylor had explained that McNamara would be bringing photos of crowded Florida airfields to the White House and asked whether the planes should disperse. LeMay thought it was best to stay on the good concrete airfields with the 450 aircraft, 150 on each of 3 fields; Notes Taken from Transcripts of Meetings of the Joint Chiefs of Staff, p. 17.

would include the low-level fighter attack. [Unclear] at all times. We have air-to-surface ships; we have surface ships, picket ships. We've done everything we can to—

President Kennedy: [Unclear] relying on that. Why don't we just [unclear, possible reference to being lined up wingtip-to-wingtip]?

Taylor: Well, they're in a checkerboard, at least the ones that I've seen. They're orderly, but they're still—

President Kennedy: How many fields are you using there?

Taylor: Four big ones, but only 2 [unclear], Homestead and Key West. If they come in low-level, they can't reach the northern [unclear]. If they get high, I don't think they'll have any problems being able to take them out.

President Kennedy: This is yesterday?

McNamara: Yeah.

I think the conclusions, Mr. President, are, as General Taylor has suggested, we should maintain a substantially smaller alert force than has been maintained, ready to go after a SAM site or a limited target in Cuba with just one to 2 hours' notice. We should go back to the original plan of 12 hours' notice for any sizable strike.

If we were to do that, the great bulk of those aircraft would move back to their home fields. And the remaining force deployed on these 4 bases would be much, much smaller. We'd leave the logistical support at the bases, in most cases. Simply move the aircraft back. This will shift our lead time from one to 2 hours for the bulk of the force to 12 hours. But I think this is an acceptable reduction in lead time.

President Kennedy: Well, all right. We'll make the decision tonight.

Taylor: Well, our problem is to create minimal confusion, and that's what the Chiefs are looking at this morning.

President Kennedy: Which picture is that?

Several: That's McDill [Air Force Base].

[Unclear group discussion; references to being "lined up" and "too far north" for the MiGs but not for the IL-28s.]

Taylor: [Unclear] . . . to the fighter-bombers. The IL-28, there's a later possibility, but they're not hooked up.

McNamara: The second problem I want to point out, Mr. President, is the present position of the Soviet vessels, and our plans for intercepting them. There are 2 vessels that I'll be discussing. One is the *Gagarin,* and the other is the *Kimovsk,* of which these are pictures.

Both of these will be approaching the barrier, by which I mean, they are about 500 miles from Cuba at approximately noon today, roughly the present time, Eastern Daylight Time. I say they will be approaching it, if our dead reckoning is correct.

[22 seconds excised as classified information.]

The *Gagarin* appears to be about 30 to 50 miles behind the *Kimovsk.*

[10 seconds excised as classified information.]

The *Gagarin* declared [its cargo as being] technical material and concrete. This is a typical declaration of an offensive weapons–carrying ship from the Soviet Union. We have checked back the records and this typical way by which this

...gerous situation. The Navy recognizes this, is fully prepared to meet it. They probably will declare radio silence. And therefore neither we know, nor the Soviets will know, where our Navy ships are for much of today.

And that, I think, summarizes our plan.

President Kennedy: Which one are they going to try to get? Both of them?

McNamara: They are concentrating on the *Kimovsk,* but we'll try to get both. The *Kimovsk,* I would say, is the fastest, and is the most likely target.

President Kennedy: What kind of ship is going to try to intercept? A destroyer?

McNamara: Well, last night, at about midnight, the plan was to try to intercept the *Kimovsk* with a destroyer. Previously it had been thought it would be wise to use a cruiser. But, because of our knowledge of the submarine, at the time of intercept, we thought it would be less dangerous to withdraw our forces to use the destroyer. The effort with antisubmarine equipment. Helicopters will be in the vicinity, and those helicopters will attempt to divert the submarine from the intercept point.

McCone: Mr. President, I have a note just handed to me. It says that we've just received information through ONI[4] that all 6 Soviet ships that are currently identified in Cuban waters—and I don't know what that means—have either stopped or reversed course.

---

4. The U.S. Navy's Office of Naval Intelligence.

Rusk: What do you mean, Cuban waters?

McCone: Well, I don't know.

McNamara: Both of these ships [the *Kimovsk* and *Gagarin*] are outbound [to] Cuba [from] the Soviet Union. There are several, and I presume that that's what that refers to. There are only—

President Kennedy: Why don't we find out [unclear]? [McCone leaves the room.]

McNamara: There were a number of ships so close to the harbor in Cuba this morning that we anticipate their entering the harbor at the present time, inbound from the Soviet Union. There were a number of ships outbound also relatively close to the harbors.

Gilpatric: Another ship, a tanker, which is now passing through one of the straits, one of the channels in the island, tankers—

President Kennedy: If this submarine should sink our destroyer, then what is our proposed reply?

Taylor: Well, our destroyer will be moving around all the time, and the submarine is going to be covered by our antisubmarine warfare patrols. Now, we have a signaling arrangement with that submarine to surface, which has been communicated I am told by CINCLANT.

Alexis Johnson: [Unclear] the identification procedures for a submarine. I sent a message to Moscow last night saying that, as a part of the President's proclamation, the Secretary of Defense has issued the following procedures for identification of submarines, and asked the embassy to communicate this to the Soviet government, and that we would just also be in communication with other governments, that this would be a general information. Whether they—I have not got acknowledgment of receipt of that. As far as our proclamation is concerned, it's been delivered to the Soviet foreign office last night and very promptly returned. It was also delivered to the embassy here last night. We have not yet received it back. But the identification procedures should be in their hands.

They are standard . . . I understand they are in the position of standard international practice.

Unidentified: Accepted by the Soviets?

McNamara: No. This is a new procedure I had them set up yesterday, Alex. [Unclear exchange.]

Here is the exact situation. We have depth charges that have such a small charge they can be dropped and they can actually hit the submarine, without damaging the submarine. Practice depth charges. We propose to use those as warning depth charges. The regulations that Alex is talking about state that, when our forces come upon an unidentified submarine, we will ask it to come to the surface for inspection by transmitting the following signals, using a depth charge of this type and also using certain sonar signals which they may not be able to accept and interpret. Therefore, it is the depth charge that is the warning notice and the instruction to surface.

It was after McNamara made this point in the discussion, Robert Kennedy jotted down later that day, that he thought "there f

Gilpatric: The time element being what it has been, I am not sure that we can assume—

McNamara: I think it's almost certain [unclear], you and I were working on at 1:30. The Soviet Union backed [unclear] the submarine. Now, I think I neglected to mention one thing about the submarine, however.

[19 seconds excised as classified information.]

President Kennedy: If he doesn't surface or if he takes some action—takes some action to assist the merchant ship, are we just going to attack him anyway? At what point are we going to attack him?

I think we ought to wait on that today. We don't want to have the first thing we attack as a Soviet submarine. I'd much rather have a merchant ship.

Taylor: Well, we won't do it unless the submarine is really in position to attack our ships in the course of an intercept. It is not pursuing them in the high seas.

McNamara: I think it would be extremely dangerous, Mr. President, to try to defer attack on this submarine in the situation we're in. We could easily lose an American ship by that means. The range of our sonar in relation to the range of his torpedo, and the inaccuracy, as you well know, of antisubmarine warfare is such that I don't have any advantage of great confidence that we can

5. Robert Kennedy's handwritten notes on the meeting, found in the Robert Kennedy Papers, are quoted in Arthur M. Schlesinger Jr., *Robert Kennedy and His Times* (New York: Random House, 1978), p. 514. See also Robert Kennedy's own later reconstruction of this part of the meeting in *Thirteen Days: A Memoir of the Cuban Missile Crisis* (New York: W. W. Norton, 1971), pp. 69–70.

push him away from our ships and make the intercept securely. Particularly, I don't have confidence to do that if we restrict the commander on the site in any way. I've looked into this in great detail last night because of your interest in the question.

Rusk: Can you impose the Soviet merchant vessel between the submarine and yourself? Or does he have torpedoes that can go around and come in from the other side [unclear], right where he wants you?

McNamara: The plan, Dean, is to send antisubmarine helicopters out to harass the submarine. And they have weapons and devices that can damage the submarine. And the plan, therefore, is to put pressure on the submarine, move it out of the area by that pressure, by the pressure of potential destruction, and then make the intercept. But this is only a plan, and there are many, many uncertainties.

Rusk: Yeah.

President Kennedy: Okay. Let's proceed.

Rusk: Mr. President, I do think it's important in our present procedures—of course, these may change later—but to make it, to be quite clear what the object of this first exercise is. And that is to stop these vessels from going to Cuba. It is not to capture them for ourselves at this stage. It is not to do anything other than keep them from going to Cuba. I take it that we all understand the present purpose.

Bundy: We have no priority concern to capture the weapons, Mr. Secretary? This is an important point to get clear.

Rusk: I would think that if we take a ship in custody at this stage we would not desert its cargo. We would simply prevent the ship from going to Cuba. I think it's very important that, at this stage in, our conduct is to show that this is the object of the quarantine exercise.

President Kennedy: Well now, is this a significant question right now?

Bundy: No. Only if we get it.

President Kennedy: Only if we get it. Then we can discuss whether we want it.

Robert Kennedy: I presume that somebody on the destroyer speaks Russian.

McNamara: We've talked about that. I don't have any answers.

Bundy: Well, the Navy undertook to make arrangements on that several days ago.

[Unclear discussion.]

Gilpatric: They have Russian-speaking personnel with the ships, but whether this specific ship has it or not, I'm not sure.

McNamara: I'm looking into that.

President Kennedy: May we get this matter of procedure as quick as possible? You can get a Russian-speaking person on every one of these ships. Ros?

Gilpatric: Yes, Mr. President.

Bundy: That is being done.

Is there other urgent business? If not, I think we should hear the committee [on communications].

President Kennedy: Yes, I want to . . . I would think that, pending of course on what we learn when Mr. McCone gets back, I would ~~[unclear]~~

~~[unclear]~~ keep the air corridor open up to the point where it looks as though this is militarily no use, in which event, if they firmly [unclear], is firmly demonstrated. Then they're going to put in overpowering air force in the air corridor.

Then we have a decision to be taken by NATO as to whether or not to proceed with this attack upon the SAM sites, on the bases from which the planes come. Or whether we want to go into phase two, and regroup, and produce more force before we go further.

[McCone returns to the Cabinet Room.]

McCone: These ships are all westbound, all inbound for Cuba. "Cuban waters" is considered west of 30 degrees [west longitude]. I just don't know where that is.

Bundy: Get a map.

McCone: Now, the ships are the *Poltava, Gagarin, Kimovsk, Dolmatovo,* the *Moscow Festival,* and the *Battle of Kursk.*

McNamara: The *Battle of Kursk* is close to the barrier, in fact, to the east of it, if I recall correctly. The *Kimovsk* and the *Gagarin* are the 2 I mentioned. They are roughly 500 to 550 miles from Cuba at the present time. The other ship I believe is one of the tankers we mentioned which is closer to Cuba, so that at least 2 of those ships are 500 miles from Cuba.

President Kennedy: Now, what do they say they're doing with those, John?

McCone: Well, they either stopped them or reversed direction. [Unclear.] I don't know. I assume this is the communication.

President Kennedy: Well, where did you hear this?

McCone: It's from ONI. It's on its way over here.

President Kennedy: Now is this all the Russian ships, or is this just selected ones?

McCone: Apparently it's selected ones, because there's 24 of them.

McNamara: It looks as though these are the group of ships that are relatively close to our barrier. There's another group of ships very close to the Cuban shore, a substantial number. So close, I'm sure they wouldn't turn them around. And there might be one in between there. There's a tanker, the *Raznitch,* which appeared to be about 100 miles from Cuba this morning. I'll see if I can get more information.

President Kennedy: Well, let's just say that, if that report is accurate, then we're not going to do anything about these ships close in to Cuba.

Bundy: The ships further in, we would not wish to stop, would we?

[There is some unclear background conversation, and then Bundy laughs. This was probably the moment at which Dean Rusk whispered to Bundy: "We are eyeball to eyeball, and I think the other fellow just blinked."][6]

President Kennedy: Now, if these ships have turned, that would mean that it isn't just they're picking out the one that might have these weapons on. That sounds like every ship that's within—at that certain distance.

We—we're not planning to grab any of those, are we?

McNamara: We're not trying to grab any ship that is not proceeding towards Cuba.

[Mixed voices; unclear exchanges.]

President Kennedy: No. I think probably they're turned around.

[Unclear comment by McNamara.]

Rusk: It's time to consider a remark made by the Cuban ambassador to the Brazilians yesterday, at the Security Council, that if we would hold off on the blockade for a day or so or until the Security Council votes, that his government was disposed to accept UN sanctions. Now, we can't rely on that. After all, it's a remark the Cuban ambassador allegedly made to the Brazilian ambassador.

Robert Kennedy: [referring to the news that Soviet ships have stopped or are turning back] Well, isn't that information we better give to the Navy?

Rusk: Yeah, we better be sure the Navy knows that they're not supposed to pursue these ships.

[Unclear exchanges.]

McNamara: It came from the Office of Naval Intelligence.

---

6. See Dean Rusk, as told to Richard Rusk, *As I Saw It,* ed. Daniel S. Papp (New York: W. W. Norton, 1990), p. 237.

[Unclear discussion. Other people come into the room.]

President Kennedy: Okay. Let's do the communications.

Unidentified: . . . clearly west of the line [30 degrees west longitude, not the quarantine line], just about even with the Azores. You see it's right down the middle of the Atlantic.

President Kennedy: [referring to something else] That being what city?

[Group discussion; people moving about and talking.]

Bundy: How many do you need?

attention because, if the crisis becomes more serious, these become pertinent.

If you look at worldwide communications available to the Defense Department, and the State Department, and we have looked at CIA, and we have looked at the communications of Latin America. I thought we would discuss the Latin American communication problem first because I think it's of major interest to many of you. We have here today Admiral Irvin and General Sampson of the Defense Communications Agency; General McDavid of the Joint Chiefs of Staff; with a career [official] in the Department of State communications—[3 seconds excised as classified information]; Dr. Baker and Dr. Lewis of the Bell Telephone Laboratories, who are members of your Science Advisory Committee's Panel on Command and Control.

The Latin American communication situation is rather special because of the Defense Department communications needs in that direction, both for traffic and technical reasons, [and it] is relatively undeveloped. The bulk of the Central and South American communications now available to the government has a limited and very different character than communications in Europe or many other parts of the world. And I'd like to describe briefly the character of this thing so you can see our difficulties, and the limitations. I think there is some very serious questions of their adequacy, and we have to consider what we should do to augment the situation both in terms of facilities and in terms of manning, if this particular crisis is sustained, because in many places we don't have adequate manpower.

A substantial number of radio telephone circuits are available to almost all points of interest commercially. But for technical reasons it's at present, it is impossible to encrypt any of these circuits. Therefore, they're open circuits. Encryption of Latin American voice circuits through technical progress or installation of cables may come, but not in time to meet our immediate needs. Voice communication in the clear will usually be available, but with rare interruptions due to radio propagation.

The Department of State has a telegraph network to the embassies in Central and South America. [8 seconds excised as classified information.] The networks are made up of several classes of circuits, and out of these networks any of these channels can be encrypted for teletype. We have circuits to Mexico, Panama, Brazil, the Argentine, and Uruguay on a 24-hour basis over a State or a Defense Department circuit.

Circuits to the remaining capitals are available either in the form of private Telex, teletype, or switch-telegraph circuits, or simply through filing cablegrams over the ordinary circuit services. In the latter case, the priority normally is given by the commercial firms to U.S. embassy messages, and the embassies have direct wires into cable offices to expedite the transmission.

[57 seconds excised as classified information.]

Now, one problem is that all of the Latin American enciphered telegraph facilities are made up of what we call off-line facilities, so that it takes a considerable amount of time to get an enciphered message from the transmitter to the receiver, and they can't be used for two-way telegraph conferences. Thus delays of a few minutes up to a half-hour or more can be encountered on the circuits.[7]

During the present crisis, for a few days more at least, the commercial companies are standing by on a 24-hour basis in order to minimize the delays that would ordinarily be encountered on these circuits. Other substantial delays may be introduced at the present time by the normal operating procedures at the embassies. There's usually only one communication officer assigned to each net, and they are not manned continuously. This is, of course, that's something we could change. During the off hours, Marine guards alert the personnel and can get them back to the station, but this takes them some time.

[Someone begins whispering information to President Kennedy, and they talk to each other at a whisper, while Wiesner pauses.]

President Kennedy: [in his side conversation] Well, the question seems to

---

7. "On-line" communication meant two-way communication in real time, as in a telephone call. "Off-line" communication meant that a message would be prepared, then possibly sent at a later time, then eventually delivered depending on the capacity or backlog in that circuit. Once received, there would then be a reply. Cable traffic is off-line.

me, if they start to turn them around . . . I would think you ought to check first. [Unclear.] Are they simultaneously turning?

[Unclear discussion.]

General, what is the—how do we get . . . What does the Navy say about this report?

[9 seconds excised as classified information.]

Taylor: Three ships are definitely turning back. One is the *Poltava,* which we are most interested in. They did not give an additional . . .

be in touch with the *Essex,*[8] and just tell them to wait an hour and see whether that ship continues on its course in view of this other intelligence. We better move quickly, because they want to intercept between 10:30 and 11:00.[9]

McNamara: We may be 500 miles from . . . This particular ship that we are scheduling for an intercept between 10:30 and 11:00 our time, which is right now, is about 500 miles from Cuba.

Robert Kennedy: Isn't that one of the ones that—

McNamara: It is the *Kimovsk,* which has 70-foot hatches.

Unidentified: Mr. President, there are a number of special people in this particular meeting this morning here. I'd like just to mention that what we have discussed has the highest classification.[10]

[Unclear discussion.]

President Kennedy: Go on with the report, Jerry.

Wiesner: Well, in summary, what we're saying is that this network that we have down there, while it may have been satisfactory for normal peacetime circumstances, and while it can be augmented temporarily by additional personnel, if the [National] Security Council believes this is desirable, it's certainly

8. The aircraft carrier U.S.S. *Essex,* a lead ship of Navy Task Force 136 commanded by Vice Admiral Alfred Ward, was directly responsible for implementing the quarantine under CIN-CLANT (Admiral Dennison) and the Chief of Naval Operations (Admiral Anderson).

9. At that moment it was about 10:40 A.M. in Washington.

10. The information from the Office of Naval Intelligence was based, at least in part, on signals intelligence and direction-finding conducted by the National Security Agency.

never going to be a network that in any way resembles the command and control network, if we should need it.

Secondly, I'd like to point out—and we can discuss this in more detail if you want—that goes into principal cities in these countries in which it goes. And if for some reason we lose your communication in those principal cities, unless the mobile equipment or portable equipment we have in the embassy is available, we will be without contact, without reliable word from those particular countries. And I think this is a matter we should give some rather considerable thought to.

And finally, the CINCCARIB[11] have stated a requirement for communication capacity into these countries which is considerably in excess of anything that we now have available, and for reliability which they don't believe is now available on these certain circuits, even if we increase the manning.

There's been discussions between DOD [Department of Defense], CIA, and the Department of State considering how such enhanced communications can be made available. But I don't believe that we have the complete resolution yet of how to do it. As I see it, we have several questions before us. Do we want an increased communication watch on the DOD/CIA nets? Do we want to try to provide enhanced communication capability? Once it is operating, are we interested in an on-line site? I believe the CINCCARIB is, for its interests from Panama to these countries. No one has expressed the need for such communication capability in Washington.

On the other hand, if we are going to provide it, one purpose may be that we should provide it for the other purposes as well. The gentlemen who represent the State Department and the CIA and the Defense Department are here and can answer any additional questions you may want to ask.

I thought I would ask General McDavid to say just an additional word about the CINCCARIB needs, because they're probably urgent at this time.

McDavid: Yes, sir. CINCCARIB actually has come in with his plan, and we have, in the Defense Department, examined it carefully, and have asked that he go ahead with it in three phases. The first phase was to go into 2 of the countries, Guatemala and Bolivia. The second phase is to take on 6 more that are right in the Caribbean. These are the urgent ones now. There are 8 of them. And these are the ones where negotiations are already under way for 2, this is Guatemala and Bolivia, and the other 6 we have yet to start up negotiations, but—

11. The Commander-in-Chief, U.S. Forces in the Caribbean, headquartered in the U.S. Canal Zone, in Panama.

President Kennedy: What will we do with each one of these?

McDavid: We want to put at least a voice circuit and a secure teletext circuit from the Panama Canal to each of these countries. We have put in a mobile radio set down in each country, manned by military personnel.

President Kennedy: Do they have personnel?

McDavid: It will be U.S. military personnel into the Caribbean. Yes, sir.

President Kennedy: And do each one in these countries give us almost instantaneous communication?

the countries. So it seems to me that if we could agree here that it is an acceptable requirement, and we'll organize to—

[Unclear interjection.]

Right, but this is a magnificent opportunity to break down a diplomatic block which has existed for years.

Wiesner: I wonder if Mr. [Prew? Crew?] would like to comment on this problem that we're going to encounter both diplomatically and operationally.

Prew or Crew?: Mr. President, I think the problems have been greatly alleviated in the last two weeks with the signing of an agreement with Brazil. But I think each one will have to be negotiated differently.

Bundy: Well, at least the—we don't want to get into the detail.

Rusk: I wonder if I could urge you to conclude now that the great United States of America can't face a series of crises without adequate communications—

[Others say: "That's right."]

—and we should not be fighting picayune problems of the budget to establish these [unclear]. And that you will tell the congressional leaders this afternoon, among other things, that this has illustrated dramatically the necessity for making a major effort.

President Kennedy: How much will this cost to do the one we're now talking about in the Caribbean?

McDavid: As far as the military personnel is concerned, it's approximately 150 people. It is equipment that we have within our stock, however. We think it will cost around a million dollars for the—

McNamara: Mr. President, the budget is not the problem. The problem is [unclear] the money. The problem is gaining the approval of the Latin American countries to install the equipment.

Ball: But there's also a budget problem.

Rusk: Yeah, but there's a budget problem, too, Bob. We had to fight desperately for any money to improve our communications.

Wiesner: A little later in the presentation we're going to talk about the State Department and CIA communications. And there I think there are some budget questions, or at least funding has been one of the limitations in developing . . .

Robert Kennedy: We went through a really horrifying experience, and I think Alex will [remember], during the Dominican[12] [unclear], which was just incredible, because we would be sitting around in meetings, 48 hours—

Rusk: I think we should also include, either directly under the White House direction or Defense or State, [that] we also have a standby task force capable of immediate reinforcement of communications in critical parts wherever they develop in the world, whether it's Congo or—

Robert Kennedy: What is the time lag? Now, if the problem is diplomatic you can put it in comparatively quickly, can you, once you get the okay?

McDavid: Once the communications end has been taken care of. Right now our commercial communications that we have are delayed all the way from 56 hours.

Bundy: If you got a go signal to put this thing in, how long would it take you to put it in?

McDavid: The first 2 are ready on standby. We have equipment in Panama.

Unidentified: The State Department is negotiating.

President Kennedy: Do you pay all these countries that you're going to start to negotiate with?

Wiesner: Mr. President, I just made a note here. I think it's important that we not duplicate. That State, and Defense, and CIA, to the extent possible, have a single communications network. Adding another network on to whatever we have, I think, is very unsound.

Rusk: It may encourage independent radio stations in other countries. However, I think that this is a favorable time for us to make arrangements with other countries, providing—

---

12. Probably a referrence to the furor set off in Washington at the end of May 1961 by the news that the dictator of the Dominican Republic, Rafael Trujillo, had been assassinated, news that led to a review of U.S. policy toward that country.

Bundy: Including military personnel, because with speedy action we're going to have to use defense measures—

Rusk: —provided we can say it won't cost us anything or cause us any problems, operationally I'm sure, for these countries. This is an illustration for a readily available OAS network.

McCone: Could I could speak for just a minute? Because I've got a USIB [U.S. Intelligence Board] meeting at 11:00. I have listened to all of the chiefs of stations[13] in Latin American countries in Central America and D

from the standpoint of the personnel that's involved, and the attitudes of certain countries with regard to the number of personnel that are located within their countries.

For that reason, I would urge: One, that it [the Defense Department plan] be supported. Two, that it be carefully coordinated. It will take some considerable time to complete it. And I think as I remember the whole thing, down to the southern part of Latin America, General [unclear]'s estimate was that it would take some 2 or 3 years to get the whole business completed.

[71 seconds excised as classified information.]

Rusk: General, what kind of money, on an order of magnitude, are we talking about?

Unidentified: Oh, I don't know.

[Mixed voices; someone states that it's "not money."]

McNamara: This is a plan that we can cover with existing appropriations. Appropriations are not the problem standing in the way of communications to Latin America. The problem is twofold. One is getting organized within the government to do it. And the second is negotiating the agreements with the Latin American countries.

Bundy: We have two problems. One is to do that, which is not going to be happening tomorrow. And the other is to beef up our media translation.

---

13. The chief of station is the head CIA officer in an American mission overseas.

McNamara: We can put a lot of this in very quickly because I have worked with that general and we have the equipment available.

At this point President Kennedy turned off the tape recorder. In his summary of the meeting, Bundy wrote that in the remaining discussion "the President directed that State and USIA[14] should give immediate attention to increasing understanding in Europe of the fact that any Berlin crisis would be fundamentally the result of Soviet ambition and pressure, and that inaction by the United States in the face of the challenge in Cuba would have been more and not less dangerous for Berlin . . . The President directed that a senior representative of USIA should regularly be present at meetings of the Executive Committee."[15]

14. The United States Information Agency, then headed by Edward R. Murrow. Murrow was in ill health at the time, and Donald Wilson acted in his stead.

15. McGeorge Bundy, "Record of Action," October 24, 1962, JFKL.

5:00 P.M.

CABINET ROOM AND OVAL OFFICE

Soviet ship movements and continued to pursue its diplomatic efforts. At 3:25 Bundy phoned Ball with news that the most significant Soviet ships had definitely turned around. He then gathered a few officials to talk about next steps. Meanwhile, Rusk reviewed the situation and his government's policies in detail with the British, French, and German ambassadors. McNamara paid close attention to the Navy's blockade plans, leading to some confrontational exchanges in which each side later remembered the other as being brusque and intemperate.

Keeping the promise he had made 2 days earlier, President Kennedy arranged to meet again that afternoon with the congressional leadership, joined by Rusk, McNamara, McCone, and Lovett. Meanwhile Robert Kennedy and other advisers were discussing the implementation of the blockade with the Vice Chief of Naval Operations, Admiral Claude Ricketts, in the White House Situation Room.

President Kennedy evidently turned on the tape recorder, possibly in the Oval Office, during some exchanges with a few officials late in the afternoon. The audio quality is poor, and only a few fragments can be meaningfully understood.

[Rusk had apparently reported on his session with the British, French, and German ambassadors.]

Nitze: They're worried about the conviction which they can give if these things are really being manned. They're also worried about this camouflage point. They said: Why didn't the Russians camouflage? Well, this [low-level reconnaissance photos] demonstrates that the Russians did do their best to camouflage. Using these pictures, I think, would be very helpful.

President Kennedy: You mean they are now camouflaged?

Nitze: They are now camouflaged, that's right.

President Kennedy: Well, I think that the line is gonna be that the Russians led us into a trap.

Bundy?: You can give a clearance on it [use of the photos]. The [unclear] have been very resistant to let us say what is fact. Now I think you're over the dam. The Russians did camouflage these things quite as standard practice. Very carefully they proceeded by night, our agents' reports now indicate, our refugee reports. They have never been good at overhead camouflage. It's just how doctrinally backwards they are. If we can break this out of intelligence, and use it [unclear].

[After a few fragments of sentences, the remaining discussion is unintelligible. The session is breaking up, and people are milling around, talking, and departing. Then there are only the sounds through an open door to Mrs. Lincoln's office as she types and answers the phone. Finally, the tape recorder is apparently turned off.]

President Kennedy turned on the tape recorder again as the 5:00 P.M. meeting in the Cabinet Room was under way with the assembled Senators and Representatives. McCone had already delivered his intelligence update. Rusk is reviewing the diplomatic situation.

Rusk: . . . the [United Nations] General Assembly well understands neutral opinion has much more weight than it does in the Security Council. But our friends in the UN, our allies, have been very helpful during this situation.

In general they're still . . . We know that there are some elements of caution in Soviet attitudes, and that speech at the UN,[1] although it was bitter and as violent as ever, did seem to go to some pains to keep the finger on the Cuban and the U.S. aspects of the matter, rather than the U.S.S.R.–U.S. aspects of the matter.

So far as we know, the Soviets have not told their own people that they have missiles in Cuba, which indicates that this is not something, that they think that their own people may be very disturbed, and create war scares there if they would give them that information.

---

1. The speech delivered by Soviet Ambassador to the UN Valerian Zorin on the afternoon of October 23.

We do think that, although the situation is highly critical and dangerous, that it is not explosive in any inevitable way at this point, and that we can continue to watch the activity of the other side and their reactions to see what is likely to happen. There is a variety of rumors, gossip, contacts, and reports. But I don't think I can give a definitive view today as to what the real attitude of the Soviet Union is on this matter. Our best judgment is that they are scratching their brains very hard at the present time, deciding just exactly how they want to play it, what th———————————————

[*Mixed speaking.*]

McNamara: Yes, Mr. President. Following a proclamation which was signed by the President at 7:00 last night, the orders to Task Force 136, which is operating under Admiral Ward, were issued to the units deployed on the quarantine stations. They were in position this morning at 10:00 Eastern Daylight Time, which was 2:00 P.M. Greenwich Time, the effective time of the quarantine. There have been no intercepts today. None were necessary.

The tours of duty of Navy personnel and Marine Corps personnel presently on active duty have been extended indefinitely to allow the fleet to be brought to full operational manning, and the Marines to achieve a higher-than-authorized strength to support the reinforcement of Guantanamo and to be prepared for any further eventualities. I have no other report to make.

Dirksen: Mr. Secretary, what are your units for intercept vessels? Destroyers?

McNamara: There are cruisers and destroyers in the intercept positions, and one or the other will be used depending upon the circumstances. There are antisubmarine warfare [aircraft] carriers available also to protect against possible submarine attack during the, at the time of, intercept.

Dirksen: If it's not a covert figure, how many [ships] are participating in the task?

McNamara: Well, roughly 25 destroyers, plus 2 cruisers, an antisubmarine warfare carrier, and certain other support ships.

Fulbright: Mr. Secretary, where are these Russian ships that were en route to Cuba?

McNamara: We can't say exactly. There's a tremendous expanse of ocean that we are endeavoring to watch, roughly from the Azores to Bermuda.

The Soviet vessels that were proceeding toward Cuba appear to fall in two categories. One category appears to have shifted course. And the other category appears to be moving toward Cuba. Those that have shifted course appear to be moving eastward. We have plots based on dead reckoning and other sources, but I wouldn't be able to say exactly where they were at a certain time.

Fulbright: When do you anticipate that there will be a confrontation if they continue their course toward Cuba?

McNamara: I can't say. It depends how they continue their course. They appear to be varying speed and direction, and for that reason I can't answer the question.

Fulbright: Do you have any information that they are under instructions that changed their direction?

McNamara: I really can't say. I would assume that, if they've changed their course, they've done so under instructions.

Rusk: Mr. President, if I may, I'd like to add that we not make any reference to the ships of special interest to the United States. This is information the Soviets might find useful.

Mansfield: Mr. President, as long as the Secretary has brought up the question of withholding information, I was deeply disturbed to read this morning, in the *Herald Tribune*, a story by Rowland Evans which I think ought to be discussed here.[2] Not that it isn't factual. It is pretty much so. But the fact is that [unclear] said a lot of things [unclear].

Russell: I haven't seen it, but I heard about it. Someone read part of it to me over the phone. I refused to talk to Mr. Evans. He tried to call me late yesterday afternoon. [Unclear] getting around to any other papers, a number of other papers. I've had so many news wires, I issued a statement that I deem it inappropriate for anyone in congressional testimony, or the White House, or Congress to discuss any details as to what transpired. Our position is that any such information should be released by the White House, particularly in the present case, it cannot serve any useful purpose, because our constitutional commander-in-chief, the President, has announced the policy of this country to the world. I shall not, therefore, comment in any way on any rumors concerning, about this Congress and the White House. The only voice to speak for the United States is the President. I'm supporting the program he's announced. But it's gotten all out, I don't know who's released it. I know I haven't.

Dirksen: What's the general nature of it, Mike?

2. An account of the meeting between President Kennedy and the congressional leadership on Monday, October 22.

Mansfield: Well, [unclear] the question of [unclear], mentions Senator Russell specifically. He [Evans] really creates the impression that it's only a matter of days until an invasion will be launched; the President, in effect, has made up his mind, and that's about it. That's the story.

Russell: Well, it didn't quote me, but it treated me very broadly and, I may say, correctly. But inasmuch as I've been devil's advocate, Mr. President, I've been at times harshly critical of the State Department, I would like to take this opportunity to heartily congratulate the S[unclear]

Russell: I hope, Mr. Secretary, that that'll take the edge off of some of what I have said. [Laughter.]

Kuchel: I must say, Mr. President, I join the congratulations. But having worked with the Secretary a little bit, I am not really astounded. I've seen him do some magnificent jobs [unclear].

Russell: [Unclear.] This was a tremendous job. [Unclear] authority of the pronouncement of the Organization of American States, the most firm commitment to armed action to protect this hemisphere that I have ever seen. I never would have believed we could have gotten it.

Kuchel: This is a highlight in our favor so far.

Russell: What?

Kuchel: This is a highlight in our favor so far.

Russell: I think so.

Rusk: I would like to say that our Latin American friends, when they realized that these were offensive long-range missiles in Cuba, realized that this was a matter of the utmost importance. And they came forward, as they had to do.

Dirksen: Mr. President, speaking of the State Department, Len just tells me about this Wadsworth[3] paper. What about it?

Hickenlooper: Well, I got a message that James Wadsworth had wanted to adopt some organization—church organization, peace organization—opposed to [the U.S. action], for a week's moratorium [on actions by either the U.S. or

---

3. James Wadsworth had been the U.S. Ambassador to the United Nations in the last years of the Eisenhower administration. We are unable to identify "Len."

U.S.S.R.], and they wanted me to stimulate it. I have to say, I told them this is junk.

Rusk: Well, we do expect U Thant,[4] sometime in the early evening, to issue a statement on his own, in which he would prefer a balanced statement calling for a 2-weeks' moratorium, during which there would be no movement of arms to Cuba and no quarantine, with rather vague references to verification, and no reference to the actual missiles in Cuba itself.

We have tried our best to get him to withhold any such statement, but he may nevertheless make it. But we'll have to get that.

President Kennedy: Get back to Stevenson.

Rusk: Yes, we'll . . . we did.

Dirksen: Excuse me, Mr. President, just a moment ago somebody overheard on the radio that Khrushchev, indirectly through Bertrand Russell, suggested a summit conference. Is there any . . . ?

President Kennedy: [to Rusk] Could you read that?

Rusk: The whole statement that he [Khrushchev] gave to Bertrand Russell: "The Soviet government will not take any decisions which will be reckless, will not allow itself to be provoked by unwarranted actions of the United States of America. We shall do everything in our power to prevent war from breaking out. We would consider a top-level meeting useful." Noting that the U.S. government should display reserve and stay the realization of its piratical threats, which have brought the most serious consequences.

And he [Khrushchev] did say that "As long as the rocket nuclear weapons have not been used, there is a possibility of averting war. When the Americans launch aggression, a meeting at the highest level would become impossible and useless." So there's quite a variety of things in there.

Dirksen: That was no direct invitation to you.

President Kennedy: No.

Dirksen: Do you want any comment on a summit meeting?

President Kennedy: I think it's useless.

Dirksen: I would too. Absolutely useless.

Humphrey: Mr. President, has there been any official information at all from the Soviet Union to either you or the Secretary of State?

President Kennedy: No. As you know, I wrote them a letter, and they sent

---

4. U Thant was then Acting Secretary General of the United Nations. The permanent representative of Burma (now Myanmar) to the UN since 1957, Thant had become the agreed compromise candidate to act as Secretary General in 1961 when the United States and the Soviet Union had been unable to agree on a successor to Dag Hammarskjold.

me back a letter which was a condensation of the statement the government put out, objecting to all the things that we were talking about doing and [unclear].

So we're right now in the midst of waiting to see whether these ships are going to, whether they're going to turn back other ships which might be carrying weapons. Or continuing with others. And whether those ships will be stopped when we . . . For example, tankers, which obviously couldn't carry

[unclear] . . . is that involved in this too? What if they try to send them by planes?

President Kennedy: Well, in the statement we made in the quarantine we said "carriers," so we can't cover planes. But the first thing we ought to do is do the ships, because the only way you can stop a plane is to shoot it down. And with our problem in Berlin, at least at the first stage we ought to just confine it to ships.

In addition, we are trying to take steps at the various places where these planes stop—Dakar, Conakry—to see if we can provide for some control over the movement of arms through there, though it's possible for them to fly nonstop but with a light load. We think we should do this, before we start shooting down those planes.

McNamara: Mr. President, there's only 7 Soviet aircraft that, to the best of our knowledge, have flown to Cuba in the last 120 days. This is a fair measure of their capability for the use of commercial-type aircraft for that purpose. They have very few.

Russell: They do have planes that are capable of flying the intermediate missiles into Cuba, though, don't they Mr. Secretary?

McNamara: It's highly questionable. They could fly in warheads, or something of that kind. Then they can fly in offensive materials. But if they were going to do any one of these, all they would have to use is their bombers for that purpose, which they might do.

We have such planes. It's questionable whether they have planes that can move missiles of this size. In any event, they don't have enough planes, enough commercial planes, to move any important quantity of trade into Cuba. They would have to use their bombers for that purpose, and they might well decide to do so.

Fulbright: Besides, is there any evidence of submarines, Mr. McNamara?

McNamara: I want to answer that. But I want to say that our knowledge of submarines, Soviet Union submarines, in the Atlantic is the most highly classified information we have in the Department.

Fulbright: If you prefer not to answer, don't do it.

McNamara:: Well, I think I'm [unclear].

Russell: I think you better leave that off, particularly in view of what happened after the previous conference with the other Congressmen, Mr. Secretary. [Unclear.]

[Mixed voices. Rusk says: "Not a large number, but a certain number."]

Dirksen: Are you surprised by the slow uptake in the Soviet Union? [Unclear.]

Rusk: We thought, and I defer to Ambassador Thompson, who's my chief adviser on this sort of thing, that this was planned for a long time.

Really, their timing, as we look back on it now, was for Khrushchev to come to the UN in late November, prepared to lay on a real crisis over Berlin in direct talks with the President. He wanted to have all this in his pocket when he had that talk.

And our impression so far is that we have not caught them with a lot of contingency plans all laid out and ready to go. This has upset their timing.

Vinson: May I ask a question of Mr. McCone?

President Kennedy: Yes.

Vinson: Mr. McCone, what was your latest estimate on the number of MiG-21s in Cuba?

McCone: Our original estimate was one that we saw and 12 possible [unclear] crates, which we suspected to be MiG-21s. The next real [unclear] was when we saw 39, which I believe was on the 17th of October.

Unidentified: Thirty-nine—

McCone: Thirty-nine MiG-21s.

Smathers: Do we have any monitoring that would indicate, by chatter or otherwise, whether these MiGs are flown by Cubans or by Russians?

McCone: Yes, we have some information on that, of MiG-21s that were airborne here a few days ago. About half of them were by Russians. One, at least, we suspect was a Czech, and the balance by Cubans.

Smathers: Mr. McCone, may I ask this question? You stated at the outset that something about "Don't shoot unless attacked." Now, is that the order to the Cubans, not to shoot unless attacked?

McCone: That's the information that we received today.

Smathers: But the other day [October 22], you said the Cubans were not in on these missiles at all, they were not in there. So . . .

McCone: That's correct. As far as we know, with the information we have, Senator, they are not in on the missile sites. Except that maybe in a very moderate way, in connection with construction of camps, or things of that kind. And in those circumstances, our information that we have developed is

McNamara: Yes. The terms of the quarantine apply to all ships equally, and we will therefore hail and stop and search ships of various nationalities proceeding through the quarantine area.

Hickenlooper: Suppose we just announce that any of those ships, for the next 5 years, couldn't come into any American port? Wouldn't that turn 'em around real fast?

Rusk: Sir, there are quite a few that are being turned around voluntarily at the moment. The Japanese have just called back their ships from Cuba, and the British government is moving now to move in on their shipping on to Cuba. That's all . . . This could very well be handled voluntarily before we get to that point.

Fulbright: What about our other alliances, Mr. Secretary?

Rusk: Well, the rest of them are in pretty good shape. The Turks, the Italians, the Germans have all taken action. The Greeks have put on various of their restrictions, but we still have tankers and a few sanctioned items that are on ships carrying cargo, and we are working on that.

We do have a problem about taking steps now that would be directed toward destroying Cuba, and limiting our steps for the moment to the Soviet weapons problem, the offensive-capability problems. We thought this first step ought to be to concentrate on the weapons problems, the military problems.

Hickenlooper: What sort of [unclear] will be in the President's report to the nation?

President Kennedy: I don't think we have one yet.

Unidentified: Huh?

President Kennedy: I don't think we have one yet, Senator, till we see what happens in the next 24 hours, whether the Soviets are going to accept it. I'd say in the next 2 or 3 days we'll know a lot more about it and we can see what to report then.

Hickenlooper: Well, I was looking at a television this afternoon. A newspaperman reported that Khrushchev had said that he had asked you, or sent a message through, to have a summit conference. And I wondered if that is true?

President Kennedy: No. I heard such a report was on the television, but that isn't true. We've received no message from him about it.

Hickenlooper: If it does come through, what's going to be the answer?

President Kennedy: Well, why don't we wait if the message comes through? But there's no such message as yet. The only message, I think they're probably referring to one of Lord Russell. But we received no message. And I think, until we do receive one and see what it says, I think it would probably be—

Hickenlooper: Do we have some information as to whether the Russian ships are proceeding toward Cuba?

President Kennedy: Not with precision, no. Some seem to be. Some may not be. But I don't think we'll know for 12 hours.

Hickenlooper: Well, yesterday it was stated that, at least came over the radio that, Khrushchev had said that he'd ordered his Russian people to resist [the quarantine]. Now, if that happens, then we're in it, aren't we?

President Kennedy: Well, we'll have to wait and see, Senator. I think in the next 24 hours we can tell what our problems are going to be on the quarantine itself.

Unidentified: Next 24 hours?

President Kennedy: I would think we should know about the . . .

Now, Everett, what's your judgment about—I don't think we have much until we know a little more about the quarantine—about the leadership.

Dirksen: I think 24 hours.

President Kennedy: Well, I think we ought to know whether they're going to stop, or whether we have to sink one, so that we'd probably know more about it, I would think much more, by morning.

Mansfield: Do you want us [congressional leaders with Congress in recess] to hang around for 24 hours?

Unidentified: That's the question, Mr. President.

Dirksen: Some members are anxious, of course, to get home.

President Kennedy: Well, now, we can do it this way: We can, obviously if we . . . It seems to me that, based on our previous experience, we [unclear] everybody get here within 6 hours, and therefore I think that, unless the leadership prefers [differently], we could break up now with the understanding that we can always get you back here before any major action is taken. That we will be in touch with you, as I said, on the same conditions we were before, come back the same day and that. In any case we ought to meet on Monday [October 29], and if we have a major problem to face in the next 2 or 3 days we could meet on Friday [October 26].

Dirksen: Well, would you like to set a Monday meeting?

President Kennedy: Why don't we set definitely a Monday meeting, with the

Why don't we do this. The Secretary raises the point that we don't look like we're putting, in any way relaxing our effort. I think, why don't we just say that we're going to meet shortly, that the leadership's on an 8-hour standby basis, on call [unclear] be meeting shortly, and then we don't . . .

Unidentified: Matter if there's any reference to Monday?

Russell: Well, I don't know if you need to say anything, Mr. President, but I don't know if there's much for us to meet on. Our course is pretty well determined. If certain events happen, it's all arranged. We will have Secretary McNamara's fleet out there sitting on Cuba for some time, so [unclear] not coming in.

President Kennedy: Well, why don't we keep it on an 8-hour basis, and I'll be in touch with the leadership as far as when we should next meet, but we might be taking a [unclear]. But we will be in touch with you.

[Unclear interjection.]

That's right, and I think we'll just say that the leadership is on an 8-hour standby basis.

Smathers: But do you intend, so far as you know, because that Monday . . . Would you like for us to be back that Monday?

President Kennedy: Why don't I get in touch with you on Friday on that. I think it's probably better not to do what the Secretary [unclear], have a day, so the 8-hour standby basis [unclear].

Humphrey: Mr. President, before we meet . . . Secretary McNamara, I heard your [October 23, 8:00 P.M.] press conference, part of it, on the television. You mentioned military equipment and associated materials, or something like that—

McNamara: The offensive weapons and associated equipment, I believe I said.

Humphrey: I just wondered, in light of what you said here in reference to tankers and so forth, if that . . .

McNamara: It was not intended to include tankers at the present time, but rather electronic parts that are associated with missile systems.

Russell: I got the impression it didn't even apply to conventional weapons. They brought in 5,000 rifles and 2 dozen [unclear].

McNamara: We meant to leave that impression, that rifles were excluded from the quarantine.

Russell: Yes, yes. When I read your statement. And I got the impression that this was something that was related to these missiles, but these were ordinary [artillery] field pieces.

McNamara: That's exactly the impression—

[Unclear interjection.]

—with the qualification that the items covered by the quarantine would be changed at certain [unclear].

Russell: Yes, well, you made that clear. [Unclear.]

Fulbright: [Unclear] 7 to 10 days you will be ready to take definite action [invasion] if conditions warrant it?

McNamara: We are prepared to do so if conditions warrant.

Fulbright: You will be prepared?

McNamara: Yes, that is correct.

Fulbright: And that's the procedure?

McNamara: That is correct.

Hickenlooper: Mr. Secretary, do I understand you to say you would permit 5,000 rifles to go through?

President Kennedy: Let me. Here's the reason.

What we want to do for the OAS and the UN and for our allies is emphasize offensive weapons. The language of the quarantine, however, can be changed at any moment. But the first collision with the Soviets, we wanted to just have it on the offensive weapons, for political reasons. If they won't accept quarantine, we're not going to let the Russians go through, but we wanted to put the whole emphasis on this missile thing, because this puts us in a much stronger position around the world. So that's where we've chosen the first clash to come. But quite obviously, if they accept the quarantine, we will not permit these weapons to go through.

Mansfield: Mr. President, may I say something on this matter of the security of these meetings? Now, we're going to be asked all kinds of leading questions by the press. I've been called all day. And I think the answer should be that we don't comment upon the matter in any shape, form, or fashion. That it will, that any release will come from the White House. We won't even tell them where somebody sat.

I remember one time when a commentator called me and wanted to know which side was President Eisenhower and the Secretary of State. And I said

Rusk: I'll say that. If I were quoted as saying the [unclear].

Kuchel: Well, sir, I've been to some of these meetings for quite a while, Mr. President. Not as long as some around here, but . . . And I trust that what Mike Mansfield brought up here doesn't require a personal disavowal on the part of each one of us.

[Unclear; several appear to agree.]

Because I have just been meticulous in refraining from talking about what's said here.

One further thing, Mr. President. As I understand it, you or the White House will make some statement to the effect that this thing's going along, and that the people who've been called in by you are now free to go on home?

President Kennedy: No, I think we'll put it in another way, that I've requested that the leadership stay on an 8-hour alert basis, and that that's what they're doing. And I think everyone is free to go on that basis, but [unclear interjection]—better just stick with the 8-hour basis.

Hickenlooper: May I ask you a question? I have received a number of wires to the effect that, why isn't this referred to the United Nations? And I have said that I am just, tell them that this thing is being taken up there. But that I advise them . . . I would more definitely let them know. And these are some very prominent people. How can I answer them?

Rusk: We'll be glad to provide answers to those people for you, and draw their attention to the proceedings in the United Nations.

[The meeting then breaks up. A couple of people say: "Give them the papers." Another refers to people "reading 3-day-old papers." The noise continues for a while as everyone leaves. Then the tape recorder is turned off, presumably by President Kennedy.

A few minutes later, the tape recorder is turned on again. This time only a few people are talking, probably in the Oval Office. President Kennedy, Bundy, Robert Lovett (who had attended the congressional meeting), and a few others are present.]

Lovett: . . . folks had a direct question, which seemed to make sense. Bill [Fulbright] went quite a lot further. And I gather from what he said that he's convinced himself that this is the proper course of action.

President Kennedy: [Unclear] he's basing his opposition to it on the grounds that the OAS wouldn't meet . . .

Lovett: And, I gather, on the same . . . that Senator Russell is a little more belligerent, or prepared for further action. And I think the answer that I made to him is perhaps one . . .

It seems to me that the wisdom, that the basic wisdom here, is to regard Cuba really as an extension of Berlin, and to consider that the Berlin reaction is the one at which the Cuban affair was, at least in part, aimed. Therefore we have to avoid an invasion of Cuba, a diversion of attention and the troops involved in the thing, at this stage.

The primary, one of the primary benefits, dividends, from this form of action which the President has decided on is that it ought to develop, rather quickly, the intentions of the Russians. We've had some indications that they seem to be off balance. It seems to me that it would not be unreasonable to expect them to stay off balance for a couple of days while they make up their own minds what their intentions are.

Therefore, any invasion, I should say any strike, any air strike, which to me is generally a result of a congenital habit of overstating the case as well as the results of an air strike.

Bundy: [apparently interrupting] Do you want Paul and Bobby to come over?

President Kennedy: No, I don't want to take them away from their work. I just want to get a . . . I'm just thinking about what the . . .

Lovett: I don't think there's any such thing as one of these quick, sanitary . . . There's no such thing as a small military action. Now the moment we start *anything* in this field, we have to be prepared to do *everything*. So under no circumstances . . .

It seems to me that the decision as to what step is taken, if there is a continuing acceleration of buildup down there, would depend on the intentions which Russia has shown at that point. And I don't think a decision has to be made now. But it has to be made in the light of what happens in the middle of these things in the next few days.

President Kennedy: There seems to be some disposition on Adenauer's part, and I might even say Macmillan.

[David [Ormsby Gore] said he shared that sense with Macmillan.[5]

thing as a small military action, that if you have a strike or a series of strikes, you've got to follow it up.

Lovett: Then you've got a second front.

McCone: What concerns me is the blockade as a whole, they don't try to penetrate it. They go ahead and complete these missile sites, with more and more missiles now under cover of warehouses and so forth. We have no way of telling what the status of warheads is. What we're gonna do, in view of the threat, in view of the situation, in view of the symbol of strength that this gives—the effect it's going to have on Latin America and all the rest.

This might happen. The pictures which we saw here today, which were taken [by overflights] yesterday, the evidence of work going on on the sites. [Unclear.]

5. Ormsby-Gore had met with Bundy, shortly before the congressional leadership meeting, to discuss President Kennedy's upcoming telephone conversation with Macmillan. In a brief note to the President, Bundy had said that Macmillan was pressing for the initiation of negotiations, starting with a moratorium on both missile construction and the blockade (also U Thant's suggestion). Ormsby-Gore was concerned about Macmillan's stance. Bundy noted: "David thinks you should make it very plain to the Prime Minister that this is not an acceptable position and that the US cannot stand down its blockade without progress toward the removal of the missiles"; Bundy to President Kennedy, October 24, 1962, National Security Files, box 170, United Kingdom—General—10/15/62–11/12/62, JFKL. For Ormsby-Gore's report on his talk with Bundy and on the Macmillan positions that concerned him, see Washington 2667, 24 October 1962, and Foreign Office to Washington 7457, 24 October 1962, PRO, PREM 11/3690, 24020.

McNamara: I thought of Cuba as our hostage. I think it's as much our hostage as Berlin is a Soviet hostage. I think if we can remain cool and calm here, we've really got the screws on them. They're being restricted from what the world—

[Unclear exchange.]

President Kennedy: Yeah, well, I think that may be, but we don't want to decide that. But it is a fact that if they put the screws on Berlin in the way that we considered they were going to, then we are bound to invade Cuba.

Unidentified: But we can also put the screws on Cuba.

[Mixed voices. McNamara can be heard saying: "Exactly. Exactly."]

Bundy: For whatever it's worth, this commitment would come out to about a billion dollars in Cuba.

President Kennedy: Well, I think [unclear] that looks like we've got it there.

Well, in any case we've got to think, and we can see in the next 24 hours more, but . . . what we've got to be thinking about is this problem, of our blockade being successful and this work going on, and being faced in November with 50 or 60 of these missiles. Well, we're faced with 30 of them now, so but anyway we'll be faced with 60 of them. Under what conditions would the Russians fire them? They might be more reluctant to fire them if they've already grabbed Berlin than they would be if we suddenly go in, there. But anyway these are what we've got to be thinking about.

Unidentified: . . . what the U Thant [proposal says]—

President Kennedy: We've got the same issue. [Reading a copy of U Thant's statement from New York:]

The following message is being sent to the President of the United States:

I have been asked by the permanent representatives of a large number of member countries of the UN to address an urgent appeal to you in the present critical situation. These representatives feel in the interests of international peace and security that all concerned should refrain from any action which may aggravate the situation and bring with it the risk of war. In their view it is important that time should be given to enable the parties to get together to resolve the situation the present crisis presented and normalize the situation in the Caribbean.

This involves on the one hand the voluntary suspension of all armed shipments to Cuba and also the voluntary suspension of the quarantine measures involving the searching of ships bound for Cuba. [Kennedy initially reads "re-searching," and someone interjects that this has been read in over the telephone.]

I believe the voluntary suspension for a period of 2 or 3 weeks will greatly ease the situation and give time to the parties . . .[6]

I'd like to [unclear]. It seems to me, we make . . .

[Mixed voices.]

Bundy: Looks like a very . . . Have you discussed this with—

. . . . . if . . . Well, I did, I talked to Stevenson. We wanted to make it equal.

on their launchers.

Dillon?: And have UN observers.

McCone: And that they have UN observers.

Bundy: At the sites.

McCone: On the location at the sites.

[Unclear exchange.]

President Kennedy: [Unclear] talk about what we want to say on this. [Unclear.]

Bundy: I'll check with the Secretary and get the statement for you.

Do you want to answer it tonight? Stevenson thinks it's an advantage to make a quick answer.

President Kennedy: Yeah, so do I.

Unidentified: Well?

Bundy: Oh yes, that's the first thing.

[Unclear discussion.]

McCone: I ought to have announced this earlier. [Mentions talking to David Lawrence, publisher of *U.S. News and World Report,* and someone else.] I went through all the [unclear].

President Kennedy: You're going to have to talk to Walker Stone, who is the editor of all the Scripps-Howard papers. [Unclear comment by McCone.]

Did you see, did you talk to [Arthur] Krock?

McCone: Yeah.

6. The document is reprinted in Larson, *"Cuban Crisis,"* p. 134.

President Kennedy: How was . . . ?

McCone: He's all right; he's all right.[7]

[The conversation trails off inaudibly as the meeting breaks up. A few fragments of conversation can be heard as people leave. After a period of silence the recording stops.]

At about 7:00 P.M. in Washington, President Kennedy and Prime Minister Macmillan spoke again on the telephone. Again, a British notetaker transcribed the conversation.[8]

Macmillan: Well, I'm all right.

President Kennedy: Well, we have no more word yet on what's going to happen out there. As you have probably heard, some of these ships, the ones we're particularly interested in, have turned around. Others are coming on. So we ought to know in the next 12 hours whether they're going to try to run it or whether they're going to submit to be searched. So we'll be wiser by tomorrow night, but maybe not happier.

Macmillan: You don't really know whether they're going back, or whether they're going to try and make it, do you?

President Kennedy: Some of the ships that have turned back are the ones that we were the most interested in and which we think would have given us some material. Others are continuing. I think they're just tankers that are continuing.

Now, I don't know whether they are going to make us sink these or whether we are going to be permitted to search them. That's still in question.

Macmillan: How do you think . . . On the whole, the fact that they are turned back is a great triumph for you. And the question is, how do we exploit that triumph?

President Kennedy: Well, I don't think we can say it is yet, because some of them are coming on. And the ones that are turning back are the ones that we felt might have offensive military equipment on them, so they probably didn't

7. The previous afternoon, October 23, McCone had met with Arthur Krock and then with David Lawrence and a Mr. Scott to discuss the evidence of Soviet activity and President Kennedy's decision. See McCone to File, "Meetings with Mr. Krock, Mr. David Lawrence, and Mr. Scott," 23 October 1962, in McAuliffe, *CIA Documents*, p. 287.

8. The following is from "Record of Telephone Message between the Prime Minister and President Kennedy, 24.10.62," PRO, PREM 11/3690, 24020. We have modified the punctuation of the original, but not the text.

want that equipment to fall into our hands. That's the reason they're turning back. But we still don't know whether the other ships will respect our quarantine or whether they will make us take action, military action, against them. That we don't know, and we won't know that for overnight.

Macmillan: That's very interesting. But, now, what do you think it means? If they're turning back, it means he's frightened a bit, doesn't it?

No. He may be turning back these, the little ones, to

of military impo-

But we won't know that, as I say, until tomorrow.

Macmillan: Well, what do you think is the next thing to do? How are you going to get the rockets out of Cuba? The ones that are there now?

President Kennedy: Well, if we go through stage one, as I say, and if they respect our quarantine, then we've got this problem of the rockets on Cuba. And the last 24 hours' film show that they are continuing to build those rockets, and then we're going to have to make the judgment as to whether we're going to invade Cuba, taking our chances, or whether we hold off and use Cuba as a sort of hostage in the matter of Berlin. Then any time he takes an action against Berlin, we take an action against Cuba. That's really the choice that we now have.

What's your judgment?

Macmillan: Well, I would like to think about that. I think it is very important, because I suppose the world feels that we shall, sometime or other, [have] to have some sort of discussion with them. But we don't want to do that in such a way that he has all these cards in his hands.

President Kennedy: He has Cuba in his hands, but he doesn't have Berlin. If he takes Berlin, then we will take Cuba. If we take Cuba now, we have the problem of course of these missiles being fired, or a general missile firing, and we certainly will have the problem of Berlin being seized.

Macmillan: Yes, I agree with that. It needs thought.

I see that he has made some proposal on the wireless in answer to Lord Russell saying that he wants a summit meeting. Have you heard that?

President Kennedy: Yes, I saw that, but he said that there would be no point in a summit if we continued our piratical actions. The implication was that he would be glad to talk, but not if we continued our quarantine or if we carry it out. It wasn't very precise.

Then the Secretary General [U Thant] has asked for a sort of cessation of our quarantine for 2 weeks, but we can't agree to that unless they would agree not to continue to work on the missile bases.

Macmillan: Yes, I think that's quite right. But all the same, I think that he [Khrushchev] is a bit wondering what to do, don't you?

President Kennedy: Well, I think that they certainly have not been very precise in the last 24 hours.

The question I would like to have you think about, Prime Minister, is this one. If they respect the quarantine, then we get the second stage of this problem, and work continues on the missiles. Do we then tell them that if they don't get the missiles out, that we're going to invade Cuba? He will then say that if we invade Cuba that there's going to be a general nuclear assault, and he will in any case grab Berlin. Or do we just let the nuclear work go on, figuring he won't ever dare fire them, and when he tries to grab Berlin, we then go into Cuba. That's what I'd like to have you think about.

Macmillan: Well, I think that's very well put, if I may say so. I'd like to think about that and send you a message back. May I do that?

President Kennedy: Fine, Prime Minister.

I understand that you are going to have a debate about this. Are you having much difficulty with the Labour Party?

Macmillan: All I have to do is to make a short statement, and they ask a few questions. It won't last more than half an hour, and then we prorogue the Parliament. So tomorrow should be fairly simple. I shall just make a statement of the facts, and supporting you, and just leave it at that. Of course they will ask me whether I propose to intervene, and all that kind of thing, but I shall say the time's not ripe for that yet.

President Kennedy: That's fine. I think you had a copy . . . The two important points seem to me: one, my statement in early September saying that we were opposed to taking any military action in Cuba unless they indulged in offensive capacity; and the second was their statement that they would never put rockets into Cuba. So this deception seems to me to be so indefensible from their point of view. And I assume you have all that material, in case you were being pressed at all by the Labour members [of Parliament].

Macmillan: Yes, very kindly you've given me that. Ambassador Bruce gave me that this morning, and I think we've got all that into the statement.

This big issue of which you have just spoken is the one I would like to think about. And then we must consider how to handle it, and how we handle the Europeans who will begin to get a bit excited—de Gaulle and Adenauer and company—and how we take the next steps.

But I feel myself pretty sure that we ought not to do anything in a hurry. We ought just to let this develop, this, a day or two.

President Kennedy: Right, Prime Minister. As I say, we are mobilizing our ... ... invade, we will be in a position to do [so] within

assurances. If we withdraw the quarantine, we have no assurances that ... won't be sent in there, number 1. And number 2, if we could get reasonable assurances that they wouldn't be sent in there, that would be satisfactory, but there's also work on the missile sites [that] would have to stop, and that the missiles that are presently pointing at us should be subjected to inspection. So that's what we'll come back with, and then we'll see what he says.

Macmillan: Will that be all public, or is that a private message to you?

President Kennedy: I think he's probably reporting it to the Security Council. I haven't seen it on the ticker yet, but he's sending it to Khrushchev. So my judgment is, he'll release it, and our answers will be released.

Macmillan: I think that's rather tiresome of him, because it looks sensible and yet it's very bad.

President Kennedy: Well, yes. I think the fact that work on the missile bases will continue . . .

I'll read you his message. I am just informed that he has not made a public statement yet. He has just given us a copy of the prospective public statement that he is going to make. Now, it may not be finally made, but I'll read it to you:

> I have been asked by the permanent representatives of a large number of member governments of the UN to address an urgent appeal to you in the present critical situation. These representatives feel in the interests of international peace and security that all concerned should refrain from any action which may aggravate the situation and bring with it the risk of war. In their view it is important that time should be given to enable the parties to get

together to resolve the situation the present crisis presented and normalize the situation in the Caribbean.

This involves on the one hand the voluntary suspension of all armed shipments to Cuba and also the voluntary suspension of the quarantine measures involving the searching of ships bound for Cuba.

I believe the voluntary suspension for a period of 2 or 3 weeks will greatly ease the situation and give time to the parties concerned to meet and discuss with a view to finding a peaceful solution to the problem. In this context I shall gladly make myself available to all parties for whatever services I may be able to perform. I urgently appeal to Your Excellency for immediate consideration of this message. I have sent an identical message to the Chairman of the Council of Ministers of the Soviet Union.

Signed, U Thant

Now, we don't know whether that['s] what he's finally going to do, but that's what he was indicating he was going to do half an hour ago.

Macmillan: I think that's a very dangerous message he's sent. I think it's very important that your reply should be good, and I have no doubt it is.

President Kennedy: Yes. Well, we're just getting it ready, and we'll point out the deficiencies in it—that there's no guarantees against a breach of the quarantine, and also the work on the missile sites will continue, and the danger will be greater within 2 weeks. So we'll point that out and send it right back to him the minute we get an indication that he's going to send it to us.

Macmillan: Well now, how do you think we shall get out of this in the long run? Do you think we ought to try and do a deal, have a meeting with him, or not? What initiative do you think ought to be taken, and by whom?

President Kennedy: Well, I think probably, at the end of this 24-hour period when we understand more of what he's going to do on the quarantine, I think we shall probably judge it better.

As I say, part of that answer, Prime Minister, seems to me to depend on the answer to the question that we were originally discussing, which was whether we ought to wait and let this buildup continue in Cuba. Because otherwise we risk war, and, equally important, at least of some importance, we risk the loss of Berlin. Otherwise we can keep on the quarantine, the buildup of missiles will continue, and then we would threaten to take action in Cuba if they go into Berlin.

Until we have really reached a judgment on that question, which is now what we're thinking about, it's hard to answer the point about whether we ought to have a meeting with him. I don't know quite what we will discuss at the meeting, because he'll be back with his same old position on Berlin, probably offer to dismantle the missiles if we'll neutralize Berlin. So that I think we would have a difficult political problem. But we ought to be thinking about it.

Macmillan: I would like to think about it. Would it be disagreeable for you, for me to come and see you or not at any stage? Do you think it would be advisable, or not?

[*President Kennedy:*] Why don't we talk on Friday [October 26] when we

be away

Macmillan: I shall stay in London. But I think it very useful to a brief talk each evening, if it's not inconvenient to you, then we can just compare notes as to how things are going on.

President Kennedy: Good. I will call you then, tomorrow evening, Prime Minister, at 6:00 my time.

Macmillan: That'll do me fine. Good night.

President Kennedy: Good night, Prime Minister. Thank you.

Later in the evening, at about 9:30, a new message arrived from Moscow for President Kennedy. The version he received read as follows:

Dear Mr. President:

I have received your letter of October 23, familiarized myself with it and am answering you.

Imagine, Mr. President, that we had posed to you those ultimative conditions which you have posed to us by your action. How would you have reacted to this? I think that you would have been indignant at such a step on our part. And that would have been comprehensible to us.

Having posed these conditions to us, you, Mr. President, have challenged us. Who asked you to do this? By what right have you done this? Our relations with the Republic of Cuba, like our relations with other states, regardless of what sort of state it may be, concern only the two countries between which those relations exist. And if one is really going to talk about a quarantine, referred to in your letter, it can be established, according to accepted international practice, only by the agreement of states between themselves, and not by any sort of third party. There exist, for example, quarantines on agricultural goods and products. But in the case at hand, the question is in no way one of quarantine, but rather of far more serious things, and you yourself understand this.

You, Mr. President, are not declaring quarantines, but advancing an ultimatum and threatening that unless we subordinate ourselves to your demands, you will use force. Consider what you are saying! And you wish to convince me to agree to this! What does agreement with such demands mean? This would mean to guide oneself in one's relations and other countries not by reason but to indulge arbitrariness. You are no longer appealing to reason, but wish to intimidate us.

And, Mr. President, I cannot agree with this and think that in your heart you recognize that I am correct. I am convinced that in my place you would act the same way.

Reference to the decision of the Organization of American States cannot in any way substantiate the demands now advanced by the United States. This organization has absolutely no authority or basis to make decisions like that of which you speak in your letter.

Consequently, we do not recognize these decisions. International law exists, generally recognized norms of conduct exist. We firmly support the principles of international law, strictly observe the norms regulating navigation on the high seas and in international waters. We observe these norms and enjoy the rights recognized by all states.

You wish to compel us to renounce the rights that every sovereign state enjoys, you are attempting to legislate in questions of international law, you are trampling upon the generally accepted norms of this law. And all this not only out of hatred for the Cuban people and its Government, but also as a result of considerations of the election campaign in the USA. What morality, what law can justify such an approach by the American Government to international affairs? You cannot find such a morality and such a law, because the actions of the USA with regard to Cuba are outright banditry, or, if you like, the folly of degenerate imperialism. Unfortunately, the peoples of all countries, and least of all the American people, can suffer gravely from such folly, since the USA has fully lost its former inaccessibility with the advent of contemporary types of armament.

Consequently, Mr. President, if you coolly weigh the situation which has developed, not giving way to passions, then you will understand that the Soviet Union cannot fail to reject the arbitrary demands of the USA. When you confront us with such conditions, try to put yourself in our situation and think how the USA would react to these conditions. I do not doubt that if someone had attempted to dictate conditions of this sort to you, the USA, you would have rejected such an attempt. And we also say—No.

The Soviet Government considers that violation of freedom of the use of international waters and international air space is an act of aggression, pushing mankind towards the abyss of a world missile-nuclear war. Consequently, the Soviet Government cannot give instructions to the captains of Soviet vessels bound for Cuba to observe the instructions of the American naval forces blockading that island. Our instructions to Soviet mariners are strictly to observe the generally recognized norms of navigation in international waters and not to retreat from them by even one step. And if the ~~~ ~~~~ ~~~~~ realize what sort of responsibility

at State, and Ball focused on the last p~~ g ~ challenge to the quarantine. He told Kennedy that the United States had no option "but to go ahead and test this thing out, in the morning."[10] Kennedy and his advisers were already thinking about whether to stop a Soviet tanker, the *Bucharest*, which was approaching the quarantine zone.

Turning to U Thant's message, now made public, Ball commented on President Kennedy's instruction to give a stern reply immediately, that night. Stevenson, said Ball, was worried that the United States might be blocking negotiations and was "kicking like a steer" about replying so soon. Kennedy did not bend. The ships the Soviets had turned around, he observed, were ones they wanted to keep out of American hands; they were moving other ships toward Cuba to challenge the quarantine.

A reply to U Thant's public message was completed for release the following morning. After more phone calls, Kennedy called Ball again with an additional idea. Perhaps U Thant "ought to give out a message in a way that gives them enough of an out to stop their shipments without looking like they completely crawled down." Kennedy suggested asking U Thant to make a public appeal to the Soviets to stop their ships for a few days, and then some preliminary talks could be arranged in New York. Worried about compromising the principle of the quarantine and showing a lack of resolve, Kennedy and his advisers wondered if they should set an example with the *Bucharest*, even though no

9. Reprinted in Larson, *"Cuban Crisis,"* pp. 127–129.

10. Memorandum of Telephone Conversation between Ball and President Kennedy at 10:30 P.M., October 24 (prepared by an anonymous State Department notetaker), in *FRUS 1961–1963*, vol. 11: *Cuban Missile Crisis and Aftermath*, pp. 188–189.

one thought Khrushchev would have time to stop the tanker, and no one was anxious to start a confrontation by boarding a ship that was not carrying prohibited cargo. McNamara was planning only to hail it and ask for identification.

Just before midnight, Ball tried out the idea of the direct appeal from U Thant with Stevenson, who was persuaded. Stevenson got U Thant out of bed (not, apparently, an easy feat) and induced him to issue a direct appeal that day, October 25. Washington officials worried about whether Stevenson would nail down the right content: "Stevenson may go down the drain" was how Bundy put it to Ball. So at 2:00 A.M. a message went to New York, giving Stevenson written instructions on what U Thant's appeal should and should not say. In essence it was: "Hope that Khrushchev will hold his ships out of interception area for limited time in order to permit discussions of modalities of agreement."[11]

Since Khrushchev's letter threatened a military confrontation when Soviet ships were stopped the next day, a quick reply to that message was also considered necessary. Kennedy and his White House staff prepared a text, and at about 2:00 A.M. on October 25, Kennedy's terse reply was sent on its way.[12]

11. See Memoranda for Telephone Conversations of President Kennedy and Ball (11:15 P.M.), Rusk and Ball (11:25 P.M.), Ball and Stevenson (11:45 P.M.), Ball and Bundy (12:30 A.M.), and the instruction, Deptel 1084, ibid., pp. 190–197, 199.

12. The reply was read aloud in full to the Executive Committee during its morning meeting on October 25.

THURSDAY, OCTOBER 25

10:00 A.M.

- --

As the sun rose in Washington on October 25, a message ᵾᵾᵾ ᵾ᷍᷍᷍ ᵾᵾᵾ ᵾ᷍᷍ arrived at the White House, conveying an answer to the question of further action against Cuba that Macmillan and Kennedy had discussed the previous evening. In Britain, large peace demonstrations had protested U.S. policy, and even comparatively moderate commentators were questioning the wisdom of Kennedy's stance. The *Evening Standard* published a cartoon with one panel showing Eisenhower holding Prime Minister Anthony Eden's coattails to prevent his going over a brink labeled "Suez"; in the other panel, Macmillan merely looked on as Kennedy started to step across a brink labeled "Cuba." Macmillan's message shows the influence of this drift in British public opinion.

Following for Bundy from de Zulueta[1]
Please pass following personal message from Prime Minister Macmillan to the President:
Message begins:
   I have been thinking over the 64,000-dollar question which you posed on the telephone. After much reflection, I think that events have gone too far. While circumstances may arise in which such action would be right and necessary, I think that we are now all in a phase where you must try to obtain your objectives by other means.
   I am going to make the point today in the House of Commons that if you had let the Russians get away with it after your September statement, none of the American guarantees to the free world would have had any value.

---

   1. Philip de Zulueta, Private Secretary to Macmillan for foreign affairs, was the closest counterpart to Bundy within the office of the Prime Minister.

This is the vital point of justification. I am also going to make the second point that in view of the Russian duplicity we cannot rest on mere words in any arrangements; we must have verification and confirmation. In these circumstances, I would suggest that in the reply which you make to U Thant today, which will be of vital importance and subject to the closest scrutiny of our friends and neutrals as well as enemies, you should concentrate on the point that there must be some system of inspection if the quarantine is called off. Such inspection must make sure that ships with arms do not in fact enter the ports. We cannot rest now upon the Russian promise. That is the first point.

You must also demand that there should be some inspection by the United Nations or other independent authority to stop work on the major military installations so long as the negotiation lasts. This would enable you to say that you had in fact obtained your objectives. For if there are no ships arriving, then the purpose of the quarantine is served; and if there is no more construction, the purpose of largely immobilising this threat is also served. In other words, such an approach as I suggest fits in with the answer to last night's questions which I feel I must give.

At the same time you will no doubt continue with your military build up for any emergency. This may be as important a factor for persuading the Cubans to accept inspection as in other directions.[2]

There had been little sleep for those watching the quarantine line and shipping in the Atlantic. McNamara's close scrutiny and constant questions had sparked more tense exchanges with Admiral Anderson, especially over where and how the Navy was monitoring Soviet submarines. A Soviet tanker, the *Bucharest*, approached the quarantine line at 7:15 A.M. and identified itself. President Kennedy directed that the ship be trailed but allowed to proceed for the time being.

The military preparations and troop movements were so rapid, peremptory, and extensive that they inevitably attracted great attention in and out of the American press. In that morning's *Washington Post*, well-known columnist and reputed Kennedy administration insider Walter Lippmann suggested that the crisis could be resolved by exchanging the withdrawal of Soviet missiles in Cuba for the U.S. missiles in Turkey.

The Executive Committee of the National Security Council reconvened in the Cabinet Room at 10:00 A.M. The meeting began with a discussion between President Kennedy and the Acting Director of the U.S. Information Agency,

---

2. PRO, PREM 11/3690, 24020. We have modified the punctuation of the original, but not the text.

Donald Wilson, about the possibility of using radio broadcasts or leaflets to tell the Cuban people what President Kennedy had said on October 22 and to give them evidence about the Soviet missiles in their country. President Kennedy turned on the tape recorder during this discussion.

Wilson: . . . Voice of America shortwave on a couple of frequencies, and ⌐ ⌐ medium-wave stations, 2 in Miami

missiles, and whether we ⌐⌐ whether we get any reports out of Cuba from the [foreign] embassies whether it is generally accepted that there are missiles, and whether the dropping of pictures of missiles would have any effect.

Wilson: All right. I believe the dropping of pictures would be very good. However, the larger question for psychological purposes would be—

President Kennedy: Whether they doubt it? They may not doubt it.

[Mixed voices.]

Taylor: Dropping pictures is a major operation.

Bundy: Well, we just have to decide to send your airplanes over to do it. [Unclear.]

[To McCone] You want to present?

McCone: Mr. President, according to our reports, there's been no change that's been noted in the scope or pace of the construction of the IRBMs and MRBM missile sites in Cuba. The recent construction is continuing and has been noted for the last several days.

Cuban armed forces continue their alert, with military aircraft on stand-downs since the morning of 23rd of October. There are indications in Cuba that known and suspected dissidents are being rounded up at the present time.

[27 seconds excised as classified information, probably a reference to 14 of 22 Soviet ships bound for Cuba having turned back.][3]

---

3. Other evidence indicates that at this stage of the briefing McCone reported: "As of 0600 Eastern Daylight Time, at least 14 of the 22 Soviet ships which were known to be en route to Cuba had turned back"; CIA Watch Committee Memo, "The Crisis USSR/Cuba," 25 October

Five of the 8 remaining are tankers. Two of the dry-cargo ships not known to have reversed course may be carrying nonmilitary cargo.

President Kennedy: [To someone else] Why don't you sit up here?

McCone: [37 seconds excised as classified information, probably a reference to the *Belovodsk,* a dry-cargo ship still on course that did have military cargo.] . . . carrying 12 MI-4 armed helicopters.

We still see no signs of any crash procedure in measures to increase the readiness of the Soviet armed forces. The Watch Committee concludes in their report this morning as follows: "We conclude that Soviet bloc armed forces are continuing to increase their state of readiness and some units are on alert. We have, however, noted no significant redeployments. So that [unclear] program, although there is a high level of alert."

Bloc media are playing up Khrushchev's 24 October statement that he would consider a top-level meeting as "useful."

There is, as yet, no reaction to the widely known turnaround of Soviet ships, which had not become widely known to the public at the time of the issuance of this report except through this morning's articles in some of the papers. But attention remains centered on the neutralist efforts in the United Nations to find machinery for easing tension, as well as the efforts of U Thant. But he is [unclear], as well as [unclear].

[21 seconds excised as classified information, probably a reference to the Canadians' search of a Cubana airliner passing through their country en route from Prague to Havana.][4]

Latin American countries are beginning to offer military units for the quarantine, and there is generally little adverse reaction in that hemisphere.

This is contained in the report, which will be circulated, and maybe we'll have a copy before this meeting's over.

[15 seconds excised as classified information. McCone is probably discussing the visit of the chair of the British Joint Intelligence Committee, Kenneth Strong, to Washington and a briefing given to Strong about the intelligence information.][5]

At first he [Strong] was quite skeptical. Later he became thoroughly convinced, and reported to his ambassador [Ormsby-Gore], and also directly to

---

1962, in McAuliffe, *CIA Documents,* p. 304. The recorded material may have referred to the communications intelligence sources of this information, mentioned in previous meetings.

4. The incident is discussed in ibid.

5. The episode is described in Dino A. Brugioni, *Eyeball to Eyeball: The Inside Story of the Cuban Missile Crisis,* ed. Robert F. McCort (New York: Random House, 1991), pp. 327–328, though the date given for Strong's visit is in error.

his government, that the evidence presented was convincing, and he thought the situation was provocative. I think this is a very useful thing that by coincidence he happened to be here.

The low-level photography of a few days ago, upon analysis, proves to be more valuable than was first thought. The U-2 flights yesterday were unsuccessful because of weather. And this morning one of the U-2s has been stood _____ _____ second flight has gone or not.

Saturday]. The list is q___ percent of it is baby food. There's a large quantity of plasma, about the annual consumption [unclear]. We have made no appreciation of our estimate of just what's involved in the list, except it's been turned over to wholesale drug companies for analysis and for a report. It's being handled directly by Donovan. No activity on our part whatsoever.

[10 seconds excised as classified information, apparently a description of an intelligence source.] He reports regularly that this deal [with Donovan for the prisoner release] is still being considered by Castro's advisers as being on. This is as of yesterday.

He also reports that there's great worry in Havana, great anxiety amongst the people and involving aircraft—antiaircraft guns on the roofs of buildings. And their military is in a high state of alert.

That's all I have this morning.

President Kennedy: I wonder if we could get from Cuba any sort of report or an analysis of . . . so we can be up to date about the state of morale of the people there, and their viewpoint on all of this.

McCone: [9 seconds excised as classified information.] I'll handle it.

There was one report of interest that might come to your attention. Santo Domingo Radio reported that 5,000 troops [unclear] in [unclear], was unconfirmed that the CIA placed a low evaluation on it.

---

6. James Donovan was serving as a private mediator in attempting to negotiate the release of Cuban exiles captured in 1961 at the Bay of Pigs. The negotiations had resulted in the Cuban request for American delivery of medical supplies, which the U.S. government would attempt to secure in private donations rather than give tax money to the Castro government.

President Kennedy: . . . ever getting the answer to these questions about their response to their knowledge of the missile sites now, their reaction to it, and their support of the regime? Have you got any—

McCone: Well, let me go into that carefully. We have quite a number of sources— [16 seconds excised as classified information.]

Bundy: Next of all, Mr. President, you ought to know the overnight military operations.

McNamara: Mr. President, early this morning, on the order of 7:00 local time, which would be approximately 6:00 Eastern Daylight Time, the naval ships, a destroyer in particular, intercepted the *Bucharest,* which is a Soviet tanker, moving within range of the barrier, queried it as to its name, destination, point of origin, and type of cargo. The *Bucharest* responded it's from the Black Sea and was bound for Havana, and was carrying petroleum products. To the best of our knowledge, no other words passed between the ships. The destroyer was instructed to maintain surveillance of the *Bucharest,* and that instruction came down.

There are, I think, a series of actions related to this that we might undertake today. At the present time our naval craft participating in the quarantine are under instructions not to board, because they are instructed to board only designated ships, and those ships haven't been designated.

I believe we should say, instruct them, to selectively query, and consequently inspect by boarding, certain nonbloc ships. This can be done very quickly. This will establish boarding as a pattern of operation in the quarantine zone.

We could then follow this, later today, by boarding the *Bucharest,* if that seems desirable. But whether it seems desirable or not, I believe we should establish a pattern of boarding as a quarantine technique, and do it immediately.

President Kennedy: Have we got any other ships we can board now?

McNamara: Well, non-Soviet ships, there are many. But in order to allow Admiral Dennison to lay on a plan for doing that, we should give the instructions, and do so very promptly. I think that would be highly desirable.

[Others agree. Someone says: "I do too."]

McNamara: Have you issue the instructions for nonbloc ship boarding, have them keep us informed of the procedure, and if they say there aren't any in range, suggest [stopping a ship flying the flag of] a SEATO country.

Unidentified: Board, or use of the [unclear].

McNamara: That's one action.

The second action, as to whether we should board the *Bucharest,* I think we ought to talk here further, and I'll pass over that for the moment because there is time—

President Kennedy: What would be the next ship? And what time would we have a—

McNamara: Next Soviet ship?

President Kennedy: Yeah.

McNamara: The next Soviet ship of real interest to us . . . I say "of interest," because this passenger ship's location is not specifically known. By dead reck-

[illegible] within the barrier area plus or minus 100 miles or so.

50 hours ago

moving directly east by turning around completely, it appears that have moved northwest. I say "might have" because some of our direction-finding equipment and other information as to how it behaved are not accurate to closer tolerances than about a 90-mile radius. And we're not absolutely sure, therefore, what happened to it. But it looks as though it might have deviated from its established course and then resumed course during the night. And it appears to be moving now towards Cuba. It's of great interest to us because it's not only a tanker, but it has a deck load. And it acquired a deck load of, as I recall, of ammonia tanks. But these could very possibly be, and as a matter of fact they probably are, missile fuel tanks on deck. In any case, it will come to the barrier at 2000 hours, 8:00 Eastern Daylight Time, day after, tomorrow night.

President Kennedy: Wait a minute, that would be—

McNamara: 8:00 P.M., Friday night [October 26]. Now that's the only other Soviet ship that could—

President Kennedy: [Unclear] Saturday morning, so that would be 48 hours.

McNamara: Or, alternatively, we could go further than the barrier in Friday daylight and intercept it. But that's the only Soviet ship moving in at the moment that we think is attractive.

There are some other actions that I think we can take that relate to this, however, Mr. President, that I'd like to mention now. I believe that we should establish a low-level surveillance pattern that is consistent with an air attack.

There is much evidence that the Soviets have instructed the Cubans to act very cautiously. I'd like to run down that because it relates to this low-level surveillance and possible further escalation of our military force. It appears that they've given instructions to Cuban nationals not to fire on U.S. aircraft. And more than that, it appears that, in a separate instruction, they gave orders to Cuban MiGs not to take off from the airfields. I'm not certain of this, but there's some evidence to believe that.

It's quite clear they have camouflaged the SAM sites, surface-to-air missile sites, thereby reducing their readiness, because they have to pull these covers off in order to fire effectively.

McCone: No question about that.

McNamara: The photographs demonstrate that exactly.

[43 seconds excised as classified information.] . . . and instructions to the KOMAR craft not to move out of port. We have pictures of the KOMAR craft inboard in port, with covers on the missiles.

[93 seconds excised as classified information.] . . . and therefore, I think that we can conduct low-level surveillance with very little risk of an incident that we did not wish to incite ourselves.

President Kennedy: What's the advantage of the low-level?

McNamara: Well, two advantages. Three advantages, really.

One, it gives us some intelligence that we can use, benefit from.

Two, it will establish a pattern of operation that is consistent with an attack, and cannot be differentiated from an attack, and therefore reduces the warning of an attack, and may make it possible to attack with lesser forces because we reduced the warning. And this, I think, is an extremely important point we can discuss later.

And three, it demonstrates to the public and the world that we are not only interested in stopping the flow of offensive weapons to Cuba, but also definitely have as our objective the removal of the weapons that are there.

Why are we justified in conducting low-level surveillance under these circumstances? We're justified in doing so because there's evidence that the Soviets are camouflaging their sites. There is tremendous evidence of this. You can see the camouflage tents drying on the ground. It's been raining and it's wet and they're drying them out. They're under instructions to camouflage immediately. And they're camouflaging not just the weapons, but various buildings, trucks—

President Kennedy: Maybe some Russian will explain to me someday why they didn't camouflage them before. And why they do it now. And at what point they thought we were going to find it out. [Unclear.]

McNamara: It's an amazing thing. But now I think we're beginning to read their minds much more clearly than was true 72 hours ago.

And there's absolutely no question but what they're under orders to camouflage and do it fast. And because the camouflage equipment is wet and spread out on the ground, it's drying. And as soon as it dries they put it on everything in sight. They're camouflaging trucks; they're camouflaging erectors; they're camouflaging missiles. It's really a fantastic sequence of action.

And I think this gives us justification if we went in and checked on what's ⋯⋯ things so we know whether they've

⋯⋯

cover the IL-28 airfields, ⋯⋯ SAM sites—not the whole island, but selected SAM sites, the ROMAN bases, and the coastal missile bases—the coastal-defense missile bases.

McCone: And the nuclear storage areas.

McNamara: Now, I think we can do this—I beg your pardon. That's exactly right, the nuclear storage areas, which they are working on with great speed and effort.

I think we can do this safely. I think it will give us valuable information that we would need and benefit from if we subsequently decide to carry out an attack. And I think it will establish a pattern of operation consistent with an attack, and therefore it will camouflage an attack.

I would suggest we do it by announcing to the Cubans that we are going to carry out unarmed surveillance today, for the reasons I've outlined, consistent with the OAS requirement and consistent with our own [unclear] views, that these planes are unarmed, but if they are attacked we will attack the attacker.

President Kennedy: It seems to me we negate one of the purposes, which is to make it possible someday to make this an attack. Why do we even bother to announce it? Why don't we just do it?

McNamara: Well, we may not [announce]. We might say we're going to carry on not just today, we're going to carry on unarmed surveillance to determine whether they are removing the weapons or whether they are proceeding to—

McCone: You said that in your speech.

McNamara: Well, because if we want to continue this pattern of low-level surveillance or close surveillance, frequent surveillance, I think it would be very useful if we could announce that it's unarmed and get it clear that it's unarmed. And they would think that it's unarmed.

Taylor: [Unclear] might want to arm it.

McNamara: Pardon me?

Taylor: Someday you may want to arm it.

McNamara: Well, we don't have to say that every day hereafter it's going to be unarmed. We simply say we're going to carry out surveillance. Well, let me put that [issue of the announcement] aside. That's a very minor factor to this whole problem.

McCone: This low-level is very desirable, Mr. President. Not only does it relate to the immediate situation, but also [unclear]. We could get much-needed information [unclear].

[Mixed conversation; brief discussion.]

McNamara: [Unclear] . . . could do that. If there's no question, I'd like to order it immediately.

[Unclear exchange.]

No announcement.

[Unclear] . . . the targets now are all 9 missile sites, the IL-28 airfields, the MiG airfields, the KOMAR bases, the coastal bases, and selected SAM sites. And I would suggest that the SAM sites being selected be—let's just say the 6 that are most directly associated with attack on the IL-28s and the missile sites.

Taylor: If you don't mind, I'd like to leave that open. Because it's most convenient, we'll set up our pattern for the other basing site, and then see what the most convenient—

President Kennedy: Don't you want to get an airplane, a single airplane—

McNamara: Let's say, if they can't get a substantial number, let us know, because [unclear] exactly . . .

President Kennedy: Okay.

McCone?: I think you might consider, if it's in the pattern of the flight, to get one or 2 of the SAM sites that we got 2 or 3 days ago, to see what the activity is.

McNamara: One fourth category: nuclear storage sites.

General Taylor left the room and passed the approval for the low-level surveillance flights to the Joint Chiefs at about 10:40 A.M.

McNamara: Now, there are quite a number of other things that I think we might consider for today, Mr. President. You might want to defer discussions—

[Unclear interjection by President Kennedy.]

One of them is, we might wish to push toward a veto at the Security Council of our proposal that UN inspectors go in and inspect the missile sites. This is a prelude to a possible subsequent attack on those sites.

There is some possibility that we're moving to the position now, where we can attack those missiles and have a fair chance of destroying them with very

missile site is 8 hours from launch, . . . indicated, then we have very little risk of going in within that 8-hour period.

And, secondly, if at the same time that that condition exists, all the Cuban forces, to the best of our knowledge, are under orders not to attack, we know at the very least there will be confusion if we come over there with a few aircraft and shoot them up.

Thirdly, if we can go in with low-level surveillance for a day or two and establish a pattern of operation, we send in the same number of ships, but now they're armed instead of unarmed.

And if the Security Council has turned down by veto our proposal—by which we send in UN inspectors—this might set up the circumstances in which we can go in and take those missiles out.

Robert Kennedy: Bob, do you think that maybe they've got instructions of nonfiring or nondefensive action, might be based on the expectation or the wish that we fire the first shot and then they'll all be [alerted?] . . .

McNamara: Possibly. I don't know.

Robert Kennedy: But that would play a role in the fact that maybe we would want to do this in the next 48 hours.

McNamara: It would. And all I'm suggesting at the minute is that we take this step that will give us the option to do it if we later choose to. And one of those steps is getting a Security Council veto. And the other step is carrying out this low-level surveillance. We don't have to do anything more today.

Robert Kennedy: Thank you.

President Kennedy: Why don't we come back then to whether the political situation of the UN and everyplace else is such that we want to let this *Bucharest* pass today without making an inspection request. What is the political effect of our letting that pass? Are we better off to make this issue come to a head today, or is there some advantage in putting it off till tomorrow?

Robert Kennedy: When will it arrive in Cuba?

McNamara: The *Bucharest,* as best we can tell, is traveling about 17 knots, is around 500 miles from Cuba, and she'd arrive therefore sometime tomorrow. If we're going to— [Unclear interjection.] Yeah. If we're going to, we have about 8 hours left, because it is now 11:30 [local time, not Daylight Savings Time], and we wouldn't want to do it at night.

Rusk: Well, the fact is that we have already hailed it [the *Bucharest*], asked it questions. It's answered. We've already passed it through.

McNamara: We haven't passed it. We just hailed it; it replied; and we're shadowing it. That, to the best of my knowledge, are the only words that were passed.

Thompson: By the time this arrives in port we will almost then be ready to tackle the other ships, and there wouldn't be much interval between its arrival—

McNamara: That's approximately correct, no.

President Kennedy: You want to . . . Is there any reason that you'd put it off, or not put it off for 24 hours, the searching of a Soviet ship?

McNamara: It actually could be put off possibly 48 hours, Mr. President.

Rusk: From my point of view, the tanker's not the best example. I mean, we haven't got POL on the [prohibited materials] list, and if there's no visible missiles on their own deck there's not much room for any other [unclear]. [Unclear.]

President Kennedy: Obviously, definitely, we don't have to turn it around. The question really is, if a vessel arrives in Havana tomorrow, and whether it arrives . . . [People] think the United States, think what happens, indicating [that we're] setting a pattern.

McNamara: Well, I think that we could say that Khrushchev in the newspaper stated that he had instructed the ship captains not to deviate from the norm of sea practice. He used the word "norm" in his message. We consider this a deviation from the norm of sea practice. It is not customary practice to ask what cargo you're carrying and to get a response. It is done sometimes; but it, I understand, it is not customary. Therefore, we could say—

President Kennedy: Well, we wouldn't want to get in and argue about whether he deviated as much as we . . .

If we decide not to, the only reason for doing it is because we wanted to give sufficient grace to the Soviet Union to get these instructions clear or for the UN to have a chance. That seems to be the best grounds to put it on if we decided to put our clear, our best case. We could say that we . . . the view of

U Thant.[7] I mean, I think the only drive we can put it on is that we looked at the vessel. It was obvious what it was carrying. If it's not carrying offensive weapons, it responded. And I think our position at this point, in view of U Thant's appeal, we let this go. But, more because of the vote in the Security Council.

~~. . . . . . got to get some explanation. Because everybody else is gonna have~~ . . . . ~~I don't think~~ we can [unclear]

[Mixed voices.]

We don't want to board any tankers, if not . . .

[Unclear discussion.]

McNamara: Oh, yes, we will be boarding tankers.

Unidentified: Not today.

Bundy: Well then, if we better board, we've got to board this one if we can't board somebody else's.

McNamara: Well, there will be ships we won't . . . There will be tankers we didn't board.

Bundy: [Unclear.] It seems pretty awful to me if we board a British tanker, and not this one.

Unidentified: If it's important to board a Russian ship, this may be [unclear] to board a ship.

President Kennedy: Well, they're not doing anything serious right now. The most serious ones [Soviet ships] have turned around. They obviously don't want us to grab any of them.

I think the whole problem is to make the judgment, with Khrushchev's message to me last night in which he said they're not going to do it—they're going to take action if we do. Combined with what is happening at the UN and so on now. Unless there is something . . . Unless more time is going to make [it] more likely that we're going to get something out of either the UN or Khrushchev, then I suppose you have to grasp the nettle. I don't know

---

7. Probably a reference to the American suggestion to U Thant, late the previous evening, that he publicly ask Soviet ships not to challenge the U.S. quarantine line in order to allow more time for a peaceful settlement.

whether 48 hours, having let this go through, having this tomorrow, when I'm going to announce to Cuba that we've let it go through and try to [unclear] . . .

McNamara: I think it's such an obvious delay in letting it go through that it would not weaken our position to have that announced, that it went through.

Robert Kennedy: Could we pick up the other one [the *Grozny*]?

McNamara: Well, we can pick it up. But it can't be done in anything less than 48 hours. It can't be done in less than 24, I would think.

President Kennedy: You couldn't pick it up this afternoon?

McNamara: No, sir.

Unidentified: Well, this ship won't be in until tomorrow. [Unclear] tomorrow.

Robert Kennedy: Well, what time? We don't know definitely what time tomorrow.

McNamara: No, but I think . . . We can't pick it up except at a considerable distance from Cuba.

President Kennedy: Now they've [the *Bucharest*] already arrived, wired back that they were accosted by a destroyer and they were left at sea. What impression do they get over there if we let this one go?

McNamara: I think their impression would be that it was not carrying prohibited cargo. It was obviously a tanker. We queried it. They told us it was carrying only fuel oil. It was not on our list. We let it go through.

Robert Kennedy: This ship [*Bucharest*] is 500 miles out. It will [not] get there till what, 8:00 tomorrow [night].

McNamara: Roughly that idea.

Robert Kennedy: Now, would we have a chance of picking this other one [the *Grozny*] up tomorrow?

McNamara: Well, we would in this sense: If you do it at 2000 hours, which is 8:00 P.M. Eastern Daylight Time, day after tomorrow [October 27] . . . And if we send a ship out immediately to meet it, we would either roughly calculate we'd intercept it around 8 or 900 miles out from Cuba sometime late tomorrow.

Dillon?: And if they turned around? What would we do with that?

Unidentified: Well, it's already proceeding.

McNamara: I doubt very much they'll change its course between now and tomorrow night. There's no reason why they should do it now, instead of earlier.

Dillon?: This is the *Grozny*?

McNamara: This is the *Grozny*. There is certain reason to believe that they're uncertain how to handle it. This is the only ship that appears to us, possibly first deviated from its established course and then resumed that course. All the other ships either continued on course to Cuba or turned around and went back.

President Kennedy: What is the advantage of letting this one pass?

McNamara: The *Bucharest?* The only advantage is avoiding a shooting incident over a ship that appears to the public to be an obvious example of a ~~ship not carrying prohibited cargo.~~

Alexis Johnson?: I don't either, but the only thing that's sort of strange is boarding someone else's tanker, but don't board the *Bucharest.*

[Unclear exchange.]

Robert Kennedy: Well, then, I think you should say we established the fact that we're not going to board tankers . . .

McNamara: For 24 hours.

Bundy: We're not going to board tankers that were dispatched before the issue came up.

Unidentified: That have no deck cargo.

Bundy: —that have no deck cargo. There's no need.

President Kennedy: Well, that will become a matter of our public information.

McNamara: No, I definitely wouldn't make this—

[Mixed voices.]

Thompson: The Russians may put out the fact that we've made contact.

Robert Kennedy: Well, I think you could probably just dismiss it, on the basis—

[Unclear exchange.]

McNamara: We can say a lot of things. We can say the *Bucharest* had hatches that were too small to allow anything other than hoses. Tankers come in several different categories. Some tankers can carry nothing but fuel oil. Other tankers can carry POLs plus dry cargo under deck. Other tankers can carry POL, dry cargo below deck, and a deck load. We can simply say that *Bucharest* was in the first category because it didn't have a deck load, hatches were such that—

[Mixed voices.]

Robert Kennedy: I suppose we can say that, as of the present time, the Russians are observing the quarantine. They've turned all their other ships back.

Rusk: We can also simply say that we've satisfied ourselves that this cargo was POL, and POL is not contraband.

[General agreement.]

Bundy: If we have already instructed the admiral—I gather we just did—to start collective interception, should we instruct him not to intercept other tankers at once?

McNamara: Yes, I think we can, but to avoid any public indication that that's the rule.

President Kennedy: In other words, then the argument for not doing it is not based on the Soviet response at the UN, but merely on the type of ship it is? Is that correct?

Rusk: Well, [unclear] during this present UN-type discussion and to feel out the Soviets a little further on this, and just what they're going to do.

Robert Kennedy: I think we have to take up the fact that we have to intercept a ship that doesn't have that contraband.

Ball: Oh, I do too. I think this one's either a cargo ship or this one [*Grozny*] with something on deck.

Bundy: I don't see how you can let an undefined cargo ship go through on the announcement of the master [declaring its type of cargo].

President Kennedy: Well, the fact of the matter is, as Bobby said, the quarantine to a degree is already successful because some of the ships have turned back. Fourteen ships have turned back as a result of the quarantine.

And that part of the problem there is that we've got to face up to the fact that we're going to have to grab a Russian ship, and that he says he's not going to permit it. Now, the question is whether it's better to have that happen today or tomorrow.

Bundy: Well, it's at least, it's conceivable that over a 48-hour period we will get the kind of thing we're asking U Thant for [Soviet agreement to stay away from the quarantine line]. It's not likely, but it's conceivable.

President Kennedy: In that case we might as well wait.

Bundy: Then we might as well wait.

President Kennedy: We can claim that 14 ships entered—

[Several unclear exchanges.]

Gilpatric?: I don't think we ought to announce that, as a general principle. Because if we get the 24 hours we're going to have to—

Robert Kennedy: No, because I don't think he [Khrushchev] is going to come forward.

President Kennedy: We don't have to announce [unclear].

The officer [who intercepted the *Bucharest*] satisfied himself, because he made sure there's no contraband. Now, by tomorrow night when this [the *Grozny*] arrives at 8:00 P.M., by then we're going to . . . I think we ought to _____ depending on what happens tomorrow afternoon,

_____ night. But what _____

can intercept them [the *Grozny*] as related to our own forces. So I think you should instruct them, Mr. President, to be prepared to intercept tomorrow during daylight, if it's at all possible. Develop a practical plan to do so.

Robert Kennedy: And that's no matter where it might be.

McNamara: No matter where it might be, exactly. And what we would then do is move our ships out—or move some ships out toward it now.

Robert Kennedy: Yeah. Will they know that?

McNamara: The *Grozny?* No.

Robert Kennedy: The Russians won't know we're moving ships?

McNamara: No.

McCone: You know, I'd like to just call your attention to this page [of the morning CIA Watch Committee report], II-4. You take the last items, 7 through 14. All these ships turned around. They are ships en route to the Baltic [rather than Cuba], probably ordered at the same time. That's in the [unclear]. Back to the Black Sea is number 9, left the Mediterranean October the 23rd and reentered the Mediterranean on the 24th. Here's one that left the Baltic on the 23rd and returned into the Baltic on the 24th. Here's one that left the Black Sea on the 23rd and reentered 20 hours later on the same day. Here's one—

President Kennedy: What's the date today?

McCone: Today's the 25th. Turned around in the Mediterranean on the 23rd of October and headed to the Black Sea. There's another turned around in the Mediterranean on the 23rd and headed to the Black Sea. And another one.

They turned these around when they were pretty far east, which is quite significant, I think. Well, it's my opinion, change in appraisal that they might just be heaving to for 24, 48 hours in the Atlantic attempting to seek cargo or something else.

Unidentified: This would suggest that they do not intend, that they're not counting on this blockade or embargo being liquidated quickly.

McCone: Yes, I would think so.

Unidentified: The other explanation might be that they're counting on taking forceful action against the [unclear] when we intercept. Afraid this will spread [unclear].

Bundy: The real question there is whether any of the ones far to the east are still proceeding westward. Do we have an answer to that?

McCone: Well, it [the Watch Committee report] refers to [ships numbered] 1 through 7, [unclear] information we have.

Dillon: What about Soviet ships in the Pacific? Have any of them turned?

President Kennedy: And ships that are not going to Cuba, whether they're all turning back.

Bundy: There's nothing, Mr. President—I've just checked the language in your speech—which requires you to stop any ships. It's simply: "If found to contain cargo of offensive weapons it would be turned back." The way in which we find this [that there is a prohibited cargo] is not . . .

Rusk: Could we get Harlan Cleveland[8] to . . .

McNamara: Mr. President, may I raise one other question? We should, I believe, have included missile fuel on the list of prohibited items. I'd like to send out an interpretation of that list today including missile fuel. This is preparation for the *Grozny* interception.

Dillon?: This might be the reason why the [*Grozny* displayed] hesitation on the course.

McNamara: Well, it might be. In any case, I'd like to cover that.

Bundy: [quietly to Dillon] More likely the quartermaster . . .

Robert Kennedy: Do we know that this one they're letting through [*Grozny*] is carrying missile fuel?

McNamara: We're almost sure the missile fuel would not be on deck load.

Unidentified: Have you ever seen missile fuel?

McNamara: No.

[Unclear exchange.]

President Kennedy: How are we going to handle the problem, if this one [*Bucharest*] proceeds, that today there's a lot of interest in what's happening

---

8. Assistant Secretary of State for International Organization Affairs, the bureau responsible for, among other things, the U.S. mission to the United Nations.

to these ships? Is it going to come out that not one ship was stopped? We all know we've got to do the defense on that for 24 hours [unclear] [until the *Grozny* is intercepted].

Bundy: Do you have a proposal, Don [Wilson]?

President Kennedy: It isn't really so much Don as it is the Pentagon.

McNamara: I would say that, we've been boarding ships that raise any [unclear] our minds about the type of cargo they're carrying. No Russian

including the *Bucharest.*

Alexis Johnson: That means presumably you would board any inbound ship, if it had deck cargo.

McNamara: Yes. This is what we were instructed to do. And we will have evidence tonight that we did it.

[Unclear comment.]

Bundy: It would be good to find a tanker with deck cargo today.

McNamara: It's extremely unusual for tankers to carry deck cargo. This is why the *Grozny* is so extraordinary.

Wilson?: Mr. President, there will certainly be a lot of speculation about these other ships and what's happened to them, the ones that have turned back. I wonder if we should give out information that they have indeed turned back.

President Kennedy: Well, I think we can let it out of the Pentagon when you've satisfied yourselves. We'll be giving answers to these other questions about every Russian ship. That's probably not so, because otherwise they'd [unclear] every ship that had come in.

I assume we are going to try to find the answer to what's happened to the other Russian ships. And we'll play that out. But I would think that the Defense Department could announce about the [unclear]. It's pretty well out, isn't it?

Unidentified: Or if we get additional supplemental information to increase the number [of Russian ships turning back].

Unidentified: Well, it's gone to 14.

Bundy: The number's gone from 6-ish to 14.

President Kennedy: Was this evidence put out yet?

Unidentified: No.

Ball: The only thing that was put out was a statement that Manning[9] put out last night, a statement we discussed, [unclear] very vague.

Rusk: I'd be very careful about putting out as a general [unclear], also going back [unclear], pick up one [unclear].

Bundy: Well, we're caught with one crowd or the other.

President Kennedy: [Unclear, amid several people speaking] . . . avoid euphoria . . . Khrushchev is much tougher than that.

McCone: I thought the statement last night was pretty good. [Unclear] the significance of it. You don't have to make any additional statement. Why don't you just say [unclear].

McNamara: I would stay away, simply stand on that, and stay away from any statement of what the Soviet ships are doing, and simply report on the day's activities: We applied the quarantine. We stopped ships that we had any reason to believe might have been carrying prohibited cargo. We queried other ships.

President Kennedy: Once we get the principle, once we stop the ship and see what happens then, then it seems to me, if we then, a day or so later, put POL on the [quarantine] list on the grounds that the missile sites are continuing, as you say . . .

McNamara: Yes, and that the IL-28s are being assembled. We put aviation gas on the list, therefore.

President Kennedy: Therefore, all tankers will cease.

McNamara: Right.

[Unclear comment by President Kennedy about the tankers.]

Yes, I think so, Mr. President.

Robert Kennedy: What's going to happen if we can't get the *Grozny,* or whatever its name is? The prospects.

Thompson?: They have a few trains on the Long Island Railroad. [Laughter.]

McNamara: . . . tankers coming along, but they're way, way east. I would seriously [unclear], Bobby, to go out there and to turn it around and board it [the *Grozny*] any time.

Robert Kennedy: If you're going to do that, I'd much rather get on that other [the *Bucharest*]. I suppose that's too late.

President Kennedy: Or get one that's turned . . .

---

9. Robert Manning, press spokesman for the Department of State.

Bundy: The *Kimovsk,* or the *Gagarin.*

Rusk: If it's gotten orders to turn it around, this, it radios Moscow that it's turned around and it's still boarded.

McNamara: Well, it depends on whether it turns around at the time we intercept it, or whether it's turned around earlier.

Bundy: If it took evasive action we could go ahead.

Unidentified: Will your missile-fuel announcement help it?

Robert Kennedy: The whole point is that you might scare them off. [Unclear] too much, waiting around [to board a ship].

McNamara: Well, I think we have to establish that missile fuel is on the list. We've got to do that today.

[Unclear discussion.]

Bundy: [Unclear.] You've got to make the legal proclamation to turn the *Grozny* around. [Agreement.]

Rusk: Isn't it our purpose to turn it around without shooting, if we can?

[Pause; then several people start speaking.]

Robert Kennedy: The point is that they may eventually have to intercept a ship. And we'd like to intercept a ship that had something other than a lot of baby food for children.

Nitze?: Establishing a precedent is secondary, or should be secondary, to turning around the ship.

President Kennedy: You think they'll [resist?] interceptions?

Nitze?: I think Dean's right. If we get all these ships, Russian ships, turned around, that's fine. But the problem is that those that do go through, I think you've got to expect . . .

Bundy: Yeah. Clearly, otherwise, they're deciding what is the meaning of our proclamation.

Ball?: Well, I think that's right. But personally it would be a great mistake to intercept a ship if it were in the process of turning around. Because that puts us in no defensible position. The purpose of the—

Bundy: Can we all think about that a little—?

President Kennedy: Well, I think the only question we've got, at least in the next 24 hours, is whether we ought to let this tanker [the *Bucharest*] go through.

Gilpatric?: We've continued to shadow her. We've got all kinds of pictures.

President Kennedy: We're not going to grab any other tankers today. And then I think the Defense Department ought to be thinking about what our explanation would be. We've got some credit on our side, the 14 ships that may have turned around.

And we've got the question of whether this procedure is a little flat. That won't become really a major problem until tomorrow night when it [the *Bucharest*] arrives [in Havana]. By then, as I assume, we may have another Russian ship [the *Grozny*].

Is there a political advantage in stretching this thing out? That's really the question. Are we going to get anything out of the UN or Khrushchev?

Bundy: Why don't we turn to the UN for a while, Mr. President, [unclear]?

President Kennedy: OK.

Rusk: Ambassador Stevenson would like to [people are checking through their papers; unclear].

[Reading Stevenson's suggestion for the U.S. response to U Thant's proposal of the previous day:][10]

> I deeply appreciate the spirit which prompted your message of October 24th and I welcome your good offices.
>
> As we made clear in the Security Council yesterday, this threat was created by the secret introduction of offensive weapons into Cuba. The first task should be to assure the nations of the Western Hemisphere against that threat. In your telegram you suggest the voluntary suspension of all arms shipments to Cuba and the voluntary suspension of the quarantine measures for 2 or 3 weeks to give time to the parties concerned to meet and discuss with a view to finding a peaceful solution to the problem. In your statement before the Security Council you also suggest the suspension of the construction and development of major military facilities and installations in Cuba during the same period.[11]

10. The original version of the suggested reply which we used to reconstruct Rusk's remarks is USUN New York 1453, 24 October 1962 (midnight), in the microfiche collection of documents titled "Cuban Missile Crisis," National Security Archive, Washington, D.C.

11. The night before (October 24), Stevenson reported that he had asked U Thant to add this particular statement. Stevenson had apparently modified his suggestion slightly that morning, in discussions with the State Department. See ibid.

I am prepared to accept these suggestions, provided the Soviet Union does the same and that the UN guarantees our compliance.

I can assure you of our desire to reach a satisfactory and a peaceful solution of this matter.

We carefully have been watching, the State Department has been [working on its own version of a reply].

preliminary talks and hopes the U.S.S.R. will do the same.

For the talks that follow, the second phase, [unclear] would be helpful for our [unclear] efforts, and that it be made clear to the Security Council that the existing threat was created by the secret introduction of offensive weapons into Cuba.

[Unclear as Rusk reads a paragraph from the draft State Department reply.]

President Kennedy: Well, the only thing I would say would be, would it be possible for us to say: If the UN can give adequate guarantees—which they can't give, but—adequate guarantees against the introduction of offensive material during this period. The quarantine can be lifted only if the UN can substitute effective guarantees against the introduction of this material during this period. They can't do that, but at least it doesn't make us look quite as negative.

It's up to the UN to provide a formula for a guarantee against the intro-duction of offensive weapons. Otherwise we say we're not going to lift the quarantine under any condition. [Unclear.]

Rusk: [suggesting language] "quarantine will continue unless the UN can provide satisfactory alternative arrangements."

[Unclear discussion.]

Rusk: [suggesting other language] "preliminary talks, which could set the arrangements by which the UN could make sure that no offensive armaments reaches Cuba during the 2-to-3-week period mentioned in your message." [Unclear.]

President Kennedy: We don't have to mention the quarantine, I would think, in the wire [to New York].

Bundy: We haven't [unclear].

Ball: During these preliminary talks we'd keep the quarantine on. I think otherwise there would be a serious misunderstanding about it. Because what, in effect, he has asked is that the quarantine be taken off in a way that we can't . . .

President Kennedy: Well, we can't take the quarantine off until he offers a substitute. He hasn't offered a substitute.

Bundy: Why don't we say that for "offensive armaments"? That's the fundamental proposition with us. The quarantine is there to prevent the introduction of offensive weapons.

[Unclear discussion.]

Rusk: [suggesting language] "The present quarantine measures will of course continue."

President Kennedy: Yeah.

Bundy: Why isn't that [continuation of the quarantine] a more sweeping proposition that covers both? It obviously covers preliminary talks when there is nothing. The quarantine doesn't come off in the longer period either.

President Kennedy: Exactly.

Unidentified: [Unclear] you don't really get beyond the preliminary talks unless there is some kind of UN—

Bundy: I understand that. I'm talking about the impact of the statement, that's all. I don't think we're differing on substance, Dean.

McNamara: Is it clear there is nothing in this statement that indicates we are taking the quarantine off? Is it simply agreed to prohibit the movement of offensive weapons into Cuba?

Bundy: No. It's a three-way thing to take the quarantine off.

[Unclear exchange.]

Effective guarantees against the movement of offensive weapons; discontinuance of development; and adequate inspection.

Rusk: [Unclear] to make sure that the offensive weapons are not operational.

President Kennedy: Yeah. In other words, it would not merely, because the Russians didn't merely think of some way not to introduce offensive weapons. That would not be sufficient.

McNamara: What the quarantine does is not to stop offensive weapons. That we always felt would happen. What the quarantine does is a form of pressure to assure the removal of those weapons.

And I think we would not want to give them any loophole by which they could get that quarantine off, before effective steps have been taken to assure the removal of those weapons.

President Kennedy: Because we're about to spread that quarantine [to prohibit more imports, such as POL].

Bundy: Well, that is the question there. Because the real problem is that a 3-week standstill which does not move towards removal tends to be self-perpetuating, and unsatisfactory.

That's for the 2-to-3-week period. But during that 2 to 3 week period, all thing that you talk about and focus upon is getting the weapons out of there.

Bundy: Well, the question I raised, and I think is on the Secretary's mind, is whether, when you get into a tangle of this kind, the status quo doesn't come to have a momentum of its own. Is that or isn't it acceptable? That's my question.

McNamara: Could I start back a bit and say, I don't see any way to get those weapons out of Cuba. I never have thought we'd get them out of Cuba without the application of substantial force.

Now, the force we can apply is of several kinds. There's economic force and there's military force. The insurance rates are rising today. This is gradually going to reduce the amount of trade moving into Cuba. This is a very important element of our course. I wouldn't want to remove the quarantine, no matter [what] kind of inspection we had there, unless they agreed to take the weapons out. Because we could never impose it again, so long as they said they had adequate procedures to ensure no more weapons moved in.

Bundy: Suppose we were to have an understanding on the part of the UN that the object is the removal of the weapons?

McNamara: Yes, something, or the agreement that that's to be done, something like that.

Bundy: Something one stage further. So that the status quo moves in our direction. Create some weight. That's what your quarantine is for, to have weight on.

Rusk: This is my point, exactly. We don't believe that there should be insuperable difficulties in reaching a solution if those responsible for the threat are prepared to remove it.

President Kennedy: I think we've got a lot of it. We're not going to get anyplace with this thing because [unclear] offensive weapons coming in.

Bundy: Could you frame this sentence around a little bit farther: "remove it, and it is with that objective that we accept this," that we make these proposals.

President Kennedy: We can accept it with . . . Why don't we get that and make sure that we [unclear] discuss it, but I think we put this in a reasonable—

Bundy: We want to restate our purpose of removal a little bit, Mr. President.

Rusk: [suggesting language] "Therefore, we accept your proposal for preliminary talks."

President Kennedy: You want to read this thing again, the first part, Mr. Secretary?

Rusk: "At the preliminary talks we should discuss the arrangements by which the UN could make sure that no offensive armament reaches Cuba during the 2-to-3-week period mentioned in your message, and the manner in which nations of this hemisphere could be assured of a suspension of work on the establishment of missiles and other offensive weapons in Cuba.

"During these preliminary talks, in the absence of effective UN measures, the present quarantine [unclear] continues. The United States therefore accepts the proposal of preliminary talks and hopes the U.S.S.R. will do the same.

"The talks that follow in the second phase should be helped by the restatement [unclear], to make clear to the Security Council and others that the existing threat was created by the secret introduction of offensive weapons into Cuba.

"The first priority should be to assure the nations of the Western Hemisphere against that threat. These nations, the Organization of American States, authorized the quarantine of offensive weapons for that purpose. Surely no one could fail to understand their insistence on effective guarantees, and that the present purpose was produced by secret action taken contrary to the most [unclear].

"Those guarantees should cover the further introduction of offensive weapons into Cuba; discontinuance of development work on existing sites; and the UN observers to ensure that offensive weapons are not operational. We do not believe that there should be technical difficulties with anything [unclear] a permanent resolution [unclear].

"The other problem is that those responsible for the threat must be prepared to remove it."

[Unclear discussion. People can be heard saying: "removal of the weapons" and "nothing in there about removing the threat."]

Rusk: [suggesting language] "The answer to this problem lies in the removal of the weapons." [Unclear] the removal of the weapons.

The message was worked on, discussed again with Stevenson, simplified further ⟦ ... ⟧ to New York at about 2:00 P.M. President Kennedy's

⟦ ... ⟧

you have made certain ⟦ ... ⟧ determine whether satisfactory arrangements can be assured.

Ambassador Stevenson is prepared to discuss these arrangements with you.

I can assure you of our desire to reach a satisfactory and a peaceful solution of the matter.

The Executive Committee turned to other diplomatic issues.

Rusk: Mr. President, there's one other point about which I'd just want to make some mention. The Brazilians have come up with a very interesting possibility, in [the idea of] declaring Latin America a nuclear-free zone.

Now, this will come forward. It's very likely to spread fast to Africans. Now, our defense colleagues are looking at this promptly with [unclear] people. But if you have a Latin American/African combination on two—

President Kennedy: Did they say "nuclear-free" or "missile-free"?

Rusk: Well, I think they wouldn't take it on just that basis. They'd insist on "nuclear-free."

President Kennedy: We don't know whether there's nuclear weapons on there [in Cuba]. And missiles, we can tell something about them. I mean, well . . .

Rusk: But see, you have a bloc of about 50 countries there.

Dillon: It means we have to get out of Morocco [unclear] time.

Rusk: No, it doesn't. Well, that's a thing we have to check. We don't have nuclear weapons in the Moroccan bases.

12. State telegram 12974, 25 October 1962, National Security Files, JFKL.

McNamara: Well, we stage through there periodically.

[Unclear discussion.]

Rusk: I wanted to mention this possibility. This could create an enormous pressure in the Assembly and around the world and aimed at the Soviet Union, on the presence of these weapons in Cuba.

President Kennedy: Okay. What else do we got?

Bundy: If we can take one second, Mr. President.

President Kennedy: We sent that letter back to Khrushchev last night, didn't we?

Bundy: Yes. If you want . . . the exchange. He wants the exchange . . . Ted Sorensen has it. It may be worth a moment. Do you want me to take time to read it?

President Kennedy: Yeah, read the pertinent paragraphs to those who haven't . . .

Bundy: It's a long letter from Khrushchev about our immorality, and that the quarantine's no good, and the OAS is no good, and their people will follow them along into combat. And the last paragraphs go like this:

> Mr. President, if you coolly weigh the situation which has developed, you will understand that the Soviet Union cannot fail to reject the arbitrary demands of the USA. When you confront us with such conditions, put yourself in our situation and think how the USA would react to these conditions. I do not doubt that if someone attempted to dictate similar conditions to you—the United States—you would say no. And we also say—no.
>
> The Soviet government considers that violation of the freedom of the use of international waters and international airspace is an act of aggression which brings mankind toward the abyss of a world missile-nuclear war. Consequently, the Soviet Government cannot give instructions to the captains of Soviet vessels bound for Cuba to observe the instructions of the American naval forces blockading that Island. Our instructions to Soviet mariners are strictly to observe the generally recognized norms of navigation in international waters and not to retreat from them by even one step. And if the American side violates these rules, it must realize what sort of responsibility will rest on it in that case. Of course we shall not be simply observers to piratical acts by American ships on the high seas. We will then be forced, for our part, to take the measures we deem necessary and adequate in order to protect our rights. For this we have all that is necessary.
>
> Respectfully yours, N. Khrushchev[13]

13. This translation of the letter, done informally as it came in, differs in subtle ways from the official State Department translation prepared later and included in most documentary compilations.

We checked this around last night, and perhaps the most interesting comment was Ambassador Thompson's. Tommy, would you read for a moment as to how you interpret that.

Thompson: Well, I thought the incoming [letter] indicated preparation for resistance by force, and is forcing us to take forcible action. [Unclear interjection.] Yeah.

. . . this answer to the president: "Dear Mr. Chairman

indicated quite plainly that the United States offensive weapons as presenting the gravest issues. After that time, this government received the most explicit assurances from your government and its representatives, both publicly and privately, that no offensive weapons were being sent to Cuba. If you will review the statement issued by TASS in September, you will see how clearly this assurance was given.

In reliance on these solemn assurances, I urged restraint upon those in this country who were urging action in this matter at that time. And then I learned beyond doubt what you have not denied—namely, that all these public assurances were false and that your military people had set out recently to establish a set of missile bases in Cuba. [Bundy adds the comment: "It should have been secret," meaning that the letter should have said: "secret missile bases."] I ask you to recognize clearly, Mr. Chairman, that it was not I who issued the first challenge in this case, and that in the light of this record these activities in Cuba required the responses I have announced.

I repeat my regret that these events should cause a deterioration in our relations. I hope that your government will take the necessary action to permit a restoration of the earlier situation.

Nitze: That suggests, though, that what he intends is to not let his ships be put in a position where they could be boarded and searched.

President Kennedy: Don't put one in there, so that . . .

Nitze: He hasn't put any [unclear].

Bundy: It's possible, it seems to me, Paul, that what you're saying is that we may be moving into some kind of de facto, unclarified quarantine.

McNamara: Well, I'd like to assume that that's the case. I think our problem is a matter of, to look ahead at least 24 hours here.

For a minute, let's make these assumptions, that (a): that the Security Council decides to sidestep our proposal or the United Nations does nothing;

(b): that we have no Soviet ship to intercept tomorrow, or that if we do intercept one it carries no prohibited weapons and submits to whatever action we apply to it;

(c): that the development of offensive missiles continues in Cuba, and we have evidence of that today from our low-level surveillance. What do we do?

Unidentified: I think we have to wait for the—

President Kennedy: Well, we first stop the Soviet ships someplace and after this see what they're going to do.

McNamara: I'm just thinking of 24 hours. Now, the possibility is we won't be able to do that, Mr. President. Maybe we can, but let's assume for the moment that we can't.

Or alternatively assume we do, and it wasn't carrying prohibited weapons, and it submitted to our quarantine procedure in any way we choose to apply it, indicating that the Soviet Union, for the time being, is going to prohibit the movement of offensive weapons to Cuba. What do we do under these circumstances?

It seems to me that, as George implied, we have to escalate. And if that's the case, how are we going to escalate?

Now, we have a number of alternatives. Now, I might suggest we consider those today, at least some of us, perhaps the same group get together before the end of the day and consider how we would escalate.

Bundy: May I suggest that we have a meeting of this committee without the President, for some examination of these . . .

[Mixed voices. Someone says: "That might well be appropriate." Someone else says: "Later" and "Later today."]

President Kennedy: [Unclear] . . . extending [the quarantine] to POL [unclear].

McNamara: No, sir, I don't think that is necessary. As a matter of fact, it would be difficult to put POL in under this. There's one way to do it, and that—it seems to me—and that is to say that today we found they were accelerating work on the preparation of the IL-28s for operations. And therefore it became essential that we add aviation gas—not POL, but just the select kind of POL for aviation gas—which would be the—or jet fuel, whatever it is, for the bombers.

Now, we could do that, but that's not much of an escalation, because . . .

Gilpatric: That means then that they can't send any tankers.

McNamara: But I was going to say it's not much of an escalation, because there aren't any tankers immediately within our grasp here. So I'm just wondering about time. It would seem to me that the timing is important. We don't want to allow any particular period of time [to] go by if it starts to freeze the situation. We want to continue to move toward this ultimate objective of removing the missiles. And in order to do that we have to keep this situation moving without being frozen at any particular point.

Bundy: Could we get a consensus on that, and especially the President's own

. . . very much, that a plateau here is the most dangerous

relationship . .

McNamara: Well, it doesn't yet. It looks as though it's [extending antine to POL] a provocative move, Mr. President, unless it's related directly to one of these offensive weapons.

McCone: Don't forget that, Bob, [unclear] construction requires that heavy machinery.

McNamara: [Unclear] by the IL-28s, jet fuel is involved in that.

Frankly, I don't think that's enough of a move, and all I would suggest at the moment is that we think of [unclear].

Unidentified: That's right. It's not enough escalation. And I would suggest, therefore, that we be directed to meet here today to consider a program of escalation that we might put into effect within 24 to 48 hours.

President Kennedy: We can always . . . We can take the *Bucharest* in the morning, if that's more risk, can't we?

[Brief, unclear discussion. Someone says: "It won't be much risk."]

President Kennedy: We could take it in the morning, just move in. Can we put air cover over our destroyers [unclear]?

McNamara: Yes. The carrier's there. The [Soviet] submarine probably won't be moving [unclear] waters. I don't think there's much risk.

[Unclear discussion.]

Bundy: . . . Mr. President, because it will then appear that we have spent 24 hours thinking about what to do about this ship. In terms of what the Secretary calls the "eyeball to eyeball,"[14] I think it's better that . . . Even if they did it now, we ought to let her go.

14. Rusk's words at the meeting the previous morning, October 24.

McNamara: I agree with that, Mr. President. I don't think the *Bucharest* is a very useful case.

President Kennedy: It's already gone across the barrier; that's the only important one.

Bundy: There's a real case to be made, that's perhaps not been made as strongly this morning as it could be, for doing it and getting it done, on the ground that this is what we said we'd do, and we are going to have to be the judges of the effectiveness of the quarantine.

Rusk: The barrier is there, though, for something else but POL. And if we have any reasonable doubts that POL . . .

Bundy: It is true that none of us doubts that it's POL.

Rusk: I personally don't think that [unclear].

President Kennedy: The object is not to stop offensive weapons, because the offensive weapons are already there, as much as it is to have a showdown with the Russians of one kind or another. Isn't that really . . .

Bundy: That's right.

[Mixed voices.]

Rusk: At the point where we have a stronger case than we have with the tanker.

McNamara: This would be my view, Mr. President. The tanker doesn't give us much of an excuse for a showdown. And if a showdown occurs, it may weaken our position till the next event.

Bundy: That's important for you to know, Mr. President, that there is a good, substantial argument, and a lot of people in the argument on the other side. All of them will fall in with whatever decision you make. [Indicates that Nitze should speak.]

[Unclear exchanges.]

Nitze: The distinction really is between whether you look at specific instances of something, whether it's a tanker or some other ship, or you look at it as the principle of a blockade. Our view, I think, yesterday afternoon was: If we declare the quarantine, apply rules, go ahead and carry out that rule indiscriminately, not selecting ships or types of ships.

Rusk: Mr. President, I think there are certain points to keep in mind and take a look at. First of all, there are a number of the ships that are no longer bound for Cuba. [Unclear] has already mentioned that.

Secondly, what the effect is on, if the present Soviet conduct on not turning back ships continues on the Cuban run. Now, under the circumstances it's already escalated very, very fast.

President Kennedy: In any case, I'll tell you what let's do. Let's wait there. But we've [unclear]. I don't . . . We can always take this ship. Your point about, show we can do that, "eyeball to eyeball" . . . We can sit around waiting for Khrushchev, or waiting for U Thant . . . We don't want to sit [unclear].

Bundy: I would think about it tomorrow morning.

President Kennedy: Okay, well, we still have then [tomorrow morning] another 6 or 7 hours [to board the *Bucharest*]. I think the only arguments are

that maybe, and, if I wrote back to Khrushchev, we could justify [could be heard saying "consider"] . . . We'll meet at 5:00 this afternoon, if that's the way. Let's think a little more about it.

Robert Kennedy: Can you take a tanker without blowing it up, Bob?

McNamara: Yes.

Bundy: Do we know when the Security Council comes to a vote?

Rusk: They meet at 4:00 this afternoon. They might come before that.

Unidentified: Can we have a meeting of our group without the President?

At this point President Kennedy turned off the tape recorder.

THURSDAY, OCTOBER 25

5:00 P.M.

CABINET ROOM

After the morning Executive Committee meeting, a Pentagon spokesman announced, as planned, that at least a dozen Soviet vessels had turned back from the quarantine. The passage of the *Bucharest* was handled by a statement that the ship had been intercepted and permitted to proceed without boarding.

During the day in New York, U Thant issued a new statement. Based on the suggestion from Stevenson, made to U Thant the previous night, at Washington's instructions, this statement appealed to Khrushchev to order his ships to stay away from the interception area for a limited time and appealed to Kennedy to order his ships to avoid any direct confrontation with Soviet ships during the next few days.

The Executive Committee reconvened at 5:00, at first without President Kennedy.[1] The meeting began with an intelligence briefing by McCone listing 15 ships still en route to Cuba, one of them being the *Grozny*. There were no unusual developments in Europe, though Dillon observed that there had been a run on gold in Germany and, to a lesser extent, in London. He thought buyers were hedging against the uncertainties of the crisis.

McNamara called attention to the *Marucla*, a Lebanese dry-cargo ship, but under Soviet charter. The Pentagon considered it a good candidate for boarding. Ships had been dispatched to meet it, but the *Marucla* appeared to be turning back from Cuba. An East German passenger ship, the *Völkerfreundschaft*, was approaching the quarantine line, perhaps with Soviet missile technicians aboard. This development troubled Taylor and Dillon.

---

1. The following summary is based on Bromley Smith, "Summary Record of NSC Executive Committee Meeting No. 5," October 25, 1962, JFKL.

Rusk stressed the need to sustain pressure on the Soviets to have any hope of gaining either removal of the missiles or UN controls over them by political means. He again mentioned the proposal at the UN for a Latin American nuclear-free zone, which might rally considerable support in the General Assembly. Rusk was also still interested in the possibility of a direct approach to Castro, appealing to him to step aside and save his country from the Soviets. Yet overall, Rusk felt there was little time for diplomacy, as the missiles and

better to knock out the missiles with an air attack rather than ... Soviets at sea. Various other measures to throttle Cuban trade were considered.

Just before joining this meeting, at about 6:00 P.M. in Washington and 11:00 P.M. in London, President Kennedy telephoned Prime Minister Macmillan, as promised the previous evening. Although it was his first opportunity to respond directly to the message he had received that morning from Macmillan, the President apparently chose not to discuss it.[2]

Macmillan: Well, Mr. President, how are you?

President Kennedy: Prime Minister, how did you do in your debate?

Macmillan: We did very well. The House was very good. I have sent you the text of what I said, and I think it was very well accepted. I made all the points I could, especially the one you gave me about your statement of September 11 [actually September 13] and the deception which the Russians have made. That was very well received.

President Kennedy: Prime Minister, we got a second message from U Thant, which you may be familiar with, which asks Khrushchev to keep his ships out of there and asks us to avoid a confrontation. Now we are sending back a message saying that if he keeps his ships out of there, of course we will avoid a confrontation.

As you know, today 14 ships turned around, and they were probably the ones with the aggressive cargo. One tanker we stopped [the *Bucharest*] and we

---

2. The following transcript is from PRO, PREM 11/3690, 24020. We have modified the punctuation, but not the text.

asked where it was going, and it said it was coming from the Black Sea to Cuba and the cargo was oil. It was obviously a tanker, and we passed that.

We have tomorrow 2 or 3 vessels, including particularly an East German vessel which has probably 6 or 700 passengers. It stopped in Leningrad on its way, and it may have 6,000 tons of cargo on it. So we are going to have to stop that, we think. That's what we are now discussing.

Now we have got two tracks running. One is that one of these ships, the selected ships which Khrushchev continues to have come towards Cuba. On the other hand we have U Thant, and we don't want to sink a ship and then right in the middle of when U Thant is supposedly arranging for the Russians to stay out. So we may have to let some hours go by, but sooner or later, probably by tomorrow evening, we'll have to accost one of these and board it.

Now, we got a message last night from Mr. Khrushchev, which I'll make sure you get, if you haven't gotten it already, which said that this is piratical, and that their ships are going to go through and not submit to this, and that if we do stop them, they have the means of action against us. That's last night. So that's about where we are.

Macmillan: Well, thank you very much. I have just seen your message to U Thant, which seems to me, if I may say so, extremely ingenious and very firm. Because you are saying that the real point is how to get rid of these weapons, and then that Ambassador Stevenson will be discussing with U Thant the arrangement. What line do you propose the Ambassador should be taking with U Thant?

President Kennedy: We had a message from U Thant about a half-hour ago which goes somewhat further than the first one went. The second one said that he is asking Khrushchev to keep his ships out of there. His first message did not do that. We are therefore going to accept that, as it comes further in our direction than his first one, and then tell him that if he will keep his ships out of there, then that's fine, that we won't have an incident. On the other hand, we do point out, in our response to him, that Soviet ships still are coming. Now that's that.

Now, if these conversations begin, we're going to point out that, in the beginning, once we get this matter of the ships straightened out—because we still haven't had our first search yet, and that's going to be a very important event, and we will then know what the Russians are going to do. But that will come tomorrow. Then, if we begin the conversations, we are going to begin to point out that work is going on, and that work must stop. Or otherwise we've got to extend this blockade, and consider other actions to stop it. But I think that's at least 24 hours away.

I think the next thing for us to do is to figure out how we will handle this first search, in view of the fact that the UN is involved in this now. In other words, I don't want to have a fight with a Russian ship tomorrow morning, and a search of it at a time when it appears that U Thant has got the Russians to agree not to continue. I hope that by tomorrow afternoon it will be clear, either that the Russians are just continuing their shipping during these pre-liminary conversations, or, if they're not, then the responsibility is on them.

these talks go on. So that if we get Russian shipping suspend, produce one situation. If Russian shipping does not suspend, then we will have to face the search and the possible sinking of the ship sometime tomorrow afternoon. That's our first problem.

Then, if we satisfactorily get through that problem, then when these conversations begin, we are going to begin to emphasize that work on these sites is continuing, and that unless it is discontinued, we must tighten the blockade and possibly take other action. That would probably begin to be emphasized if the talks begin, but even if the talks don't begin we are going to begin to say it on Saturday [October 27] anyway.

Macmillan: Yes, I quite understand that. I think that's what you must do. But I quite see that it's in two stages. First question is the ships, and then the actual question of the weapons in Cuba.

President Kennedy: As I say, the 14 ships that have turned back are obviously the ones that have the sensitive cargo that he does not want us to be able to produce. The ships that are continuing probably are the ones that don't have anything important in them, but we cannot permit him to establish the principle that he determines which ships will go and which will not. But, as I say, I think tomorrow night we will know a lot better about this matter of the UN's actions and Khrushchev's attitude about continuing his shipping, and also what attitude he will take in regard to our searching them.

Macmillan: Well, I think that's a great help. Perhaps it would be a good thing if I could give you a ring tomorrow night, Mr. President. Would that be all right?

President Kennedy: We will know tomorrow night whether Khrushchev will accept U Thant's proposal to cease all shipping going to Cuba during the period of these talks, number one.

Number two, if he doesn't do that, we'll know what their reaction will be to our searching of a vessel. So I think I could call you tomorrow night at the same time, if that's not too late for you.

Macmillan: That's very nice indeed, and it'll suit me very well. I am very much obliged to you. We'll have a talk tomorrow night. Good night.

President Kennedy: Good night, Prime Minister. I'll send you Khrushchev's message of last evening. Good night.

President Kennedy then joined the meeting of the Executive Committee. He turned on the tape recorder in the Cabinet Room as McNamara was returning to the issue of what to do with the East German passenger ship that was approaching the quarantine line.

McNamara: . . . all about the ship. And what we know, as of this evening, is the *Völkerfreundschaft* appears to have left Rostock on the 11th of October, stopping at Leningrad and departing there on the 13th. It is said to be a passenger ship of 12,000 tons, 525 feet long, 2 cargo holds forward, 3 aft, and said to have a 6- or 7,000-ton cargo capacity. Normally a passenger capacity of 392 tourist-type passengers, but certainly could be 1,300 industrial workers on board, including 550 Czech technicians, plus 25 East German students—[34 seconds excised as classified information.] This should pass through the barrier today, and we have the destroyer [U.S.S.] *Pierce* following it.

The question is, should we ask it to halt and submit to inspection? If it did not halt, should we pass it without forcing it to halt, or should we force it to halt? If we were to force it to halt, should we use fire, or should we put a Navy ship in front of it? If we use fire, and damage the ship, with 1,500 people on board, and find that it's hard to explain, does not include items on the prohibited list, have we not weakened our position? And these considerations led me to conclude this afternoon that I should recommend to this group and to you that we not ask that ship to stop.

President Kennedy: I think the only problem really is this U Thant second message where he's saying to us that we not, that we avoid an incident if Khrushchev keeps his ships out. But now we don't think Khrushchev will agree to that, but I—

Bundy: You might want to point this out, Mr. President. The U Thant message doesn't cover this ship. It talks about Soviet ships.

Sorensen: There's one way to show that our response to U Thant's message is not a soft one at all. The East German ship came up, so we stopped it. At the same time, we did not engage the prestige of the Soviets.

President Kennedy: [Unclear], what time is the latest we can make—

McNamara: The latest we can make a decision is probably 1:00 or 2:00 this morning, tomorrow morning—

President Kennedy: —We have to stop—

McNamara: —We have to give orders to the Navy and it's moving in—

McNamara: Allegedly the 13th of October.

Taylor: Well, there's a question of the accuracy of this intelligence we've been talking about. [Unclear.]

[82 seconds excised as classified information.]

McCone: But we have no positive information that technicians are on board [unclear].

Robert Kennedy: That'll be fine.

Unidentified: We ought to let it through.

Nitze: How do you tell a missile technician from an agricultural technician?

McNamara: What do we gain by [unclear]? Let's put it that way. What do we gain if we stop it?

[Mixed voices.]

Dillon: What do you lose? Well, I think you do lose something if you let it go through without . . . if it comes out that they've . . .

Bundy: [Unclear] what you lose, the most dangerous thing you lose is the evidence to the bloc [unclear].

President Kennedy: Well, I think the only argument for not stopping it, actually, is this U Thant thing, where we have an incident of a kind tomorrow morning on the ship at a time when supposedly he's asking the Russians to stay out of the area, before we've got an answer. Then if we get an answer from them, or not an answer, I would say then we have to pick up some ship tomorrow, [unclear].

McNamara: I think to start with a passenger ship, sir, I think there's big problems.

[Unclear comment by President Kennedy.]

Yeah, seriously disabled and loss of life, under circumstances that indicate we'd acted irresponsibly. This, I think, would be absurd.

[Mixed voices.]

President Kennedy: The only reason for picking this ship up is because we've got to prove sooner or later that the blockade works.

McNamara: Right. Now, there is the possibility—just a second here—of picking the *Grozny* up, which is a Soviet tanker with a deck cargo, is now we think is about 1,000 miles from Cuba. There's some question as to whether it's continuing to move forward to Cuba. SAC aircraft reported it dead in the water. But it may well be moving in.

In any event, we can send a ship out tonight if we need it tomorrow. We can maintain radar surveillance over it tonight with aircraft, and unless it turns tail, we can intercept that tomorrow. It will be at that point 7 to 800 miles from Cuba. Now, I would strongly recommend we do just that.

President Kennedy: Tomorrow afternoon, though.

McNamara: Afternoon.

President Kennedy: We'll be seeing what's happening with his answer [to U Thant's appeal]. Either Khrushchev's accepted it or denied it.

McNamara: That is correct.

Robert Kennedy: Can I give another side of it? Stepping in? The fact is you're going to increase surveillance. And you're going to be more tough-edged on POL and some of these other things. That if you let this ship go through—the *Grozny,* whatever it is, the tanker, the Russian ship—that all of the other Russian ships for the next, at least the next 3 or 4 days, have turned back. There isn't any Russian ship coming along.

If you go along and you say that the quarantine has been effective—that we're not interested at this time in POL, we let the tanker [*Bucharest*] through—And now on the third day we let this [*Völkerfreundschaft*] through just like the tanker. Tomorrow night perhaps they take these pictures, and they say, we have Bob McNamara announce that after this one's gone through we're not going to let tankers go through anymore. So it shows that we're tightening it. We're not backing off at all from it.

In the meantime, we haven't had a confrontation with the Russians. In the meantime, we are in the United Nations and we are elsewhere, and we're also showing the Cubans that we mean business by running surveillances over the island. And then we put out announcements that they're continuing their buildup.

Ultimately, we might decide that it would be better, rather than have the confrontation with the Russians at sea, that it might be better if you have, knock out their missile base. That's the first step. I don't know, it might [unclear] more with the Cubans than with them. And we go look through and we tell them [the Soviets] to get out of that vicinity in 10 minutes, and then we go through and hit the base.

I don't know, I think it's got some advantage in the fact that it gives you a little bit more time to play with. I think you can show through announcements

now fully effective.

[Several people say: "Right."]

Bundy: But I don't think that can be said about the East German ship, which went through Leningrad and picked up a lot of cargo.

Robert Kennedy: I think it's an excuse. If you wanted to really wait, without losing face—

McNamara: I think the question is twofold. One, it's a question of timing. And the second is whom do you want to confront first.

Now, the timing, we could well postpone the confrontation with either party for 48 hours, and during this time we could appear to be forceful by conducting surveillance. Mr. President, before you came in we suggested that we conduct tomorrow, or at least be prepared to conduct tomorrow, 2 separate surveillance operations. One in the daytime, with 8 or 10 aircraft going in again on essentially the same targets as we surveilled today. And, by the way, those aircraft we believe all came back successfully. And so far we've had no unusual response to either the low-level surveillance the day before yesterday or that of today. So we propose tomorrow to be ready to do that again, and to announce publicly the results of that surveillance tomorrow.

Secondly, we have proposed tomorrow to have the capability of conducting a similar surveillance at night, using the flares. And these are really quite startling. And this would allow us: (1) to show that we were forceful in maintaining surveillance; (2) to get additional information we need on the site; (3) to determine whether they were carrying on activity on those sites at night.

So we . . . These two items, I think in themselves, will convince both our public and the world that we are maintaining a forceful position.

President Kennedy: We don't know what they're doing with their planes on that airfield where—

McNamara: The pilot who flew over the IL-28 field the other day reported that visually he sighted additional IL-28s out of the crates. We haven't had any other intelligence.

President Kennedy: Well then, if we followed your points, Bob, we'd let the East German ship go on the grounds that it's a passenger [ship]. We announce tomorrow that the Soviets . . . Tomorrow afternoon we ought to have a Soviet response to U Thant which will affect this, *Grozny.* And in any case, we can announce that all the shipments are being suspended at that point. He [Khrushchev] doesn't announce the ships are being suspended. And I don't think he will, probably.

Then we would announce that in view of the fact that he hasn't, we're putting the . . .

Robert Kennedy: In view of the surveillances which show that they continue to work, in view of the fact that there are in fact—

President Kennedy: We put POL [on the prohibited list].

McNamara: We'll put jet bomber fuel on the list.

[Mixed voices. Someone says: "They'll stop the tanker and check the ship." Another: ". . . looked in the tanker"]

McCone: Bob, have you checked on the Cuban San [unclear] site? Are they importing jet fuel or are they make—?

McNamara: No, they're making their own. We'll put jet fuel and the raw materials from which it is made. We'll break it that way.

[Unclear discussion.]

President Kennedy: But then, the point is that . . . Bobby, under the proposal that you were talking about, you would assume that once we announce that, they'll turn this *Grozny* off around?

Robert Kennedy: No. You let that through just as we let that one [the *Bucharest*] go through today. You let the tanker through.

President Kennedy: We don't announce then the POL?

Robert Kennedy: Yeah. You wait till after—

[Mixed voices.]

McNamara: Yeah, you do, but it's about 40 hours from now.

Robert Kennedy: It's like the *Bucharest*—

President Kennedy: And then what do you do?

Robert Kennedy: —then there's not a Russian ship coming along for 4 or 5 days, and you announce that this thing has been a success and all.

President Kennedy: And then what do we do? Do we announce—

[Robert Kennedy begins to interrupt.]

Then you need to decide about this air strike again, or we then put POL on the thing, or—

[Robert Kennedy and McNamara speak simultaneously about "a lot of other things we can do".]

McNamara: We have a lot of harassing actions we could carry out that ~~would provoke~~ if we wished to.

through, and stopping the East German?

Robert Kennedy: I don't get the feeling on the East Germans taking the lead; I don't think they play a role in . . .

[Unclear interjection.]

I just think that Bob's point, about the fact that it has got 1,500 people on it . . .

Rusk: Mr. President, Bobby, I recommended a blockade. And I haven't been very helpful in not [unclear]. I suppose we make our best case with a Russian ship that had deck cargo that was highly suspicious, or a blind ship that hadn't—you just had to look at because you couldn't tell what the kind of cargo on there was.

I said the other day that I thought the tanker was not the best case for the first instance of confrontation. I think even less is the big passenger ship. If we fire into that ship or we have to disable it, or if we in some way think about any of that stuff, we're picking up people [unclear].

Robert Kennedy: We don't have to.

Rostow: On the other hand, if we get a negative from the Russian [unclear], aside from generalized discussion we have two reports [from his planning subcommittee]. One of them is the buildup of [unclear] flying, of doing it in a direct nature. And the other is to pick up from the IL-14s [actually IL-28s], and with that put a fuel-oil blockade on, which is another [unclear] way to [unclear].

Robert Kennedy: Then you get what the Secretary said you're going to be doing [unclear] anyway.

Rostow: That would be another round. It would be a round against the background. The POL thing is very serious to them. It's a 100 percent reliant economy, in very short supply, and the clock would be ticking on absolutely 99 percent coming to a halt from the moment that you put that on.

[Mixed voices.]

Unidentified: I think it would be quite a long time.

[Unclear discussion of the effectiveness of an oil cutoff.]

Rostow: We had this experience in the German war [unclear]. As soon as it was cut, it had the most drastic effect.

Ball: As soon as they hit the hydrogenation plants, the German air force fell apart because they couldn't do any [unclear].

[Unclear discussion.]

President Kennedy: Have we got a good analysis of what the POL blockade would do to them?

Rostow: I have a general paper and a supplementary one, in detail on the POL point.

[Mixed voices. Though we cannot hear McNamara mentioning it, his civilian analysts in the Pentagon had prepared their own analysis of a POL blockade. They thought Rostow was wrong and that such a blockade would be ineffective, or worse.]³

President Kennedy: I think that, it seems to me that, given the U Thant appeal to the world to give them a chance of easing this, I think it's an obvious mistake when we combine that with the East German cargo [and passenger] ship, which even though we tried to disable it we might sink it, there's no doubt if you try to shoot a rudder off, you either sink it or let it pass by. I would think that the combination of that, with negotiation with U Thant, really we don't want it tomorrow morning. We don't want to sink that ship. So I think we let that one go.

Now, I would think tomorrow afternoon we ought to get an answer from Khrushchev. He's either going through [the quarantine line] or not. Then we have . . . That he's not going to do what he says [in his letter of October 24].

---

3. Adam Yarmolinsky led the analysis, which concluded that "nothing sort of direct attacks on Cuban resources (crop destruction, contamination of raw materials by sabotage, etc.) would produce immediate and drastic results, and all of these measures seem less desirable than direct military action." The POL stoppage would take 2 to 6 months to be effective, they thought. "In general, these economic measures would appear to insure only an escalation of our objectives [by undermining Castro's government in Cuba] while reducing the means available to accomplish them." Yarmolinsky to McNamara, "Possible Economic Measures in the Cuban Situation," 25 October 1962, pp. 1, 4, Cuban Missile Crisis Files, 1992 Releases box, National Security Archive, Washington, D.C.

It would seem to me we then make our judgment whether we grab the *Grozny* thing, whether we grab this *Grozny*. We've got 2 days. Well, I think all we're really doing is holding our hand on this East German one, because [we] don't want the incident tomorrow morning at a time when we are involved in this back-and-forth.

Then, I think we have to decide whether we take this, or whether we are ~~POL~~ ~~Because~~ I think if the work continues, we either have to

bombing? Are these pathfinder kind of flares?

McNamara: They're basically pathfinder flares, but they're not—

Unidentified: Could this be regarded by the people seeing it as though they were probably a bombing run?

McNamara: No, I don't believe so. We weren't doing anything ahead of time, except to simply say we're going on regular reconnaissance missions night and day.

Robert Kennedy: If they hear that explosion from the night flares, I think that they'll think some [unclear] . . .

[Mixed voices.]

Robert Kennedy: Although it's probably a good idea.

[Unclear exchanges. The meeting is beginning to break up.]

President Kennedy: Your point, Walt, is that if we go to POL that's a very strong act.

Rostow: It's a very strong act, sir. The clock begins to tick. On the other hand, it still gives them time to negotiate. His attitudes would be—off in the background, especially.

President Kennedy: Well, I'm just trying to think about whether, if we let this ship go, don't relax on them.

As I say, we still could pick up beginning tomorrow night. We'll know a little more of Khrushchev's response. We still get this *Grozny*. Don't have to emphasize the East Germans. We'll just let that go.

[Others agree.]

What do you think, Tommy?

Thompson: I'm a little troubled by Khrushchev's strong letter yesterday, that he [unclear] that we're not backing away from [unclear]. On the other hand, he is backing away and that [unclear]. We'll just have to [unclear].

[Unclear exchanges.]

Thompson: [Unclear] talked to the Yugoslav ambassador after the briefing the other day, and he volunteered, without my bringing it up: "I just want to tell you one thing. I don't think I agree with your damned [unclear] papers, that Khrushchev thinks you're afraid to act, or are weak. I've had a lot of private conversations with him. And he said he doesn't think that." So that [unclear].

Rusk: [Unclear] says that [Soviet-]bloc shipping is acting normally, except for the Cuban trade.

President Kennedy: About that thing, before this [unclear] over Cuba, that isn't what has caused him to do this. It's his frustration over Berlin. This idea of [unclear] abandon [unclear], this choice [unclear].

President Kennedy then turned off the tape recorder.

The UN Security Council began its meeting at 4:00 P.M. During televised coverage of the deliberations that evening Stevenson delivered a spirited defense of the U.S. position, at one point dramatically challenging the Soviet ambassador, Zorin, to state plainly whether the missiles were in Cuba or not: "Yes or no—don't wait for the translation—yes or no." When Zorin said that Stevenson would have to wait for his answer, Stevenson declared: "I am prepared to wait for my answer until hell freezes over." Kennedy, watching the confrontation, commented: "Terrific."[4]

4. Richard Reeves, *President Kennedy: Profile of Power* (New York: Simon and Schuster, 1993), p. 406.

FRIDAY, OCTOBER 26

10:00 A.M.

CABINET ROOM

During the night of October 25–26, both the United States and the Soviet Union replied to U Thant's appeal that the two countries avoid a confrontation at the quarantine line. Kennedy's message, sent late on October 25, said that the United States would do everything possible to avoid a direct confrontation so long as Soviet ships stayed away from the interception area during preliminary talks. "I must inform you, however, that this is a matter of great urgency in view of the fact that certain Soviet ships are still proceeding toward Cuba and the interception area." On the morning of October 26 news arrived that Khrushchev had also accepted U Thant's appeal, saying he had "ordered the masters of Soviet vessels bound for Cuba but not yet within the area of the American warships' piratical activities to stay out of the interception area," though only for a temporary period. Khrushchev then renewed his call for negotiations.[1]

During the night of October 25–26, surveillance aircraft had pinpointed the location of the *Marucla,* the Lebanese ship carrying dry cargo to Cuba under Soviet charter, and determined that it was underway toward Cuba. This ship was an ideal answer to the dilemmas that the White House had wrestled with on October 25, and the destroyers *Pierce* and *Kennedy* trailed the vessel during the night and boarded her after sunrise the next morning.[2] The Greek crew complied with all requests.

---

1. Correspondence published in Larson, *"Cuban Crisis,"* pp. 154, 167–171.

2. Destroyers are commonly named after war heroes, and these were no exception. The full names of the destroyers were U.S.S. *John R. Pierce* (DD 753) and U.S.S. *Joseph P. Kennedy, Jr.* (DD 850). The latter had been named after President Kennedy's elder brother, a pilot who had lost his

On the 25th President Kennedy had focused almost exclusively on the operation of the quarantine and the related diplomacy involving U Thant. His senior advisers had, however, been working on what to do, beyond the quarantine, about the missiles already in Cuba. On the morning of October 26, all the advisers arrived armed with folders of papers prepared by their staffs.

These advisers included Stevenson and John J. McCloy, both of whom had come down from New York. On October 20 Kennedy had tracked down McCloy in Europe and flown him back to the United States to act as Stevenson's assistant. Ostensibly, the aim was to make the U.S. UN delegation more bipartisan, McCloy being a prominent Republican. In reality, it was done, at Lovett's suggestion, because of fear that Stevenson might be too weak a negotiator. McCloy, a Wall Street lawyer with extensive government service, had the reputation of being a very tough negotiator.

The Security Council debate had ended in an impasse, given the Soviet Union's veto power. Yet Stevenson would be seeing U Thant that afternoon for possible informal discussion. The State Department also thought the Latin American nuclear-free zone resolution in the General Assembly might help show the strength of world opinion in support of the U.S. cause. Other political alternatives were being analyzed at State, including a direct approach to Castro and possible bargains that could be struck at a summit meeting with Khrushchev.

A political-military strategy was also being prepared, one that would use military means to increase political pressure on Cuba or the Soviet Union. Here the main idea was to extend the quarantine, possibly to include POL, the idea that Rostow had presented the previous evening.

Military preparations had also advanced. The largest concentration of U.S. armed forces since the Korean War was massing in the southeastern United States. Several different options for air strikes had been readied. Under the contingency plan prepared and preferred by the Joint Chiefs of Staff, designated Operation Scabbards, a massive air strike would hit Cuba 12 hours after the President gave the order. Strikes would continue for 7 days, at which point U.S. troops would begin going ashore. These preparations had fueled widespread speculation in the morning newspapers about an imminent invasion.

Intelligence analysts had been working in shifts around the clock to com-

---

life after volunteering to fly an exceptionally dangerous mission in Western Europe during World War II. That a ship so named should be carrying out the first boarding of a vessel was a coincidence, but one that was certainly noticed.

prehend the miles of film delivered by the U-2 and low-level reconnaissance flights. Castro had also delivered another speech on the evening of October 25, denouncing the U.S. actions and warning that the reconnaissance flights would not be tolerated.

The meeting began with a substantial intelligence briefing by McCone. Though Kennedy had not turned on the tape recorder yet, notes of the meeting show that McCone again read the highlights of that morning's Watch Com-

been expecting there. . . .

twice as much and take considerably longer to add to its ICBM strike capability from the USSR as great an increment as the potential salvo from Cuban launching sites.

Only 2 Soviet freighters, and 5 tankers, 1 of them already past the quarantine line, still are headed for Cuba. The *Belovodsk*, with 12 MI-4 helicopters, is in the North Atlantic; the *Pugachev* appears to have slowed or stopped several days west of the Panama Canal. A total of 16 dry cargo ships now are carried as having turned back toward the USSR on 23 October.

Two Soviet civil air flights are scheduled for Havana with passengers; cargo, if any, is not known. One may be turned back by Guinea today. A TU-114 is scheduled via Senegal to reach Havana 1 November.

There are further indications that some Soviet and satellite elements, particularly air and ground elements in Eastern Europe and European Russia, are on an alert or readiness status. No major deployments have been detected, however . . . There is some evidence that additional tactical aircraft have been placed on 5 minute alert in East Germany, where 2 areas along the West German border have been closed off for exercises.

Moscow highlights Khrushchev's acceptance of U Thant's appeal in a bid to start US-Soviet negotiations. Peiping [Beijing], however, is irritated that the Soviet response to US action is not stronger. The Communists still deny there are any offensive weapons in Cuba.

There is no major change or significant new development in non-bloc reaction to the crisis. Most of the OAS nations have offered to participate

3. CIA, "The Crisis: USSR/Cuba," 26 October 1962, in McAuliffe, *CIA Documents*, p. 316.

in some form in the quarantine, and NATO members have agreed with minor reservations to deny landing and overflight rights to Soviet planes bound for Cuba.

McCone then distributed and summarized another intelligence memorandum and provided a bit more detail on the status of the missiles in Cuba. He reviewed the latest interagency appraisal, which emphasized that "rapid construction activity" was continuing. The "activity apparently continues to be directed toward achieving a full operational capability as soon as possible. Camouflage and canvas covering of critical equipment is also continuing. As yet there is *no* evidence indicating any intention to move or dismantle these sites."[4] He then described the movements of nonbloc ships to Cuba, emphasizing that such ships could also be used as arms carriers by the Soviets. As requested the previous day, he also reviewed intelligence analysis of Cuban internal reaction to the crisis. He reported on the celebration that took place in Havana when the *Bucharest* arrived.

While on the subject of Cuban internal opinion, McCone turned to the status of Operation Mongoose. Responding to pressure, especially from Robert Kennedy, to do more with it, the CIA had developed a plan to land by submarine ten 5-man teams of Cuban exiles to collect intelligence in Cuba. The project was prepared hastily, outside the normal Mongoose supervision channels, and by October 25 it had become tangled in disagreements between the CIA operator running the particular project, the man nominally running Mongoose—Edward Lansdale—and the Pentagon. On this point, McCone recalled that he

> posed two operational problems. One, the CIA plan to have ten teams go into Cuba by submarine to gather intelligence on missile bases and other points of interest. McCone stated that CIA was prepared to use its assets to support Mongoose operations under Lansdale's direction; that the objective was to take Cuba from Castro and turn it over to the Cuban people or alternatively to secure intelligence in support of possible military activities and, in this instance, the requirement should be established by [the Secretary of Defense] and JCS.
>
> McCone stated there was an organizational problem with Lansdale under current conditions and a meeting had been called for this afternoon to

---

4. GMAIC, JAEIC, NPIC, "Summary," in "Supplement 6 to Joint Evaluation of Soviet Missile Threat in Cuba," 26 October 1962, ibid., p. 314.

resolve this problem and to establish a course of action on the Lansdale Mongoose organization.[5]

At about this point in the discussion President Kennedy turned on the tape recorder.

_____

McCone: . . . unilaterally, and this is what we're gonna do, and get this thing

ment [there should be in Cuba]. That was all part of Mongoose.

President Kennedy: Yes. I called Mr. McCone last night and I told him to tell Mr. [Edwin] Martin that I thought we ought to be making a crash program on . . . The problem becomes, what if there's an invasion? What kind of people—how many Cubans we'll have, what will be the civil government arrangement and all that?

Bundy: These are very important matters.

President Kennedy: Well now, who will take on that?

Bundy: Mr. President, I think if we could make that a part of the discussion at the Mongoose meeting this afternoon, because it really is . . . the paramilitary, the civil government, the correlated activities to the main show that we need to reorganize.

President Kennedy: We need to get somebody in charge at State, CIA, and Defense, on this question of—

Bundy: Castro/Cuba is the most [unclear].

McCone: [Unclear] working group. And we put that in operation this morning, in order to meet your requirement of having something at 6:00 tonight. However, this is a subject that we're going to pick up at the meeting this afternoon.

President Kennedy: And the other thing is that now we may [unclear] in

5. McCone to File, "Meeting of the NSC Executive Committee, 26 October 1962, 10:00 A.M.," 26 October 1962, ibid., p. 317.

the Cuban community in greater Miami if those Cubans who would be doctors, and all the rest who would be useful, if we have an invasion of Cuba, [could] be useful during the immediate invasion period in various functions. I would think probably the CIA. But this would all be part of the matters that I hope would be discussed today.

McCone: I don't think that . . . I think we ought to have a plan under which [unclear].

[9 seconds excised as classified information.] . . . the problem there is we'll have to get within 12 miles and intercept their high-frequency communications.[6] If it gets out [beyond 12 miles, reception] deteriorates pretty rapidly. [Unclear.]

McNamara: I think, Mr. President, that this is an operational matter we ought to watch very carefully. In my frequent contacts between Defense and CIA, the Navy was very much concerned about the vulnerability of this ship and the loss of security if its personnel are captured. It's been standing 10 miles off of the island of Cuba and in the midst of the possible operations, and it seems wise to draw it out 20, 30 miles and take it out of the range of capture, at least temporarily. I think perhaps we should put it back in if the activities quiet down. But I think this is an operational problem.

Unidentified: I agree we ought to—

[22 seconds excised as classified information.]

[Unclear exchange between President Kennedy and Bundy; President appears to leave the room.]

Bundy: [Unclear] take a couple of minutes on administrative business which I think we can do while the President [unclear].

I want to be sure that the whole committee knows that we have three operating subcommittees now: One on Berlin under Mr. Nitze. One on forward plans under Mr. Rostow. One on communications in which Mr. Ohrig is the chairman, but we expect most of the executive and operating work to be done through the Defense Communications Agency.[7]

This last is a matter of real interest. We are hoping to get action while everybody is steamed up to break a number of bottlenecks, in and outside, national and international, which affect the command and control problem of our foreign affairs.

There is a problem of civil defense. Mr. Pittman would like authority to

6. Apparently a reference to the electronic intelligence ship U.S.S. *Oxford,* located in international waters just outside the 12-mile territorial limit.

7. We have been unable to identify Ohrig.

announce acceleration of the current defense program at a meeting tomorrow. This has been reviewed, I think, with Mr. Gilpatric, and has been reviewed on our side. The general guideline is that we should look as if we would now [unclear] time do all the things we wanted to do, but not create a crash or panicked atmosphere which would make louder noise. Is that all right with you, Ros?

[Gilpatric appears to agree.]

was a problem, and we were not under pressure to discuss it with large g....

Now, this [quarantine] is a major operation, in which from day to day the difference between everybody knowing about that, and nobody knowing what we're now deciding to do next, is a very serious and difficult one. And I think it means that those concerned with action choices will have to be even more guarded than they were last week, or we should find ourselves tipping our hand as to the kinds of alternatives that were under committee discussion yesterday.

[President Kennedy returns to the room.]

I've gotten past item 2, Mr. President.

President Kennedy: All right, we have, Secretary McNamara?

McNamara: Yes, Mr. President, first the state of the quarantine. We are on board, at the present time, the *Marucla,* a Lebanese freighter, chosen yesterday because it was a nonbloc ship. We wanted to indicate quarantine procedures by stopping it and boarding it with the least possible chance of violence. It turned out later that this ship was under charter to the Soviet Union. We are, in any event, on board at the present time.

The boarding was successful. The ship cooperated by making boarding arrangements. It will be some time before we determine what is on board. I would suggest, Mr. President, that we release now the information that we are on board. It won't be held long. There is information that is being transmitted in the clear. Single sideband radio.

Unidentified: We fully agree with—

President Kennedy: The only question I have is, how do we justify stopping this ship and then letting the [unclear] ship go? What do we say?

McNamara: A general cargo ship. It loaded at Riga. It loaded at Riga in the Soviet Union.

McCone: Yes, it loaded at Riga with Soviet cargo.

President Kennedy: This Lebanese one [the *Marucla*]?

McCone: Yes, this Lebanese ship.

President Kennedy: All right. Want to have Pierre [Salinger] to come in here, Mrs. Lincoln?

Lincoln: Yes.

President Kennedy: The Defense Department ought to announce this. Want to just tell Pierre to call [Defense Department spokesman] Arthur Sylvester.

Now, the only question I've got is how do we still justify this ship. Do we have to announce we have let the other ones through?[8]

McNamara: I don't believe we have announced it.

Bundy: We have tried to limit that. When it does come up, that we don't want to begin with a passenger ship seems to be the best way of explaining it. That is exactly what controlled the decision, as I remember the discussion.

McNamara: I wouldn't go so far as to say we don't want to begin if it's a passenger ship.

President Kennedy: Just say that it was a passenger ship.

Ball?: We made no decisions not to stop that thing. It was a passenger ship. That's all we have to say.

Unidentified: This was the first dry-cargo ship originating in a Soviet port that's gone through the line. Is this correct?

Bundy: That's right.

McNamara: I believe that might be the case. I won't guarantee that it is so.

Unidentified: Mr. President, we've had an eye on [unclear].

McNamara: Exactly.

In any case, it was successful and I think the destroyers [unclear].

Looking at possible interceptions today, there appear to be none. There are no nonbloc ships; nor are there any bloc ships within easy range of the quarantine ships. There are 4 Soviet ships approaching the quarantine zone, but many of them are far, far away, some as far away as 3,000 miles. We anticipate that the *Grozny,* which appeared to be dead in the water yesterday at the time the SAC airplane passed over, will reach the barrier tomorrow

---

8. In addition to the *Bucharest* and the *Völkerfreundschaft,* the British tanker *Suiaco,* bound for Jamaica, and a Polish ship bound for New Orleans had been allowed to proceed through the quarantine line without inspection.

night at 11:00 P.M. This is the tanker with the deck load. We have considered the possibility of advancing to meet her today. We have done nothing further to accomplish that. We can still work on it, but it is unlikely that we can intercept her today even if we went all out to do so. So I would suggest no action on that.

The [name unclear], another tanker, will reach the barrier on the 31st of October at 2:00 A.M., Eastern Daylight Time. The *Belovodsk*, a cargo ship, will

buildup of offensive weapons in Cuba. Based on that surveillance [illegible] the assembly of IL-28s has continued at an accelerated pace. Therefore, acting under your authority, I am adding to the prohibited list bomber fuel, and the materials from which it is manufactured.

President Kennedy: We couldn't . . . What we're trying to get at now is tankers?

McNamara: Exactly. We're thinking of POL.

Bundy: This is POL.

President Kennedy: Couldn't we . . . What about tying it in to the missiles; they're the more dramatic offensive weapons. There are going to be such bombers everyplace. So is there some way that we could probably tie it into the destruction of these missile sites, rather than just the bombers?

McNamara: Well, we could do bomber fuel and associated petroleum products.

Bundy: You don't want at the end to have the bombers there. If you want to get them out, this is as good a time as any—

President Kennedy: No, I'd rather . . . What we're dealing with once again is the same problem, of stopping tankers, and I would rather tie that, if I could, to the missiles.

McNamara: Can't we do them both?

[Unclear exchange.]

President Kennedy: Yeah, that's what I would prefer.

I would say that we ought to tie . . . It seems to me, that in view of the fact that the missile work is going on, the sites are going on, we are tying up that fuel which contributes to that work. And, in view of the fact that the work on the missile sites is going on, we are also tying up aviation because of the bombers. So that we—I think the missiles are the dramatic point. Bombers—they might say: "Just throw out your bombers everyplace."

Rusk: Mr. President, can we break that into two pieces? I think that there would be some advantage in having a real shot at the U Thant talks for 24 hours before we consider putting on the POL. We really need to have another round there, to see if—

President Kennedy: Wouldn't we be better, then, to say something about, that the work is going on, and that this must come to a stop, and then tomorrow say it isn't stopped, and therefore move to POL?

Bundy: Well, the 24 hours, I think that's a problem that the Secretary brings up. The point is not losing the momentum that we've—[unclear].

Ball: Mr. President, can we announce every day that when we have that evidence, of that work that continues, [unclear] mounting indignation, [unclear reference to talks at UN].

President Kennedy: Well, that's why it seems to me that what we're gonna do is maybe give them a 24-hour notice that if they don't stop the work with assurances, that we're going to stop . . .

Bundy: The [unclear] consideration here is, we might . . . If we agree that this is the next step on the line of pressure, we might leave the timing until we've talked about the attack thing, and see at just what moment—

[Unclear exchange.]

McNamara: There's a report on that.

Dillon: I'd like to raise one thing about agreeing that this is the next step on the line of pressure.

I think we've got to decide very quickly whether we want to proceed down this area, or this track, or not. Because I think it leads to quite different consequences. If we follow this track [moving to blockade POL] we'll be sort of caught up in events, not of our own control. We will have to stop a Soviet ship with what appears to be peaceful cargo on it. We will run into Soviet reactions around the world, which could be similar. I don't mean they might shoot the American ships. We might wind up in some sort of a naval encounter all around the world with the Soviet Union which would have nothing to do with the buildup of the missile bases in Cuba.

The end result of that would be, we either go on to a possible general war, or the pressure gets so extreme that we have to stop, both sides, doing this sort of thing. Meanwhile the missiles continue in Cuba. This is the problem of this alternative track, of getting back on to the basic thing, that this work does not stop. This is not stopping. That our primary effort of acceleration, it ends up increasing our confrontation direct with the Soviet Union at sea, which is not as clearly connected with these missile bases. Difficult to do, what you said, to connect this with the missile bases, with Cuba.

[I suggest] that we put the confrontation there by preparing for air action to hit these bases if there is no, if they continue working. This decision would mean that we consider very seriously that if we color the way we handle the U Thant negotiations, we put great pressure on to do something to get inspectors

Bundy: I'm not sure it's as sharp as you make it, but this isn't the right

McNamara: Nor am I. I don't believe . . . There are alternative courses.

Let me go to another subject then. We conducted a daylight surveillance yesterday with approximately 10 aircraft at missile sites and the IL-28s area. There's no question but what—construction work is continuing. We can measure it. We can show it.

I would suggest that today we do two things. One, announce that it is our policy to continue surveillance day and night.

Secondly, that we send out immediately, and issue orders from here to do so, 8 to 10 aircraft to go on daylight surveillance today. They are on alert status. They can be off and over the targets by noon time, Cuban time.

And thirdly, that following our announcement that we are carrying out daylight and nighttime surveillance, that we send out 4 aircraft tonight on nighttime surveillance. These would be using flares, roughly 10 flares per target. It's thrown out of the airplane at about 5,000 feet, opening and becoming, operating at about 2,000 feet, illuminating the target area and the surrounding territory and serving as the basis for photographs.

And further I would suggest that we state that it is our intention to continue surveillance in order to determine the extent to which the development of offensive weapon systems is continuing.

Rusk: Mr. President, I wonder really again, on the nighttime reconnaissance, whether we ought to start that tonight, until we've had a crack at the U Thant discussions.

Ball: Why the provocative . . . ?

Rusk: Well, these flares are pathfinder flares, typically. They are frequently used with bombs like in London.[9] And we don't . . . We're not sure what the interpretation of the other side would be.

Unidentified: There won't be any bombs.

McNamara: There won't be any bombs tonight. We would tell them in advance that they were for—

[Unclear exchange, someone refers to "coming in advance."]

President Kennedy: I don't see anything wrong with there being that type of surveillance.

Unidentified: You're not afraid to announce it at all.

Bundy: Very important to announce it, because otherwise the danger the Secretary speaks of is real, in my opinion.

Unidentified: [Unclear] to announce any surveillance, continuous, and by announcement.

President Kennedy: But what we're trying to do is to build up this case that they're continuing the work. Because sooner or later we're going to have to do something about that. So that's all we're trying do. [Unclear.]

Unidentified: On the other hand, [unclear] one part of this thing, and that is to simulate an attack.

Bundy: They'll never believe it until it happens.

Stevenson: I don't see any point in announcing it, Mr. President. I should think that would be the last thing you would want to do—

President Kennedy: Why?

Stevenson: I would continue it and then make your announcements, from time to time, on the status—

President Kennedy: Well, what we're trying to do is to emphasize the fact that this buildup is going on and that we're observing it. But why wouldn't we announce it?

Stevenson: You shouldn't . . . You haven't announced it. You said you're going to continue—

Bundy: We're doing it under OAS requirements.

McNamara: And I would go further, and periodically release information resulting from it.

---

9. During night bombing raids in World War II, an initial wave of scout aircraft would drop flares or other devices to mark the targets for the oncoming bombers. He may have been referring to German use of such devices in bombing raids against London in 1940–41, or to British use of the devices (since the British relied on bombing raids at night) in their missions against German targets. The adjective "pathfinder" comes from the British use of such flares.

President Kennedy: If we're going to . . . The question will come as to what our surveillance of the last 4 days has shown.

Unidentified: Yes.

President Kennedy: Why don't we wait on this surveillance until we get the political talks, because what . . . It really depends on whether we're going to issue a statement this morning saying work is going on and must cease and . . . the day ones on [unclear, authorizing the proposed

I did want to go . . . with the Cubans.

Wilson: Yes, sir.

Rusk: Because we do . . . One of the possible outcomes here is to produce such pressures there, in Cuba, as to cause something to crack on the [unclear]—

President Kennedy: Those leaflets dropped. When do you think that'll happen?

Wilson: Well, whenever you order.

[Unclear exchange. Wilson says: "No, sir."]

President Kennedy: The problems about the drop of the leaflets are, that if we have decided to do an air strike, we may want to drop the leaflets, some leaflets, 15 minutes ahead of time. We don't want to get them so used to leaflets dropping so that they don't bother to read them when we come over then.

I'm not sure I'd drop these leaflets over the missile sites. I think I'd drop them in Havana, Santiago, and a few other places just to have warned them what we're going to do.

Bundy: No need telling the people on the missile sites that there are missiles in Cuba.

Wilson: The question is now with the leaflets, there is one major problem. I showed you last night the outlines of the leaflets. We are using one of the pictures that has been released of an intermediate-range site, and it just isn't very good. I mean the leaflet is this size; that's the way they make them at Fort Bragg.[10]

---

10. Fort Bragg, in North Carolina, was the headquarters for the U.S. Special Forces as well as for the Army's psychological warfare activities.

What I would like to recommend, if you want to go ahead and have a leaflet drop, we've got the wording, we have the older picture down there. I got a report this morning [that] it looks very bad.

President Kennedy: How about that one that appeared in the front pages of the [*Washington*] *Post,* with that square in the lefthand corner which shows that—

Wilson: It doesn't come up too well. What I would like to request is that the one that Ambassador Stevenson showed yesterday be sent immediately to Fort Bragg by CIA with a man accompanying it, and the negative, if we want to do this right away. Pierre [Salinger] tells me—I have not seen it, but Pierre tells me it is a very convincing . . .

President Kennedy: Then why don't you pick, of all the pictures we've put out and those that you did [referring to Stevenson], why don't you pick . . . ?

Wilson: The ones we've put out so far, Mr. President, I am not . . . There's only been 4 that we put out on the offensive sites and none of them are [unclear].

McCone?: Donny, there are special restrictions on some of these pictures. But I think because of, the decision is, that everything is weighed, and you get the one you like best.

President Kennedy: Among those that have been, in one place or another, released?

Bundy: Including any yesterday at the UN.

McCloy: I may just make a suggestion on that, because I'm talking to these delegations up there, going over this briefing of those sites there, with some effect I think. They're rather taken aback by the speed with which these things occurred. But one of the things that's been most impressive to them, that we didn't have the second time but we had the first time,[11] was that picture of the big bomb going through Red Square. Now, that isn't the [unclear] bomb, the [unclear] missiles that we have down there, but it's a smaller, it looks as if it's half a city block long. And I'd stick that in there. Because that thing will raise their eyebrows; there's nothing defensive about this. How this works, in terms of size. They ought to go back up again and look that up along with that second briefing we had yesterday.

The other thing that I think we ought to do is to stress just as strongly as we can—I assume that you're intensifying all your pressure on the island of Cuba now—but to give them a political [unclear]. Because if they don't give

---

11. The first briefings, on Tuesday, October 23, and the briefings on Thursday, October 25.

a damn, if you want, all these fools would rather have a Castro government, you can have him. But at this point I don't think you ought to give them a chance [unclear] by trying to attack the government. Because this is where this man is bringing you. But one thing that we're not going to . . . But "he's [Castro] bringing you [the Cuban people] to a point of disaster, and a point of risk."

President Kennedy: They got a pretty good message. In any case, you can

President Kennedy: Who has that?

[Several voices answer: "Pierre."]

Wilson: All right, sir.[12]

Rusk: Let's start with the . . . First of all, Mac, we've moved the briefing [unclear]. First is the substance of the [unclear], of the views we'll be handing to the Secretary General [U Thant] in the next day or two beginning this afternoon, I believe.

Bundy: Mr. Yost[13] will be seeing him, beginning at 11:30 this morning.

[Unclear interjection.]

Rusk: We need instructions on that part urgently, now we—

President Kennedy: I asked Pierre about this. [To Stevenson] You're gonna see him at 4:00? Is that correct?

Stevenson: I'm going to go back and see him, but meanwhile he had sent for us at 11:30, and I didn't want to appear to be indifferent to his request, so I'm sending someone else.

Rusk: These are [unclear] talks, preliminary talks, to set up a situation in which further discussion could occur. But it should be essential that there be minimum requirements before any talks can go forward.

These would be: no more offensive arms delivered to Cuba; no further buildup of missile sites or long-range bomber facilities; and any existing Cuban

---

12. By Saturday, October 27, millions of leaflets had been produced, ready to be airdropped over Cuba. Developments that day put planning for the leaflet drop on hold; then the issue was overtaken by events.

13. Charles Yost was a member of the U.S. mission at the United Nations.

nuclear strike capability would be rendered inoperable. In other words, there has to be a UN takeover of the, insurance on the sites, that they are not in operating condition. Now, we have to insist upon that very hard, because the whole object here has to be to get rid of this nuclear threat in Cuba.

Now, this is going to be very difficult to achieve, because the other side is going to be very resistant to UN inspectors coming into Cuba. So we estimate that we shall [unclear] at that point. Otherwise, what will happen is that the Soviets will go down and blow up the path of talking, talking indefinitely, while the missile sites [unclear] operational, especially the intermediate range. And then we are nowhere. And we are faced with an even more difficult problem on the sites than we are at the present time.

Now, this will involve a considerable effort on the part of the Secretary General, even if the Soviets and the Cubans accept it. He would have to have a UN observer corps, in Cuba. It would have to include up to 300 personnel at a minimum, drawing from countries that have a capacity, a technical capacity, to know what they're looking at and what directions must be taken to insure inoperability. That would mean countries like Sweden, Switzerland, perhaps Austria, and a limited number of, perhaps Brazil, countries of that sort. That's Canada. We can't have Burmese or Cambodians going in there, or other countries, in the face of 3 regiments of Soviet missile technicians, being led down the garden path on the operational problem.

Further, on the quarantine itself, we think that the UN should put a quarantine into operation, but that ours must remain in position until the UN has an effective one in position. Now, they could do this in several ways. They could establish, at the designated Havana ports, inspection personnel to inspect every incoming ship; these turn in at about 2 a day at different ports. We ourselves have maintained complete Navy surveillance of the area and insure that no ships come into any other port, and that we have full information on what is on board each ship.

There are a lot of detailed arrangements on both these items that would have to be considered. But we would have to keep our forces in the immediate background, and move promptly if the UN arrangements are not trustworthy.

An alternative would be to have this inspection occur offshore. The Defense Department and my colleagues have been talking about that, and that doesn't seem to be as feasible as having an in-port inspection.

But this is the general nature of the instructions that we have been honing, and Ambassador Stevenson will have a detailed draft there by State and Defense on these views later today. But I think we ought to talk about the general policy questions involved now.

First, that the arrangements must include no further arms shipments, no continued buildup, and a defanging of the sites that are already there.

Dillon: [Unclear] evidence that the key thing is that if they refuse that consistently, that gives you your excuse to take further action.

Nitze?: The most immediate thing that we could do, or they could do, would be to move the missiles from the missile sites. They could put the missiles on the IL-28 fields, separated from the erectors, and then move the fuel trucks

McCloy: I feel very strongly, Mr. President, that that's the thing to stress. I wouldn't put it in the order that the Secretary put it. I'd put it in just the reverse order. The critical thing, I think we're all resigned, that this thing was for a sinister purpose. The thing, this buildup, makes it look to me as if it was according to the time schedule, and perhaps for an adventure in some other area.

And I think we know we can't reintroduce the blockade once we let it drop. They [the diplomats] won't get the OAS in back of us again, and this is the one thing that the country's behind, everybody's behind. I mean, there's a growing momentum of opinion developing, perhaps a little slowly, but right now it's crystallizing. But this is the danger. This has got the—

Rusk: One of the problems to understand is that the quarantine is related to the presence of the missiles, the missile sites. And not just to the shipment of missile arms.

President Kennedy: Yes, because even if the quarantine's 100 percent effective, [unclear] because the missile sites go on being constructed. It's only a first step. [Unclear interjection.] Only a first step, the quarantine.

Rusk: Perhaps a removal of these things from Cuba is something that could be worked out in the 2 to 3 weeks.

President Kennedy: Obviously we can't expect them to remove them at this point without a long negotiation. Of course you won't get [unclear] unless you take them out. But at least, for the purposes of the negotiation . . .

Now, [unclear], do you have any thoughts about what our presentation—

Rusk: I wonder if I could [unclear] outline the other two [ideas] very briefly so that we can get the whole presentation.

We also would think it wise, from the State Department point of view, and I think the Defense Department has some utterly far-reaching objections to it, to encourage the Brazilians and hopefully the Mexicans, [unclear], to put [a proposal] forward for an atom-free Latin America.

Now, this involves some very complicated problems for us. They would not, I think, involve Puerto Rico, because that is a part of the United States. It would not involve actual transit through the [Panama] Canal, because that's available to warships and everything else in time of peace. It could involve, Bob, the business of our storing nuclear weapons in the Canal Zone. I just wanted to flag that to you because it could be an important problem. And it could also involve the actual use of Latin American airfields for transit in peacetime.

Now, I'm not worried about what the commitments would be in time of war. In time of war any such arrangements go by the board. But it could involve, it in effect could bar, the actual transit of weapons to Latin American bases in peacetime.

Unidentified: ASW [antisubmarine warfare] [unclear] also.

[Mixed voices, quietly in background.]

Rusk: I wonder if we could get Mr. Foster[14] [unclear] also.

Unidentified: [To an aide] Would you get Mr. Foster in for a moment? He's [unclear].

McNamara: We need to study and consider this possibility. The Chiefs are very cool toward it, for a variety of reasons that General Taylor can outline. I'm inclined to favor it.

Rusk: Mr. President, the political situation on this is as follows: If you can get a large number, a large part of the membership of the UN, supporting an atom-free Latin America, then you, on the one side, may get the—

[Quiet, unclear aside to President Kennedy by Bundy.]

—you may give the other side an occasion for pulling back, because they've been supporting nuclear-free zones for years. And they may find in this a face-saving point where they can do something about it.

Secondly, if they are not going to yield, then it is just as well to have their rejection of this situation and this possibility well on the record, before any forcible action has to be taken.

McNamara: I think you might like to hear General Taylor's comments on the Chiefs' views, and then I'd like to make some comments.

14. William C. Foster, Director of the Arms Control and Disarmament Agency, was a veteran executive in the steel and chemical industries and had been Deputy Secretary of Defense from 1951 to 1953.

Taylor: Well, we [the Chiefs] have just had a chance to talk around the table. We have not taken a formal position on it. I would say there is great skepticism that this would be effective, but we realize that you're [unclear].

Secondly, it would seem to us to divert the UN attention to a secondary or a tertiary issue, when we should be bearing down on the removal of missiles.

[Someone appears to agree.]

Rusk: These proposals would require the removal of missiles.

Rusk: Well, if the African states themselves brought in Africa, then I think that [unclear] we would not discuss . . . The question has just been raised on this, on what happens if Africa is included. I think we can expect in the General Assembly the Africans to want to add Africa to the list, because this could be a temporary problem for President de Gaulle.

We don't know exactly what his [de Gaulle's nuclear weapons] testing program is. We do know that he has concluded that Algeria is not going to be a testing site. [Unclear] possible; he is shifting to the South Pacific. It may become necessary, to meet a French objection, to tell him that so long as we are not subject to a nuclear test ban, or we are not testing, that he could use our own site for any particular testing he has in mind in the immediate future, pending [unclear]. We may have to give him some help on that.

But the other side possibly could object to this. And if they turn it down, our intentions are much clearer to everybody.

McNamara: Let me stipulate, Dean, that I'm in favor of that, so long as it is clearly linked to the first point you made. I don't believe we should allow ourselves to be maneuvered into a position in which this is *the* approach we take in order to achieve the elimination of the missiles from Cuba. With that single qualification, which is an extremely important qualification, I would strongly favor that.

Dillon: There's also, it could take too long, and that's what—

Rusk: Well, I would think there would be ways in which you could detect—

[Audio quality deteriorates suddenly while Rusk is speaking.]

Unidentified: . . . might wish to add to that Ed Martin, who does support UN action on that. The OAS has passed such a resolution, under the Rio Pact, that would view Cuba's possession of these missiles as another violation of the Rio Pact, and thereby give a stronger [unclear] in the UN or create a [unclear] for our attack option.

Rusk: We have had some discussion of that [unclear]. We are a member of the OAS. And there is some advantage in this being done by the other countries, without our direct participation. The smaller countries wanted to take themselves out of the great power confrontation.

President Kennedy: This is Brazilian?

Rusk: This is a Brazilian initiative.

President Kennedy: Is it part of the Brazilian initiative that the OAS or UN, or somebody else, would guarantee Cuba?

[Unclear answer from Rusk.]

I thought the proposal was that they would remove these weapons if the U.S. guaranteed the territorial integrity of Cuba.

[Unclear replies, but others appear to agree.]

Well, obviously we're going to have to pay a price. How are we going to get those missiles out of there without your fighting them? Get them out, or . . .

Rusk: Mr. President, unless there is some violent action by Cuba, along the lines of these offensive weapons, Cuba has all sorts of existing guarantees of territorial integrity. We've got that policy in your message. I think we had [unclear]. They've got the UN Charter; they've got the Rio Pact; they've got [unclear] . . .

President Kennedy: Obviously, [unclear] political, [unclear]. We've been talking about these actions we've got to take to get these out of there [unclear].

Rusk: Well, here is a way in which that [unclear] more urgently.

[Unclear; Rusk is raising the idea of a direct contact with Castro, through the Brazilian ambassador to Cuba, in Havana] . . . and I'd like to read these paragraphs, which would hopefully be sent as instructions to this ambassador, to the Brazilian ambassador in Havana [quoting from draft State Department cable to the Brazilian government as the message they hope the Brazilian ambassador will pass to Castro]:

"The world now knows without any question and in great detail the nature and size of the buildup of Soviet offensive missile capability in Cuba. There can be no valid question in anyone's mind on this point.

"The action of the Soviet Union in using Cuban soil as sites for offensive nuclear missiles capable of striking most of the Western Hemisphere has placed the future of the Castro regime and the well-being of the Cuban people in great jeopardy.

"The countries of the Inter-American system have unanimously called for their removal and approved and are participating in the measures being taken to eliminate this Soviet threat to all of them.

"The Soviet Union is turning around its cargo ships in face of the U.S. blockade which the countries of the hemisphere have authorized. Not only is the Soviet Union failing to support Cuba on this matter, but numerous feelers have been put out by high Soviet officials to allied governments for exchanges of their position in Cuba for concessions by the NATO countries in other parts

[Rusk adds a brief, inaudible comment on this sentence, then resumes.]

"Castro might recall that President Kennedy has said publicly that only two issues were nonnegotiable between Castro and the U.S.—the military-political ties to the U.S.S.R. and the aggressive attitude toward the internal affairs of other Latin American countries. This view will be shared by other members of the Inter-American system. Of course this means giving up the offensive nuclear capability being established in Cuba and sending home Soviet military personnel, on which help can certainly be given if needed. From such actions many changes in the relations between Cuba and the OAS countries, including the U.S., could flow.

"Time is very short for Cuba and for Castro to decide whether to devote his great leadership abilities to the service of his Cuban people or to serving as a Soviet pawn in their desperately risky struggle for world domination by force and threat of force.

"If Castro tries to rationalize the presence of these missiles as due to Cuban fear of a U.S. invasion, Ambassador Batian[15] should reply that he is confident that the OAS would not accept an invasion of Cuba once the missiles were removed and that the U.S. would not risk upsetting Hemispheric solidarity by invading a Cuba so clearly committed to a peaceful course."

Although [unclear], as far as Castro is concerned I would say that there is a minimum of two things. First, get the Russians out. And second, [unclear.]

Dillon: You made the changes which I thought were necessary.

---

15. Luis Batian Pinto, Brazil's ambassador to Cuba.

President Kennedy: [Unclear.] But I don't think there's enough evidence that we could achieve that, but I think probably the [unclear] of it would be regarded as rather of some importance.

[Unclear exchange between Rusk and President Kennedy.]

President Kennedy: Well then, what do you do? Send that down to them [the Brazilian government]?

Rusk: We thought we would get this off right away.

So, this relates to that point, of the atom-free proposal that the Brazilians are asking for help on. If they [the Cubans] get rid of these offensive weapons, then it is not our purpose to take . . .

Nitze: The question here is *when* they're going to get them out. This suggests that there will be long-drawn-out negotiations, both with respect to the Latin American connection and with respect to this. It seems to me that we've got to make clear in some way or another—

[Mixed voices. President Kennedy says: "First out of all this discussion"; Bundy appears to say: "Inspectors have to be there."]

Dillon: We originally had a 24-hour time limit, not as a thing but as a "perhaps not more than 24 hours remains," which is an indication of . . . We dropped that out.

Rusk: I don't like to put a 24-hour thing, because you pass the 24th hour without having taken the action, then you've undermined the whole message, you've . . .

Dillon?: "Perhaps not more than a few days."

Rusk: That would get in there some element of—

[Unclear exchange.]

McCone: The thing I don't like about this, this would sort of insulate Castro from further actions. Long before these missiles were there, I hear the link with the Soviet Union, and the use of Cuba as a base for operations to undermine all Latin America, was a matter of great concern. Now, what this does is more or less leave him in that position. The missiles aren't there, but still this situation that has worried us so much for the last 2 or 3 years goes on.

I bring that up because I think there's two things we have to consider here. One is getting rid of these missiles. And the other is to have the Cuban people take over Cuba, and take it away from Castro. Well, this does not impel a break between Castro and the Soviet Union.

Rusk: Well, this message itself would repeat the President's statement that the military-political connection with Moscow is nonnegotiable, as well as the actions taken against other Latin American countries.

Now, if Castro were, through some miracle, to get his wits together and turn on the Soviets, on these missiles, then this problem is solved there, as far as the Soviets are concerned. If they were to get this message. On the off chance. That's the purpose of this operation, if possible.

Robert Kennedy: What happens in the future in either one of these things, we discussed earlier . . . Now, to get rid of the nuclear weapons and have a major operation, that gets a large amount of time . . . All those weapons they

Rusk: The draft [message to Castro] that we have does not give assurances against any kind of rascality.

Ball: Nuclear weapons. It refers to nuclear weapons and nuclear-capable . . .

Robert Kennedy: Do you think we should get something there?

[Unclear exchange.]

Bundy: Mr. President, I believe myself that all of these things need to be measured in terms of the very simple, basic structural purpose of this whole enterprise, which is to get these missiles out. Castro is a problem. If we can bring Castro down in the process, dandy. If we can get in some other people, dandy. But if we can get the missiles out . . .

President Kennedy: My priority is to get the missiles out. We can take care of dumping Castro, [unclear] and do something in Berlin, and all this too, if this changes, and our commitments. So I think we ought to concentrate on the missiles right now.

[Quietly, to an aide] I'll call back. In about an hour.

Thompson: [Unclear.] In my opinion, the Soviets will find it far easier to remove these weapons or to [unclear] their support for removal, than they would to accept inspections. I'm saying Soviet technicians under UN people would . . .

Bundy: If we could verify their disappearance . . .

[Unclear exchange.]

Rusk: [Unclear] . . . for our part, to have in mind during these talks.

President Kennedy: All right, let's do . . . Let's get moving. Let's get this message action [to Castro], one more look at it, Mr. Secretary. Let's send this off. It probably won't get anyplace. But I think for now we've got to put in the greatest urgency, because time's running out for us, and [unclear] work on these things while these conversations go on.[16]

We've got to be saying that work has to cease, which we're verifying every day, during these negotiations. We have to be saying that to U Thant; the Brazilian to Castro, throughout the 2 weeks [of preliminary talks].

Governor, do you want to talk a little and give us your thoughts?

Stevenson: Well, sir, I've just seen this proposed track on the political procedures. I think it's well for you all to bear in mind that the concept of this proposal [from U Thant] is a standstill. That is to say, no one was to take further action for—we could work out the modalities—for 2 or 3 weeks while we negotiated a final settlement.

This includes in the immediate modality as one of the objectives of the final negotiations, which is to make the weapons inoperable. I would be very much troubled by trying to get that included in the original 24-, 48-, 36-hour negotiations, because it includes something that is not a standstill. It includes a reverse, a reversal of something that has already taken place.

I think it would be quite proper to include in our original demands that the weapons be *kept* inoperable.

President Kennedy: Work on the sites would be ceased?

Stevenson: Work on the sites, of course. Now, the three points that we've talked about are suspending the—

Bundy: Excuse me, you're going to have to be clear. Are we talking about the first 2 days or about—

Stevenson: We're talking about the first 2 days. I'll outline to you the first 2 days and the subsequent days, if you wish.

The first 2 days the objectives were, on our side, that no ships go to Cuba carrying arms. This included all arms, not just offensive arms. That's what U Thant said. That's one place that we have to determine whether we're willing to apply this only to offensive weapons or whether we want to insist, as he put it, on all arms.

The second point is how that's to be done. The second point is that there should be no further construction on the bases, and how that is to be policed.

16. The message to Brazil was sent at 2:00 that afternoon. After further discussion between the U.S. embassy in Rio de Janeiro and Washington, the message was discussed with Brazil's foreign minister on the night of October 27. The Brazilian agreed to help, but the plan was overtaken by the events of October 28. See Deptel 1055, October 26, 1962; Rio 902, October 28, 1962, in *FRUS 1961–1963*, vol. 11, pp. 228–229, 278.

The third point is that we would then suspend our quarantine, pending the 2 or 3 weeks' negotiation.

Rusk: The work on the bases must include the inoperability of the missiles.

Stevenson: I think that it would be quite proper to attempt to do that, but to *keep* them inoperable. [Unclear] to say that they should be *rendered* inoperable, because that requires—

Rusk: Keep them inoperable.

open whether it's a standstill.

Rusk: If they turn out to be operable, then that means something altogether different.

Stevenson: I'm suggesting that we might include in the initial modalities of the negotiation that all the weapons be kept inoperable, and find out what that means in response from the other side. But I don't think that there should be any misunderstanding about what was intended here, which was a standstill and only a standstill.

Unidentified: Well, it should remain inoperable.

[Mixed voices. Someone says: "the first 2 days."]

Stevenson: The next point is for the . . . Well, then comes the long-term negotiation. What we wanted to obtain in the long-term negotiation, I assume—this is the 2-week negotiation—is the withdrawal from the hemisphere of these weapons, and the dismantling of the existing bases for these weapons.

And what they will want in return is, I anticipate, a new guarantee of the territorial integrity of Cuba. They need that; that's what they said these weapons were for. And the territorial integrity of Cuba.

It is possible that the price that might be asked of us in the long-term negotiation, 2-week negotiation, might include dismantling bases of ours, such as Italy and Turkey, that we have talked about.

We might also include, in the long-term negotiations, Cuba's agreement to a Latin American free nuclear zone.

We might include, you might attempt to include, something like defanging Cuba for subversion and penetration. I'm not sure how we can do that, or whether we can do that, or should do that. That certainly is open for discussion.

But I would conclude by making it very clear that the intention here was a standstill, not positive acts. And the standstill was to include the discontinuance of construction, discontinuance of shipping, discontinuance of the quarantine, which we, we'd have to agree to do that in 48 hours.

After that, we negotiate a final settlement which would relate to the withdrawal of the weapons, or the inoperability of the weapons already inoperable. I would think "inoperable" becomes meaningless, because during the long-term negotiations we're concerned with the withdrawal of the weapons from the hemisphere.

McCone: I don't believe, I don't agree with that, Mr. President. I feel very strongly about it. And I think that the real crux of this matter is the fact that he's got these pointed, for all you know, right now at our hearts. And this is going to produce I think, it may produce, a situation when we get to Berlin after the elections, which changes the entire balance of world power.

It puts us under a very great handicap in carrying out our obligations, not only to our Western European allies, but to the hemisphere. And I think that we've got the momentum now. We've got the feeling that these things are serious and that they must be . . .

That threat must be removed before we can drop the quarantine. If we drop that quarantine once, we're never going to be able to put it in effect again. And I feel that we *must* say that the quarantine goes on until we are satisfied that these are inoperable.

President Kennedy: Well, our quarantine itself won't remove the weapons. So we've only got two ways of removing the weapons. One is to negotiate them out, or we trade them out. And the other is to go over and just take them out. I don't see any other way we're going to get the weapons out.

McCone: I say that we have to send inspections down there to see what [unclear] state they are in. I feel that if we lose that . . . But this is the security of the United States! I believe the strategic situation has greatly changed with the presence of these weapons in Cuba.

President Kennedy: That's right. The only thing that I am saying is, that we're not going to get them out with the quarantine. I'm not saying we should lift the quarantine or what we should do about the quarantine. But we have to all now realize that we're not going to get them out. We're either going trade them out, or we're going to have to go in and get them out ourselves. I don't know of any other way to do it.

Bundy?: The point about the first 2 days is, if I understand Governor Stevenson, or the sense of his proposal, or the proposal which is before us from the UN, it does involve a dropping of the quarantine, without what I would call adequate momentum. Very far from it.

Rusk: Mr. President, I do think you have, the UN people [planned inspectors] have these [unclear]. And they are required to report in to their center every hour. If the [report is] negative, of the figures they receive on our report of the condition of the site, [this] will immediately cause us to send planes ~~~~~~~~ look. So that we would be in a position, if we needed to, that

Unidentified: They're not going to take them out. So we're going to have to—

McNamara: I wasn't even aware that the first 2 days, after which the quarantine would be lifted, would be accompanied by UN inspectors. That wasn't part of the 2-day plan.

[Quick exchange: "Not in the first 2 days."]

McNamara: That's my point.

Stevenson?: During the first 2 days we'd just discuss how to do it.

[Unclear exchange.]

McNamara: You say, with these things you'd take the quarantine off, but was it your thought to take it off before the UN inspectors are in Cuba?

Stevenson: No. [Unclear.] They'd inspect all shipments and be satisfied that there are no ships moving, and that we'd be satisfied that there's no construction on the bases.

McNamara: And we'd have UN inspectors down there to do that.

Stevenson: Yeah, but that's going to be a problem, that Dean mentioned a moment ago. How we're going to mobilize these fellows and recruit them, and that's one of the things we have to start talking about today.

McCone: Well, on that point I think it seems to me pretty clear, though, as the Secretary says, that we can't expect a bunch of Burmese to go down there and take the security of the United States in his hands. I think we've got to insist upon having our own people down there. [Unclear] the Soviets are already there. They take this seriously.

[Unclear comment.]

Bundy: If we're talking about inoperability, we have to be there.

McCone: You have to have technicians. You have to have somebody that knows what these things mean.

President Kennedy: The only thing is, as I say, it isn't as if what we're now doing is going to get them out of there.

Bundy?: No, sir, but we are on a course . . . We have the intent to get them out of there, and if we adopt a course at the UN which presumes that they might stay there, we've had it.

President Kennedy: Fine, but as I understand the Governor's proposal, what he's suggesting is that we give this thing the time to try to negotiate them out of there. Now, we won't be able to negotiate them out of there. But otherwise I don't see that we're going to get them out of there unless we go in and get them out.

Stevenson?: I think it serves a [unclear] to determine that.

Rusk: Sir, I'm not too optimistic that we will get these necessary preconditions in these first 2 days of talks. I think we will . . . If the Soviets were to come that far, this would be a major backdown.

Dillon: Well, they can't back down that much.

McCone: The difficulty, it seems to me, is going in these 2 days, and within an 8-hour period that they could put these things on their stands, and we're looking at them.

Bundy: Look, the quarantine isn't going to prevent that.

McCone: No. But I think we ought to have a [unclear] action, [unclear]. We have, during the 2-day period, and [unclear] during the 2-week period. We can take such action as necessary.

Stevenson: If there is any violation of the standstill during the 2-week period of negotiations for a settlement, then of course we would have to, then all bets are off. We're back to status quo.

Rusk: We are taking some risks on that for the next day or two. Offensive weapons.

Nitze: The settlement ought to really give you some security during the period while these negotiations go on.

President Kennedy: What's that you say, Paul?

Nitze: A settlement separating the missiles from the erectors.

[Several people talk at once. One person refers to the IL-28s. Other discussion about making the missiles inoperable.]

Stevenson?: You're trying to work out, in the modalities, the long-term negotiation.

Nitze: No, no. During the negotiations they disassemble them, so we're not negotiating under the threat. [Unclear.]

Unidentified: Have we seen a missile on a launcher?

Unidentified: Right next to them.

[Unclear exchange.]

Nitze: [Unclear] a way that it would take a day to get them up, by having those missiles all in the same place as the IL-28s.

down, is *not* in our interests.

Unidentified: I think it would be [unclear] appropriate for you to invite the Cuban ambassador in this regard to get their point of view on [unclear].

Unidentified: It may be [unclear] a radio to send there, a UN inspection force down there to determine the existence of the missiles if there are any questions about it, [unclear].

Dillon: I just don't see how you can negotiate for 2 weeks with these things sitting on, right next to the launchers.

Unidentified: The IRBMs will be becoming operational.

Dillon: If we drop the demand that they be made inoperable we'll be going back on our statement that we wouldn't negotiate under threat.

Rusk: The fact that you have personnel at the sites, with regular reporting, if they change into an actual operating position you would know about it.

President Kennedy: Ambassador, does Mr. Yost know what he's supposed to say at 11:30 [in his meeting with U Thant]?

Stevenson: To tell him I'll be back at 4:30.

[Unclear exchange. Yost may be phoning in from New York.]

President Kennedy: Excuse me a second.

Stevenson: Could I be excused, sir? I did want to say one other thing to him for a moment.

President Kennedy: Okay, sure. [Unclear] in my office.

McCone?: Don't you think we ought to have sophisticated people on this mission? We ought to be able to nominate the people that go.

Dillon: The British would be all right.

McCone: British, French. [Unclear] these Swedes or Austrians, I want some-body that knows something about this business.

Robert Kennedy: I can't *believe* that they would allow a whole lot of foreign-ers running around these missiles.

Bundy: What they are going to try to do is to sustain various forms of discussion while the thing goes—

Unidentified: As a practical matter—

Dillon: They can as a practical matter remove the missiles from the erectors, and let people see, as Paul said, and then we could read that by putting in a different place, and then you don't have—

Robert Kennedy: I know that that's . . . You know, they could put 12 missiles out on the lawn, and 16 back in the woods. You've got to know where all the others are. How are you going to know—

Taylor: We could make them account for the ones we've actually seen, but those aren't everything, and we haven't . . .

President Kennedy: The point is, that we really haven't got to in this thing is, what we've really got to do is, at least, we've got to see if he [Stevenson] has this proposal for feeling . . . which nobody is very much interested in.

But the point is that the blockade is not going to accomplish the job either. So we've got to have some other alternatives to accomplish what Governor Stevenson suggests may or may not be accomplished by negotiations. We haven't had any proposal on the other side except to continue the blockade, which isn't going to accomplish, except it's going to bring the confrontation closer, which may or may not be desirable, but—

Dillon: It may bring it [the confrontation] in the wrong place.

President Kennedy: Well, I think we have to be thinking, what are we going to do on the other track, if we're not going to do the negotiating track. What other devices are we going to use to get them out of there?

McNamara: Mr. President, can't we negotiate *and* keep the blockade? As I understood Secretary Rusk's proposal—

Rusk: Well, we're not going to pull out of the blockade until . . . Our point is that we don't pull out of the blockade in any way, until we get the modalities that [unclear] I was talking about, which includes: no more arms sent to Cuba; no further buildup of missile sites or long-range bomber facilities; any existing Cuban nuclear site capabilities must be rendered inoperable.

McNamara: Now, and you could define that as separating the missiles from the sites, and having inspectors there.

They may not agree to that, but—

[Mixed voices.]

Bundy: The inoperable point is very important, that the Governor must, he's got to clearly express.

[Unclear exchange.]

McNamara: You've got to separate the missiles from the launchers.

In any case, if we could link together, in the initial proposal, UN inspection and separation of the [unclear] . . .

President Kennedy: [Unclear] in 48 hours, if he would agree to that, I would

[Unclear exchange between Bundy and President Kennedy about planning another presentation to bipartisan congressional leadership.]

Taylor: During that negotiation, Mr. President, shouldn't we be raising the noise level of our indignation over this?

President Kennedy: That's something for the next . . . Let's move on then to the next question, which is whether we ought to sometime today say that photographic evidence taken yesterday indicates that work is going on. And that therefore—which we know is unsatisfactory, some [unclear] like that. You've got photographs of this thing?

McNamara: They do indeed. I have the evidence here.

President Kennedy: Say that this is going on and we can't accept that.

But I would think that tomorrow, we would then be in the position of deciding if we're going to go with [expanding the blockade to include] POL or if we're going to decide to go the other route, the force route.

Taylor: We can have a lot of planes in the air over them, Mr. President. Do we increase our activities? We have fighters. We can have night photography of Havana, for example. We can do many things. There is mounting activity—

Bundy: It's like the problems of last week, Mr. President. The more we begin to look under these things, the less apt to be clear it is that they're sharply separated.

We need to work on that today. And with your permission we would constitute a working group, working in the State Department, of this committee on this problem.

Rusk: Well, I do think it would be important to pursue the possibility of the political thing, to be sure that the Soviets have turned down these three conditions before we put on the night reconnaissance.

President Kennedy: [Unclear, agrees.] I'd rather, I would go with this. Now, do we today put out for the world opinion, giving an idea about the work continuing? And that comes out of, I would think, the White House, rather than the Defense Department, because otherwise [unclear].

Bundy: There is stuff on the wires that the Soviets are saying the U.S. military is taking over. It may be even advantageous for the State Department . . .

President Kennedy: Let's this afternoon have a statement which broadly presents, which Mac can work on, saying about the work going on, and indicating—we'll have to draw this with care, with the State Department and Tommy—with what severity which we judge this.

This way we start the . . . We perfected the blockade, but that's only half the job. This will lead us then to the POL or to the . . .

Bundy: My suggestion would be, Mr. President, that we have a White House spokesman simply say that there are problems—

President Kennedy: Okay, why don't you get it out.

Bundy: —that the work is going on, and we call attention to the President's speech.

President Kennedy: Something like that..

Unidentified: [Unclear] whether you drop leaflets . . .

President Kennedy: We've got to arrange the leaflets, and we would like to tell them to drop [unclear].

Unidentified: [Unclear] which is a decision to drop them.

President Kennedy: I've said, but if you've got some sort of reservation [unclear].

Unidentified: I have a feeling that this [unclear] may be the time to stir up things.

President Kennedy: Let me just say the only other question here is a matter which [unclear] brought up yesterday. I thought that we ought to get somebody . . . I don't know whether we ought to get a presentation tomorrow by the Defense Department on air action again, whether that is [unclear, mixed voices]. [Unclear] a week ago. I'd like to have us to take a look now at whether that—

[Unclear reassurance that this will be provided.]

Okay.

[Meeting starts breaking up.]

Bundy: If [unclear] were available, it would be a great help if you could chair this planning operation with the State Department, identify a Department officer, and [unclear].

Robert Kennedy: Are we going to go right now, Mac?

Unidentified: People are going to assemble over there . . .

The meeting then broke up, and the tape recorder was turned off.

AFTERNOON AND EVENING

OVAL OFFICE

After the members of the Executive Committee departed, President Kennedy returned a phone call from David Ormsby-Gore.[1] The British ambassador asked how long President Kennedy felt he could wait for U Thant to try for an adequate, verified standstill. President Kennedy told him that the Soviets were pushing ahead to finish the missile sites. The United States could not, therefore, wait much longer.

At the State Department several Executive Committee members discussed a possible air strike against Cuba. Taylor reported back to the Chiefs that a consensus seemed to be emerging in favor of starting with a limited strike just against the missile sites and the IL-28s. The air defenses in Florida were now so strong that fears of a retaliatory air strike by the MiGs had apparently diminished. Taylor and the Chiefs continued to favor a larger air strike, at least extending to the SAM sites as well.

More ominous intelligence news had been digested during the morning, however, especially from the low-level photography mission flown on October 25. The photos gave new evidence about the pace of Soviet preparations to ready the MRBM sites for firing, and the possible deployment of tactical nuclear weapons. Intelligence analysts concluded that the MRBMs were becoming fully operational, readied for imminent possible use. McCone, with Lundahl, sought and received a private meeting with President Ken-

---

1. This may have been the call he was told about during the meeting, which he asked his secretary to say he would return in an hour.

nedy to brief him on this information. Robert Kennedy may also have been present.[2]

President Kennedy: [looking at imagery] . . . and if we hadn't? Isn't this peculiar? If we hadn't gotten those early pictures, we might have missed them.[3] Wonder why they didn't put a cover over it. They think they're so smart that . . . Here's another similar one.

McCone: This is the missile stand. There's the blocks. Here are the 2 missile

Unidentified: [Unclear] Strong. I gave him a debriefing on that yesterday [unclear].

President Kennedy: He actually said: "I guess they're missile sites." But what he said were missiles were actually ground to air. But now you don't see any people, do you?

Unidentified: I don't see any people here.

President Kennedy: What would be a good question, it seems to me, in the future is to find out what our pilots see themselves compared to what the pictures show.

Unidentified: Well, they don't see much.

President Kennedy: If we're going to do an air strike—whether the fellows can pick this up themselves—

McCone: I don't know what this shows here. This picture unfortunately doesn't show it very well. Let's get one or two others.

There's a whole complex here. See, here is the missile erector. Here's a cable that goes over into a power source. Then, in other parts of the pictures, there are the fueling trucks, of which there are two types. And there's—and then

2. Robert Kennedy's memoir includes an accurate quotation from McCone's briefing, though it is placed incorrectly in the morning Executive Committee meeting; *Thirteen Days: A Memoir of the Cuban Missile Crisis* (New York: W. W. Norton, 1971), pp. 85–86. So we presume that he either sat in on this briefing, later listened to a recording of it, or both.

3. The missiles were now being concealed by much more aggressive camouflage efforts, which troubled them. The analysts were now able to spot the missiles only with the aid of the photographs taken of them earlier in October.

there's the missile stored over in the missiles building. I've concluded that it isn't possible to really hide these things as we have sometimes thought. They're mobile, but they're not quite as mobile as a tractor-trailer. Furthermore, they're big.

President Kennedy: Is this all there is in this thing which can be fired now?

Unidentified: No, this can be fired. I'll have to ask him to bring in [Lundahl]. Bring in Art.

McCone: It's quite an extensive installation, even though it's portable. And hence it is, first, a larger target and a more sensitive target than [an IRBM].

We've had our people make a study of it quite independently. We have, as you know, a lot of military people that are seconded to the Agency so that amateurs aren't in military billets. We conclude that—we feel that—[there is a] higher probability of immobilizing these missiles, all of them in the strike, than I think our thinking has tended in the last few days. Now, it won't be final because we don't see all the missiles for which there are launchers and SAM sites. Therefore, there are some that have been able to move them. And also those in repair. Now, I would see that picture that shows the extent of the complex—

President Kennedy: Have we got a mobile missile that's transportable by plane that has a range of 1,000 miles?

Unidentified: I don't believe so. I take that back. Mr. McNamara said something about that the other day at the meeting which was news to me. But I think he said it tentatively. I don't know whether this—

President Kennedy: It couldn't fly. We could—if we ever have to fly, say, 15 into Berlin—if we wanted to—

McCone: I would think so, yes.

[Lundahl has come in. Unclear exchange.]

Well, let the President see, Art, if one or two of those pictures would show those, the low-level pictures, would show how extensive the complex is.

Lundahl: I displayed some of these.

Unidentified: Yesterday?

Lundahl: Yes. The 23rd, sir [actually the 25th].

President Kennedy: Is this one of the places that we had earlier, pictures that show—?

Unidentified: Yes, sir.

Unidentified: We hadn't released these at the time, have we?

Unidentified: No, sir.

McCone: This is a picture—this is a picture that we released for use in the pamphlet [to be dropped over Cuba]. Now, you see? Here is your launcher.

Your missile's stored here. Here are the oxidizer-tank trailers. Here are the fuel tanks.

President Kennedy: There wouldn't be much to that. [Unclear.] Did it blow or just—?

Lundahl: Assuming red nitric acid, sir, very heavily lined trucks, so if they're opened up, they might make some real trouble for those who are trying to contain it. That's the oxidizer that they use with their SAMs, the mediums

[unclear section]

camouflaged again over here. Here's something, we don't know what that is.

President Kennedy: Just a question, how much [unclear]? I don't see any people there, so . . .

Lundahl: The ground is so wet they have to lay their cables above ground on little stanchions. And they have to put catwalks around it because there's all kind of water. There's been lots of rain there in just the last couple of days. Here's some of their advanced equipment.

Unidentified: Now, this is interesting.

[38 seconds excised as classified information. From the context this appears to be a briefing about the discovery of possible Soviet tactical nuclear weapons, in the form of a short-range nuclear missile called the FROG.][4]

President Kennedy: But you couldn't shoot these up much, could you? Just guess. No, it shows. Is this the only place we've got with sort of an armory?

Unidentified: So far, sir. We have others, but we haven't made—

President Kennedy: It would indicate that.

McCone: There's a real concentration of effort now. Here are your launchers. Here are those 2 pads for the wheel chocks. There's another erector here. Here's

4. The FROG missile launchers were discovered by the same low-level photography of October 25 that was a main subject of this briefing. The next day's GMAIC, JAEIC, NPIC joint report included the following: "Photography (Mission 5012 of 25 October) confirmed the presence of a FROG missile launcher in a vehicle park near Remedios. (The FROG is a tactical unguided rocket of 40,000 to 50,000 yard range, and is similar to the US Honest John)"; "Supplement 7 to Joint Evaluation of Soviet Missile Threat in Cuba," 27 October 1962, in McAuliffe, *CIA Documents,* p. 325.

your cable that comes through some kind of a cutoff switch here and then over to a launch-control building and a generator. So there—in addition to the launcher and the missile, there are a number of trucks and trailers and interrelated equipment, much of which is quite sensitive but would go to make this installation a workable installation.

President Kennedy: We don't know how many people there are in each one of these guard [houses], do we?

McCone: No, we don't. No, we don't. We have some information that on some sites there are as many as 500 personnel on-site with 300 additional Soviet guards, which you'll probably find in a very large restricted area.

President Kennedy: What conclusion does this lead you to?

McCone: Well, it leads me to . . . Well, I guess this is why there's a need [unclear].

Unidentified: Is your car at the west entrance, sir?

[Unclear group discussion.]

McCone: Thanks very much, Art.

The thing is, there's a very great deal of concern about this thing. I think that they've got a substantial number of these, that they could start at dark and have missiles pointing at us the following morning.

For that reason, I'm growing increasingly concerned about following a political route which, unless the initial act is to ensure that these missiles are immobilized by the physical separation of the missile, which is on a truck and trailer, from the launcher, which is itself a truck and trailer. One of them can be hauled on land by the other. This, I think, would be—

President Kennedy: Well now, the only problem is . . . I agree, that that's what we want. The alternative, of course, is to do the air strike or an invasion. We still are going to face the fact that, if we invade, by the time we get to these sites after a very bloody fight, they will still be pointing at us. So it still comes down to a question of whether they're going to fire the missiles.

McCone: That's correct. That's correct.

President Kennedy: There's no action that, other than diplomatic, that we can take. It is not easy to get rid of these. There are only two ways to do this, as I said this morning. One is the diplomatic way. I doubt [it] is going to be successful. The other way is, I think, a combination of an air strike and probably invasion, which means that we would have to carry out both of those with the prospect that they [the missiles] might be fired.

McCone: Invading has got to be the much more serious undertaking of those two, you realize.

President Kennedy: Because of the equipment they are going to have?

McCone: Because of the equipment; because they had a hell of a lot of equipment before they got these things [the FROG tactical nuclear weapons] that you just saw pictures of. That's very useful stuff they've got there. They've got missile carriers, gun carriers, half-tracks, and all such things as that. If they're equipped with even half of what we presume—with what the Russians will have, they'll give an invading force a pretty bad time.

President Kennedy: Of course, if you had control of the air, you could chew

President Kennedy: We're getting in touch with the Pentagon? Who's in charge with respect to invading? Do we have a fellow? Wheeler is the one who is working on that?

McCone: Yes, I think Wheeler is working just now. And there's a General Truman(?), whom I don't know, who I think is the man under Wheeler, under Anderson, who is responsible for preparing the invasion forces.

President Kennedy: What about the air strike?

McCone: I don't know who has that.

President Kennedy: Well, but I mean, what about the—what course of action would this lead you to?

McCone: Well, this would lead me . . . This would lead me to move quickly on an air strike if we . . .

At this point the recording stopped. President Kennedy turned to other work, including updates on the operation of the quarantine. Two Soviet submarines had finally been obliged to surface under pressure from the U.S. ships shadowing them. A Swedish dry-cargo ship, the *Coalangatta,* which had docked in the Soviet Union and was en route to Cuba under Soviet charter, proceeded to the quarantine line and then refused to stop when it was intercepted by an American destroyer. Faced with this curiously defiant behavior by a ship that had not been on the list of suspect vessels, and despite Khrushchev's pledge to U Thant that Soviet ships would avoid the quarantine area, the destroyer asked for instructions. The matter was bumped up to Washington. Ultimately the signal came back: "Don't fire. Let the Swedish ship pass." The matter seemed odd, even troubling.

At 2:30 a number of President Kennedy's top advisers gathered again, this time in the JCS Operations Room of the Pentagon, to discuss Operation Mongoose. McCone explained that, although the CIA was totally behind Lansdale as the head of Operation Mongoose, the Agency had not adequately informed Lansdale as it concurrently tried to support the U.S. military's operational planning against Cuba. The planned infiltration of 50 Cuban exiles into Cuba was postponed, pending a reexamination by Defense and State of what they needed. The other major item from the morning Executive Committee meeting, planning for a possible post-Castro government in the aftermath of a U.S. invasion, was turned over to the State Department.

Late in the afternoon Stevenson met with U Thant. He presented the three points agreed upon at the morning meeting: no more arms ships; no further work on missile sites; and missile sites rendered inoperable. This must happen in 48 hours. If it happened, then there could be 2 or 3 weeks for negotiations, though the quarantine would stay in force until compliance with these points could be verified. U Thant and Stevenson talked through the details of possible verification arrangements, but U Thant doubted that the Soviets or Cubans would accept what the Americans wanted, especially the measures to keep the missiles inoperable.

Yet U Thant was hopeful that a settlement could be found through a deal in which the United States would guarantee the territorial integrity of Cuba, and, in return, all missile sites and other offensive weapons would be dismantled and removed. U Thant claimed to have got the idea from the speech of Cuban President Osvaldo Dorticos to the General Assembly. U Thant telephoned Rusk directly to convey the same idea for a deal, this time described as trading a verified standstill that met all American conditions only for American agreement not to attack Cuba during the 2 or 3 weeks of negotiation on a final settlement. Rusk was receptive. U Thant also thought the Russians would want to have some face-saving reciprocal right of inspection, perhaps of Cuban refugee camps in the United States. On this point, Rusk was noncommittal.

From an informal source Rusk heard more evidence of Soviet interest in trading removal of missiles for a noninvasion pledge. The ABC News journalist John Scali had been contacted by a Soviet KGB officer based in Washington under cover as a journalist, Alexander Fomin. Fomin told Scali that he thought his government would be interested in a deal in which Soviet bases would be dismantled under UN supervision; Castro would promise not to accept offensive weapons of any kind; and the United States would pledge not to invade Cuba. Scali promptly reported this to the State Department and to Rusk.

Thinking that the Soviet government might be using Fomin as an informal channel to feel out U.S. interest in this bargain, Rusk encouraged Scali to pursue the matter further with Fomin.[5]

The new intelligence information prompted President Kennedy and Bundy to rework the White House announcement that had been discussed at the morning Executive Committee meeting. The final statement was read out by Pierre Salinger at 6:15. It said:[6]

tion activity was being engaged in at the intermediate range ballistic missile sites. Bulldozers and cranes were observed as late as Thursday actively clearing new areas within the sites and improving the approach roads to the launch pads.

Since Tuesday, October 23, missile-related activities have continued at the medium range ballistic missile sites resulting in progressive refinements at these facilities. For example, missiles were observed parked in the open on October 23. Surveillance on October 25 revealed that some of these missiles have now moved from their original parked positions. Cabling can be seen running from missile-ready tents to powered generators nearby.

In summary, there is no evidence to date indicating that there is any intention to dismantle or discontinue work on these missile sites. On the contrary the Soviets are rapidly continuing their construction of missile support and launch facilities and serious attempts are underway to camouflage their efforts.

While Salinger was reading this statement to the press corps, President Kennedy was in another meeting, in the Oval Office, with India's ambassador to the United States, B. K. Nehru, discussing China's recent invasion of India. This meeting, too, was secretly recorded. Although the Cuban crisis was not

5. Fomin's real name was Feklisov. The text presents the story as it was then understood by Rusk and others in the U.S. government. The real story is murkier, but it is plain that Feklisov was not actually acting as an agent of his government in this matter. See Alexander Fursenko and Timothy Naftali, "Using KGB Documents: The Scali-Feklisov Channel in the Cuban Missile Crisis," *Cold War International History Project Bulletin*, no. 5 (Spring 1995), 58.

6. Reprinted in Larson, *"Cuban Crisis,"* pp. 171–172.

the topic of discussion, during their conversation Kennedy mused about the Soviet enigma. "Does anybody know the mystery of the Communist system?" he asked, half rhetorically. Why would China attack India? "What is it they're getting out of this? They take on you. Why don't they take on us in Vietnam or something? Why did they take you on?" Ambassador Nehru said he did not know, and speculated that China might be trying to exploit U.S. preoccupation with the Cuban crisis. Before the Chinese attack, Khrushchev had been building better relations with India by promising military supplies. Kennedy told Nehru that India ought to see if Khrushchev would now keep his promise. Thinking of Cuba, Kennedy then commented on the lower standard of behavior accorded to people like Khrushchev. "If you're a son of a bitch [like Khrushchev], then every time he even looks at all agreeable everybody falls down with pleasure."

The meeting with Nehru ended at about 6:20. Immediately afterward Kennedy put through his daily call to Prime Minister Macmillan.[7]

President Kennedy: Hello, Prime Minister.

Macmillan: Hello, what's the news now?

President Kennedy: Well, Governor Stevenson saw U Thant this afternoon and made our proposals about the importation of arms ceasing, and that work on these bases stopping, and leading to eventual dismemberment.

There are some reports around, some Russian conversations, but it's rather unofficial and unreliable, about some thought that it's possible they might do something about withdrawing the weapons if they could get a territorial guarantee of Cuba. But that is so unofficial that I'm not in a position now to know whether there's anything to it or not.

Khrushchev told U Thant that he would keep his ships out of there for the time being, but he wouldn't do it very long. He isn't giving us very much because actually he's got no ships in the area anyway. But at least he's made that announcement; he's keeping his ships out of there for the time being.

We are continuing the quarantine. The buildup of the sites continues, however. And I put a statement out this afternoon describing how the buildup is going on so that, unless in the next 48 hours we get some political suggestions as to dismantling the base, we're then going to be faced with a problem of what to do about this buildup.

7. The following transcript combines the American notes (through the end of Kennedy's initial statement) and the British record for the remainder. See National Security Files, box 37, Cuba—General—Macmillan Telephone Conversations, 10/62–11/62, JFKL; PRO, PREM 11/3690, 24020. We have modified the punctuation, but not the text.

Macmillan: The idea that you have just mentioned is that Cuba might be made like Belgium was by international guarantee—an inviolable country, and all of us would guarantee its neutrality and inviolability. Is that a possibility?

President Kennedy: That is a matter which seems to me we ought to be thinking about, and we will be talking about that in the next 24 hours as to whether there is any room for a settlement on that basis.

Probably with Castro in power it would leave the Russians, perhaps, free to

himself propose to the United Nations, which I believe they would accept, that he should go with a team and ensure that these missiles were made inoperable during the period of any conference or discussion.

President Kennedy: Yes, that is correct. There would have to be some technical way of determining that these weapons were being made inoperable and that work on the sites was ceasing during these conversations, that is correct.

Macmillan: Yes. But do you think that U Thant . . . I am quite sure that Hammarskjold[8] would have done such a thing.

Mightn't he [U Thant] suggest to the United Nations that he would do this? He would go and do it with a team, and see that they were not operable during the period of the talks.

President Kennedy: Yes, there is some suggestion of that. Also, they want to inspect some of the refugee camps in Florida and Nicaragua, Guatemala and Swan Island. That was the summing up of the conversation with the Governor [Stevenson], and I am looking into it. I don't think we have got anything going there that would be difficult to inspect, but this is all part of the political proposals which are now being looked at in view of the Governor's conversation.

So I would sum it up, Prime Minister, by saying that by tomorrow morning or noon, we should be in a position of knowing whether there is some political proposal that we would agree to, and whether the Russians are interested in it or not. We will know a little more, I think, by tomorrow afternoon.

8. Dag Hammarskjold, the previous Secretary General of the United Nations, had died in an airplane crash in Africa in 1961.

In the meanwhile, the quarantine stays, if he doesn't send ships in. We let a ship pass this afternoon [the *Coalangatta*]. But there are no other ships within 48 hours or so, so we don't expect any problems on the sea.

The problem that concerns us is the continued buildup, and I issued a statement on that today. I think I can probably get you a little more precise information on the various political proposals and U Thant's conversation with Stevenson. I'll send you a report of that tonight, and then you will have it in the morning.

Macmillan: There is just a third point that occurred to us. If we want to help the Russians to save face, would it be worthwhile our undertaking to immobilize our Thor missiles which are here in England during the same period?[9] During the conference?

President Kennedy: Well, let me put that into the machinery and then I'll be in touch with you on that.

Macmillan: I think it is just an idea, that it might help the Russians to accept . . .

President Kennedy: Sure, Prime Minister, let me send that over to the Department. I think we don't want to have too many dismantlings. But it is possible that that proposal might help. They might also insist on Greece, on Turkey, and Italy. But I will keep in mind your suggestion here, so that if it gets into that, it may be advantageous.

Macmillan: Yes, I don't see why they should ask for more, because we have got 60 [Thor missiles]. So that missile for missile, you see, there wouldn't be as many as that in Cuba.

President Kennedy: Yes. That is correct. After listening to Adlai Stevenson's report you will have that in mind in the conversation.

Macmillan: Well now, if there are any other suggestions that we can make, you will probably send me a message tonight and we can get in touch with you tomorrow.

President Kennedy: That is correct, Prime Minister. I think we will just have to wait until we have analyzed this conversation [between Stevenson and U Thant]. I haven't seen the entire conversation, but I think that the prospect of a trade of these missiles for some guarantee for Cuba is still so vague that I

9. The Thor missiles, deployed in the United Kingdom in 1959, had soon been deemed obsolescent, and by the time of this call the U.S. and Britain had already agreed that they would be withdrawn later in 1962. Macmillan's offer was, however, symbolically significant, since there was no precedent for such an outside intrusion into the defensive arrangements of a NATO country.

am not really in a position to say that there is any possibility of an easing up. Maybe by tomorrow evening at this time I'll know better.

Macmillan: Yes. Because, of course, at this stage any movement by you may produce a result in Berlin which would be very bad for us all. That's the danger now.

President Kennedy: Well, we are not going to have any problems, because he is keeping his ships out of there and, as I say, we let one ship pass today

than we have done, up till now.

But of course, on the other hand, if the missile sites continue, and get constructed, and we don't do anything about it, then I would suppose that it would have quite an effect on Berlin anyway.

Macmillan: Yes. I think that is the difficulty.

But anyway there are three political plans which we have now got going, and if I may I'll send you a message concerning them, and you will send me the result of the U Thant conversation.

President Kennedy: I'll send you a memorandum, based on the topic of the conversation Stevenson had with U Thant.

I will also keep in touch with you tomorrow at this time, or otherwise I'll send you a message tomorrow. Or maybe I'll send you a message, unless we get something immediate.

And, number three, we will not take any further action until I have talked to you, in any case.

I won't bother to call you tomorrow, because I may be away from here tomorrow evening, and I assume you may be too. But I will send you a message if there is anything new. And, in any case, I'll talk to you on the phone before we do anything of a drastic nature.

Macmillan: Thank you. I'll be here all day, so you can get me any time of the day tomorrow, or Sunday [October 28].

President Kennedy: Prime Minister, I am going to send you a note tonight, or tomorrow morning, about asking, if it's agreeable with you, if General Norstad [can] stay on till January 1 and let there be an overlap with Lemnitzer's tour of duty, and Lemnitzer go on and take over the American forces, and be there and have a 60-day period to be sort of adjusted to his new responsibilities. You will be getting a formal letter, and I didn't want to say anything about it because we haven't been in touch with General de Gaulle as yet, who is very sensitive in these NATO matters. But I will be in touch with you, and I will assume probably that that suggestion will be agreeable to you.

Macmillan: That seems, indeed, very sensible.

President Kennedy: Well, I will be in touch in a formal way with you tomorrow on that matter, and I'll send tonight the memorandum of the U Thant conversation. And I hope all goes well.

Macmillan: Well, thank you very much. And of course Bundy can always ring up de Zulueta here. They can speak to each other, so it is quite easy to have a talk.

President Kennedy: Fine, Prime Minister. And I'll be in touch with you very shortly. Thank you, and good night.

Macmillan: Good night.

———————

Very soon after this conversation Macmillan sent off the following message to President Kennedy to clarify the British position:[10]

My dear Friend,

I thought it would be useful just to confirm the main points of our talk tonight, and I shall expect to get from you a report of the conversations between Stevenson and U Thant and the situation as you see it following these talks. This will be very helpful to me and I am grateful. In the political field there were three possibilities which we mentioned:

1. The inviolability of Cuba might become subject to an international guarantee by all the great powers, provided that it was demilitarized. I was wrong in making the analogy with Belgium before 1914, it is more nearly an analogy with Austria today under the State Treaty.[11]

2. If no settlement can be reached out of U Thant's present conversations, U Thant should make a proposal to the Security Council and/or to the [General] Assembly informing them that he intends to go to Cuba himself, with a suitable team, to see the situation and to secure the immobilization of the missiles and the stopping of further work on the sites to allow discussions to open.

3. I put in the proposal that it might be helpful to save the Russians' face

———————

10. PRO, PREM 11/3690, 24020. Though the message is dated October 27, it in fact arrived in Washington later in the evening of October 26 Washington time.

11. The State Treaty, concluded in 1955 among Austria, the Soviet Union, the United States, Great Britain, and France, provided for the neutralization of Austria in exchange for the withdrawal of the occupying forces of the 4 powers.

if we undertook during the same period to allow the immobilization of our Thor missiles, of which there are 60, under United Nations supervision. This has, of course, the disadvantage that it brings in the concept of bargaining bases in Europe against those in Cuba. Nevertheless if it would turn the scale I would be willing to propose it to U Thant and it might be less invidious for us to take the lead rather than place the burden on the Turks. You said you would have this idea looked at.

Dear Mr. President,

I have received your letter of October 25. From your letter, I got the feeling that you have some understanding of the situation which has developed and [some] sense of responsibility. I value this.

Now we have already publicly exchanged our evaluations of the events around Cuba and each of us has set forth his explanation and his under-standing of these events. Consequently, I would think that, apparently, a continuation of an exchange of opinions at such a distance, even in the form of secret letters, would hardly add anything to that which one side has already said to the other.

I think you will understand me correctly if you are really concerned about the welfare of the world. Everyone needs peace: both capitalists, if they have not lost their reason, and, still more, communists, people who know to value not only their own lives but, more than anything, the lives of the peoples. We, communists, are against all wars between states in general and have been defending the cause of peace since we came into the world. We have always regarded war as a calamity, and not as a game or as a means of attainment of definite goals, nor, all the more, as a goal in itself. Our goals are clear, and the means to attain them is labor. War is our enemy and a calamity for all of the peoples.

12. What follows is the version of the letter actually read and relied on by the decisionmakers at the time, namely the unofficial translation made by the U.S. embassy in Moscow when it transmitted the letter to Washington. It is reprinted, with some notes about later corrections, in Larson, "Cuban Crisis," pp. 175–180. It differs in various, subtle ways from the official State Department translation that was prepared later and appears in many of the documentary compilations.

It is thus that, we, Soviet people, and, together with us, other peoples as well, understand the questions of war and peace. I can, in any case, firmly say this for the peoples of the Socialist countries, as well as for all progressive people who want peace, happiness, and friendship among the peoples.

I see, Mr. President, that you are not devoid of a sense of anxiety for the fate of the world, of understanding, and of what war entails. What would war give you? You are threatening us with war. But you well know that the very least which you would receive in reply would be that you would experience the same consequences as those which you send us. And that must be clear to us, people invested with authority, trust, and responsibilities. We must not succumb to intoxication and petty passions, regardless of whether elections are impending in this or that country, or not impending. These are all transient things, but if indeed war should break out, then it would not be in our power to stop it, for such is the logic of war. I have participated in two wars and I know that war ends when it has rolled through cities and villages, everywhere sowing death and destruction.

In the name of the Soviet Government and the Soviet people, I assure you that your conclusions regarding offensive weapons in Cuba are groundless. It is apparent from what you have written me that our conceptions are different on this score, or rather, we have different estimates of these or those military means. Indeed, in reality, the same forms of weapons can have different interpretations.

You are a military man and, I hope, will understand me. Let us take, for example, a simple cannon. What kind of means is this: offensive or defensive? A cannon is a defensive means if it is set up to defend boundaries or a fortified area. But if one concentrates artillery, and adds to it the necessary number of troops, then the same cannons do become an offensive means, because they prepare and clear the way for infantry to attack. The same happens with missile-nuclear weapons as well, with any type of this weapon.

You are mistaken if you think that any of our means on Cuba are offensive. However, let us not quarrel now. It is apparent that I will not be able to convince you of this. But I say to you: You, Mr. President, are a military man and should understand: Can one attack, if one has on one's territory even an enormous quantity of missiles of various effective radiuses and various power, but using only these means. These missiles are a means of extermination and destruction. But one cannot attack with these missiles, even nuclear missiles of a power of 100 megatons because only people, troops, can attack. Without people, any means, however powerful, cannot be offensive.

How can one, consequently, give such a completely incorrect interpretation as you are now giving, to the effect that some sort of means on Cuba are offensive. All the means located there, and I assure you of this, have a defensive character, are on Cuba solely for the purpose of defense, and we have sent them to Cuba at the request of the Cuban Government. You, however, say that these are offensive means.

But, Mr. President, do you really seriously think that Cuba can attack the United States and that even we together with Cuba can attack you from the territory of Cuba? Can you really think that way? How is it possible? We do not understand this. Has something so new appeared in military strategy

Vienna gives me the right to talk to you this way.[13]

This indicated that we are normal people, that we correctly understand and evaluate the situation. Consequently, how can we permit the incorrect actions that you ascribe to us? Only lunatics or suicides, who themselves want to perish and to destroy the whole world before they die, could do this. We, however, want to live and do not at all want to destroy your country. We want something quite different: to compete with your country on a peaceful basis. We quarrel with you; we have differences on ideological questions. But our view of the world consists in this, that ideological questions, as well as economic problems, should be solved not by military means, they must be solved on the basis of peaceful competition, i.e., as this is understood in capitalist society, on the basis of competition. We have proceeded and are proceeding from the fact that the peaceful coexistence of the two different social-political systems, now existing in the world, is necessary, that it is necessary to assure a stable peace. That is the sort of principle we hold.

You have now proclaimed piratical measures, which were employed in the Middle Ages, when ships proceeding in international waters were attacked, and you have called this "a quarantine" around Cuba. Our vessels, apparently will soon enter the zone which your Navy is patrolling. I assure you that these vessels, now bound for Cuba, are carrying the most innocent peaceful cargoes. Do you really think that we only occupy ourselves with the carriage of so-called offensive weapons, atomic and hydrogen bombs? Although perhaps your military people imagine that these [cargos] are some sort of

13. The confrontational summit conference in June 1961, the only time the two men talked in person.

special type of weapon, I assure you that they are the most ordinary peaceful products.

Consequently, Mr. President, let us show good sense. I assure you that on those ships, which are bound for Cuba, there are no weapons at all. The weapons which were necessary for the defense of Cuba are already there. I do not want to say that there were no shipments of any weapons at all. No, there were such shipments. But now Cuba has already received the necessary means of defense.

I don't know whether you can understand me and believe me. But I should like to have you believe in yourself and to agree that one cannot give way to passions; it is necessary to control them. And in what direction are events now developing? If you stop the vessels, then, as you yourself know, that would be piracy. If we started to do that with regard to your ships, then you would also be as indignant as we and the whole world now are. One cannot give another interpretation to such actions, because one cannot legalize lawlessness. If this were permitted then, there would be no peace, there would also be no peaceful coexistence. We should then be forced to put into effect the necessary measures of a defensive character to protect our interests in accordance with international law. Why should this be done? To what would it all this lead?

Let us normalize relations. We have received an appeal from U Thant, Acting Secretary General of the U.N., with his proposals. I have already answered him. His proposals come to this, that our side should not transport armaments of any kind to Cuba for a certain period of time, while negotiations are being conducted—and we are ready to enter such negotiations—and the other side should not undertake any sort of piratical actions against vessels engaged in navigation on the high seas. I consider these proposals reasonable. This would be a way out of the situation which has been created, which would give the peoples the possibility of breathing calmly. You have asked what happened, what evoked the delivery of weapons to Cuba? You have spoken about this to our Minister of Foreign Affairs.[14] I will tell you frankly, Mr. President, what evoked it.

We were very grieved by the fact—I spoke about it in Vienna—that a landing took place, that an attack on Cuba was committed, as a result of which many Cubans perished. You yourself told me then that this had been a mistake. I respected that explanation. You repeated it to me several times, pointing out that not everybody occupying a high position would acknowledge his mistakes as you had done. I value such frankness. For my part, I told you that we too possess no less courage; we also acknowledged those

14. At the October 18 meeting in Washington between Kennedy and Gromyko.

mistakes which had been committed during the history of our state, and not only acknowledged, but sharply condemned them.[15]

If you are really concerned about the peace and welfare of your people, and this is your responsibility as President, then I, as the Chairman of the Council of Ministers, am concerned for my people. Moreover, the preservation of world peace should be our joint concern, since if, under contemporary conditions, war should break out, it would be a war not only between the reciprocal claims, but a worldwide cruel and destructive war.

time, commanded the US expeditionary corps during the "American Adventure in Siberia."

We know how difficult it is to accomplish a revolution and how difficult it is to reconstruct a country on new foundations. We sincerely sympathize with Cuba and the Cuban people, but we are not interfering in questions of domestic structure; we are not interfering in their affairs. The Soviet Union desires to help the Cubans build their life as they themselves wish and that others should not hinder them.

You once said that the United States was not preparing an invasion. But you also declared that you sympathized with the Cuban counterrevolutionary emigrants, that you support them and would help them to realize their plans against the present government of Cuba. It is also not a secret to anyone that the threat of armed attack, aggression, has constantly hung, and continues to hang over Cuba. It is only this which impelled us to respond to the request of the Cuban government to furnish it aid for the strengthening of the defensive capacity of this country.

If assurances were given by the President and the government of the United States that the USA itself would not participate in an attack on Cuba and would restrain others from actions of this sort, if you would recall your fleet, this would immediately change everything. I am not speaking for Fidel Castro, but I think that he and the Government of Cuba, evidently, would

15. A reference to Khrushchev's celebrated denunciation of Stalin's excesses, in 1956.

16. During the civil war following the 1917 Russian revolution, Britain and France intervened against the Bolsheviks in 1918 in the Arctic and near the Black Sea. In 1919 and 1920 Japan, the United States, and other countries dispatched troops that briefly intervened in the fighting in Siberia.

declare demobilization and would appeal to the people to get down to peaceful labor. Then, too, the question of armaments would disappear, since, if there is no threat, then armaments are a burden for every people. Then, too, the question of the destruction, not only of the armaments which you call offensive, but of all other armaments as well, would look different.

I spoke in the name of the Soviet government in the United Nations and introduced a proposal for the disbandment of all armies and for the destruction of all armaments. How then can I now count on those armaments?

Armaments bring only disasters. When one accumulates them, this damages the economy, and if one puts them to use, then they destroy people on both sides. Consequently, only a madman can believe that armaments are the principal means in the life of society. No, they are an enforced loss of human energy, and what is more are for the destruction of man himself. If people do not show wisdom, then in the final analysis they will come to a clash, like blind moles, and then reciprocal extermination will begin.

Let us therefore show statesmanlike wisdom. I propose: we, for our part, will declare that our ships, bound for Cuba, will not carry any kind of armaments. You would declare that the United States will not invade Cuba with its forces and will not support any sort of forces which might intend to carry out an invasion of Cuba. Then the necessity for the presence of our military specialists in Cuba would disappear.

Mr. President, I appeal to you to weigh well what the aggressive, piratical actions, which you have declared the USA intends to carry out in international waters, would lead to. You yourself know that any sensible man simply cannot agree with this, cannot recognize your right to such actions.

If you did this as the first step towards the unleashing of war, well then, it is evident that nothing else is left to us but to accept this challenge of yours. If, however, you have not lost your self-control and sensibly conceive what this might lead to, then, Mr. President, we and you ought not now to pull on the ends of the rope in which you have tied the knots of war, because the more the two of us pull, the tighter this knot will be tied. And a moment may come when that knot will be tied so tight that even he who tied will not have the strength to untie it, and then it will be necessary to cut that knot. And what that would mean is not for me to explain to you, because you yourself understand perfectly of what terrible forces our countries dispose.

Consequently, if there is no intention to tighten that knot and thereby to doom the world to the catastrophe of thermonuclear war, then let us not only relax the forces pulling on the ends of the rope, let us take measures to untie that knot. We are ready for this.

We welcome all forces which stand on positions of peace. Consequently, I expressed gratitude to Mr. Bertrand Russell, too, who manifests alarm and concern for the fate of the world, and I readily responded to the appeal of the Acting Secretary General of the U.N., U Thant.

These, Mr. President, are my thoughts, which, if you agreed with them, could put an end to that tense situation which is disturbing all peoples.

These thoughts are dictated by a sincere desire to relieve the situation, to remove the threat of war.

Respectfully yours, N. Khrushchev

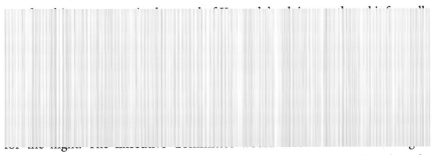

consider how the United States should respond to the letter and explore the apparent Soviet proposal.

SATURDAY, OCTOBER 27

10:00 A.M.

CABINET ROOM

The Executive Committee began what would become the longest day of the crisis with an intelligence briefing. McCone emphasized again the rapid pace of continuing work at the missile sites as well as the fact that almost all the MRBMs were now ready for action. Analysts were worried by the observation of tracks that seemed to indicate that missiles were being moved into the ready position and had been checked out during the night, but we do not know whether McCone mentioned this in his briefing. He did highlight the key points from that morning's Watch Committee report, which were:[1]

Based on the latest low-level reconnaissance mission, 3 of the 4 MRBM sites at San Cristobal and the 2 sites at Sagua La Grande appear to be fully operational. No further sites or missiles have been identified.[2]

The mobilization of Cuban military forces continues at a high rate. However, they remain under orders not to take any hostile action unless attacked.

Steps toward establishing an integrated air defense system are under way. On the diplomatic front, Cuban representatives are trying to plant the idea that Havana would be receptive to U.N. mediation. They indicate, however, that a prerequisite must be "proof" that the US does not intend to attack Cuba.

Despite Khrushchev's declaration to U Thant that Soviet ships would temporarily avoid the quarantine area, we have no information as yet that

---

1. CIA, "The Crisis USSR/Cuba," 27 October 1962, in McAuliffe, *CIA Documents*, p. 328.
2. The identification of the FROG tactical nuclear rockets was mentioned prominently in that morning's interagency estimate on missile readiness. The President had already been briefed on them the previous day.

the 6 Soviet and 3 satellite ships en route have changed course. A Swedish vessel, believed to be under charter to the USSR [the *Coalangatta*], refused to stop yesterday when intercepted by a US destroyer and was allowed to continue to Havana.

No significant redeployment of Soviet ground, air or naval forces have been noted. However, there are continuing indications of increased readiness among some units. Three F-class submarines have been identified on the surface inside or near the quarantine line.

After the briefing from McCone, McNamara reported on the status of the quarantine and the positions of Soviet-bloc ships moving toward Cuba. The *Grozny*, about 600 miles from Cuba, was finally approaching the quarantine line.[3] He recommended that ships be ordered to stand by in readiness to board the vessel.

Ball pointed out that the Soviets might not know just where the quarantine line was being drawn. The group agreed that a message should be sent quickly to U Thant, asking him to be sure to tell the Soviet representatives in New York where the line was being drawn, so that they could decide whether to turn back the *Grozny*. Toward the end of the discussion of this message, President Kennedy turned on the tape recorder.

President Kennedy: We've got to be in a position to put it out [the message to U Thant].

Sorensen: We could be in position in an hour.

President Kennedy: Okay. Put it out. Send it over to him.

Bundy: Any other ships besides the *Grozny*, Bob?

McNamara: No, I don't . . . I believe we'll find the *Grozny* does not carry prohibited material.

Unidentified: That's what I think, too. It's scheduled.

---

3. The location of the *Grozny* had been lost for a time, and the ship was found again that morning by SAC reconnaissance aircraft. In these efforts one of the aircraft, an RB-47, crashed at takeoff and its 4-man crew was killed.

McNamara: But I think we ought to stop it anyhow, and use force if necessary.

Unidentified: You've given us the information we should give to the cutoff [the quarantine line], where it should be.

McNamara: Yes. Yes. I'll get that. Now, other [matters], Mr. President.

We would recommend 2 daylight surveillance missions today. We're prepared to send one flight out of approximately 8 aircraft. I say approximately because it might be 7 or 9. [Send it out] immediately and have it over the target at about 11:30 Cuban time, and send another flight out this afternoon about 4:00.

President Kennedy: Different place?

McNamara: Same targets.

President Kennedy: Well, let me ask two questions, Bob. First, are you sending different pilots who have experience?

McNamara: We've got our—the fighter pilots we instructed last night to try to rotate some fighter pilots through this reconnaissance, so we'll get some people . . .

President Kennedy: Now, the other thing is we've got to [have them] eyeball for us. And then we're going to have them interrogated afterwards and [unclear] see how much they can pick up.

Taylor?: I'll leave it to the lead pilot. He'll know what the purpose of it is, and if you need to be able to make a swing around, take another look, we will.

President Kennedy: [apparently reading from news ticker copy handed him by Sorensen] "Premier Khrushchev told President Kennedy yesterday he would withdraw offensive weapons from Cuba if the United States withdrew rockets from Turkey."

Bundy: No he didn't.

Sorensen: That's how it is read by both of the associations that put it out so far. Reuters said the same thing.

Unidentified: He didn't really say that, did he?

President Kennedy: That may not be . . . He may be putting out another letter. What is our explanation? But anyway, they've got this clear about how . . .

Let's just go on, then. Are you finished there, Mr. Secretary?

Pierre? That wasn't in the letter we received, was it?

Salinger: No. I read it pretty carefully. It did not read that way to me.

President Kennedy: Is he supposed to be putting out a letter he's written to me or putting out a statement?

Salinger: Putting out a letter he wrote to you.

President Kennedy: Well, let's just sit tight on it [unclear].

Bundy: Is it a different statement?

Rusk: I think we'd better get [the text]. Will you go and check and be sure that the letter that's coming in on the ticker is the letter that we were seeing last night?

McNamara: Okay. Then may we issue the orders, then, for 2 mission [surveillances]? Mac [Bundy], would you do that?

President Kennedy: What's the advantage of the second mission?

Unidentified: Okay.

Unidentified: All right, sir.

McNamara: Two in daylight, one tonight.

Bundy: The night is laid on but not finally authorized?

Unidentified: Not exactly, but if you want to do it, that's all right.

Bundy: Well, then we believe there ought to be an announcement of that or at least as of yesterday.

Rusk: I really think we ought to talk about the political part of this thing, because if we prolong it more than a few days on the basis of the withdrawal of these missiles from Turkey—not from Turkey, from Cuba—the Turkish thing hasn't been injected into the conversation in New York, and it wasn't in the letter last night. It thus appears to be something quite new.

McNamara: This is what worries me about the whole deal. If you go through that letter, to a layman it looks to be full of holes. I think my proposal would be to keep—

Bundy: Keeping the heat on.

McNamara: Keep the heat on. This is why I would recommend the 2 daylight and one night missions, and I fully agree we ought to put out an announcement that we *are* going to send the night mission over.

Bundy: Which way do you want it to stand? That we approved it [the night reconnaissance mission], Mr. President, subject to appeal, or do you want to hold it?

McNamara: We can hold it, Mr. President.

President Kennedy: I think what I'd like to do is . . . I think we ought to go ahead, so it's all right with me. I think we might have one more conversation about it, however, at about 6:00, just in case during the day we get something more.

McNamara: There's plenty of time. We'll keep it on alert.

President Kennedy: That's right. We plan to put it on unless there's something in the daytime.

Bundy: Well, the announcement can . . . That is a complication. We can't very well make the announcement and not do it [the night reconnaissance].

McNamara: We won't make the announcement. But at that time we'll make it.

Bundy: Well, I would suggest we review it at 4:00 and make the announcement.

McNamara: Or we'll have the announcement prepared, and how we're going to get it out.

Bundy: If you make the announcement late it's not much good. So have the announcement all ready to go from the Pentagon at 4:00.

McNamara: And we'll have some time to chat over it.

Bundy: We'll talk to the President at that time.

Unidentified: Okay.

Vice President Johnson: Does that involve these flares dropping and so on?

McNamara: Yes, it does, Mr. Vice President.

Unidentified: Will you be ready to beam it in?

Unidentified: Yes, sir, if I get the word on the radio.

President Kennedy: In case this [newly reported Khrushchev proposal] *is* an accurate statement, where are we with our conversations with the Turks about the withdrawal of these . . .?

Nitze: Hare says this is absolutely anathema and is a matter of prestige and politics.[4] George [Ball] has read the report from Finletter.[5]

---

4. Raymond Hare was U.S. Ambassador to Turkey. A few days earlier the State Department had cabled him to ask how he thought the Turks would react to a deal involving the withdrawal of the Jupiter missiles from Turkey. Hare was not instructed to approach the Turks, just to offer his opinion. Hare was sure the Turks would object. "Problem would be partly psycho-political, partly substantive; psycho-political, in sense that Turks are proud, courageous people who do not understand concept or process of compromise . . . Problem is also substantive in sense that Turks . . . set great store on arms which they feel necessary meet their needs and were adamant in refusing our suggestion last year that Jupiter project not be implemented . . . if we insist to contrary, demand for arms to fill vacuum would be specific and sizeable"; Ankara 587, 26 October 1962, National Security Files, box 226, NATO—Weapons, Cables—Turkey, JFKL.

In the second section of his cable, received in Washington as this meeting was getting underway, Hare suggested 4 alternatives (elaborated in a third section that came in during the early

Ball: We have a report from Finletter, and we've also gotten a report from Rome on the Italians which indicates that that would be relatively easy.

Turkey creates more of a problem. We would have to work it out with the Turks on the basis of putting a Polaris [submarine] in the waters, and even that might not be enough according to the judgment that we've had on the spot. We've got one paper on it already, and we're having more work done right now.[6] It is a complicated problem because these [Jupiter missiles] were

Bundy: It's very odd, Mr. President. If he's changed his terms from a long letter to you and an urgent appeal from the Counselor [Fomin] only last night, set in the purely Cuban context, it seems to me we're well within our . . . There's nothing wrong with our posture in sticking to that line.

---

afternoon): (1) no deal, which would be easiest; (2) unilateral phaseout of Jupiters to be replaced by some NATO multilateral seaborne deterrent force in Polaris submarines; (3) a trade with Soviets on Turkey and Cuba but one that was kept on a "strictly secret basis with Soviets"; Hare wondered if the Soviets could be trusted to keep the secret and noted that the Turks would still need to be placated with other arms; (4) a deal that became public, which "would be most difficult of all."

The Turks' initial reaction to the crisis had been completely supportive; they had asked only for accelerated deliveries of F-104 fighter aircraft and spare parts for F-100 fighter bombers. A day later, on October 24, the Turkish foreign minister expressed shock about public comparisons between Turkey and Cuba, and renewed the request for the military equipment. Two days later the foreign minister's line was the same, and he was "in exceedingly good and confident mood"; Ankara 576, 23 October 1962; Ankara 581, 24 October 1962; and Ankara 585, 26 October 1962; ibid.

5. Thomas Finletter was the U.S. permanent representative to NATO's North Atlantic Council, in effect, the U.S. ambassador to NATO, then headquartered in Paris. In the same October 24 message that asked for Hare's opinion on a Cuba-Turkey trade, the State Department also asked for Finletter's view of the matter. Finletter thought the Turks would attach great symbolic value to the Jupiter missiles, and he also mentioned the possibility of trying to offer some sort of alternative based on the new Polaris submarines; Paris Polto 506, 25 October 1962, ibid.

6. Ball was probably referring to a memo from the relevant State officials that used this situation to renew the idea of a multilateral MRBM force, phasing out Turkish Jupiters once this force—based at sea—could take its place. See Tyler, Rostow, and Talbot to Rusk, "Cuba," 24 October 1962, Cuban Missile Crisis Files, 1992 Releases box, National Security Archive, Washington, D.C.

7. A public decision of NATO ministers in December 1957, reiterated in subsequent communiqués.

President Kennedy: But let's wait, and let's assume that this is an accurate report of what he's now proposing this morning. There may have been some changes over there.

Bundy: I still think he's in a difficult position to change it overnight, having sent you a personal communication on the other line.

President Kennedy: Well now, let's say he has changed it. This is his latest position.

Bundy: Well, I would answer back saying that "I would prefer to deal with your—with your interesting proposals of last night."

President Kennedy: Well now, that's what we ought to think about.

We're going to be in an insupportable position on this matter if this becomes his proposal. In the first place, we last year tried to get the missiles out of there because they're not militarily useful, number one.

Number two, it's going to—to any man at the United Nations or any other rational man, it will look like a very fair trade.

Nitze: I don't think so. I don't think . . . I think you would get support from the United Nations on the proposition: "Deal with this Cuban thing. We'll talk about other things later." I think everybody else is worried that they'll be included in this great big trade if it goes beyond Cuba.

Rusk: That's true of the allies. It would not be true of the neutrals.

Bundy: No.

Rusk: But let's go on for a moment to think about this. One possibility would be to, if this is persistent—

Sorensen?: Why are you stopping, Mr. Secretary?

[Unclear response by Rusk.]

President Kennedy: [apparently reading from a news ticker] "A special message appeared to call for negotiations, and both nations, Cuba and Turkey, should give their consent to the United Nations to visit their territories. Mr. Khrushchev said that, in the Security Council, the Soviet Union would solemnly pledge not to use its territory as a bridgehead for an attack on Turkey, called for a similar pledge from the United States not to let its territory be used as a bridgehead for an attack on Cuba. A broadcast shortly after said it was out of the question for the U.S. to abandon its Turkish military bases . . ."

Now, we've known this was coming for a week. We can't. It's going to be hung up here now.

Unidentified: We might just request negotiations.

Unidentified: We've done it.

Unidentified: No, we have not.

Rusk: We haven't talked with the Turks. The Turks have talked with us—in NATO.

President Kennedy: Well, have we gone to the Turkish government before this came out this week? I've talked about it now for a week. Have we had any conversations in Turkey, with the Turks?

Rusk: We've asked Finletter and Hare to give us their judgments on it. We've not actually talked with the Turks.

why we are going to take hostile military action in Cuba, against these sites, what we've been thinking about. [I'm] saying that he's saying: "If you'll get yours out of Turkey, we'll get ours out of Cuba." I think we've got a very touchy point here.

Bundy: I don't see why we pick that track when he's offered us the other track within the last 24 hours. You think the public one is serious?

President Kennedy: I think you have to assume that this is their new and latest position, and it's a public one.

Ball: What would you think of releasing the letter of yesterday?

Bundy: I think it has a good deal of virtue.

President Kennedy: Yeah, but I think we have to be now thinking about what our position is going to be on *this* one, because this is the one that's before us, and before the world.

Sorensen: As between the two, I think it's clear that practically everyone here would favor the private proposal.

Rusk: We're not being offered a choice. We *may* not be offered the (a) choice [referring to the private proposal].

President Kennedy: But seriously, there are disadvantages also to the private one, which is this guarantee of Cuba.

But in any case, this is now his official one. And we can release his other one, and it's different, but this is the one that the Soviet government obviously is going on.

Nitze: Isn't it possible that they're going on a dual track, one a public track and the other a private track? The private track is related to the Soviets and

Cuba, and the public track is one that's in order to confuse the public scene with additional pressures.

President Kennedy: It's possible.

Thompson: I think, personally, that statement is one that the Soviets take seriously.

Rusk: Well, I think, yes. I think that the NATO–Warsaw Pact arms problem is a separate problem, and that ought to be discussed between NATO and the Warsaw Pact. They've got hundreds of missiles looking down the throat of every NATO country. And [long pause] I think this is—we have to get it into *that context.* The Cuba thing is a Western Hemisphere problem, an intrusion into the Western Hemisphere.

[Unclear group discussion.]

Nitze: I think we ought to stand as much as we can on a separate basis.

Unidentified: Absolutely.

Nitze: Fight the Turkish one with the best arguments we can. I'd handle this thing so that we continue on the real track, which is to try to get the missiles out of Cuba pursuant to the private negotiation.

Bundy: The other way, it seems to me, is, if we accept the notion of a trade at this stage, our position will come apart very fast.

We are in a very difficult position. It isn't as if we'd got the missiles out, Mr. President. It would be different. Or if we had any understanding with the Turks that they ought to come out, it would be different. Neither of these is the case.

President Kennedy: Well, I'd like to know how much we've done about it and how much did we talk about it.

Bundy: We decided *not* to, Mr. President. We decided *not* to play it directly with the Turks.

Rusk: —our own representatives to their—

Ball: If we talked to the Turks, they would bring it up in NATO. This thing will be all over Western Europe, and our position would have been undermined.

Bundy: That's right.

Ball: Because immediately the Soviet Union would know that this thing was being discussed. The Turks feel very strongly about this. We persuaded them that this *was* an essential requirement, and they feel that it's a matter of prestige and a matter of real [unclear].

Bundy: In our own terms it would already be clear that we were trying to sell our allies for our interests. That would be the view in all of NATO. Now, it's irrational and it's crazy, but it's a *terribly* powerful fact.

Thompson: Particularly in the case that this is a message to you and to U Thant. It seems to me we ought to get word to Stevenson that, if this is put up up there, he should immediately say we will not discuss the Turkish bases.

Bundy: The problem is Cuba. The Turks are not a threat to the peace. Nobody smells the Turks as—

President Kennedy: I think it would be better, rather than saying that, until we've got time to think about it . . . Than saying: "Well, the fact of the matter

It leaves the steering in the hands . . . Well, we know what the problem is here.

Rusk: Well, I think that it's relevant here to be able to say that we supported the declaration of Iran that they would not accept foreign missiles in Iran. The Turkish problem is a NATO–Warsaw Pact problem. And it's an arms problem between these two groups that is something for these two groups to talk about with *each other* as a problem of disarmament with respect to NATO and Warsaw Pact.

Dillon: Well, there's also this thing of upsetting the status quo, and we did not upset it in Iran [unclear].

President Kennedy: He's put this out in a way to cause maximum tension and embarrassment. It's not as if it was a private proposal, which would give us an opportunity to negotiate with the Turks. He has put it out in a way that the Turks are bound to say that they don't agree to this. And therefore—

Dillon: There's another military thing to it. It may be preparations for counteraction against those particular bases once we leave Cuba again. Could be that.

[Unclear discussion.]

President Kennedy: Until we have gotten our position a little clearer, we ought to go with this last night's business, so that that gives us about an hour or two—we don't have Khrushchev.

Rusk: There's nothing coming in yet on *our* tickers. I don't know whether—

President Kennedy: He says he'd like to consider the following statement be issued—this is Stevenson [proposing the following statement]:

"The United States never had any territorial designs against Cuba, but of course we cannot tolerate Soviet Cuban aggression against us or our sister republics. The Soviet offer to withdraw weapons in Cuba is welcome, and we give assurance of our peaceful intentions towards Cuba. In the meantime, it is imperative that further developments of Soviet bases stop and discussions proceed with the Secretary General of the United Nations in New York." Governor Stevenson recommends that such a statement be made in order to prevent the Soviets from capturing the peace offensive.

Governor Stevenson also recommends that we not consider the Turkish offer as reported in the attached Reuters dispatch as an alternative or an addition to the Khrushchev proposal in his letter.

I think that we ought to get a statement *ready* which will—which would make references to *last night's*—back on that, number one. Number two, something about the work on the bases stopping while we have a chance to discuss these matters. I don't know *what* we're going to do about the Turkish matter.

[President Kennedy and Sorensen leave the room.]

Thompson: Khrushchev may have picked up a statement which [Bruno] Kreisky, the Austrian foreign minister, made day before yesterday—has made, and which he [Khrushchev] may think was inspired by *us*—in which he raised the question of Turkish bases.

Unidentified: Of course, maybe the Russians got Kreisky to do it, too.

[Sounds of papers being shuffled; unclear conversations.]

Rusk: And if we publish the letter of last night, Tommy, what other letters will get published on that?

Thompson: I think probably this whole exchange. This [Khrushchev letter of October 26] refers—starting with this crisis—this refers to the previous letters. It starts out by saying: "I have received your letter." I've got the feeling that if you have someone explaining the [current] situation, you have to publish the exchange.

President Kennedy: I don't know. Perhaps we don't have to put out the letter as much as we do the three proposals or so. All right. Why don't you . . .

Dillon: [Unclear] Berlin. We've got to say that presently Cuba and the whole gamut of NATO–Warsaw Pact things would be . . . It would be better just to discuss Cuba.

[Unclear discussion.]

Thompson: . . . this has been delayed [in] transmission . . .

Robert Kennedy: The first point being that this is a question of Cuba and the bases, [and] must be resolved within the next few days. It can't wait. The negotiations and discussions must get on. And the work that is continuing despite our protests has been going on. So therefore it's got to be resolved quickly. This action that has been taken is not an action just by the United

Nations [meant to say States?], but it is an action by all Latin American countries plus the United States.

This has nothing to do with the security of the countries of Europe, which do have their own problems. We would obviously consider negotiating the giving up of bases in Turkey if we can assure the Turks and the other European countries for whom these bases were emplaced, if there can be some assurances given to them for their own security. This will entail inspection, as we anticipate

the UN]. We ought to get the summaries.

Bundy: I know it. Ask them to bring it in if they can get it.

Rusk: I think that we must insist [unclear] all agencies.

Robert Kennedy: Sure. Well, I think that the wording [in Stevenson's proposed statement] is nearly acceptable. I don't see how we can ask the Turks to give up their defense.

Unidentified: What do you think they could—

Robert Kennedy: No, I didn't. Unless the Soviet Union is also going to give up their weapons that threaten the Turks.

McNamara: You mean not only weapons, but agree not to invade Turkey. And allow inspection to ensure that they haven't.

Robert Kennedy: We would be glad for it. We think that's a very good point made by the Russians, and we would be glad to—and we finally feel that this is a major breakthrough, and we would be glad to discuss that.

In the meantime this [missiles in Cuba] is a threat to the United States and not just that—to all of Latin America, and let's get that done.

Unidentified: I think that's tough on [the Turks] to say that this is what we want.

Bundy: And I think we have to find a way.

Unidentified: [Unclear] start up a second inspection [unclear] inspect in Europe?

Robert Kennedy: Well, we do it with Cuba first. That will be taken [first], and then if we want the Turks out, we have got to have them inspected—reverse the [unclear] now.

Unidentified: We ought to check with the President first.

McNamara: We ought to really check the time. These are absolutely contradictory. Check the time.

McNamara: Well, Khrushchev's statement to U Thant is absolutely contradictory to his statement to the President. The question is, which came first? I thought the reply to U Thant came first.

Rusk: What's the statement to the President?

McNamara: The long letter of last night.

Unidentified: Yeah. And this one is just—

McNamara: We ought to mention this in the reply, because this has—

Thompson: It [Khrushchev's October 26 letter] was delivered [to the U.S. embassy in Moscow] at 4:43 [P.M.]. Moscow time was 9:43 yesterday morning. Now, because that letter was sent—

McNamara: Can we call up there and find out what time we got the message from Khrushchev?

Unidentified: Yes, you can do that.

Unidentified: Yes.

Thompson: You can never be sure when they were sent from Moscow. Delivery time is certainly indicated. It's after.

[Unclear conversation]

Unidentified: Well, call the Russian embassy [unclear] . . .

Unidentified: No.

Unidentified: In what way?

Unidentified: Just saying we're not going to do that.

Bundy: Yeah, I agree. There has to be [unclear] situation. Direct attention to that, the fact that the Cuban [buildup] is continuing. Ships have not yet obeyed instructions on which Mr. Khrushchev gave assurances to U Thant.

Now, what is the 4-step program [for removing missiles, possibly referring to Stevenson's message]? That is the really . . .

Unidentified: It's about construction.

Bundy: About construction.

McNamara: For sure, not operability.

At this point the group, or at least Rusk, apparently got some copies of the text of Khrushchev's message to President Kennedy, being broadcast and carried by the press. The text of the message, as the Executive Committee received it, was:[8]

---

8. Unofficial translation, reprinted in Larson, *"Cuban Crisis,"* pp. 183–186.

Dear Mr. President:

It is with great satisfaction that I studied your reply to Mr. U Thant on the adoption of measures in order to avoid contact by our ships and thus avoid irreparable fatal consequences. This reasonable step on your part persuades me that you are showing solicitude for the preservation of peace, and I note this with satisfaction.

I have already said that the only concern of our people and government and myself personally as chairman of the Council of Ministers is to develop

sequently a deepening of the crisis, which because of this contact can spark off the fire of military conflict after which any talks would be superfluous because other forces and other laws would begin to operate—the laws of war. I agree with you that this is only a first step. The main thing is to normalize and stabilize the situation in the world between states and between people.

I understand your concern for the security of the United States, Mr. President, because this is the first duty of the president. However, these questions are also uppermost in our minds. The same duties rest with me as chairman of the USSR Council of Ministers. You have been worried over our assisting Cuba with arms designed to strengthen its defensive potential—precisely defensive potential—because Cuba, no matter what weapons it had, could not compare with you since these are different dimensions, the more so given up-to-date means of extermination.

Our purpose has been and is to help Cuba, and no one can challenge the humanity of our motives aimed at allowing Cuba to live peacefully and develop as its people desire. You want to relieve your country from danger and this is understandable. However, Cuba also wants this. All countries want to relieve themselves from danger. But how can we, the Soviet Union and our government, assess your actions which, in effect, mean that you have surrounded the Soviet Union with military bases, surrounded our allies with military bases, set up military bases literally around our country, and stationed your rocket weapons at them? This is no secret. High-placed American officials demonstratively declare this. Your rockets are stationed in Britain and in Italy and pointed at us. Your rockets are stationed in Turkey.

You are worried over Cuba. You say that it worries you because it lies at a distance of 90 miles across the sea from the shores of the United States. However, Turkey lies next to us. Our sentinels are pacing up and down and watching each other. Do you believe that you have the right to demand security for your country and the removal of such weapons that you qualify as offensive, while not recognizing this right for us?

You have stationed devastating rocket weapons, which you call offensive, in Turkey literally right next to us. How then does recognition of our equal military possibilities tally with such unequal relations between our great states? This does not tally at all.

It is good, Mr. President, that you agreed for our representatives to meet and begin talks, apparently with the participation of U.N. Acting Secretary General U Thant. Consequently, to some extent, he assumes the role of intermediary, and we believe that he can cope with the responsible mission if, of course, every side that is drawn into this conflict shows good will.

I think that one could rapidly eliminate this conflict and normalize the situation. Then people would heave a sigh of relief, considering that the statesmen who bear the responsibility have sober minds, an awareness of their responsibility, and an ability to solve complicated problems and not allow matters to slide to the disaster of war.

This is why I make this proposal: We agree to remove those weapons from Cuba which you regard as offensive weapons. We agree to do this and to state this commitment in the United Nations. Your representatives will make a statement to the effect that the United States, on its part, bearing in mind the anxiety and concern of the Soviet state, will evacuate its analogous weapons from Turkey. Let us reach an understanding on what time you and we need to put this into effect.

After this, representatives of the U.N. Security Council could control on-the-spot the fulfillment of these commitments. Of course, it is necessary that the Governments of Cuba and Turkey would allow these representatives to come to their countries and check fulfillment of this commitment, which each side undertakes. Apparently, it would be better if these representatives enjoyed the trust of the Security Council and ours—the United States and the Soviet Union—as well as of Turkey and Cuba. I think that it will not be difficult to find such people who enjoy the trust and respect of all interested sides.

We, having assumed this commitment in order to give satisfaction and hope to the peoples of Cuba and Turkey and to increase their confidence in their security, will make a statement in the Security Council to the effect that the Soviet Government gives a solemn pledge to respect the integrity of the frontiers and the sovereignty of Turkey, not to intervene in its domestic affairs, not to invade Turkey, not to make available its territory as a *place d'armes* for such invasion, and also will restrain those who would think of launching an aggression against Turkey either from Soviet territory or from the territory of other states bordering on Turkey.

The U.S. Government will make the same statement in the Security Council with regard to Cuba. It will declare that the United States will respect the integrity of the frontiers of Cuba, its sovereignty, undertakes not to intervene in its domestic affairs, not to invade and not to make its

alarm you, are in the hands of Soviet officers. Therefore any accidental use of them whatsoever to the detriment of the United States of America is excluded. These means are stationed in Cuba at the request of the Cuban Government and only in defensive aims. Therefore, if there is no invasion of Cuba, or an attack on the Soviet Union, or other of our allies then, of course, these means do not threaten anyone and will not threaten. For they do not pursue offensive aims.

If you accept my proposal, Mr. President, we would send our representatives to New York, to the United Nations, and would give them exhaustive instructions to order to come to terms sooner. If you would also appoint your men and give them appropriate instructions, this problem could be solved soon.

Why would I like to achieve this? Because the entire world is now agitated and expects reasonable actions from us. The greatest pleasure for all the peoples would be an announcement on our agreement, on nipping in the bud the conflict that has arisen. I attach a great importance to such understanding because it might be a good beginning and, specifically, facilitate a nuclear test ban agreement. The problem of tests could be solved simultaneously, not linking one with the other, because they are different problems. However, it is important to reach an understanding to both these problems in order to make a good gift to the people, to let them rejoice in the news that a nuclear test ban agreement has also been reached and thus there will be no further contamination of the atmosphere. Your and our positions on this issue are very close.

All this, possibly, would serve as a good impetus to searching for mutually acceptable agreements on other disputed issues, too, on which there is an exchange of opinion between us. These problems have not yet been solved, but they wait for an urgent solution which would clear the international atmosphere. We are ready for this.

These are my proposals, Mr. President.

Respectfully yours, Nikita Khrushchev

Discussion then focused on specific points and phrases in Khrushchev's message.

Rusk: [reading and paraphrasing from Khrushchev's broadcast message] It is with great satisfaction that I studied your reply to U Thant. This reasonable step on your part shows that you are concerned with the preservation of peace as all our people are concerned with the preservation of peace. The statement [unclear] is not to prevent [unclear]. He says that the main thing is not to prevent [unclear] [but] is to avoid a crisis in which negotiation would be useless.

I agree with you; this is only a first step. The main thing is to secure prerequisites for peace. You are alarmed that we have helped people with arms for defense. I repeat, defense of Cuba. But how are we to react when you've surrounded our country with bases about which your military speak demonstratively. [You say] Cuba is only 90 miles from your border. Turkey is close to our border, so you can demand the removal of aggressive weapons, but you do not recognize our right to have the same concern. These do not tally.

It is a good thing that you have agreed that our representatives should meet. I am entirely supportive of using U Thant as intermediary. He is capable of being one.

I propose that you agree to remove from Cuba the means which we consider aggressive. You represent yourself as facing a threat from our missiles in Turkey. Let us set a time for our representatives to meet to control this. I expect a statement in the Security Council that you respect the sovereignty of Turkey and will not allow your territory to be used for aggression against Turkey. Send a statement within the framework of the Security Council for debate with the United States with regard to Cuba. With this we would of course have to agree on a time limit. Let's do so. But not a long time, 2 or 3 weeks or a month. We agree we should send our representatives to the United States. Why do I want this? Because the entire world awaits. [Rusk now appears to begin a sarcastic rewording of the letter.] Khrushchev, who speaks of disarmament, continues nuclear tests. He continues all over the world. All of this would be a good starting point to agree on other controversial questions which arise in the atmosphere. Such are my proposals. With respect, Khrushchev.

McNamara: How do you interpret the addition of still another condition over and above the letter that came in last night? We had one deal in the letter; now we've got a different deal.

Unidentified: [Unclear] wants to assign this [unclear].

Unidentified: Shouldn't we point this out in a letter?

Unidentified: We've got three positions.

Thompson: My idea is that the letter—the long letter of last night—he wrote himself and sent out without clearance.

[Unclear group discussion.]

McNamara: This really changes the character of the deal we're likely to be able to make, and also, therefore, our action in the interim must be really to keep the pressure on.

Unidentified: I agree.

Bundy: This should be knocked down publicly. A private . . .

Let me suggest this scenario. We knock this down publicly in the way we just described, separating the issues, keeping attention on Cuba, with a 4-point requirement involved. Privately, we say to Khrushchev: "Look, your public statement is a very dangerous one because it makes impossible immediate discussion of your private proposals and requires us to proceed urgently with the things that we have in mind. You'd better get straightened out."

McNamara: This is exactly what I think.

Unidentified: Yeah.

Unidentified: And we release the fact that there was the other letter?

Bundy: No. No. We say we are reluctant to release this letter which displayed an inconsistency in your position, but we don't have very much time.

[At about this time, President Kennedy returns to the Cabinet Room.]

McNamara: Our point ought to be that he's changed the deal. Well, no sooner had we gotten the first letter translated, he added a completely new deal and released it publicly. And under these circumstances.

Robert Kennedy: What is the advantage? I don't know which way we are 24 hours from now. So we win that argument. But before 24 hours—

McNamara: We incorporated his deal in our letter.

Unidentified: We give it full attention. We have to take [unclear].

Unidentified: Well, his missiles can't be made alert. Remove the missiles, have inspection sites, and then have the inspection.

Robert Kennedy: Now the problem is going to be, not the fact that we have this exchange with him, but the fact that he's going to have a ploy publicly that's going to look rather satisfactory at the present. How are we going to have him do anything but take the ball away from us publicly, if we don't agree, if we just write him a talkative letter?

Bundy: In the letter, Bobby, should we surface his earlier message?

Robert Kennedy: Well, I think all of that. I think we're going to have to, in the next 3 or 4 hours, not just put the ball completely in his hands and allow him to do whatever he wants. We can have an exchange with him and say: "You double-crossed us, and you"—and we don't know which deal to accept. And then he writes back in the meantime. He's got all the play throughout the world on the fact that he—

Unidentified: Just turn him down publicly.

Robert Kennedy: Yeah, but I think that's awful tough.

[Unclear discussion.]

McCone: I don't think you can surface this publicly without referring publicly to his letter of yesterday.

Robert Kennedy: I'd like to have a consideration of my thought about saying that he—I haven't refined this at all—but that he's offered this arrangement in Cuba—that he will withdraw the bases in Cuba for assurances that we don't intend to invade Cuba. We've always given those assurances. We'd be glad to give them again. That, in his letter to me, he said that he would permit inspection. Obviously that entails inspection not only of Cuba but entails inspection of the United States to ensure that we're not—by United Nations observers—to ensure that we're not getting ready to invade. Now, this is one of the things for U Thant.

The bases in Cuba involve the security of the Western Hemisphere. This is not just a question of the United States. This is a question of all Latin American countries. All have joined together in this effort. Time is running out on us. This must be brought to fruition. The question of the Turkish bases—which is excellent that you brought that up—in that there should be disarmament of the Turkish bases. But that has nothing to do with the security of the Western Hemisphere. It does have to do with the security of Turkey, and we would be happy to assure the Turks that we are making a similar arrangement in Turkey. We will withdraw the bases from Turkey if—and allow inspection of Turkey to make sure that we've done that. And you withdraw your invasion bases of the Soviet Union and permit inspection there.

Bundy: I think it's too complicated, Bobby.

Robert Kennedy: [sharply] Well, I don't think it is.

President Kennedy: It seems to me the first thing we ought to try to do is

Cuba seems to set the groundwork for something to do in Turkey.

So I think we ought to have the Turks . . . We ought to have a talk with the Turks, because I think they've got to understand the peril that we are going to move into in the case we take some action in Cuba. Chances are that he'll take some action in Turkey. They don't understand that. And in fact they may even not say that [unclear]. [It may be] more of a—[if] we try to do any more about Cuba then he's going to do it to Turkey. So I think the Turks ought to think a little. We ought to try to get them not to respond to this until we've had a chance to consider what action we'll take. Now, how long will it take for us to get in touch with the Turks?

Unidentified: I'll find out today, Mr. President. We'll see.

Unidentified: I think it's going to be awfully hard to get the Turks not to say this.

Unidentified: They'll have to say something.

Unidentified: And this is NATO's problem.

Rusk: I think this is the thing. The Turks ought to always say that the military [position] and the security of Turkey and military arrangements in Turkey is part of the NATO.

Bundy: Part of the Atlantic, part of the Western Alliance, and doesn't have anything to do with Cuba. They ought to—they can certainly make a statement disassociating this.

Unidentified: It should be discussed in a different context.

Bundy: It seems to me it's important that they *should*. If anyone pulls them in, it will be us. They can't be expected to do that.

President Kennedy: No, but we want to give them some guidance. These are

American missiles, not Turkish missiles. They are under American control, not Turkish control.

Unidentified: So the missiles [unclear].

McNamara: The missles belong to the Turks, and they're manned by Turks, but the warheads are in U.S. custody. And they're committed to NATO.

President Kennedy: In other words, we couldn't destroy the missiles anyway, because they belong to Turkey.

McNamara: They belong to Turkey.

President Kennedy: All we can destroy is the warheads.

McNamara: And we can't even really withdraw the warheads. We simply are custodians of the warheads for the account of the Turks, in recognition that you [President Kennedy] must release them [under NATO nuclear release procedures].

President Kennedy: Well now, what we have to do first is get, I would think, very quickly to get a chance to think a little more about it.

But what we ought to say is that we have had several publicly and privately different proposals, or differing proposals from the Soviet Union. They are all about complicated matters. They all involve some discussion to get their true meaning. We cannot permit ourselves to be impaled on a long negotiating hook while the work goes on on these bases. I therefore suggest that the United Nations immediately, with the cooperation of the Soviet Union, take steps to provide for cessation of the work, and then we can talk about all these matters, which are very complicated.

Bundy: I think it will be very important to say at least that the current threat to peace is not in Turkey; it is in Cuba. There's no pain in saying that, even if you're going to make a trade later on.

I think also that we ought to say that we have an immediate threat. What is going on in Cuba: that is what has got to stop. Then I think we *should* say that the public Soviet, the broadcast, message is at variance with other proposals which have been put forward within the last 12 hours. We could surface those for background.

President Kennedy: That being so, until we find out what is really being suggested and what can really be discussed, we have to get something in words. Maybe we can see if the work's going on.

Bundy: That's right.

President Kennedy: There isn't any doubt. Let's not kid ourselves. They've got a very good proposal, which is the reason they made it public—

Bundy: What's going on, while you were out of the room, Mr. President, we reached an informal consensus that—I don't know whether Tommy agrees—

that this last night's message was Khrushchev's. And this one is his own hard-nosed people overruling him, this public one. They didn't like what he said to you last night. Nor would I, if I were a Soviet hard-nose.

Thompson: I think the view is, the Kreisky speech, they may have thought this was our underground way of suggesting this, and they felt that—

Unidentified: Who said this?

President Kennedy: The only thing is, Tommy, why wouldn't they say it

They've got a very good product. This one is going to be very tough, I think, for us. It's going to be tough in England, I'm sure, as well as other places on the continent. If we are forced to take action, this will be, in my opinion, not a blank check, but a pretty good check [for the Soviets] to take action in Berlin on the grounds that we are only unreasonable, emotional people. That this is a reasonable trade, and we ought to take advantage of it. Therefore, it makes it much more difficult for us to move [against Cuba] with world support. These are all the things that—why this is a pretty good play of his.

That being so, I think that the only thing we've got him on is the fact that, while they put forward various proposals in short periods of time, all of which are complicated, under that shield this work goes on. Until we can get somewhat of an agreement on the cessation of work, how can we possibly negotiate [with proposals] coming as fast as the waters [run]?

Bundy: And the ships still, in spite of his assurances to U Thant, his ships still—

President Kennedy: Are still coming.

Dillon: There is one other very—might be a very dangerous sentence in this thing that no one has particularly mentioned. But it's a thing I've been afraid of all along in the Cuban trade. Where he says: How are we to react when you have surrounded our country with bases about which your military speak "demonstratively." That will affect our whole base system.

President Kennedy: Somebody said that of Turkey?

Dillon: Well, no. Then he goes on and says . . . But he's left it open to be able to say it's—

President Kennedy: But the direct trade is suggested with Turkey.

Thompson: Mr. President, it's far beyond the missiles, because this says "the means which you consider aggressive." This includes the planes, the missiles, the technicians, and everything, anything else, which means the real abandonment of our base in Turkey as far as he is concerned.

Bundy: Obviously that's subject to various shades. He could take missile for missile, which wouldn't be good enough from our point of view with respect to Cuba. It would be tough.

President Kennedy: Well, we can talk in 3 weeks on that, couldn't we?

But the problem is here. Work on their bases should stop. That, in my opinion, is what our defensible position is.

McNamara: Start to suspend the operability of it [missile sites in Cuba], Mr. President. It isn't enough to stop work on a base that is already operable.

President Kennedy: All right. I've seen that. Let's see what Stevenson is suggesting. What did you say, Paul?

Nitze: I don't think it's a strong line to suggest confusion in the various translations of just what the public is aware of in Cuba.

President Kennedy: The only thing—what I'm trying to suggest is all these proposals come, they're all complicated, and what we can do is hang this up in negotiations on different proposals while the work goes on.

Nitze: That looks like a rationalization of our own confusion. I think we've got to take a firmer line than that.

Bundy: I myself would send back word by phone, for example, that last night's stuff was pretty good. This is impossible at this stage of the game. And that time is getting very short.

President Kennedy: What is our public position?

Bundy: The public position is as you outlined it. But I think it's very important to get *them* to get the message that if they want to stop something further in Cuba, they have to do better than this public statement.

President Kennedy: [to an aide] I want you to get Stevenson on the phone.

Bundy: Mr. Secretary, have you got a draft typed?

Rusk: No, I'm just scribbling off something here. But I think we ought to say something very quickly.

Bundy: That's right.

Unidentified: Sure.

Sorensen: Right in here is something that I'm confused with [unclear]. Get Pierre—

[Unclear discussion.]

President Kennedy: Do you have any idea how many missiles may be facing Turkey—intermediates?

Unidentified: I don't know offhand, Mr. President. I would guess it is on the order of at least 100 within range . . .

Unidentified: We have 15 Jupiter missiles.

President Kennedy: We have 15 Jupiters in Turkey?

Unidentified: But we have a lot of nuclear weapons. There are 100 bombers.[9] These are analogous weapons that you are speaking about. If you take the bombers out of Cuba, we could get the nuclear weapons and planes out of

Nitze. Are we sure that the Russians might not have . . . The Russian language used might not have applied, might be interpreted on the part of the Russians that they were talking [in the reply to U Thant] about ships carrying proclaimed nuclear material.

Thompson: [on the two messages from Khrushchev to Kennedy] He [Stevenson] says he doesn't have the text of any new letter but he heard the broadcast.

President Kennedy: Hello? Oh, Governor, I got your message. What?

There's a letter that I received last night which is different than this. What's your judgment? [Long pause.] Right. [Long pause.] Good. [Long pause.] All right. [Long pause.] Yes. [Long pause.]—is to act against Cuba, but in addition—[Long pause.]

I think we have been around and around too much on that. Oh, fine. Well, I think the only . . . What we've got to do is get them to agree to stop work

---

9. Nuclear-capable F-100 fighter-bombers were stationed in Turkey, along with a stockpile of nuclear bombs.

10. Stevenson is still trying to sort out the time of Khrushchev's reply to U Thant's appeal, promising that he would keep his ships away from the quarantine line, in relation to the time of his long message to President Kennedy on October 26, which was more defiant in its discussion of the quarantine. They are concerned because of the apparent discrepancy between the promise to U Thant and the continued movement of Soviet ships toward the quarantine line.

This source of confusion is separate from the concern occasioned by the apparent contradiction between the proposed deal for removal of missiles from Cuba in Khrushchev's October 26 letter to Kennedy, and the different proposal contained in the message to Kennedy that had just been broadcast around the world.

while we talk about all these phony propositions. OK. [Long pause.] Good. [Long pause.] All right. Fine. Thank you. [Hangs up.]

What about our putting something in about Berlin?

Dillon: Well, that's the tragedy. If you start talking about Cuba—about Turkey.

President Kennedy: Let's get it out of this problem, then you might as well—I mean, we might put sand in his gears for a few minutes.

Bundy: In what way?

President Kennedy: Well, what about satisfactory guarantees for Berlin?

Unidentified: He's not going to give.

President Kennedy: I'm just trying to think of what the public problem is, because everybody is going to think this is very reasonable.

Dillon: This Turkish thing has got to be thrown in—you are quite right, Mr. President—into the overall European context. Then you can bring in Berlin, and I think it's fine, because it's not only the Turks that are going to be answering to this. The Germans are going to be making statements in the next few hours. And various other people, about this, when they're asked. And they're going to take a very strong position.

President Kennedy: They're getting calls from Hare there [at the State Department], aren't they?

Dillon: I mean, you can have statements out of Bonn.

Unidentified: I'll try to find out where he [Ambassador Hare, in Ankara] is, Mr. President, and I'll put the—do you want to put the call in right away?

President Kennedy: Who has talked to the Turks? Has Finletter talked to them?

Unidentified: No.

Rusk: The [Turkish] prime minister talked yesterday to Hare. He has yet to be heard from.

Dillon: I would say that the Turkish proposal opens the way to a major discussion of our connections in Europe, including Berlin.

Unidentified: I think that we mention Berlin.

Nitze: Oh, no, no. If you mention that, you've lost the Germans.

Unidentified: That's right.

Nitze: Right then and there. If we start [bringing in Berlin], if we are the first ones.

At this point the recording stops, possibly because the tape had run out and no one was standing by to replace it.

According to the notes of several present, the group turned to drafting the press statement that would offer a public response to Khrushchev's public letter. Bundy and Gilpatric read drafts that they had prepared. Alexis Johnson then reported that, as President Kennedy had expected, the Turkish government had already issued a public statement sharply rejecting the Soviet proposal.

Sorensen then described his own draft for the U.S. statement. The group concentrated, however, on the Gilpatric draft, revised it, and agreed on it. The White House later issued the following:

current crisis—the action of the Soviet Government in secretly introducing offensive weapons into Cuba. Work on these offensive weapons is still proceeding at a rapid pace. The first imperative must be to deal with this immediate threat, under which no sensible negotiations can proceed.

It is therefore the position of the United States that as an urgent preliminary to consideration of any proposals work on the Cuban bases must stop; offensive weapons must be rendered inoperable; and further shipment of offensive weapons to Cuba must cease—all under effective international verification.

As to proposals concerning the security of nations outside this hemisphere, the United States and its allies have long taken the lead in seeking properly inspected arms limitation, on both sides. These efforts can continue as soon as the present Soviet-created threat is ended.[12]

As discussion in the Executive Committee continued, both Robert Kennedy and Gilpatric emphasized that the issues of Cuba and Turkey must be kept separate and dealt with separately. Negotiations on other issues could not proceed until the missile threat in Cuba was removed.

President Kennedy then recalled that in the spring of 1961 the U.S. government had wanted to get the Jupiter missiles out of Turkey because they had become obsolete and had little military value. If the missiles in Cuba added

---

11. Reprinted in Larson, *"Cuban Crisis,"* pp. 186–187.

12. Several accounts assert that this statement was released by the White House Press Office at 4:30 P.M. It was, however, released in the morning and discussed during the day in New York and foreign capitals, as well as in the Executive Committee, where it was referred to as the "morning statement."

50 percent to the entire Soviet nuclear-missile strike capability against the United States, then trading their removal against the missiles in Turkey would be of great military advantage to the United States.

President Kennedy reiterated the points he had made earlier, that the United States was in the position of risking war in Cuba and in Berlin over missiles in Turkey that had little military value. He also repeated his view that, from the political point of view, it would be hard to get allied support for an air strike against Cuba because many would think the Cuba-Turkey trade was a good deal. The United States would be in a bad position if it appeared to attack Cuba in order to keep useless missiles in Turkey.

President Kennedy also reiterated his previous position on the Turks: the United States could not propose to withdraw Turkish missiles from Turkey, but the Turks could offer to do it. This was why the Turks should be informed of the great danger in which they would live during the coming week, and urged to face the possibility of some kind of a trade over missiles.

At about noon President Kennedy left the meeting to confer with a group of state governors, including Nelson Rockefeller of New York and Pat Brown of California, who had been brought to Washington to be briefed on the crisis and on their states' role in the necessary civil-defense preparations. McCone and Gilpatric had reviewed the situation with them earlier in the morning at the Pentagon. Now, after the discussion of civil-defense measures, President Kennedy talked briefly with them at the White House.

The Executive Committee continued to work. Study of Khrushchev's message created more uncertainty about whether his proposal included all NATO bases or was confined to Turkey. The possibility of another press release was considered and rejected.

Meanwhile, Thompson had drafted a possible reply from President Kennedy directly to Khrushchev. This was discussed with a view to presenting it to the President later. The group then broke up, agreeing to reconvene at 2:30 at the State Department without President Kennedy, then to return to the White House at 4:00 to resume discussions with the President.

McNamara returned to the Defense Department at about 4:00 and asked the Joint Staff of the JCS to prepare two additional plans. One would involve moving a Polaris ballistic-missile submarine into a firing position off the Turkish coast before America attacked Cuba; if the Jupiters were attacked, the United States would still then have 16 invulnerable missiles based offshore. He also asked for a detailed U.S. response to a Soviet attack on Jupiter bases in Turkey with conventional weapons.

Meanwhile the Joint Chiefs of Staff (absent Taylor) had decided, on the basis of their previous views and the morning's intelligence, to draft a formal, written recommendation to the President that he promptly order a massive air strike against Cuba on Sunday, October 28, or Monday, October 29, and prepare to invade. Probably over the phone, McNamara then reviewed the recommendation with President Kennedy.

In the early afternoon, news arrived that a U-2 on a mission to collect atmospheric samples from Soviet nuclear testing near the North Pole had been reported lost near Alaska. Expressing sharp alarm about the danger of a war, McNamara left the Pentagon briefly to tell Rusk. They learned that as a result of navigation difficulties near the Pole, the U-2 had gone off course into Soviet airspace. Soviet MiG fighters had attempted to intercept the aircraft. American fighters based in Alaska had been sent aloft to protect the U-2 once it reentered U.S. airspace, which it did.[1] The Soviet leadership, already aware of the constant

1. Because of the state of nuclear alert then prevailing as a result of the crisis, the U.S. fighter aircraft carried fully armed Falcon air-to-air missiles, which had nuclear warheads. See Scott

patrolling by U.S. strategic bombers on flight paths that would lead into the U.S.S.R., could be presumed to have noticed this incident.

When McNamara returned to the Pentagon, he learned that a U-2 overflying Cuba for that day's photography was 30–40 minutes overdue. He then went to the State Department for his 2:30 meeting. The Chiefs finalized their recommendation to the President. Taylor would present it when the Executive Committee reconvened.

The session at the State Department reached no consensus on next steps. Discussion dwelled increasingly on planning for an air strike against Cuba.

While the advisers deliberated at State, worrisome news came in from the Navy: the *Grozny* continued to move toward the interception zone. At the State Department, Robert Kennedy argued for avoiding a clash over the *Grozny*. Rather than trigger a confrontation immediately, at sea, he urged that the government now buy time in order to launch an air attack against Cuba on Monday, October 29, or Tuesday, October 30.

The next news to arrive, as the meeting continued, was even worse. The assumption that air defenses in Cuba would not shoot at the unarmed U.S. reconnaissance aircraft was no longer valid. Intelligence analysts had already noticed that Soviet officers appeared to be taking control of the command network for all Cuban air defenses. The U-2 that had flown over Cuba that morning was still overdue. As Washington frantically tried to figure out what had happened to it, the pilots returning from the low-level reconnaissance flights reported that gunners in Cuba had tried to shoot them down. The Pentagon press statement on the legal basis of the Jupiter deployment was amended to add that any interference with U.S. surveillance would meet counteraction. This statement was released at about 3:30.

The Executive Committee resumed work in the Cabinet Room at 4:00 P.M. President Kennedy turned on the tape recorder as the meeting began with McNamara's report on the latest developments.

Unidentified: . . . low-flying aircraft?

McNamara: Low-flying aircraft. And by abort I simply mean that they turned away from their targets and are returning to base.

Taylor: They told me that they were running into resistance. I assume they saw somebody in the [unclear].

Sagan, *The Limits of Safety: Organizations, Accidents, and Nuclear Weapons* (Princeton: Princeton University Press, 1993), pp. 136–138.

McNamara: So it looks like we'll have to make a statement today as to what we do about that, as far as surveillance is concerned.

President Kennedy: Well, we better wait till we hear more about why they aborted. We might have to [stop] because they are too hostile right now.

McNamara: Mr. President, I wonder if it wouldn't be wise to put out the announcement about night surveillance, whether we decide to carry it out or not. This is the announcement that we would propose.

this communiqué [won't do].

[Unclear group conversation.]

Bundy: What paragraph? What page?

McNamara: There are two drafts of this resolution.

President Kennedy: Just say: "The OAS has provided for"—

McNamara: Well, you used the word "organization" earlier today, for example.

Wilson: Mr. President, on that announcement, we were wondering about the Voice of America in Spanish [broadcasting into Cuba]. Should we just handle this regularly until you have made a decision to make a nighttime reconnaissance?

We have a statement that will be repeated every 5 to 10 minutes on the radio if there is to be a nighttime surveillance flight—in other words, telling the people that the light in the sky, the explosion, is harmless. I presume that we would not want to go with anything like that?

President Kennedy: I think we had better wait. I don't know whether tonight is the night to do that. You may not want to do it. It would not be that much of a . . .

Taylor: We had better evaluate this before we let them go.

President Kennedy: I think we had better wait on that.

Wilson: Nothing is that [unclear]. I suppose when this is made public we could report it, of course. I see no harm in that, but it is very low-key.

President Kennedy: I think we had better wait to find out what happens when . . . I think we better wait till we find out what happens before we put this out for tonight.

McNamara: I want a board meeting called.

President Kennedy: Meaning?

McNamara: COMOR.

President Kennedy: [Not] the other one?[2]

McNamara: No.

President Kennedy: What time . . .

McNamara: I think we should put it out right now. We don't have to do it tonight. This simply says that night surveillance is required.

President Kennedy: The Defense Department [will] put that out?

McNamara: Yes.

Unidentified: It says, "Future surveillance will also include"—

McNamara: Yes. I don't—That way we are committed to it.

President Kennedy: Yes, but I don't think we ought to go every 5 minutes with it though [on Voice of America broadcasts].

Unidentified: Oh, no.

Robert Kennedy: What he—what he was going to do, the night you do it, he was going to tell people in more detail about it. Not—this has nothing to do with the blockade.

Unidentified: All right.

Unidentified: I'm going to wait here and make sure that nobody does anything wrong . . .

[Pause; rattling of papers and coffee cups.]

Rusk: [referring to the draft letter from President Kennedy to Khrushchev] Now, it has been brought up on page 2, paragraph 4, that Khrushchev was talking about [getting] assurances not to invade Cuba and that limited kind of [unclear].

Dillon: Not to invade Cuba or support forces planning to undertake it. That is the exact language he uses.

President Kennedy: . . . have to use that language to give assurances?

Rusk: Not to invade Cuba.

Dillon: Or support those forces intending to carry out an invasion.

Rusk: [still describing language in the draft letter] Then, in the end [the United States would pledge not] "to take aggressive action against other American states through military aggression or subversion, or take other aggressive action against other American states."

---

2. McNamara was referring to the interagency Committee on Overhead Reconnaissance. President Kennedy may have thought he was referring to the U.S. Intelligence Board, which had somewhat broader responsibilities.

Sorensen: In other words, "military aggression or subversion."

Rusk: "We will not seek through military aggression or subversion—to take aggressive action against other American states."

Sorensen: Do they [the Cubans or Soviets] ever admit that any of their actions are aggressive?

Rusk: Well, interfering in the affairs of other American states is so very broad and so very vague that they would be afraid that you would say—compare it with the radio broadcasts as an excuse for an invasion.

Unidentified: All bets are off.

President Kennedy: I don't think we can use this language.

Robert Kennedy: Well, this is just assurances.

Rusk: Gentlemen, if they fail, I am more concerned.

Robert Kennedy: Well, it is sufficient to give assurances—

Sorensen: We just assume that their assurances have become invalid on analogy to [unclear].

President Kennedy: Now, this last paragraph, Mr. Secretary, I think we ought to say: "As I was preparing this letter, which was prepared in response to your private letter of last night, I learned of your—this immediate crisis in Cuba," and so forth. When we get action there, I shall certainly be ready to discuss the matters you mentioned in your public message.

You see, that's more forthcoming. What we are saying here is that we are rejecting his public message, but we might as well—

Dillon: Be prepared to discuss the actions that—the detailed thinking—

President Kennedy: Well, "We would be prepared to discuss your [Khrushchev's] public message," "the matters in your public message" or "the issues in your public message."

This is not going to be successful. We might as well realize that. That's why I am just wondering whether he's going to come back to us.

Robert Kennedy: After he has rejected the deal, then where are we going to be?

President Kennedy: Tomorrow he will come back and say that the United States has rejected this proposal he has made. So I think that we ought to be thinking also of saying that we are going to discuss all these matters if he'll cease work. That is the only place where we have got him.

So I think we ought to be able to say that the matter of Turkey and so on, in fact, all these matters, can be discussed if he'll cease work. Otherwise, he's going to announce that we've rejected his proposal. And then where are we?

We're all right, if he would cease work and dismantle the missiles. Then we could talk for 2 weeks. But until we get that . . .

So I think we ought to put that in. Just say: I learned of your public message accepting the connection [unclear] to bases in Cuba and saying that there is no immediate need of a crisis. Contact is necessary, period. You must realize that these other matters involving NATO and the Warsaw Pact countries will require time for discussion.

Unless we also mean to announce that we've rejected it [a possible Turkey deal], I don't think that we ought to leave it this way. I think we ought to say that, if we are going to discuss this, we're going to have to have a cessation of work, and therefore the burden is on him.

That is our only, it seems to me, defense against the appeal of his trade. I think that our message ought to be that we'd be glad to discuss this and other matters but we've got to get a suspension of work.

Robert Kennedy: And the bases being observed and dismantled.

President Kennedy: In the public message you [Khrushchev] [talk about] missile bases in Cuba.

Alexis Johnson?: Mr. Zorin has been to U Thant [in New York]. And one of the people who was there just came out and said that the position that Zorin had taken was, that the first letter [from Khrushchev on October 26] was confidential and it was designed to reduce tension, but, so far as he was concerned, the second letter [of October 27] contained the substantive proposal.

Sorensen: The second letter is the public letter? [It was.]

President Kennedy: I think we ought to say to U Thant this afternoon that, can he give us any assurances, can he get any assurances from the Soviet Union, that work has ceased?

We ought to get that before the end of the afternoon. Just that simple message to U Thant. He ought to call Zorin in before we discuss these other matters.

Unidentified: All right, that is a good idea.

Unidentified: All right with me.

President Kennedy: Why don't we send that up to U Thant right now, before we discuss these other matters which are complicated and involve other countries and which are bound to take time, and everybody will recognize that they are going to take time.

Unidentified: This is Stevenson's feeling too, that this [removal of missiles in Cuba] ought to be a condition before we go [on to discuss Turkey]—

President Kennedy: Well, why don't we just make that, why don't we just send that message to U Thant. If we get an assurance from—which can be inspected—that they will cease the work. And then we will discuss these

morning introduces—I think we ought to release this later today—introduces matters not involved in the Cuba issue but involving the relationships of countries other than the Western Hemisphere, which are complicated and unfamiliar and will take some time.

If we are going to discuss these, we would like to have some assurances that can be verified that the Soviet Union will cease work on the missiles and that the missiles which are presently there have been made inoperable. Would the Secretary General get from the Soviet Union these assurances. In that case, the United States would be prepared to discuss any proposals of the Soviet Union.

Rusk: Is anybody a shorthand expert in here?

[Pause.]

Sorensen: [reading] "The proposal made by the Soviet Union this morning involves a number of countries and complicated issues unrelated to the existing threat to peace posed by Soviet planes and missile bases in Cuba.

"The lengthy discussions required for any possible settlement of these matters cannot be undertaken by this country until it is assured that work on these bases is halted and the bases, themselves, are inoperable."

President Kennedy: I wouldn't say "lengthy" because that sounds [unclear].

[Rewords] "The Soviet Union's message of this morning has introduced issues which are not directly related to the Cuban crisis. The United States will be glad to discuss these matters with the Secretary General and the Soviet Union, but they do involve the interests of the 15 countries of NATO and, obviously, would take, therefore, some time."

I would like the Secretary to add—I ask, therefore, the Secretary General whether he can get assurances from the Soviet Union—assurances from the Soviet Union which can be verified by the United Nations—that the missiles and so on and so on and about the missile bases that they have been rendered inoperable.

If this can be done then the conversations can take place in an atmosphere which will be more fruitful.

Dillon: Couldn't they say that they're not interested in these 15 other countries that you say would require consultation [unclear]?

President Kennedy: Ted, why don't you [prepare the message]? Is that agreeable, Mr. Secretary [speaking to Rusk]? Why don't you send that right to U Thant and see if we could get assurances, all verified [unclear].

Unidentified: George Ball is getting him on the phone right now.

President Kennedy: U Thant?

Unidentified: Yes.

President Kennedy: I'd like to get that out of the way. I'd like to have a written message which could be released if necessary.

[Unclear group discussion.]

Robert Kennedy: I would think, Jack, it would be well to get that out pretty quick.

President Kennedy: Right. By tomorrow morning.

Robert Kennedy: Yeah, so that the [unclear] can make it into a big story.

Bundy: I talked to Bohlen in Paris. He said the knockdown of the Cuba trick [in the morning statement] had been very well received there. He thought there was no problem in France. He said to tell us—

Rusk: What we probably need is a revolt in NATO to say that, yes, we do need it [the Jupiters in Turkey].

Bundy: Well, I've also talked to Finletter, and I asked him to check the permreps [permanent representatives of member states to NATO] and say that the United States stands for this position [against involving Turkish missiles in the Cuban issue].

But if the NATO countries should feel that it places them in unusual hazard, he is authorized to elicit their points of view. [Laughter.] Maybe we could stir them on that point.

Taylor: We have some more information on the afternoon [low-level reconnaissance] flight, Mr. President.

These planes took off at 1541. There were 4 in the afternoon flight—from the 1541 takeoff. One developed mechanical trouble, so for repair it turned back. So 6 approached the Cuban coast in 3 flight plans. One in the flight plan was fired upon and so had to turn back, leaving 4 [actually 5] planes, who presumably succeeded. They will be back on base at 1638, 1738, and 1740. I would expect that it would be around 6:00 before [unclear, referring to getting reports from pilots].

President Kennedy: Indicate fired on by what?

Unidentified: It did not say. Presumably low-level antiaircraft fire.

Robert Kennedy?: 1700, what time?

[unclear discussion.]

President Kennedy: Just have it ready, and then we will just call the Secretary to verify.

Unidentified: Night flights . . . It doesn't say there were 12.

President Kennedy: I suspect we might have one more conversation about the details of this firing on.

Unidentified: Do you want to hold another meeting, Mr. President?

President Kennedy: Yes, I think we're going to do that until I talk to . . . I just want to talk to the Secretary a little more about it before we put it out [the proposed announcement of night reconnaissance flights]. He might want to do something else.

Unidentified: [turning to the issue of the U-2 that strayed into Soviet airspace near Alaska] We haven't had any U-2s fly over Russia. They were [unclear] in the next day or so.

The question before us is whether it's to our advantage or not to our advantage to say that it was a flight engaged in routine air-sampling operations, assigned to an area normally 100 miles away. But it had an instrument failure that caused it to go off course. Ground stations tried to recall the aircraft to its course but did not succeed in time to prevent its overflying a portion of the Soviet Union. Whether we should use—

President Kennedy: I think we are better off not to do it if we can get away with not having some leak. Because I think our problem is [to maintain] our credibility with Khrushchev.

Bundy: We didn't do it even then until he commented to us, last time.

President Kennedy: Well, [we came] very close—didn't we?

Bundy: No, sir.

President Kennedy: Well, I don't think there's any advantage. It gives him a story tomorrow and makes it look like we're, maybe, the offenders. I don't see the advantage in that.

Unidentified: There may not be.

McNamara: Mr. President, may I say in relation to that, I think that if we haven't announced already, and I know we haven't, we shouldn't do it now.

One of our afternoon [low-level reconnaissance] aircraft was hit by a 37-millimeter shell. It's coming back. It's all right, but it simply indicates that there's been quite a change in the character of the orders given to the Cuban defenders. I don't think we ought to confuse the issue by issuing a White House—

President Kennedy: I agree. Let's let it go.

Unidentified: I don't know enough about—

Rusk: Mr. President, here's another [draft] letter to Mr. Khrushchev that is rather longer.

President Kennedy: I think we've got two questions [for the letter to Khrushchev]. One is, do we want to have these conversations go on about Turkey and these other matters while there's a sort of standstill in Cuba, or do we want to say that we won't talk about Turkey and these other matters until they've settled the Cuban crisis? I think these are two separate positions.

And I don't think we're going to get there. They are not going to announce that [once] they have taken a public position. Obviously, they're not going to settle the Cuban question until they get some compensation on Cuba.

That being true, I think the best position now, with him and publicly, is to say we're glad to discuss this matter [Turkey], and this whole question of verification, and all the rest once we get a positive indication that they have ceased their work in Cuba.

Otherwise, what we're really saying is: We won't discuss Turkey until they settle Cuba. And I think that he will then come back and say that the United States has refused his offer. I don't think that that is as good a position as saying that we'd be glad to discuss his offer, if we can get a standstill in Cuba. That puts us in a much stronger world position, because most people will think his offer is rather reasonable.

I think we ought to put our emphasis, right now, on the fact that we want an indication from him in the next 24 hours that he's going to stand still and disarm these weapons. Then we will say that under those conditions, we'll be *glad* to discuss these matters. But I think that if we don't say that, he's going to say that we rejected his offer, and therefore he's going to have public opinion with him. So, I think our only hope to escape from that is to say that we insist that he should stand still now.

We don't think he'll do that. Therefore, we're in a much better shape to put our case on that, rather than that Turkey is irrelevant.

[Unclear group discussion.]

President Kennedy: I think we ought to say: "if this proposal."

[Again reviewing the draft message to be passed to U Thant, reading the

however, will require time for consultation with the countries whose interests—with these countries—and cannot be undertaken by this country until it is assured that work on these bases in Cuba has halted and the bases, themselves, are inoperable.

"I, therefore, request with the utmost urgency that you seek such assurances from the Soviet Union in order that negotiations can go forward."

Does anybody object to that?

Unidentified: No, it's fine.

President Kennedy: OK. We'll send that now. We ought to ask Adlai to deliver it right away and ask for an answer, don't you think?

Unidentified: The only question I would like to raise about that is that it really sets Turkey as a quid pro quo—

Unidentified: That's my worry about it.

President Kennedy: Well, the negotiations . . . The point is that we are not in a position today to make a trade; that is number one. And we won't be. The trade may be made in 3 or 4 days. I don't know. We have to wait and see what the Turks say. We don't want the Soviet Union or the United Nations to be able to say that the United States rejected it. So I think we're better off to stick on the question of a freeze, and then we'll discuss it.

Bundy: Well, there are two different audiences here, Mr. President. There really are. And I think that if we sound as if we wanted to make this trade, to our NATO people and to all the people who are tied to us by alliance, we are in real trouble. I think that, we'll all join in doing this if it is the decision. But I think we should tell you that that is the universal assessment of everyone in the government that's connected with these alliance problems.

Robert Kennedy: Now what report did you get from Chip Bohlen saying that what—

Bundy: That the knockdown [of Khrushchev's public message] in this White House statement this morning was well received.

Finletter's report is in. Hare's long telegram [about probable Turkish reaction to removal of the Jupiter missiles] is in. They all make the same proposition, that if we appear to be trading the defense of Turkey for a threat to Cuba, we'll just have to face a radical decline in the effectiveness [of the NATO alliance].

President Kennedy: Yes, but I should say that, also, as the situation is moving there fast, Mac. And if we don't [accept it]—if for the next 24 or 48 hours—this trade has appeal. Now, if we reject it out of hand, and then have to take military action against Cuba, then we'll also face a decline [in the alliance].

Now, the only thing we've got, for which I think we'd be able to hold general support, would be [keeping the door open to subsequent discussion of the trade] . . .

Well, let's try to word it so that we don't harm NATO. But the thing that I think everybody would agree to is that while these matters, which are complicated, are discussed, there should be a cessation of work. Then I think we can hold general support for that. If they won't agree to that—the Soviet Union—then we retain the initiative. That's my response.

Sorensen: I have a suggestion, Mr. President. When we come to the sentence where we say we'll be glad to discuss this matter, we put in the phrase "Inasmuch as they—that is, these initiatives—relate to disarmament proposals this nation has previously put forward, the United States will be glad to discuss this matter."

President Kennedy: I don't think that's much [unclear].

McCone: When you separate out those discussions with Cuba, nobody wants to talk about those at all for that purpose, Mr. President.

McNamara: Couldn't we just add in there "Inasmuch as they relate to"—you want to make it the entire issue of NATO, not just Turkey. Or is that clear? "Inasmuch as they relate to the defense of NATO bases in Italy, Turkey, the U.K, and elsewhere," then you can go on. So you link it all together, and you take away the attention from Turkey. In that case, I don't see anything wrong with it.

Unidentified: It's a big world.

Robert Kennedy: You got another copy of this?

Rusk: Now, there are assurances in the final paragraph [of the draft letter to Khrushchev] for U.S. verification—"seeks such assurances" or "gives us verbal assurance."

President Kennedy: Yeah. That sounds good.

[Unclear group conversation.]

Robert Kennedy: I think that the Republicans can just turn on the radio today. People are going to be questioning [unclear], therefore we can't, the fact that we just out of hand reject it isn't going to make it all right for the world

Unidentified: This morning's statement—

Sorensen: After we've talked about the required consultation with NATO and so on, simply say: "I repeat, however, the position of the United States that preliminary to consideration of any proposals . . ."[3]

Robert Kennedy: Yes, but he [President Kennedy] wants to find out—perhaps take the initiative away—by saying to the Soviet Union tonight: President Kennedy—the United States government—wants to know that, prior to having any discussions about any matters, that you will give us assurances that work on the bases has stopped.

Unidentified: That's right.

Robert Kennedy: No, but I don't think that that does. I think that that is the point that has to be made in the statement. Will you give the United States government assurances that, before we try to negotiate this—

McNamara: No, that's the last sentence, which I am in favor of.

Rusk: What about the next-to-last sentence: "The discussions of these other matters now will require some time and cannot be undertaken by this country until we are assured through international verification that work on the bases— all offensive weapons bases in Cuba—is halted and the bases, themselves, are inoperable. We therefore request you" . . . Then the last sentence.

---

3. The line in the morning White House statement read: "It is therefore the position of the United States that as an urgent preliminary to consideration of any proposals work on the Cuban bases must stop; offensive weapons must be rendered inoperable; and further shipment of offensive weapons to Cuba must cease—all under effective international verification."

Unidentified: Now, this morning—

Robert Kennedy: What can we add on?

McCone: This morning we had a shipment in . . .[4]

Unidentified: I think there is something in what Mr. McCone says. This does sound as if we were equating the two. What it really should say is—

McNamara: We've already said it this morning. This morning we said [in the White House press statement]: "Preliminary to consideration of any of your proposals on Turkey, or on Cuba, or on anything else" . . .

Unidentified: Yes.

Thompson: Mr. Secretary, the second word shouldn't be "Turkey." The question is raised about—the proposal is for a swap with Cuba.

McNamara: Yes, and that is why I said what I said, [which] is that Turkey is still the object. We ought to broaden this out, to make certain that we are not talking solely about Turkey. "We must discuss these matters with you."

[Unclear group conversation.]

McNamara: There should be no question that we are talking beyond Turkey. This involves the entire defense of NATO, our bases in Turkey, Italy, and the United Kingdom, and a number of other complicated issues relating to a number of countries.

Rusk: It involves the entire membership of NATO and the Warsaw Pact.

McNamara: . . . entire membership of NATO with respect to Turkey's bases.

Unidentified: Well, they are involved.

McNamara: Turkey's bases. It involves the entire defense of NATO, bases in Turkey, Italy, and the U.K.

Nitze: He hasn't said anything regarding [unclear].

McNamara: Oh, he certainly did. Yes, he did.

Dillon: Just look at his proposal.

Unidentified: Which one? This one?

[About 2 minutes of largely inaudible group conversation. President Kennedy leaves the room for a time, in part to place a secure telephone call to General Norstad at NATO.]

Rusk: [reading another draft message to U Thant] "The problems raised by the Soviet Union's broadcast this morning involve many countries and complicated issues not directly related to the threat to peace posed by Soviet offensive missile bases in Cuba. They can be fully resolved only in relation to NATO defense arrangements as well as Soviet force deployments. The United

---

4. The meaning of this reference is unclear to us.

States will be glad to discuss these matters with you subject to consultation with members of NATO whose interests are also involved.

"Discussions of these other matters, however, will require some time and cannot be undertaken by this country until it is assured under effective international verification that work on offensive-weapons bases in Cuba has halted and the bases, themselves, rendered inoperable. Therefore"—

Unidentified: Now, we dropped "shipments" out of there.

New York—as very—

Unidentified: Well, I—

Unidentified: This morning's statement—

Rusk: With regard to the Soviet Union, in paragraph 2 of the attached statement—

McNamara: I think that the President's feeling was that he wanted to indicate that he was willing to negotiate on, in a sense, Turkish bases, but only after we have the assurances. You know, we asked for them [the assurances] in this morning's statement.

Robert Kennedy: I think it almost said that he [President Kennedy] would be willing to discuss Turkish bases or anything that they want to discuss.

McNamara: Yeah, but the point was he wanted to appear reasonable. He didn't want to appear to turn down the proposal because some people in the world would think [it] was a reasonable proposal. He wanted to turn it down—he wanted to defer consideration of it—but do it with a good excuse, which was that they hadn't yet given us this assurance.

Dillon: Why can't you just start with the first sentence that Dean has and then follow with the second paragraph without the "therefore" of our original statement—this morning's statement? "It is the position of the United States" and so forth. And then finish up: If this is accomplished, we will be prepared to discuss all these other things.

Robert Kennedy: [apparently reacting to a quiet suggestion from Thompson] Tommy brings up the point about whether this—he [Khrushchev] sends this kind of a telegram, a wire, to get the message across—whether it [the second, public, message] blows the whole other operation on Cuba contained in this other letter [the first, private, message] that he's sending. The idea is not to get this whole matter—

Bundy: How do you mean, Tommy?

Thompson: Well, he's [Robert Kennedy's] speaking of the letter of last night.

He [Khrushchev] made this proposal that the whole problem is raised by our threat to Cuba. We're prepared to remove that threat. This point [in the second, public, letter involving Turkey] undercuts that effort entirely. If we start talking about this with Zorin—

Bundy: If we start talking about what?

Thompson: That we are willing to discuss the question of these bases with only a freeze in Cuba.

Bundy: Yeah.

Thompson: You see, then this other thing—

Unidentified: What did Zorin say this morning?

Dillon: That the first was for public consumption.[5] It was not the real Soviet public position.

For one of two reasons they changed their minds on this. One was that they may have picked up this Kreisky thing [suggesting the trade with Turkey], and they thought they could get more. The other is that Khrushchev may have been overruled. In either case, we have to change that. We have to take a tough line.

Rusk: Why don't we go back to the original idea of putting a final paragraph [suggesting other matters can be negotiated if there is a standstill in Cuba] on this letter [to Khrushchev] that we have written?

Unidentified: That's what I—

Rusk: Because we really ought to leave U Thant a chance to work on the original draft if possible. If we heat up the situation a bit in Cuba, then Khrushchev may find it heating up again. It looks more dangerous then.

Dillon: What is the situation going in Cuba with this fellow [in the low-level reconnaissance flight] being shot at? We haven't got but one more day.

Bundy: That's right.

Thompson: I much prefer this draft of this letter [to U Thant], especially, indeed, the last part of it.

Nitze?: The real question is whether it is Khrushchev [that is the object of the message] or whether it's the UN.

---

5. Zorin reportedly explained that the first, private, letter was aimed at reducing tensions. Thompson is equating that goal with "public consumption" in Zorin's view, even though Khrushchev's first letter was actually private, not public.

Bundy: That's the point. It seems to me that Turkey and Cuba are all very well for us to discuss. Turkey and Cuba are not relevant for us except in the context of our doing a violent thing. And after we've done a violent thing we, none of us, know where to go.

The one chance of avoiding that is to impress Khrushchev and get him back where he was last night.

Thompson: We have to operate on Khrushchev with a public warning. We

of changing our whole policy for a public-relations effect is that if we have decided that definitely we are going in, then we have— Otherwise, it is—

Rusk: What about *them?* Look at the last paragraph of the proposed letter [to Khrushchev] that we were working on:

"As I was preparing this letter, I read your broadcast message. That message raises problems affecting many countries and complicated issues unrelated to the existing tension caused by your offensive deployments to Cuba. They can be fully resolved only in relation to NATO defense arrangements as well as the strength and deployment of Soviet forces. The United States will be glad to discuss these matters with you and others—after consultation with other interested governments."

Vice President Johnson: I don't see why you don't [in] the last paragraph— after the first sentence—the last paragraph here on page 3—just add the last paragraph of the statement this morning. That is what you want to say:

"We are preparing this letter, which was prepared in response to your letter of last night, and have learned of your public message attempting to connect NATO with bases in Cuba. As this proposal affects the security of nations outside this hemisphere, the United States and its allies have long taken the lead to promote discussion on both sides. These efforts can continue as soon as the presence of Soviet missiles there has ended."

That is the proposal. That we can and will just as soon as you get rid of these bases and—

Bundy: Well, I see no reason why a private message to the chairman shouldn't be a touch more forthcoming. I think that—I don't see any reason why we can't say: "We understand your sensitivity on this matter but we can't get at this until we get past the Cuba problem."

Robert Kennedy: Well, I think what Bob says is what concerns the President. The fact that this [public Soviet offer] is very reasonable, and we just turned it down. And people are going to start thinking about the two things: Turkey and the bases in Cuba; and we just turned it down; and suddenly we drop the bomb on Cuba.

Vice President Johnson: Well, we didn't turn it down. We'll continue just as soon as you stop work.

Rusk: Why don't we see if we can agree on this language for the Secretary General's appeal and maybe that will give us some ideas of the language [for the letter to Khrushchev].

[President Kennedy returns to the Cabinet Room accompanied by General Lyman Lemnitzer, who has just completed his term as Chairman of the Joint Chiefs of Staff (replaced by Taylor) and is waiting to take Norstad's place at NATO.]

Robert Kennedy: We really cut it up while you've been out of the room.

[Unclear group conversation.]

Unidentified: If anybody has it, I want to read it.

Unidentified: You're going to end up with Soviet missiles in Cuba and none [of ours] in Turkey.

Unidentified: Is there any . . . Mr. Secretary?

Bundy: The real question, of course, comes back to the action in question. The justification for this message is that we expect it to be turned down, and we expect to be acting tomorrow or the next day. That's what it's for, and it's no good unless that's what happens.

Rusk: I think we have to make a judgment here as to whether—Tommy and everybody else—whether the Soviet Union is putting this further demand forward this morning as a real sticking point up to the point of shooting, or whether it is an attempt at the last minute to try to get something more. In fact they indicated last night they would settle for something less.

Robert Kennedy: [returning to the draft message to U Thant] Could you do it this way?

Rusk: The second point is they are trying to get some more at the last minute.

Robert Kennedy: Couldn't you say that: "A number of proposals have been made to you, U Thant, and to the United States in the last 36 hours. Would you find out from the Russian representative whether, while these proposals are being considered, work on the bases could be discontinued and the missile bases remain inoperative?"

Unidentified: That's not bad.

Unidentified: That's not bad.

Unidentified: Better watch out. Quick!

Robert Kennedy: That would get—I think it might resolve the . . . [The message could say:] "A number of proposals have been made to you and to

Robert Kennedy: I don't know how you can put that [phrase]. While they [these proposals] are being considered and discussed" . . .

Bundy: "While various solutions are being considered and discussed." "While these and other proposals are being discussed."

Robert Kennedy: Would you find out—

Bundy: We don't need to concentrate just on Soviet proposals.

Sorensen: "Various solutions." I think that Bobby said so in the proposal. "While various solutions are being discussed."

[Unclear group conversation.]

Rusk: We're going to have to revise the [draft] letter to Khrushchev [to conform with the language being used with U Thant].

Bundy: Not very much, do we?

Ball: Is this letter to Khrushchev going to be appropriate, Bobby?

Rusk: It's likely to become public.

Unidentified: It shouldn't be. I mean—

Rusk: U Thant would have to make that public along with the other of last night.

Unidentified: He should make it public. We shouldn't make it public.

Dillon: Well, what I'm thinking of is some public longer letter from us that would counteract the Soviet propaganda in the press about Turkey.

Unidentified: What is the military plan?

McNamara: Well, the military plan now is very clear. A limited strike is out. We can't go on a limited strike without the reconnaissance aircraft.

So the military plan now is basically invasion, because we've set a large strike. We might try a large strike without starting the invasion, or without committing ourselves, because we can't carry it out anyway for a period of X days. So we have time to cancel invasion plans. But they should be put on from start to start. Call out the reserves. We also need to have the air units for the invasion in any case. We need the army units in reserve and our strategic reserve in relation to actions elsewhere in the world.

But we shouldn't start this until we do two things: one, until we minimize the Soviet response against NATO, and there is a possible way to do that. And two, until we know how we are going to respond to a Soviet response against NATO.

I would suggest that to minimize the Soviet response against NATO following a U.S. attack on Cuba, we get those Jupiters out of Turkey before the Cuban attack. I say out of Turkey; I mean inoperable. And let the Soviets know that before the Cuban attack.

Now, on that basis, I don't believe the Soviets would strike Turkey. They might take other actions, but I don't think they'd take that action.

Rusk: Then—it is my feeling that they would act on Berlin.

McNamara: They might.

Thompson: It's possible that—the fact that one [low-level reconnaissance] plane was fired on. The others weren't. This doesn't indicate necessarily that they [are] generally going to fire.

McCone: I would say it's getting awfully close.

McNamara: I am not prepared at the moment to recommend air attacks against Cuba. I'm just saying that I think we must now begin to look at it more—

Dillon: You might say, more realistically than we have before. You might say "these Jupiters" just to indicate the fact that we have no intention of doing anything else—that we have rendered these Jupiters inoperable.

McNamara: Well, I could do this only by replacing it with Polaris.

Unidentified: Well, you can't replace them by Polaris.

McNamara: Oh, yes you can.

Unidentified: In 24 hours?

McNamara: Well, we can say: "We've done it." We say that the Polaris in the Mediterranean is deploying off the coast of Turkey..

Unidentified: You could cover some of the targets.

Thompson: There is a dilemma in this formula, and that is: If you advertise the Polaris publicly as a substitute to the Soviet Union, [you] may have achieved nothing [toward persuading the Soviets to trade out their missiles in Cuba] by getting rid of the Jupiters.

McNamara: Well, you may not have achieved anything, but they sure have less of a basis for striking Turkey.

Unidentified: That's right.

McNamara: What I would try to avoid, if I could, [is an] immediate Soviet military response to a U.S. attack on Cuba.

Thompson: Well, we had better reply.

Unidentified: That's right.

Unidentified: We'd have to ask him to find out

volving the interests of a number of countries." Was that it?

[Unclear group discussion.]

Unidentified: So that these various—

Bundy: No. [Reading language:] "So that these various solutions can be discussed."[7]

President Kennedy: Now, what about releasing this? Should we give it to him and then put it out?

Robert Kennedy: It should get out within the next hour or so.

The message to U Thant was passed along to be phoned to Stevenson in New York. The Executive Committee then turned to alliance issues and President Kennedy's telephone conversation with General Norstad.

President Kennedy: I just talked to General Norstad. He thinks that we ought to have a meeting of the NATO Council tomorrow morning to present this to them so that they all have a piece of it. Otherwise, no matter what we do . . . If we don't take it [the Cuba-Turkey deal], we'll be blamed. If we do take it, we'll be blamed. Very right.

---

6. Bundy is referring to the sentence that at this point began: "Find out from the Russian delegate whether, while various solutions are being discussed, work will stop."

7. Hence the sentence sets discussions about other ideas *after* the Soviets take the desired steps in Cuba, and begins: "Find out from the Russian delegate whether, so that these various solutions can be discussed, work will stop."

Bundy: I talked to Finletter and asked him to present it individually [to each NATO ambassador]. Would you prefer to have a meeting?

President Kennedy: Yes, I think we ought to have one. And I think the United States' position ought to be that here it is [the proposed deal, and the consequences of rejecting it]. And we ought to have the . . . if we don't take [into account] what the prospects will be, as well as what we do. Otherwise it's too easy to say: Well, let's not take it.

We ought to get up a message to Finletter, instructions, and we ought to call for a meeting about it at 9:00 or 10:00 in the morning.

Robert Kennedy: That, I think, blows the possibility of this other one, doesn't it?

President Kennedy: What?

Robert Kennedy: It blows the possibility in your first letter.

President Kennedy: Of what?

Robert Kennedy: Of getting an acceptance of the proposal that goes up in your letter now, which is that it [a trade of withdrawing missiles for a pledge not to invade Cuba] has nothing to do with that [Turkey]. I think that if they understand you have a meeting in NATO . . .

Unidentified: That is the disadvantage of a Council meeting.

Rusk: Why does the report . . . ? It doesn't have to be known that that is the only purpose of the discussion.

Robert Kennedy: They are going to know that.

Dillon: It's pretty obvious that they made a suggestion about Turkey that the NATO Council would be interested in meeting about.

Bundy: I don't think that there is any pain in the meeting. Why don't we get the meeting called?

President Kennedy: The advantage of the meeting is that, if we reject it [Khrushchev's Cuba-Turkey deal], they participate in it. And, if we accept it, they participate in it. I think we ought to.

Bundy: I'm going to call Finletter and call a meeting.

President Kennedy: I think he ought to—

Robert Kennedy: The other possibility is that, if you wait 24 hours and see if they accept this other thing [Kennedy's draft reply that would offer the pledge not to invade Cuba], or that they're not going to accept it . . .

President Kennedy: You mean the meeting?

Robert Kennedy: The [October 26] letter that he offered which we accepted today. We wrote him in this [draft] letter, that you've approved, where we say that we won't invade Cuba in return for—

Ball: You see, the way the record would stand, Mr. President, is this.

We got out a blast this morning in which we said: "Look, we don't think this [Turkish issue] is really relevant." Then you send a query [to U Thant] this afternoon as to whether they're going to stop work.

Then, if we send a letter this afternoon, along the lines of the letter we were proposing, which ties it back to his message of last night . . . If this [public offer of a Cuba-Turkey deal] was simply a kind of fishing expedition in Moscow to see if they could get beyond what he'd put in his last night's letter, they may

Ball: We have a letter, a telegram, from Freddy Reinhardt[8] saying that the Italians really don't care at all about . . .

Thompson: There was supposed to be a message coming through from Tompkins[?].

Unidentified: Oh! I don't know.

Rusk: Well now, in view of that message just gone up to U Thant, [how do] we wind up this letter [from President Kennedy to Khrushchev]? [Reading] "As I was preparing this letter, I learned of your broadcast message. That message raises complicated issues not related to Cuba or the Western Hemisphere. The United States would be glad to discuss these matters with you and the other governments concerned. The immediate crisis is in Cuba and it is there that very prompt action is necessary. With that behind us, we can make progress on other, wider issues." We still don't have a suggestion.

President Kennedy: In this language, are you really rejecting their proposal of this morning?

Bundy: I don't think so. It is rejecting—

Rusk: I wouldn't think so.

Dillon: It is rejecting the immediate tie-in [to Turkey].

President Kennedy: Well, we just have to ask. We don't have to reject the tie-in. If we're going to reject it, we ought to have all of NATO rejecting it.

What we want to insist on now is a cessation of work et cetera while we

8. G. Frederick Reinhardt, the U.S. Ambassador to Italy.

discuss it. Then we may reject it, but NATO ought to reject it because I think the reprisal is going to be on all NATO. And I don't want them around saying—

President Kennedy: Well, that is the problem. It's just a question of timing, isn't it?

Ball: I would suggest this, Mr. President. If you have a NATO Council meeting in the morning, I think you are going to get a flat rejection of this [deal involving Turkey], which then ties our hands. I mean, then you can't go forward very easily in the face of this, because the NATO ambassadors [to the UN] met this afternoon in New York, and they took a very strong line against any discussion of this.[9]

President Kennedy: I don't think the alternative has been explained to them. You see, they just think it's a continuation of the quarantine. They don't have any notion that we're about to do something [militarily]. That's got to be on them. You see, that hasn't been explained to NATO, and I'm not going to get into that before they reject it [the Cuba-Turkey trade].

Unidentified: Or a warning.

Dillon: If you have a [NATO] Council you'll probably get a strong reaction from a great many of the members of NATO against our taking any action against Cuba. I think they would say: "Don't trade." But they would also say: "Don't do anything in Cuba."

Robert Kennedy: Exactly.

McNamara: Mr. President, I wonder if we should not take certain actions with respect to the Jupiters in Turkey and Italy before we act in Cuba. And if we decided to take that action with respect to the Jupiters in Turkey and Italy before we acted in Cuba, then we could tell NATO that, at the time we talked to them about this proposal from Khrushchev and our response to it.

If we act in Cuba, the only way we can act now is with a full attack. I don't think we can make any of these limited attacks when they are shooting at our reconnaissance aircraft because we would—we would not dare go in with the

9. Stevenson had met that afternoon with NATO ambassadors as well as ambassadors from friendly Latin American countries. He had repeated the position he had given to U Thant: that other matters might be discussed, but only after the problem in Cuba had been addressed. He had implied that Turkish bases might be discussed in later talks, but the Turkish ambassador rejected this notion so vehemently that, as the British ambassador (Sir Patrick Dean) reported later, Stevenson "drew in his horns a little before the Turkish delegate's obvious unhappiness at any prospect of negotiations over Turkey." The group agreed that the situation was becoming very urgent and that the introduction of Turkey and NATO bases would lead to an intolerable delay in resolving the underlying problem in Cuba. UK Mission UN 1801, "Cuba," 28 October 1962, PRO, PREM 11/3691, 24020.

kind of limited attack that we've been thinking about the last 24 hours without taking out their SAM sites.

The moment we take out the SAM sites and the MiG airfields, we're up to the 500-sortie program. If we send 500 sorties in against Cuba, we must be prepared to follow up with an invasion in about 7 days. If we start out on that kind of a program, it seems to me that the Soviets are very likely to feel forced to reply with military action someplace, particularly if these missiles—Jupiter missiles—are still in Turkey

targets the Jupiters were directed to, in order to reduce the risk to those two nations but maintain the full defense of NATO.

Now, if we were willing to undertake . . . In the first place, I think that that kind of action is desirable prior to an invasion of Cuba. In the second place, if we are willing to decide to do that, we're in a much better position to present this whole thing to NATO.

Ball: What would be the reaction if the Soviet Union was to reply that they were going to maintain 3 atomic [-missile] submarines off the United States coast?

Unidentified: We would send in [unclear] anyhow.

McNamara: We have already detected 3 submarines off the U.S. coast in the last 48 hours. Now they, as far as we know, don't carry missiles, but that's just happenstance.

President Kennedy: The Turks won't take them [the Jupiters] out, will they?

McNamara: I think, I think we could. In the first place, we can tell the Turks—

President Kennedy: Except, if we took them out [of Turkey], we'd get the trade the Russians have offered us. If we take them out, they'll take them out [of Cuba].

McNamara: Well, I think we have to say to the Turks we're going to cover the targets with Polaris missiles.

President Kennedy: Yes, but I think, if we're going to take them out of Turkey, they say they will take them out of—

Bundy: It's one thing to stand them down, Mr. President, in political terms.

It is one thing to stand them down as a favor to the Turks, while we hit Cuba, and it's quite another thing to trade them out.

McNamara: But what we could do is unilaterally . . . Bilaterally with Turkey, we would agree to defuse them [the Jupiters] and replace them with Polaris.

Then we would go back to the Soviet Union and say: "Now, [you said] the threat is there. The threat is gone. You don't have to worry about that. We're going back to your letter of last night, and this is the proposal we make. We agree not to invade. You agree to take your"—

Bundy: But the incentive to them?

McNamara: Turkey is gone.

Bundy: It could lead the Soviet Union to come back to the next problem.

Unidentified: [unclear] just made them an offer.

Robert Kennedy: You made an offer—up there now—and you also ask U Thant to find an answer to this. Now, if U Thant should come back and say, number one, that they are going to continue the work on the bases, in which case, I suppose we have to move in some way.

Or they are going to say that they are going to discontinue the work on the bases. If they say they are going to discontinue the work on the bases, they can either accept our proposal, or they can reject the proposal and say we still want Turkey for Cuba.

If they reject the proposal and say they want Turkey for Cuba but they are going to discontinue the work on the bases, then, I would think, would be the time to bring NATO in and say: "This is the proposal, do you want to consider it?" We haven't lost anything, and they have discontinued the work on the bases.

If they say they are going to continue the work on the bases, I think then we've got to decide whether, if they have said by tomorrow morning that they are going to continue the work on the bases, whether we are going to have a military strike.

I think if you have a meeting of NATO tomorrow morning, I don't see that that is going to—I think it's going to shoot this other possibility which U Thant has suggested [on October 26], of going forward with this letter [from Khrushchev the previous night], and see if we can trade the noninvasion of Cuba for this, and I think we are keeping the pressure on. We don't look like we're weakening on the whole Turkey complex. I mean, I don't see that you are losing anything by not having the meeting tomorrow morning except the fact—I admit you are risking something, because some of the allies are going to say that you're out of your mind.

Bundy: I would prefer to let Finletter find out for a day what people think.

President Kennedy: It's going to be . . . You see, they haven't had the alternatives presented to them. They'll say: "Well, God, we don't want to trade them off!"

They don't realize that in 2 or 3 days we may have a military strike which would bring perhaps the seizure of Berlin or a strike on Turkey. And then they'll say: "My God, we should have taken it!"

would seem to me the NATO meeting ought to be held before the strike. If it's necessary to strike tomorrow, there ought to be a NATO meeting tomorrow morning.

Robert Kennedy: May I just say—what if he says: "We're going to discontinue the work on the bases, now we are going to make the missiles inoperative, and we'll work out with you United Nations supervision." That could take 3 weeks just to work that problem out. And what are we doing for that?

McNamara: If he said he was going to discontinue work on the bases and make them inoperable?

Robert Kennedy: Yes.

Unidentified: We would carry on surveillance.

Robert Kennedy: And we would continue the—

Unidentified: The blockade.

Robert Kennedy: —the blockade.

McNamara: That's the good course of action. No, that's an excellent course of action, which I don't believe he is going to accept. The probability is, he won't say that he'll stop work on the bases. And we're faced with a decision tomorrow of what to do.

Robert Kennedy: Yes, of course. But before the world we're in much better shape.

Thompson: It seems to me we ought to surface all of this correspondence with him, including this [private] letter [of October 26]. He broke his proposal before you got it. Now do the same thing [ignore Khrushchev's latest proposal].

Then you've got the focus back on Cuba and Latin America and the fact that we're prepared not to invade. And this makes it much tougher for him to go ahead and—

Unidentified: Good point.

President Kennedy: What I'm concerned [about] is that NATO . . . Norstad said that BBC radio or TV said that there's no connection [between Cuba and Turkey]. There's going to be a lot of tough talk in New York saying that they [the allied ambassadors] all said it. And they are going to say [at NATO] in Paris, there is no connection. They don't realize what's coming up.

Rusk: Mr. President, if NATO seems solid on this, this has a chance of shaking Khrushchev off his pony.

Ball: Suppose that we give him [Khrushchev] a letter which is addressed to his letter of yesterday, and ask U Thant to release them both. Then he releases correspondence which consists really of an offer from Khrushchev but at least we come back [with]: "Why, thank you, yes." We say: "Why, thank you, yes." And it doesn't mention Turkey. Then, it seems to me that he is in a difficult position.

Gilpatric?: How much will Finletter be allowed to tell the NATO people to get their view of the alternatives? Would the bombing be referred to in their presence?

President Kennedy: Well, I think he would probably just say: "The work is going on. If you are not going to take this, if you are not interested in this [Cuba-Turkey] deal, then I think we are going to have to do something." He doesn't have to say what it is, but the escalation is going to go on. We think it is very likely that there will be some reply against, possibly, Turkey and, possibly, against Berlin. They should be aware of that.

What we don't want is for the deal to be turned down by them without realizing that the turndown puts us in a position of them having to do something. What we are going to be faced with is that, because we wouldn't take the missiles out of Turkey, we are either going to have to invade or [have] a massive strike on Cuba which may lose Berlin. That's what concerns me.

Rusk: One other variation here, that Mr. Foster talked to, is that we say the missiles in Cuba and the missiles in Turkey be turned over to the UN for destruction. And that the nuclear defense of NATO, including Turkey, is provided by other means. An actual disarmament step. Turn them over for destruction on both sides.

Thompson: The Soviets don't want to let anybody get out there and see what their technology is.

President Kennedy: Take them out.

I think the real problem is what we do with the Turks first. If we follow Secretary McNamara, what we are going to do is say to the Turks, which they are bound to think is under Soviet pressure: "We want to get your missiles out of there."

McNamara: What I would say to the Turks is: "Look here, we're going to have to invade Cuba. You are in mortal danger. We want to reduce your danger while at the same time maintaining your defense. We propose that you defuse

respond to Soviet military pressure on NATO. And I'm not prepared to answer that question.

Unidentified: Are the Soviets going to take their missiles out if we take them out of Turkey?

President Kennedy: Well, that is a possible position.

McNamara: Well, I don't know what we'd do. If we work this out with Turkey first, and then we announce it to the world, and then say to the Soviets: "Yes, now we accept your deal of last night [only trading for a pledge not to invade Cuba]."

President Kennedy: The question is whether we can get the Turks to do it.

Taylor: You're deeply in trouble with NATO by [taking] this bilateral kind of approach.

McNamara: Well, the other course of action is not to have the bilateral course of approach, invade Cuba, and have Turkey . . .

Bundy: We haven't tried the enlargement of the blockade. We haven't even thought about it for some hours, and it's been on my mind a good deal. POL we still have to—

Rusk: If we get a negative answer to the message that has just gone up to U Thant, we really ought to consider whether in as low-key as possible—although there'll be a tremendous flap about it—in order to give you necessary authority to call up additional units, beyond those provided by the 150,000 legislation, you'd declare a state of national emergency.

McNamara: I'd call a requisition of 29 ships.

Rusk: I think some mobilization measures, not only here but in other NATO countries, might be very timely here in shaking Khrushchev off this position at this point. His change in position in a matter of hours here means either that—

Bundy: Ted [Sorensen] points out that his message of last night is not categorical about taking the missiles out. It says the specialists would go out.

Unidentified: That's right.

Thompson: It's very loose.

President Kennedy: This morning's [public message from Khrushchev] is more precise, isn't it?

Unidentified: Yeah.

Unidentified: Well, it's not in exchange of a card. He knows the difference.

Thompson: Mr. President, if we go on the basis of a trade, which I gather is somewhat in your mind, we end up, it seems to me, with the Soviets still in Cuba with planes and technicians and so on, even though the missiles are out. And that would surely be unacceptable and put you in a worse position.

President Kennedy: Yeah, but our technicians and planes and guarantees would still exist for Turkey. I'm just thinking about what we're going to have to do in a day or so, which is 500 sorties, and 7 days, and possibly an invasion, all because we wouldn't take the missiles out of Turkey.

We all know how quickly everybody's courage goes when the blood starts to flow, and that's what's going to happen to NATO. When we start these things and they grab Berlin, everybody's going to say: "Well, that was a pretty good proposition."

Let's not kid ourselves that we've got . . . That's the difficulty. Today it sounds great to reject it, but it's not going to, after we do something.

Nitze: I think there are two alternatives. One of them is to plan whether we're going to make these 500 sorties and whether it's going to result in an attack by them someplace if we do. The other alternative is to make the blockade total [including POL and everything else].

[Unclear group discussion, during which someone apparently reports to President Kennedy some further communication from Adlai Stevenson.]

President Kennedy: I think we're in pretty good shape [at the UN] with this morning's message [the White House statement] about the work ceasing. So I think, if he [Stevenson] feels that strongly, we better . . .

Does he mind our sending the message [to U Thant]?

Unidentified: No, he thought the message is good. But he says that this is what U Thant is trying—

President Kennedy: Well now, what I'm concerned [about] is that the NATO

groups will all take a hard position on this before they've understood what our
. . . They've met already in New York. They're going to be talking in Paris. And
the word's going to be coming out that this is unacceptable, pretty soon, before
they have a chance to realize that the—

Nitze: Yesterday, I had a meeting with the Four[10] and brought them right
up to the point of seeing how serious this was, and I think Dean talked to
them about the alternatives they face.

to be . . . We've got to have NATO have a hand on this thing, or otherwise
we'll find no matter [what] . . . If we take no action or if we take action, they're
all going to be saying we should have done the reverse. And we've got to get
them with us.

Now, the question really is—two questions: First, whether we go immediately to the Turks and see if they are receptive to the kind of deal which the
Secretary [McNamara] talked about. If they are not receptive, then we ought
to go to the general NATO meeting because the NATO meeting may put
enough pressure on them.

I just tell you, I think we're better off to get those missiles out of Turkey
and out of Cuba because I think the way of getting them out of Turkey and
out of Cuba is going to be very, very difficult and very bloody, in one place or
another.

Nitze: The Turks will not agree to take them out, except under NATO
pressure.

Dillon: I don't see any point in talking to the Turks in the White House. I
think you have to do it through NATO.

Bundy: Well, I'm not sure. Let's speculate with this, Mr. President. If you

10. A group of representatives, also called the Quadripartite Group, from Britain, France, West
Germany, and the United States, habitually conferred on Berlin/German issues.

11. Dirk Stikker, from the Netherlands, was Secretary General of NATO, the organization's top
civilian office.

have that conviction, and you are yourself sure that this is the best way out, then I would say that an immediate personal telegram of acceptance [of Khrushchev's public offer] was the best thing to do.

President Kennedy: Well, I don't think we accept it [the Soviet offer]. What I think we have to do is get the Turks to agree. Accepting it over their opposition and NATO opposition, I think would be . . .

I'd rather go the total blockade route, which is a lesser step than military action. What I'd like to do is have the Turks and NATO equally feel that this is the wise move.

Sorensen: I wonder, Mr. President, inasmuch as your statement this morning does give some [public] answer to the public statement of the Soviets, whether we can't defer this for 24 or 48 hours while we try the private-letter route in answer to his private letter of last night. There's always a chance that he will still accept that.

The problems will be deferred [if we go ahead with the planned NATO consultation]. We meanwhile will have broken up NATO over something that never would have come to NATO.

Rusk: Bearing in mind that our specific arrangement has already been set forth in New York to U Thant. Adlai Stevenson has suggested a letter here that may not be bad in this particular context.

[Reading Stevenson's proposed letter for Kennedy to send to Khrushchev] "I have read your letter of October 26 with great care and find in it an indication of a willingness on your part to seek a calm solution of the problem. I wrote the letter[12] to assure you that my desire is the same. The first thing that needs to be done, however, is for work to cease on the offensive missile bases in Cuba, and for all weapon systems in Cuba capable of offensive use to be rendered inoperable.

"Assuming this is done promptly"—you have to have something about UN action here—"I have given my representatives in New York instructions that will permit them this weekend to work out an arrangement for a permanent solution of the Cuban problem with the Acting Secretary General and with your representative.

"If you will give your representative similar instructions, there is no reason why we should not complete these arrangements and announce them to the world within a couple of days. I note and welcome indications in your second

12. Probably a reference to President Kennedy's letter to Khrushchev sent in the early morning of October 25.

letter, which you have made public, that you would like to work toward a more general arrangement as regards other elements. I would like to say again that we very much want to move in this direction. If your mention of Turkey and other countries signifies that you are prepared to discuss a detente affecting the whole of Europe, we are of course quite prepared to consider with our allies the suggestions that you and your partners in the Warsaw Pact might have in mind. I think that the mutual explanations in which you and I have been engaged in the past few days, and the discussion in New York . . .

[portion of text illegible]

. . . of the world, as you have described in your letter of yesterday. I therefore most earnestly urge you to join us in a rapid settlement of the Cuban crisis, as your letter of October 26th suggests is possible, so that we can then go on to an early solution of other serious problems, which I am convinced are not insoluble."

Unidentified: Adlai just told me that he has been talking along these lines to all our representatives up there, and they're all—

President Kennedy: But he's going to come back and say: "What about that proposal I made this morning?" So we . . .

Don't you think we ought to say very hard that what we've got to do in the end is that we've got to get an understanding in the next—on the question of the cessation of work.

Rusk: That could be done on the basis of your message to U Thant that you just sent up there. But the—

Unidentified: Let's get this settled first. Then we'll go on to other things.

Unidentified: It [the message to U Thant] more or less implies that.

Rusk: What I wanted to do was to have a letter in hand always which would give him [U Thant] a chance to work it out without relation to Turkey.

President Kennedy: This [proposal from Stevenson] is to Khrushchev.

Rusk: No, he wanted a copy of the letter to Khrushchev. That [the current draft letter to Khrushchev] does not really make much of a point on the Turkish point.

Robert Kennedy: That's the letter here?

Rusk: Yes.

Sorensen: Why not put in the specific points that are in this letter [proposed by Stevenson], though? Otherwise, it's about the same.

President Kennedy: The point of the matter is that Khrushchev is going to come back and refer to his thing this morning on Turkey. And then we're going to be screwing around for another 48 hours.

I think what we've got to do is say that we've got to make the key of this letter the cessation of work. That we're all in agreement on that. There's no question about that.

Then the question [is] whether Turkey's in or just Cuba. Otherwise he'll just come back and say: "Well, we're glad to settle the Cuban matter. What is your opinion of our proposal about Turkey?" So then we're on to Monday afternoon, and the work goes on, and we haven't had a chance to specifically gauge his good faith on the cessation of work. We haven't got an answer to that question. So I think that we ought to make that the key question—the cessation of work. Then if we get the cessation of work, we can settle the Cuban question and we can do other things. Otherwise he can hang us up for 3 days while he goes on with the work.

Rusk: I don't think Adlai and U Thant have yet abandoned the possibility of working this out without direct relation to Turkey though.

Robert Kennedy: You haven't got those points that we had in this letter [the Washington draft to Khrushchev] in that letter [proposed by Stevenson].

President Kennedy: Let's go with this letter [drafted in Washington], Mr. Secretary. Let's start with our letter. Let's start with that, because otherwise we'll never get an answer. We're going to take the "cease work" and [unclear]. I think our letter is specific that it's desirable.

And I think we then go to page 3 [of the draft]: "I have given my representatives instructions to permit them to work out"—and so on, so on, and so on. "If you give your representatives similar instructions, there's no reason why there should not be a complete announcement to the world no later than tomorrow. I learned of your public messages"—and so on, so on, and so on—"crisis in Cuba. When we get agreement there, I shall certainly be ready to discuss the matter."

Now, the only problem with this letter—again on page 3—is: "when we get agreement on Cuba," which he isn't going to give us. He's now moved on to the Turkish thing; so we're just going to get a letter back saying: "Well, we'll be glad to settle Cuba when we've settled Turkey."

So I think we have to make the crucial point in this letter, without opening up Turkey, is the question will he—at least in the next 24 hours, while we discuss all these matters—will he agree with me to stop the work on the bases. That's the only the thing we can, because we have—because he either has to say yes or no. If he says no to that, then we are—at least, we have some indication. Then we're—

McNamara: Take out paragraph one and put it at the end. Make that . . . That isn't part of the deal. The deal is: They remove the weapons. We guarantee not to invade. And then put paragraph one at the end.

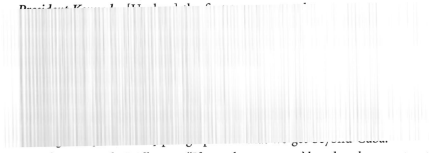

President Kennedy: Well, now, "If, number one, you'd undertake agreement to cease work on offensive missile bases in Cuba and promptly to render inoperable all weapons systems in Cuba and permit UN verification of this action"—that would be number one.

McNamara: Right.

President Kennedy: Then we would get into discussion of all those matters.

McNamara: Right.

Bundy: But I think that that ought to be made as a separate matter in the letter.

Sorensen: I just raise the question to make sure that we do insist on UN verification, because I understand from the Defense Department that we could verify it by ourselves, and even, they say—

President Kennedy: We can't get the UN in?

Sorensen: Yeah.

Robert Kennedy: Well, I think actually—if they put them under trees as we were expecting a week ago, or 10 days, would that—?

Sorensen: A week ago—the work has stopped.

McNamara: If the Cubans would agree not to interfere with reconnaissance.

Robert Kennedy: It said "under international verification." I think we'd better stick with that.

President Kennedy: Well, let's see what he comes back with here. I mean, I don't think we're going to get as much [unclear]. Let's make it as reasonable as possible. You're not yet—

Rusk: See if you don't think you can use Adlai's draft and put in the specific things down there where the arrow is.

President Kennedy: Yeah, his second paragraph is useful. Just put in "this needs to be verified"—"this needs to be satisfactorily verified"—"this needs to be verified under" . . .

Unidentified: Right.

Rusk: What Adlai says about what to do about Turkey and other problems is pretty good.

President Kennedy: The only thing is . . . What he's saying is that they've got to get the weapons out of Cuba before we'll discuss the general detente. Now, we're not going to be able to effect that. He is not going to agree to that.

Rusk: Let a couple of us go out and try to put the specifics of this [Washington draft] letter in between the paragraphs of Adlai's.

President Kennedy: It seems to me what we ought to—to be reasonable. We're not going to get these weapons out of Cuba, probably, anyway. But I mean—by negotiation. We're going to have to take our weapons out of Turkey. I don't think there's any doubt he's not going to, now that he made that public.

Tommy, he's not going to take them out of Cuba if we—

Thompson: I don't agree, Mr. President. I think there's still a chance that we can get this line going.

President Kennedy: That he'll back down?

Thompson: Well, because he's already got this other proposal which he put forward [to remove missiles for a pledge not to invade Cuba].

President Kennedy: [Unclear.] Now, this other public one, it seems to me, has become their public position, hasn't it?

Thompson: This is maybe just pressure on us. I mean to accept the other, I mean so far— We'd accepted noninvasion of Cuba.

[Unclear group discussion.]

Thompson: The important thing for Khrushchev, it seems to me, is to be able to say: "I saved Cuba. I stopped an invasion."

And he can get away with this if he wants to, and he's had a go at this Turkey thing, and that we'll discuss later. And then, in that discussion, he will probably take—

President Kennedy: All right, what about, at the end, we use this letter and say: "will be a grave risk to peace. I urge you to join us in a rapid settlement of the Cuban crisis as your letter suggests [unclear] which is not insoluble [unclear].

"But the first ingredient, let me emphasize, for any solution is a cessation of the work and inoperability of the missiles under reasonable standards." I mean, I want to just come back to that. Otherwise time ticks away on us [unclear].

Sorensen: In other words, Mr. President, your position is that once he meets this condition of the halting work and the inoperability, you're then prepared to go ahead on either the specific Cuban track or what we call a general detente track?

President Kennedy: Yeah, now it all comes down . . . I think it's a substantive question because it really depends on what is and what is

[unclear].

President Kennedy: He's going to want to have that spelled out a little.

Thompson: His position, even in the public statement, is that this is all started by our threat to Cuba. Now he's [able to say he] removed that threat.

Robert Kennedy: He must be a little shaken up, or he wouldn't have sent the message to you in the first place.

President Kennedy: Well, that's last night.

Robert Kennedy: Yeah, but I mean—so that you can—it's pretty conceivable that you could get him back to that. [Unclear.] I don't think we should abandon it.

President Kennedy: All right. Well, I think that Adlai's letter is all right then [on the Turkey/detente point].

Robert Kennedy: I think we can always go to that.

Unidentified: Yeah.

[Unclear group discussion.]

Robert Kennedy: Well, I think they're more confused.

[Unclear group discussion.]

President Kennedy: All right. Let's send this. Now, the other two things that we have to decide are, one, about the NATO meeting. And the second is, what we are going to do about the Turks. In this case, then, we won't have a NATO meeting tomorrow morning because we won't get an answer back—

Robert Kennedy: Are we going to put this one [letter to Khrushchev] out [for public release]? Is this one of the ones we put out?

[Unclear group discussion.]

Unidentified: I don't know about that.

Sorensen: We'll give it to U Thant.

Bundy: We can't use the secret message—Khrushchev's of last night.

Unidentified: Yes.

President Kennedy: Yes.

Unidentified: You going to put that out?

Unidentified: No.

Unidentified: It would be desirable to.

Ball: The Governor's—Adlai's—suggestion was that we release this and then let them put the pressure on the Soviets to—

Robert Kennedy: Well, the only thing is, we are proposing in here the abandonment [unclear].

President Kennedy: What? What? What are we proposing?

Robert Kennedy: The abandonment of Cuba.

Sorensen: No, we're just promising not to invade.

McNamara: Not to invade. We changed that language.

President Kennedy: We're going to put that one [sentence] out and put another one down.

[Unclear exchange.]

Robert Kennedy: Do you think it would be worthwhile talking to Eisenhower?

President Kennedy: What is the advantage of putting it [the letter] out?

Bundy: You know it puts some heat on him if you put it out. If you can get his message out of last night.

Robert Kennedy: How about if you put it [the pledge not to invade Cuba]: "As you have said before—as you have publicly assured the world before—there will be no change in this policy."

President Kennedy: Well, I'd rather say that the United States has no hostile intentions towards Cuba, just so we state it as an obvious fact.

Robert Kennedy: Then they can come back—

President Kennedy: I don't see really what is the obvious advantage [of publicly releasing the letter to Khrushchev]. Why is U Thant going to publish this?

Ball: To force out the Khrushchev letter to which this is a response.

President Kennedy: This is U Thant?

Ball: Well, this was Stevenson's—

Alexis Johnson: This was Stevenson's proposal. Stevenson's proposal is that we release this letter—this letter be released—in order to get this back on the Cuba track, and the focus away from his letter of this morning about Turkey.

Dillon: His long letter.

President Kennedy: [Unclear.] [The current draft letter to Khrushchev conditions the U.S. pledge of no invasion] "upon removal of the weapons in Cuba and peace in the Caribbean" [unclear]. Can we say that?

Rusk: They're going to be worried about that, because you're not dealing precisely here with an agreement. We're simply talking about a concrete agenda of peace.

Rusk: Yes.

President Kennedy: Here we go.

Rusk: [reading] "Dear Mr. Chairman:

"I have read your letter of October 26th with great care and find in it the indication of a willingness on your part to seek a calm solution to the problem. I welcome that and assure you that my desire is the same. The first thing that needs to be done, however, is for work to cease on offensive missile bases in Cuba, and all weapon systems in Cuba capable of offensive use rendered inoperable under effective United Nations arrangements."

Bundy: The sentence isn't quite complete—"to be rendered inoperable."

Rusk: "to be rendered."

President Kennedy: I'd just change line 2, that finds an indication of his willingness. Just "statement of your willingness" or "welcome your statement of your desire," because we don't really find willingness.

Robert Kennedy: What's the rest of that? I thought that was only 2 lines.

President Kennedy: Change a little—start again, Mr. Secretary.

Rusk: "I have read your letter of October 26 with great care and find in it a statement"—

President Kennedy: "and welcome your statement."

Bundy: I think we can cut the next sentence.

President Kennedy: "and welcome your statement of your desire."

Rusk: Say how they—what is our final—"of desire on your part to seek a calm solution to the problem."

President Kennedy: "statement of your desire."

Rusk: "the statement of your desire."

Thompson: Then perhaps we just say: "My desire is the same."

President Kennedy: Why not just say my desire is the same as his. "I can assure you of the great interest of the people of the United States to find a satisfactory solution to this"—

[Loud noises, clanking.]

Rusk: "The first thing that needs to be done, however, is for work to cease on the offensive missile bases in Cuba and for all weapons systems in Cuba capable of offensive use to be rendered inoperable, under effective United Nations arrangements.

"Assuming this is done promptly, I have given my representatives in New York instructions that will permit them this weekend to work out an arrangement for a permanent solution to the Cuban problem with the Acting Secretary General and with your representative.

"If you will give your representative similar instructions, there is no reason why we should not be able to complete these arrangements and announce them to the world within a couple of days. I note and welcome indications in your second letter which you have made public that you would like to work toward a more general arrangement as regards other armaments."

President Kennedy: Now, wait a second. That second letter is the one on Turkey: "note and welcome"—"I note your second letter." I don't think we ought to welcome it. "I note the indication."

Rusk: "I note the indication in your second letter which you have made public that you would like to work toward a more general arrangement as regards other armaments. I would like to say once again that we very much want to move in this direction. If your mention of Turkey signifies"—

President Kennedy: Well now, let's see—"move this in this direction." It seems to me that should be more general. I don't know about the . . .

I'd like to, I would like to state that the United States is very much interested in—what?

Nitze: "such discussion."

President Kennedy: "sees Turkey and"—I'd like to say that the United States is—

Ball: "general reduction of armaments."

Sorensen: Yes—"general reduction of armaments." And so forth.

Ball: Or "the nuclear threat."

[Unclear group discussion.]

Rusk: I think we'd better change this specific reference to Turkey: "If your mention of Turkey and other countries."

President Kennedy: Why don't we just say "other countries"? Leave Turkey out.

Rusk: "your mention of other countries signifies that you are prepared to discuss a detente affecting the whole of Europe."

McNamara: "If your mention of the defenses of NATO signifies your"—

McCone: But in that letter he tied it very specifically to the Turkish situation. I don't think he tied it in that public letter as an example of—

fortunately, because we haven't cleared it with Turkey or NATO. So I suppose we have to fudge it somewhat. But I agree with you. He's just talking about Turkey.

Rusk: "If your mention of NATO bases signifies that you are prepared to discuss a detente affecting the whole of NATO and the Warsaw Pact, we are of course quite prepared to consider with our allies the suggestions that you and your partners in the Warsaw Pact might have in mind. I think that the mutual explanations in which you and I have been engaged in the past few days, and the discussions in New York, have gone far enough to set forth a concrete agenda for peace"—

Bundy: Could I interrupt that? Do we have to talk about their "partners in the Warsaw Pact"? It's really what you have in mind.

Unidentified: It's really for NATO.

Bundy: What *you* [Khrushchev, not his allies] have in mind.

President Kennedy: Yeah, I think you ought to—

Rusk: "I think the mutual explanations in which you and I have been engaged in the past few days, and the discussions in New York, have gone far enough to set forth a concrete agenda for peace, depending upon the removal of the weapons in Cuba and assurance of peace in the Caribbean.

"But the continued work on the missile bases, or prolonged discussion of removing missiles and other offensive weapons from Cuba while linking these problems with the broader questions of European and world security, would intensify the Cuban crisis and will be a grave risk to the peace to the world which you described in your letter of yesterday. I therefore most earnestly urge you to join us in a rapid settlement of the Cuban crisis as your letter of October 26th suggests is possible, so that we can then go on to an early solution of other serious problems which I am convinced are not insoluble."

President Kennedy: Well now, if you put another paragraph [on the specific bargain described in the Washington draft] . . . As I say, this letter says nothing that the first one doesn't.

Robert Kennedy: I don't understand. Can I just say? What's wrong? What are all the points that we make in this letter? What do we suggest?

Rusk: Well, these are points that have already been set out up there.

Robert Kennedy: Yeah, but I thought that the answer—that this letter was accepting his proposal for—

Rusk: The reason for the . . . The actual reason we didn't add those points to this letter was the President's desire not to get his hands tied with respect to the Turkish problem.

Robert Kennedy: Well, I don't think this does that—

Sorensen: One, two, three, four [specifics in the Washington draft], particularly if this letter is going to be made public, are pretty good to have on the record.

President Kennedy: Well, at 4(b), we undertake to give assurance with respect to the territorial integrity and independence of Cuba.

Sorensen: No, we changed that. We refer to the Caribbean.

President Kennedy: Well, that's what we did here, but I don't know.

Robert Kennedy: But that's not—I think you changed that in there. Send this letter and say you're accepting his offer [in his private letter of October 26]. He's made an offer and you're in fact accepting it.

And I think that letter sounds slightly defensive about the fact. "God, don't bring in Turkey now; we want to settle Cuba." I don't know whether it adds anything. And I think this letter—he made an offer last night. This letter [the Washington draft] accepts the offer.

Rusk: By the way, there's another—there's another paragraph to be added: "But the first ingredient, let me emphasize, is the cessation of work on missile sites and measures to render such weapons inoperable, under effective international guarantees."

President Kennedy: Well, in any case, the two letters are more or less—there's no policy difference, is there?

Robert Kennedy: Well, I think there's an entirely different quality.

President Kennedy: All right, look, if we go back to this [Washington draft] letter, all we'd want to change would be 4(b), where we "undertake to give assurances with respect to territorial integrity and political independence."

We'd just substitute "would undertake to give assurances regarding peace in the Caribbean."

Sorensen: No, I thought we said we'd promised not to invade Cuba. That's the language he asked for.

President Kennedy: That's correct. But I don't think, if we're going to make this public at this point, until we know how much we're going to get, we don't want to get into that fight.

President Kennedy: Governor Stevenson's version—he likes his draft so much better. He's going to have to conduct it. I don't see that there's a substantive difference about it, do you?

Robert Kennedy: Well, I think that there was.

President Kennedy: Why?

Robert Kennedy: Because I think, one, it's just, in general terms, rather defensive. And it just says we don't want to get in—please don't get into discussions of NATO or Turkey because we want to talk about Cuba.

The other one says: "You made an offer to us, and we accept it. And you've also made a second offer, which has to do with NATO, and we'll be glad to discuss that at a later time."

The other, first letter—of Adlai—I don't think says anything. I don't think we're any further along, except we don't like what you said.

[Unclear discussion.]

Sorensen: It may be possible to take [unclear] elements of his, part of ours.

Robert Kennedy: I wouldn't repeat about the NATO thing twice. You've got it in once, twice. I think it sounds rather defensive about this. It has really thrown us off by the fact that you've brought this thing up.

I think we just say: He made an offer. We accept the offer. And it's silly bringing up NATO at this time, based on whatever their explanations have [unclear].

President Kennedy: What is the reason that Adlai's unhappy about our first letter?

Unidentified: He feels our first letter sounds too much like an ultimatum—that it's making demands.

Robert Kennedy: I think it's just an acceptance of what he [Khrushchev] says [in his letter of October 26]. Don't you think?

President Kennedy: Well, we can't. I'll tell you.

Ball: I tell you, Mr. President, I think Adlai . . . I think if we could take our letter, introduce some of the elements of his letter in the last part of it, that might do it. I'm not sure how yet.

Robert Kennedy: Why do we bother you [President Kennedy] with it? Why don't you guys work it out?

President Kennedy: I think we ought to move. I don't . . . There's no question bothering me. I just think we're going to have to decide which letter we send.

Robert Kennedy: Why don't we try to work it out without you being able to pick it apart.

[Prolonged laughter.]

President Kennedy: The one you're going to have to worry about is Adlai, so you might as well work it out with him.

[Louder laughter.]

Sorensen: Actually, I think Bobby's formula is a good one. Does it sound like an ultimatum if we say: "And we are accepting your offer in your letter last night. And therefore there's no need to talk about these other things."

Rusk: There's a major second part.

President Kennedy: What do you say?

Rusk: [reading] "I think the mutual explanations in which you and I have been engaged in the past few days, and the discussion in New York, have gone far enough to set forth a concrete agenda for peace, depending upon the removal of the weapons in Cuba and assurance of peace in the Caribbean. I read your letter to mean that this is acceptable."

President Kennedy: Your [Khrushchev's] letter of October 26th?

Rusk: "I read your letter of October 26th to mean that this will be acceptable."

Bundy: This is acceptable.

Unidentified: So be it.

Unidentified: Second.

McCone: [reading from the Washington draft] "The elements of the proposal which you have put forth seem to me to be as follows."

[Unclear group discussion.]

Unidentified: Yeah. I think we've got to list all the things which we can accept.

Rusk: "These are, it seems to me, to be as follows." And write them down.

President Kennedy: As I say, he's not going to now [agree to what he proposed in his private letter] . . . Tommy isn't so sure [that he won't agree].

But anyway, we can try this thing. But he's going to come back, I'm certain. But the only thing is, I don't want him to . . . That's why we've got to end with saying, whatever we're going to do, that we've got to get a cessation of work.

Bundy: That's right, Mr. President. But I think Bobby's notion of a concrete acceptance on our part of how we read last night's telegram is very important.

Taylor: Mr. President . . . [Conversation unclear.]

. . . irrefutable evidence in the meantime that offensive weapons are being dismantled and rendered inoperable.

That the execution of the strike plan be followed by the execution of 316, the invasion plan, 7 days later.

Robert Kennedy: Well, that was a surprise. [Laughter.]

President Kennedy: Well, that's the next place to go. But let's get this letter [to Khrushchev]—

Taylor: Monday morning and the invasion are just something to think about. It does look now, from a military point of view . . .

President Kennedy: What are the reasons why?

Robert Kennedy: Can you find out about that?

Taylor: They just feel that the longer we wait now . . .

President Kennedy: But there's no . . .?

Taylor: Right.

President Kennedy: OK.

Dillon: Well, also, we're getting shot at as we go in for our surveillance. The Cubans are not just talking about it.

President Kennedy: [aside, probably to Rusk] Let's get this letter phoned. [Then louder] Bobby, you want to go out now and get this letter set with Adlai?

[Louder still] Our next question is the Turkish one and NATO. We've got Secretary McNamara's proposal and . . . Did we ever send that message to Hare, Mac, that you and I talked . . .?

Bundy: No, we have a long message in from Hare, which arrived this afternoon, in which he responds to the message sent to him, on Wednesday, at great length.[13] He'll do his damnedest, but it's very difficult, which is in essence what he—the way it comes out.

President Kennedy: Well, now we have the question of a choice between the bilateral arrangement with Turkey, in which we more or less do it [arrange to pull out the Jupiters and replace with Polaris], or whether we go through NATO and let NATO put the pressure on, and also explain to the Turks what's going to happen to them if it does—if they end up slow in this matter.

Dillon: All of this is going to take an awful lot more time than [to be ready for a strike on] Monday morning.

Unidentified: Yeah, yeah.

McNamara: There is a way to shorten it. If you're going to deal directly with the Turks, the President simply sends a message to the prime minister and says: "This is the problem, and this is the way I think it ought to be solved, and I'm prepared to do it tonight. And I need an answer from you within 6 hours," or 8 hours, or something like that. That's one way to do this.

Now, let me tell you my conversation with Andreotti because it bears on this.

President Kennedy: Who's Andreotti?

McNamara: [Giulio] Andreotti's the defense minister of Italy. I talked to him just 2 weeks ago about these Jupiters in Italy, and the Italians would be happy to get rid of them if we want them out of there.

Bundy: The difference between Reinhardt's report [from Rome] and Hare's [from Ankara] is between night and day.

McNamara: I realize that. But there are . . . What I'm suggesting is, we can do this with both Italy and Turkey, and get Italy to go along with us, I think. And this will put some additional pressure on Turkey. [Interruption.] No, but [explaining] the aftereffects of the case [an attack on Cuba] . . .

President Kennedy: We want to do it—if we're going to do that, Bob, and that may be the way we ought to do it, the effect of that, of course.

I don't know how you . . . Not having had it explained to NATO what's going to be the effects of continuing the [Jupiter] missiles, it's going to look like we're caving in. Now, do we want to go through NATO to do that, or do we want to do it bilaterally?

To get it done, you probably have to do it bilaterally, to take all the political effects of the cave-in of NATO. Do we want to have a meeting, in the morning, of NATO and say: "If we don't do it, here's the problem."

13. Bundy is referring to Raymond Hare, U.S. Ambassador to Turkey, and his cable, Ankara 587. The message is described in detail on page 496, note 4.

Bundy: I think you have to do it simultaneously.

Bundy: I think the disadvantage of having a NATO meeting and going to the Turks tonight and tomorrow, is that you don't give this track a fair run that you just tried out.

McNamara: Yes, I agree, Mac. I really don't think we have to move immediately on a Turkish track, but I think we have to get—

Bundy: Wound up [prepared] to do so.

McNamara: We b̶ ̶ ̶ ̶ ̶ ̶ ̶ ̶ ̶ ̶

̶ ̶ ̶ ̶ ̶ ̶ ̶p in front of the night, and they veered away.

McCone: One was hit.

Taylor: That's not been determined.

McNamara: No. Did the Chiefs talk later?

Gilpatric: Well, I heard this conversation. I talked to [Deputy Assistant Secretary of Defense Edward L.] Katzenbach, but there's some difference [in what the pilots said]. I think you have to wait until a little later.

McNamara: Let's put it this way. We had fire on the surveillance.

Now, the first question we have to face tomorrow morning is, are we going to send surveillance flights in? And I think we have basically two alternatives. Either we decide not to send them in at all, or we decide to send them in with proper cover. If we send them in with proper cover and they're attacked, we must attack back, either the SAMs and/or MiG aircraft that would come against them or the ground fire that comes up.

We have another problem tomorrow—the *Grozny* is approaching the zone. We sent out a message today outlining the interception zone.

Ball: Was this publicly released?

McNamara: We sent it to U Thant, and it's released publicly. The *Grozny* will be coming into this zone. Khrushchev has said he is ordering his ships to stay out of the zone. If a Russian ship moves into the zone after he says that publicly, we have two choices: stop it and board it or don't. Now, when you—when you put the two of these together—the question of stopping surveillance and not stopping the ship—it seems to me we're too weak.

Unidentified: Yeah.

Taylor: I'd say we must continue surveillance. That's far more important than the ships.

McNamara: Well, my main point is, I don't think at this particular point we should show a weakness to Khrushchev. And I think we would show a weakness if we failed on both of these actions.

Taylor: And we mustn't fail on surveillance. We can't give up 24 hours at this stage.

McNamara: I fully agree, Max. I was just trying to lay out the problem. Therefore, I would recommend that tomorrow we carry on surveillance but that we defer the decision as late as possible in the day to give a little more time. Because if we go in with surveillance, we have to put a cover on, and if we start shooting back we have escalated substantially.

President Kennedy: When would you shoot?

Dillon: What cover on it? I don't understand that.

McNamara: Well, we can't send these low-altitude aircraft in.

Dillon: They're going to attack that.

President Kennedy: If you're going to take a reprisal, the cover isn't much good, because you've got the antiaircraft guns. You've got somebody up there at 10,000 feet and actually they can't give much cover.

What you'd really, it seems to me, have is a justification for more elaborate action, wouldn't you? Do we want to worry about whether we're going to shoot up that one gun, or do we want to just use this as a reason for doing a lot of other shooting at SAMs?

Taylor: The main thing is to ensure effective reconnaissance—whatever that implies. We won't really know till we . . .

President Kennedy: I would think we ought to take a chance on reconnaissance tomorrow, without the cover, because I don't think the cover is really going to do you much good. You can't protect, hide them, from ground fire tomorrow.

If we don't get an answer from U Thant, then we ought to consider whether Monday morning [October 29] we . . . I'm not convinced yet of an invasion, because I think that's a bit much. I think we may . . .

Taylor: I agree with that. My personal view is that we should be ready to go Monday [with the air strike] and also ready to invade, but make no advance decisions.

McNamara: Well, I doubt.

President Kennedy: I don't think your cover's going to do much good.

McNamara: No. I fully agree.

My point is, I don't think we should stop the surveillance tomorrow. That I want to underline.

Point number two is, if we do carry on a surveillance tomorrow and they fire on us—

Taylor: Well, that's a decision of theirs. Then we'll know.

McNamara: Then I think we ought either to do one of two things. We ought to decide at that moment that we're either going to return that fire, tomorrow, in a limited fashion against the thing that fired on us . . .

. . . prepared for either one tomorrow. Let's wait and see if they fire on us tomorrow and meanwhile we've got this message to U Thant—and we're— So let's be prepared.

Dillon: We've got to be very clear then that, if we're doing this tomorrow, and then they do shoot weapons, then we do need to have the general response. There's no time to do what you're talking about with Turkey, and then we do that.

President Kennedy: Well, that's why I think we ought to get to that. I think what we ought to do is not worry too much about the cover. Do the reconnaissance tomorrow.

If we get fired on, then we meet here and we decide whether to do a much more general response to being fired on. [We would] Announce that the work is going ahead. Announce that we haven't gotten an answer from the Soviets. Then we decide that we're going to do a much more general one than just shooting up some guns down there.

Dillon: Yes, but what about moving ahead with this Turkish—?

President Kennedy: Well, that's what I want to come to now. Now let's get on with the Turkish thing.

Nitze: How about . . . I don't think we're going to be able to get the NATO meeting the following night in Paris. How about getting the NATO ambassadors in here?

Dillon: Why can't you get the NATO meeting in Paris?

Nitze: How are you going to get the instructions to them?

President Kennedy: Well, 11:00 [P.M.] now [in Paris]. We can get them to Finletter in 6, 7, or 8 hours, 9 hours.

Nitze: I'd have a heck of a time—Sunday.

Thompson: Wouldn't it be possible to send something short of what Bob suggested to the Turks and Italians, their prime ministers, saying that, as things are developing—our planes were fired on today—as things are developing, it may become necessary for us to take forceful action in Cuba?

"There is the risk that this would involve an attack on the missiles" in Turkey or Italy, depending on who you're talking to. "We are therefore considering whether or not it would be in your interest for us to remove these, taking other steps to do this, and we may be having to take this up in NATO." Now, this is a preliminary—

President Kennedy: Well now, that's what we suggested to Hare—not only their interests independently—but that's what we were talking about doing. We ought to send that to the Turks, because it's their neck.

And, of course, they're liable to say: "Well, we can take it." So we've got to have it look to the general interest as well as theirs, and a more effective defense for you [Turkey]. Now, they're not going to want to do it, but we may just decide we have to do it in our interest.

Now, the question is, if we decide we have to take it out, wouldn't we much rather have NATO saying it rather than—

Bundy: I don't think we would get that [from NATO], Mr. President. I don't think we should expect—

President Kennedy: You don't think, if once we start explaining it to them— What would happen . . . ?

Bundy: I doubt if the Council will recommend that we stand down Turkish missiles.

Thompson: Even with an offer of Polaris?

Unidentified: Who would oppose it other than the Turks?

McCone: Well, those missiles kind of make us a hostage. We have to go through NATO. I think that's the way I interpret the Turks' position now and also a couple of years ago.

Rusk: When we talked [in the spring of 1961] about Polaris in place of the missiles, the Turkish reaction was: "The missiles are here. And as long as they're here, you're here."

President Kennedy: Well, I tell you, there's a few members of NATO who won't like it much. Most of the NATO members aren't going to be very happy about it because the problem is . . . I think it's Berlin or something.

McNamara: Well, here's one way to put it. The Jupiter missile is obsolete. It's more obsolete than the Thor missile. The British have recognized the obsolescence of the Thor and have decided to take it out and replace it with other systems, of which the Polaris is an effective one. And we propose the same thing be done for Turkey.

Unidentified: And Italy, too.

McNamara: And Italy, too. Exactly. Both of them are obsolete.

Thompson: The Turks have asked for planes and plane parts—

McNamara: We can say we'll send more planes.

President Kennedy: Now, they will—as I say—it's bound to be looked on, though, as [if] the United States—they'll say that this is

McNamara: Well, I don't see that. Much of the . . . We have our air squadrons there with nuclear weapons. There's at least as much [nuclear striking power] . . .

President Kennedy: We want . . . In other words, Bob, we want to send a message to our ambassadors to begin this track, which would then send a message to NATO to explain to them what the facts of life are. You see, they don't know what's coming up. It's not going to be so happy.

If they decide—if the Turks say no to us [on withdrawing the Jupiters], it would be much better if NATO was also saying no, than it will be if everybody will say, which is what always happens a few days later when the trouble comes, that we should have asked them and they would have told us to get them out.

Robert Kennedy: Do we have to make . . . ? What if we had until Wednesday or Thursday for . . .

President Kennedy: Early on Thursday [November 1] to decide on the air strike?

Robert Kennedy: Yeah, I mean, that you could do—I think there's some danger, as I said earlier, in calling a NATO meeting.

Rusk: Particularly [since] a Sunday meeting would attract a lot of attention.

Robert Kennedy: I think if you waited until tomorrow morning and he's rejected it, our offer, our acceptance of his other offer, and then you know whether the work's going to continue and you know some of these other things.

And then Monday morning you call a meeting of NATO, and you say: "This is what we're up against. They're going ahead with this, and this is what we suggest." By then we'd know what we would want to do. I don't think we really know what—know exactly what we want to do.

President Kennedy: Well, one, it seems to me, we ought to begin a negotiation with the Turks now.

Robert Kennedy: I think somebody perhaps should go over.

Bundy: I think it's very difficult to negotiate with the Turks as long as we think there's anything in last night's track [being able to strike a deal just with the pledge not to invade Cuba]. Now, I think that's what's dividing us at the moment.

Robert Kennedy: But by tomorrow morning you could send somebody over to them and say: "Now, this is what" . . . I mean, you'd get there tomorrow morning and you'd say: "Now, this is what we think."

[6 seconds excised as classified information.]

McCone: I think it's very probable that that initial discussion that Ray Hare had with the Turks leaked in some way—by reading or otherwise.

Bundy: He didn't talk to the Turks.

McCone: Well, he reported it.

Bundy: No, no. Not to the Turks.

McCone: Well, I had the impression that—

Bundy: The letter [cable] doesn't . . . He was not talking to the Turks. He was estimating the situation himself.

I think it's—

Robert Kennedy: There was an early conversation.

Nitze: Ismet[14] raised the question with him. That was in news reports.

Bundy: That's different.

Ball: He had specific instructions not to talk to the Turks. We told him. Neither he nor Reinhardt was supposed to.

President Kennedy: First of all, are the Turks more likely to take them out if we have a bilateral or a NATO decision?

Bundy: I think NATO.

Dillon: NATO, as part of an overall decision.

McCone: That's the way they were put in. It was through NATO.

Thompson: Are we saying that they'll go along with whatever is decided within NATO?

Robert Kennedy: What is the rush about this, other than the fact that we have to make a choice?

---

14. Ismet Inonu, Prime Minister of Turkey.

McNamara: I think the rush is what do we do. A U-2 was shot down. The fire against our low-altitude surveillance.

Robert Kennedy: A U-2 was shot down?

McNamara: Yes. [Unclear name] said it got shot down.

Robert Kennedy: Was the pilot killed?

Taylor: It was shot down over Banes, which is right near a SAM-2 site in eastern Cuba.

Unidentified: A SAM site.

. . . . that fires against a surveillance aircraft, and only if we maintain a tight blockade in this interim period. If we're willing to do those two things, I think we can defer the air attack until Wednesday or Thursday and take time to go to NATO.

President Kennedy: How do we explain the effect of this Khrushchev message of last night? And their decision [to shoot down U.S. planes], in view of their previous orders [to fire only if attacked], the change of orders? We've both had flak and a SAM site operation. How do we . . . ? I mean, that's a . . .

McNamara: How do we interpret this? I don't know how to interpret it.

Taylor: They [the Soviets] feel they must respond now. The whole world knows where we're flying.

That raises the question of retaliation against the SAM sites. We think we—we have various other reasons to believe that we know the SAM sites [that shot down the U-2]. Two days ago—

President Kennedy: How can we send a U-2 fellow over there tomorrow unless we take out all the SAM sites?

Taylor: This is exactly the effect.

McNamara: I don't think we can.

[Unclear group discussion.]

Unidentified: It's on the ground?

Taylor: It's on the ground. The wreckage is on the ground and the pilot's dead.

McNamara: It's in the water, isn't it?

15. The pilot was Major Rudolph Anderson, of South Carolina.

Taylor: I didn't get the water part.

Bundy: If we know it, it must be either on friendly land or in the water.

McNamara: It is on Cuban land at this point?

Taylor: That's what I've got.

McCone: I wonder if this shouldn't cause a most violent protest. Write a letter right to Khrushchev. Here's, here's an action they've taken against— against us, a new order in defiance of public statements he made. I think—

Unidentified: They've fired the first shot.

McCone: If there's any continuation of this, we've got to take those SAM sites out of there.

Taylor: We should retaliate against the SAM site, and announce that if any other planes are fired on we will come back and take it.

[Unclear group discussion.]

Unidentified: One sentence. For 2 or 3 days, it looked good there.

Unidentified: It looked good to me. Isn't this what we told the NATO people we'd do—the Quadripartite Group?

Nitze: Yes. We told the Quadripartite Group we would [unclear] the missiles.

Bundy: You can go against one [SAM site], can you? Now, tonight?

McNamara: No, it's too late [with daylight fading]. This is why it gets into tomorrow, and I . . . Without thinking about retaliation today, what are we going to do if we want to defer the air attack to Wednesday or Thursday.

Taylor: It will be very dangerous, I would say, Mr. Secretary, unless we can reconnoiter each day—reconnoiter each day. That's the difficulty of reconnaissance.

McNamara: And if we're going to [do] reconnaissance, carry out surveillance each day, we must be prepared to fire each day.

Taylor: That's correct.

President Kennedy: We can't very well send a U-2 over there, can we now, and have a guy killed again tomorrow?

Taylor: We certainly shouldn't do it until we retaliate and say that if they fire again on one of our planes that we will come back with great force.

Nitze?: I think you've just got to take out that SAM site. You can't continue with them.

President Kennedy: Well, except that we've still got the problem of—even if we take out this SAM site, the fellow still is going to be awfully vulnerable tomorrow from all the others, isn't he?

Bundy: If you take one out, you got to try again.

McNamara: I think we can forget the U-2 for the moment.

Rusk: It builds up, though, on a somewhat different plane than the all-out attack plan.

Unidentified: Yeah.

McNamara: We can carry out low-altitude surveillance tomorrow, take out this SAM site, and take out more SAM sites tomorrow, and make aircraft go in at low altitude.

President Kennedy: Well now, do we want to announce tonight that this U-2 was shot down?

Gilpatric: No, no. This is a general statement that we would enforce surveillance.

President Kennedy: Well now, do we want to just announce that an American plane was shot down—a surveillance plane was shot down in Cuba? It seems to me that's been—

Ball: I would announce it after you've taken further action.

Unidentified: I understand, sir, that Havana has announced it. That's how we . . .

President Kennedy: Well, I think that we ought to announce it because it shows off Khrushchev's protestations about Cuba.

Unidentified: Came from over there?

Bundy: This about the pilot is from Havana.

Sorensen: Oh, that's Havana!

President Kennedy: We haven't confirmed that, have we. There are so goddamn many . . . We could stay here all day.

Well now, let's say if we're sure the U-2 has been shot down, it seems to me we've got to announce it, or it's going to dribble out. Havana's announced it anyway. We ought to announce it.

Sorensen: We don't know that yet.

President Kennedy: Then we ought to not say anything, don't you think? And just take the reprisal without making any announcement? We don't want

---

16. Gilpatric is referring to the statement issued by the Defense Department's press spokesman at about 3:30 P.M., in reaction to the hostile fire upon the low-level reconnaissance aircraft.

to announce that we're going to take a reprisal against that SAM site tomorrow, or would that make our reprisal more difficult?

McNamara: It would certainly make it more difficult.

President Kennedy: I think we ought to announce that action is being taken—action will be taken to protect our various aircraft.

McNamara: Exactly. Then we ought to go in at dawn and take out that SAM site. And we ought to send a surveillance aircraft in tomorrow with the regular flights early in the morning, and we ought to be prepared to take out more SAM sites and knock out the—

President Kennedy: Well, what we want to do, then, is get this announcement written.

Ros, why don't you write this out, plus this thing about what we're going to do. Then we'll get back to what we're going to do about the Turks.

[Overlapping voices.]

McNamara: Well, I think he was shot coming in.

Robert Kennedy: But he came in.

Rusk: There's a map I have showed him the other way around.

McNamara: Now, he was to go up here.

President Kennedy: Well, can we take that SAM site out?

Rusk: Here's the chart that was just handed us. It shows he was on his way out. Because that's the Banes site.

Robert Kennedy: In addition, there was one other shooting at the low-level, wasn't there?

Unidentified: Yes.

Unidentified: Where was that, Bob, do you know?

McNamara: I haven't the detail.

Unidentified: Near [unclear name]?

Unidentified: Possibly.

Taylor: They started the shooting.

President Kennedy: Well now, we're going to get out an announcement about the earlier thing, and we're going to say that . . .

McNamara: We're going to say that it was shot down, and we're going to continue our surveillance protected by U.S. fighter aircraft.

Dillon: Suitable protection.

Unidentified: The assumption is—

McNamara: Well, I'd just say "U.S. fighter aircraft" so you don't leave any doubt about it.

Robert Kennedy: Tomorrow morning, add POL [to the quarantine]?

McNamara: I wouldn't do it tonight, Bobby. I'd just announce this one.

I think tomorrow morning we ought to go in and take out that SAM site, and send our surveillance in with proper protection immediately following it or on top of it, or whatever way the—

Taylor: [3 seconds excised as classified information, possibly because the information came from intercepted Cuban communications.] The plane is on the ground. It is not in the water.

Unidentified: In Cuba?

Robert Kennedy: In Cuba. Well . . .

in any case. It may be we don't know it was shot down.

Bundy: We don't know it.

McNamara: I think—certainly I'd say—it was shot down. Because the probabilities are that it was shot down, and we want an excuse to go in tomorrow and shoot up that SAM site and send in our—

Dillon: If the plane's on the ground there, it was shot down. It didn't just come down and land.

McNamara: Well, there might have been mechanical failure problems.

President Kennedy: The only point is—the only thing that troubles us—is the other plane was shot at.

McNamara: That's right. Exactly.

President Kennedy: They say—that's why I'd like to find out whether Havana says they did shoot it down.

Unidentified: We don't have anything from Havana yet, do we?

Gilpatric: We assume these SAM sites are manned by Soviets.

Unidentified: Yes.

Gilpatric: That's the significant part, if it is the SAM site.

Unidentified: You might have Cubans—

Unidentified: No, but they'd be inoperative.

McNamara: You had antiaircraft. This is a change of pattern. Now, why it's a change of pattern, we don't know.

Robert Kennedy: Yeah.

Unidentified: I think the important thing to find out is, if we possibly can, whether this is a SAM site.

McNamara: There's no way to find out. What we know is that that particular SAM is the one that had the Fruitcake radar, which is required for control of the missiles.

Unidentified: Will we know whether it's in operation today?

McNamara: It was in operation, we believe, at the same time that the U-2 was over. We checked it this morning. We checked it.

Alexis Johnson: It's a very different thing. You could have an undisciplined antiaircraft, Cuban antiaircraft outfit, fire. But to have a SAM site, with a Russian crew, fire is not any accident.

Unidentified: Well, if he had been at altitude and had any type of a failure, he could fly to Puerto Rico or Mexico.

Unidentified: He could have had an engine failure of some type that was—

Dillon: But even then he could fly out.

Unidentified: I mean that destroyed him.

Unidentified: But if he blew up they're not going to be recovering his box from the aircraft, not likely.

[Unclear discussion; much clatter; possible sound of song—a cleaning crew? a radio?]

President Kennedy: What we got to do is—let's just see if we can get this. Announce the plane that from a base in Cuba was fired upon.

Let's see if . . . George, come up and sit here now. Let's talk a little more about the Turks, how we're going to handle that. NATO and the Turks, that's the one matter we haven't settled today.

Dillon: I am very much concerned that this Castro announcement was late. The reason eludes me.

President Kennedy: I think we ought to . . . Why don't we send an instruction to Hare to have a conversation [with the Turks], but also have the NATO meeting? And to explain to them what's happening over here? Otherwise, we're going to be carrying a hell of a bag.

Dillon: I think you're going to have great pressure internally within the United States, too, to act quickly, with our planes always being shot down while we sit around here.

President Kennedy: Therefore, we've got to move. That's why I think we'd better have a NATO meeting tomorrow.

Dillon: I think the fact that something's shot down is no reason to have a NATO meeting tomorrow morning.

President Kennedy: Explain to them where we are. I'm just afraid of what's going to happen in NATO, and Europe, when we get into this thing more and more, and I think they ought to feel that they were part of it. Even if we don't do anything about the Turks, they ought to feel that they know what . . .

McNamara: I would agree, but I think we ought to know what we want NATO to do tomorrow, which means that we have to have a proposition. NATO itself won't initiate anything.

Unidentified: There will be 15 voices without instructions.

McNamara: Without instructions from the governments, so that . . .

. . . that we might do would be to send a, get a NIACT[17] message off to these governments—the embassies in the capitals. And get hold of Finletter and tell him to call a NATO meeting for the end of the afternoon tomorrow which would enable, hopefully, at least for some of them to have some instructions.

Dillon: And send a message to the capitals saying we are doing this, and that we want the representatives to be instructed.

President Kennedy: Of course, it would be relatively easy if we wanted to get NATO to reject this thing [the Soviet proposal for a Cuba-Turkey trade]. But that isn't necessarily what we want right now.

Unidentified: If they rejected it—

Unidentified: It's kind of a briefing.

McNamara: I don't think you can go to NATO. I don't think you can send any messages out to the capitals until we decide what we want to do.

Unidentified: That's right.

McNamara: When we decide that, I think we can force them, and I think we can do it in such a way that the aftereffects will not—not be too severe. But I think we've got to decide ahead of time what it is we want to do, and what I would suggest we decide is that we want those missiles taken out of

---

17. NIACT: "night action." Sending a cable with this designation of precedence sets off procedures to alert the receiving embassy that the message requires immediate action without waiting until the normal opening of business in the morning.

Turkey. And we simply say that we believe this is, as I do believe, in the interest of the alliance, and that we will replace those missiles with other fire.

President Kennedy: What they're going to say is we've taken the trade of the Russians, aren't they?

McNamara: But I would say: "We may have to attack Cuba. If we attack Cuba, they're holding Turkey as a hostage and they're likely to attack Turkey and this" . . .

Bundy: "To free our hands in Cuba, we must get these missiles out of Turkey," is what we say.

McNamara: Yeah. "Without endangering you, the alliance." This is the theme we give to them.

McCone: That is the point that always has to be made to these countries— that, after all, the menace of these missiles like these in Cuba is a menace to the retaliatory power of the United States, which is the central defense of the whole free world, including Turkey.

McNamara: Yeah, well, I would put it like this. "We're not trading Turkish missiles for Cuban missiles."

Bundy: No, no.

McNamara: Not a bit. We're relieving the alliance of a threat that is presently upon them.

Bundy: Of a local threat—

President Kennedy: But they will say, it's going to be regarded in the NATO meeting as a trade, isn't it? They're going to say: "Well now, are you going to do a deal with the Russians? We'll take them out of Turkey?"

Bundy: It will be seen as a trade by a great many people, Mr. President. There's no doubt about that. We've looked that one in the eye. If you don't buy that, then it seems to me Bob has the best way of dealing with it.

President Kennedy: Of course, what we would like to do is have the Turks come and offer this.

Unidentified: Yeah.

McNamara: Given time, we might work that out, but you can't work it out with the Turks in a short time. I'm certain of that. They are a terribly stubborn people to talk to on this kind of a point.

Unidentified: This [letter to Khrushchev] is ready to go.

Sorensen: We have one last line, Mr. President, that Bobby thought you would want to look at—the last line on the first page.

President Kennedy: Also, "invasion." Do you think we ought to say that? It depends on—yeah, but I think you speak of a chance for peace in the Caribbean. I think that's all we have to say at this point. He understands.

Bundy: Ted?

Sorensen: Yes.

Bundy: Do you want any help getting that sent?

[Unclear group discussion.]

McNamara: George and Mac, we could sit down and try to draft an instruction, first to the governments tonight, then to Hare, and then to NATO. They're all the same, in effect.

Bundy: The instruction will be one based

Unidentified: Well, I'd say we'd withdraw the warheads, wouldn't we?

President Kennedy: The warheads. The Turks would charge this is the only thing. As I say, is if this is going to come, we ought to . . . The Turks and NATO, this is on the cheap for them, they will say the United States is pulling out in order to try to make a deal on Cuba. No, it's not a matter of whether we say it's to protect Turkey or not. That's the way they're going to think about it.

Dillon: Well, we can put in "provided that NATO agrees."

McNamara: I was going to say, we can put it on an either/or basis. We can say we're in a position where we believe we're going to have to attack Cuba. If we attack Cuba, there's great likelihood that the Soviets will attack the missiles in Turkey.

Unidentified: Or in Italy.

McNamara: "We are willing, if you would wish us to do so, to give you [Turkey] additional guarantees, move Polaris submarines there, place additional planes in, and to state beforehand that the missiles in Turkey and Italy have been rendered inoperable before we attack Cuba, thereby increasing your safety, if you wish us to do so," and put it on that basis.

Bundy: If they don't take it—

McNamara: If they don't take it, that's their decision.

President Kennedy: Yeah, and if they don't take it, we feel they should recognize the danger, accept the danger.

Unidentified: Yes, yes.

Dillon: Put yourself in . . .

McNamara: Right. Let's try to work that out.

President Kennedy: This will be for a [NATO Council] meeting tomorrow. Don't you think we ought to have them get in touch with us as soon as possible?

Bundy: No, I think I would not do it tomorrow, Mr. President, myself.

President Kennedy: I think we ought to get something tomorrow afternoon. You see, it's already midnight there. That's tomorrow afternoon.

McNamara: We send it to the governments tonight and then in preparation for a meeting late tomorrow.

Robert Kennedy: Who do you send it? Who do you send?

Dillon: Sending it to the heads of all the NATO governments.

President Kennedy: Because time's running out on you [Turkey].

McCone: That's why we want to offer, in any event, to give the additional assistance in view of the added stress, because—

McNamara: Oh, oh, yes. That's part of it.

McCone: Whether they agree with you or not, offer the assistance. We'll say: "It's much better for you."

Ball: It's very difficult. Because you can't be in a position where we'll render these things [the Jupiters] inoperable or take them out and don't get a Cuban deal, and don't get anything else except Cuban elections.

McNamara: Well, that's quite a bit.

McCone: All we're doing on this one—we are achieving what is the equivalent to Khrushchev's price.

Dillon: The only time that we say that we render them [the Jupiters] inoperable is when we've determined that we're going to attack in Cuba.

McNamara: This is the point. If we attack in Cuba—

Dillon: We don't say this publicly before we've attacked. We say this just a few hours before we attack, and then we attack.

[At approximately this point, at about 6:30, President Kennedy leaves the room. The discussion continues, more informally.]

Unidentified: Let's go down this track. Take one more look at it.

Unidentified: Yes, let's draft the message [to U.S. ambassadors in NATO capitals] then.

Unidentified: I really don't think we're very clear on that.

Vice President Johnson: What you're saying is that you're willing to give them up, as McNamara proposes. Why not trade?

Unidentified: No, that isn't what he said.

McNamara: Let me start my proposition over again.

Vice President Johnson: And save a few hundred thousand [lives].

McNamara: Let me start my proposition over again.

We must be in a position to attack quickly. We've been fired on today. We're going to send surveillance aircraft in tomorrow. Those are going to be fired on without question. We're going to respond. You can't do this very long. We're going to lose airplanes. We'll be shooting up Cuba bit by bit, but we're going to lose airplanes every day. You just can't maintain this position very long. So we must be prepared to attack Cuba quickly. That's the first proposition.

Now, the second proposition. When we attack Cuba, we are going to have to attack with an all-out attack, and that means 500 ... ...

missiles in Turkey, the Soviet Union may, and I think probably will, attack the Turkish missiles.

Now the fourth proposition is, if the Soviet Union attacks the Turkish missiles, we must respond. We cannot allow a Soviet attack on the Jupiter missiles in Turkey without a military response by NATO.

Thompson: Somewhere.

McNamara: Somewhere. That's right. Now, that's the next proposition—

[Others begin talking.]

Well, I've got a . . . Why don't I get through. Then let's go back and attack each one of my propositions.

Now, the minimum military response by NATO to a Soviet attack on the Turkish Jupiter missiles would be a response with conventional weapons by NATO forces in Turkey. That is to say, Turkish and U.S. aircraft against Soviet warships and/or naval bases in the Black Sea area. Now, that to me is the absolute minimum. And I would say that it is *damn* dangerous to have had a Soviet attack on Turkey and a NATO response on the Soviet Union. This is extremely dangerous.

Now, I'm not sure we can avoid anything like that if we attack Cuba. But I think we should make every effort to avoid it. And one way to avoid it is to defuse the Turkish missiles before we attack Cuba. Now, this is the sequence of thought.

[Unclear group discussion.]

McCone: I don't see . . . Why don't we make the trade then?

[Unclear group discussion.]

Ball: I would say that, on the assumption that if you defuse the Turkish missiles, this saves you from a reprisal. But it may mean a reprisal elsewhere.

McNamara: Oh, I think it doesn't save you from a reprisal.

Ball: In Berlin or somewhere.

Unidentified: No, no! [Other voices raised.]

Ball: You're in a position where you've gotten rid of your [Jupiter] missiles for nothing.

McNamara: Well, wait a minute. Now, I didn't say it saves you from a reprisal. I simply said it reduces the chance of military action against Turkey.

Ball: But what good does that do you if you get action against Berlin or somewhere else?

McNamara: Well in the meantime . . . Wait a minute, you have to go back to my proposition and say: "If there aren't Jupiter missiles in Turkey to attack, they're going to apply military force elsewhere." I'm not at all certain of that.

Ball: Oh, I am.

Vice President Johnson: Bob, if you're willing to give up your missiles in Turkey, you think you ought to defuse them, why don't you say that to him and say we're cutting a trade, make the trade there, [and] save all the invasion, lives, and everything else?

McCone: Day and night we've talked about this. And we said we'd be *delighted* to trade those missiles in Turkey for the same in Cuba.

McNamara: I said I thought it was the realistic solution to the problem.

McCone: Sure. Right. What we were afraid of was he would never offer this, and what he would want to do is trade *Berlin.*

Unidentified: Right.

McCone: We regarded this as just the kind of thing that—

McNamara: I'm not opposed to it now. All I'm suggesting is, don't push us into a position where we *haven't* traded it, and we *are* forced to attack Cuba and the missiles remain in Turkey. That's all I'm suggesting. Let's avoid that position. We're fast moving into that.

Ball: Well, I mean, we're now back at the point which I wanted—

Bundy: We were going to *let* him have his strike in Turkey, as I understood it last week. At one point, at least, that was the way we talked about it.

McNamara: That's right. That was one alternative.

Ball: Actually, what we were thinking was that what he was doing was to trade this against Berlin—or nothing. We thought that if we could trade it out for Turkey this would be an easy trade and a very advantageous deal. Now we've made that offer to him.

Bundy: It doesn't look so good.

Ball: And we don't want it. And we're talking about a course of action which involves military action with enormous casualties and a great, great risk of escalation. I really don't think this is—we ought to shift this one.

McNamara: Well, why don't we look at two courses of action?

Bundy: Let's see what consequences George draws.

Ball: Well, I would far rather, if we're going to get the damn missiles out of Turkey anyway, say: "We'll trade you the missiles. We're ___ ___ ___" I ___

McNamara: Well, I think you have two alternatives.

Bundy: George, I missed your statement. I have to ask you to say it again.

Ball: I'd say: "Sure, we'll accept your offer. If this is a matter of grave concern to you, and you equate these things—which we don't, but if you do, OK—we can work it out. We're going to put Polaris in the Mediterranean because you've got the whole sea to range in, and we can't keep you out of the ocean."

Bundy: And what's left of NATO?

Ball: I don't think NATO is going to be wrecked. If NATO isn't any better than that, it isn't that good to us.

Dillon: What happens, though, to the missiles in Cuba over the next 3 weeks while this is going on?

Ball: Well, I mean, if you do this, you do it on the basis of an immediate trade, and they immediately—

Bundy: And surveillance.

Ball: And surveillance, which is one of the conditions.

Bundy: What you do is you go with the Turks and NATO—you go through the propositions that Bob has outlined here.

McNamara: I would suggest this. Let's get the message [to U.S. ambassadors in NATO capitals] ready on the assumption that either the Soviets don't want to trade or we don't want to trade, one or the other. And hence the trade route of Jupiters in Turkey for missiles in Cuba is not acceptable and therefore we're going to attack Cuba.

Now, let's follow that [other path of making the Jupiters in Turkey inoperable], and get a message written on that basis. Before we attack Cuba we're going to reduce the danger to Turkey to a minimum.

Bundy: I'd like to see both of these messages written. I think they both need to be written.

McNamara: But the fact is this other course [rendering the Jupiters inoperable] will essentially be that [Cuba-Turkey trade]. So let's get first the message written on the assumption that it doesn't.

Ball: Why don't you write that, and I'll go write the other one.

Bundy: George, let me speak to you for a moment.

Robert Kennedy: If there's a chance to do it [work it out with the Turks] openly like that, I think it's worthwhile.

Write it up anyway?

Unidentified: Yeah.

Bundy: Do you want to write one? Or do you want me to draft it, or what do you want to do? All right. I'll get a draft.

Ball: Have you got a piece of paper?

Gilpatric: Who's it to, Bob?

McNamara: Well, it's going to go to three parties. It's going to go to the Turks, to the heads of government of NATO countries, and to the North Atlantic Council. Same message, effectively.

Bundy: Do people want dinner downstairs, do they want trays, or do they want to wait?

Unidentified: We'll wait.

McNamara: We probably ought to think about a course of action in the next 2 or 3 days. What we're going to—[clatter]

Max is going back to work out the surveillance plan for tomorrow with the Chiefs and see how much cover we need and so on. So we're just going to get shot up, sure as hell. There's no question about it. We're going to have to go in and shoot. Now, we can carry this on, I would think, a couple of days, maybe 3 days, possibly 4, but we're going to lose planes.

We had 8 [low-level reconnaissance] planes went out today. Two aborted for mechanical reasons. Two went through safely and returned, and 4 ran into fire—

Taylor: And had to abort.

McNamara: —and had to abort.

Dillon: What was it they ran into?

McNamara: Low-altitude fire.

McCone: You know, it seems to me we're missing a bet here. I think that we ought to take this occasion to send directly to Khrushchev, by fast wire, the most violent protest, and demand that he stop this business and stop it right away, or we're going to take those SAM sites out immediately. This is what I'd tell him. I'd tell him this is a . . . I'd just use one of the messages that he's sent to us, and I'd send it right off. And if he won't . . .

And I would trade these Turkish things out right now. I wouldn't be talking to anybody about it. We sat for a week in which everybody was in favor of doing it. And I would make that part of the message. Tell him . . .

conduct . . . . What do we do here?

Dillon: Well, I mean, this is a job for the—

McCone: That's what I said.

McNamara: Let's assume that the approach [for a Cuba-Turkey trade] is made.

Dillon: And he doesn't do it.

McNamara: And either he doesn't do it or he comes back . . .

Let me go back a second. When I read that [Khrushchev's] message of last night this morning, I thought, my God! I'd never sell, I would never base a transaction on that contract. Hell, that's no offer. There's not a damn thing in it that's an offer. You read that message carefully. He didn't propose to take the missiles out. Not once is there a single word in it that proposes to take the missiles out. It's 12 pages of fluff.

McCone: Well, his message this morning offered a trade—his published message.

McNamara: Well, no. I'm speaking of the last night message. The last night message was 12 pages of fluff. That's no contract. You couldn't sign that and say we know what we signed.

And before we got the damn thing read, the whole deal changed—*completely* changed. All of which leads me to conclude that the probabilities are that nothing is going to be signed quickly.

Now, my question is, assuming nothing is signed quickly, what do we do? Well, I don't think attack is the only answer. I think we ought to be prepared for attack, all-out attack. And I think we ought to know how far we can postpone that. But I don't think that's the only answer, and we ought to think of some other answers here. Now, John's suggestion, I think, is obviously one, to try to negotiate a deal.

McCone: I wouldn't try to negotiate a deal. I would send him a threatening letter.

I'd say: "You made public an offer. Now, we'll accept that offer. But you shot down planes today before we even had a chance to send you a letter, despite the fact that you knew that we were sending unarmed planes on a publicly announced surveillance. Now, we're telling you, Mr. Khrushchev"—this is just one thing—"that we are sending unarmed planes over Cuba. If one of them is shot up, we're going to take your installations out, and you can expect it. And therefore, you issue an order immediately."

Unidentified: Right.

McCone: And be prepared to follow that up.

McNamara: But what I'd do is disassociate that from the Turkish missiles, John. That's part of your message that I would . . .

McCone: No, I wouldn't, because when the pressure lets up, you'll get another proposal. You'll have Berlin thrown in. That's the point I want to make, Bob. You'll get something else thrown in tomorrow. You'll get Berlin.

McNamara: Oh, I think that's possible. It's highly possible. That's why I think we have to be prepared for attack.

Well, let's go down and try and get this message [to NATO capitals] drafted, so that later tonight we have some alternatives.

McCone: Let's do a little drafting and meet here later.

Dillon: Why don't you write up your kind?

McCone: What?

Dillon: Why don't you write up your kind of proposal?

Sorensen: What about this one [draft letter to Khrushchev] that was designed to go down this morning, Bob?

McNamara: What?

Sorensen: What about the one that was turned down this morning— the one that Tommy had drafted that was revised to include the shooting down.

Bundy: Well, it's just pretty much the same thing [as the message approved earlier in the meeting]. Just saying that missiles were getting—

[Unclear group discussion.]

Unidentified: Make this a public announcement?

Unidentified: I'd make it a public announcement.

[Unclear group discussion.]

Unidentified: The fact that this U-2 was shot down, is that public? Is that on the wire?

Unidentified: Not that I know of. It hasn't hit it yet. The President hasn't said anything.

Unidentified: Or the fact of its getting lost?

Unidentified: Should we put it in?

[Silence, sounds of papers rustling.]

Vice President Johnson: In general, the trading of a Polaris for the Jupiters would . . .

. . . . why he wouldn't buy it, but it hasn't been tried on NATO, so far as I know.

Vice President Johnson: But suppose you were prime minister. What would you do about it? Wouldn't you rather have Polaris? I think the reason why he wouldn't buy it would be fear that that meant that we wouldn't come [to defend Turkey].

Ball: That would be one of the worries . . . If we give him an assurance, it certainly wouldn't be a valid one.

Vice President Johnson: If we gave him assurance that, if we hit Cuba at the same time, what have we got to get there with?

Unidentified: They probably [unclear].

Vice President Johnson: My impression is that we're having to retreat. We're backing down. I think if we retreat gradually from the President's speech . . . It's not like this.

They [the Turks] know how many countries are concerned and how much fear. Every damn place you go, there's fear. If you walk into Turkey, they've got to be insecure. Berlin. People feel it. They don't know why they feel it and how. But they feel it. We got a blockade and we're doing this and that and the [Soviet] ships are coming through.

Unidentified: No, the ships aren't coming through.

Unidentified: Okay.

[Unclear discussion.]

Gilpatric: No, but I would think that they would think quite to the contrary. The Russians are retreating. They've stopped their ships.

[Unclear group discussion.]

Unidentified: Did we get off this letter to U Thant this afternoon—the first part of it Adlai's and the rest of it ours?

Beg pardon?

Rusk: It went off to Adlai and U Thant.

Vice President Johnson: All that summarizes what has gone today. We sent U Thant . . . What went out this morning? What has been done today?

Let's just see how he [Khrushchev] was looking at our performance today before he shot down this plane. Well, last night he sent us a long letter. Before we could read it, he made the public trade proposal, didn't he? That was his. Those were the last two things we heard from him before the shot, right?

Unidentified: Right.

Vice President Johnson: First thing we did to him was send this proposal to U Thant, saying find out if he will stop the work and disable the missiles.

Rusk: Well, in the meantime we . . . The first thing was his letter, and we announced [in the afternoon Defense Department announcement] that we would enforce surveillance.

Vice President Johnson: That's right. And we made the [White House] announcement this morning and called attention again to the necessity of his stopping his missile work. That announcement, that's the first thing. And the second thing, we sent U Thant a very short message, that paragraph 5. Wasn't that the second thing we did?

Rusk: Well, the first thing was the comment that—the first comment on the broadcast message [in the morning White House statement].

The second thing was an announcement [in the afternoon at the Pentagon] that we would enforce surveillance and take counteraction if they shot at us.

The third thing was the short message to U Thant.

The fourth thing was the longer message to Khrushchev.

Unidentified: All right.

Vice President Johnson: I've lost the second one. I don't remember it.

Rusk: I think tomorrow we—

Vice President Johnson: Is this what you called the second one? [Reading from the morning White House press statement] "Several inconsistent and conflicting proposals have been made by the USSR here in the last 24 hours . . ."?

Rusk: That's right.[18] And [unclear].

---

18. It was not right. The previous list had put the White House statement first, not second.

Now, in the morning we've got to try to get him back on last night's track—to concentrate on Cuba.

Thompson: If this ship [the *Grozny*] comes in, I think you should stop it.

Unidentified: Is the ship still proceeding as far as we know?

Unidentified: No. And so is surveillance.

Unidentified: He also notes about the surveillance, but didn't we also mention night surveillance?

Unidentified: Yeah.

Imagine some crazy Russian captain doing it. The damn thing [the flare] goes "blooey" and lights up the skies. He might just pull a trigger. Looks like we're playing Fourth of July over there or something. I'm scared of that.

And I don't see what you get with that photograph that's so much more important than what you . . . You know they're working at night, and you can see them working at night. Now, what do you do?

Psychologically, you scare them [the Soviets]. Well, hell, it's like the fellow telling me in Congress: "Go on and put the monkey on his back." Every time I tried to put a monkey on somebody else's back, I got one. If you're going to try to psychologically scare them with a flare, you're liable to get your bottom shot at.

Rusk: What is George Ball doing?

Vice President Johnson: He's drafting his view of the trade with the Turks. He [Ball] says that if you're going to [make the Jupiters inoperable], you ought to accept the trade. If you're going to give up the Turkish bases, that you ought to say: "OK, we'll give them up for Cuba."

McNamara says: "Tell them we'll give them up for nothing." That's the way I see it to do that. There are two sides. McNamara says: "If we're going to hit Cuba, we've got to say to the Turks that we want you to give up your Jupiters, and we'll give you Polaris instead." Ball said: "Well, if you're going to do that, just say to Mr. Khrushchev: 'Yes to your proposal today.'" So he's there drafting one of the two proposals. McNamara's drafting one, Ball drafting the other, both of them coming back with the two.

Dillon: Here is the third thing, which is really the Ball line, plus McCone's idea about surveillance, which is [reading]: "Mr. Chairman:

"We have reached a moment of utmost gravity. Your forces in Cuba have fired on one of our unarmed planes conducting surveillance in accordance with the resolution of the OAS. You have done this before I had an opportunity to reply to your letter of this morning, offering to remove your offensive weapons in Cuba in return for the removal of similar weapons from Turkey. This suggestion of yours requires consultations with our NATO allies. I am undertaking such consultation and recommending that our allies agree to the removal of the Jupiter missiles from Turkey at the same time that your missiles are removed from Cuba. Meanwhile, it is essential that these weapons [in Cuba] be made inoperable immediately. Until this is done"—

Rusk: The weapons in Cuba.

Dillon: Yeah. "these weapons in Cuba be made inoperable immediately. Until this is done, subject to reasonable international control, we must continue our unarmed aerial surveillance of Cuba. If these planes," or again, "these unarmed planes" . . .

"If these unarmed planes are again fired upon, we will be required to respond with all the necessary force. The decision, Mr. Chairman, is yours. If you give orders to your forces in Cuba to cease interference with our unarmed planes and if you agree to immediately render the offensive weapons in Cuba inoperable, the way to peace is open. Otherwise, we will be forced to act."

Rusk: What do you think?

Vice President Johnson: I think he's got a point.

I think you're going to have a big problem right here, internally, in a few more hours in this country. This autumn, the wires [telegrams from citizens] are stacked high all over the country. State of the Union—"But where have you been? What are you doing?" "What have you done?" "The President made a fine speech. What else have you done?"

Rusk: What, you mean about more action?

Vice President Johnson: They want to know what we're doing. They see that there's some ships coming through [the quarantine]. There's a great feeling of insecurity. I told you the other day, before these fellows [congressional leaders] came in here [October 24], they're reflecting it. They're going to be saying: "I told you so." Tomorrow or the next day.

Rusk: What would be the effect in the country of accepting the Turkish thing?

Vice President Johnson: I don't know.

[Possible brief gap in recording as tape reels were changed.]

What would [Ismet] Inonu say if you said: "Now, you've got these Jupiters, and they're lighted up there. The searchlights are on them, and everybody knows about them. They're not worth a damn. And we'll take that old Model T out, and we'll give you a Polaris, a much better job. And how will you feel?"

Well, he might feel that we wouldn't come to [aid] him [in a crisis].

Rusk: We've got 17,000 men there [in Turkey].

Vice President Johnson: We've got 20,000 men there.

So we could say: "Now, we're going to come. But we're ...

... sick, don't you think?

Thompson: There may be one angle to it, Mr. Vice President, that may bother him a little bit. A Polaris submarine would strictly be a U.S. organization.

Vice President Johnson: I think what will bother them is that this man in the United States is not coming [to his aid in a crisis].

Rusk: But the point is, the point there, is that we're there. Our NATO detachment is there. The nuclear aircraft carrier. Are those our planes?

Dillon: Yes. Always. There are both U.S.—there are both U.S. aircraft and [other NATO].[19]

Unidentified: No, I mean, though, if they hit us.

Unidentified: Fire from a nuclear aircraft carrier—those are our planes?

Unidentified: Yes, totally.

Unidentified: Both U.S. and—they're both U.S. aircraft and—

Vice President Johnson: Well then, if we're going to do this, why don't we try to sell them on that, Mr. Secretary? Have Hare talk to him and just say: "Now, you're more likely to get hit this way than you are the other way."

Isn't that true, Tommy?

---

19. Both U.S. and Turkish aircraft were based on land in Turkey, capable of carrying nuclear bombs and with the U.S. aircraft certified as ready to carry them. Nuclear bombs for these aircraft were also stockpiled in Turkey under U.S. control. The speakers may also be referring to the nuclear-powered (and nuclear-armed) aircraft carrier that was part of the U.S. Sixth Fleet, stationed in the Mediterranean.

Thompson: Yeah. Actually, we'd have better protection. They're totally obsolete. But I think we can . . .

The trouble with all this is that, unless we're absolutely decided we're going to hit Cuba, bomb them, then this leaves us in a very difficult position. They'll take their guided missiles, but they'll leave their technicians in Cuba, and their bombing planes in Cuba, and we're in a hell of a mess.

Unidentified: They take whatever you . . .

Unidentified: Say [in U.S. demands to the Soviets]: "nuclear weapons, nuclear delivery systems."

Dillon: Well now, we're just talking about missiles. Because we can't talk about planes, because then we have to take our planes out of Turkey, you see, and we don't want to do that.

Thompson: The only possible, it seems to me, justification for this [approach to Turkey] is if you're going to bomb.

Vice President Johnson: Look, the whole thing is they [the Soviets] shot down one plane, and they [the Americans] gave up Turkey. Then they [the Soviets] shoot down another, and they [the Americans] give up Berlin. You know, like a mad dog—he tastes a little blood and he . . .

Thompson: You see, I think they could put off the missile thing. It occurs to me that we really aren't prepared to talk Turkey for Cuba.

Dillon: Well, we have something of a basic thing. All of us talked about this less than a week ago. We all said that was fine, and we would . . .

Thompson: Not the base [in Turkey].

Dillon: Well not the base, just the missiles.

Thompson: He's now definitely getting the idea that he can get a lot more. This proposal is: whatever you want out of Cuba, you take out of Turkey.

Dillon: Oh, I see what you were talking about. A week ago, it was that they'd take everything out of Cuba and we'd just take the missiles out of Turkey, whereas now he's [going to be] saying: "I'll take the missiles out of Cuba. You take missiles out of here. I take airplanes out. You take airplanes out." So . . .

Unidentified: Technicians for technicians.

Unidentified: Well, they are different things. They are not alike.

Dillon: There's everything in Turkey.

[Tape volume goes down.]

Unidentified: They don't match. They are not alike.

Thompson: That's why I think any suggestion that we're willing to accept this [Cuba-Turkey trade], unless we have made an irrevocable decision that we're to take these out by bombing, it's very dangerous. Because then we're really getting nothing but defeat, as far as I am concerned.

I can't believe it's [the Cuba-Turkey trade] necessary. You know, the night before he was willing to take this other line [asking only for a U.S. pledge not to invade Cuba].

Vice President Johnson: So what happened? Is somebody forcing him to up his ante? Or did he try to just see: Maybe they'll give up more; let's try it; and I can always come back to my, the original position.

Thompson: Well, I think it's one of two things. Either Khrushchev was overruled and . . . Or Khrushchev and/or his colleagues

Unidentified: Unless he ceases doing anything in Cuba or Turkey—

Thompson: . . . or at least there are negotiations on these bases in Turkey.

Unidentified: He suggests—

Vice President Johnson: One gets a feeling now where he's been at all the time. This was what—

Dillon: Well, he made the Turkey-Cuba trade proposal when he thought that that was what we would do.

[Unclear exchanges.]

Thompson: [Khrushchev is saying:] "These boys are beginning to give way. Let's push harder."

I think they'll change their minds when we take any forceful action, stopping their ship or taking out a SAM site or killing a Russian somewhere. But if we . . . Other than that, I'd rather shoot at any plane that comes up or shoot[s at] some of our [reconnaissance aircraft] . . .

Dillon: Or would you rather send them a thing like this which says if they shoot at all, you're going to take all of them out. Or would you rather just go in and take one SAM site out?

Thompson: I'm inclined to take one site out. I don't think giving an ultimatum of this kind . . . I don't necessarily—

Unidentified: If he's given an ultimatum—

20. Lippmann had suggested a Cuba-Turkey trade in his column in the *Washington Post* on the morning of October 25.

Rusk: I think somebody should make him realize that there is going to be some action.

[Unclear group discussion.]

Vice President Johnson: You warhawks ought to get together. [Laughter.]

Well, what if he's—if he was motivated by Lippmann's message, why? Is it your theory that he got it after he sent this letter last night and before this one this morning?

Thompson: No. I think the decision was made after he sent that first letter. In the first letter he was wobbling around and going on about Cuba. Everything else was outside the main core.

Unidentified: But the attack [on the U-2] is not to be ignored. We can state something publicly.

Rusk: So therefore we can dictate something.

Unidentified: Everybody's downstairs.[21]

McCone: I propose, Mr. Secretary—

Unidentified: They're in the Situation Room, aren't they?

McCone: [reading] "I think that it is the responsibility of the United States to make the necessary provisions to order surveillance of the missile sites you have been secretly installing in Cuba. This I announced to the world on last Monday night in a statement with which you are familiar.

"As a result, unarmed United States planes have conducted regular surveillance flights over Cuba, and from these I have learned and have informed the American public that you were persisting in the construction of these missile bases. Today your forces have fired on our planes, damaging some of them"—

Dillon: "unarmed plane."

McCone: —yes, "unarmed planes, damaging some of them and shooting down one, killing a pilot. This shocking further provocation on your part coming to my attention, as I was drafting a response to your recent messages, causes me to advise you that further attacks on our unarmed reconnaissance planes cannot be tolerated and that, if they occur again, there is no course open to me than to order such action as is necessary to ensure the safety of United States planes.

"Obviously, you cannot expect me, in view of the highly secret nature of

---

21. Most of the other members of the Executive Committee had gone downstairs in the West Wing of the White House, to the area around the White House Situation Room, where they were working on the various messages.

your Cuban operation, to do other than to learn, by all means available to me, the nature of the threat against my country you have secretly created"—

[Short break in tape.]

Rusk: —"and to the Hemisphere"—"to the Western Hemisphere."

McCone: Yes, I have that. "[threat against] this nation and the Hemisphere, if I am to discharge my responsibility, which you so clearly recognize.

"Yesterday, Secretary General U Thant received one proposal from you. In the evening I received another quite diff

removed.

"Until the United Nations or other agreed means of verification are established, no course is open to me [other] than aerial surveillance as publicly announced, and any action on your part to halt this will necessitate such actions by the United States as I deem necessary."

Rusk: That's very good. Can we get it back?

Dillon: Well, that's very good, but you don't talk about giving up [missiles in Turkey] . . .

McCone: No. I do say that all three of them [Khrushchev's proposals] are worthy of talking about.

Dillon: There's a case for talking to U Thant, too.

McCone: No. That comes later, apart from it. I think we ought to send him—I don't think we ought to send it to him that way.

[Inaudible group discussion.]

Rusk: [Unclear] thoughts around Cuba. Again, I think the Cubans are beginning to realize that something serious is about—

Vice President Johnson: I'm surprised that they have been allowing these planes to go in all these days anyway without any action. That's what the concern of a lot of people has been for the last couple of days in the papers. I mean, all the old appearances—and I don't think that's good for us. He's looking at it the same as behind the eight-ball a little bit, and he's got to get a little blood. And he's got it.

Now, when they realize that they shot down one of our pilots, we're letting this ship go through and that ship go through, and we've had a hell of a . . . They'll want to know what we are going to be doing.

I guess it will be done tomorrow. I guess it will be done tomorrow. Put the blanket [surveillance] down. And they'll shoot, and we'll shoot, and that's—

Unidentified: That's their main concern.

Rusk: All right, and down at the [unclear] there's a ship loaded with Cubans.[22]

Unidentified: Is that a fact?

Unidentified: Keep them out.

Vice President Johnson: Just tell the Russians about them.

Unidentified: Keep that one out of Cuba.

Unidentified: What we're doing is invading . . .

Vice President Johnson: Actually, the Russians have done it [unclear], but it's too late now.

Dillon: We would have to change it unless we prevail over the bombing of Cuba.

Thompson: The only thing that bothers me at all about it is that you can see that we have two conflicting things here. One is to prepare for action in Cuba, and the other is to get a peaceful solution along the lines which we have proposed. And the purposes are conflicting because, if we want to get him to accept the thing that he put in his letter last night, then we shouldn't give any indication we're ready to talk about the Turkish thing. Because if we do, and put it forward, then we have to take one of those two courses [of action in Cuba].

[Pause.]

[Unclear exchange.]

Unidentified: On Monday?

Unidentified: Are you talking about our proposal?

[Unclear discussion.]

At this point, at about 7:20 P.M., President Kennedy returned to the Cabinet Room. During the approximately 50 minutes that he had been away, Robert Kennedy and Sorensen had hammered out the final version of the letter to Khrushchev, and the President had approved it. Perhaps while it was being

---

22. An apparent reference to the ongoing CIA-Defense plans, readied but not executed, to send about 50 Cuban exiles to Cuba by submarine, infiltrate them into the country, and use them to collect intelligence.

typed and prepared for transmission to the U.S. embassy in Moscow, President Kennedy and his brother talked about the death of the U-2 pilot. President Kennedy commented, his brother remembered, on how it is always the brave and the best who die.

President Kennedy and his brother also apparently then decided that Robert Kennedy would arrange to see Soviet ambassador Dobrynin and personally deliver a copy of the letter to Khrushchev. Robert Kennedy called Dobrynin at about 7:15 and arranged to see him, at the Attorney G̶ ̶ ̶ ̶" ̶

Unidentified: Depending on the [unclear].

Robert Kennedy: Has anybody got a [unclear]?

[Laughter.]

Vice President Johnson: . . . those damn planes he had going.

Thompson: They've [the Soviets have] done two things. They've put up the price and they have escalated the action.

Vice President Johnson: The action?

Thompson: The action. And I think that to mention, as McCone does [in his new draft message to Khrushchev], that we can discuss these other things may be to give them a further ground for incitement, and would have a bad effect on Khrushchev. I think it's a further sign of weakness.

Unidentified: Tommy?

Thompson: It's a further sign of weakness to indicate a willingness to talk about this thing which he put up which was, I think, comparatively unacceptable to us. This is missile for missile, and technician for technician, and plane for plane.

Vice President Johnson: I guess what he's [Khrushchev is] really saying: "I'm going to reason . . . I'm going to dismantle the foreign policy of the United States for the last 15 years in order to let you get these missiles out of Cuba." Then we say: "We're glad, and we appreciate it, and we want to discuss it with you."

Thompson: How is it left about this last letter saying to U Thant—after Khrushchev's letter to U Thant. Because if we get that [President Kennedy's letter to Khrushchev] out in public, I think that offsets a lot of things where we're worried, at present, about the public posture. It [the message to U Thant unbalanced by release of the letter to Khrushchev] would make the Cuban thing—I mean the Turkish deal—look good. And the thing was put forward by Khrushchev, and that we can put this forward, then suddenly he shifts. The public will realize this, that he suddenly sets up the [new] deal [over Turkey].

[There is some background noise. At this point President Kennedy and his brother may have left the room again for a short time.]

Vice President Johnson: They shoot down this plane, it won't make the folks too anxious to trade anyway.

Dillon: Well, I think that it would be very good to have this letter be sent to [both] Khrushchev and U Thant [effectively making it public]. If it's not gone out [to the public] tomorrow, it looks like we had the advantage of 24 hours and done nothing.

Bundy: Well, the letter we need . . . The letter [to Khrushchev] leaves at 7:30.

Dillon: It has? The one you [President Kennedy] just sent?

Rusk: The one we've just sent to U Thant?

Bundy: The one to Khrushchev leaves at 7:30.

And the answer to the inevitable questions about it: "Are you going to tell us what was in the letter Mr. Khrushchev sent to Mr. Kennedy [referred to in Kennedy's letter]?" We have instructed Pierre to say: "You can draw your own conclusions from the letter President Kennedy wrote."

Thompson: Do you suppose that's why Khrushchev put his last letter on the wire before he sent it?

Vice President Johnson: Mr. Khrushchev's letter of last night still is [confidential] . . .

[Inaudible group discussion.]

Dillon: I don't think we should publish it. If you ever want to keep the channel that way.

Bundy: Well, I think the whole thing actually—

Rusk: What time do you think we ought to reassemble, Mac, before this thing here about getting off the letters to [unclear].

Vice President Johnson: We should ask Mr. McNamara how far along he is with his draft. He and Ros ought to be over with the different one they did.

[Unclear group discussion.]

Dillon: . . . take out a SAM site tomorrow.

Unidentified: In what [unclear] statement?

Unidentified: Has it [the U-2 shootdown] been announced?

Unidentified: Take it out . . .

Vice President Johnson: You just ask yourself what made the greatest impression on you today, whether it was his letter last night, or whether his letter this morning, or whether it was that U-2 boy going down.

Dillon: The U-2 boy.

Vice President Johnson: That's exactly right, what did it. That's when everybody started to change, and that's [attacking a SAM site] what's going to make an impression on him—a signal that each one of us is right. He's an expert at that palaver.

[unclear] substantial difference [unclear].

Vice President Johnson: Secretary McNamara is drafting that message.

[Inaudible group discussion.]

President Kennedy: Let's see what the difference is, and then we can think about that. What is the difference?

Bundy: Well, I haven't been in as much of the discussion as some others, Mr. President, but I'll ask Mr. Thompson to speak.

Thompson: Well, I can't express his view better than Bob McNamara could do, but I think we clearly have a choice here, that either we go on the line that we've decided to attack Cuba and therefore are terribly bound to do that.

Or we try to get Khrushchev back on a peaceful solution, in which case we shouldn't give any indication that we're going to accept anything on Turkey because the Turkish proposal is, I should think, clearly unacceptable. It's missile for missile, plane for plane, technician for technician, and it leaves, if it worked out, it would leave the Russians installed in Cuba. And I think that that is unacceptable.

It seems to me there are many indications that they suddenly thought that they could get—upped the price. They've upped the price, and they've upped the action. And I think that we have to bring them back by upping our action, and by getting them back to this other thing [the no-invasion pledge proposal] without any mention of Turkey. Because this is bad, maybe, from the point of view that you said . . . It seems to me you meant . . . But we're necessarily going to have to cover that [the Jupiters] later.

But [in the current letter to Khrushchev] we're going to surface his first proposal [of October 26], which will help the public position and would get them back on, centered on, Cuba and our willingness to accept it. And that somewhat diminishes the need for any talk about Turkey. It seems to me the public will be pretty solid on that, and that we ought to keep the heat on him and get him back on the line which he was obviously on the night before.

That message [of October 26] was almost incoherent, and showed that they were quite worried. And the Lippmann article and maybe the Kreisky speech has made them think they can get more, and they backed away.

President Kennedy: When did Kreisky make his suggestions about Turkey?

Thompson: In a public speech to a party group, maybe.

President Kennedy: And Lippmann had it when?

Bundy: Two days ago.

President Kennedy: Two days ago?

Sorensen: It was in the *Washington Post.*

President Kennedy: Well, I think—

Thompson: Oh, excuse me. Go ahead.

President Kennedy: Well, I'm just saying that I'll say: "Of course we ought to try to go the first route which you suggest." Get him back. That's what our letter's doing. That's what we're going to do by one means or another.

But then it seems to me we ought to have a discussion with NATO about these Turkish missiles, but more generally about sort of an up-to-date briefing about where we're going.

Vice President Johnson: We have two alternatives. Secretary McNamara suggests that we draft a message to the Turks and to the NATO people, saying that "We will give you Polaris for the Jupiters in Turkey. And then we're going to hit Cuba, and therefore we ought to do this because then it means that you're safer than you would be." That's what he thinks.

Ball takes the position that you shouldn't. You should get something for your trade. If you're going to give up the Jupiters, why, you ought to get him to take care of Cuba.

President Kennedy: Well . . . There's a third view, which is that you take this [October 26 proposal] back to him . . .

Vice President Johnson: McCone's got one [draft message] that lays down an ultimatum, that just says we're going to . . . "You shot our man there, and we aren't going to take any more of this."

President Kennedy: Well, what do you do on Cuba on that one?

Rusk: Mr. President, I think that the trouble with Ball's track is that their public statements today—plane for plane, man for man, missile for missile . . .

Unidentified: Who said this?

Rusk: That's Ball's track. A sort of acceptance, in effect, of the broadcast speech [actually message] of this morning. It would just get us completely out of Turkey in every respect or leave the Soviets very much in Cuba. It's the track of last night we want to get them back to. I think if we step up our actions tomorrow against Cuba, not against—not necessarily against the Soviet Union . . .

Dillon: Ambassador Thompson has another idea, which was that instead of the ultimatum, a lot of talk about "if you shoot any m—— f——

. . . . We know approximately.

President Kennedy: But we don't know where it was shot down yet, do we? [4 seconds excised as classified information.]

Bundy: The Cubans have command of the ground, but [do] they give us back any . . . ?

Unidentified: That's correct.

Unidentified: What kind of a place . . . Or where he went off our track. Or where the Cubans are saying that, there is still no evidence, I feel . . .

President Kennedy: That he was shot down.

Bundy: We can't get any more evidence than that. That's what the intercepts say.

Unidentified: Havana might announce it, which would be—

Unidentified: Havana has announced it, that he was shot down by antiaircraft fire.

President Kennedy: Oh, they have? I didn't know that yet.

Unidentified: Havana radio has announced that.

President Kennedy: Well, we ought to get that, because I'm not sure that Secretary McNamara knows that. Can we get that program?

Unidentified: That came from Scoville. Let me double-check the message on that.

Thompson: I also think that we ought to . . . If that Soviet ship [the *Grozny*] comes in within this line, we ought to stop it.

Thompson: Do we have any idea what that ship is carrying?

Unidentified: No.

Unidentified: Deck cargo?

Thompson: If we don't stop it, and let it go through, then—

President Kennedy: In his [Khrushchev's] message this morning on Turkey, did he say [if] we took out the missiles in Turkey, he'd take out the missiles in Cuba?

Dillon: Yes. He said: "analogous things." We take out what we considered offensive, and analogous "means" would have to come out of Turkey.

Thompson: [reading from his version of the message] "I therefore make this proposal. We agree to remove from Cuba those means which you regard as offensive means. We agree to see this carried out and make" . . . the UN. "Your representatives will make a declaration to the effect that the U.S., on its part, . . . will remove the similar means from Turkey."[23]

That's why I think it's very dangerous to indicate any tentative play on this thing. He's really got us there. As the Secretary says, it's either/or, if we go along this path. We either get out of Turkey completely, or we leave the Soviets in Cuba and have only missiles out.

Bundy: Well, we could make a counterproposal, obviously—

Thompson: Yes.

Bundy: "Get everything out of Cuba, and we will negotiate with the Turks with the same objective, even if the Turks don't agree."

Unidentified: Can't do that.

President Kennedy: We can't very well invade Cuba, with all the toil and blood it's going to be, when we could have gotten them [the Soviet missiles] out by making a deal on the same missiles in Turkey. If that's part of the record, then I don't see how we'll have a very good war.

But other than that, it is really a question of what to say to NATO. I don't . . .

Vice President Johnson: It doesn't mean just missiles. He takes his missiles out of Cuba, and takes his men out of Cuba, and takes his planes out of Cuba. Why, then your whole foreign policy is gone. You take everything out of Turkey: 20,000 men, all your technicians, and all your planes, and all your missiles. And crumple.

Unidentified: Especially if you take the men out.

Vice President Johnson: It won't. It won't . . .

President Kennedy: How else are we going to get those missiles out of there, then? That's the problem.

---

23. Because the message had been broadcast, different U.S. officials were using unofficial translations prepared by assorted press agencies or wire services. The term "weapons" was also often translated as "means." Thompson's version translated "analogous" as "similar."

Rusk: Well, last night, he was prepared to trade them for a promise not to invade. Now he's . . .

Vice President Johnson: Somebody told him to try to get a little more. Every time we send him a message . . .

President Kennedy: We already sent him one.

Vice President Johnson: Well, send him another one, then. Do you have a copy of it?

Dillon: Here it is.

"I et m

. . . see about what we do about our plane. We see about our two messages to the UN—I mean—[unclear] Turkey, and probably think about that. And I think it would be better at, say, 9:00.

[The marathon Executive Committee meeting, after more than 3½ hours, breaks up. There is some unclear discussion. A woman asks: "When are you coming back?" The answer comes back: "Nine."]

President Kennedy's message to Khrushchev was transmitted to Moscow at about 8:00 P.M. Robert Kennedy was preparing to deliver it personally to Dobrynin. The message was being simultaneously released to the press. The final message read as follows:[24]

Dear Mr. Chairman:

I have read your letter of October 26 with great care and welcomed the statement of your desire to seek a prompt solution to the problem. The first thing that needs to be done, however, is for work to cease on offensive missile bases in Cuba and for all weapons systems in Cuba capable of offensive use to be rendered inoperable, under effective United Nations arrangements.

Assuming this is done promptly, I have given my representatives in New York instructions that will permit them to work out this weekend—in cooperation with the Acting Secretary General and your representative—an arrangement for a permanent solution to the Cuban problem along the lines suggested in your letter of October 26. As I read your letter, the key elements

24. Reprinted in Larson, "*Cuban Crisis*," pp. 187–188.

of your proposals—which seem generally acceptable as I understand them—are as follows:

1. You would agree to remove these weapons systems from Cuba under appropriate United Nations observation and supervision; and undertake, with suitable safeguards, to halt the further introduction of such weapons systems into Cuba.

2. We, on our part, would agree—upon the establishment of adequate arrangements through the United Nations to ensure the carrying out and continuation of these commitments—(a) to remove promptly the quarantine measures now in effect and (b) to give assurances against an invasion of Cuba. I am confident that other nations of the Western Hemisphere would be prepared to do likewise.

If you will give your representative similar instructions, there is no reason why we should not be able to complete these arrangements and announce them to the world within a couple of days. The effect of such a settlement on easing world tensions would enable us to work toward a more general arrangement regarding "other armaments," as proposed in your second letter which you made public. I would like to say that the United States is very much interested in reducing tensions and halting the arms race; and if your letter signifies that you are prepared to discuss a detente affecting NATO and the Warsaw Pact, we are quite prepared to consider with our allies any useful proposals.

But the first ingredient, let me emphasize, is the cessation of work on missile sites in Cuba and measures to render such weapons inoperable, under effective international guarantees. The continuation of this threat, or a prolonging of this discussion concerning Cuba by linking these problems to the broader questions of European and world security, would surely lead to an intensification of the Cuban crisis and a grave risk to the peace of the world. For this reason I hope we can quickly agree along the lines outlined in this letter and in your letter of October 26.

John F. Kennedy

As the members of the Executive Committee filed out of the Cabinet Room, some of them were asked to stay behind and join President Kennedy in the Oval Office for another, brief, discussion on just how Robert Kennedy should deliver this letter to Ambassador Dobrynin.

9:00 P.M.

OVAL OFFICE AND CABINET ROOM

Dobrynin would be waiting for Robert Kennedy at the Justice Department. President Kennedy gathered some of his advisers in the Oval Office for a brief discussion about what his brother should say to Dobrynin, to amplify on the contents of the letter to Khrushchev.

Bundy, who refreshed his memory by listening to these recordings for many hours, recalled:[1]

> . . . a smaller group moved from the Cabinet Room to the Oval Office to talk over the second means of communication—an oral message to be conveyed to Ambassador Dobrynin. As I remember it, those present in the discussion that followed with the president were Dean Rusk, Robert McNamara, Robert Kennedy, George Ball, Roswell Gilpatric, Llewellyn Thompson, Theodore Sorensen, and I. One part of the oral message we discussed was simple, stern, and quickly decided—that the time had come to agree on the basis set out in the president's new letter: no Soviet missiles in Cuba, and no U.S. invasion. Otherwise further American action was unavoidable. This stern part of the message was implicit in what we had been discussing all day, and I do not recall that we had difficulty in agreeing on it. The president in particular was clear and insistent on this part of the message.
>
> The other part of the oral message was proposed by Dean Rusk: that we should tell Khrushchev that while there could be no deal over the Turkish

---

1. McGeorge Bundy, *Danger and Survival: Choices about the Bomb in the First Fifty Years* (New York: Random House, 1988), pp. 432–433.

missiles, the president was determined to get them out and would do so once the Cuban crisis was resolved. The proposal was quickly supported by the rest of us and approved by the president . . . Concerned as we all were by the cost of a public bargain struck under pressure at the apparent expense of the Turks, and aware as we were from the day's discussion that for some, even in our closest councils, even this unilateral private assurance might appear to betray an ally, we agreed without hesitation that no one not in the room was to be informed of this additional message. Robert Kennedy was instructed to make it plain to Dobrynin that the same secrecy must be observed on the other side, and that any Soviet reference to our assurance would simply make it null and void.

. . . The meeting in the Oval Office lasted perhaps 20 minutes. The moment Dean Rusk made his suggestion it became apparent to all of us that we should agree. It would allow us to respond to Khrushchev's second proposal in a way that he might well regard as helpful, while at the same time it did not require us to engage NATO or the Turks in a public trade of "their" interests for "ours."[2] No one could be sure it would work, but all of us believed it was worth a try.[3]

The concept Rusk suggested would not have been new to at least several officials in the room. In the portion of his message that had arrived from Ankara early in the afternoon, Ambassador Hare had suggested a secret deal with the Soviets, provided that they could be trusted to keep it secret (which

---

2. Rusk's proposal thus also answered the argument that Thompson had voiced so strongly, and that had been so persuasive to Vice President Johnson, among others, about the danger of reciprocal bargains in Turkey—plane for plane, man for man. By offering only a unilateral statement of general intent and expressly ruling out a formal trade, the United States was delinking the details of its Turkish assurance from the carefully worded specifics of the demands in Cuba.

3. Much later, Rusk said that during the evening President Kennedy had talked privately with him about another diplomatic contingency plan. Rusk would telephone the president of Columbia University, Andrew Cordier. Cordier was very close to U Thant (he later edited U Thant's papers) and would be in a position to suggest discreetly to him that Washington might be receptive to a proposal involving the Turkish missiles in order to gain removal of the Soviet installations in Cuba. If Khrushchev rejected President Kennedy's offers, then Rusk could call Cordier and give him the go-ahead to prime U Thant to propose the trade. Mark White has argued, using British evidence about an analogous Rusk-Cordier contact, that, 25 years after the event, Rusk forgot that he had actually talked to Cordier on October 24–25, and that the idea had concerned the possibility of UN monitoring of Turkish missile sites in exchange for UN monitoring of Cuban missile sites to be sure they were inoperable; Mark J. White, *The Cuban Missile Crisis* (London: Macmillan, 1996), pp. 202–203. The actual outcome was that Cordier's intervention with U Thant was not requested for any purpose. Given the sophistication of the discussion about how to approach the Turks, such a U.S. move, under Rusk's version of the story, would, we think, have been both preceded and followed by prolonged and skeptical discussion in the Executive Committee.

he doubted). From both the recordings and other evidence, it is plain that Rusk and Bundy, at least, had read Hare's cable.[4]

Robert Kennedy immediately left for the Justice Department, where he met with Dobrynin. A few days later he prepared the following account of his conversation with the Soviet ambassador:[5]

We met in my office. I told him [Dobrynin] first that we understood that the work was continuing on the Soviet missile bases in Cuba. Further. I

matter.

He raised the point that the argument the Cubans were making was that we were violating Cuban air space. I replied that if we had not been violating Cuban air space then we would still be believing what he and Khrushchev had said—that there were no long-range missiles in Cuba. In any case I said that this matter was far more serious than the air space over Cuba and involved peoples all over the world.

I said that he had better understand the situation and he had better communicate that understanding to Mr. Khrushchev. Mr. Khrushchev and he had misled us. The Soviet Union had secretly established missile bases in Cuba while at the same time proclaiming, privately and publicly, that this would never be done. I said those missile bases had to go and they had to go right away. We had to have a commitment by at least tomorrow that those bases would be removed. This was not an ultimatum, I said, but just a

---

4. See Bundy, *Danger and Survival,* p. 434 and n. 75.

5. Robert Kennedy to Rusk, 30 October 1962, President's Office Files, JFKL. Robert Kennedy relied on this account in preparing his memoir, *Thirteen Days,* but a few sentences in this part of his draft were edited and rewritten by Sorensen when the book was prepared for its posthumous publication. We consider his original memo, declassified in 1991, to be reliable, especially since his description of the meeting is substantively identical with the report of the talk sent back to Moscow that night by Dobrynin. The Dobrynin cable is published in *Bulletin of the Cold War International History Project,* no. 5 (Spring 1995), 79–80 (the authors of the article and comments on Dobrynin's cable were evidently unaware that Robert Kennedy's unedited account of the meeting was available). On the circumstances that prompted Robert Kennedy to write this account, see Arthur M. Schlesinger, Jr., *Robert Kennedy and His Times* (Boston: Houghton Mifflin, 1978), pp. 522–523. Schlesinger's 1978 book quotes some of Kennedy's notes on the matter, accurately describing the substance of the Jupiter discussion.

statement of fact. He should understand that if they did not remove those bases then we would remove them. His country might take retaliatory action but he should understand that before this was over, while there might be dead Americans there would also be dead Russians.

He asked me then what offer we were making. I said a letter had just been transmitted to the Soviet Embassy [U.S. Embassy in Moscow] which stated in substance that the missile bases should be dismantled and all offensive weapons should be removed from Cuba. In return, if Cuba and Castro and the Communists ended their subversive activities in other Central and Latin-American countries, we would agree to keep peace in the Caribbean and not permit an invasion from American soil.[6]

He then asked me about Khrushchev's other proposal dealing with the removal of the missiles from Turkey. I replied that there could be no *quid pro quo*—no deal of this kind could be made. This was a matter that had to be considered by NATO and that it was up to NATO to make the decision. I said it was completely impossible for NATO to take such a step under the present threatening position of the Soviet Union. If some time elapsed—and per your [Rusk's] instructions, I mentioned 4 or 5 months—I said I was sure that these matters could be resolved satisfactorily.[7]

Per your instructions I repeated that there could be no deal of any kind and that any steps toward easing tensions in other parts of the world largely depended on the Soviet Union and Mr. Khrushchev taking action in Cuba and taking it immediately.

I repeated to him that this matter could not wait and that he had better contact Mr. Khrushchev and have a commitment from [him] by the next

6. Note Robert Kennedy's reference to an additional condition, about Cuban subversion. Such a condition was in the original draft letter to Khrushchev discussed in the afternoon, using the phrase "peace in the Caribbean," but the language was dropped in the final editing of the message. Possibly Robert Kennedy had forgotten that the condition had been dropped from the final version of the letter approved by the President. Rusk was later asked by Martin, who had not attended the 4:00 Executive Committee meeting, what had happened to this language, and Rusk said he did not know. As a result an urgent cable was sent to U.S. embassies in Latin America telling them that the U.S. pledge not to invade in Kennedy's letter (now public) was "subject to Cuba behaving herself as required under Hemisphere treaties to which she is committed"; Edwin McCammon Martin, *Kennedy and Latin America* (Lanham, Md.: University Press of America, 1994), pp. 435–436.

7. In the original of this document, on Justice Department letterhead, a line is drawn through this last sentence. The original is in the President's Office Files of JFKL, not in the Robert Kennedy Papers. Since the memo does not appear in Rusk's files, it is possible that Robert Kennedy drafted the memo to Rusk, showed it to his brother, and that the paper was then kept in the President's files and never sent to Rusk. We cannot tell who drew the line through this sentence, or when or why, but the sentence is certainly accurate, as it was echoed in both Dobrynin's report and the handwritten notes quoted by Schlesinger.

day to withdraw the missile bases under United Nations supervision for otherwise, I said, there would be drastic consequences.

When Robert Kennedy returned to the White House, possibly around 8:30 P.M., after delivering the message to Ambassador Dobrynin, he found President Kennedy had just finished a brief swim and was having a light dinner with a close aide, Dave Powers. Powers remembered Robert Kennedy giving a pessimistic account of the meeting with Dobrynin. Powers was gobbling down his food. "God, Dave," Presid

...p ac ~uiucia. Dunay placed a brief call at about 8:30, Washington time. He urged, on behalf of President Kennedy, that the British government hold off on any public offer involving the Thor missiles, on the ground that "there would be opposition from the more extreme members of the NATO Alliance to what might appear to be giving in to Soviet pressure."[9] Bundy promised to call again after the 9:00 White House meeting.[10]

The Defense Department was preoccupied with what to do about the downed U-2 flight and what to say about it to a clamoring press.

At the State Department some additional news had come in, none of it good. With some Soviet ships continuing to steam toward the quarantine line, the government wanted to be sure there was no misunderstanding about the location of the line. Stevenson had offered a formal, written clarification of the contours of the interception zone to Zorin. Zorin had refused to accept the document. Castro had publicly answered the previous day's appeal to him from U Thant, asking for a temporary suspension of missile-site construction. Washington now received a copy of Castro's message refusing the appeal and demanding an immediate halt to the quarantine.

---

8. Kenneth P. O'Donnell and David F. Powers, with Joe McCarthy, *"Johnny, We Hardly Knew Ye"* (New York: Pocket Books, 1972), p. 394.

9. The previous day Macmillan had told Kennedy he might try to break the stalemate by making a public offer to accept outside supervision of the withdrawal of Thor missiles from Britain (already planned), if that would help the Soviets accept the supervised withdrawal of their missiles from Cuba.

10. "Summary Record of a Conversation . . . ," 28 October 1962, PRO, PREM 11/3691, 24020. The call took place at 1:30 A.M. London time.

Castro did, however, invite U Thant to come to Havana for direct talks about the crisis. Castro also delivered another speech to the Cuban people, which was being digested in Washington as the 9:00 meeting of the Executive Committee began.

President Kennedy apparently turned on the tape recorder as Rusk was completing his status report.

_____

Rusk: . . . Certainly he's [Khrushchev] made a public speech on the subject [actually a message]. But we've also made some public speeches, and I think we're in such a confrontation that he's got to worry very much, as the telegram that came in last night, that came in late, obviously showed. He's got to worry a great deal about how far he wants to push this thing.

He's pushing on his relations with the United States, his relations with you, the actual strategic situation. I would think that tomorrow we take certain steps to build up the pressure. We have the enforced surveillance. We shoot anybody who gets in our way. We see whether U Thant produces any results tonight, for when we're here in the morning. We intercept that Soviet ship [the *Grozny*]. We consider, tomorrow afternoon, putting POL on the blockade.

In the firing that goes on in Cuba, we keep the focus on the Cubans. I had suggestions in John McCone's draft [message] that would tend to do that—the message to Khrushchev about the necessity for enforced surveillance, that would keep the monkey on Cuba's back in this regard. If we do have to enforce our right to overfly and to have a look, it's an accidental fact that some Russian technicians may be around at the time we have to shoot, since they've already fired the first shot. It is something that is regrettable, but it is not something that we can make a very public issue out of. We are enforcing this with respect to Cuba, not the Soviet Union—the surveillance business.

Dillon: Do you do anything about the SAM site that shot down our plane?

President Kennedy: We don't know if it did yet, Doug.

Rusk: If we are going in tomorrow with the message through U Thant that we are going to enforce the right of surveillance . . .

Bundy: If we can't get assurances that allow him to proceed to Havana . . .

Unidentified: Would you like to discuss the surveillance?

[Unclear group discussion.]

President Kennedy: Yes.

Taylor: The Chiefs have been . . . I went back this evening and talked this over with the Chiefs. The problem of low-level surveillance is becoming difficult because in all the flights today around the SAM sites and certain missile sites there is low-level ack-ack [antiaircraft artillery].

Unidentified: And we go flying into it.

Taylor: Quite a bit. The planes are turning back. They got over the first of the missile sites and then, at the second, turned back and cut out. We have some photography.

So I would say by tonight, by the end of the day, we probably have seen some of the [antiaircraft] dispositions around these ~~sites. U~~ ~~of 30 milli~~

~~going~~

~~also to prove~~ we're still on the job.

But we're approaching the point, I think, Mr. President, where low-level reconnaissance will be entirely impossible. And if we reach that point, and if we're going to continue reconnaissance, without actually taking out the whole works, we're faced with taking out a number of the SAM sites that—say 10—can get us [unclear] coming in again at medium- and high-level reconnaissance. But low-level reconnaissance probably is on its way out, and I think we'll learn that tomorrow.

McNamara: I would add to that, I don't believe we should carry out tomorrow's U-2 mission. The U-2 is due to go tomorrow.

But I do believe we should carry out the low-level reconnaissance with the necessary fighter escorts and preparations for following reconnaissance, if it's attacked, with attack on the attackers.

Unidentified: You don't think that fighter escort on the low level will help tomorrow?

Taylor: These [fighter escort] planes are off the coast now, in case they have a cripple [a damaged reconnaissance aircraft] coming out, but this was a case again of trying to put rush crews on certain targets because we know, we don't think . . .

Dillon: I wasn't quite clear. Is the antiaircraft shooting at these things around the missile sites themselves?

Taylor: Either side of the missile site.

McNamara: I think that the point is, that if our planes are fired on tomorrow, we ought to fire back. That's what I'd have, as far as . . . The best indication of the antiaircraft sites that we have is around the missile sites—

Rusk: But why fire back at the missiles on the ground bases on the basis that you're firing back at the antiaircraft [guns]?

Dillon: Because that's where they are.

President Kennedy: Let me say, I think we ought to wait till tomorrow afternoon, to see whether we get any answers if U Thant goes down there [to Havana].

We're rapidly approaching a real . . . I don't think that firing back at a 20-millimeter [gun] coming off the ground is good. I think we ought to figure that Monday [October 29], if tomorrow they fire at us and we don't have any answer from the Russians, then Monday, it seems to me, we can, ought to, maybe, consider making a statement tomorrow about the firing and regarding [the fact that] we'll take action now any place in Cuba, on those areas which can fire. And then go in and take all of the SAM sites out. I'd rather take . . . I don't think that it does any good to take out, to try to fire at a 20-millimeter on the ground. You just hazard our planes, and the people on the ground have the advantage.

On the other hand, I don't want, I don't think we do any good to begin to sort of *half* do it. I think we ought to keep tomorrow clean, do the best we can with the surveillance. If they still fire and we haven't got a satisfactory answer back from the Russians, I think we ought to put a statement out tomorrow that we are fired upon. We are therefore considering the island of Cuba as an open territory, and then take out all these SAM sites.

Otherwise, what we're going to do is find this buildup of the protection for the SAM sites low [with guns to fire at low-flying planes], and the SAM sites high [missiles for high-flying aircraft], and we'll find ourselves without . . . Our reply will be so limited that we'll find ourselves with all the disadvantages.

I think we ought to, tomorrow, let's get U Thant our messages: "If they fire on us, tell them we'll take them all out." And then if we don't get some satisfaction from the Russians or U Thant or Cuba tomorrow night, figure that Monday we're going to do something about the SAM sites. What do you think?

McNamara: I would say only that we ought to keep some type of pressure on tonight and tomorrow night that indicates we're firm. If we call off these air strikes tonight, I think that settles . . .

Unidentified: I have a paper here, Mr. President, that we haven't discussed yet.

McNamara: Let me say first, I believe we should issue an order tonight calling up the 24 air reserve squadrons, roughly 300 troop-carrier transports, which are required for an invasion. And this would both be a preparatory move, and also a strong indication of what lies ahead.

President Kennedy: I think we ought to do it.

Taylor: I might say this, that as a part of the help to cutting the time short of an invasion, shipping is really more important than this, although I'm entirely for this.

President K------ ---- --

... to put that out. I can do it under the Executive Order which you signed granting me the authority [unclear]. I would like this too. Let me read this [draft press statement]:

"Today, U.S. unarmed reconnaissance aircraft, conducting surveillance of the buildup of offensive weapons secretly introduced into Cuba by the Soviet Union, were fired upon. Such surveillance operations were in accordance with the resolution adopted on October 23rd, by the Organ of Consultation of the Inter-American System under the provisions of the Rio Treaty of 1947. To ensure that the nations of the Western Hemisphere continue to be informed of the status of the threat to their security, it is essential that such reconnaissance flights continue. To protect these flights against attack, they will henceforth be accompanied by fighter escorts. The possibility of further attack on our aircraft and the continuous buildup of the offensive-weapon systems in Cuba require that we be prepared for any eventuality. Therefore, tonight, acting under the authority granted to me by Executive Order such and such, I have instructed the Secretary of the Air Force to order to active duty 24 troop-carrier squadrons of the Air Force Reserve and their associated support units."

Gilpatric: You might want to take out the sentence about the fighter escorts.

Unidentified: Yes. I'd leave that out.

Taylor: When you're talking about fighter escorts, at the low level it really isn't a fix.

President Kennedy: Do we call up any fighters, or it'll just be troop carriers?

Unidentified: Just the troop carriers.

McNamara: We could call up some fighters. But they're just cats and dogs, Mr. President. It isn't worth it.

Rusk: I think more from the public point of view, and from the effect on Khrushchev, you should add some fighters even if you don't call up . . .

Taylor: We have them off the coast looking for cripples, but they haven't been coming over because of the danger of the SAM sites.

McNamara: Dean, it isn't worthwhile.

Rusk: I just wanted to be sure.

President Kennedy: Now, who announces this? The Defense Department?

McNamara: Yeah, I'll do this.

McNamara then left the meeting and went back to the Pentagon. At about 9:20 he gave a press conference and read the statement that the President had just approved.

Discussion in the Executive Committee then turned to the problem of intercepting the Soviet ship *Grozny* at the quarantine line.

[Unclear exchanges. Someone mentions "8:30." Someone else, possibly referring to a possible U Thant visit to Havana, says: "It gives him a loophole giving Castro about 48 hours." Someone else, evidently referring to Moscow, says: "It will be at his doorstep at 12:00 tomorrow, noon; it will be 4:00 in the morning our time."]

Robert Kennedy: It's just a question of whether we want to intercept that [the *Grozny*] or let it go through. I think there is an argument against it [the interception].

On the one hand [with the U-2], they fired and the complications come from them. But we end up tomorrow afternoon, or the next day, firing on a Russian ship, and Monday [October 29] we're going to perhaps fire on all of Cuba. Other than ships getting in and out, it's not really going to count in the big picture.

President Kennedy: Well, we ought to wait and see tomorrow, and then announce that the ship, contrary to his assurances,[11] came through and therefore no ships went through at this point.

Robert Kennedy: The POL, and the fact that we left tankers and POL alone . . . Obviously doesn't have—

---

11. In his October 26 reply to U Thant's appeal to avoid a confrontation, Khrushchev promised to order Soviet ships to avoid the quarantine line temporarily.

President Kennedy: In addition it's not really his assurance to us, it's his assurance to U Thant and the United Nations.

Unidentified: But in regards to you, interestingly, is, his assurance to you is very different.

Bundy: U Thant got his [Khrushchev's] assurance.

Unidentified: Well, then shouldn't we provide—bring attention to U Thant about this thing, the ship coming along?

[Inaudible group discussion.]

assurance was to U Thant, not to me, that they'd keep them out of there. So, for the UN, the record is clearer.

Taylor: Mr. President, with regard to reconnaissance, the Chiefs talked this over at great length. We would say there is no great [unclear] need [unclear] for reconnaissance tomorrow, except for the fact that we know that we should check on whether they're working or not.

And secondly, we think that it would be a mistake to back away to an alternative time. So they think the reconnaissance in daylight is based largely on the need to . . .

President Kennedy: We also want to find out if they're firing tomorrow. If they're firing tomorrow, we better announce that.

[McNamara returns to the Cabinet Room from his brief press conference at the Pentagon.]

I think, Mr. Secretary, we were talking about this ship [the *Grozny*].

McNamara: Yes.

President Kennedy: He gave U Thant assurance he wouldn't send these ships. So I think that we ought to tonight call Stevenson to inform U Thant that this ship is continuing to approach, and that we'd like to get some answer from them, whether this is going to be called back. Or otherwise the confrontation must take place. It needs to be—we ought to have a little bit—the record a little better. Do you have any objection now to our calling Stevenson?

Unidentified: No. In fact, I would like to say something—

[Inaudible group discussion.]

Robert Kennedy: Could we have a couple of minutes, just a minute's discussion as to whether we should intercept it or not. I don't know whether we think that that's advisable if we are going to face firing, if they are firing on us. I should think the argument could go . . .

Rusk: Well, I was just making a list here of the things that have happened today. By the way, the [formal clarification of the] intercept area business was available last night, I think.

President Kennedy: I just want to call them [at the UN], Bobby, and tell them about the ship. We don't have to say what we are going to do about it. But I think we ought to tell them.

Robert Kennedy: Okay.

[Unclear comment.]

President Kennedy: Okay. Can we find out where it [the *Grozny*] is, Mac, in a technical way, and give them the latitude and longitude?

Bundy: I was just talking to Harlan Cleveland—

President Kennedy: We don't need to say what we're going to do about it, but we ought to say it is approaching and we'd like to have him [U Thant] know about it. If you want to go ahead and bother telling him.

Robert Kennedy: Well, if we decide tomorrow morning, is it possible to decide tomorrow?

Unidentified: Yes.

McNamara: Yeah, we can wait until about noon tomorrow.

Robert Kennedy: We can even discuss it now.

Rusk: Mr. President, just to remind us that 7 things have happened today. They, by the way, are building up the pressures on Khrushchev with an impact that we can live with.

One was the [White House] statement this morning on the broadcast [message from Moscow].

The second was this business on the intercept for U Thant [formally clarifying the contours of the interception zone].

Third was an announcement [from the Pentagon] on enforced surveillance.

Fourth was our short message to U Thant giving our answer [to Khrushchev's public message] number two.

Five was our answer to K's letter of October 26th [the letter Kennedy sent to Khrushchev].

Six was a callup of air squadrons.

Seven will be a warning to U Thant of an approaching ship.

Now, in general, I think perhaps for one day, that's building up. But I think tomorrow we'll need to be sure that the pressures continue to build up, if we . . .

President Kennedy: Well, we've got two things [we can do]. First place we've got the POL [blockade].

Secondly, we've got the announcement about these [air-defense sites] . . .

Whatever happens, if we don't take this ship [the *Grozny*], we announce that the agreement has been broken, and from now on it's POL, all ships, and so on. Call up the 29 [reserve] ships in addition [to] our own ships. So it seems to me we've got two or three things tomorrow that—

President Kennedy: I thought tomorrow we'd do that. But to add ships, it's a little late tonight, and I think probably tomorrow . . .

Unidentified: I think it's a separate action.

Unidentified: Are we going to call up the National Guard?

Gilpatric: No.

McNamara: No. I don't think that we need to talk to the governors about that today. It may become necessary later.

President Kennedy: What we'd better do now is figure out these messages to NATO and Turkey and . . . Has everybody seen Norstad's message?[12]

Bundy: No, sir. It was in private, for you.

President Kennedy: I'll read it.

Dear Mr. President:

I just talked to Finletter, who is arranging for the NAC [North Atlantic Council] meeting in the morning. He might be instructed to give details of Khrushchev's communication to you, to state that regardless of the merit or lack of merit of the proposal, the seriousness of the situation requires [momentary break in tape].

Finletter's presentation should be brief, factual and should be cool and skeptical, without suggesting that you have established a firm and final position. The resulting discussion would, I hope, be useful to you as an indication of European opinion and might develop some aspects of the

---

12. President Kennedy had spoken with General Lauris Norstad, Supreme Allied Commander of NATO Forces, over a secure telephone line during the afternoon.

problem of importance to you in making your decision. In any event, it should help to avoid a situation, in which you can be wrong, whatever you do, and your allies can be right and wise regardless of developments. It also of course helps meet the consultation commitment. No matter how productive and useful a NAC discussion may be, it will not, I fear, substantially relieve you of the burden of making a difficult decision. Many questions will arise as this subject is considered. Among these are:

A. The missiles in Cuba. Are missiles in Cuba on the same basis as those in Turkey? Clearly the answer is, no.
B. Can Turkey be treated as a satellite? Even if Khrushchev seems now publicly to have placed Cuba in that category.
C. Although accepting the Khrushchev proposal may bring short-term relief, if such action be taken as a sign of weakness in any case, will it contribute to strengthening our longer-range position?
D. Would an acceptance of the proposal indicate that the threat of missiles posed to the U.S. enforced the weakening of our NATO defenses under Soviet pressure, where MRBMs sited against Europe had strengthened our defense and our resolve?
E. What would be the effect on Greece and Turkey, both of whom live in constant fear of being left alone?

This is a very incomplete list of the questions which come to mind as one considers this problem. The answers seem to me to add up to a rejection of Khrushchev's proposal. And I believe Finletter should be instructed to indicate this as the general direction of U.S. thinking.

That's General Norstad.

You've got the prospective draft [cable of instruction to Finletter and other ambassadors to affected NATO countries]?

Rusk: There is one. We have . . . We have one on the basis that . . .

[Very long pause as papers are distributed.]

Mr. President, I wonder if, in a matter of this sort, whether it is necessary for the United States to give its first choice at the time that we first discuss this problem with the NAC. We could let them know that we've got to take action with Cuba if this thing continues. And this will create dangers in the NATO area. Remind them that the Soviets have raised this question of Turkey. We'd genuinely like to consult Europe—the NATO allies.

Now, there are three possibilities. The one is that we in NATO take the position that they cannot connect the defenses of NATO with the situation, the security situation, in another part of the world. Because these defenses relate to the Soviet military position regarding NATO, with hundreds of missiles aimed at NATO. Therefore, we have to stand firm in NATO and make sure that the Soviet Union realizes that we have to combine with NATO on this issue.

The second alternative would be, on straight security grounds, take Bob McNamara's point, here on page 3 [urging immediate replacement of Jupiters with Polaris to reduce the likelihood of an attack against Turkey should the United States attack Cuba].

The third would be to take George Bell's proposed draft [_____

_____

_____

_____]

If we were asked for an especial preference, of course the preference is one—that we go ahead with this Cuban business without regard to bargaining with NATO. But that NATO must understand the nature of the risks that are involved for NATO.

President Kennedy: Well, if you're going to really present it to them that way, you wouldn't want to state a position, I don't think, Mr. Secretary, would you? Because they'll feel compelled then to agree with that. It sounds sort of strong and firm and clear, and then they . . . Unless we're sure that that's the direction we want to steer them. I think we can steer them in that direction. It's initially the easiest position, but I think we ought be sure that that's what we want to do.

Unidentified: We have to—what we want to do . . .

President Kennedy: It seems to me, Mr. Secretary, that even if we want them to end up that way, we don't want it to look like that's where we urged them and therefore they have accepted, some reluctantly, some eagerly, the United States' opinion. Then it goes bad, which it may well. Then they say: "Well, we followed you, and you bitched it up."

But so far all that really gets involved are us, the Russians, and Cuba. Beginning with the offer on Turkey, then they're really in it. I don't think we ought even to indicate . . . All we're doing is saying: "This is it. The situation is getting worse, and we're going to have to take some action. And we want you to know. We want you to have an opportunity, and we're consulting with you, definitely." Is there any merit in this?

And if we don't take it [the proffered Cuba-Turkey trade], then we want everybody to understand what we think may be the alternative if we're going to have to move. I think that's probably what this first meeting ought to be, and then we might have another one the next morning.

But I think this is . . . Otherwise, I'm afraid they will say: "Well, we worked with you, but . . ."

Dillon: We ought to state very clearly that we aren't pushing them either way. We aren't.

Gilpatric: We ought to leave out the penultimate paragraph, the first—around the top of page 3, and the last paragraph, which could mean many things.

[Inaudible group discussion.]

Rusk: Some of them may come up with an idea that would unlock this damn thing, something that we haven't thought of. It's just possible.

Thompson: Can't we just report to them all these actions that are being taken, and not anything further?

President Kennedy: Well now, with the introduction of Turkey, we think that if we take an action which we may have to take, I don't think we ought to say . . .

Which we may well have to take, the way it's escalating, if they hit Turkey and if they hit Berlin, we want them—if they want to get off, now's the time to speak up.

McNamara: Mr. President, do we believe that we will be able to settle Cuba more easily with or without the Jupiters in Turkey? I think we ought to decide this point before we—

Robert Kennedy: I think—

McNamara: —open our doors to NATO.

Robert Kennedy: That's what . . . Can't we wait? Isn't it possible to get through tomorrow at 3:00 or 4:00 without even getting into NATO with the Turkey business?

Unidentified: Yeah.

Robert Kennedy: And then figuring—I mean, if we lose the gamble with [Khrushchev]—I think that's one.

If once they find us playing around and figuring on Turkey, and that we're willing to make some deal, and if I were they, I'd push on that. And then I'd push on Italy, figuring that, well, if they are going to go on that, they are going to carry the decisions one step further.

But if we are hard on this thing, the gains that we have, we know that we've got some respite. We may see some way in Moscow, or they wouldn't have made the offer [of October 26] initially. Why don't we just wait another 18 hours. See if that's been seized at all. We're hard and tough on this. We call up the planes tonight, and we wait. We find out if U Thant is successful.

Then we find that he's not successful, the whole thing looks like it's collapsing, and we're going to have to go in there. So then we call them [the NATO allies] together. And we say: "This is what the problem is."

President Kennedy: Have we called the [NATO] meeting yet?

Unidentified: Yes, we have.

Bundy: I think it says in Norstad's message, 10:00. That's 3:00 our time

obligation, and we'll meet with you again, raising this irrelevance [the Turkey offer], at 10:00 tomorrow morning."

Robert Kennedy: Yeah, and that "we'll meet with you again"—

Bundy: "raising this irrelevance."

Robert Kennedy:—"at 10:00 tomorrow morning [Paris time]." Then, if the thing blows tomorrow, then we go at 10:00 the next morning and say that . . .

Dillon: That may be a little late.

Robert Kennedy: Well, I think you've got to figure that's another 24 hours. We could do it, OK. Well, one day, I can't believe it's going to make that much difference.

Taylor: This [air strike] is going up on Tuesday [October 30]. It's possible that—

Robert Kennedy: I mean, but I think you've got to give them a chance. But I think if we indicate to them [the Soviets] tomorrow that we're willing to make a deal on Turkey, if they're [the allies] willing to make a deal, that half of them are going to be willing to make it, half aren't, or a third aren't. I would think then you would be in a—

President Kennedy: Well, but the only thing is: Have we lost anything?

Do we want Finletter to indicate we want to close [rule] the deal out tomorrow, or he shouldn't discuss the Turkey deal tomorrow?

Robert Kennedy: No, I think you just keep silent. Tell them what has happened today. Go through the whole thing. This is just to report to them what we've done, what steps we're taking, and then they're . . . That we called up the air and we're thinking of calling up the ships, or we're calling up the ships. This is what happened. We sent the U-2 over. It looks like it got shot down. We got some of these . . . And this is the offer that they made to us with these messages that came through Scali and through the other people. We've accepted this and the President is very hopeful.

Then they suddenly came in with the Turkey business. We haven't considered that because we think it should be restricted to the Western Hemisphere. We made that [reply to Khrushchev]. We said that we would accept that [original offer]. We haven't heard yet. We will report to them when we hear, and we suggest that we meet at 10:00 tomorrow morning [Monday, October 29].

And then if the Russians come back and say: "We're only going to do it if you can get the bases out of Turkey." And then we come in and we talk to them [the NATO allies], and say: "Now, this is what our suggestion is. What do you want to do?" And they say: "We want to hold fast," and then on Tuesday [October 30] we go into [military action] . . . I think if we indicate tomorrow, suddenly there will be a mess.

Thompson: It will become public.

Unidentified: Become public.

President Kennedy: All right, does anybody . . . Mr. Secretary, what do you think of that?

Rusk: No, I think that's right.

President Kennedy: Mac, can you draw the [message] . . . ?

Bundy: Yes, sir.

President Kennedy: You and Ted draw up the instructions based on what Bobby said.

Unidentified: It would combine these two [drafts].

Unidentified: With what General Norstad said.

Bundy: It simply leaves out, as I understand it, the recommendations section of both messages. [Three people agree.]

[Unclear exchanges about the text.]

Gilpatric: I think we have got to say whatever we say [in NATO] in the capitals also.

Dillon: Whatever we say there is going to be known.

Unidentified: Oh, yes.

[Mixed voices.]

President Kennedy: And then he [Finletter] can take the temperature. But we have to instruct Finletter not to try to get them to move on a position.

Dillon: If it's a very serious briefing, this could serve as an indirect warning to the Russians.

Unidentified: Yeah, that might be.

Unidentified: Yeah, yeah.

Bundy: How much—what noise do we want at the end of it [the instructions] in terms of welcoming discussion? Do we want—?

Rusk: We want to put the situation to them and indicate that we welcome their views on it. I tend to hope that they might have some ideas about the alternatives.

President Kennedy: Well, no, what I think . . . I don't think . . . .

President Kennedy: Well, I think this is just a draft.

Robert Kennedy: Do you think, Mr. President, that somebody that's been involved in these discussions and knows as much about the background— like—should be there and explain all of this?

Bundy: Mr. President, it's only 7 hours until the [NATO] meeting. I don't—

President Kennedy: Is it?

Sorensen: [presenting the rewritten instructions cable] It's essentially Ros's draft, and there's one paragraph dropped. You're not recommending any policy. I wonder, though, whether you want to raise, not a policy question, but a military question. Ask them to examine how valuable are the Jupiters.

McNamara: I would suggest that we not lead into discussion of this. This is a report. We don't want discussion tomorrow [on the Jupiters], because they may split up, and you may have chaos.

President Kennedy: And that would be fatal.

We won't. We'd better ask for a meeting on Monday on it.

Bundy: In that case, you better cut out the last paragraph, go over the last paragraph. You might want to—

[Inaudible group discussion.]

President Kennedy: I think we'd better give them [the U.S. ambassadors] some of this stuff—for your eyes [only]—about not bringing up the Jupiters at this point, because it will leak and so on. Mac [getting his attention while Bundy is drafting], I say, I think we shouldn't bring up the question of Jupiters at this point because it may leak, and our efforts to get the Russians—

Bundy: I think the message should begin that it is now decided that your briefing should not be related to the Soviet proposal but to the situation. I think that that's really what's concluded, especially in the light of the fact that tomorrow is the day of signals to the Soviet Union. Is that right?

Robert Kennedy: I think it could go into much more detail. I think you really put that in.

McCone: [returning to his draft message] Are we going to have any communications with Khrushchev on this provocation?

President Kennedy: The plane going down? The plane going down? That's the next one.

Rusk: There's a [draft] message there that would keep the finger pointed on Cuba on this business of surveillance, but I gather that those points have already been covered.

President Kennedy: What are we going to announce in regard to tomorrow's planes?

McNamara: We shouldn't announce anything.

President Kennedy: Not whether we are continuing or—

Gilpatric: We've already announced that we are going to continue.

President Kennedy: This evening?

McNamara: But we didn't say tomorrow. We said we're going to continue surveillance.

President Kennedy: We've got enough messages right now, John. I think that he knows about the plane. He's announced it, so I think that the . . .

Sorensen: I think in some ways it's a sign of weakness if we keep resorting to messages.

President Kennedy: I think we shouldn't send him one again. I think we ought to just let that one go tonight. The boat [the *Grozny*] is going to be the important thing. Is he going to turn that boat around. Or—

Who's notified Stevenson?

Ball: We're trying to. Alex [Johnson] has talked to New York, and they're going to call back. Whether U Thant goes down [to Havana] or not apparently isn't clear—quite clear yet.

Rusk: Goes down where?

Unidentified: To Havana.

President Kennedy: Well, I was thinking about that ship, because we're going to be faced with the problem of that ship tomorrow. Do we have a . . .? Do we announce it [that the ship is approaching the quarantine line] or do we just send—

Unidentified: In an announcement or—

Bundy: It is approaching the intercept area?

Ball: I'm not sure. Alex was talking about [unclear].

Unidentified: Let's find that out.

[Unclear group discussion.]

President Kennedy: I think we ought to send a letter to de Gaulle. I think we ought to send a letter to de Gaulle, stating sort of what the situation is.

Unidentified: It shouldn't go to de Gaulle, when Adenauer is . . .

President Kennedy: I'm in constant touch with Macmillan. Ball . . .

giving the résumé about what the situation is. I'm thinking that I should send it to de Gaulle.

What about the Turks now? What are we going to say to Hare?

Rusk: Well, we should say to him what we say to NATO.

Unidentified: He'll get exactly the same—

President Kennedy: I think we ought to have an "eyes only" [cable] in which we tell him to . . .

I mean, at least in the next 24 hours, we shouldn't even suggest to Hare that there's any possibility of the [unclear].

Unidentified: No, you don't want to talk—

Rusk: You've seen that long telegram [from Hare] giving the four alternatives.[13]

President Kennedy: From him [Hare]?

Rusk: From him.

President Kennedy: From Hare.

Thompson: He's done a very good job on the Turkish situation.

[Inaudible discussion.]

President Kennedy: Let's just say that it seems to me, that on Hare, if we don't want to try to get the Russians off the Turkish trade, then we probably don't want to do anything with Hare for 24 hours until we get some sort of an answer.

13. See page 496, note 4.

Thompson: This is Hare's telegram. I don't know if you saw it or not. I think we ought to send him something.

President Kennedy: Well, let's see.

Let's give him an explanation of what we're trying to do. We're trying to get it back on the original proposition of last night because we don't want to get into this trade. If we are unsuccessful, then we—it is possible that we may have to get back on the Jupiter thing. If we do, then we would of course want it to come from the Turks themselves and NATO, rather than just the United States. We're hopeful, however, that that won't come. If it does, his judgment on how should it be handled with the Turks, if we're prepared to do the Polaris and others, does he think this thing can be made? We'll be in touch with him in 24 hours, when we find out if we are successful in putting, bringing, the Russians back on the original track.

Thompson: All right. We will get that.

President Kennedy: OK?

Bundy: Now, you want a quick letter to de Gaulle.

Dillon: You can send a personal one to de Gaulle, Adenauer, and Macmillan, if you want to, in view of the special relationship with them.

President Kennedy: We've sent a message to Macmillan tonight already. Let's send one to Adenauer and de Gaulle, writing the same to both.

Question to George.

Ball: The only problem is that, as John suggests, when some of these NATO, NAC ambassadors, report to their own capitals, and when they break—

Robert Kennedy: No, but I mean the message you're going to send to the ambassador really is—

Unidentified: No, no, no [unclear].

Robert Kennedy: It will go right to him and won't go to anybody else?

[Unclear exchanges about planning the next day's reconnaissance flights.]

Taylor: No, that's all right. We have two major decisions we have to make by 11:00 today.

[Unclear group discussion.]

President Kennedy: They say they shot down our U-2. They stated they shot it down.

[Unclear exchange. 11 seconds excised as classified information.]

Taylor: They say they shot down planes.

Robert Kennedy: Then I think then we ought to . . . If we get shot at tomorrow—

McNamara: Mr. President, if we go in at low level tomorrow, we have to be prepared, it seems to me, to attack MiGs if they attack our aircraft.

Taylor: What we always have to . . .

McNamara: This time we would make it perfectly clear that if they attack our aircraft, we're going in after some of their MiGs.

President Kennedy: It won't be the ground. We'll save that [antiaircraft guns] for a real operation, which would . . . Under the schedule, we couldn't do it till Tuesday morning [October 30], because we'll have to go back to NATO again Monday, in which we say the situation is getting worse and so on and so forth. Give them that last chance.

McNamara: There's a task group of some kind working on it. We ought to take the time tomorrow to talk about that.

Bundy: . . . the plan.

Taylor: The plan is all the whole thing and has several defense activities.

Robert Kennedy: Are you thinking of going from Mississippi to Cuba?[14] [Laughter.]

[Unclear group discussion.]

Sorensen: What time did we decide on [meeting] tomorrow morning?

McNamara: Eleven in the morning.

Sorensen: I'll be here.

[Inaudible group discussion; laughter.]

McNamara: Mac, Ted, there's something to be done right now.

[Unclear discussion.]

Robert Kennedy: How are you doing, Bob?

McNamara: Well. How about yourself?

Robert Kennedy: All right.

McNamara: You got any doubts?

---

14. The Kennedy administration had just endured a crisis at the end of September over the integration of a black student, James Meredith, into the University of Mississippi. Large numbers of U.S. marshals and federal troops were deployed to Mississippi to protect Meredith and his supporters and attempt to keep the peace.

Robert Kennedy: Well, no. I think that we're doing the only thing we can do, and well, you know.

[Inaudible group discussion.]

McNamara: I think the one thing, Bobby, we ought to seriously do before we act is be *damned* sure they understand the consequences. In other words, we need to really show them where we are now, because we need to have two things ready: a government for Cuba, because we're going to need one— we go in with bombing aircraft; and, secondly, plans for how to respond to the Soviet Union in Europe, because sure as hell they're going to do something there.

Dillon: You have to pick out the things they might—

McNamara: Well, I think, that's right.

[Unclear reply from Dillon.]

McNamara: I would suggest that it will be an eye for an eye.

Dillon: That's the mission.

McCone: I'd take Cuba back. I'd take Cuba away from Castro.

Sorensen?: Suppose we make Bobby mayor of Havana?

The Executive Committee meeting then broke up for the night. Work went on, however. The first task was to send off the instructions to NATO and selected U.S. ambassadors in allied capitals. The cable that had been discussed was sent out around midnight. It told the envoys that Khrushchev's October 26 message to President Kennedy and other contacts had "seemed to offer real hope solution could be found," but that as a result of Khrushchev's new, public message, "these hopes have been diminished." The United States would "continue to press for solution in Cuban framework alone." Using President Kennedy's language, the cable said the situation was "deteriorating." Given the activity at the missile sites and continued movement of Soviet ships into the interception zone, the ambassadors were warned that the United States might find it necessary "within a very short time" to "take whatever military action may be necessary to remove this growing threat to the Hemisphere." The ambassadors were also cryptically advised, so that they could take the temperature of their foreign contacts, that "U.S. action in Cuba may result in some Soviet moves against NATO."[15]

---

15. State telegram ToPol 578 to Finletter at NATO, 28 October 1962 (dated 26 October, but actually sent in the early morning of the 28th), National Security Files, Meetings and Memoranda, ExComm Meetings 6–10, 10/26/62–10/28/62, JFKL.

Bundy, as he had promised, telephoned de Zulueta in London at about 11:00 P.M. (4:00 A.M. in London), after debriefing David Ormsby-Gore on the latest developments. Bundy detailed the contents of the message that had just been sent to Finletter and the others. He again urged that Macmillan hold off for a while on issuing a public offer on Thors in Britain, unless perhaps the situation became extremely tense in a day or so. Bundy also said that U Thant was working very hard to persuade the Soviets not to shoot at U.S. planes and not to challenge the U.S. quarantine line.[16]

...... Macmillan to the President. Begins:

I have had the report of Bundy's talks through our night.

The trial of wills is now approaching a climax. Khrushchev's first message, unhappily not published to the world, seemed to go a long way to meet you. His second message, widely broadcast and artfully contrived, adding the Turkey proposal, was a recovery on his part. It has made a considerable impact.

We must now wait to see what Khrushchev does. I shall expect to hear from you how things are developing. I agree that the use of any initiative by me is all a matter of timing.[17]

Many officials besides Bundy spent the night at their offices. President Kennedy was restless too. He and Dave Powers stayed up and watched a screening of a movie Kennedy liked, *Roman Holiday,* starring Audrey Hepburn and Gregory Peck.

SAC bombers continued their round-the-clock circling in Arctic skies. Nearly 100 warships maintained the quarantine, and more ships readied for invasion. U.S. destroyers patrolled constantly over Soviet submarines in the Atlantic. The 5th Marine Expeditionary Brigade began boarding the ships that would carry it to the invasion staging areas. The 14,000 Air Force reservists who had been called up that night were moving to their active-duty stations.

16. "Telephone Conversation between Mr. Bundy and Mr. de Zulueta . . . ," PRO, PREM 11/3691, 24020.

17. From PRO, FO 371/162388, 25000.

MONDAY, OCTOBER 29

10:10 A.M.

CABINET ROOM AND OVAL OFFICE

On the morning of October 28 the *Grozny,* en route into the interception zone, stopped dead in the water. At about 9:00 A.M. in Washington, wire services announced that Khrushchev was sending a new message to Washington. The message, broadcast to the world over Radio Moscow, soon began coming off the ticker. The summaries announced that the Soviet government would dismantle and remove its missiles from Cuba. The full text of the message followed, as translated unofficially by the U.S. agency that monitored foreign broadcasts:[1]

Esteemed Mr. President:

I have received your message of October 27, 1962. I express my satisfaction and gratitude for the sense of proportion and understanding of the responsibility borne by you at present for the preservation of peace throughout the world which you have shown. I very well understand your anxiety and the anxiety of the United States people in connection with the fact that the weapons which you describe as "offensive" are, in fact, grim weapons. Both you and I understand what kind of weapon they are.

In order to complete with greater speed the liquidation of the conflict dangerous to the cause of peace, to give confidence to all people longing for peace, and to calm the American people, who, I am certain, want peace as much as the people of the Soviet Union, the Soviet government, in addition

---

1. Foreign Broadcast Information Service translation of text broadcast on Moscow Domestic Service, reprinted in Lawrence Chang and Peter Kornbluh, *The Cuban Missile Crisis 1962: A National Security Archive Documents Reader* (New York: New Press, 1992), pp. 226–229.

to previously issued instructions on the cessation of further work at building sites for the weapons,[2] has issued a new order on the dismantling of the weapons which you describe as "offensive," and their crating and return to the Soviet Union.

Mr. President, I would like to repeat once more what I had already written to you in my preceding letters—that the Soviet government has placed at the disposal of the Cuban government economic aid, as well as arms, inasmuch as Cuba and the Cuban people have constantly been under the

It is unthinkable in our time not to notice a pirate ship, particularly if one takes into account such a saturation of American ships in the Caribbean from which actually all this is watched and observed. In such circumstances, piratic ships are freely moving around Cuba, shelling Cuba, and carrying out piratic attacks upon peaceful transport vessels! It is, after all, known that they even shelled a British freighter!

In short, Cuba has been under the constant threat of aggressive forces which did not conceal their intentions to invade Cuban territory.

The Cuban people want to build their life in their own interest without interference from without. You are right in this, and one cannot blame them because they want to be masters of their own country and dispose of the fruits of their labor. The threat of Cuba's invasion and all the other ventures aimed at bringing about tensions around Cuba are designed to engender uncertainty in the Cuban people, intimidate them, and hinder them in building their new life undisturbed.

Mr. President, I want to say clearly again that we could not be indifferent to this. The Soviet government decided to help Cuba with means of defense

2. U.S. intelligence analysts, after studying photography from the reconnaissance flights of October 27, judged, however, that activity at the missile sites had been continuing at least during the day of October 27.

3. Khrushchev is referring to shots fired at Havana from a boat offshore manned by Cuban exiles. Though Cuban exile groups carried out various raids from time to time, there is no mention of such an episode in the CIA Watch Committee daily reports, in McCone's briefings, or in the Executive Committee discussions.

against aggression—and only with means for purposes of defense. We stationed defense means there which you call offensive. We stationed them there in order that no attack should be made against Cuba and that no rash action should be permitted to take place.

I regard with respect and trust your statement in your message of October 27, 1962 that no attack will be made on Cuba—that no invasion will take place—not only by the United States, but also by other countries of the Western Hemisphere, as your message pointed out. Then the motives which promoted us to give aid of this nature to Cuba cease. They are no longer applicable. Hence we have instructed our officers—and these means, as I have already stated, are in the hands of Soviet officers—to take necessary measures for stopping the building of the said projects and their dismantling and return to the Soviet Union.

As I already told you in my letter of October 27, we both agree to come to an agreement that United Nations representatives could verify the dismantling of these means.

In this way, if one is to rely on your assurances which you have made and on our orders to dismantle, then all necessary conditions for liquidation of the conflict which has arisen appear to exist.

I note with satisfaction that you have responded to my wish that the said dangerous situation should be liquidated and also that conditions should be created for a more thoughtful appraisal of the international situation which is fraught with great dangers in our age of thermonuclear weapons, rocket technology, space ships, global rockets, and other lethal weapons. All people are interested in insuring peace. Therefore, we who are invested with trust and great responsibility must not permit an exacerbation of the situation and must liquidate the breeding grounds where a dangerous situation has been created fraught with serious consequences for the cause of peace. If we succeed along with you and with the aid of other people of good will in liquidating this tense situation, we must also concern ourselves to see that other dangerous conflicts do not arise which might lead to a world thermonuclear catastrophe.

In conclusion, I wish to speak of the regulation of relation[s] between NATO and states of the Warsaw Treaty, which you mention. We have long ago spoken of this and are ready to continue an exchange of opinions with you on this question and find a reasonable solution. I also wish to continue an exchange of opinions on the prohibition of atomic and thermonuclear weapons, general disarmament, and other questions concerning the lessening of international tension.

Mr. President, I trust your statement. However, on the other hand, there are [ir]responsible people who would like to carry out an invasion of Cuba at this time, and in such a way to spark off a war. If we take practical steps and announce the dismantling and evacuation of the appropriate means from Cuba, then, doing that, we wish to establish at the same time the confidence of the Cuban people that we are with them and are not divesting ourselves of the responsibility of granting help to them.

We are convinced that the people of all countries, like yourself, Mr. President, will understand me correctly. We do not issue threats. We desire only peace. Our country is now on the upsurge. Our people are enjoying the fruits of their peaceful labor

place.[4]

In 1960, we shot down your U-2 aircraft, the reconnaissance flight of which over the USSR led to the wrecking of the meeting of the Powers in Paris. You then took a correct position in condemning that criminal action by the former United States government. However, during the period of your tenure of office as president, a second instance of the violation of our frontier by an American U-2 aircraft took place in the Sakhalin area. We wrote you about this violation on August 30. You replied that this violation had taken place as the result of bad weather and gave an assurance that it would not be repeated. We gave credence to your assurance because there was indeed bad weather in that area at that time. However, if your aircraft did not have the task of flying near our territory, then even bad weather could not cause an American aircraft to enter our airspace.

The conclusion follows from this that it is done with the knowledge of the Pentagon, which tramples on international practices and violates the frontiers of other states.

An even more dangerous case occurred on October 28 [27] when your reconnaissance aircraft intruded into the territory of the Soviet Union in the north, in the area of the Chukotka Peninsula, and flew over our territory.

One asks, Mr. President, how should we regard this? What is it? A provocation? Your aircraft violates our frontier and at times as anxious as those which we are now experiencing when everything has been placed in a

---

4. A reference to the U-2 that strayed over Soviet airspace early on October 27.

state of combat readiness. For an intruding American aircraft can easily be taken for a bomber with nuclear weapons, and this could push us toward a fatal step—all the more so because both the United States government and Pentagon have long been saying that bombers with atomic bombs are constantly on duty in your country.

Therefore, you can imagine what kind of responsibilities you assume, especially now during the anxious times we are now experiencing.

I would like to ask you to assess this correctly and take steps accordingly in order that it would not serve as a provocation for unleashing war.

I would also like to express the following wish. Of course, it is a matter for the Cuban people. You do not at present maintain any diplomatic relations but through my officers on Cuba I have reports that flights of American aircraft over Cuba are being carried out. We are interested that there should not be any war at all in the world; and that the Cuban people should live quietly. However, Mr. President, it is no secret that we have our people on Cuba. According to the treaty with the Cuban government, we have officers and instructors there who are training the Cubans. They are mainly ordinary people—experts, agronomists, zoo technicians, irrigation and soil improvement experts, ordinary workers, tractor drivers, and others. We are concerned about them.

I would like to ask you, Mr. President, to bear in mind that a violation of Cuban airspace by American aircraft may also have dangerous consequences. If you do not want this, then no pretext should be given for the creation of a dangerous situation.

We must be now very cautious and not take such steps which will be of no use for the defense of the states involved in the conflict, but which are likely to arouse only irritation and even prove a provocation leading to the baneful step. We must, therefore, display sobriety and wisdom and refrain from steps of this sort.

We value peace, perhaps even more than other people, because we experienced the terrible war against Hitler. However, our people will not flinch in the face of any ordeal. Our people trust their government, and we assure our people and the world public that the Soviet government will not allow itself to be provoked.

Should the provocateurs unleash a war, they would not escape the grave consequences of such a war. However, we are confident that reason will triumph. War will not be unleashed and the peace and security of people will be insured.

In connection with negotiations in progress between U.N. Acting Secretary General U Thant and representatives of the Soviet Union, the United States, and the Cuban Republic, the Soviet government has sent to New York

USSR First Deputy Minister of Foreign Affairs [Vasily] Kuznetsov[5] with a view to assisting U Thant in his noble efforts aimed at liquidation of the present dangerous situation.

With respect for you,

Khrushchev. October 28, 1962

At the Pentagon, the Joint Chiefs were skeptical of Khrushchev's offer. They approved a memorandum to President Kennedy saying: "The JCS interpret the Khrushchev statement . . . . g about the good result.

As he was speaking President Kennedy turned on the tape recorder.

Rusk: . . . [Earlier President Kennedy] remarked that whichever line of action you adopt, those who were in favor of it were going to regret it. In this situation, I think there is some gratification for everyone's line of action, except to do nothing.

Those who were in favor of invasion were getting ready for the thing which turned out to be the major quid pro quo to getting these weapons out of Cuba. Those who wanted a first strike—

At this point President Kennedy switched off the tape recorder through the remainder of the meeting.

After Rusk's comment, Bundy added that some had been hawks and some had been doves, but today was the day of the doves.

The group agreed to suspend further air reconnaissance for the day. They then discussed possible UN inspection alternatives. President Kennedy suggested telling the UN that either they would carry out reconnaissance or the

---

5. As Andrei Gromyko's top deputy, Kuznetsov was Ball's counterpart. He arrived in New York on October 29.

6. JCS to President Kennedy, "Recommendation for Execution of CINCLANT OPLANS 312 and 316," JCSM-844–62, 28 October 1962; Taylor to McNamara, CM-61–62, 28 October 1962, OSD records, 71-A-2896, National Records Center.

United States would do it. He authorized the sharing of necessary intelligence information with UN officials. President Kennedy mentioned, and the group agreed, that though he would prefer not to get "hung up" over the withdrawal of IL-28 bombers too, the U.S. should work to get them out.

President Kennedy asked his advisers to be reserved in their public comments and cautioned that no one should be under the illusion that the problem of Soviet weapons in Cuba was now solved. The quarantine would remain in force while negotiations continued. Much work remained to be done, including efforts to prevent other Communist subversion in Latin America. He directed the preparation of a reply to Khrushchev's letter, which was sent that afternoon:[7]

> Dear Mr. Chairman:
>
> I am replying at once to your broadcast message of October 28 even though the official text has not yet reached me because of the great importance I attach to moving forward promptly to the settlement of the Cuban crisis. I think that you and I, with our heavy responsibilities for the maintenance of peace, were aware that developments were approaching a point where events could have become unmanageable. So I welcome this message and consider it an important contribution to peace.
>
> The distinguished efforts of Acting Secretary General U Thant have greatly facilitated both our tasks. I consider my letter to you of October 27th and your reply of today as firm undertakings on the part of both our governments which should be promptly carried out. I hope that the necessary measures can at once be taken through the United Nations as your message says, so that the United States in turn can remove the quarantine measures now in effect. I have already made arrangements to report all these matters to the Organization of American States, whose members share a deep interest in a genuine peace in the Caribbean area.
>
> You referred in your letter to a violation of your frontier by an American aircraft in the area of the Chukotsk Peninsula. I have learned that this plane, without arms or photographic equipment, was engaged in an air sampling mission in connection with your nuclear tests. Its course was direct from Eielson Air Force Base in Alaska to the North Pole and return. In turning south, the pilot made a serious navigational error which carried him over Soviet territory. He immediately made an emergency call on open radio for navigational assistance and was guided back to his home base by the most

---

7. From outgoing telegram to Embassy Moscow, reprinted in Chang and Kornbluh, *The Cuban Missile Crisis*, pp. 230–232.

direct route. I regret this incident and will see to it that every precaution is taken to prevent recurrence.

Mr. Chairman, both of our countries have great unfinished tasks and I know that your people as well as those of the United States can ask for nothing better than to pursue them free from the fear of war. Modern science and technology have given us the possibility of making labor fruitful beyond anything that could have been dreamed of a few decades ago.

I agree with you that we must devote urgent attention to the problem of

or elsewhere.

John F. Kennedy

The Executive Committee gathered again on Monday morning, October 29. The press was full of news of an American triumph. But the previous day Castro, obviously furious about Khrushchev's decision, had written to U Thant saying that the U.S. pledge not to invade Cuba would be ineffective unless the United States ended all economic pressure against Cuba of any kind, stopped activity of exiles against Cuba, stopped all overflights, and liquidated the base at Guantanamo.

McCone also pointed out, in his intelligence briefing that morning, that construction at the Soviet sites appeared to be continuing. President Kennedy turned on the tape recorder during the briefing.[8]

McCone:—the Chinese passed this note to the Cuban ambassador, on page 8[?], implying that the U.S.S.R. was an untrustworthy ally.

In particular they said that since 1959 Moscow had refused to give China technical information concerning production of nuclear arms. This is a year earlier than our previous estimates.

Thompson: Could you repeat that, John?

McCone: Yes, sir.

---

8. The portion of tape preceding this meeting has background noise, silence, and some brief exchanges among maintenance workers.

Peiping [Beijing], the Chinese Communists, sent a note to the Cuban ambassador in Peiping implying that the U.S.S.R. was an untrustworthy ally. In particular they said that since 1959 Moscow had refused to give China technical information concerning production of nuclear arms.

Turning for a moment to the India–Communist China situation, we have noted in India the presence of a Chicom [Chinese Communist] division which saw service in North Korea.

Carter: The unique feature about this division is that they wear blue uniforms, in contrast with the khaki uniforms that the Chinese army normally wears.

McCone: We have been impressed by the discipline and firepower with automatic weapons of this division. Chicom strength in the Northeast Frontier Area appears to be one division of approximately 10,000 men against 21,000 Indians. The Indians are reinforced with another 15,000, making 36,000 in all.

With respect to Soviet missile, weapons testing, the Soviets fired three 1,100-mile missiles yesterday at [the test range at] Kapustin Yar, where [unclear]. The first missile carried a 200-kiloton [thermonuclear] payload. The other 2 missiles were fired through the burst [explosion] in order to test elements of an antimissile system in a nuclear-burst environment. This is turning into another exercise, which is somewhat different than we have noted in the same area.

President [João] Goulart of Brazil is sending a personal emissary, General Alvino Silva, chief of the military cabinet, to Cuba to see Fidel Castro. The purpose is to report [unclear] which will ensure the integrity and sovereignty of Cuba. The plane carrying Silva is the same as one that carried U Thant to New York [unclear].

On the messages, just to repeat, these three messages that we have received on Cuban orders not to fire unless fired upon.

[2 minutes, 37 seconds of recording excised as classified information. This excision covers the remainder of McCone's briefing.]

Other evidence indicates that McCone may have discussed intelligence describing varied messages to Cuban air-defense forces telling them not to fire unless fired upon, changing those instructions, and then restoring them.

The intelligence reports of October 29 also reportedly included information that 2 days earlier, on October 27, Cuban authorities had ordered sabotage operations to be carried out in Venezuela. These sabotage efforts had been devastating. Aimed at oil refineries, they had reportedly destroyed or disrupted one-sixth of the refining capacity of Venezuela, a major oil-exporting country.

President Kennedy: All right. We have this proposal now, I might as well read it.

"The President has established a Coordinating Committee to give full-time attention to the matters involved in the conclusion of the Cuban crisis. The

two. Kuznetsov is seeing U Thant at 11:00, and U Thant will be calling Stevenson at 12:00. I think we really ought not to make decisions on surveillance, for example, unless we get some reading out on whether Kuznetsov is throwing in some major monkey wrenches into this thing. I do think we need surveillance today. But I think we ought to make the decision as to how many, what kind, where, after we find out what his first impression is, as to what Kuznetsov is up to. For example, if it seems quite clear that the CIA report, that the conclusion is correct, that there does not appear to be much danger that the Soviets will attempt to delay implementation of the [unclear] dismantle [unclear], I think that would affect our decision to some extent.

President Kennedy: Well, we've got the long-range, as well as the question of whether we do it today or not. We might want to do it tomorrow, if necessary, but I think the longer-range problem of how this surveillance . . . is one of the matters which the committee ought to meet on right away.

How we are going to maintain a satisfactory degree of knowledge about Cuba? We can't rely on the UN to do it. Now, we have these SAM sites—

McNamara: Mr. President, it is a very difficult problem.

Dr. Charyk[9] is here this morning. He discussed the matter with the Secretary General [U Thant] and General Rikhye[10] yesterday, and I think you might like

9. Joseph Charyk, Under Secretary of the Air Force, was the top civilian official managing Air Force conduct of U-2 overflights.

10. Brigadier General Indar Jit Rikhye, of the Indian Army, was U Thant's military adviser.

to hear briefly his report. And then we can consider how to approach the problem. We have several suggestions.

Joe, would you briefly summarize your discussions.

Charyk: Mr. President, the meeting was initiated by a suggestion that we attempt to make available to the United Nations, by this morning, a means by which they could conduct the United Nations reconnaissance over target areas, and a means by which that could be continued over a period of time that was involved in this mapping of the missile sites.

We made various suggestions. The one that we spent the most time discussing was the possibility of making available to the United Nations an RC-130 aircraft, which is completely equipped with camera equipment, which is painted white with the UN insignia, and we could fly tomorrow morning.

We went into this in considerable detail with Rikhye. He did not express concern as to the use of American aircraft. He expressed grave concern as to the use of an American air crew. And he also indicated that in the time available it was just impossible to make the appropriate arrangements.

It turns out that there are three countries, in addition to the United States, that have qualified air crews on this aircraft. These include Canadians, the South Africans, and the Indonesians. Apparently during the day he [Rikhye] had inquired as to the availability of air crews, and he did not make reference to either the Canadians or the South Africans, but indicated he attempted to assess the availability of Indonesian air crews. But it was clearly impossible, on the basis of going this morning.

He also indicated that he had made attempts to obtain UN observers that could go aboard any aircraft that would be flown, and he had made several contacts, but again it was impossible to make such an arrangement in order to be effective this morning.

President Kennedy: Rikhye's nationality is what?

Charyk: Indian.

He also indicated that the Secretary General would be on the scene [in Cuba] tomorrow [October 30]. He is leaving at 10:00 to discuss the arrangements that have been made for his transportation, and indicated that they had made arrangements for a Cessna aircraft which would be available in Havana, hopefully, on Tuesday night or not later than Wednesday. And that this aircraft would be used to take observers to the sites to observe the actual status of the dismantling operation.

Rikhye had been a field officer in an armored unit in Italy during World War II and had worked on UN peacekeeping missions in Gaza, the Congo, and Netherlands New Guinea.

And he [Rikhye] felt at the time that the UN observers were on the scene, that it was incomprehensible that the Soviets would fail to comply with their commitment to dismantle. And that, furthermore, it would be extremely . . . It would create serious problems if, during the time that the Secretary General were in Cuba, that actual reconnaissance was being undertaken.

We went into a rather detailed discussion of the importance of aerial reconnaissance. I attempted to make the point that aerial reconnaissance

altitudes, types of airplanes, and so on, but then came back always with the same point that, of course, for tomorrow morning there is absolutely nothing that can be done. And it would be most unfortunate if flights were conducted during the time the Secretary General were there.

President Kennedy: How long is the Secretary General going to be there?

Charyk: The indication was that he would be there on Tuesday and Wednesday [October 30 and 31].

President Kennedy: Well, that does not [unclear] today.

McNamara: No, no, sir.

Charyk: Now, he expects [Soviet/Cuban] gratification with the fact that we had called off our reconnaissance yesterday, that is yesterday, and thought that would have a salutary effect.

We specifically avoided a discussion of reconnaissance today. They neither asked the question nor did we indicate that we would, or would not, conduct the surveillance today.

Purely [unclear], but if the statement were actually raised, then we would, of course, make some sort of response and decide if it was desirable to avoid the direct confrontation. So although it was hinted at, there was no specific discussion of reconnaissance today. But they were quite explicit on the reconnaissance on Tuesday and on Wednesday during the time that the Secretary General would be there.

We then went into the discussion of the suggestion of a voluntary suspension of the blockade on Tuesday, simultaneous with the arrival of the Secretary General, and they would hope that we would agree to this, and we would keep the ships on station, and that we would indicate to the UN observers the specific ships of which we were concerned. They would have the UN inspectors—and I understand these are UN guards—at the ports, and they would pay primary attention to the vessels with which we were primarily concerned, and they would then report back to us on the results of their inspection. And in the event that material was being passed which was on the prohibited list, they would notify us not later than Wednesday night [October 31]. So this was the suggestion relative to the blockade.

Rikhye indicated that, in any event, he felt that it was quite important that Kuznetsov, who was arriving at 8:55 last night, be informed as to what our decisions were.

President Kennedy: Thank you very much, Mr. Charyk.

Rusk: Decisions on the quarantine?

Charyk: Well, we have discussed both surveillance and the quarantine, and it was not clear to me whether the reference to informing Kuznetsov referred to the blockade alone, or whether it referred to both. I rather got the idea that it referred to both.

President Kennedy: Does U Thant go [to Cuba] tomorrow morning?

Charyk: He goes tomorrow morning at 10:00.

President Kennedy: I think we want to have our, Ros and George up there.

McNamara: I would recommend, Mr. President, that we agree now that we will send the reconnaissance out late in the afternoon [today], after notification of Kuznetsov and the Cuban ambassador through Ambassador Stevenson with this understanding: That if at 12:00, or shortly thereafter, whatever has been said by or through Kuznetsov indicates this is an incorrect decision, then we'll get back to you and change it if necessary.

Secondly, that we get Dr. Charyk, with this committee that's just been set up today, up to New York to work out detailed plans for continuing reconnaissance.

Rusk: On the quarantine, are we likely to have a problem today or tomorrow, in terms of the location of the Soviet ships?

McNamara: Probably not. The *Grozny* is circling and/or staying dead in the water, orbiting or such tactics, at the perimeter of the interception zone. One of the other ships that has been carrying cargo for the Soviet Union, a Czech ship, appears to be skirting the edge of the interception zone on a northerly course. A third ship will be at the barrier tomorrow, a Russian ship carrying helicopters. But in each of these cases, there is ample time to take any action we wish to, without deciding what that action should be today or early tomorrow.

Rusk: Mr. President, I do think that we have to keep emphasizing that the measures that we have taken are to continue into effect until UN machinery can effectively replace them.

McNamara: Exactly.

Rusk: Because if we give up that point, we may get sucked into a massive trick here.

President Kennedy: When are you guys going? You have planes standing by?

Unidentified: We've already got . . .

McNamara: Of course.

President Kennedy: Now, what are we thinking about as far as the long-range [surveillance plan]. What is this committee going to . . .? What proposal are you going to make to Kuznetsov, as far as long-range surveillance? Once a week we'll make these flights? Or how do we sort of organize it?

Charyk: First we ought to give the UN the capability so that they'll have the kind of equipment to make any frequency—

President Kennedy: Not the Indonesians. I think we ought to say the Canadians.

[Unclear exchange.]

Charyk:—by the U.S. Air Force and we'd have U.S. people aboard although they wouldn't be operating the planes.

President Kennedy: Where would they be? I think we'd have to have U.S. in order to put them in the hands of the Indonesians completely.

McNamara: They object very strongly to the use of American air crews.

[Unclear exchange.]

But he would accept U.S. observers?

Charyk: We discussed camera operators, and there they were not very strong on who would actually operate them. They expressed strong preference for another nationality, but they did not appear to resist that the idea of American instructors at least would be necessary initially.

President Kennedy: I think we ought to . . . This is one of those things the committee ought to do. We ought to be very hard that there's going to be an American on that plane.

Charyk: The long-range plan—

[Unclear exchange.]

McCone:—that kind of a job and do it well.

Carter?: What about the processing of film?

Charyk: Yes. We spent some time discussing processing of film, discussing the type of facilities that would be required for processing.

They asked who would own the film. I indicated that under these conditions, if they were accepted by this government, the basic film would belong to the United Nations but copies would be made available to all the nations, the organized states. And that we would be very happy to assist in the establishment of the proper kind of processing facilities, wherever they might be desired.

President Kennedy: And we would make, one of the things this committee would be making arrangements for, would be weekly flights or twice-weekly flights for an indefinite period, with at least an American aboard who knows how to operate the camera, and with all the film—would at least get a copy to us. That would be one of the conditions.

McCone: That would be one of them.

President Kennedy: And as you say, it's the least intrusive, least offended— least offensive in intent to the sovereignty of Cuba, because one way or another it's going to be inspected. And this is—these flights were regularized. It seems to me, they'll probably insist that a Cuban be on this plane.

McNamara: Rikhye would be quite happy to have a Russian and a Cuban.

Unidentified: Rikhye would regard this a supplement to ground inspection. [Others agree.]

McCone: I think, as Joe points out, it will make ground inspection much more effective.

President Kennedy: Now as far as our . . . Pierre [Salinger] is asked: "What is the status of our quarantine?" I think we ought to say our ships are on station. And leave it just at that. I mean, just say our ships are on station and just try to leave it that ambiguous, I would think, for the next 24 hours. Would you have any thoughts, any objection, to that?

Taylor: [unclear] agreed on the objectives of the quarantine.

President Kennedy: No. Nor should we say any [unclear], other than to say that our ships are on station.

Unidentified: That might be creating a problem with U Thant, so that he can do something.

President Kennedy: All right. Why don't we say that—yes?

Rusk: Ships are on station pending the transfer of effective supervision to the United Nations.

President Kennedy: Pending the arrangement in the United Nations for effective—

Rusk: Pending United Nations arrangements.

President Kennedy: The ships stay on station there.

The reserve callup. Are you going to reverse what you did Saturday

Charyk?: No Canadians.

Unidentified: Wouldn't it be possible to get one?

[Mixed voices.]

President Kennedy: That's another thing the Coordinating Committee . . . It seems to me that it would be all right. We said we'd let a Russian go, but let's send an American. If [we can] not get an American, then we shouldn't have a Russian. But we should try to get a Canadian.

Rusk: Howard [name unclear], and Adlai Stevenson, [unclear] is urging him to offer F-101 pilots to the UN.

Those Canadians could at least for a few days put in crews, that would be then substituted for by other crews later if there's something that was possible. To use Canadian crews . . .

President Kennedy: What else is there?

McNamara: One other subject the committee should work on, I imagine, Mr. President, is the protection against covert aggression [from Cuba], some formula to reintroduce into the language the protection we had in some of the drafts on . . .[11]

President Kennedy: I talked yesterday with Governor Stevenson about putting that . . . [unclear] to introduce the new conditions. So we finally got him to say something about peace in the Caribbean. That's a bad image.

11. The original draft letters to Khrushchev considered on the afternoon of October 27 made "peace in the Caribbean" a condition of a U.S. pledge of noninvasion.

Should have in, [what] I define as a cessation of subversion. He [Stevenson] said he would tell that to U Thant. I think we ought to see how much we can get back in of that language, because if they begin to continue what they did in Venezuela, we're going to be doing things. And so . . .

Rusk: I assured the members of the OAS yesterday, when I briefed them, that no arrangement we make on this situation which, [unclear] doubt in any way on the responsibility of securing the hemisphere and the Rio Pact. If these fellows cause trouble, we'd have to cause trouble there.

President Kennedy: This can all be changed, I think. I think we can try to get that in.

McNamara: I have nothing further, Mr. President.

President Kennedy: What about you?

Rusk: I don't think there's anything.

President Kennedy: Let's see whether, we've got to be able to straighten this [unclear], with Stevenson. Pile in some cars, and you ought to leave right now. The quicker you get up there the better, I think.

[Ball and Gilpatric leave to go to New York.]

Gilpatric: We've got a helicopter from the Pentagon, if you'll come with me, and [unclear] Charyk.

Taylor: On the surveillance [unclear] status, we have rarin' to go, to observe all the offensive-weapon sites that we've been looking at.

President Kennedy: With the U-2, it'd be a high-level?

Taylor: No, it would be low-level.

Rusk: This could make a point of difference, politically. I realize that we noticed them [the Cubans] stand down, not necessarily the SAM sites. This is something we need to think very hard about.

But I think also there's a further element that I'm interested in. The U-2 is more likely to discover if they're building, if they're digging a hole, nearby to bury some of these damn things before the UN gets there. I don't think the low-level . . . it's too pinpointed to discover—

McNamara: Dean, there's a real question whether the U-2 can discover a hole of that kind. And there are further questions as to whether the U-2 can show the detail of the equipment that we need to see, to compare [with] recent low-level. So I think from a reconnaissance point of view, we'll learn more from low-level.

Now, there may be political reasons why we should not go in at low-level.

Rusk: Just wait and see what the reaction is. What Kuznetsov says we do . . .

Taylor: Let me just tell you, I would say U-2 would not do it, Dean, because of the danger of cloud cover. The only sure way—

President Kennedy: Would you send 6 [low-level reconnaissance aircraft] in?

Taylor: Pardon?

President Kennedy: Six? How many would you send in?

Taylor: Eight, I'm sorry.

McNamara: Six to 8.

Unidentified: Six is the minimum, preferably 8.

President Kennedy: There isn't any doubt that it's a hazard, we're doing this. Not to the planes so much as politically. [Unclear.] What is the

on Sunday, Mr. President.

And we found on Saturday, some indication that they are moving equipment, missile support equipment, into the IRBM bases. We could not find that out with U-2, I'm certain.

President Kennedy: We ought to check it and announce it in advance?

McNamara: Yes.

President Kennedy: "Awaiting the arrival of the UN,"—"pending the arrival,"—"pending the organization of effective"—

McNamara: . . . "effective UN capability, we would carry this out." "We are carrying it out today."

[Unclear exchange.]

"Unarmed aircraft," right.

[Several people begin talking, working over the draft statement to be released, and making arrangements for the reconnaissance flights. Someone says, probably to Salinger: "Be sure this word 'pending' comes through in what you're going to say."]

Taylor: I have one other comment, on the importance of air surveillance. Someone, I believe, mentioned that this would supplement the ground observers. I am sure, in my own mind, that this will have to be the backbone of our surveillance. I never have . . .

Charyk?: This is the point that I was trying to make to Rikhye, to accept that the concept of having a few observers on the set and going from site to site is ridiculous. But that, on the other hand, a relatively small ground corps could be effective if you had effective aerial surveillance.

Taylor: That combination is the cheapest and the easiest. But you must have effective aerial surveillance.

President Kennedy: Have we got a longer-range plan of how we can survey this place through other means? What is that?

Nitze: You could exploit the thing that U Thant said to Cuba. After all, that "you Cubans don't have to fear photographs." [Unclear.] We can now justify continuing surveillance more than we are now doing. This is why I have a hesitation about saying we're going to do this, *pending* UN substitution therefor. I think we ought to attack the general principle of the propriety of surveillance.

Unidentified: On the other hand, the Brazilian nuclear-free-zone proposal, with inspection provisions on there, would offer a means of including long-range surveillance.

Nitze: I think it's very important what we do today on this, as to the background we lay on the long-range thing.

President Kennedy: But he [Khrushchev] made a specific mention of this sort of low-flying reconnaissance in his message? The Soviet [unclear].

Bundy: He said to wait on that.

President Kennedy: What, he [unclear]?

Rusk: Yes, but he didn't make it a condition, see.

Nitze: He didn't make it a condition.

Rusk: Just a wish.

McCone: If it would help, I think we could offer to have UN observers be with us while we process the film. As long as we do that [unclear].

President Kennedy: Well, they probably wouldn't want to be involved with this.

Charyk: We discussed that. We'd be happy to have the observers follow the processing all the way through. They didn't seem to think that was a particularly good idea. But on the other hand, Dr. Wentworth, who was sitting here [unclear].[12]

[Unclear exchange.]

Rusk: . . . to convince [U Thant] to bring this [inspection] thing home. One is Kuznetsov and the other is Castro. And he's going to have more trouble with Castro than he's going to have with Kuznetsov, and so we've got to think a little bit about that.

---

12. We have not been able to identify Wentworth.

[Unclear exchange.]

Unidentified: We ought to consider not making a public announcement.

President Kennedy: What'd you say?

Nitze: We ought to consider not making a public announcement. Just informing Kuznetsov, and the Cubans through the Cuban ambassador up there, and not making a public announcement.

Dillon: To save their face?

[Text obscured]

Unidentified: Then you're going to notify.

Unidentified: That's right.

Unidentified: Otherwise you just go without notification.

McNamara: Well, we shouldn't do that. We ought to notify them in advance if we're going to go.

President Kennedy: I think we would have to say to them in order—otherwise, they would say this is just [a] whole reversal of the direction [announced the previous day, suspending surveillance flights]. You don't want to bitch this thing up, just to, just to fight.

Unidentified: We could accompany [the surveillance with an announcement].

President Kennedy: I think we ought to say "pending an arrangement, a satisfactory UN response." Now we can argue about what a satisfactory response is.

Taylor: Air reconnaissance, I think.

President Kennedy: Satisfactory air reconnaissance.

Let's get on to something else.

Mr. Secretary [McNamara], we have to think about whether or not we want to do this today or not, total.

Rusk: I'd like to know that after we hear what Kuznetsov has to say.

President Kennedy: What time is . . .

Rusk: He's seeing U Thant at 11:00.

President Kennedy: Is anybody seeing Kuznetsov Monday night?

Rusk: No. U Thant is seeing Stevenson, immediately after.

Dillon: Vis-à-vis Castro, it may be helpful to us, because of this with the Cuban [unclear].

President Kennedy?: He fires at our plane. Now what do we do then?

McNamara: Well, it won't be easy to fire on it. It'll be more likely that the Soviets . . . The Soviet antiaircraft batteries around the missile sites were firing on the planes the other day.

Unidentified: Are those Soviet-manned?

McNamara: We're almost certain they were.

Rusk: Mr. President, there is another point here. If we notify Kuznetsov of this flight, there will be some point in letting the *Grozny* go on through. We don't think it has any harm in it.

McNamara: Well, the *Grozny* is being controlled by the Russians for the moment. It's just there, quite clearly awaiting instructions from the Soviets.

Taylor: I'm impressed with the great difficulty of resuming reconnaissance, to get people to act on it.

President Kennedy: Tell me again now, General, tell me why these are important.

Taylor: To find out whether the Soviets really mean what they told you in the letter. Whether they stopped work.

President Kennedy: Well, [unclear] to do much yet.

What?

Thompson: Wasn't the report that there were 24 of them [MRBMs] all ready to go?

If they're going to be dismantling them, they'll be working around the sites on the dismantling. We want to see that. The main justification is to make sure that they're not loading them up—

Unidentified: Can you tell whether they're dismantling or—

Unidentified: Oh, yes.

McNamara: U Thant's guess was that by Wednesday, when his inspectors arrive at the sites, there will be no missiles available to be inspected. I think he's probably right. And if that's true, we should certainly see a lot of change between Saturday and today.

Taylor: We'll have to have them [surveillance flights] tomorrow.

Rusk: Can we, in any event, take the peripheral U-2 pictures at Havana airport? That's a tiny little sliver of land out there. Couldn't we see them from a peripheral picture?

President Kennedy: If U Thant shows up there on Wednesday and there's no missiles there, and there's evidence of . . .

Your judgment is, your statement is, General, that U Thant can't tell whether there's any dismantling because he won't have sophisticated enough people?

Taylor: If they stop work in expanding, the next step is to begin work to dismantle them. The two are not quite the same, and I think that if they are photographed, it will give us some, some partial [unclear].

President Kennedy: But, of course, what we need from U Thant are the photographs on Wednesday [October 31]. But if I can be getting these assurances that he's going to photograph it Wednesday the photographs will it "

technical people.

Rusk: To what extent can ground photography be an indication here?

McCone: Well, very good.

Rusk: I think that's the one thing that we can insist that he take along is a good—

Gilpatric?: You'd need an army to cover all the sites, to take all the pictures. It would be an extraordinary position.

McNamara: He's taking down 10 to 15 people, I believe. That would be the total UN force he's likely to have.

Gilpatric?: He's taking a Caravel aircraft, and that'll be the upper limit.

President Kennedy: Well, I think that the UN, and George and them, ought to be thinking about what it is that we do with the limitations of U Thant and the personnel [unclear] to take these pictures. You ought to make sure he got 5 photographers.

[The meeting breaks up. People begin leaving, arranging rides back to their offices. After a few minutes, President Kennedy, in a different part of the room, begins talking again with a small number of officials, including Rusk, McNamara, Bundy, and Taylor.]

McNamara: We make a decision here by 2:30 P.M., and we'll be over the target around 4:00 or 5:00.

President Kennedy: Let's see if we can get some assurances about photographs. If we can get some assurances from U Thant by Wednesday.

[Unclear] what U Thant will be able to do. So I think we need . . . [unclear] potential to try to establish the principle.

We're not sure ourselves that we can get the photography today. Say they're going ahead with the work. Well then, that means the whole deal blows. Whether it blows today or Wednesday, we're going to be faced with the same problem.

McNamara: I think, Mr. President . . .

Taylor: Wait, wait . . . I think what everyone is looking here for is to verify [unclear].

President Kennedy: I agree, but I don't think that we can get much [unclear] between today and yesterday noon. This message came in today [yesterday].

Taylor: Well, he's had 24 hours, and all indications are [unclear] there's no doubt in our minds are [unclear] and experienced, very energetic in improving work. Yet if they stop the work how do we [unclear]. If they really start the work again that might get a little hard, and I don't [unclear].

McNamara: Mr. President, I think there are three points. First, I don't believe there'll be UN reconnaissance flights. I think it's so impossible the way they're working, and talking. I don't think there will be a UN capability right away.

Secondly, the main requirement today, I think—

President Kennedy: [to someone else] Have somebody call him up and tell him that Ros Gilpatric is leaving . . .

Bundy: They're going up to New York? All right.

McNamara: The main requirement—I think we really need to show our people that we're protecting their interests.

Then there is this third advantage. I don't think it's absolutely essential to know what happened between Saturday and Monday, but it is of some value.

Rusk: There are a number of political consequences, which were summarized in Mr. McCone's statement this morning, which indicated that this was for real. [Unclear reference to historical Soviet desire to "show people that they were all unified," contrasted with evidence of obvious discord] . . . and the Chinese organization, and the Castro revolt. So I'm not discouraged yet about the possibility that this may be for real.

[Mixed voices, nearly inaudible. Someone says: "I was thinking about the longer-range."]

President Kennedy: I think they're going to dismantle these . . . Now with the mobile ones, they may be hiding in the woods, we're not ready to tell that. But I don't think there's any doubts here that [unclear].

[Unclear discussion.]

I think we're going to find a cessation of work. That's what I think you'll find, more or less.

I think what we've got to do is to have set up this week a [unclear], through the UN or other [unclear]. That is essential.

Today's mission, in my opinion, is not as important. It's the this week's mission that is important. So I think U Thant has to give us the assurances that he is going to have, this week, photographic reconnaissance or we're going to do it ourselves. Today's mission is, I think, more questionable. I don't think we're going to see a hell of a lot, and I do think that if we get 6 or 8 planes going to go down over those things

then we're going to desist, pending setting it up by the UN." And if they don't do it, we're going to have to continue the surveillance.

McNamara: I think it's extremely important, we did not tell them yesterday that either we do it today or they do it today. I don't think we'll ever get U Thant to do it.

[Mixed voices.]

Bundy: Forrestal was there.[13] They will not be surprised if we do it today. I think they'll be surprised if we don't.

President Kennedy: All right, well, let's go ahead. We ought to first tell U Thant. We ought to tell Kuznetsov. Say what we're doing is, doing this in order to give our own people and others, including the OAS and others, some evidence of [unclear] . . . to confirm our confidence in them [unclear].

And then say to them: "We can only desist on this thing, after our experience would be, if you set up a capacity. But otherwise we're going to go ahead." And we give them, "either we're going to do it or the UN's going to do it." If the UN goes with the procedure, we'll withdraw.

Now, who wants to take on the job of notifying?

Rusk: Well, I think we ought to hear from Kuznetsov first.

President Kennedy: Well, how are we going to hear from him?

[Unclear exchange.]

---

13. Michael Forrestal, a member of the staff of the National Security Council, working for Bundy.

Rusk: U Thant is telephoning Stevenson just as soon as Kuznetsov leaves. Stevenson thought, U Thant thought it would be around 12:00.

President Kennedy: I'll tell you what let's do: Mr. Secretary, we're going to get this thing [the low-level reconnaissance mission] laid on. Go ahead with the notifications you want. If for some reason, after our conversations . . .

We ought to get it to U Thant before he leaves.

The group breaks up and leaves the Cabinet Room. After a period of silence, the tape recorder is turned off. Sometime later the tape recorder is turned on in the Oval Office. President Kennedy is receiving a military briefing from several officers on plans for an invasion of Cuba. At the point when he turns on the tape recorder, the officers appear to be discussing how to deal with possible Soviet tactical nuclear weapons in the overall invasion plan.

Dennison?: . . . and all the pieces of equipment are gone. And we don't know how many are in how many other places. But they are searching the previous U-2 photos now, that can get a signature of like camps, and they found 2 more. But, of course, in that photo you can't tell what's in there. It takes the low-level job to get that. [Unclear.]

So we really don't know how much they got and we have to find out, which can be done. And it's done at a price. After you do your air, you continue to do your air, everything available, you take them out, every airplane, and then you can take that place, absolutely.

Unidentified: Now, what they would do with a nuclear weapon if they had them?

Dennison?: I don't know. I think they'd shoot them. Then the question is: Are they at nuclear war?

President Kennedy: Now, what if they didn't use their nuclear weapons, but used those armored vehicles, self-propelled and all the rest, given the fact that probably the younger Cubans are loyal to Castro and have enough national spirit, even ones that don't like Castro, so that we would certainly run into a hard-core situation and a lot of guerrilla [activity] and, as well as . . . You think that, your judgment is, that it's not a major military effort or—

Dennison?: It would be a major military effort, yes, sir. But once you hit this place, then you go at night, you take on every troop movement. See, they [the armored vehicles] have to find the one longitudinal highway, about two tracks, which means that if they're moving, any sizable tanks or anything, that you can take them on at night, with a flare. And you can get pictures of what they're doing.

You see, at the Guantanamo end [of Cuba], for example, our people be-lieve—well, I think they pretty well know from their . . . I believe that they've [the Cubans] got positions prepared back there about, oh, maybe, about 15 miles, and then inland. But they feel that they have the troops and all the stuff that they would move in there, including, perhaps, this kind of stuff that we saw in the regimental area.

It would take [the Cubans] 2 nights' march to get into those positions. They're not occupied. But they've got them and of course the thing is

Unidentified: There's a family of 250-pound low-glide bombs, which we carry a lot of on our planes. But we would really make a shambles of it.

But the three things that concern me was:

First, did we find all of these missiles and weapons?

Second, what would they do in the course, in the way of demolitions, which might impede the—getting to shore with the armor, particularly for the Army.

And, third, whether they might have a very elaborate demolition plan on these airfields. These things we really wouldn't know until we got in there.

Dennison?: Not until our last pictures did they receive [audio quality sud-denly deteriorates for about 10 seconds], but the way the pictures read out on that shows them busy constructing defenses at the beach. Of course, mines can cause you some trouble. But you find out before you go in, and you take some measures to get rid of the damn mines. You can go in and unarm them, you see. Go swim in the water and unarm them.

President Kennedy: Well, we just have to watch, and if they continue this conventional buildup into Cuba, then we just have to draw conclusions from that. So I think we just stay on it because it's . . . With the Russians, it just shows the last 2 months that whole operation that they've run which was, you know, complete.

They have their ambassador telling us, I mean it just shows how they're willing to liquidate—this Dobrynin is regarded very well in Russia, supposedly, served in here and has some reputation . . . He's around telling both the Attorney General and he told Rusk they would never send missiles there. That was 2 weeks ago. So now he's liquidated as a source and nobody believes him anymore, and the chances are he probably didn't know! He looked so *shocked* that day. When Rusk showed him, he still wouldn't believe it. So it's probable they didn't even tell him.

When you're dealing under those conditions where there is no basis . . . We just have to assume that we're going to be back with Cuba in 2 or 3 months if they start to build up their conventional forces. Then I think we'll have to say this is a breach of the . . .

Well, I just thought the Navy and the Marines and the preparedness, I think, was what we'd do this week.

Anderson?: Well, thank you very much. We need to beat Pittsburgh [in football]. We need to beat Pittsburgh. [Laughter.]

[The briefers depart. A few people remain in the Oval Office with President Kennedy.]

President Kennedy: [Unclear.] But I saw Pittsburgh has a pretty good team today.

Anderson?: Yeah?

President Kennedy: They beat them 47 to something?

Anderson?: 32 to 9, I think it was; 32 to 9.

President Kennedy: Is this the first game they've won? Have they won a lot?

Anderson?: We won last week. We beat Cornell. Cornell, and William and Mary, and one other one. They're playing another game on Saturday, in Philadelphia. But maybe Navy isn't too good this year.

President Kennedy: You're not going—

Anderson?: Yeah, I'm going to get up there. Yeah, sure.

President Kennedy: I imagine the airports must be looking bad, aren't they, with everything moving out?

Anderson?: No, actually all cooperation has been split up.

President Kennedy: So they did a good job on those photographs.

Anderson?: Oh, yeah.

President Kennedy: We had decided Saturday night to begin this air strike on Tuesday [October 30]. And it may have been one of the reasons why the Russians finally did this.

[Unclear.]

Anderson?: Well, they may have thought we were going to do it on Monday.

President Kennedy: Well, General Taylor said that they felt Tuesday [October 30] was the better.

[Someone comes into the office. Unclear comment by President Kennedy.]

President Kennedy: Those bluejackets, I saw them down there last some months ago.

Shoup?: They're pretty good. The Marines have trained them.

[Unclear exchanges. Some silence. President Kennedy talks quietly in a different part of the office.]

President Kennedy: The problem is that we have them in some places where you can't use them [nuclear weapons]. It's past their mobility[?].

Wheeler?: That's right. Can't use them up in the Himalayas.

President Kennedy: Those are the places you get [unclear].

Shoup?: The 64 dollar question is so to speak, the ....

[President Kennedy appears to agree.]

If that joker [Castro] ever had control, now . . . 'Course they're [the Soviets] telling him they got the keys, like we've got the keys—

President Kennedy: I'm sure they do.

Shoup?: The Russians say [to the Americans]: "We got the keys; you got the keys. You trust us; we trust you" . . .

President Kennedy: No, we don't trust each other. But we figure that they're never going to give them to the Cubans, anymore than we'd give them to, you know, the Turks. Because we know that . . . I don't think anybody wants that weapon to escape from their control. It's just too . . .

Wheeler?: Well, it won't be too long now, before you'll see Khrushchev on the run down [unclear].

President Kennedy: [Unclear.] I thought what we're trying to do is think of something about Berlin. You have given some degree of initiative, and just to see if we can get a proposal which could . . . Because Berlin really is a paralyzing . . .

Anderson?: That's right.

President Kennedy: Because everything you want to do, you say: "Oh, well it will screw us in Berlin." And I think if we can ever get any kind of decent deal on Berlin . . . It's just the worst place for us to let them always . . .

Anderson?: That's right.

President Kennedy: It gives them the initiative all the time; it always makes us look like it divides the allies.

So I instructed them this morning. I said: "You really ought to look and see if there is *some* proposal, because this is a completely" . . .

In the first place you're not even serving the long-range interests of West Berliners. Because there's 2 million of them. They could be blocked off at any day, and they would never get out of there. You have to [unclear] off on that Autobahn, and . . .

So Berlin is a . . . You know, Rusk told me George Marshall, the other day he said at the UN [unclear]—this was back in '43. If we could get the UN to get us out of Berlin. I think Marshall saw that it was going to become an impossible situation over the years. It gives the Soviets such a chance to . . . So that's what, I think, what we ought to do now. We ought to get some initiative here.

Wheeler?: Well, it's nice of you to receive us.

[The remaining guests depart. Someone else comes in, or remains. Unclear exchanges. Someone says, "Always available."]

Unidentified: Philip[?] wanted me to tell you how grateful he was, for your coming out to . . .

President Kennedy: Oh, well, fine.

[Silence. The President appears to be writing at his desk. Someone comes in.]

Sorensen?: Just think about this. If we don't do this tonight, then I'd do it with the press, it would be a good basis for a press conference.

[Unclear exchanges; the President is away from his desk.]

Unidentified: [Unclear] is working a number of people that you may remember, who have to be held. And I thought you'd want to send that out.

President Kennedy: How are you doing it? I saw the *New York Times* had some reports this morning on [unclear].

[Unclear exchanges about what to tell the press.]

President Kennedy: Now, have we got it all clear about up there, Adlai's in charge up there, no problem about this thing.[14]

Ball: Well, I don't think, I heard . . . Mac and I talked to Adlai, and then I talked to McCloy. I think McCloy understands he's got [unclear].

President Kennedy: Adlai's in charge of the UN delegation. I'll get to McCloy this afternoon. I just want to be sure that there's no press. What we're here trying to do is just the technical details of setting up McCloy up there. I know that it's 7 days before the election. I know what the charge is going to

---

14. Possibly a reference to speculation about the slight to Stevenson implied by sending McCloy to New York as chair of the new Coordinating Committee to negotiate the Cuban settlement, aided by Ball and Gilpatric.

be—[Adlai's] inadequate and all the rest. Therefore, we're protecting ourselves. We should not look at all like . . . He's in charge up there. McCloy's going to be working under him. And there's no real problem about it, as long as we don't make it look like it's a problem.

The whole UN delegation [unclear] comes from Adlai. [Unclear references to Stevenson.] Just the technical details—what are you going to do about verification, what are you going to do about the target areas . . . [unclear], that George Ball is going to do, . . .

Unidentified: I think they'll make it a problem.

[Unclear exchanges.]

President Kennedy: . . . He's working under Adlai's supervision. But you've got to have a defense man, some guy up there who's just doing this. But we want you [unclear] to know that Adlai is our voice.

So I think that that's the general line.

[President Kennedy apparently picks up a phone line in his office.]

Hello? I'll come right over. Yeah.

Can you get [unclear] for a second?

Lincoln: He's out at lunch. We're trying to track him down.

President Kennedy: OK.

[Unclear, fragmentary conversation.]

President Kennedy: What I've got to do, I've got to decorate that widow, some time.

[Fragmentary conversation about U.S. versus UN verification and a press conference. Rusk has apparently come into the Oval Office.]

President Kennedy: [harsh and rapid] Now listen, we've got to get some policy down and I'm going to say this privately. When the Soviets came in, I told them on Sunday, and I have the notes to show it, on this Turkish thing, and if they were going to come in on that they ought to be [unclear]. When they [the Soviets] came in on Saturday [with the proposed Cuba-Turkey deal], there was nothing [planned] there, really. There was a wire sent to Hare, asked his opinion about it, one sent to Finletter. But we were not really prepared to know what we were going to say, and we weren't prepared. We would have negotiations with the Turks in case this should really prove to be desirable, and we would adjust it so that we could do it if we wanted to do it.

Now it seems to me that it was obvious, [unclear], as I say in my notes, the notes of a [unclear] conversation last Saturday shows that I asked them to review this, and I particularly asked Nitze because it was a NATO commitment. Now it seems to me that somewhere in the State Department [someone] ought to be about a week ahead, not just to be drawing plans up for 6 months ahead.

[Unclear reply by Rusk.]

President Kennedy: We had it for 24 hours, and for an hour tried to figure out how—whether we turn it down, and nobody had any idea really what the Turks would go for and all the rest.

I'm just thinking, what is going to be our problem next this week?

[Unclear reply by Rusk, referring to papers.]

President Kennedy: Well, I'd like to get them. I never get your stuff. Go talk to Mac now, and have somebody over at the White House who is responsible for liaison with you, so I can get some of these things.

[Unclear reply by Rusk.]

President Kennedy: Could you get them to me more?

[Unclear exchange. Rusk leaves. Silence.]

President Kennedy: What do we got?

[Unclear discussion.]

[5 minutes and 28 seconds excised as being outside of the deed of gift to the JFK Library, concerning personal or family matters.]

[Unclear] Do you have anything you want me to sign?

[Unclear conversation between President Kennedy and Mrs. Lincoln.]

President Kennedy: [pushes a button on his phone] Dick, I want to get a President's commemorative for the Executive Committee of the National Security Council who've been involved in this matter.

And what I thought of was something that would have the month of October on it. And the 10 days—would have a line drawn around the calendar days; yeah, it would be a calendar. [Unclear.]

Now . . . Yeah. Yeah. You see, just like a page out of a calendar, with a line drawn in there [unclear].

How could I get that so it wouldn't be too expensive?

You want to get at that?

It's about 12, about 12. The days with the line drawn around it. Let's see,

Tuesday, Thursday, October—what is it? That's the 29th, I would say, so it would be the 28th. Yeah. Right. That's right. [Unclear.]

Thank you. Okay.

The tape recording then stopped. The commemorative was prepared in silver, by Tiffany's, for about 30 officials of the U.S. government.

CONCLUSION

deal work out? Second: What do we know now about the Soviet behavior? Kennedy said on the first day of the crisis, "It's a goddamn mystery to me." Is it less so now? Third: What do the tapes tell us? What about the missile crisis do we learn from them that is new, and of what possible use now or in the future is this unique record of concentrated, high-level decision-making?

AFTERMATH

Though anxiety gave way to euphoria after Khrushchev's broadcast of Sunday, October 28, the crisis was not over. Low-level reconnaissance on October 29 appeared to detect continuing construction. The Joint Chiefs suspected Khrushchev of simply trying to buy time. If Kennedy stopped aerial surveillance, as U Thant had requested, how would he know whether the Chiefs were right or wrong?

President Kennedy's position remained awkward through the last days of October. Led to believe that the crisis was essentially over, reporters expected evidence that the missiles were being pulled out. The government had no such evidence to release. Kennedy had little to go on except his own belief that Khrushchev was sincere, a belief reinforced by intelligence of Cuban and Chinese anger at what they seemed to regard as Soviet betrayal.

On October 28 Khrushchev sent a private message to President Kennedy, trying to nail down the deal on withdrawal of the Jupiter missiles. Khrushchev said he understood the need to handle this matter confidentially. He had respected that need in his public message agreeing to withdraw the missiles from Cuba. But the Soviet leader said his concessions "took into account" the American agreement to resolve the Jupiter problem.[1]

Dobrynin delivered this letter to Robert Kennedy on October 29. The next day Robert Kennedy called in Dobrynin and gave the letter back, refusing to accept it. Robert Kennedy's handwritten notes for this meeting say: "No quid pro quo as I told you. The letter makes it appear that there was." The missiles would leave Turkey; "you have my word on this & that is sufficient . . . ; if you should publish any document indicating a deal then it is off." Dobrynin said his government would never publish anything. Robert Kennedy reminded Dobrynin that his government had also said it would never put missiles in Cuba. Dobrynin took the letter back, and the U.S. government kept no record of the letter or its receipt.[2]

On October 30 Khrushchev sent another private letter to President Kennedy congratulating them both on having "in the main liquidated" a "dangerous crisis"; but in the same letter he suggested immediate removal of the quarantine and U.S. abandonment of Guantanamo.[3]

Not surprisingly, President Kennedy remained wary. He continued to review invasion plans, leaving in place forces to execute an air strike and invasion. Though McNamara and others predicted that nothing would come of U Thant's mission to Havana, Kennedy waited on its outcome.

When U Thant met with Castro in Havana on October 30, he found a Cuban leader whose fury covered all points of the compass. U Thant later told the Americans that Castro had been in an "impossible and intractable mood"—"extremely bitter" toward the Soviets, the Americans, and even U Thant himself, whom he seemed to regard as a lackey of the imperialists. U Thant said he had never had a more trying encounter in all his experience. Castro refused any cooperation in verification.[4] Given Castro's mood, U.S. resumption of aerial reconnaissance involved risk of further shootdowns and further debates about appropriate forms of reprisal. Nonetheless, Kennedy authorized new U-2 and low-level reconnaissance flights.

Meanwhile in New York the U.S. negotiating team of Stevenson and McCloy found that Kuznetsov did not count the IL-28 bombers as offensive weapons. Kuznetsov was instructed to say that the bombers had no military value, and Khrushchev wrote to Kennedy denying that the bombers could threaten anyone.[5] At the beginning of October the Kennedy administration had been willing to overlook these aircraft rather than provoke a crisis. Now they had become part of the threat President Kennedy had publicly pledged to erase.

These two problems, lack of verification and the status of the IL-28s, were the principal issues dogging November talks in New York. Khrushchev sent there one of his more trusted Presidium colleagues, Anastas Mikoyan. He also exchanged further confidential letters with Kennedy. By November 20, Kennedy could announce at a press conference that the outstanding issues had been resolved. The IL-28s would come out of Cuba within 30 days. Though there would be no UN inspection, U.S. forces would be allowed to observe the departing Soviet ships. Their cargos of offensive weapons would be on deck and could be observed by passing U.S. ships or aircraft. The United States would keep flying reconnaissance planes over Cuba. When the offensive weap-

... the quarantine would finally be lifted. American forces would

There would be no noninvasion pledge beyond the safeguards any country enjoyed under international law. Thus the United States was back to its old precrisis position that if Cuba did not interfere with anyone else's security, it would have nothing to fear from the United States. President Kennedy told Mikoyan directly that if the original agreement with UN inspection was not upheld to the letter, the President could "only act in the best way the situation permits."[6]

The U.S. intelligence community thought that it saw hard evidence of Cuban readiness to shoot again at U.S. reconnaissance aircraft. The intelligence was accurate, and the Soviet government bluntly instructed its envoy to tell the Cubans that this time Soviet forces would not help to shoot down any American planes. Periodic U-2 flights continued (invulnerable to the guns controlled by the Cubans) until satellite photography took their place. The Executive Committee agreed to keep forces poised to attack Cuban antiaircraft sites if a U.S. plane was shot down.[7]

Covert harassment of the Castro government resumed, spurred by discoveries of new Cuban attempts to subvert the governments in Venezuela and other South American countries. By the summer of 1963 these CIA operations had returned to about where they had been in the summer of 1962, before the Soviet arms shipments began. Washington was again back to a policy judged to have low risk and a low return—petty harassment that was probably not enough to bring down Castro, but also not enough to drag the United States into an open or direct intervention in Cuba.

Also left out of President Kennedy's November 20 press conference was any mention of the Jupiter missiles. The matter was not forgotten, but was handled in broader reviews of NATO's nuclear force posture, including a meeting in Paris in December 1962 marked, as one delegate put it, by almost "intolerable serenity," stemming from the outcome of the Cuban crisis. The Turks agreed to removal of the Jupiters. The missiles were dismantled by the end of April 1963. A Polaris missile submarine took up station in the Mediterranean.[8]

THE SOVIET SIDE OF THE STORY

Throughout the crisis, the Americans asked themselves repeatedly why the Soviets had decided to put missiles in Cuba despite Kennedy's explicit and repeated warnings. They differed in their guesses as to how the Soviets would react to U.S. statements and actions and why the Soviets did what they actually did. Why, for example, did most ships subject to Moscow's orders stop sailing for Cuba while some, particularly the *Grozny*, kept going? Why did Soviet-manned SAM crews do nothing about U-2 flights from October 14 through October 26, then shoot one down on October 27? Why did Khrushchev change his terms for withdrawing the missiles? In the long private message received late on October 26, he seemed to say his only condition was a U.S. promise not to invade Cuba. In the message publicly broadcast on the morning of October 27 (U.S. time), he called in addition for removal of U.S. "offensive means" from Turkey. Why? And why, having publicly adopted this position, did Khrushchev back down on October 28?

Owing to the passage of time, the publication of memoirs by Khrushchev and others, and, most recently, a study by Aleksandr Fursenko and Timothy Naftali, based not only on newly opened archives but on Presidium and KGB files not yet accessible to other scholars, we have information on these questions well beyond that available to Kennedy and his circle.[9] The two main findings are these. First, Kennedy and his advisers did not make any serious misjudgments about the Soviets; most of what we know now confirms what was surmised by Kennedy's "demonologists," especially Thompson. Second, our best retrospective judgments about the Soviet side still entail guesswork; in all probability, no one will ever be able to answer with complete confidence *any* of the questions about the Soviets that bothered Kennedy and his advisers.

With these caveats, let us summarize what can now be said about each of the major puzzles, beginning with the question of why the Soviets put the missiles into Cuba and thus brought on the crisis. This actually separates, like a Russian doll, into several parts. Why did Khrushchev order in May 1962 that the Soviet Strategic Rocket Forces set up MRBM and IRBM launchers in Cuba, and why did he make such a secret of it? Had he announced his intentions or even told Kennedy privately that he planned to base IRBMs in Cuba, the crisis would have unfolded differently. Conceivably, there might have been no crisis at all. In the second meeting on October 16, Kennedy said, "Last month I should have said that we don't care." Looking back years later, Sorensen speculated that, if Kennedy had had foreknowledge, he might not have taken

the President drew the line precisely where the

mettle and the

least *consider* telling Kennedy what he had in mind?

Since the missiles were only en route to Cuba when Kennedy issued his September 4 warning, why did Khrushchev not at least pause to reconsider what he was doing? Since the Soviets understood the U-2's capabilities and knew that the United States conducted reconnaissance over Cuba, what made any of them think the secret could be kept? What did they plan to do if the secret were not to be kept? And, if the secret were kept, what did they plan to do, once the missiles were fully in place?

To explain the original Soviet decision, Kennedy and his advisers considered several hypotheses. Their favorite was that Khrushchev intended the missiles in Cuba as levers to loosen U.S. concessions regarding Berlin. A second hypothesis focused on the strategic balance. The Joint Chiefs of Staff, for example, presumed that Khrushchev had gambled as he did in order to get wider target coverage against the United States and offset the American lead in ICBMs. A third hypothesis was that Khrushchev had acted in order to protect Cuba from invasion. The only person in the Executive Committee who came close to asserting this view was Thompson, who argued, in the afternoon meeting of October 27, that the Jupiters in Turkey were of secondary interest to the Soviets. "The important thing for Khrushchev," he said, "is to be able to say: I saved Cuba. I stopped an invasion." (But Thompson was speaking then of how Khrushchev could save face; he was not necessarily saying that defense of Cuba had been uppermost among Khrushchev's original motives.) A fourth hypothesis presumed factional interplay in the Kremlin. Thus, whatever the motive or motives, they might not be Khrushchev's own. To account for the difference in content between Khrushchev's private letter and broadcast message, Bundy hazarded that the former was Khrushchev's, the latter that of "hard-nosed people overruling him."

Since 1962 no other hypotheses have been advanced to supplement the four voiced by Kennedy and his advisers. But they have had different fates. Berlin, oddly, dropped from sight. Hardly anyone writing retrospectively about the crisis, except the participants, stressed Berlin as a possible primary factor in Soviet decisions. The strategic-balance hypothesis proved more hardy. Two RAND analysts wrote a book not long after the crisis, developing at length the strategic-balance rationale for Khrushchev's actions. This argument has remained an important strain in writings about the crisis by historians and political scientists specializing in international relations or security studies. But the defense-of-Cuba hypothesis has proved the most robust and longest-lived, especially among historians. This view has derived its strength and longevity not only from the United States' demonstrated "arrogance of power" (in Senator Fulbright's phrase) before, during, and since the Vietnam War but also from documentary revelations concerning Operation Mongoose and pre-crisis invasion planning, as well as testimony from Khrushchev and other Russians.[11]

What we now know indicates that Kennedy and his advisers understood the reasoning in the Kremlin better than have most scholars writing about the crisis in retrospect. While Khrushchev and his colleagues did indeed care a great deal about Cuba, the thought of deterring a U.S. invasion figured only incidentally in their discussions about the missile deployments. Calculations about the strategic nuclear balance were much more in evidence. Berlin was an omnipresent and dominating concern.

To summarize what we now know about Soviet deliberations in 1962 is not, however, to state a final verdict on the motives guiding Soviet behavior before and during the crisis. The more we learn about Soviet decision-making in the Khrushchev era, the less confidence we can feel in any analyses that explain decisions in terms of a hierarchy of interest calculations. Eight points emerge from the accumulating evidence:

1. To interpret Soviet decisions is to interpret Khrushchev. He alone decided on policy. Other members of the Soviet elite who favored other policies could have their way only when Khrushchev was not around or not paying attention. No one could overrule him—yet.

2. Khrushchev made decisions largely on his own. Now and then, he would talk over a question with a fellow member of the Politburo or someone from the bureaucracy, but he did not systematically seek even advice, let alone policy analysis. He looked upon other members of the Politburo as potential enemies.

He may have had some respect for military leaders; he treasured memories of working with generals on the Ukrainian front in World War II. But he probably heeded military men only with regard to narrowly military issues. Khrushchev never obtained advice and analysis such as Kennedy obtained from his Executive Committee, and, given the quality of the rest of the Soviet leadership, he ~~~ld not have got it if he had tried.

than from calculation. Whether

chips has disappeared. ~~~~~~~

terize him, Fyodor Burlatsky and Georgi Shaknazarov, who had been Khrushchev, agreed on the word *azartnyi,* which means, in Russian, "reckless" or "hotheaded."[12]

4. Khrushchev's instincts in foreign affairs were disciplined by relatively little experience or knowledge. Sixty-eight in 1962, he had been a coal miner as a youth and then a party functionary for most of his life. He was party boss in Moscow at the time of Stalin's death, when, by outmaneuvering better-educated and less plebeian rivals, he became number one in the hierarchy. For practical purposes, he did not think at all about the world outside the Soviet Union until the mid-1950s, when it fell to him to test whether Stalin had been right in prophesying that the capitalist-imperialists would wring the necks of his successors. His first encounter with capitalist-imperialist leaders came when he met Eisenhower at the Geneva summit conference in 1955.

5. The framework into which Khrushchev fitted what he learned about the outside world was built around a rather simplistic version of Marxism-Leninism. Although he was intelligent, quick, shrewd, and capable of subtlety, his observations of the outside world were influenced by tenets he had absorbed and taught in his decades of party work. When he visited the United States in 1959, he was eager to meet Wall Streeters because he had grown up believing that they called the tunes for U.S. political leaders. He seems to have assumed that U.S. decisions would usually be governed by crass interest. By the same token, although he knew of and had participated in the brutalities of Stalinism, he retained a romantic belief that Soviet-style socialism did ride the wave of the future and did promise eventual happiness for humankind. This viewpoint helps to account for his "secret speech" at the Twentieth Party

Congress in 1956, exposing Stalin's crimes, as well as for his boastful prophecies that movements of national liberation would eventually bury the West.

6. Because of his narrow experience of the outside world, Khrushchev probably misread Kennedy. At Geneva in 1955, he had been a bit awed by Eisenhower. He changed his estimate a bit when he visited the United States in 1959 and saw an Eisenhower weakened by medical problems and on his way out of power. When he saw Kennedy in 1961 at Vienna, Khrushchev was more impressed than he had expected to be by the "young millionaire and . . . son of a millionaire," but whereas he had come away from Geneva crediting Eisenhower with toughness, he came away from Vienna crediting Kennedy with "flexibility." He would later praise Kennedy for being "realistic enough to see that now the might of the socialist world equaled that of the capitalist world."[13]

7. Khrushchev's thinking about foreign affairs had been molded by the Suez-Hungary crisis of 1956. Before that crisis, the United States had treated the Soviet Union as on a par with Britain and France. During the crisis, the United States temporarily broke with the British and French, deploring their surprise attack on Egypt and demanding that they desist. Khrushchev joined in this demand. Blustering, he threatened the British that, if they did not pull out of Egypt, the Soviet Union might use its "modern destructive weapons." The British and French did withdraw, largely because of diplomatic and economic pressure from Washington, but Khrushchev credited his threats with having had decisive effect.[14]

Because Britain thereafter abandoned its previous pretensions, and France did so until General Charles de Gaulle came to power in 1958, the Soviet Union became by default the other superpower, even at the moment of brutally crushing opposition in Hungary. Thereafter, it became Khrushchev's standard practice to make demands and talk loudly about Soviet rockets. Though he had had to back down more than once when he found the West united with regard to Berlin, and the Americans unflinching, Khrushchev still derived from the Suez experience the lesson that the way to succeed with foreign powers was to rattle rockets in their faces.

8. Khrushchev's decisions were influenced by Kremlin politics, but not in the way suggested by Bundy's reference to his "hard-nosed people." Although Khrushchev was in absolute control in Moscow, he knew that he might on almost any day find himself absolutely not in control. After Stalin's death, police head Lavrenti Beria and Premier Georgi Malenkov had formed, along with Khrushchev, a ruling triumvirate. Beria had been removed from power by gunfire, arranged for him by Khrushchev and Malenkov. As indication that Soviet politics were becoming more humane, Malenkov's removal involved

mere demotion. Similar things happened to other Khrushchev opponents. Murder went out of fashion. But Khrushchev could never for a single day forget that he, too, might receive the Soviet equivalent of the black spot. In the spring of 1962, forced to admit the failure of his programs to increase croplands and farm output, he had to announce 20–30 percent increases in the state-control-ed prices of basic foods. This move triggered protests that, in one city near ~~~~~~~~~~~~~~~~~~~~~~ only through machine-gun fire

A few years later, as ne dictated ~~~~~~~ during an official visit to Bulgaria, from May 14 to 20, 1962, one thought hammering at my brain: what will happen if we lose Cuba?"[17] We now know that Soviet-Cuban relations were deeper and much more complex than Americans realized. The Soviets had begun providing covert assistance to the Castro government in the spring of 1959, and secretly arranged the first sales of arms that autumn, well before the U.S. government had decided whether Castro would be a friend or foe. Some Americans and many Cubans suspected that the Castro regime harbored a secret radical agenda, that the security ministries were being brought under the control of pro-Soviet Communists in order to pursue this revolutionary agenda at home and abroad, and that this faction included Fidel Castro's brother, Raul, and Che Guevara, if not Fidel himself. Evidence from Soviet files shows that these suspicions were well founded.[18]

From 1960 onward Castro repeatedly predicted horrific scenarios involving U.S. action against him, then took actions that made his prophecies self-fulfilling. In March 1960, blaming American agents for the catastrophic explosion of a ship carrying arms into Havana from Belgium (there is no evidence of any U.S. involvement in the event), he denounced Washington publicly and privately and tightened his relations with Moscow. In anticipation of nationalizing U.S. property and liquidating his domestic opponents, he sought further Soviet military, economic, and intelligence assistance to contend with the U.S. intervention that he asserted would surely follow. The Kremlin obliged with "a blank check to buy whatever he needed," including direct cash payments to Fidel.[19] Though Washington did not know all this, Castro's March 1960 attacks did catalyze the Eisenhower administration's decision to begin preparing covert operations to overthrow the Cuban leader.

In June 1960 Castro nationalized U.S. oil refineries (which had refused to refine Soviet crude oil) and again told the Soviets that an invasion was imminent. At about the same time Khrushchev received an intelligence report from a Soviet spy at NATO that the "chiefs at the Pentagon" were hoping to launch a preventive strike against the Soviet Union (the report was untrue). Apparently this report was taken seriously, for in early July Khrushchev gave a speech stressing Soviet capabilities for nuclear attack on the United States. In his best Suez-crisis vein, Khrushchev threatened that Soviet rockets might fly if Washington chose to invade Cuba. The speech delighted the Cuban leader, who told the Soviets they had deterred an American attack.[20] Castro then publicized his closer friendship with Moscow.

There was another invasion scare in October 1960, Fursenko and Naftali discovered, this time based on rumors that Cuban exiles were being trained by the CIA in Guatemala. (Such training was in fact taking place, but the force was still months from being ready.) The Soviet and Cuban governments, however, genuinely believing an attack to be imminent, mobilized troops and sounded loud public alarms. Moscow again threatened use of its nuclear missiles. When the invasion did not come, the Cubans again believed the Soviet threats had deterred it. In early November, in a private address heard by Cuban Communists and the Soviet KGB resident, Castro extolled Marxism, professed always to have been a Marxist, and said again and again: "Moscow is our brain and our great leader, and we must pay attention to its voice."[21]

Both the Cubans and the Soviets were caught by surprise when the Cuban exiles actually invaded, in April 1961. Khrushchev again thundered support for Castro and warnings to Washington, adding this time the threat that the flames ignited in Cuba could touch off a chain reaction leading to conflict across the globe.[22] Again the Soviets took some credit for deterring Kennedy from providing the military support that might have made the invasion succeed. And the Americans still failed to grasp that the Soviets and Cubans credited Soviet missiles for an apparent series of deterrent successes.

Increasingly, Khrushchev and the Soviet government linked their prestige with Castro's. They held out Cuba as the prime example of success in their newly announced global strategy of undermining capitalism through wars of national liberation in the less developed world. It offered the chief proof that the Soviet Union, not China, remained the vanguard of world revolution. Loss of Cuba, Khrushchev acknowledged, "would have been a terrible blow to Marxism-Leninism" and "would gravely diminish our stature throughout the world, but especially in Latin America."[23]

In the fall of 1961 Castro asked for much larger arms shipments and especially for large numbers of the most modern antiaircraft missile, the SA-2. Khrushchev did not immediately act on this costly request. In the interval, Castro purged his government of perceived rivals, criticized the Soviets for not acting with sufficient revolutionary boldness, and began talking with China about possible economic assistance. Particularly alarming from the standpoint

Castro's ousting of Anibal Escalante, the leader of the Cuban

pro-Moscow cadres. Oc-

sion. They

by the U.S. military. Khrushchev's son-in-law,

have heard President Kennedy say that he viewed Cuba much as Khrushchev viewed Hungary. Though KGB sources in Washington downplayed chances of an invasion, Khrushchev and others in the Soviet government paid more attention to whispers of danger. Khrushchev later explained why. "I'm not saying we had any documentary proof that the Americans were preparing a second invasion," he wrote in his memoirs, "we didn't need documentary proof. We knew the class affiliation, the class blindness of the United States, and that was enough to make us expect the worst."[25] Hence, on April 12 the Presidium approved the delivery of about 180 SA-2 missiles to Cuba and a battery of Soviet coastal-defense cruise missiles, along with trainers and a regiment of regular Soviet troops. A military mission was to survey additional needs.[26] The United States knew nothing of this.

No new information about threats to Cuba seems to have arrived in Moscow between April 12, when the Presidium approved the SA-2s, and May 24, when the Presidium authorized sending to Cuba an entire Group of Soviet Forces, including the ballistic missiles. On May 18 Castro did ask the military mission for more coastal-defense missiles, and possibly for more Soviet troops (his own later testimony is vague on this point). But neither Castro nor any other Cuban nor any Soviet representative in Cuba mentioned nuclear weapons.[27] Knowing that the presence of nuclear weapons in his country could both provoke and legitimize an American attack, Castro had stated repeatedly that Cuba had "no intention to offer any part of its territory to any state for the establishment of military bases."[28]

Khrushchev, however, had begun to ponder this possibility not long after the decision on the SA-2s. Anastas Mikoyan, who had served with Khrushchev under Stalin, had the dacha just next to Khrushchev's in the Lenin Hills. He was probably the member of the Politburo whom Khrushchev came nearest to trusting, and in late April, in one of their one-on-one backyard chats, Khrushchev mentioned to Mikoyan that he was thinking of basing ballistic missiles in Cuba. Mikoyan's son, from whom we have the report of this conversation, says that his father reacted negatively. He had been to Cuba and had helped cement relations with Castro, and he predicted that Castro would reject the idea out of fear of the U.S. reaction.[29] If Mikoyan did indeed try to discourage Khrushchev, he did not succeed. Khrushchev broached his idea to Defense Minister Rodion Malinovsky, who instantly became an enthusiastic supporter. Knowing not only that the Soviet Union was far behind the United States in ICBMs but that the existing ICBMs (SS-6s) were monstrous weapons of doubtful reliability and that successor models (SS-7s and SS-8s) were stalled in the two missile design bureaus, Malinovsky recognized in Khrushchev's proposal a way of shortening the time required to even the strategic balance. And Khrushchev was apparently enthusiastic. "Why not throw a hedgehog at Uncle Sam's pants?" he asked Malinovsky.[30]

Certainly the Americans did not fully grasp how deeply, in the spring of 1962, Khrushchev and his colleagues felt that, in Malinovsky's words, "our inferior position was impossible to us."[31] The United States touched the Soviets on the raw by completing the long-delayed deployment of 15 Jupiter IRBMs at 5 launch sites in Turkey. The first was set up in November 1961, the last in March 1962. The Soviets had known all about the planned deployment for years. Moscow had complained loudly about NATO's public decision, especially during 1958 and 1959, and probably knew that the missiles had finally been put in place. Although there is no evidence that Soviet planners attached any particular strategic significance to these obsolete systems or even to the nuclear-armed U.S. aircraft based in Turkey, which should have been more worrisome militarily, the deployment may have made it easier for Khrushchev and others to rationalize the decision concerning the missiles in Cuba.[32]

In March and April 1962 the aspect of the nuclear standoff that most fully engaged both the Soviets and the Americans was their intense negotiation, centered in Geneva, about the possibility of banning any further test explosions of nuclear weapons. The Soviets had resumed above-ground testing with a dramatic series of detonations in September 1961. Kennedy had been under constant pressure to reciprocate in kind but had held back. The key issue was the verification of a ban. Rusk and Gromyko wrangled over the issue in Geneva and got nowhere. On April 25 the United States began tests in the Pacific. These were going on at about the time Khrushchev began privately exploring with Mikoyan and Malinovsky the idea of deploying missiles to Cuba.[33]

The Soviets equated nuclear testing with improvements in a nation's nuclear arsenal. From their perspective, the U.S. resumption of testing was a statement ⸻ ⸻ing advantage rather than let the Soviet Union catch ⸻ ⸻ough May 1962, when

Khrushchev. ⸻ ⸻ what it feels like to have her own land and her ⸻ the United States was already threatened by Soviet bombers and ICBMs, ⸻ or primitive though they might be, Khrushchev was surely thinking of the more visceral sense of threat created by missiles just across one's own borders. Yuri Andropov, then a senior adviser to Khrushchev, privately told Khrushchev that the Soviet deployment of missiles to Cuba was a way to "sight them at the soft underbelly of the Americans."[36] Kennedy certainly felt it just that way. "A knife stuck right in our guts" was the metaphor he used to the Joint Chiefs of Staff on the morning of October 19.

What happened after Khrushchev's initial talks with Mikoyan and Malinovsky remains murky. Apparently Khrushchev put together a small group of top officials to consider the idea. Malinovsky's newly appointed deputy, also newly appointed as head of the Soviet Strategic Rocket Forces, Marshal Sergei S. Biryuzov, not only supported Malinovsky's view regarding the strategic advantages of missiles in Cuba but ventured the opinion that the missiles could be deployed without being discovered by the Americans. Mikoyan's son says that his father, who knew Cuban geography at first hand, regarded Biryuzov as "a fool" and was amazed that the marshal "thought there were places in the mountains where the Americans would not discover the missiles."[37]

At the end of April the most trusted Soviet envoy in Havana, Alexander Alexeev (then the KGB resident), was recalled to Moscow, without knowing why. On May 7 Khrushchev told him that he would become the new ambassador to Cuba. On May 20, after returning from a weeklong trip to Bulgaria, Khrushchev summoned Alexeev and asked him how Castro would respond to a Soviet deployment of nuclear missiles to Cuba. A bit dumbfounded and intimidated, Alexeev, Moscow's premier expert on Fidel Castro, said he "could never suppose that Fidel Castro would agree to such a thing." Cuba was relying on its own defenses, built with Soviet aid. If the Soviet government "installed missiles, I thought this would provoke a rejection of the Cuban Revolution from the rest of the hemisphere."[38]

Malinovsky immediately took issue with Alekseev, refusing to believe that "a socialist country could refuse our aid." Khrushchev said nothing, and then informed Alekseev that he and Marshal Biryuzov would be joining a delegation to Havana to explain matters to Castro. On May 21 Khrushchev formally presented his plan to the Defense Council, consisting of top civilian and military leaders (no uniformed military men were members of the Presidium), and received its unanimous approval. The initiative was then formally drafted by General Staff officers and presented by Malinovsky at a combined meeting of the Presidium and the Defense Council on May 24. Khrushchev offered his comments. After a pro forma discussion everyone agreed to the proposal. Five days later the delegation was in Havana.

Castro reluctantly agreed to the deployment. Though he was told over and over that the deployment was only for his own good, he and his colleagues always thought, and often said, that they were helping the Soviets change the global balance of military power in favor of socialism. Castro expected that the deployment would produce an intense crisis, but "we really trusted that they [the Soviets] were acting with knowledge of the entire situation."[39]

Several other options were available to the Soviets. They could have signed a defense treaty with Cuba without deploying forces;[40] deployed purely conventional forces, as already planned, forcing U.S. invaders to risk direct conflict with Soviet forces; deployed conventional forces armed with purely tactical nuclear weapons that could reach offshore targets but not the continental United States; or deployed nuclear-armed bombers, presenting a slower-moving and less nerve-racking challenge to the Americans. But apparently, none of these options had been analyzed except the flow of conventional arms authorized by the Presidium decision of April 12 and discussed by the subsequent military mission to Cuba. Certainly Khrushchev did not analyze them in any visible way.[41] For the Soviet General Staff, Khrushchev's plan "was like a roll of thunder in a clear sky."[42]

In addition to the deployments of arms and forces envisioned by the earlier decisions to aid Cuba (including the 140 air-defense missile launchers), Moscow followed up Castro's agreement with plans, approved in June, to deploy 40 land-based ballistic-missile launchers and 60 missiles in 5 missile regiments.

These would be part of a full-size Group of Soviet Forces, more than 45,000 strong, with 4 motorized rifle regiments (and more than 250 armored fighting vehicles), a wing of the latest Soviet fighter aircraft (the MiG-21), about 80 nuclear-capable cruise missiles for coastal defense, and a regiment of more

...that the Soviets intended to develop

The operation also

nuclear forces.

In addition to the nuclear warheads for the ba... nuclear weapons, each with an explosive power comparable to that of the atomic bombs used against Japan in 1945, would be provided for the coastal-defense cruise missiles. The Americans did not know that these cruise missiles were deployed with nuclear warheads. Nor did the Soviets plan to reveal this fact to them.

Khrushchev also checked his judgment, mainly with Biryuzov, on whether the deployment could be concealed, given that U.S. surveillance aircraft frequently overflew Cuba. After traveling to Cuba, Biryuzov and his delegation reported back that the terrain and camouflage efforts would indeed shield the missile sites from U.S. surveillance.[44]

In July 1962 Raul Castro visited Moscow carrying one question for Khrushchev from Fidel: What would happen if the operation was discovered while in progress? Khrushchev answered that there was nothing to worry about; if there was trouble he would send out the Baltic fleet as a show of support. Castro later acknowledged that the Cubans "did not think that it was the Baltic fleet that would solve the problem. What we were thinking about was Soviet will and determination, about Soviet strength. And we got the statement of the top leader of the Soviet Union that there was nothing to worry about, that he would not allow it. So what was really protecting us was the global strategic might of the USSR, not the rockets here."[45] Castro was presuming that Khrushchev had thought through how he would handle a nuclear confrontation if the missile deployment was discovered before it was complete. As Castro himself later realized, there is no evidence that Khrushchev ever seriously considered this question.

Khrushchev did have an image of what would happen if he succeeded in presenting the United States with a *fait accompli.* The Kennedy administration, he believed, would "swallow this bitter pill . . . I knew that the United States could knock out some of our installations, but not all of them. If a quarter or even a tenth of our missiles survived—even if only one or two big ones were left—we could still hit New York, and there wouldn't be much of New York left." [46] Viewing Kennedy as a young, inexperienced intellectual presiding over a dangerously bellicose military establishment, Khrushchev apparently thought that Kennedy would let him get away with trickery, and that he would end up with both the Soviet Union and Cuba better protected against the "chiefs in the Pentagon." [47]

Khrushchev did not ask whether his ambassador in Washington or any other experts shared his estimate of the United States. Gromyko claimed later to have warned Khrushchev privately that "putting our missiles in Cuba would cause a political explosion in the United States," but that Khrushchev was unmoved by this advice. Commenting that Khrushchev "grossly misunderstood the psychology of his opponents," Ambassador Anatoly Dobrynin complained later: "Had he asked the embassy beforehand, we could have predicted the violent American reaction to his adventure once it became known. It is worth noting that Castro understood this . . . But Khrushchev wanted to spring a surprise on Washington; it was he who got the surprise in the end when his secret plan was uncovered." [48]

On May 12, in the midst of the key decisions about sending missiles to Cuba, Khrushchev spent about 14 hours with Kennedy's press aide, Pierre Salinger, then visiting Moscow. He barely mentioned Cuba. The central issue, Khrushchev said, was Berlin. Dobrynin, who took up his post at about this time, remembered that "Germany and Berlin overshadowed everything." [49] Describing what he expected to be his position when negotiations on Berlin resumed, Khrushchev had written to Kennedy in 1961: "You have to understand, I have no ground to retreat further, there is a precipice behind." [50]

The expression "precipice behind" vividly conveys the value Khrushchev now attached to success on Berlin. [51] In another letter to Kennedy, Khrushchev protested that Washington's willingness to threaten a nuclear war to protect Berlin "can rest, excuse my harsh judgments, only on the megalomania, on an intention to act from the position of strength." [52] In March 1962 he had promised Kennedy that "one way or another" he would force the Western troops out. [53] In late April the negotiations in Geneva between Gromyko and Rusk had reached a stalemate over Berlin. Angering his West German allies,

Kennedy had been willing to offer a *modus vivendi* that might allow the status quo to continue. But this had not been good enough for the Soviet government, which denounced the failure of the talks at the end of April.[54]

Thus, in late April and early May 1962, when Khrushchev was in the final ... to send missiles to Cuba, Berlin clearly had a large place ... in 1958 and again in 1961, demand- ... having let those

Dobrynin, just ... the principal issue in U.S.-Soviet rela... arrogant" about its nuclear deterrent, and concluded, ... arms were cut shorter." He liked Kennedy and considered him a man of character, yet he also clearly believed "that putting pressure on Kennedy might bring us some success."[57]

In Moscow, Ambassador Thompson, ignorant of Khrushchev's plans to send missiles to Cuba, was puzzled. No American knew Khrushchev better or had followed his positions more closely. Thompson could not understand why Khrushchev was increasing pressure on Berlin. "He must surely know our position is firm," and "it does not seem reasonable that he would wish further to commit his personal prestige which [is] already deeply engaged." And the pressure just kept increasing.[58] The Soviets began telling Americans that, though they would wait until after the U.S. congressional elections, the Berlin issue would be forced to a conclusion in November.[59]

By the beginning of September 1962 Khrushchev had arranged to unveil the existence of the missiles in Cuba and publicly sign a treaty with Castro in late November, after the congressional elections. He also planned, probably in a speech to the United Nations on the same trip, to renew his ultimatum for final resolution of the Berlin crisis, demanding the withdrawal of Western troops from their sectors. Khrushchev knew the United States would threaten war if he carried out his ultimatum. But by that time Khrushchev would have the missiles, poised in Cuba, to help him call America's bluff and finally carry his 4-year-old Berlin policy to a successful conclusion.

Khrushchev practically spelled out these plans to a senior U.S. visitor, Stewart Udall, on September 6. On September 28 Khrushchev wrote directly to Kennedy and told him that a settlement of the Berlin issue would come after the U.S. elections, probably "in the second half of November."[60] When Khrushchev's foreign minister, Gromyko, met with Kennedy on October 18, the message was the same.

When the missiles were discovered, Llewellyn Thompson (now recalled from Moscow to serve as the State Department's special adviser on the Soviet Union) immediately understood why Khrushchev in July had seemed to be staking even more of his prestige on a policy that would meet unaltered U.S. resistance. Now Thompson solved his puzzle. Circumstances had changed; it remained to be seen whether U.S. policy would change too.[61]

Khrushchev's plans began to go awry at the end of August, when a U-2 overflight discovered the installation of some of the SA-2 air-defense missiles. President Kennedy then issued his September 4 warning to Khrushchev against placing "offensive weapons" in Cuba (an ambiguous term, but the Soviets knew what the Americans meant). The Americans, at least Bundy, speculated in the White House meetings that Khrushchev had not reacted to the warning because the decision to deploy the missiles had already been made. Bundy was half right.

The decision had been made, but the nuclear weapons themselves had still not been shipped. Khrushchev feared that the Americans might attack Cuba before the nuclear deterrent could be put in place. So, rather than abandon the deployment, he decided to add to it by rushing tactical nuclear weapons to Cuba that could immediately be used against invading ground forces. These rockets were called Lunas by the Soviets and FROGs in the West (for Free Rocket Over Ground). Khrushchev, vacationing at the Black Sea resort at Pitsunda, bullied the U.S. visitor, Stewart Udall, threatening that he could "swat your [America's] ass" if the United States chose to fight for Berlin. On the same day he received a visit from Mikoyan, bearing a report on how to get more nuclear weapons to Cuba. On September 7 Khrushchev approved the dispatch of 6 Luna rocket launchers with 12 nuclear-armed rockets, and 6 nuclear bombs for the IL-28s already being sent to Cuba. The Defense Ministry dissuaded Khrushchev from sending these weapons by airplane to Cuba. Instead they would be added to the shipment of MRBM warheads that would leave the Soviet Union on September 15.[62] The ship left on schedule and arrived in Cuba on October 4. Khrushchev's other reaction to Kennedy's warning was the September 11 TASS statement that promised to defend Cuba while saying there was no need to send any missiles there.

Kennedy's renewed, personal warning on September 13, prompted by the discovery of the coastal-defense cruise missiles, did not deter Khrushchev from proceeding with the deployment, though he did decide to postpone setting up the base for Soviet missile submarines, fearing that the related ship movements and construction would be too visible.[63] Near the end of September 1962, as Khrushchev was getting progress reports on the missile deployment, he turned ...ide. saying: "Soon hell will break loose." The aide replied: "I hope the ...ita Sergeyevich." Khrushchev thought for a moment, ...nvthing."[64]

...vko reported

discovery of the ...

discovery and the blockade. The reas...

at the time and remain puzzling to this day.

To provide defense against U-2 surveillance, Khrushchev had suggested ... July that the SA-2 air-defense missiles go in first so they could shoot down U-2s and thwart detection of the missile installation. The vast plan for the shipments was reorganized accordingly,[66] and the SA-2 missiles were in place and operational by late September. American fears of a U-2 shootdown had, after some discussion, deterred direct overflights of Cuba for more than a month, but they resumed in mid-October.

Soviet troops in Cuba had tracked the U-2 overflights of October 14, 15, and 17, but, strangely, they had orders not to fire at U.S. planes unless attacked.[67] The missiles to shoot down the U-2s were in place, but were not allowed to fire at them. We have no evidence on why this was so. Perhaps in the aftermath of Kennedy's September warnings, the central authorities in Moscow did not want any clash and, for this or other reasons, had left in place standing orders not to fire, without covering the U-2 contingency. The Soviet forces in Cuba realized at the time of the overflights that the missile sites and IL-28s could well have been discovered. Fingers were pointed about adequate camouflage, though the construction of such complex sites for such large missiles was inherently hard to conceal. Yet, in a further mystery, there is no evidence that the commanders in Cuba ever dared to tell Moscow that the missile sites had been overflown and that the Americans probably knew about the missiles.

The Kremlin plunged into its own crisis deliberations on October 22, with news of the impending Kennedy speech. Unlike Kennedy, Khrushchev continued his usual foreign-policy process, consulting a small group of Presidium members aided by the defense and foreign ministers and the leading international expert from the Communist Party's Central Committee. When a formal decision was needed, Khrushchev convened the full Presidium. At this point the 36 MRBMs (for 24 launchers) were in Cuba, with their nuclear warheads. So were nearly 100 other nuclear warheads for the coastal-defense missiles, short-range rockets, and IL-28 bombers. Nuclear warheads to be carried on the IRBMs (for the 18 launch sites still under construction) were also in Cuba. The IRBMs themselves were still at sea.[68]

Khrushchev worried that the Americans would attack Cuba. He considered turning the nuclear weapons over to the Cubans and letting them respond. But he assured his colleagues he would not let Castro use the MRBMs against the United States. Perhaps the Cubans could deter an invasion simply by threatening use of the short-range tactical nuclear weapons against an invading force.[69] In such a case, of course, a U.S. air strike, by itself, would in effect be uncontested.

The Presidium first decided that Malinovsky should cable General Issa Pliyev, the commander of Soviet troops in Cuba, ordering him to bring his troops to combat readiness and to use all Cuban and Soviet forces, except the nuclear arms, to meet an attack. Then, changing its mind, it considered a message authorizing use of the tactical nuclear weapons but not the ballistic missiles. Malinovsky was uneasy about this instruction, worrying that the Americans might intercept it and use it as a pretext for striking with their own nuclear weapons. So the Kremlin sent the first draft, withholding final authorization for use of the nuclear weapons.[70]

News of Kennedy's speech, announcing the quarantine, was greeted with relief when it arrived in the early morning of October 23. Reports also arrived from Soviet envoys. Dobrynin characterized the U.S. move as a general effort to reverse a decline in its world power, partly as a result of fears about Berlin. He warned that the Americans were preparing for a real test of strength, and then recommended that Moscow threaten a move against Berlin, starting with a ground blockade and "leaving out for the time being air routes so as not to give grounds for a quick confrontation." Yet Dobrynin added that Moscow should not be in a hurry actually to implement a blockade, "since an extreme aggravation of the situation, it goes without saying, would not be in our interests." Alexeev meanwhile reported from Havana that the Cubans had mobilized, would not fire on U.S. planes unless they fired first, would await the Soviet response, "and are placing their hopes on the wisdom of our decisions."[71]

Relieved that the Americans had not attacked Cuba, and considering the U.S. imposition of a blockade a weaker response that left room for political maneuver, the Kremlin issued its flat, tough response on October 23. Khrushchev and his Presidium did decide to halt most of the 30 ships en route to Cuba, but they directed that the 4 carrying IRBMs and a fifth, loaded with nuclear warheads for these missiles, continue on course. They ordered that the 4 nuclear-armed submarines headed for Cuba also keep going. When Kuznet- _____ _____ -tion of countering the blockade with pressure _____ _____ ould "do without

unyielding demand _____ brought Dobrynin's cable, reporting Robert Kennedy, to stop your ships." Replying defiantly to Kennedy, Khrushchev declared that Soviet captains would run the blockade. At the same time, however, the Presidium decision of the previous day was apparently reversed. As McCone reported on the morning of October 24, a fresh burst of signals had gone out to Soviet ships at sea in midmorning (Moscow time). The ships carrying the IRBMs now halted. A few ships with more innocent cargos, including the *Bucharest* and *Grozny*, became the ones sailing ahead to test the quarantine. (The ship carrying the nuclear warheads had already made it to a Cuban port.) It is possible but unlikely that this occurred without Khrushchev's knowledge, though he did not advise the Presidium of any change in orders and, indeed, spoke at its meeting on October 25 as if the ships carrying IRBMs were continuing on their way.[73] Actual Soviet behavior justified Rusk's conclusion that, in the face of American firmness, Khrushchev "blinked."

As in past crises, Khrushchev made an attempt to open prolonged negotiations. Zorin, his ambassador to the United Nations, had begun such an effort as soon as the crisis broke, and Moscow had done nothing to discourage him. On October 24, Khrushchev supplemented his harsh message to Kennedy with a candid open letter to the philosopher Bertrand Russell, who had been leading anti-American demonstrations in London. In this open letter, Khrushchev suggested a possible summit meeting.[74] Calling in a visiting American businessman, William Knox, Khrushchev made the same proposal. Talking with Knox for more than three hours, Khrushchev had said that if the United States stopped and searched a Soviet merchant ship, he would instruct his submarines to sink the U.S. vessels.

Khrushchev also criticized Kennedy's handling of the crisis, observing that

Eisenhower would have handled it in a more mature way and remarking that Kennedy was younger than his eldest son. Khrushchev also said: "You cannot now take over Cuba." He admitted that ballistic missiles with nuclear warheads had been supplied to Cuba, but said the Cubans were volatile people and all the weapons were under the control of Soviet officers and would be used only if Cuba was attacked. If the United States really wanted to know what kind of weapons could defend Cuba, the Americans only had to attack, and they would find out very quickly. He said, according to Knox's report, that he was not interested in the destruction of the world, but if we all wanted to meet in hell, it was up to them.

According to Knox, Khrushchev also related an anecdote: A man came upon hard times and found it necessary to live with a goat. Even though the man became used to the smell, he did not like it. Still, it soon became a way of life. Russians, Khrushchev said, had been living with a goat in the form of certain NATO countries such as Turkey, Greece, and Spain. Americans had a goat in the form of Cuba. "You are not happy about it and you won't like it, but you'll learn to live with it."[75]

On the morning of October 25 the Soviet leadership had Kennedy's tough, terse reply to Khrushchev's message. Khrushchev reconvened the Presidium. He told them he did not want to trade "caustic remarks" any longer with Kennedy. Instead he wanted to turn around 4 ships that were still carrying IRBMs to Cuba and try to resolve the crisis. Conciliation had supplanted the previous day's defiance. Khrushchev announced to the Presidium his readiness to "dismantle the missiles to make Cuba into a zone of peace." He suggested sending a message including the words "Give us a pledge not to invade Cuba, and we will remove the missiles." He was also prepared to allow UN inspection of the missile sites. First, though, he wanted to be able to "look around" and be sure Kennedy really would not yield.[76]

There is little evidence to explain why Khrushchev had changed his mind and decided to give in. Perhaps the tone of Kennedy's letter had underscored the certainty of a confrontation that Moscow could not hope to win without threatening nuclear retaliation, and Khrushchev was unwilling to make this threat. In any event, the Presidium approved his plan with the usual unanimous vote.[77]

Later on October 25 the Soviets presumably received news that the *Bucharest* had been allowed to proceed toward Cuba. They may also have received news that the Americans had begun low-level reconnaissance flights over Cuba. On that day U Thant also issued his new appeal that Khrushchev keep his ships away from the quarantine line and that the United States avoid a direct confrontation. Khrushchev sent no messages to the U.S. government.

Khrushchev was stirred to action on October 26. That morning, according to Fursenko and Naftali, he received a series of intelligence reports of increased ̶ ̶diness and preparations. Among these a KGB report from ̶ ̶ ̶ ̶rding to a well-connected American ̶ ̶ ̶l" and "could

of Sovi.. ̶

Khrushchev presumably a̶l̶s̶o̶ ̶ ̶ ̶ Alexeev in Havana. Alexeev said that Castro had app̶i̶u̶v̶.̶ ̶ to avoid a confrontation on the quarantine line. However, Castro now wan̶i̶c̶u̶ to shoot down "one or two piratic American planes over Cuban territory" (that is, U.S. reconnaissance planes), and the Cuban leader did not take rumors of a possible U.S. invasion very seriously.[79]

Khrushchev promptly made several moves. He sent instructions to accept U Thant's proposal for avoiding a confrontation at the quarantine line, thereby promising to keep Soviet ships away from this line. He also dictated the long letter to Kennedy suggesting a peaceful resolution of the crisis: if the United States would promise not to invade Cuba, "the necessity for the presence of our military specialists in Cuba would disappear." More a hint than a concrete proposal, this message was well within the guidelines approved by the Presidium the previous day, so Khrushchev did not seek that body's formal approval, but merely sent copies of the letter to the members.[80] Khrushchev may also have suggested that a Soviet official in New York (probably KGB) urge U Thant to suggest a deal trading a noninvasion pledge for withdrawal of the missiles, though this cannot be confirmed. When the KGB resident in Washington, Feklisov, broached this idea to journalist John Scali that day, he was acting on his own initiative, perhaps prompted by his own worries about the ominous indicators that he had been reporting to Moscow.

There is no evidence that Khrushchev reacted to Alexeev's message reporting Castro's hopes to shoot down some U.S. planes. Nor is there any evidence of Soviet interest in the American boarding of their chartered cargo ship, the *Marucla*. During the day on October 26 Khrushchev might have heard that the Swedish cargo ship under Soviet charter had successfully defied the blockade. That it passed through the line at all seemed to the Americans to contradict Khrushchev's promise to U Thant, but we have no evidence about any Soviet consideration or even awareness of this matter. Nor do we have any evidence about Soviet consideration of the movement of the *Grozny* toward the quarantine line, though this was a continuing concern in Washington.

With his October 26 letter to Kennedy, Khrushchev had moved to defuse the threat of an imminent invasion, but he had still not conceded anything concrete. Moreover, by keeping the correspondence private, he had hidden his tentative move from Castro. Soviet military activity in Cuba continued without respite. By the next morning, October 27, Khrushchev came to a judgment, for reasons that are still obscure, that the Americans could be pushed harder. Perhaps he misjudged the signals being sent by the way they were enforcing the quarantine.[81] In direct contrast to Castro, whose relaxed attitude about a U.S. invasion had switched to alarm on October 26, Khrushchev had switched from alarm on October 26 to a more relaxed attitude on October 27.

The Soviet commander in Cuba, General Issa Pliyev, reported to the Defense Ministry that the Cubans had concluded that a U.S. air strike would begin that night or at dawn on October 27 and that Castro had ordered air-defense units to fire at American aircraft if there was an attack. Pliyev said that he had dispersed nuclear warheads closer to their launchers. The Soviet leaders endorsed Pliyev's plans.[82]

Nevertheless, when Khrushchev convened the Presidium he told them that the United States would not dare to attack Cuba. Five days had passed since Kennedy's speech, and nothing had happened. "To my mind they are not ready to do it now." Since, however, there was no guarantee against a U.S. attack, Khrushchev would make another, more concrete offer that both acknowledged the presence of missiles in Cuba and added the U.S. missiles in Turkey to the bargain. With that, he said, "we would win."[83]

Just as there is little evidence to explain why Khrushchev reversed his assessment of U.S. intentions, there is little evidence to explain why he now chose to add the Turkish missiles as a bargaining point. The missiles in Turkey had not been an important topic in any of the previous Presidium discussions during the crisis.

There are some signs that Khrushchev took his cue from a report about Lippmann's column of October 25 and from some other scattered hints of U.S. willingness to contemplate such an offer. Had he included the idea in his private letter of October 26, the U.S. reaction might have been different; no one, including Dillon and McCone, had much use for the Jupiter missiles. Yet introducing the idea at this point raised some obvious questions. Wouldn't the

Americans perceive this as a change in the Soviet negotiating position, plainly inconsistent with the October 26 letter (and even more inconsistent with the positions being floated, without Khrushchev's knowledge, by KGB agents in Washington and perhaps New York too)? The Americans might think the Soviet ꞏ ꞏ ꞏ ꞏ ꞏ had reneged on his previous offer.

ꞏ ꞏ ꞏ ꞏ ꞏ would have suggested that there was at least ꞏ ꞏ ꞏ ꞏ ꞏ ꞏ ꞏ ting the new

Khrushchev then furth ꞏ ꞏ ꞏ initiative by making his offer public. This move made ꞏ ꞏ ꞏ tremely unlikely, especially given the implications for NATO of such a public trade. A public deal might save face for Khrushchev, but no face would be saved if the Americans rejected it—which almost any analyst would have predicted. The Turks publicly rejected the trade just as the Americans started to discuss it. Castro certainly expected the Americans to reject such a deal, and Alexeev reported to Moscow that Castro was comforted by that very prospect.[85]

There is no evidence that Khrushchev or any member of the Presidium analyzed this point. Apparently the new proposal was broadcast over the radio in the interest of reducing transmission time, and "nobody foresaw that by making public the Turkish angle of the deal we created additional difficulties to the White House."[86] Of course, Khrushchev's actions may not have been thoughtless. He could have offered a deal in order to stalemate the negotiations, not further them. The position was well designed for public consumption, if not for U.S. acceptance. Khrushchev may have hoped that the Americans would effectively back down by virtue of entering into prolonged and fruitless negotiations. But if this was Khrushchev's gambit, it was another example of recklessness, for the U.S. reaction could well have been to abandon negotiations and turn to the use of military force. In fact, this was how most of President Kennedy's advisers did react.

Having dictated the message to President Kennedy, Khrushchev and his colleagues had second thoughts about Pliyev's dispersal of nuclear weapons. An order was quickly sent to Pliyev not to employ any nuclear weapons without express authorization from Moscow. Khrushchev also sent a message to Havana urging Alexeev to caution Castro against any rash actions.[87]

Events during October 27 must have battered Khrushchev's complacency. A message from Castro, sent from Cuba on October 26, announced that a massive U.S. air strike, and possibly also an invasion, was "almost inevitable" in the next 24 to 72 hours. In the event of invasion, Castro urged Khrushchev to consider "elimination of such a danger," plainly referring to use of Soviet nuclear weapons against the United States. "However difficult and horrifying this decision may be," Castro wrote, "there is, I believe, no other recourse."[88]

The same day brought news about the incursion of the American U-2 into Siberian airspace. Aside from the reproach in his October 28 letter to Kennedy, we have no evidence about how Khrushchev viewed that episode.

Then the Cubans shot at unarmed U.S. low-level reconnaissance aircraft. On October 26 Castro had given the order to fire on any aircraft entering Cuban airspace.[89] Alexeev had reported this intention on October 25, but Moscow seems not to have noticed. Castro discussed his order with Soviet commanders on October 26; this fact may have been reported to Moscow too. On October 27 Khrushchev sent instructions to Alexeev to suggest that Castro rescind the order; but by then, of course, it was too late, even if Castro had wished to heed the advice.

When the U-2 came over it too was apparently, and falsely, perceived as posing a threat. Authority to fire had been delegated in the event of an American attack, and the local Soviet commanders (below Pliyev himself, who was temporarily unavailable) chose to interpret their instructions liberally in order to aid their excited Cuban comrades.[90] Although a Soviet missile actually downed the plane, Khrushchev seems not to have fully grasped this fact until some time later.[91]

Late in the afternoon of October 27 Khrushchev would have heard that the Americans had immediately rejected his public proposal with a press statement of their own. Alexeev reported telling Castro that "in the present circumstances it would not be fitting to aggravate the situation and initiate provocations." Castro understood, but "considering the rise in the army's martial spirit and the Americans' warning, our friends were compelled to take such a step."[92]

Khrushchev was reportedly quite worried about the shootdown of the U-2. He was certainly a bit unnerved by Castro's urging to prepare for using nuclear weapons against the United States. A few days later, in another message to Castro, Khrushchev referred to this "very alarming" message in which "you proposed that we be the first to carry out a nuclear strike against the enemy's territory." "Naturally," Khrushchev added, "you understand where that would lead us. It would not be a simple strike, but the start of a thermonuclear world war."[93]

Kennedy's message to Khrushchev arrived late that evening, laying out the deal that would entail the verified withdrawal of Soviet "offensive weapons" in exchange for the noninvasion pledge. Khrushchev opened the Presidium ses-
... on the morning of October 28 with a very different assessment from the
... his colleagues that they were "face to face with the
... the possible result of destroying
... retreat."[94]

the Presidium. ...
words by the President's brother, as ...,
prompted the conclusion that the time of reckoning had ...
later told Castro that his warning of an imminent U.S. attack had been confirmed by other sources and that he had hurried to prevent it.[95]

Khrushchev's resolve to yield was redoubled by Robert Kennedy's reported warning, and by his assurance that Jupiters would eventually be withdrawn from Turkey. Reportedly only Khrushchev, Gromyko, and Mikoyan had much to say at this Presidium session. "Others preferred to keep silent as if hinting to Khrushchev that since he had made his bed, he could sleep on it."[96]

The tension was compounded by a report that at 5:00 P.M. Moscow time (9:00 A.M. in Washington), President Kennedy would be making another speech to the American people. In fact this was only going to be a rebroadcast of Kennedy's October 22 speech, but Khrushchev and his advisers feared an imminent announcement of U.S. military action. An urgent, conciliatory reply was prepared and hurriedly broadcast over the radio to be sure it reached Washington in time. Another message was rushed to Dobrynin in Washington, directing him to "quickly get in touch with R. Kennedy" and to pass on the following "urgent response: The thoughts which R. Kennedy expressed at the instruction of the President finds understanding in Moscow. Today, an answer will be given by radio . . . and that response will be the most favorable. The main thing which disturbs the President, precisely the issue of the dismantling under international control of the rocket bases in Cuba, meets no objection and will be explained in detail." Pliyev received a cable chiding him for having been in such a "hurry" to shoot down the U-2. He was ordered to ground all Soviet jets in Cuba to avoid any further clashes with U.S. reconnaissance aircraft.[97]

There was no time to consult with Castro. He learned of Khrushchev's decision over the radio, along with the rest of the world.

After the missile crisis was over, in January 1963, Khrushchev began walking away from his failed Berlin policy, by simply declaring victory. He began to argue that he had really won because in 1961 he had forced the West to accept the construction of the Berlin Wall and to live with a divided Berlin.[98] This had not, of course, been his position in 1962.

Khrushchev still could not stop wondering whether the Americans would really have gone to nuclear war over Berlin. Surely they would not have made such a threat unless they were incredibly complacent about their nuclear superiority. His Cuban deployment would have punctured that complacency. It would have vividly demonstrated the vulnerability he wanted the Americans to feel, the vulnerability that should, would restrain them. After the Cuban venture failed, even after he had then also abandoned his 1962 plan of action on Berlin, Khrushchev still wanted to know: Had Washington been bluffing? In August 1963 Khrushchev asked Rusk point-blank: "Why should I believe that you Americans would fight a nuclear war over Berlin?" Rusk remembered, "That was quite a question . . . So I stared back at him and said, 'Mr. Chairman, you will have to take into account the possibility that we Americans are just goddamn fools.' We glared at each other, unblinking, and then he changed the subject and gave me three gold watches to take home to my children."[99]

In November 1963 President Kennedy was murdered by a gunman who had long harbored grievances about Kennedy's hostility toward Castro's Cuba. In October 1964 Khrushchev was ousted from power by his Presidium colleagues. "You insisted that we deploy our missiles in Cuba," one of his Presidium accusers thundered. "This provoked the deepest crisis, carried the world to the brink of nuclear war, and even frightened terribly the organizer of this very danger." Khrushchev was blamed for the humiliating defeat.[100]

FURTHER REFLECTIONS ON THE TAPES

The material in this book offers the most complete set of data available on how a modern government actually made a set of important decisions. President Kennedy certainly had discussions that he did not record. Yet much of the analysis lying behind all the major policy choices can be reconstructed from the recordings and other available material. The most secret move, Rusk's idea of providing a unilateral assurance on the withdrawal of the Jupiters from Turkey, emerged from deliberations that had already covered the range of possibilities. Kennedy did not make any impulsive decisions during the crisis.

He invariably opened up much of his reasoning about the pros, cons, and likely consequences of his choices before he made them. He exposed his thinking to a range of analyses and critiques from formal advisers, informal advisers, and representatives of the British government.

There are some large revelations in the recordings. One is the close connection [...] the stalemated East-West struggle over Berlin. We
[...] to Khrush-

Berlin. It is not [...]
and Midway of the Cold War. Never again, even in the [...]
1983, would the Soviet challenge or the Western response be so direct and so intense.

Certainly Berlin was never far from President Kennedy's thoughts. He refers to it constantly, calculating every move in light of its probable impact there. Only after the peak of the crisis does he voice his frustration with the ways Berlin has constrained his freedom of action at every turn. The creative solution Kennedy sought to this problem never really emerged. During the crisis Walt Rostow had suggested moving tactical nuclear weapons into Berlin to deter a Soviet countermove, but the idea was quashed before it reached the White House. After the crisis Nitze suggested (perhaps remembering a similar idea that George Kennan had developed, and Nitze had supported, in 1948) that the United States propose a unified but demilitarized Germany. This idea, too, was quashed before it reached the White House.[101]

Another revelation is the extent of President Kennedy's own role in the management of the crisis. Naturally this role is enhanced by the fact of recordings made at the White House, with the President selectively choosing what to record for posterity. Kennedy is also reticent during the first day of the crisis, mostly letting others reason through the problems. Yet by the meeting of October 18 he is shaping the discussion and thinking ahead, and the results of this are apparent in his October 19 meeting with the Joint Chiefs of Staff, in which, alone, he takes on the combined weight of their arguments and has apparently gone far toward making up his mind, even before the oft-recounted discussions later that day at the State Department. From October 22 onward Kennedy is dominating the meetings.

Saturday, October 27, may well have been the finest hours of John F.

Kennedy's public life. To us he seems more alive to the possibilities and consequences of each new development than anyone else. He remains calm, lucid, and is constantly a step, or several steps, ahead of his advisers. He is the only one in the room who is determined not to go to war over obsolete missiles in Turkey. Yet he fully understands and is trying to work around the large consequences of appearing to sell out the Turks. We can understand why, after celebrating Khrushchev's announcement that the missiles would be withdrawn from Cuba, Kennedy kept Rusk behind and privately, but witheringly, dressed him down for not having better planned to cope with Khrushchev's predictable move.

The recordings subtly but significantly alter our understanding of practically every major question about U.S. policy during the crisis, sometimes by validating one interpretation over another, sometimes by spotlighting overlooked aspects of the deliberations. We think the material largely speaks for itself, but we can note a few examples.

The decision not to launch an air strike during the first few days was restrained, in substantial part, by the belief that such a strike had to include a wide attack on Cuban airfields as well as SAM sites. The reasoning behind such a wider strike plan was careful. It derived less from reflexive routine than from reasonable fear of MiG strikes against Florida, at a time when air defenses in the American Southeast were flimsy. Concern about Berlin also weighed on Kennedy as he considered the air strike, for he had to worry about how U.S. allies would behave if called upon to deal with a Soviet response against Berlin.

The concentration on military moves and countermoves during the crisis is natural. Yet diplomatic maneuvers are equally central. U Thant plainly played an important role that has been largely forgotten by participants and has never received much attention from historians. It is also obvious from these records that Macmillan and Ormsby-Gore became de facto members of Kennedy's Executive Committee, though we suspect that by October 26 Kennedy had become skeptical of the quality of Macmillan's advice.

Classification restrictions are almost entirely gone, and the general content of material that remains restricted can be readily imagined. So we now have a much clearer picture of the role of military plans and intelligence concerns in the deliberations. The military discussions range from Kennedy's grimly amusing October 22 exchange with Nitze about the standing orders for use of the Jupiter missiles in Turkey, to the timing and detailed preparation of plans for managing the blockade or attacking Cuba or preparing an occupation government, to the horrific talk of how to protect Americans against fallout after U.S. cities have been devastated by a Soviet nuclear strike.

The intelligence issues are everywhere, often interlocked with dilemmas about military plans. The bad news about the missiles in Cuba did not come all at once but broke in waves, and the wave of news about the IRBMs, disseminated on October 18, strengthened the momentum favoring military

⸺ The yield from intelligence gathering and organizations such as the

⸺ Center is impressive. Enlarged, one day's

⸺ noted at one

There are regular discuss⸺

do if one is shot down, then about what to do when one ⸺

there is the question of low-level reconnaissance, then the question of low-level reconnaissance at night, aided by explosive flares. We keep remembering Lyndon Johnson's pithy summary: "Blooey!"

Collecting intelligence only began the problem of analyzing what it meant, and what to do about it. We come to know Kennedy better in these recordings, and his advisers too. Robert Kennedy, whether alone with his brother or in a group, is quick and insightful. Sorensen usually stays in the background. Bundy is unsettled during the first week about what to do, offering many questions but fewer answers, but seems to become stronger and more focused as the crisis develops.

Rusk, too, seems to offer clearer advice later in the crisis. He is often the voice of caution. Though at the outset of the crisis McNamara slows the rush toward military action with his pointed questions and forceful presentations, he becomes increasingly consumed, as the crisis wears on, by the task of managing the spiraling military preparations, and he becomes more expectant of the need to use them. Referring to the missiles, he comments on October 25, "I'd never have thought we'd get them out of Cuba without the application of substantial force."[102]

Taylor and McCone have a consistent stand that President Kennedy understands, and for which he always has some sympathy. Kennedy respects their professional opinion. He apparently has little faith in the judgment of Taylor's colleagues, who, unlike Taylor, appear to make little effort to understand the President's problems. This quality of empathy was one that President Kennedy valued highly and often practiced in his clinical, ironic way.

Once the blockade is securely in place, after October 24, the crisis moves toward the climactic issue of whether or not Khrushchev will agree to stop construction and pull out the "offensive weapons" he has already deployed in Cuba. The Americans are plainly feeling time pressure to resolve the matter, with the military planning for a strike before the end of the month. The pressure seems to be related to the missile buildup.

Why the rush? It is still hard to know. At first, of course, they are concerned about when the MRBMs will become operational. But by October 26 and 27 it is too late; the MRBMs are judged to be ready for action. The IRBMs are still projected to be weeks away from completion, and (unknown to the Americans) the missiles to go on those launch pads have been kept out by the blockade. Nuclear warheads, though not yet found, are always assumed to be already on the island.

The question "Why the rush?" will probably never have a complete answer. Some officials fear that the missiles are becoming more elusive, harder to hit, as frantic Soviet efforts belie some of Lundahl's early optimism about the futility of camouflage. There also seems to be a strong sense that if the momentum relaxes, and negotiations string out, then the world might realize that the MRBMs really are a *fait accompli*. That fact was obscured only by the lack of general knowledge that the missiles were complete, and by the Americans' robust exercise of diplomatic initiative. Yet, as time passed, American insistence that the finished missiles be removed might become increasingly hollow and incredible. Bundy, McNamara, and others warn about letting the situation "freeze" or reach a "plateau," constantly urging that momentum be sustained.

President Kennedy and the advisers who had favored starting with a blockade may have sensed, consciously or semiconsciously, that perhaps they had already waited too long. By October 27 the Soviet MRBMs were deployed and ready. The country was galvanized by the crisis, anxious and expectant, and congressional elections were only 10 days away.

The turning point of the crisis may have been October 25, the day that Khrushchev decided that he would withdraw the missiles on terms that would abandon his most important original goals for the deployment. At that moment Khrushchev had made the fundamental decision that he could not so readily change the strategic balance of missile power; nor would he be able to use this new position to break the stalemate over Berlin. The Americans talked with relief about being able to discuss trading useless Jupiters rather than trading Berlin. What would have happened, had Khrushchev not made this bitter choice, is awful to contemplate.

Even having made the choice, Khrushchev hesitated. He did nothing on

October 25, and little on the day following. When no invasion materialized he hardened his stance, constantly holding open the possibility of keeping the missiles in Cuba until he was convinced—again—that U.S. military action ~lly be imminent.[103]

~ recordings, we feel confident that the White ~ on the Soviets. Kennedy ~ followed

acqu~

ened or spotlighted th~ ~ stance by Khrushchev would have made U.S. ~ very likely.

All these steps would have carried grave dangers of further escalation, as Kennedy knew. The shootdown of the U-2 on October 27 should, according to the agreed plan, have prompted an immediate U.S. air strike; but Kennedy overrode the contingency plan and held back the planes. Had Khrushchev's acceptance of Kennedy's offer not come through, President Kennedy probably would have authorized more reconnaissance flights on October 28, along with renewed readiness to respond to another shootdown with a general air strike.

The Americans were also already worried about an encounter with the *Grozny* at the quarantine line on October 28. A total blockade would have extended the issue from the missiles to the whole survival of the Castro government, and Soviet officials could then have been expected to renew suggestions that Khrushchev counter with a blockade of Berlin. We doubt that the weary, impatient American officials, already pressed by the sense that time was against them, would have waited long for a tighter blockade of Cuba to produce results, if they had bothered with it at all. McNamara's civilian experts at the Pentagon had already told him that such a blockade would be inadequate and would even make matters worse.

On the other hand, President Kennedy would certainly have paused and talked through the original military plan to follow a strike with an invasion of Cuba. Intelligence had discovered the tactical nuclear arms on October 25, and Kennedy was briefed about them the next day. On October 28 the JCS formally asked Admiral Dennison to revise his invasion planning accordingly, though they turned down his request to provide the invasion force with counterpart tactical nuclear missiles of its own. Reviewing military contingency plans on

October 29, Kennedy was already diverted, we think, by the question of how to deal with this tactical nuclear danger.

In any case an invasion would be preceded by 7 days of air strikes, and McNamara had become more confident about the efficacy of the strikes (if continued air reconnaissance could be maintained). So it seems likely that President Kennedy would have ordered the air strikes and withheld final judgment on the invasion until the last possible moment, seeing first what damage the air strikes had done, how the Soviets reacted worldwide, and how the diplomatic picture had changed.

The outcome of Khrushchev's gambit would in all likelihood have been very different—perhaps inconceivably different—if someone else had been President of the United States. But to speculate about such possibilities seems to us idle. We can content ourselves with the observation that Khrushchev might also have adopted quite different policies if he had had a different president to deal with or had gauged Kennedy's character differently. Given the circumstances that existed on October 16, though, it is hard to imagine that any president (in a list of those who could imaginably have been elected) would have adopted a more peaceful course than the one Kennedy chose. It seems fortunate that, given the circumstances that he had helped create, Kennedy was the president charged with managing the crisis.

Given what we now know, Soviet processes seem to offer a model of how not to make sensible decisions. Kennedy was right to treat Khrushchev as if he was in complete charge of his government. Khrushchev *was* fully in charge. Yet if a government or a leader consistently relies on false intelligence reports, makes little effort to assess other governments, does not analyze policy alternatives, and has little open debate among senior officials who are overawed by an insecure and impulsive risk taker, we should not expect very good results unless the other relevant actors are weak, equally incompetent, or extraordinarily unlucky.

We therefore close with some broader remarks on American decision-making. Both of us can call upon some direct experience to attest that White House deliberations during the Cuban missile crisis were unique in some respects but by no means in all. This record captures the feel of such discussions, so obvious to those who have participated in many of them, so difficult to describe to those who have not.

First, critical meetings have an inherently disorderly character. Rarely do they fall neatly into place around an "options paper." These 1962 meetings are more disorderly than some, less so than others. There is more structure to them than might meet the eye at first glance. They ordinarily begin with an intelligence briefing. Kennedy turns to Rusk, then to McNamara, or in reverse order, for reports on developments and issues needing decision in their areas of responsibility. Then, especially as the crisis wears on, he draws the participants toward questions that seem most salient to him in preparing for the next ⟨...⟩ digressing to handle various specific action items.

⟨...⟩ the surfeit of issues and associ⟨...⟩ meeting.

meetings ⟨...⟩
On these occasions Kennedy does ⟨...⟩
himself rarely says 10 words if he thinks he has made his poi⟨...⟩

One way to try to trace the many threads of analysis that interweave in the meetings transcribed here is to imagine for a moment that you are a notetaker at the meeting, jotting down summaries in real time. Consider the problem of summarizing, for someone who was not there, what has happened—not just what was decided, but the contrasting chains of reasoning and clash of personalities. Think too about the information and analysis provided (or not provided) before people came to these meetings and presented in the reports or recommendations that you read. Think finally about the analytical problems and action issues that arise from what has been raised, that should be addressed before the next meeting or action-forcing event.[104]

There are countless details and bits of information affecting the plans for action. The details require someone to take time to master them, or to work them out, or to act upon them, often by drafting a letter or paper, making a call, or talking with someone not present at the meeting. Someone usually assumes the responsibility for that action. People go off, sometimes during a meeting, to take the action. Bohlen, publicly expected to appear in New York and Paris, leaves the deliberations completely. On Thursday night, October 18, Rusk and Thompson miss the White House meeting because they must attend a dinner with Gromyko. On October 27, Robert Kennedy and Sorensen go off to complete a draft of a message to Khrushchev and see that it is typed up properly. That night McNamara goes off to make a press announcement at the Pentagon, then he comes back. And so on.

People with action responsibility have greater control, greater influence, over "their" issue. They may be influenced by an agenda of their own. State Department officials, challenged to think about the Turkish problem, sought a solution that would advance their long-standing project for a NATO multilateral nuclear force, though such a scheme could not possibly be readied within the time frame of the crisis.[105] One result was that little useful analytical help was available to Kennedy when the Turkish issue arose on October 27, a void that prompted his private outburst to Rusk on October 29.

Yet action responsibility also takes people out of meetings, takes them "out of the loop," takes them away from other issues or information, tiring them and tying them down. McNamara is vital to Kennedy's management of the crisis. The Defense Secretary voraciously takes on responsibilities. To us, one result is that by the end of the crisis his analyses and judgments seem narrower, less helpful to President Kennedy, than they were when the crisis began.

Perhaps, above all, we observe in this record—more clearly than in any other documents we have ever seen—the contrary pulls of detail on the one hand and belief (or conviction or ideology) on the other. Almost from minute to minute, new information or recognition of some previously unperceived implication in information already at hand or a new argument will change in subtle or sometimes not subtle ways the form or even the character of the issue being addressed. When Kennedy and his advisers learn that the Soviets are putting up IRBMs as well as MRBMs, their understanding of what is at stake clearly changes, though they might have been hard put to explain how or why. Similarly, though they have talked about the possibility of a U-2 being attacked, they have to take stock anew when they face the reality that Major Anderson's plane actually has been shot down.

These are large examples of how details drive debate. The records here are particularly rich because they show the extent to which this is a constant process, with even small bits of information or slight alterations in atmosphere affecting the delicate processes of issue definition and decision-making. Nothing is harder to relate about experience in government than this sense of being driven by daily detail, because students or interested citizens removed from the event cannot comprehend all these details, do not have time to know them. They tend much more to see an episode like the Cuban missile crisis as a single event, with a problem, one or two key choices, and an outcome. Such a level of understanding may well be accurate, as far as it goes.

Often it does not go far enough. Participants themselves often remember decision-making in a blurred way. They forget how they saw an issue before the details or atmosphere changed. As a result, the world usually learns little or nothing about courses of action that were considered but not pursued. For example, on October 26 and again on October 27, McNamara strongly advocates low-level reconnaissance missions at night, with flares to light up the earth. The reasons for this turn in part on intelligence details, the day's worries about nighttime construction activity or concealments. Other agendas are also engaged. Both the recommendation and the information that prompted it are ~~~tically unknown, half-forgotten by the participants themselves. But if the ~~~~ ~~~~ accepted, the activity might have been misread by ~~~~ ~~~~ imminent attack (which was ~~~~ ~~~~ assess-

of its delivery— ~~~ ~~~ time McNamara is sent out to annou~~~~ complex combination of judgments resulted in a particular ~~~ to Khrushchev, inadequately captured by the conventional assertion: "Kennedy chose to accept Khrushchev's initial offer of October 26." We know that the particular set of signals sent from the White House helped drive Khrushchev to a particular action. He had decided to give in *before* the report came in of Robert Kennedy's talk with Dobrynin. The actual terms of the subsequent settlement were driven, too, by the particular way the American position had been crafted in Kennedy's letter of October 27.

But the constant flow of detail, with continual pressure to act, works on the conscious and unconscious minds of decisionmakers, who see facts and form presumptions within frameworks of understanding shaped both by their personal interests and by their accumulated experience. Thus Kennedy probably never forgets about the impending congressional election, even though he seldom alludes to it and even though only sophomoric analysis would suppose that it dominated his thinking. Nor did Rusk and McNamara ever entirely lose sight of their parochial concerns as heads of cabinet departments. In the morning meeting of October 24, Rusk tries to use the crisis to get a permanent increase in the budget for State Department communications, while McNamara argues that the defense budget is adequate to cover all needs.

Auxiliary interests, political, bureaucratic, or personal, probably had less to do with how the decisionmakers acted than did filters in their minds formed by their own past experiences. Intellect and conscience alike tell Kennedy and Rusk and others that they cannot be—or seem to be—"appeasers." Kennedy, however, is not unsettled, as someone else might have been, when LeMay says to him on the morning of October 19 regarding the quarantine option, "This is almost as bad as the appeasement at Munich." The author of *Why England*

Slept knows that the quarantine is not "Munich." The son of Joe Kennedy also probably feels some empathy when he reads Adlai Stevenson's agonized plea that *everything* be considered negotiable. And Stevenson probably felt steeled to give such advice because he, after all, had been an arch anti-appeaser back when Munich had been news, not shibboleth.

The Kennedy tapes are instructive not only for what they contain but for what they do not contain, despite their constituting a nearly complete record of almost 2 weeks of deliberations. Listening to the tapes or reading the transcripts, one is struck by the decreasing frequency with which Kennedy and his advisers refer to historical landmarks. In the first day or two, such references abound. Participants try to make sense of the crisis by likening it to the Berlin blockade or "Suez-Hungary" or Korea or by invoking Pearl Harbor. This is a natural tendency when busy persons of active temperament confront unfamiliar circumstances. The more Kennedy and his advisers become immersed in the details of the crisis before them, the less they resort to such intellectual shortcutting; the more they apply to the unique problems at hand a sort of explanatory knowledge—a sense of possibilities—derived from and informed by many such experiences.[106]

In Rusk's remarks one can detect implicit lessons drawn from painful but proud recollections of both Pearl Harbor and the Korean War. Don't presume too heavily on the adversary's acting rationally, according to *our* standards of rationality, he cautions. At the very first White House meeting, he comments: "I'm beginning to wonder whether maybe Mr. Khrushchev is entirely rational about Berlin." Don't lose patience, Rusk also advises; and don't yield to temptation to solve one problem by making it a larger problem. Thus, he cautions against stopping a tanker just for the sake of stopping some Soviet ship, and he develops the formula for trading away the Jupiters by sleight of hand. In Taylor's remarks, one can see enduring effects of his analysis of the Korean War as one in which the United States forgot that military and diplomatic measures need not be alternatives but could complement one another. And McNamara's shifts back and forth from urging caution to urging action one is tempted to attribute in part to lack of moorings such as those in the minds of Kennedy, Rusk, or Taylor. McNamara's long preoccupation with problems of financial control and with management of the Ford Motor Company had equipped him with few precepts applicable to the missile crisis.

Someone who wants to learn all that can be learned from this extraordinary record of decision-making needs not only to notice how the process stutters and veers amid barrages of detail but also to infer how individuals of different backgrounds and temperaments are sorting the detail, discerning choices, and selecting among those choices, often guided by inner beacons of which they themselves may be incompletely aware. These tapes and transcripts form an almost inexhaustible resource for analyzing not only the mechanics but also the psychology of decision-making.

this study convinced that major policymaking episodes examination can reconstruct

Only by

grips with the part able to handle our own.

2. Robert F. Kennedy, *Thirteen Days: A Memoir of the Cuban Missile Crisis* (New York: W. W. Norton, 1969).

3. See McAuliffe, *CIA Documents;* and Kevin C. Ruffner, ed., *CORONA: America's First Satellite Program* (Washington, D.C.: Central Intelligence Agency, 1995).

4. More precisely, the expert used the monaural audio cassettes released by the JFKL with an SSP Sonic Solutions full-stereo NONOISE system, configured in a cascaded dual monaural real-time signal path, so that the material was, in essence, processed or denoised twice. Some compression and equalization were also utilized.

INTRODUCTION

1. On the Kennedy family, see Richard J. Whalen, *The Founding Father: The Story of Joseph P. Kennedy* (New York: New American Library, 1964); David E. Koskoff, *Joseph P. Kennedy: A Life and Times* (Englewood Cliffs, N.J.: Prentice-Hall, 1974); and especially Doris Kearns Goodwin, *The Fitzgeralds and the Kennedys: An American Saga* (New York: Simon and Schuster, 1987).

2. In the enormous literature on John Kennedy, the fullest account of the early years is Nigel Hamilton, *JFK: Reckless Youth* (New York: Random House, 1992); the most balanced is Herbert Parmet, *Jack: The Struggles of John F. Kennedy* (New York: Dial Press, 1980).

3. David Halberstam, *The Best and the Brightest* (New York: Random House, 1972), p. 9.

4. George W. Ball, *The Past Has Another Pattern: Memoirs* (New York: W. W. Norton, 1982), pp. 165–166.

5. Dean Rusk, as told to Richard Rusk, *As I Saw It*, ed. Daniel S. Papp (New York: W. W. Norton, 1990), pp. 36–37, 74–83. On Rusk also: Warren Cohen, *Dean Rusk* (Totowa, N.J.: Cooper Square, 1980); and Thomas J. Schoenbaum, *Waging Peace and War: Dean Rusk in the Truman, Kennedy, and Johnson Years* (New York: Simon and Schuster, 1988).

6. Hamilton, *JFK: Reckless Youth*, pp. 424–425.

7. Joan Blair and Clay Blair Jr., *The Search for JFK* (New York: Berkley, 1976), p. 114.

8. John Bartlow Martin, *The Life of Adlai E. Stevenson*, 2 vols. (Garden City, N.Y.: Doubleday, 1976–77), is the best and fullest biography.

9. On Robert Kennedy, see Arthur M. Schlesinger Jr., *Robert Kennedy and His Times* (New York: Random House, 1978).

10. Peter Collier and David Horowitz, *The Kennedys: An American Drama* (New York: Simon and Schuster, 1984), p. 155.

11. Hamilton, *JFK: Reckless Youth*, pp. 694–696.

12. Ibid.

13. Deborah Shapley, *Promise and Power: The Life and Times of Robert McNamara* (Boston: Little, Brown, 1993), pp. 31–35.

14. Curtis E. LeMay, with MacKinlay Kantor, *Mission with LeMay: My Story* (Garden City, N.Y.: Doubleday, 1965), p. 10.

15. Ibid., pp. 380–381.

16. On the Cold War, see various works by John Lewis Gaddis, most recently *We Now Know: Rewriting Cold War History* (New York: Oxford University Press, 1997).

17. Winston S. Churchill, speech at Fulton, Missouri, *New York Times*, March 6, 1946.

18. Hamilton, *JFK: Reckless Youth*, p. 700.

19. John F. Kennedy, speech of January 4, 1947, quoted from the *Congressional Record* in Collier and Horowitz, *The Kennedys*, p. 196.

20. Kennedy's understanding of the history of the blockade and airlift was imperfect. As of 1948, the United States had only a few nuclear weapons and very limited capabilities for using them against the Soviet Union. See McGeorge Bundy, *Danger and Survival: Choices about the Bomb in the First Fifty Years* (New York: Random House, 1988), pp. 383–385.

21. John F. Kennedy, speech of February 21, 1949, quoted from the *Congressional Record* in Parmet, *Jack*, p. 210.

22. *Mission with LeMay*, p. 382.

23. Maxwell Taylor, *Swords and Plowshares* (New York: W. W. Norton, 1972), is an autobiography; John M. Taylor, *General Maxwell Taylor: The Sword and the Pen* (New York: Doubleday, 1989), is a family biography.

24. This development is surveyed in Michael S. Sherry, *In the Shadow of War: The United States since the 1930s* (New Haven: Yale University Press, 1995).

25. Richard Reeves, *President Kennedy: Profile of Power* (New York: Simon and Schuster, 1993), p. 305. This work draws on sources not available to previous writers on the Kennedy presidency, but it does not supersede, either in detail or in insight, Theodore Sorensen, *Kennedy* (New York: Harper & Row, 1965); or Arthur M. Schlesinger Jr., *A Thousand Days: John F. Kennedy in the White House* (Boston: Houghton Mifflin, 1965).

26. The best introduction to this phenomenon is Stephen J. Whitfield, *The Culture of the Cold War* (Baltimore: Johns Hopkins University Press, 1991). See also Ellen Schrecker, *The Age of McCarthyism* (Boston: Bedford Books, 1994).

27. Ball, *The Past Has Another Pattern*, p. 112.

28. Schlesinger, *Robert Kennedy*, p. 135.

29. For the best-informed and coolest analysis of the issues, as well as a firsthand account of the missile crisis, see Bundy, *Danger and Survival.*

30. Details about nuclear weapons can be found in the Natural Resources Defense Council's *Nuclear Weapons Databook,* vol. 1: Thomas B. Cochran, William M. Arkin, and Milton M. Hoenig, *U.S. Nuclear Forces and Capabilities* (Cambridge, Mass.: Ballinger, 1984).

34. Maxwell Taylor, *The Uncertain Trumpet* (New York: Harper, 1959), p. 142.

35. The most thoughtful general survey is Jorge Dominguez, *Cuba: Order and Revolution* (Cambridge, Mass.: Harvard University Press, 1978). See also Andres Suarez, *Cuba: Castroism and Communism, 1959–1966* (Cambridge, Mass.: MIT Press, 1967); Maurice Halperin, *The Rise and Fall of Fidel Castro* (Berkeley: University of California Press, 1972); Tad Szulc, *Fidel: A Critical Portrait* (New York: William Morrow, 1986); and Robert E. Quirk, *Fidel Castro* (New York: W. W. Norton, 1993), pp. 137–152 and 402–403. Extraordinary new information, chiefly from Russian sources, appears in Aleksandr Fursenko and Timothy Naftali, *"One Hell of a Gamble": Khrushchev, Castro, and Kennedy* (New York: W. W. Norton, 1997).

36. See Ernest R. May, *American Cold War Strategy: Interpreting NSC 68* (New York: Bedford Books, 1993).

37. Schlesinger, *A Thousand Days,* p. 127.

38. Shapley, *Promise and Power,* pp. 131, 53, 70, 83–86.

39. Reeves, *President Kennedy,* p. 33. On the difference between Eisenhower's public and private personae, the landmark work is Fred I. Greenstein, *The Hidden-Hand Presidency: Eisenhower as Leader* (New York: Basic Books, 1982).

40. See, in addition to the works on Cuba mentioned in an earlier note, Peter Wyden, *Bay of Pigs: The Untold Story* (New York: Simon and Schuster, 1979).

41. Reeves, *President Kennedy,* p. 103.

42. John Ranelagh, *The Agency: The Rise and Decline of the CIA* (New York: Simon and Schuster, 1986), pp. 383–390; Lawrence Chang and Peter Kornbluh, eds., *The Cuban Missile Crisis 1962: A National Security Archive Documents Reader* (New York: New Press, 1992), nos. 5 and 6.

43. Chang and Kornbluh, *Cuban Missile Crisis,* pp. 355–359.

44. Reeves, *President Kennedy,* p. 103.

45. Ibid., pp. 102–103, 113–114.

46. Ibid., p. 116.

47. The best account is Michael Beschloss, *Mayday: Eisenhower, Khrushchev, and the U-2 Affair* (New York: HarperCollins, 1986).

48. Reeves, *President Kennedy*, p. 174. Khrushchev dictated his memoirs after his fall from power, and they were smuggled to the West. His reminiscences have been published in three volumes: *Khrushchev Remembers*, trans. and ed. Strobe Talbott (Boston: Little, Brown, 1970); *Khrushchev Remembers: The Last Testament*, trans. and ed. Strobe Talbott (Boston: Little, Brown, 1974); and *Khrushchev Remembers: The Glasnost Tapes*, trans. and ed. Jerrold Schecter with Vyacheslav Luchkov (Boston: Little, Brown, 1990). The best overview of governance in the Soviet Union during the period of Khrushchev's rise to supreme power is still Merle Fainsod, *How Russia Is Ruled*, rev. ed. (Cambridge, Mass.: Harvard University Press, 1970). On Soviet politics and foreign policy generally, the most important recent works are Vladislav Zubok and Constantine Pleshakov, *Inside the Kremlin's Cold War: From Stalin to Khrushchev* (Cambridge, Mass.: Harvard University Press, 1996); and Fursenko and Naftali, *"One Hell of a Gamble."*

49. Memorandum of Conversation, Vienna, June 4, 1961, in *FRUS 1961–1963*, vol. 14: *Berlin 1961–1962*, pp. 87–96.

50. Paper prepared by Thomas C. Schelling, July 5, 1961, ibid., pp. 170–172.

51. Reeves, *President Kennedy*, pp. 193–195.

52. See Jerrold L. Schechter and Peter S. Deriabin, *The Spy Who Saved the World: How a Soviet Colonel Changed the Course of the Cold War* (New York: Charles Scribner's Sons, 1992).

53. Kevin C. Ruffner, ed., *CORONA: America's First Satellite Program* (Washington, D.C.: Central Intelligence Agency, 1995), pp. 24, 28; NIE 11–8–62, "Soviet Capabilities for Long Range Attack," July 6, 1962, in *FRUS 1961–1963*, vol. 8: *National Security Policy*, pp. 332–342.

54. Reeves, *President Kennedy*, p. 247.

55. Kennedy to Khrushchev, October 8, 1962, in *FRUS 1961–1963*, vol. 6: *Kennedy-Khrushchev Exchanges*, pp. 163–164.

56. Schlesinger, *Robert Kennedy*, p. 471.

57. Khrushchev to Kennedy, April 22, 1961, in *FRUS 1961–1963*, vol. 6, pp. 10–16.

58. Chang and Kornbluh, *Cuban Missile Crisis*, p. 350.

59. Ibid., p. 351.

60. Passavoy to Record, "Topics Discussed during Meeting of Dr. Miro Cardona with the President," 25 April 1962; and Goodwin to President Kennedy, 17 April 1963, both in National Security Files, box 45, "Cuba: Subjects, Miro Cardona, Material Sent to Palm Beach," JFKL.

61. Memorandum of Conversation, February 19, 1962, 4:30 P.M., in *FRUS 1961–1963*, vol. 14, no. 300.

62. Memorandum of Conference with President Kennedy—Bi-Partisan Congressional Leaders—Off the Record, February 21, 1962, ibid., no. 304.

63. Khrushchev to Kennedy, March 10, 1962, and Khrushchev to Kennedy, undated but received July 5, 1962, in *FRUS 1961–1963*, vol. 6, pp. 118–126, 137–141; Weiss to U. A. Johnson, July 11, 1962, ibid., vol. 15: *Berlin Crisis 1962–1963*, pp. 213–214.

64. Michael Beschloss, *The Crisis Years: Kennedy and Khrushchev, 1960–1963* (New York: HarperCollins, 1991), p. 371.

65. Chang and Kornbluh, *Cuban Missile Crisis*, pp. 350, 352; John McCone, "Memorandum on Cuba," August 20, 1962, in McAuliffe, *CIA Documents*, pp. 19–20.

66. McCone, "Memorandum of Meeting with the President," August 23, 1962, ibid., pp. 27–29.

67. Chang and Kornbluh, *Cuban Missile Crisis*, pp. 354–355; Robert F. Kennedy, *Thirteen Days: A Memoir of the Cuban Missile Crisis* (New York: W. W. Norton, 1971), pp. 24–26.

72. Khrushchev to Kennedy, September 28, 1962, ... 161.

73. Editorial note, ibid., vol. 15, p. 336.

74. Zubok and Pleshakov, *Inside the Kremlin's Cold War*, pp. 263–265.

75. Memcon between Udall and Khrushchev, September 6, 1962, in *FRUS 1961–1963*, vol. 15, pp. 308–310.

76. Reeves, *President Kennedy*, p. 351.

77. Edwin McCammon Martin, *Kennedy and Latin America* (Lanham, Md.: University Press of America, 1994), pp. v–vi.

78. David Mayers, *The Ambassadors and America's Soviet Policy* (New York: Oxford University Press, 1995), pp. 200–202.

79. Shapley, *Promise and Power*, p. 78.

80. Paul H. Nitze, *From Hiroshima to Glasnost: At the Center of Decision, a Memoir* (New York: Grove Weidenfeld, 1989); and David Callahan, *Dangerous Capabilities: Paul Nitze and the Cold War* (New York: HarperCollins, 1990).

CONCLUSION

1. Khrushchev to Kennedy, October 28, 1962, in *FRUS 1961–1963*, vol. 6: *Kennedy-Khrushchev Correspondence*, pp. 189–190. A copy of this letter was released from Russian archives in 1992 and is included in the collection for the sake of completeness. It was never officially received by the Kennedy administration, and no copy exists in U.S. archives.

2. On Robert Kennedy's notes and the memo to Rusk on his October 30 meeting, see Arthur M. Schlesinger Jr., *Robert Kennedy and His Times* (New York: Random House, 1978), p. 523. We have found no evidence that this memo was ever sent to Rusk.

Dobrynin's account of this unpleasant meeting differs from Robert Kennedy's. In a report to Moscow, Dobrynin described the Attorney General as saying that he could not be party to an exchange of letters because it "could cause irreparable harm to my political career in the future." According to Dobrynin, Robert Kennedy gave assurances that President Kennedy would keep his promise by mentioning that, in connection with the Laos neutralization arrangements of the preceding summer, Kennedy had made, and kept, a secret promise to pull out U.S. troops deployed to Thailand. Dobrynin to Foreign Ministry, October 30, 1962, in a set of documents obtained by the Cold War International History Project, Woodrow Wilson International Center, and translated at Harvard, hereafter cited as CWIHP/Harvard Collection. On the troops in Thailand, see Michael Beschloss, *The Crisis Years: Kennedy and Khrushchev, 1960–1963* (New York: HarperCollins, 1991), pp. 397–398.

3. October 30, 1962, *FRUS 1961–1963*, vol. 6, pp. 190–198.

4. USUN New York 1585, November 1, 1962, reprinted in Lawrence Chang and Peter Kornbluh, *The Cuban Missile Crisis, 1962: A National Security Archive Documents Reader* (New York: New Press, 1992), pp. 249–251.

5. November 14, 1962, *FRUS 1961–1963*, vol. 6, pp. 209–212.

6. See, for example, Martin to Alexis Johnson, "Invasion," October 30, 1962; Ball through Bundy to President Kennedy, "Suggested Policy Line for Cuban Crisis," November 10, 1962; the State briefing papers for the press conference; and President Kennedy's explanation on this point to Mikoyan in the Memorandum of Conversation for their meeting, November 29, 1962, all in Cuban Missile Crisis Files, 1992 Releases box, National Security Archive, Washington, D.C.

7. See Bromley Smith to File, "Summary Record of Executive Committee Meeting No. 27," November 19, 1962, in Executive Committee Meetings, vol. 3, Meetings 25–32a, National Security Files, box 316, JFKL; and Gromyko to Mikoyan (then in Havana), November 18, 1962, CWIHP/Harvard Collection.

8. See Ankara 619, November 13, 1962, State Department Decimal Central Files, 782.56311/11–1362, National Archives, Washington, D.C.; Deptel 1151, "Jupiter Missiles," December 18, 1962, in *FRUS 1961–1963*, vol. 13: *West Europe and Canada*, pp. 460–461. On the "intolerable serenity" see Paris Secto 22 (Eyes Only from Rusk to President Kennedy and Ball), December 15, 1962, pp. 458–459.

9. Aleksandr Fursenko and Timothy Naftali, *"One Hell of a Gamble": Khrushchev, Castro, and Kennedy, 1958–1964* (New York: W. W. Norton, 1997).

10. James G. Blight and David A. Welch, *On the Brink: Americans and Soviets Reexamine the Cuban Missile Crisis* (New York: Hill and Wang, 1989), p. 43.

11. For the first, see Arnold L. Horelick and Myron Rush, *Strategic Power and Soviet Policy* (Santa Monica, Calif.: RAND Corporation, 1965); Alexander George and Richard Smoke, *Deterrence in American Foreign Policy: Theory and Practice* (New York: Columbia University Press, 1974); and Marc Trachtenberg, *History and Strategy* (Princeton: Princeton University Press, 1991), pp. 253–260. For the second, see Thomas G. Paterson and William G. Brophy, "October Missiles and November Elections: The Cuban Missile Crisis and American Politics, 1962," *Journal of American History*, 73, no. 1 (1986), 87–119; Thomas G. Paterson, *Kennedy's Quest for Victory: American Foreign Policy, 1961–1963* (New York: Oxford University Press, 1989); Blight and Welch, *On the Brink*, pp. 294–295; a panel

discussion on the missile crisis in *Diplomatic History,* 14, no. 2 (1990); and Russell
D. Buhite, "From Kennedy to Nixon: The End of Consensus," in Gordon Martel,
ed., *American Foreign Relations Reconsidered, 1890–1993* (London: Routledge,
1994), pp. 125–144.

12. Blight and Welch, *On the Brink,* p. 235.

13. Nikita S. Khrushchev, *Khrushchev Remembers: The Last Testament,* trans. and ed.

that his action had been the cause. Thompson may not have been fully conscious
of the significance of Suez for Khrushchev. He had been serving in Austria at the
time and had not been on top of Soviet affairs. His predecessor, Bohlen, had not
been close to Khrushchev and, judging from his cables, was so focused on Soviet
relations with Poland and Hungary that he didn't notice much of the larger
context. The scholar who has done most to call attention to Suez as a turning
point in Soviet foreign policy is Adam B. Ulam, but his writings on the subject
did not appear until the late 1960s. See his *Expansion and Coexistence: The
History of Soviet Foreign Policy, 1917–1967* (New York: Frederick A. Praeger, 1968),
pp. 586–589, and *The Rivals: America & Russia since World War II* (New York:
Viking, 1971), pp. 253–266.

15. Twenty-three protesters were killed in fighting in the city of Novocherkassk; 87
others were seriously wounded; hundreds were arrested, and, of these, at least
a dozen were later executed. Massive new internal security measures were secretly put in place throughout the country. Vladislav M. Zubok and Constantine
Pleshakov, *Inside the Kremlin's Cold War: From Stalin to Khrushchev* (Cambridge,
Mass.: Harvard University Press, 1996), pp. 263–265. For background see also
Merle Fainsod, *How Russia Is Ruled,* rev. ed. (Cambridge, Mass.: Harvard University Press, 1970), pp. 545–558, 611–612 (on developments in agriculture and the
significance of the decisions on resource allocation).

16. Though in not quite the same terms, this point is made in Richard Ned Lebow
and Janice Gross Stein, *We All Lost the Cold War* (Princeton: Princeton University
Press, 1994), pp. 19–66.

17. Khrushchev, *Khrushchev Remembers* (1970), p. 493.

18. Fursenko and Naftali, *"One Hell of a Gamble,"* pp. 3–38.

19. Ibid., p. 44.

20. Ibid., pp. 49–53.

21. Ibid., p. 70.

22. Ibid., pp. 92–94; Khrushchev to Kennedy, April 18, 1961, in *FRUS 1961–1963,*
vol. 6, pp. 7–8.

23. Khrushchev, *Khrushchev Remembers* (1970), p. 493. Khrushchev's colleague in the

Presidium, Mikoyan, later described Soviet interests in Cuba by explaining that "a defeat of the Cuban revolution would mean a two or three times larger defeat of the whole socialist camp. Such a defeat would throw back the revolutionary movement in many countries. Such a defeat would bear witness to the supremacy of imperialist forces in the entire world. That would be an incredible blow which would change the correlation of forces between the two systems." Memcon for Meeting between Castro and Mikoyan, 4 November 1962, in *CWIHP Bulletin*, no. 5 (Spring 1995), 96. In other words, there was a Soviet version of what was known, in America, as the "domino" theory.

24. Fursenko and Naftali, *"One Hell of a Gamble,"* pp. 158–163. Background and context can be found in two books by Jorge Dominguez: *Cuba: Order and Revolution* (Cambridge, Mass.: Harvard University Press, 1978), pp. 210–218, and *To Make a World Safe for Revolution: Cuba's Foreign Policy* (Cambridge, Mass.: Harvard University Press, 1989), pp. 72–77. See also Tad Szulc, *Fidel: A Critical Portrait* (New York: William Morrow, 1986), pp. 569–570, 610–613; Maurice Halperin, *The Rise and Decline of Fidel Castro* (Berkeley: University of California Press, 1972), pp. 132–154; Robert E. Quirk, *Fidel Castro* (New York: W. W. Norton, 1993), pp. 402–403; and Andres Suarez, *Cuba: Castroism and Communism, 1959–1966* (Cambridge, Mass.: MIT Press, 1967), pp. 137–152.

25. Khrushchev, *Last Testament*, p. 511. See Fursenko and Naftali, *"One Hell of a Gamble,"* pp. 148–163.

26. Fursenko and Naftali, *"One Hell of a Gamble,"* pp. 167–168.

27. Ibid., p. 177.

28. Reprinted, significantly, in *Pravda*, February 26, 1962; quoted in Yuri Pavlov, *Soviet-Cuban Alliance: 1959–1991* (New Brunswick, N.J.: Transaction, 1994), p. 37.

29. Blight and Welch, *On the Brink*, p. 238.

30. Dmitri Volkogonov, *Sem Vozhdei* [Seven Leaders], quoted in Fursenko and Naftali, *"One Hell of a Gamble,"* p. 169. At the time, the Soviet ICBM force totaled about 20. So adding at least 40 more launchers with 60 missiles would at least double the missile striking power for an initial salvo against the United States. As General Anatoli Gribkov pointed out, "In one stroke he [Khrushchev] could redress the imbalance in strategic nuclear forces." "The View from Moscow and Havana," in Anatoli I. Gribkov and William Y. Smith, *Operation ANADYR: U.S. and Soviet Generals Recount the Cuban Missile Crisis*, ed. Alfred Friendly Jr. (Chicago: Edition Q, 1994), p. 13.

31. Malinovsky quoted in Beschloss, *The Crisis Years*, p. 332.

32. The best study of the Jupiter deployment is Philip Nash, *The Other Missiles of October: Eisenhower, Kennedy, and the Jupiters, 1957–1963* (Chapel Hill: University of North Carolina Press, 1997). See also the pathbreaking work on this topic by Barton J. Bernstein, "Reconsidering the Missile Crisis: Dealing with the Problems of the American Jupiters in Turkey," in *The Cuban Missile Crisis Revisited*, ed. James A. Nathan (New York: St. Martin's Press, 1992), pp. 55–67. On Soviet perceptions, see Fursenko and Naftali, *"One Hell of a Gamble,"* pp. 195–196.

33. For Rusk's report on his talks with Gromyko, see Minutes of Meeting of the National Security Council, March 28, 1962, in *FRUS 1961–1963*, vol. 7: *Arms*

Control and Disarmament, p. 411; see also Memcon of Meeting between Rusk and Dobrynin, April 23, 1962, ibid., p. 443. The nuclear test series, Dominic I, involved 36 detonations in the Pacific, in the vicinity of Christmas Island and Johnston Island, beginning on April 25. The Soviets followed with a further series of their own atmospheric tests, beginning in August 1962.

34. Memcon of Meeting between Rusk and Dobrynin, May 30, 1962, ibid., p. 460.

35. Khrushchev, *Khrushchev Remembers* (1970), p. 494.

36. Andropov quoted in Oleg Troyanovsky, "The Caribbean Crisis: A View from the Kremlin," *International Affairs (Moscow),* April–May 1992, pp. 147, 148.

37. Blight and Welch, *On the Brink,* p. 239. Mikoyan's son identifies five people as having been in the group consulted by Khrushchev. In addition to Mikoyan père, Malinovsky, and Biryuzov, it included Frol Kozlov (the Presidium member responsible for party personnel and organization) and Foreign Minister Gromyko. But Gromyko claims that Khrushchev first informed him about the planned deployment on the flight home from Bulgaria on May 20. Andrei A. Gromyko, "The Caribbean Crisis: On *Glasnost* Now and Secrecy Then," *Izvestiya,* April 15, 1989, p. 5.

38. This paragraph and the next draw upon Fursenko and Naftali, "One Hell of a Gamble," ... Fursenko and Naftali, partly on the basis of their own interviews with Alexeev, date it to May 20.

39. Castro quoted in Szulc, *Fidel,* pp. 579–583. For the recollections from the member of Castro's Secretariat, Emilio Aragones, and another Cuban official, Jorge Risquet, see Allyn, Blight, and Welch, *Back to the Brink,* pp. 51, 26. See also Castro's account in Blight, Allyn, and Welch, *Cuba on the Brink,* pp. 197–198; and Alexeev, in *Back to the Brink,* pp. 151–152. On Cuban reluctance, see also Pavlov, *Soviet-Cuban Alliance,* pp. 38–40. See also Blight, Allyn, and Welch's discussion of Castro's real motives for accepting the missiles in *Cuba on the Brink,* pp. 345–347.

40. A defense pact, drafted and initialed by Malinovsky and Che Guevara, was to be signed triumphantly by Khrushchev in Cuba in November 1962, at the time the operational missiles were unveiled to the world. The signing ceremony never took place. When Guevara and Emilio Aragones went to Moscow at the end of August to finalize the pact, they asked Khrushchev to publicize the preparation of the treaty and end the attempted deception, hoping the treaty would be enough to deter the United States: they could insist on their right openly to accept a Soviet base, much as the United States had handled its overseas nuclear deployments (for example, in Turkey). Khrushchev said no. See Castro in Blight, Allyn, and Welch, *Cuba on the Brink,* pp. 85–86; Emilio Aragones in Allyn, Blight, and Welch, *Back to the Brink,* p. 52; and Gribkov, "The View from Moscow and Havana," p. 23.

41. Fursenko and Naftali, *"One Hell of a Gamble,"* pp. 169–172.
42. Gribkov, "The View from Moscow and Havana," p. 13.
43. Fursenko and Naftali, *"One Hell of a Gamble,"* pp. 186–187.
44. Gribkov, "The View from Moscow and Havana," pp. 15–16.
45. Castro, in Blight, Allyn, and Welch, *Cuba on the Brink,* pp. 83–84. Alekseev provided a similar account at the same meeting.
46. Khrushchev, *Khrushchev Remembers* (1970), p. 494.
47. The best compilation of this evidence is Beschloss, *The Crisis Years,* e.g., pp. 223–234 (on the Vienna meeting). For new details on Khrushchev's perception of Kennedy see Zubok and Pleshakov, *Inside the Kremlin's Cold War,* pp. 239–248, 257–258.
48. Gromyko, "The Caribbean Crisis"; Anatoly Dobrynin, *In Confidence* (New York: Random House, 1995), pp. 79–80.
49. Fursenko and Naftali, *"One Hell of a Gamble,"* p. 174; Dobrynin, *In Confidence,* p. 63.
50. Khrushchev to Kennedy, November 9, 1961, in *FRUS 1961–1963,* vol. 6, p. 57; see also Hans S. Kroll, *Lebenserinnerungen eines Botschafters* (Cologne: Kiepenheuer & Witsch, 1967), pp. 524–527.
51. For more on Khrushchev's difficult domestic and international position by late 1961, see James G. Richter, *Khrushchev's Double Bind: International Pressures and Domestic Coalition Politics* (Baltimore: Johns Hopkins University Press, 1994), pp. 142–147; Michel Tatu, *Power in the Kremlin,* trans. Helen Katel (New York: Viking, 1969), pp. 148–214; and Robert M. Slusser, *The Berlin Crisis of 1961: Soviet-American Relations and the Struggle for Power in the Kremlin, June–November 1961* (Baltimore: Johns Hopkins University Press, 1973).
52. Khrushchev to Kennedy, December 13, 1961, in *FRUS 1961–1963,* vol. 14: *Berlin Crisis 1961–1962,* pp. 683–684, 690.
53. Khrushchev to Kennedy, March 10, 1962, ibid., vol. 15: *Berlin Crisis 1962–1963,* p. 11. Kennedy sought a conciliatory *modus vivendi* with Khrushchev; see Kennedy to Rusk, March 11, 1962, ibid., p. 15.
54. On the Dobrynin-Rusk meeting of April 23, see ibid., p. 119, n. 5; State 2964, April 28, 1962, ibid., p. 121; Richter, *Khrushchev's Double Bind,* p. 148; and Tatu, *Power in the Kremlin,* pp. 233–234.
55. See, based on research in East German archives, Michael Lemke, *Die Berlinkrise 1958 bis 1963: Interessen und Handlungsspielräume der SED im Ost-West Konflikt* (Berlin: Akademie Verlag, 1995), pp. 186–190.
56. McNamara certainly believed that evident U.S. nuclear superiority was keeping the Soviets from returning to direct confrontation over Berlin. He explained the point to Kennedy in detail; McNamara to Kennedy, "US and Soviet Military Buildup and Probable Effects on Berlin Situation," June 21, 1962, in *FRUS 1961–1963,* vol. 15, pp. 192–195.
57. Dobrynin, *In Confidence,* p. 52.
58. Moscow 187, July 20, 1962, in *FRUS 1961–1963,* vol. 15, p. 234. By this time the sense of impending crisis was becoming general, and U.S. allies were also anxious to consider contingency plans. See Weiss to Johnson, "Berlin," July 11, 1962, and

Secto 13 (Rusk to Kennedy and Ball), July 22, 1962, both in ibid., pp. 213–214, 236–237.

59. See Moscow 225, July 25, 1962; Moscow 228, July 26, 1962; and Copenhagen 76 (Thompson to Rusk), all in ibid., pp. 252–255. On communications in Washington see Bundy to Sorensen, "Berlin," August 23, 1962, ibid., pp. 284–285; and Dobrynin, *In Confidence,* pp. 67–68.

60. *FRUS 1961–1963,* vol. 6, p. 157.

61. Thompson set down this analysis, already well understood in Washington, for the ⟨...⟩ October 24, 1962, ibid., vol. 15,

leverage in negotiations ⟨...⟩ year"; London 1696, October 26, 1962, conveying the ⟨...⟩ provided to the British Cabinet's Joint Intelligence Committee, in Cuban Missile Crisis Files, 1992 Releases box, National Security Archive.

62. Fursenko and Naftali, *"One Hell of a Gamble,"* pp. 206–212.

63. Ibid., pp. 211–212. This alteration in the plan was apparently made on September 25. Moscow proceeded with deployment of 4 diesel attack submarines. On each of these one of the 22 torpedoes was armed with a nuclear warhead. These were the 4 submarines detected by the Americans, tracked near the quarantine area, discussed in the White House meetings, and harassed by U.S. antisubmarine vessels.

64. Troyanovsky, "The Caribbean Crisis," p. 150.

65. Gromyko cabled report to the Central Committee of the Communist Party of the Soviet Union, October 19, 1962, in "Russian Foreign Ministry Documents on the Cuban Missile Crisis," *CWIHP Bulletin,* no. 5 (Spring 1995), 66–67; see also the gloating tone and complete misreading of both Kennedy and Rusk apparent in the final paragraph of Gromyko's longer report on his conversation with Rusk, Gromyko to Central Committee, October 20, 1962, ibid., p. 69.

66. Fursenko and Naftali, *"One Hell of a Gamble,"* p. 190.

67. Gribkov, "The View from Moscow and Havana," p. 52.

68. Ibid., pp. 45–46.

69. Fursenko and Naftali, *"One Hell of a Gamble,"* pp. 238–239, 245–246.

70. Ibid., pp. 240–241. This account supersedes the reported instruction in Gribkov, "The View from Moscow and Havana," p. 62, which was apparently prepared for the Presidium but not used.

71. Dobrynin to Foreign Ministry, October 23, 1962, in "Russian Foreign Ministry Documents," pp. 70–71; Alexeev to Foreign Ministry, October 23, 1962, CWIHP/Harvard Collection.

72. Fursenko and Naftali, *"One Hell of a Gamble,"* pp. 247–248; Troyanovsky, "The Caribbean Crisis," p. 152.

73. Fursenko and Naftali, *"One Hell of a Gamble,"* pp. 252–253.

74. Ibid., p. 253.

75. "Report on William E. Knox's Meeting during the Cuban Missile Crisis" (misdated as occurring on October 25), John F. Kennedy Library Oral History Project.

76. Fursenko and Naftali, *"One Hell of a Gamble,"* p. 257.

77. Ibid., p. 258. The Presidium and KGB files specially available to the authors apparently shed no light.

78. Ibid., pp. 255–256, 258–260.

79. Alexeev to Foreign Ministry, October 25, 1962, CWIHP/Harvard Collection.

80. Fursenko and Naftali, *"One Hell of a Gamble,"* p. 261.

81. See ibid., pp. 273–278; Lebow and Stein, *We All Lost the Cold War,* p. 115; Raymond L. Garthoff, *Reflections on the Cuban Missile Crisis,* rev. ed. (Washington, D.C.: Brookings Institution, 1989), p. 67 n. 107.

82. Fursenko and Naftali, *"One Hell of a Gamble,"* pp. 269–271.

83. Ibid., p. 272.

84. Troyanovsky, "The Caribbean Crisis," p. 153.

85. Alexeev to Foreign Ministry, October 27, 1962, CWIHP/Harvard Collection.

86. Troyanovsky, "The Caribbean Crisis," p. 153.

87. Gribkov, "The View from Moscow and Havana," p. 63; Fursenko and Naftali, *"One Hell of a Gamble,"* pp. 274–275.

88. Alexeev to Foreign Ministry, October 25, 1962; Castro to Khrushchev, October 26, 1962, both in CWIHP/Harvard collection.

89. Fursenko and Naftali, *"One Hell of a Gamble,"* p. 266.

90. Alexeev in Allyn, Blight, and Welch, *Back to the Brink,* p. 30; Garthoff, *Reflections on the Cuban Missile Crisis,* pp. 84–85.

91. The next day Khrushchev sent a message to Castro that said "you shot down" one of the provocative U.S. overflights. Khrushchev warned Castro that such steps "will be used by aggressors to their advantage, to further their aims." At that time Castro explained that he had mobilized all his antiaircraft batteries "to support the positions of the Soviet forces" and that "if we wanted to prevent the risk of a surprise attack, the crews had to have orders to shoot." Castro cryptically added: "The Soviet Forces Command can give you further details on what happened with the plane that was shot down." Khrushchev to Castro, October 28, 1962, and Castro to Khrushchev, October 28, 1962. This correspondence was published by the Cuban government in 1990, and Soviet sources verified its accuracy. Copies are available from the JFKL.

92. Alexeev to Foreign Ministry, October 27, 1962, CWIHP/Harvard Collection. Alexeev's report was oddly ambiguous about whether Soviets or Cubans had shot down the U-2.

93. Khrushchev to Castro, October 30, 1962, in released correspondence at the JFKL.

94. Fursenko and Naftali, *"One Hell of a Gamble,"* p. 282.

95. Ibid.; and Troyanovsky, "The Caribbean Crisis," p. 154.

96. Troyanovsky, "The Caribbean Crisis," p. 154.

97. See ibid.; Foreign Ministry to Washington (handwritten by Gromyko in Soviet

archives), October 28, 1962, in "Russian Foreign Ministry Documents," p. 76; Fursenko and Naftali, *"One Hell of a Gamble,"* p. 284.

98. By April 1963 Khrushchev was explaining to one American visitor, Averell Harriman, that the socialist countries had actually gained more from the Wall than they would have gained from signing a peace treaty with East Germany. "Berlin," he said, "is no longer a source of any trouble"; Memcon of Meeting between Harriman and Khrushchev, April 26, 1963, in *FRUS 1961–1963*, vol. 15, p. 510.

99. Dean Rusk as told to Richard Rusk, *As I Saw It,* ed. Daniel S. Papp (New York:

quiet efforts are being made to try and get the Nitze Committee phased out." It was. See Record of Meeting no. 1, NSC/ExCom/BER-NATO, October 24, 1962, in *FRUS 1961–1963*, vol. 15, pp. 395–397; Kitchen to Alexis Johnson, "Nitze Subcommittee," 1 November 1962, in Cuban Missile Crisis Files, 1992 Releases box, National Security Archive. Nitze sent President Kennedy a memo on "Berlin in light of Cuba" that contained suggestions for adjusting East-West relations throughout the world, including a dramatic suggestion to reduce all East and West nuclear delivery vehicles to a total of 500 on each side, with warheads of a combined yield of no more than 50 megatons. All other types of nuclear weapons would be banned. Nitze to Kennedy, undated but returned for filing from the President's office on November 5, 1962, in *FRUS 1961–1963*, vol. 15, pp. 411–419.

102. At the time McNamara said this could mean either military force or economic force, but we think the quotation fairly represents his thinking, and helps explain why he urged his colleagues to reevaluate the merits of at least an air strike against Cuba.

103. On the relative importance of nuclear and conventional forces in persuading Khrushchev, McNamara testified: "I realize that there is a kind of chicken-and-the-egg debate going on about which was preeminent. To me that is like trying to argue about which blade of the scissors really cut the paper"; McNamara testimony to the House Armed Services Committee, January 12, 1963, in files of the Office of the Secretary of Defense.

104. A typical list of things to do, jotted down by Gilpatric on October 18 and left in his files, has 13 major sets of needed actions, from legal analysis of a blockade or state of war, to planning responses if Berlin is blockaded, to handling domestic political aspects (assigned to Robert Kennedy and Sorensen).

105. See Tyler to Rusk, "Nuclear Sharing with France," October 25, 1962, on State's panicked reaction to Nitze's paper, "U.S.-French Reconciliation on Defense Matters," partly because it conflicted with State's multilateral answer for Turkey,

described in Tyler, Rostow, and Talbot to Rusk, "Cuba," October 24, 1962, both in Cuban Missile Crisis Files, 1992 Releases box, National Security Archive.

106. This point is developed at some length in Ernest R. May, *"Lessons" of the Past: The Use and Misuse of History in American Foreign Policy* (New York: Oxford University Press, 1973); Robert Jervis, *Perception and Misperception in International Politics* (Princeton: Princeton University Press, 1976); and Richard E. Neustadt and Ernest R. May, *Thinking in Time: Uses of History for Decision-makers* (New York: Free Press, 1986). On "explanatory knowledge" see Philip D. Zelikow, "Scientific Generalizations and International Policy," manuscript pending publication.